NETWORKING ARGUMENT

This edited volume presents selected works from the 20th Biennial Alta Argumentation Conference, sponsored by the National Communication Association and the American Forensics Association in 2017. The conference brought together scholars from Europe, Asia, and North America to engage in intensive conversations about how argument functions in our increasingly networked society.

The essays discuss four aspects of networked argument. Some examine arguments occurring in online networks, seeking to both understand and respond more effectively to the acute changes underway in the information age. Others focus on offline networks to identify historical and contemporary resources available to advocates in the modern day. Still others discuss the value added of including argumentation scholars on interdisciplinary research teams analyzing a diverse range of subjects, including science, education, health, law, economics, history, security, and media. Finally, the remaining network argumentation theories explore how the interactions between and among existing theories offer fruitful ground for new insights for the field of argumentation studies.

The wide range of disciplinary backgrounds and methodological approaches employed in *Networking Argument* make this volume a unique compilation of perspectives for understanding urgent and sustaining issues facing our society.

Carol Winkler is Professor of Communication Studies at Georgia State University, USA, where she leads the interdisciplinary Transcultural Conflict and Violence Initiative and is a former Associate Dean of Humanities. A former President of the American Forensics Association, she served as Principal Investigator on grants that funded urban debate programs in Atlanta and Milwaukee, including the Computer Assisted Debate Program selected as the signature school program for the 2005 White House's Helping America's Youth initiative. She has also served as an invited technical consultant for the U.S. Bureau of Justice Administration to expand the benefits of debate to low-income communities. Her current research program focuses on presidential rhetoric, extremist discourse, and visual arguments related to terrorism. Her book, *In the Name of Terrorism* (2006), won the National Communication Association's Outstanding Book Award in Political Communication, and her co-authored article on how certain visual images stand as ideological markers of the culture won that same organization's Visual Communication Excellence in Research Award. She is currently working as co-principal investigator on a Minerva funded project, "Mobilizing Media," which analyzes the media campaign of violent extremist groups in the Middle East and North Africa.

EDITORIAL BOARD

Jennifer Bevan, Chapman University
Ronald Walter Greene, University of Minnesota
Dale Hample, University of Maryland
E. Johanna Hartelius, University of Pittsburgh
David B. Hingstman, University of Iowa
Casey R. Kelly, University of Nebraska at Lincoln
Susan Kline, The Ohio State University
Robert E. Mills, Northwestern University
Gordon R. Mitchell, University of Pittsburgh
Catherine Helen Palczewski, University of Northern Iowa
Samuel P. Perry, Baylor University
Damien S. Pfister, University of Maryland
Gordon Stables, University of Southern California
Rachel Avon Whidden, Lake Forest College

Research Coordinator and Editorial Assistant
Yennhi Luu, Georgia State University

Editorial Assistant
Lyshandra Holmes-Bennett, Georgia State University

NETWORKING ARGUMENT

Edited by Carol Winkler

Routledge
Taylor & Francis Group

LONDON AND NEW YORK

First published 2020
by Routledge
2 Park Square, Milton Park, Abingdon, Oxon, OX14 4RN, UK

and by Routledge
52 Vanderbilt Avenue, New York, NY 10017

Routledge is an imprint of the Taylor & Francis Group, an informa business

First issued in paperback 2021

© 2020 Alta Conference Steering Committee

The right of Carol Winkler to be identified as the editor of this work has been asserted by her in accordance with sections 77 and 78 of the Copyright, Designs and Patents Act 1988.

All rights reserved. No part of this book may be reprinted or reproduced or utilised in any form or by any electronic, mechanical, or other means, now known or hereafter invented, including photocopying and recording, or in any information storage or retrieval system, without permission in writing from the publishers.

Trademark notice: Product or corporate names may be trademarks or registered trademarks, and are used only for identification and explanation without intent to infringe.

British Library Cataloguing-in-Publication Data
A catalogue record for this book is available from the British Library

Library of Congress Cataloging-in-Publication Data
A catalog record for this book has been requested

Disclaimer
Every effort has been made to contact copyright holders for their permission to reprint material in this book. The publishers would be grateful to hear from any copyright holder who is not here acknowledged and will undertake to rectify any errors or omissions in future editions of this book.

ISBN: 978-0-367-34702-4 (hbk)
ISBN: 978-1-03-208497-8 (pbk)
ISBN: 978-0-429-32726-1 (ebk)

Typeset in Bembo
by Swales & Willis, Exeter, Devon, UK

CONTENTS

Contents

Contents

NOTES ON CONTRIBUTORS

Alley Agee, Independent Scholar, Salt Lake City, USA.
Research Interests: Collective Resistance Rhetoric, Social Media, Feminist Rhetoric

R. Brandon Anderson, Visiting Assistant Professor, Department of Communication Studies, Gustavus Adolphus College, USA.
Research Interests: Narrative Argument, U.S. Nuclear Discourses and Public Memory, Lost Cause Social Movement Rhetoric

Karen Anderson-Lain, Principal Lecturer and Basic Communication Course Director, Department of Communication Studies, University of North Texas, USA.
Research Interests: Pedagogy and Communication, Service-learning and Community Engagement, Assessment, Critical Pedagogy, Debate and Argumentation Pedagogy

Satoru Aonuma, Professor of Communication Studies, Department of Society, Culture, and Media, International Christian University, Japan.
Research Interests: Argumentation Theory, Critical Theory, Social Movement Rhetoric, Rhetoric of Popular Culture, Modern Japanese Rhetoric, Forensics

Robert Asen, Professor of Rhetoric, Politics, and Culture, Department of Communication Arts, University of Wisconsin-Madison, USA.
Research Interests: Public Sphere Theory, Rhetoric and Critical Theory, Rhetoric and Public Policy

Timothy Barouch, Assistant Professor of Communication Studies, Department of Communication, Georgia State University, USA.
Research Interests: Public Argument, Legal Communication, Rhetoric and Political Liberalism, Communication Pedagogy

Megan A. Bassick, Ph.D. Candidate, Department of Communication, University of Oklahoma, USA.
Research Interests: Dark Side of Intimate Relationships, Long-Distance Relationships, Serial Arguments, Use of Communication Technology in Intimate Relationships

Ruth J. Beerman, Assistant Professor, Department of Communication Studies, Randolph-Macon College, USA.
>   *Research Interests*: Visual Argument, Controversy, Body Rhetoric, Gender, Citizenship

Adam Blood, Graduate Assistant in Rhetoric and Public Culture, Department of Communication Studies, University of Nebraska at Lincoln, USA.
>   *Research Interests:* Argument Studies, Loyalty Rhetoric, Ideology and Myth

Emma Frances Bloomfield, Assistant Professor, Department of Communication Studies, University of Nevada, Las Vegas, USA.
>   *Research Interests*: Rhetorical Theory and Criticism, Science and Religion, Controversy and Public Argument, The Environment and Climate Change

Allison Blumling, Masters Student, Department of Communication, University of Utah, USA.
>   *Research interests:* Critical Health Communication, Gender, Intersectionality, Critical and Collective Rhetoric

Beth L. Boser, Assistant Professor, Department of Communication Studies, University of Wisconsin-La Crosse, USA.
>   *Research Interests*: Rhetorics of Reproduction, Birth, and Motherhood; Political and Social Change Discourse

Eryn N. Bostwick, Assistant College Lecturer, School of Communication, Cleveland State University, USA.
>   *Research Interests*: Implications of Negative Disclosures, Family Communication Processes, Conflict and Argumentation in Interpersonal Relationships

David Botting, Postdoctoral Research Fellow, ArgLab, FCSH, Universidade Nova de Lisboa, Portugal.
>   *Research Interests*: Reasoning, Moral Reasoning, Moral Responsibility, Logic, Rationality

Maegan Parker Brooks, Assistant Professor, Department of Civic Communication and Media, Willamette University, USA.
>   *Research Interests*: Rhetorical Theory, African American Public Discourse, Critical Whiteness Studies, Educational Policy Deliberation, Collective Memory Studies

Daniel C. Brouwer, Associate Professor, Hugh Downs School of Human Communication, Arizona State University, USA.
>   *Research Interests*: Publics and Counterpublics, Social Movement Rhetoric, Cultural Performance, Genders and Sexualities, HIV/AIDS

Elizabeth Brunner, Assistant Professor, Department of Communication, Media and Persuasion, Idaho State University, USA.
>   *Research Interests*: Social Movements, Social Media, Visual Rhetoric, Environmental Communication, and China Studies

Ann E. Burnette, Associate Professor, Department of Communication Studies, Texas State University, USA.
>   *Research Interests*: U.S. Presidential Rhetoric, U.S. Foreign Policy Discourse, Campaign Persuasion, Rhetoric and Gender

M. Kelly Carr, Assistant Professor, Department of Communication, University of West Florida, USA.

    Research Interests: Legal Argument, Public Address, Supreme Court Opinions, Rhetorical Invention

Jonathan S. Carter, Assistant Professor, Department of Communication, Eastern Michigan University, USA.

    Research Interests: Networked Rhetorical Theory, Technics as Rhetoric, Modalities of Networked Argument, Contemporary Shifts in Publics and Publicity

David M. Cheshier, Director and Associate Professor, Creative Media Industries Institute, Georgia State University, USA.

    Research Interests: Argumentation Theory, Rhetoric and the Affective Turn, Critical (especially Frankfurt School) Theory

Ioana A. Cionea, Assistant Professor, Department of Communication, University of Oklahoma, USA.

    Research Interests: Interpersonal Argumentation, Intercultural/Cross-Cultural Communication, Quantitative Research Methods

Dana L. Cloud, Professor, Department of Communication and Rhetorical Studies, Syracuse University, USA.

    Research Interests: Marxist, Feminist, and Public Sphere Theory; Social Movements

Robert T. Craig, Professor Emeritus, Department of Communication, University of Colorado Boulder, USA.

    Research Interests: Communication Theory and Philosophy, Discourse Studies, Grounded Practical Theory, Critical Analysis of Public Metadiscourse on Communication Problems

Kareem El Damanhoury, Ph.D. Candidate, Department of Communication, Georgia State University, USA.

    Research Interests: Visual Framing, Strategic Communication of Militant Groups, Propaganda, Middle East Media, Content Analysis

Amber Davisson, Assistant Professor of Communication, Department of Communication and Philosophy, Keene State College, USA.

    Research Interests: Media and Digital Ethics, Political Communication, Popular Culture, and Digital Rhetoric

Aaron Dicker, Ph.D. Candidate, Department of Communication, Georgia State University, USA.

    Research Interests: Visual Argument, Social Movements, Extremist Groups, Counter-publics

Sara A. Mehltretter Drury, Director of Wabash Democracy and Public Discourse and Associate Professor, Department of Rhetoric, Wabash College, USA.

    Research Interests: Political Communication, Campaign Rhetoric, Debates, Democratic Deliberation, Public Address

Justin Eckstein, Assistant Professor and Director of Forensics, Department of Communication and Theatre, Pacific Lutheran University, USA.

    Research Interests: Argument, Sound, and Food

Danielle Endres, Professor, Department of Communication, University of Utah, USA.
  Research Interests: Environmental & Science Rhetoric, Social Movements, Native American Rhetoric, Rhetorical Fieldwork

Joshua P. Ewalt, Assistant Professor, Department of Communication, University of Utah, USA.
  Research Interests: Space and Place, Regional and Local Rhetorics, Social Theory, Advocacy, Public Memory, Cartography, Environmental Rhetoric

Seth Fendley, Ph.D. Candidate, Department of Communication Studies, University of Southern Mississippi, USA.
  Research Interests: Media Criticism, Digital Argument, Public Sphere, Native Advertising, Decision Making Processes of Debate Judges

Jay Frank, Ph.D. Candidate, Department of Communication Studies, University of Minnesota, USA.
  Research Interests: Climate Change; Scientific Controversy; Public Participation; Environmental Justice; Communicative Labor; Rhetorical Theory; Debate.

John Fritch, Dean, College of Humanities, Arts and Sciences and Professor, Communication Studies, University of Northern Iowa, USA.
  Research Interests: Argumentation, Forensics, Forensics Pedagogy. Rhetorical Theory

Eric Gander, Associate Professor of Public Argument, Department of Communication Studies, Baruch College, City University of New York, USA.
  Research Interests: Science and Public Discourse, the First Amendment, Communication Law; Game Theory, and Persuasion

G. Thomas Goodnight, Professor, Annenberg School of Communication, University of Southern California, USA.
  Research Intereests: Argument Spheres, Controversies, Classical Rhetoric, Rhetoric of Science, Philosophies of Communication, Globalized Networks

Ronald Walter Greene, Professor, Department of Communication Studies, University of Minnesota (Twin Cities), USA.
  Research Interests: Rhetorical Approaches to Argument, International Policy Discourse, Protest Rhetoric, Communicative Labor, Debate Education, Cultural Materialism

Allison Hahn, Assistant Professor, Department of Communication Studies, Baruch College, City University of New York, USA.
  Research Interests: Public Argument, International Communication, Environmental Deliberation, Pastoral Nomadic Participation in Environmental Policymaking

Heidi E. Hamilton, Professor, Department of Communication & Theatre, Director of Ethnic and Gender Studies Program, Emporia State University, USA.
  Research Interests: Foreign Policy Discourse, Gendered Political Communication, Social Movements

Dale Hample, Associate Professor, Department of Communication, University of Maryland, USA.
  Research Interests: Interpersonal Arguing, Argumentation Theory, Interpersonal Communication, Communication Theory

Andrew J. Hart, Ph.D. Candidate, Department of Communication Studies, University of Georgia, USA.

> *Research Interests*: Environmental Rhetoric, Climate Change, Visual Argument, Science Rhetoric/Rhetoric of Science, Celebrity Studies, Public Policy Rhetoric

Craig Hayden, Chair, Diplomatic Mastery Program, Foreign Service Institute, USA.

> *Research Interests*: International Communication, Media Technology, Rhetoric and Foreign Policy

Dale A. Herbeck, Professor and Chair, Department of Communication Studies, Northeastern University, USA.

> *Research Interests*: Argumentation Theory, Political Debate, Freedom of Speech, Communication Law and Ethics

Brian Heslop, Assistant Professor of Communication, Department of Communication, Language & Literature, Coker College, USA.

> *Research Interests*: Political and Religious Rhetoric, Civic Controversy

Aaron Hess, Assistant Professor of Rhetoric and Communication, College of Integrative Sciences and Arts, Arizona State University, USA.

> *Research Interests*: Digital Rhetoric, Critical Rhetoric, Participatory Methods, Community Advocacy and Argumentation, Public Memory

Tyler Hiebert, Ph.D. Candidate, Annenberg School of Communication, University of Southern California, USA.

> *Research Interests*: Rhetoric, Transitional Justice, Cultural Studies, Genocide Studies

David B. Hingstman, Associate Professor and Director, A. Craig Baird Center for Debate and Public Advocacy, Department of Communication Studies, University of Iowa, USA.

> *Research Interests*: Argumentation and Debate, Rhetorical Criticism, Legal Rhetorics and Freedom of Expression

Linda Diane Horwitz, Associate Professor, Department of Communication, Lake Forest College, USA.

> *Research Interests*: Public Memory, Visual Culture, Civic Pedagogy, Feminist Argumentation and Criticism

Kelsey Jackson, B.A. in Communication Studies, Keene State College, USA.

> *Research Interests:* Evolution of Social Media related to Online Sorority Platforms, Feminism in Advertising, Feminism in the Workplace

Michael Janas, Department Chair and Associate Professor, Department of Communication Studies, Samford University, USA.

> *Research Interests*: Motivated Cognition, Public Argument, Debate, Forensic Pedagogy

Jeffrey W. Jarman, Director, Elliott School of Communication, Wichita State University, USA.

> *Research Interests*: Political Debates, Public Sphere, Fact-checking, Motivated Reasoning, Neuroscience, Debate and Forensics Pedagogy

James Jasinski, Professor, Department of Communication Studies, University of Puget Sound, USA.

Research Interests: Legal Argument, U.S. Constitutional Discourse, Dissociation, Phronesis and Practical Reason/Wisdom

Amy Janan Johnson, Professor, Department of Communication, University of Oklahoma, USA.

Research Interests: Interpersonal Argumentation, Relational Communication, Conflict, Family Communication

Jeremy David Johnson, Ph.D. Candidate, Department of Communication Arts & Sciences, Penn State University, USA.

Research Interests: Digital Rhetoric, Networked Argumentation, Publics Theory, Information Theory, Speech & Debate Education

Kevin A. Johnson, Associate Professor, Department of Communication Studies/Director, Center for First Amendment Studies, California State University, Long Beach, USA.

Research Interests: First Amendment, Rhetorical Theory and Criticism

Paul Elliott Johnson, Assistant Professor, Department of Communication, University of Pittsburgh, USA.

Research Interests: Argumentation, Populism, American Conservatism, Political Theory, Biopolitics, Masculinity, Victimhood, Neoliberalism

Jason Jordan, Ph.D. Candidate, Department of Communication, University of Utah, USA.

Research Interests: Cultural Ruralism, Communication Pedagogy, Gun Rights Rhetoric

Naoki Kambe, Assistant Professor of Communication Studies, College of Intercultural Communication, Rikkyo University, Japan.

Research Interests: Visual Argument, Digital Rhetoric, Masculinities and Nature, Feminist Pedagogy, Representations of Japanese Culture

Casey Ryan Kelly, Associate Professor, Department of Rhetoric and Public Culture, University of Nebraska-Lincoln, USA.

Research Interests: Masculinity & Gender Studies, Argument Controversy, Indigenous Rhetoric, Film, Cultural Studies, Food Studies

Zornitsa Keremidchieva, Assistant Professor, Department of Communication Studies, University of Minnesota, USA.

Research Interests: Feminist Theory, Rhetorical Modalities of Governance and Political Organization

Susan L. Kline, Associate Professor, School of Communication, The Ohio State University, USA.

Research Interests: Communication Theory, Interpersonal Argument, Persuasive Communication Competencies

James F. Klumpp, Professor Emeritus, Department of Communication, University of Maryland, USA.

Research Interests: Argumentation, Communication and Social Change, Contemporary Rhetorical Theory, American Rhetorical Discourse

Katsuya Koresawa, Advisor at the Learning Support Center, Hiroshima Shudo University, Japan.

Research Interests: Debate Pedagogy, Rhetoric and Critical Theory, Rhetorical Criticism

Wayne L. Kraemer, Senior Lecturer, Department of Communication Studies, Texas State University, USA.

> *Research Interests*: U.S. Presidential Rhetoric, U.S. Foreign Policy Discourse, Campaign Persuasion, Argumentation and Debate

Brian Lain, Associate Professor/Director of Debate, Department of Communication Studies, University of North Texas, USA.

> *Research Interests*: Debate and Civic Engagement, Public Advocacy, Apocalyptic Rhetoric, Collective Memory and Commemorative Culture

Randall A. Lake, Associate Professor, Annenberg School of Communication, University of Southern California, USA.

> *Research Interests*: Public Argument; Visual Argument; Indigenous Studies; Gender, Race, and Ethnicity in Communication; Rhetoric and Criticism

Candice L. Lanius, Lecturer, Department of Communication Arts, University of Alabama in Huntsville, USA.

> *Research Interests*: Big Data Theory, Digital Rhetoric, Rhetoric of Inquiry, Human Computer Interaction

Ilon Lauer, Associate Professor, Department of Communication, Western Illinois University, USA.

> *Research Interests*: Classical Rhetoric, History of Rhetoric, Argumentation

Ronald Lee, Professor, Department of Communication Studies, University of Nebraska-Lincoln, USA.

> *Research Interests*: Arguing about Civic Virtue, Myth and Ritual in American Politics, Race-Card Play in Post-Civil-Rights Era Political Discourse

Sarah T. Partlow Lefevre, Professor/Director of Debate, Department of Communication, Media, and Persuasion, Idaho State University, USA.

> *Research Interests*: Argumentation, Kenneth Burke, Gun Debates, Fairy Tales and Socialization, Second Wave Feminism, Rhetoric and Violence

Nathan J. Lindsey, Ph.D. Candidate, Department of Communication, University of Oklahoma, USA.

> *Research Interests*: Social Influence, Interpersonal Communication, Cognitive Processing

Chandra A. Maldonado, Ph.D. Candidate, Department of Communication, Rhetoric and Digital Media, North Carolina State University, USA.

> *Research Interests*: Visual Rhetoric, Memory and Commemoration Studies, Presidential Rhetoric, National Identity, Circulation Studies

José Ángel Maldonado, Assistant Professor, Department of Communication Studies, University of Nebraska-Lincoln, USA.

> *Research Interests*: Critical Theory, Cultural Studies, Mexican and Latin American Rhetoric, Modernity and Globalization, and Transnational Indigeneity

Joan Faber McAlister, Associate Professor, Program of Rhetoric, Media, and Social Change, Drake University, USA.

> *Research Interests*: Spatial and Material Rhetorics, Visual Culture, Aesthetics, Feminist Criticism, Queer Theory

Margret McCue-Enser, Associate Professor, Department of Communication Studies, Saint Catherine University, USA.
> *Research Interests*: Native American Argument, Intersectionality in Political and Activist Discourse, Presidential Campaign Discourse, Integrity and Longevity of Liberal Arts Education

George F. (Guy) McHendry, Jr., Assistant Professor, Department of Communication Studies, Creighton University, USA.
> *Research Interests*: Surveillance, Material Rhetoric, Postdialectic Argumentation, Visual Argument, Cultural Studies, Performance Studies

Michael K. Middleton, Assistant Professor of Argumentation and Public Discourse/Director, John R. Park Debate Society, Department of Communication, University of Utah, Salt Lake City, USA.
> *Research Interests*: Social Movements, Homelessness, Rhetorical Theory and Criticism

Robert Elliot Mills, Ph.D. Candidate, Program in Rhetoric and Public Culture, Northwestern University, USA.
> *Research Interests*: Legal Rhetoric, Sovereignty, Maritime Piracy, Political Theory, Continental Philosophy

Gordon R. Mitchell, Associate Professor, Department of Communication, University of Pittsburgh, USA.
> *Research Interests*: Argumentation, Debate, Rhetoric of Science, Pedagogy, Eutrapelia

Kaori Miyawaki, Instructor, Language Education Center, Ritsumeikan University, Japan.
> *Research Interests*: Civic Engagement, Social Protests, Memory, Debate as Pedagogy, Intercultural Communication

Junya Morooka, Associate Professor, Department of Communication Studies, Rikkyo University, Tokyo, Japan.
> *Research Interests*: The History of Rhetoric and Communication Studies in Modern Japan

William Mosley-Jensen, Assistant Professor of Human Communication/Director of Debate, Department of Human Communication and Theatre, Trinity University, USA.
> *Research Interests*: Argumentation & Debate, The Public Sphere, Political Communication, Emotion & Pathos Studies, Economic Rhetoric

Meredith Neville-Shepard, Clinical Assistant Professor, Department of Communication, University of Arkansas, USA.
> *Research Interests*: Rhetorical Criticism, Argumentation, Protest, Violence, Political Rhetoric

Jaclyn Nolan, Lecturer, Department of Communication Studies, University of Georgia, USA.
> *Research Interests*: Discourses of Gender in Sex and Sport, Rhetoric of Civil Rights Movements, Rhetorics of Contemporary Feminism

Hiroko Okuda, Associate Professor, Department of Communication, Kanto Gakuin University, Japan.
> *Research Interests*: Japan's War Memories, Foreign Policy Discourse, Peace Studies, Public Address, Japan's Political Argumentation

Catherine Helen Palczewski, Professor, Department of Communication Studies, University of Northern Iowa, USA.

> *Research Interests*: Visual Argument, Gender Rhetoric and Feminist Theory-Historical and Contemporary, Rhetoric in Civic Life, Social Protests

Nicholas S. Paliewicz, Assistant Professor, Department of Communication, University of Louisville, USA.

> *Research Interests*: Environmental Communication, Public Memory, Social Movements, Argumentation Theory

Dakota Park-Ozee, M.A. Candidate, Department of Communication, University of Utah, USA.

> *Research Interests*: Political Rhetoric, Press-state Relations, and Public Discourse

Samuel P. Perry, Associate Professor, Baylor Interdisciplinary Core, Baylor University, USA.

> *Research Interests*: Race, Visual Rhetoric, Violence, Terrorism

Damien Smith Pfister, Associate Professor, Department of Communication, University of Maryland, USA.

> *Research Interests*: Public Argument and Deliberation, Networked Rhetorics, Rhetoric and/of/as Technology, Visual Culture

Angela G. Ray, Associate Professor, School of Communication Studies, Northwestern University, USA.

> *Research Interests*: Nineteenth-century U.S. Rhetorical History, Popular Learning, Lecture and Performance Culture

John J. Rief, Assistant Professor, Department of Communication & Rhetorical Studies, Duquesne University, USA.

> *Research Interests*: Rhetoric and Medicine, Health Communication, Argumentation Theory, History and Pedagogy of Intercollegiate Academic Debate

Chris Robbins, Doctoral Fellow, Annenberg School for Communication & Journalism, University of Southern California, USA.

> *Research Interests*: Material Rhetoric, Social Network Analysis, Diffusion of Innovations, Digital Communities

Robert C. Rowland, Professor/Director of Graduate Studies, Department of Communication Studies, University of Kansas, USA.

> *Research Interests*: Presidential Rhetoric, Public Sphere, Myth, Narrative, Argumentation Theory, Rhetorical Methods, Israeli-Palestinian Conflict

Monica Renae Scott, B.A. Honors Student, Department of Sociology, University of Utah, USA.

> *Research Interests:* Rhetoric of Science, Intimate Partner Violence

Kazuhiko Seno, Vice President, Japan Debate Association, Japan.

> *Research Interests*: Debate Education for Business Persons, Logical Communication Skills, Critical Thinking

Zachary Sheldon, M.A. Candidate, Department of Communication Studies, Baylor University, USA.

Research Interests: Visual Rhetoric and Argument, Film, Phenomenology and Communicology, Media Ecology, and Media Rhetoric

L. Paul Strait, Assistant Professor/Director of Forensics, Department of Communication Studies, University of Southern Mississippi, USA.
Research Interests: Rhetoric of Science and Medicine, Argument Theory, Public Sphere

Ian Summers, Ph.D. Candidate, Department of Communication, University of Utah, USA.
Research Interests: Argumentation, Protest Rhetoric and Scientific Controversies.

Noriaki Tajima, Associate Professor, Department of International Communication, Kanda University of International Studies, Japan.
Research Interests: Argumentation and Debate, Rhetorical Studies, and Critical Pedagogy

Karen Tracy, Professor, Department of Communication, University of Colorado-Boulder, USA.
Research Interests: Language and Social Interaction, Institutional Interaction of Justice and Governance, Discourse Analysis, Face and Identity Practices

Don Waisanen, Associate Professor, Department of Communication Studies, Baruch College, City University of New York, USA.
Research Interests: Strategic Public Communication, Civic Engagement, Rhetoric and Public Affairs, Public Deliberation and Argumentation, Communication Training and Development

David Cratis Williams, Professor of Communication Studies, Florida Atlantic University, USA.
Research Interests: Argumentation Theory and Definitional Argument, Argument Criticism, Kenneth Burke, Russian and Eurasian Political Argument

Rachel Wilson, M.A. Candidate, Department of Communication and Rhetorical Studies, Duquesne University, USA.
Research Interests: Identity, Communication and Mental Health, Community Engagement, Protest Rhetoric, Rhetoric of Religion

Carly S. Woods, Assistant Professor, Department of Communication, University of Maryland, USA.
Research Interests: History of Argumentation and Debate, Rhetoric and Public Address, Social Change, Women's and Gender Studies

David Zarefsky, Owen L. Coon Professor Emeritus, School of Communication, Northwestern University, USA.
Research Interests: Public Argument, Lincoln and Slavery, Rhetoric of the 1960s, Presidential Rhetoric, Argumentation Theory, American Public Address

ACKNOWLEDGMENTS

All who have ever attended the Alta Argumentation Conference recognize the biennial meeting as a unique opportunity to experience deep engagement with scholarly colleagues interested in argument. They also know that the conference occurs in a setting so serene that they will leave feeling recharged and fortunate to have made new friends. In 2017, the conference celebrated its 40th year, an event made all the more special by the presence of three scholars, G. Thomas Goodnight, Marilyn Young, and David Zarefsky, who not only attended the first (among many) Alta conferences, but also dedicated much of their long and distinguished careers to building the field of argumentation studies and supporting those associated within it.

The sponsors of the 2017 Alta Conference—the National Communication Association and the American Forensics Association—contributed in substantial ways to creating a successful experience for the attendees. Due to the generous contributions of those two organizations, an unprecedented number of graduate students and international scholars received competitive scholarships to attend the conference. The Alta Steering Committee, led by Dr. Patricia Riley, established the priorities for awarding the two categories of participants eligible to receive scholarships, as well as providing useful oversight of conference-related decisions.

As always, the University of Utah served as an outstanding local host for the Alta conference. Malcolm Sillars, professor emeritus and former chair of the University of Utah Communication Department, served as founder and local host of the first Alta Argumentation Conference. Since then, the Utah Communication Department has maintained an unfailing, welcoming environment for argumentation scholars to gather from around the world in the furtherance of the field of argumentation studies. Danielle Endres, the current chair of the University of Utah, continued that tradition. In addition to negotiating a housing contract for participants, she appointed Professor Robin Jensen as the point person for local arrangements, made the department's talented Business Manager Jennifer Duigan available to assist with conference finances, encouraged her department's graduate students to serve as on-site conference staff, and hosted a welcoming reception for participants. Local host Robin Jensen efficiently and effectively responded to numerous inquiries about how to maximize the conference experience for participants. The always courteous and helpful onsite staff of the University of Utah graduate students included: Alley Agee, Dakota Park-Ozee, Allison

Blumling, Ian Summers, Diana Zulli, Chandra Maldonado, José Maldonado, Marsha Maxwell, and Benjamin Mann.

The editorial board members listed at the front of this volume contributed significant time, needed expertise, and focused effort to evaluate and improve the panels, abstracts, and papers presented at the conference, as well as the essays included in this volume. Their insightful commentary helped strengthen the caliber of the experience of the conference participants and the readers of *Networking Argument*. Most of the board members attended a two-day editorial "boot camp," where they showed great care in their recommendations for what work belonged in the selected proceedings and how they communicated helpful feedback that I, in turn, forwarded on to contributors.

Two previous conference directors, Catherine (Cate) Palczweski and Randall Lake, functioned as constant support, ready and willing to answer all questions no matter how great or small. They always offered timely responses, strong guidance, and a wry sense of humor. Cate, whose clear eye and genuine appreciation of the beauty of the Alta setting and conference, photographed the cover image for *Networking Argument*. Jeff Jarman served as the conference webmaster. His patience with yet another new director and his quick turnaround time for making changes was instrumental to effective communications with conference attendees. Jim Klumpp served as the webmaster for the Alta Conference website, as he has done for too many years to count. His services will be sorely missed as he moves on to cabin life. Taylor and Francis also provided much needed support in the publication process. Commissioning Editor Lydia de Cruz and Colin Morgan, Senior Production Editor of Swales & Willis were both responsive to our inquiries and helpful in resolving all issues related to the volume's publication.

Five faculty members, who will remain unnamed at their own request, volunteered to serve on the Michael C. McGee Outstanding Graduate Student Paper Award selection committee. Having had a particularly competitive year of eligible recipients, I am indebted to each of them for making such a difficult decision. I also want to once again congratulate Jeremy Johnson from Pennsylvania State University for receiving the award for the 2017 Alta Conference.

Georgia State University also provided essential support that allowed me to serve the Alta conference community. Dean William Long originally agreed to allow me the necessary time to serve as conference director and editor of the selected proceedings. His successor, Dean Sara Rosen, honored that initial agreement when she took over leadership in the College of Arts and Sciences. Greg Lisby, Chair of the Communication Department at Georgia State University, generously provided support needed to obtain sufficient editorial assistance to permit the timely production of this volume. Research Coordinator Lyshandra Holmes helped organize the 2017 conference panels, just one of many invaluable research support services she has provided to me over the years. Research Coordinator Monerah Almahmoud provided much needed support in the final check of the galleys of this manuscript.

Last, and by no means least, I want to express my heartfelt thanks Yennhi Luu, the research coordinator and editorial assistant for the 2017 Alta Conference and *Networking Argument*. Her dedication to the task and attention to detail went far beyond what any director could reasonably expect from someone in her role. Her intellectual curiosity led her to not only complete her assigned "quote check" role, but also to deeply explore the nature and content of many of the citations included in this volume. Her consistently cheerful disposition, her unwavering professionalism, and her genuine interest in the conference participants and their essays made working with her on this project a true partnership.

NETWORKING ARGUMENT

An Introduction

Carol Winkler

Networks and arguments have a longstanding, intertwined relationship. At the most fundamental level, every argument functions as a network connecting claims to evidence and reasoning as well as other arguments. The network connections within an argument and between arguments may be explicit or implied. As the size and nature of these of networked argument chains expand, they take on added complexities and nuance.

All arguments also require a network of two or more parties, either real or imagined, engaged in a matter of contestation. Arguments perform constitutive functions for networks, as beliefs in certain arguments often form the foundational and sustaining principles of group alignment. Networks serve as fertile ground for argumentative invention, as collectives generate new forms of evidence, reasoning, and claims to justify their own existence, establish the parameters for participation in the network, or garner standing in relation to other competing networks, among many other desired ends. Networks also help define and provide normative guidelines for determining the appropriate and acceptable form and structure of specific arguments. The multifaceted, ever changing, interconnections between argumentation and networks continue to inspire scholarly inquiry and practical applications.

A number of recent factors, however, have caused some to question the ongoing relevance of argumentation studies for understanding contemporary networks. The rampant spread of fake news, alternative facts, and the post-truth era arguably belies conventional understandings of how argument works. The rising prominence of emotional appeals to attract, engage, and hold the loyalties of network participants have seemingly minimized the traditional standing, if not the ongoing value, of logical appeals. The tendency of networked individuals to narrowly select only facts, values, and opinions that are consistent with their current thinking holds the potential to make productive, dialectical engagement a relic of the past. Moreover, the rising appeal of charismatic leaders who eschew standard argumentative conventions may serve as models for some.

Networking Argument examines the questions related to the continuing relevance and changing applications of argumentation studies for understanding online and offline networked communication in the present day. Authors of the essays first presented their ideas at the 20th National Communication Association/American Forensics Association Summer Conference on Argumentation held in Alta, Utah during July of 2017. Each essay, with the exception of the keynote address and spotlight papers, underwent competitive editorial

1

board selection in a double-review process—once for inclusion in the conference program and once for inclusion in this volume.

The authors in *Networking Argument* certainly found no shortage of opportunities for applying argumentation studies to a wide range of contemporary networks. A brief scan of the volume reveals that scholars find fruitful areas of analysis of networked argument in the contexts of sports, health, criminal justice, politics, religion, security, popular culture, the courts, history, economics, memorials, physics, environmental science, intercultural communication, genocide, race, gender, foreign and domestic policy, big data, indigenous societies, general science, academic and community debate, and social protests. The breadth of analyses alone suggests that the central question should shift from whether argumentation continues to play a role in contemporary societies and cultures to how it functions within rapidly changing, online and offline environments.

Organizationally, *Networking Argument* begins with a series of eight featured essays presented at the 2017 conference from well-established scholars working in the fields of argumentation, rhetoric, and cultural studies. It then moves to a series of essays that apply and expand upon core strategic concepts from the field of argumentation studies with special attention to the interactive roles those concepts have within networked contexts. The third group of essays examines notions of argument circulation in online and offline networks. Finally, the volume concludes with evaluative studies of argumentation and debate networks. Clear overlap exists between these four categories, with the result that single essays provide insights that cut across the structural makeup of the volume.

Robert Asen's keynote address, "Disavowing Networks, Affirming Networks: Neoliberalism and Its Challenge to Democratic Deliberation," opens *Networking Argument* with an analysis of how argument functions within "market-inspired visions of people and their connections." Recognizing the far-reaching influence of neoliberalism on the landscape of governing structures and societal institutions, Asen explores how such a perspective defines who can argue, establishes criteria for judging contemporary arguments, and introduces built-in biases into the argumentative terrain. He concludes with a discussion of how networked argument can insert needed public engagement into debates about the value and consequences of the neoliberalism perspective.

The "Spotlighted Theories and Practices of Networking Argument" section of this volume provides model illustrations of the theoretical and practical contributions of argumentation for understanding networked communication. Each of the first four authors demonstrates how argumentation theory can adapt to the changing nature of the current, networked environment. In brief, these authors recommend that those interested in argument and argumentation should renew their focus on substance rather than fact; emphasize affect, myth, narrative, and spectacle as essential modalities of argument; view argumentation as a social productive, human technology where argument serves as one mode of communicative labor; and place added attention towards understanding the dark side of disingenuous controversies. The final three essays in this section examine argumentation's practical applicability for understanding and navigating Silicon Valley's digital culture, the #BlackLivesMatter/#Blue Lives Matter controversy, and the unpredictability of U.S. public diplomacy outcomes in the 21st century.

The next three sections of *Networking Argument* explore how traditional concepts of argument—definition, association/dissociation, and authority—function strategically within and between networked contexts. Collectively, the essays that make up "Strategic Use of Definition in Networked Argument" display a wide range of available methodological approaches for discovering how and why various entities utilize definitional arguments. The authors employ historical analogs, archival documents, news content, online debates, critical analyses, popular culture content, and the etymology of terms to help reveal definitional arguments and the reasons behind their use. The essays in this section illustrate the key contribution that definitional arguments make for understanding a broad range of subject matter, including ideologies (conservatism and populism), global threats (cybercrime, climate change), groups (female Olympic athletes, mass shooters, nuclear protesters, U.S. citizens), and actions (medicalized births and murders). Key questions explored in these essays include: how can definitional argument function as an instrument of power for authorities and those challenging established institutions? How do definitional arguments differ within the public, personal, and technical spheres? Who (or what) qualifies as central actors in definitional disputes, and how are those actors determined? What are appropriate definitional boundaries for the field of argumentation studies in networked contexts?

The authors in "Strategic Use of Association and Dissociation in Networked Argument" explore how arguments that emphasize similarity and difference can deepen understandings of current phenomena, generate novel ways of thinking about how to prompt and/or resist change, and identify the contextual limits of applying such approaches. Examining arguments in both online and offline networks, these studies apply argument by association or dissociation to politics, the courts, scientific communities, religious communities, matters of security, diplomacy, and social media. Key questions explored in these essays include: Are new types of analogy available and unexplored? Can networks themselves function as analogical arguments? What factors contribute to the success and failure of arguments by association in networked contexts? Can expansions of our previous conceptions of dissociative argument help explain outcomes with particular networks?

"Strategic Use of Authority in Networked Argument" examines how advocates use argument to challenge or sustain existing authoritative structures and practices. The first five essays explore the argumentation strategies of those seeking to overturn existing centers of power: anti-nuclear community activists, the media producers for ISIS, local protesters at the January 2017 Women's March, city collectives fighting against the Trump administration's decision to pull out of the Paris climate accords, and celebrity activities fighting against climate change. The final seven essays explore how argument functions in the maintenance of existing authority structures and practices, with a focus on banks, administrative health agencies, the police, white males, the Christian right, big data, and general science. Core questions examined in these essays include: What argumentative strategies have worked historically to challenge existing, authoritative networks and their appeals? What argumentative strategies have worked historically to bolster existing and emerging power centers? What contextual factors should those seeking to employ arguments for or against authority utilize to maximize impact on their targeted audiences?

The next two sections of *Networking Argument* address the distribution and circulation practices associated with arguments within the networked environment. Essays in "Argument Circulation in Online Networks" explore opportunities and constraints for spreading online arguments. These essays examine arguments related to exclusively online networks (a religion based exclusively online, Twitter group followers, online websites curated for college fraternity and sorority audiences, or blogging military service members) and those related to online networks that have interactions with offline networks (e.g., linkages between corporate entities, television advertisements, online search engines, and academic publications outlets). The section concludes with an essay that encourages a combined consideration of both big data and cultural studies approaches for understanding the motivations for engaging online social media, the behavior of those online, and the popularity of viral artifacts. Core questions addressed in these essays include: What factors (e.g., curator practices, legal parameters, security concerns, mediums, and genres of discourse) account for argumentative norms in the online environment?

What argumentative practices contribute to enhanced forms of audience engagement in online environments?

"Argument Circulation in Offline Networks" examines the use of historical artifacts, memory, and memorials to demonstrate the flow of arguments across time. The first essays in the section address various argumentative approaches for memorializing and remembering groups who had previously experienced genocides or ethnic cleansings (e.g., Jewish populations during World War II, Canadian aborigines from the late 1800s through end of the 20th century, the Dakota Indians in Minnesota River Valley, and the Feminicido, a group of over 1400 impoverished Mexican women who experienced rape and murder over the past 20 years without an identified perpetrator). The remaining essays in the section examine the argumentative legacy of political figures (Barbara Jordan, Franklin D. Roosevelt), Supreme Court decisions (*Regents v. Bakke*), and political campaign events (the 1960 Kennedy-Nixon debate, Reagan's Morning in America advertisement). Key questions addressed in the essays include: What contextual factors need consideration (or produce benefits) for those interested in networked arguments related to memory, memorialization, or other forms of legacy creation? What are the available argumentative strategies for shaping memory, memorializations, and other forms of legacy? What are the productive contributions of style and substance to such efforts?

The final two sections of *Networking Argument* evaluate arguments in practice. The first, "Evaluating Argumentation Networks," explores approaches for evaluating particular forms and argumentative practices that recur in a variety of interpersonal and public contexts. These essays examine evaluation criteria relevant to particular argument types (sweeping generalizations, ad hominem arguments, serial arguments, exhortations) and argumentation-related practices in specified contexts (global use of argumentative assertiveness and aggressiveness, fact-checking practices of media outlets, advocacy in small claims courts, fascist argumentation in online networks, dialectic engagement in online environments, and argument in public school board meetings and academic colloquiums). They offer a wide variety of productive approaches for developing appropriate evaluation criteria for argument in practice. Core questions addressed in these essays include: What are appropriate standards for formulating ethical, effective, or otherwise beneficial argument in certain contexts? What contextual factors need consideration in the evaluation of particular argument forms or practices? Are networks and dialectic exchange complementary or in competition?

"Evaluating Debate Networks" examines how debate influences civic and community engagement, both locally and globally. Assessing the potential impact of debate for civic engagement, the first four essays address various approaches for enhancing the intersection between debate, local community engagement, and community impact. These studies analyze the impact of intensive, summer debate workshops on student attitudes toward civic engagement, the comparative impact of differing formats on audience perceptions based on public debates held in the community, the potential usefulness of the *Text, Talk, Vote* technology for enhancing the public's critical thinking in response to political debates, and the potential relevance and additive value of lessons from the health field's Community Based Participatory Research program. The last five papers in this section provide perhaps the most extensive analysis conducted to date on the intercultural debate exchange program between the United States and Japan in operation since the 1990s. The papers provide a detailed analysis and breakdown of Japanese debate participation by educational levels, language and gender; an assessment of current Japanese debate theory and practice preferences; a comparative study of the similarities and differences of U.S. and Japanese debate publications; and an evaluation of the level of U.S. influence on Japanese debate based on participant interviews and debate observations. A response by a former U.S. participant in the U.S.-Japanese debate exchange concludes the section. Key questions addressed in this section include: What debate formats best maximize the effects of local and global engagement? What debate technologies and other types of debate materials best maximize local and global engagement? In general, what are the best practices for maximizing local and global engagement?

Networking Argument underscores the pressing need to understand argument and argumentative practice in networked environments. As many facets of society grapple with the challenges and opportunities available through the rapid expansion of local, national, and global networks, the central role of understanding, utilizing, and evaluating argument becomes more acute. At the same time, however, the field of argumentation studies must rigorously search for the best ways to adapt to the expansive growth and changing nature of online and offline networks.

KEYNOTE ADDRESS

1

DISAVOWING NETWORKS, AFFIRMING NETWORKS

Neoliberalism and Its Challenge to Democratic Deliberation

Robert Asen

More than forty years ago, Brockriede (1975) famously proclaimed that "arguments are not in statements but in people" (p. 179). Resisting a conception of argument as strictly propositional, Brockriede envisioned argument as a process through which interlocutors constituted themselves as subjects. On this point, other prominent argument scholars of his era joined him, such as Johnstone (1965), who wrote previously that "argument does seem to me to be constitutive of those who participate in it" (p. 6). Both scholars saw argument, in Brockriede's (1986) terms, as "a relational activity" (p. 58). As this reference to relationships suggests, argument's constitutive force does not operate as a discrete, intrinsic capacity of an individual. Only by engaging others may we enact the creative power of argument. Argument arises through human interaction and orients human interaction. Even solitary arguers—composing, perhaps, Facebook status updates—place themselves in a relationship by imagining an audience for their argument. In these ways, argument depends on relationships. And not just any relationship.

Argument invokes particular relationships among interlocutors that enable coordinated action on mutually recognized issues, interests, and concerns. For many contemporary scholars, investigations of argument and its relations have appeared under the heading of public sphere scholarship. To be clear, argument is only one mode of communication in the public sphere, but many scholars have employed this framework to understand the dynamics of public argument. In his foundational essay on the topic, Goodnight (2012b) intimated the relational character of publics. He considered how people's interactions may change when they engage in argument as a personal, technical, and/or public activity.[1]

My focus in this address will be on relationships—the potentially critical, democracy-building relationships that argument may construct, as well as the alternative models of relationships that market-inspired visions of people and their connections promote. The contemporary model of the multiple public sphere underscores the importance of relationships—within publics as well as across publics and counterpublics. Reacting to the unitary vision of publicity that the bourgeois public sphere propagates, and inspired by the efforts of people excluded from publics to fight for inclusion and effective participation, the model of a multiple public sphere envisions a network of directly and indirectly connected, contesting, and partially overlapping sites of discourse (Benhabib, 1996; Hauser, 1999). Across this network, people may engage a range of publics and counterpublics that reflect the fluidity of their daily lives (Brouwer, 2006). From various perspectives within this network, publics may appear as mainstream or marginal, welcoming or discouraging varied participation (Dunn, 2010). Approaching public sphere theory as critical theory, scholars have embraced the framework of multiplicity to recognize the dynamics of social complexity and diversity, to critique limitations of existing publics, and to appreciate struggles for justice and equality (Pezzullo, 2003; Squires, 2002).

This critical project faces a serious challenge in the contemporary rise of the market as a model of human relations and society. Known to many scholars as neoliberalism, this market model purports to account fully for human motivation and behavior. It asserts a supposed economic truth about our interests, values, and aspirations, as well as our responsibilities and obligations to one another. Brown (2015) noted that a "neoliberal rationality disseminates the *model of the market* to all domains and activities—even where money is not at issue—and configures human beings exhaustively as market actors, always, only, and everywhere as *homo oeconomicus*" (p. 31). We can see and hear signs of neoliberalism everywhere in our daily lives, from calls to make ourselves attractive to employers by investing in education, to policy programs of tax cuts, deregulation, and privatization, to assertions that market competition always produces efficiencies and innovation. Neoliberalism may flatten or displace the practice of argumentation as it shapes people's actions in the public sphere, for argumentation calls for modes of engagement that stress competencies and values that neoliberalism discounts, namely, judgment, perspective-taking, and more. We need to attend to the subjects that neoliberalism may constitute, and how these subjects may frustrate democratic practice.

The pervasiveness and polysemy of the term "neoliberalism" itself complicates this task. In a critical review of scholarship on the topic, Springer (2012) identified four prominent versions of neoliberalism: neoliberalism as dominant ideology, neoliberalism as policy framework, neoliberalism as state form, and neoliberalism as mode of self-governance. I believe that these approaches converge in important ways for scholarship on argument and the public sphere. In terms of self-governance, neoliberalism inculcates modes of public subjectivity that may contravene the qualities and practices that we associate with subjects who may engage in democratic deliberation (see, e.g., Gehrke, 2009; Keith, 2007; Kock & Villadsen, 2012). Yet the neoliberal subject, as an individual market actor, does not exist outside of contexts. Neoliberal ideologies promote this modality by confidently asserting the superiority of markets over democratic forms of action and association. A celebration of putative market virtues—and a warning of dire consequences for those who refuse—provides the rationale for reinventing oneself as a neoliberal subject. And if the asserted superiority of markets is an insufficient motive, then neoliberal policies and state actions may incentivize or compel market behavior. If, for example, a policy program of privatization threatens the accessibility and affordability of key social supports like health care and education, and if state agencies respond to citizens primarily as taxpayers and/or customers, then individuals may feel as if they have no choice but to compete with others in a zero-sum game for resources and comparative advantage.

Neoliberalism presents a fundamental challenge to democratic relationships that value coordinated action and the reciprocal development of the individual and community. Insofar as public argument may build these relationships, public argument also faces a threat in neoliberalism. However, neoliberalism does not operate outside of relationships or, for that matter, multiple public spheres. Historical collaborations between intellectuals like Friedrich Hayek, funders like the

Volker Fund, and politicians like Margaret Thatcher enabled its growth and circulation (Van Horn & Mirowski, 2009; Wapshott, 2011). Present-day collaborations among think-tanks like the Heritage Foundation, elected officials like Paul Ryan and Scott Walker, and funders like the Koch brothers sustain its hegemony. Yet even as neoliberal advocates work together to advance their interests, they often repudiate and seek to weaken others' relationships, undermining the formation of publics and the articulation of a collective "we." In a neoliberal world, we are all on our own.

Neoliberalism threatens public argument, but public argument may contribute to a potentially powerful response. My address unfolds in four sections. First, I engage argument scholarship to reconstruct the figure of the "familiar argument subject." This familiar figure, who embodies the virtues we associate with argument, has important lessons to teach us. To heed these lessons, we must revise this familiar figure in light of contemporary scholarship on the public sphere, which emphasizes themes of power and difference to address issues of multiplicity, inclusion, and equality, as I address in my second section. In the third section, I turn to the homogeneous, competition-driven neoliberal subject and its relations to others. Finally, in my fourth and concluding section, I consider briefly how argumentative subjects populating deliberative publics may provide some response to neoliberalism.

Argument's Familiar Subject and Its Relationships

Scholars have offered a familiar account of the subject who engages in argument. The familiar argument subject seeks to reach judgment about shared concerns under conditions of uncertainty by engaging others and risking oneself in a potentially transformative encounter. Linking scholarship and pedagogy, this figure justifies claims of argument's democratic promise, connecting the inquiries of scholars like Brockriede (1975) and Johnstone (1965) to more contemporary concerns with deliberative democracy. This figure is not universal, all-encompassing, or exhaustive, but its familiarity elicits recognition. As its promise suggests, this familiar arguer conveys clear normative force. Sometimes, this figure may illustrate practices of argument; at others, it serves as a critical perspective for analyzing existing arguments. We may add detail to the familiar argument subject by considering five qualities of this figure and its relations: judgment, contingency, reciprocal engagement, perspective-taking, and transformation/risk.

Judgment orients argument, offering an end toward which interlocutors may reference their interactions. Hauser (2007) maintained that the "public" of the public sphere directs scholars to attend to those "processes of interaction" in which people participate "in a form of collective reasoning eventuating in practical judgment" (p. 335). Hauser suggested that public argument situates interlocutors in contexts of decision-making. These contexts may be more or less instrumental, involving judgments about specific policies, values, cultural practices, differences, and more. As this range suggests, judgment need not produce agreement. Interlocutors may enact judgment when they better understand their disagreements, for example, or when they come to appreciate diverse views. Judgment suggests a considered, reflected viewpoint, one that weighs options and possibilities. Its dynamism resists formulaic application. Instead, judgment involves creativity and imagination; it may proceed differently in different situations.

Formulas cannot substitute for creative engagement because the judgments that arguers seek occur in situations of contingency. Arguers cannot know the potential outcomes of their decision-making with certainty, but they nevertheless strive to make decisions and plan their futures purposefully. The contingency of argument reflects the contingency of lives lived together. Individuals cannot guarantee their hopes and plans, and they do not all think alike. Johnstone (1965) held that argument places interlocutors "beyond the scope of effective control" (p. 1). Brockriede (1975) characterized the contingency of argument as operating in the "midrange of the more-or-less continuum" (p. 180). If issues and events seem too certain (such that particular outcomes seem destined) or if uncertainty appears overwhelming (such that purposeful engagement appears ineffective), then people may have no need for argument.

Argument entails reciprocal engagement, even if asynchronous and dispersed across a network. Reciprocal engagement refers to the active participation of all parties to an argument, which may entail attending to others' claims, values, identities, and more. Hauser (2007) discerned the emergence of publics in people's "active participation" (p. 335) in deliberative processes that develop around specific issues. Through their participation in such processes, people build and sustain the relationships that enable mutual recognition of the self and other. Recognition itself is a relational concept that requires acknowledgment of an other. For our subjectivities to appear as public, they must emerge as a collaborative project. These relationships may vary, exhibiting degrees of conciliation and conflict. If active participation entails attending to and recognizing other interlocutors, then the shape of participation itself also appears as a joint construction.

In the relationships of the familiar argument subject, perspective-taking plays a key role. Perspective-taking involves recognizing multiple perspectives on issues, events, and the world, and situating one's own perspective among these elements. Recognition entails active efforts to consider how these multiple perspectives may offer different, reasonable ways of thinking and acting that, even if not grounding for oneself, may be grounding for others. To achieve this understanding, arguers often must learn not just what other people believe, but why they believe it. Johnstone (1965) maintained that the person willing to consider others' arguments may encounter new possibilities: "Making [oneself] available to arguments, [a person] transcends the horizons of [their] own perceptions, emotions, and instincts" (p. 3). Perspective-taking does not eliminate judgment, but enables more flexible, creative judgments. Illuminating the normative force of this process, Hicks (2002) wrote that deliberation may successfully mediate multiple perspectives when "stakeholders transform their interests by hearing the ways in which the problem being addressed and the proposed solution affect others, by recognizing how their interests contribute to others' misery, and by realizing how reformulating those interests" (p. 225) may lead to a workable solution. Leading an arguer to attend to others, perspective-taking manifests active participation in argument.

As Hicks suggested, the promise of argument is the promise of transformation, although this promise entails risk. When individuals engage others in argument, their ideas, interests, positions, preferences, interpretations, and more may change. They may see themselves, their place in the world, and others differently. Yet change is risky, especially when that change concerns oneself. Natanson (1965) observed that a person risks oneself in argument because a person cannot control argument. Contingency remains. As Goodnight (2012a) explained, "Symbolic action cannot take away uncertainty as its basic enabling and constraining condition" (p. 259). Transformation and risk persist in tension. The reason is that transformation serves as an enticement to argument. Through argument, individuals may persuade others to adopt views and undertake actions they deem important. They may enable others to understand them and accept their differences as valuable. But individuals cannot exclude themselves from these same possibilities. When individuals argue, they build relationships that require the participation of others. Loving or hating their interlocutors, individuals may end an argumentative encounter as different people than when they began.

Reconceptualizing the Familiar Argument Subject Through a Multiple Public Sphere

The familiar argument subject carries important lessons that may enable argumentation scholars to imagine democratically oriented alternatives to neoliberal publics and subjects. Yet, to apply these lessons today, the field needs to reconceptualize the familiar argument subject in light of contemporary models of a multiple public sphere, which highlight difference and power to address issues of inclusion-exclusion and equality-inequality. My purpose is not to treat the familiar argument subject as a straw figure, charging it with naiveté or rebuking it as a cover for entrenched interests. Rather, argumentation studies need to reconsider this figure in light of contemporary concerns, practices, and developments. In this spirit, in her Alta keynote address, Palczewski (2002) called on scholars to expand our research into the dynamics of contemporary public argument. She discerned in counterpublic theory a critical project that would "expand not only the space for argument, but also what counts in argument" (p. 4). Reflecting on the 30th anniversary of the publication of his original "Spheres" article, Goodnight (2012a) called for "greater sensitivity to the hybrid range of vernacular and oppositional discourses constituting diverse publics" (p. 262). A reconceptualized argument subject heeds these calls.

Contemporary public sphere scholarship demonstrates that even as scholars may associate important qualities with arguers, they cannot assume that these qualities operate similarly for differently situated subjects. Instead, scholars need to attend to power and difference to illuminate the opportunities and constraints, advantages and disadvantages of diverse participants in a multiple public sphere. Scholars have foregrounded multiplicity to explore how people engage variously across networks of publics and counterpublics. Habermas (1996), responding to critics of his historical account of the bourgeois public sphere, conceptualized the public sphere as a "network" (p. 360). Across the networks of the public sphere, multiplicity facilitates engagement of different backgrounds, beliefs, and cultural traditions on public issues. No single individual can imagine all the perspectives that a group could generate. And, importantly, the identity of a person articulating a perspective may influence its meaning and uptake.[2] Far from innocent, degrees of influence may signal the operation of power.

Reconceptualizing the familiar argument subject, then, entails doing away with the universality and neutrality that appear in some of its articulations. For instance, in explicating the relationship of arguers, Brockriede (1986) identified interlocutors' goal as "warranted assertibility," which he described as "reaching consensus through reasoned arguments. Assertions must be warranted" (p. 62). Deemphasizing context, Brockriede (1986) associated his project with Perelman's notion of the "universal audience" and Habermas's "consensus theory of truth" as exhibiting a "drive toward universality" (p. 62). To the extent to which these theories move in this direction, they deflect attention from difference and power. Argumentation scholars may attend to these issues by complementing the micro-level, dyadic focus of scholars like Brockriede, Johnstone, and Natanson with the macro-level orientation that a multiple public sphere affords.

Whereas micro-level approaches take an argumentative encounter as their starting point, a macro-level orientation enables consideration of issues of inclusion-exclusion, that is, how interlocutors may access argument in the first place. Questions of access do not stop with formal participation, but consider who participates, when they may participate, and how they may participate. Even if advocates successfully remove formal barriers to entry of particular publics, they encounter implicitly and explicitly sustained modes of engagement. Some modes, such as a dispassionate style of speech, may serve as standard, while others function as irregular. Some issues may appear as subject to debate, while others may not appear on a public's agenda. Argumentation scholars should ask these questions of the familiar argument subject itself. For instance, discussing open-mindedness, which may motivate a person to seek out other perspectives, Johnstone (1965) attributed a world-making force to this quality: "The world is revealed only to an open-minded person" (p. 3). Even as scholars may endorse the practice of perspective-taking, they should consider how this practice may unfold. If perspective-taking facilitates learning, might some people be disproportionately tasked with learning about (and accommodating) other people, while these other people remain ignorant of their values, cultures, and beliefs? The modes of engagement that inform dominant publics may limit the reach of the open-mindedness that our field values in arguers.

Questions of inclusion-exclusion raise questions of equality-inequality, since conditions of access and the comparative standing of interlocutors are mutually informative. Moving between micro-level and macro-levels of argument, scholars may better understand how larger social contexts shape particular interactions, and how interlocutors may encounter one another on unequal ground. On this point, Brouwer (2006) explained how counterpublic theory *"requires recognition of resource disparities among social actors"* (p. 200). Illuminating material and symbolic disparities, the field of argumentation studies may better illuminate the dynamics of public engagement. In contrast to this move, Brockriede (1986) imagined an "ideal relationship" of arguers who seek "to establish power parity" as they "strive toward equality and at least *as persons* are peers" (p. 59). This exhortation recalls the status-bracketing of the bourgeois public sphere, by which interlocutors presumably ignore their inequalities (Fraser, 1992, p. 120). It reveals, too, the limits of an exclusive micro-level focus, since, as social formations, inequalities shaping any interaction extend beyond the interaction itself, thereby limiting the ability of interlocutors to strive toward equality. Any effort by interlocutors to strive towards equality in unequal conditions may downplay differences as unimportant. Striving towards equality may presume to level uneven burdens on interlocutors even as less powerful interlocutors often must assimilate to guiding norms and practices. A better approach may involve attending to inequalities and the larger social relationships that sustain them.

Inequality also may frustrate the familiar argument subject's ability to practice the characteristics scholars associate with this figure in relationship to others. Noting the tension attending transformation and risk, Johnstone (1965) nonetheless saw risk as essential for constituting the self: "There is a self only when there is risk [....] When people argue, they take risks that raise them above the level of immediate experience and put them on the map" (p. 6). Johnstone insisted that we all must take risks to appear as subjects, but, considering resource disparities, we should ask if risks are evenly shared across the networks of a multiple public sphere. Might resource disparities make differently situated people more or less willing to engage in argument? For example, societies may force people experiencing economic insecurity to assume greater risk in debating some issues than more prosperous potential interlocutors.[3] In this way, a neoliberal public may exacerbate the uneven practicing of risk.

A Neoliberal Public and Its Subjects

The neoliberal subject contrasts the qualities and virtues of the reconceptualized argument subject, lacking the motive and means to construct the democratic relationships that arguers may build together. As I mentioned in my introduction, scholars have invoked neoliberalism to refer to various ideas and developments. In some cases, neoliberalism names historical events. In others, it illuminates our contemporary era. With regard to history, the deployment of neoliberalism references the ideas of figures like Milton Friedman and Friedrich Hayek. Alarmed by the rise of the modern welfare state, they committed themselves to protecting individual liberty and free markets (Turner, 2007). Initially marginalized in place of the reigning Keynesianism of economics, their views of markets as social organizing principles eventually gained influence with politicians like Ronald Reagan and Margaret Thatcher (Jones, 2012; Peck, 2010). As a contemporary force, neoliberalism circulates through the networks of a multiple public sphere as its advocates argue for market solutions to public problems and promote market models of individual behavior. To the degree to which individuals readily accept claims about the innovative and empowering dynamics of markets, neoliberalism obtains the status of a common sense.[4]

While visions of deliberative democracy draw on some version of the familiar argument subject, a neoliberal public places the atomized individual at its center. In this spirit, in his 1962 book *Capitalism and Freedom*, Friedman (1962) wrote:

> To the free man, the country is the collection of individuals who compose it, not something over and above them [....] He recognizes no national purpose except as it is the consensus of the purposes for which the citizens severally strive.
>
> *(pp. 1-2)*

Disavowing anything "over and above" the individual, Friedman disavowed people's ability and interest in engaging one another to construct a collective "we." He dismissed people's ability and desire to develop shared purpose, coordinate action, and reach common judgments. Although involved in market activity, the neoliberal individual appears inimical to growth and development through human relationships. The neoliberal subject approaches the marketplace, which extends to the whole of society, from a strategic vantage point of relative advantage (Gershon, 2011; McNay, 2009; Mirowski, 2013). The neoliberal subject does not risk transformation. It may not always succeed in securing advantage, but it does not leave interactions as a transformed self. Others do not influence the self-understanding of the neoliberal subject. Other individuals' perspectives appear not as something that the neoliberal subject seeks to understand, but as information to factor into negotiating and deal-making. Judgment takes shape narrowly as calculation.

A neoliberal public defends freedom as its preeminent value, but this defense of freedom operates narrowly as the freedom of market actors. Joining together freedom and the individual, Friedman (1962) identified "freedom as the ultimate goal and the individual as the ultimate entity in society" (p. 5). Exemplifying the narrow application of these commitments, House Speaker Paul Ryan, in a February 2017 post on the need to repeal Obamacare, said, "Freedom is the ability to buy what you want to fit what you need. Obamacare is Washington telling you what to buy regardless of your needs." In this tweet, Ryan invokes freedom narrowly as the freedom of the consumer. His juxtaposition of "you" determining "what you need" against a "Washington telling you what to buy" asserts the primacy of the individual against the specter of the collective. By distributing costs and risks across populations, in this view, insurance actually coerces individuals to act against their interests. Insurance perpetuates a dangerous "over and above," in Friedman's terms. Neo-liberalism dissociates freedom from other democratic values of equality and justice, which underscore connections among individuals (Brown, 2015). Neoliberal freedom imagines a world of individuals alone shaping their destiny through autonomous action and voluntary interaction. Unlike the reconceptualized argument subject, neoliberal freedom takes no account of power relations: All individuals presumably have the same opportunities to enact freedom.

Without a conception of networked relationships that enable the formation of a collective "we" and coordinated action, a neoliberal public cannot account for engagement that exists beyond individual volition and voluntary contract. This failure to acknowledge the possibility of social change serves as an obfuscating move that entrenches powerful inter-ests, since it leaves such considerations as "the rules of the game" and the distribution of resources off public agendas for discussion and possible redress. The neoliberal subject can act *in* the market but cannot act to *change* the market. Instead, social change turns inward: The neoliberal public subject should change oneself to make oneself a more competitive market actor or, put another way, a better investment. With the market serving as the model for society generally, all of an individual's activities become meaningful through a self-investment lens. Economic activity encompasses "personal discipline" (Dardot & Laval, 2013, p. 165).

Insisting that the market treats everyone equally, and presuming that the same calcula-tions of advantage/disadvantage motivate all subjects, a neoliberal public recalls the bour-geois public in asserting its universality. The neoliberal public actor supposedly accounts for everyone: All members of a neoliberal public approach the market from the same place, act according to the same logic, and pursue the same goals. To be clear, these are stipulations, not empirical observations. Yet, whereas the bourgeoisie, according to Habermas, expressed some equivocation in the recognition that their universalism did not include access, contem-porary neoliberal advocates, like House Speaker Paul Ryan, charge ahead confidently in their belief that markets work the same way for everyone. Even as the neoliberal subject acts in a multiple public sphere, unlike the reconceptualized argument subject, the neoliberal subject represents its own mode of engagement as all-encompassing, effectively asserting a singular public.

In this move, the neoliberal subject ignores the uneven burdens that people differently situated in society face in trying to adopt its "universal" mode of engagement. With respect to gender, for instance, Brown (2015; see also Dingo, 2012; McKinnon, 2016) explained that neoliberal policies make life more difficult for women as they try to adopt the position of market actor. Disproportionately responsible for the familial activities that neoliberal advocates regard as outside of the market, women depend on the public infrastructure of childcare, healthcare, and other areas that neoliberal policy seeks to privatize. This type of work does not disappear under neoliberal policies, but is made invisible. On race, neoliberal ideology asserts a post-racial market society that reduces charges of racism to individual excuse-making (Jones & Mukherjee, 2010; Wingard, 2017). Recognizing and redressing racism requires recognition of broader categories that implicate agency in structure. Focusing on the atomistic individual, neoliberalism replaces a dialectic of agency and structure with an exclusive focus on agency.

In a neoliberal public, people relate to each other through the principle of competition, which treats social relations as a zero-sum game. An advantage one person acquires necessar-ily comes at the expense of another. As Mirowski (2013) observed, with competition as "the primary virtue," solidarity appears as "a sign of weakness" (p. 92). Neoliberal public subjects relate to others not as agents to engage reciprocally, but as obstacles to overcome. With fixed interests and without the potential for transformation with others, people relate to one another externally; they do not influence each other constitutively. Further, a neoliberal public draws upon and perpetuates inequality. In a context in which markets necessarily produce winners and losers, inequality serves as the motivation and end of public participation. Lazzarato (2009) observed that "only inequality has the capacity to sharpen appetites, instincts and minds, driving individuals to rivalries" (p. 117). By competing against others, members of a neoliberal public achieve hierarchical positioning. Dispensing with laissez-faire understandings of the state and economy, neoliberal advocates and policymakers enlist the state as an active agent in the fostering of competition by creating and expanding markets, and compelling people to behave as market actors (Schram, 2015).

How Argument Subjects and Deliberative Publics May Respond to Neoliberal Publics

The emergence of a neoliberal public is portentous, but its force is not totalizing.[5] I have critiqued a neoliberal public from the perspective of a democratic alternative. Argument scholars have demonstrated the power of democratic deliberation. In communities across the United States and elsewhere, ordinary citizens have resisted the encroachment and imposition of market models in what they have regarded as (properly) non-market activities. Advocates of deliberative publics may draw inspiration from movements like Black Lives Matter, from the willingness of people to fight for accessible and affordable health care, compassionate and just immigration policies, empowering and community-oriented public education, and more. Amidst these efforts, argument scholarship and pedagogy can play a positive role.

To the degree to which the field of argumentation studies illuminates the relationships among reconceptualized argument subjects in deliberative publics, both in terms of studies of actual practices as well as conceptual models, scholars may clarify the stakes of what neoliberalism portends for democracy. Individuals should understand that the neoliberal subject's putative disavowal of coordinated action does not preclude people from coordinating action, but may exacerbate obstacles for socially marginalized people to advocate for political change. Denying coordinated action and reciprocal relations hardens social life, heightens conflict among groups, and lessens the perceived value in accounting for people different from oneself. In denying the learning that public engagement may produce, one denies the productive power of difference. Denying judgment and perspective-taking denies personal reflection and increases the likelihood of self-alienation.

Democracy, in contrast, needs subjects who are willing to engage critically about their own views and the views of others. Democracy needs subjects committed to ideas and actions—that is, principled, purposeful—but who may see the limits of their perspectives and change their views when presented with compelling reasons by others. Democracy needs subjects who are willing to think about the potential consequences of their views and actions on others. In short, democracy needs the reconceptualized argument subject. To operate, this figure needs tending. We must explicitly construct and cultivate our relationships with others as argument subjects. Among other meanings, *tend* invokes attention, care, stewardship, cultivation, purpose, and expectation ("Tend," 2017). Tending to relationships, individuals may consider how to build them—with what values, qualities, and capacities and towards which ends.

If individuals tend to relationships, the limits of the neoliberal public provide opportunities for crafting deliberative publics. Opportunities arise because even as a neoliberal public revives the universalizing impulses of the bourgeois public sphere by envisioning "a world in which the only relationships are ones of competition," as Massey (2013, p. 11) observed, this vision cannot hold. Beyond competition, individuals find strength, joy, and affection in others (Chaput, 2010; Hawhee, 2015; Johnson, 2016). Individuals often want to coordinate their action with others. They identify with others in ways that exceed market logics. These feelings, actions, and identifications intimate solidarities that people may cultivate politically. The reciprocal relationships of argument may serve as a means of cultivation. Through the engagement of the reconceptualized argument subject, relationships may arise through the networks of the multiple public sphere.

Against the one-dimensional relationships of a neoliberal public, arguers may build variegated and enriching relationships within and across networked locals, as one potential site for change. By networked locals, I refer to directly and indirectly connected, spatially and temporally differentiated, offline and online sites of engagement that may resonate with the fluidity and dynamism of a multiple public sphere. My historical inspiration for turning to networked locals comes from Dewey (1954), who envisioned a remedy for the public's problems in the emergence of a Great Community, a diverse network of engaged local communities. Dewey hoped that a vibrant network of communities would productively draw on difference while guarding against the prejudice and provincialism that sometimes characterizes locales. My contemporary inspiration for turning to networked locals comes from witnessing the powerful advocacy of groups like Black Lives Matter and public education advocates in my state of Wisconsin. Challenging market orientations to public life, these advocates have practiced relationships that evince solidarity and reciprocal engagement. Practicing judgment and perspective-taking, they have articulated democratically oriented relationships that connect people as citizens and compatriots and coordinate action to address shared concerns.[6]

I conclude my address with a hopeful vignette that reveals both the pervasiveness of a market-oriented commonsense to public life and the potential for powerful responses to circulate widely (Selk, 2017). As Americans continue to debate the availability and affordability of health insurance, one argument circulating against its public provision is that people should pay only for services they use. For example, during a town hall held in a Dubuque, Iowa in May 2017, Rep. Rod Blum, an opponent of the Affordable Care Act, asked his constituents: "Why should a 62-year-old man have to pay for maternity care?" In response, Dubuque resident Barbara Rank wrote a letter to the local paper repeating the representative's question, then asking some more. Rank (2017) queried:

> I ask, why should I pay for a bridge I don't cross, a sidewalk I don't walk on, a library book I don't read? Why should I pay for a flower I won't smell, a park I don't visit, or art I can't appreciate? Why should I pay the salaries of politicians I didn't vote for, a tax cut that doesn't affect me, or a loophole [that] I can't take advantage of? It's called democracy, a civil society, the greater good. That's what we pay for.
>
> *(para. 1-4)*

Rebuking the individualist orientation of her representative, Rank called for judgment, perspective-taking, and reciprocal engagement. Building from the concrete local to a wider set of relations, she imagined robust, democratically oriented publics.

Notes

1 In a follow-up essay on public discourse published five years later, Goodnight (1987) explicitly brought together constitutive force and relationships, indicating that individual interaction and social formations may work together in "constituting human relationships in some ways and not others" (p. 428).

2 Young (2000, pp. 136-139) noted that "social perspectives" engender varied experiences, concerns, and questions for public deliberation.

3 Lenard (2010) argued that increasing economic inequality makes people more and less likely to make themselves vulnerable to others.

4 On this point, Hall and O'Shea (2013) wrote: "Everything becomes a commodity, and this aspect of our activities over-rides everything. In this way, a whole new way of seeing society (as a market) is coming into play. If developed, it could provide the cornerstone for a new kind of (neoliberal) common sense" (p. 11).

5 Among these lines, Honig critiqued Brown's account of neoliberalism for granting it too much power. Honig (2017) retorted, "if, as Brown thinks, again with good reason, we have *only homo oeconomicus* to guide us, then we will never work our way out of this mess" (p. 27).

6 Flower (2016) characterized "local publics" as "democracy's generative rhetorical space in which competing concerns arising out of lived experience are translated into controversial issues, which initiate local deliberation and set the process of change in motion" (p. 320).

References

Benhabib, S. (1996). Toward a deliberative model of democratic legitimacy. In S. Benhabib (Ed.), *Democracy and difference: Contesting the boundaries of the political* (pp. 67–94). Princeton, NJ: Princeton University Press.

Brockriede, W. (1975). Where is argument? *Journal of the American Forensic Association, 55*, 179–182.

Brockriede, W. (1986). Arguing: The art of being human. In J. L. Golden & J. L. Pilotta (Eds.), *Practical reasoning in human affairs: Studies in honor of Chaïm Perelman* (pp. 53–67). Dordrecht, The Netherlands: D. Reidel.

Brouwer, D. C. (2006). Communication as counterpublic. In G. J. Shepherd, J. St. John, & T. Striphas (Eds.), *Communication as…: Perspectives on theory* (pp. 195–208). Thousand Oaks, CA: SAGE.

Brown, W. (2015). *Undoing the demos: Neoliberalism's stealth revolution.* New York, NY: Zone.

Chaput, C. (2010). Rhetorical circulation in late capitalism: Neoliberalism and the overdetermination of affective energy. *Philosophy and Rhetoric, 43*(1), 1–25. doi:10.1353/par.0.0047

Dardot, P., & Laval, C. (2013). *The new way of the world: On neoliberal society* (G. Elliott, Trans.). London, United Kingdom: Verso Books.

Dewey, J. (1954). *The public and its problems.* Athens, OH: Swallow Press.

Dingo, R. (2012). *Networking arguments: Rhetoric, transnational feminism, and public policy writing.* Pittsburgh, PA: University of Pittsburgh Press.

Dunn, T. R. (2010). Remembering Matthew Shepard: Violence, identity, and queer counterpublic memories. *Rhetoric & Public Affairs, 13*(4), 611–652. doi:10.1353/rap.2010.0212

Flower, L. (2016). Difference-driven inquiry: A working theory of local public deliberation. *Rhetoric Society Quarterly, 46*(4), 308-330. doi:10.1080/02773945.2016.1194451

Fraser, N. (1992). Rethinking the public sphere: A contribution to the critique of actually existing democracy. In C. Calhoun (Ed.), *Habermas and the public sphere* (pp. 109–142). Cambridge, MA: The MIT Press.

Friedman, M. (1962). *Capitalism and freedom.* Chicago, IL: University of Chicago Press.

Gehrke, P. J. (2009). *The ethics and politics of speech: Communication and rhetoric in the twentieth century.* Carbondale, IL: Southern Illinois University Press.

Gershon, I. (2011). Neoliberal agency. *Cultural Anthropology, 52*(4), 537–555. doi:10.1086/660866

Goodnight, G. T. (1987). Public discourse. *Critical Studies in Mass Communication, 4*(4), 428–431. doi:10.1080/15295038709360154

Goodnight, G. T. (2012a). The personal, technical, and public spheres: A note on 21st century critical communication inquiry [Special issue]. *Argumentation and Advocacy, 48*(4), 258–267. Retieved from http://tandfonline.com

Goodnight, G. T. (2012b). The personal, technical, and public spheres of argument: A speculative inquiry into the art of public deliberation [Special issue]. *Argumentation and Advocacy, 48*(4), 198–210. Retrieved from http://tandfonline.com

Habermas, J. (1996). *Between facts and norms: Contributions to a discourse theory of law and democracy* (W. Rehg, Trans.). Cambridge, MA: The MIT Press.

Hall, S., & O'Shea, A. (2013). Common-sense neoliberalism. *Soundings: A journal of politics and culture, 55*(1), 8–24. Retrieved from Project MUSE database.

Hauser, G. A. (1999). *Vernacular voices: The rhetoric of publics and public spheres.* Columbia, SC: University of South Carolina Press.

Hauser, G. A. (2007). Vernacular discourse and the epistemic dimension of public opinion. *Communication Theory, 17*(4), 333–339. doi:10.1111/j.1468-2885.2007.00299.x

Hawhee, D. (2015). Rhetoric's sensorium. *Quarterly Journal of Speech, 101*(1), 2–17. doi:10.1080/00335630.2015.995925

Hicks, D. (2002). The promise(s) of deliberative democracy. *Rhetoric & Public Affairs, 5*(2), 223–260. doi:10.1353/rap.2002.0030

Honig, B. (2017). *Public things: Democracy in disrepair.* New York, NY: Fordham University Press.

Johnson, J. (2016). "A man's mouth is his castle": The midcentury fluoridation controversy and the visceral public. *Quarterly Journal of Speech, 102*(1), 1–20. doi:10.1080/00335630.2015.1135506

Johnstone, H. W., Jr. (1965). Some reflections on argumentation. In M. Natanson & H. W. Johnstone, Jr. (Eds.), *Philosophy, rhetoric, and argumentation* (pp. 1–9). University Park, PA: The Pennsylvania State University Press.

Jones, B., & Mukherjee, R. (2010). From California to Michigan: Race, rationality, and neoliberal governmentality. *Communication and Critical/Cultural Studies, 7*(4), 401–422. doi:10.1080/14791420.2010.523431

Jones, D. S. (2012). *Masters of the universe: Hayek, Friedman, and the birth of neoliberal politics.* Princeton, NJ: Princeton University Press.

Keith, W. M. (2007). *Democracy as discussion: Civic education and the American forum movement.* Lanham, MD: Lexington Books.

Kock, C., & Villadsen, L. (Eds.). (2012). *Rhetorical citizenship and public deliberation.* University Park, PA: The Pennsylvania State University Press.

Lazzarato, M. (2009). Neoliberalism in action: Inequality, insecurity, and the reconstitution of the social. *Theory, Culture & Society, 26*(6), 109–133. doi:10.1177/0263276409350283

Lenard, P. T. (2010). Rebuilding trust in an era of widening wealth inequality. *Journal of Social Philosophy, 41*(1), 73–91. doi:10.1111/j.1467-9833.2009.01479.x

Massey, D. (2013). Vocabularies of the economy. *Soundings, 54,* 9–22. doi:10.3898/136266213807299023

McKinnon, S. L. (2016). *Gendered asylum: Race and violence in U.S. law and politics.* Urbana, IL: University of Illinois Press.

McNay, L. (2009). Self as enterprise: Dilemmas of control and resistance in Foucault's *The birth of biopolitics. Theory, Culture & Society, 26*(6), 55–77. doi:10.1177/0263276409347697

Mirowski, P. (2013). *Never let a serious crisis go to waste: How neoliberalism survived the financial meltdown.* London, United Kingdom: Verso Books.

Natanson, M. (1965). The claims of immediacy. In M. Natanson & H. W. Johnstone, Jr. (Eds.), *Philosophy, rhetoric, and argumentation* (pp. 10–19). University Park, PA: Pennsylvania State University Press.

Palczewski, C. H. (2002). Argument in an off key: Playing with the productive limits of argument. In. G. T. Goodnight (Ed.), *Arguing communication and culture* (pp. 1–23). Washington, DC: National Communication Association.

Peck, J. (2010). *Constructions of neoliberal reason.* Oxford, United Kingdom: Oxford University Press.

Pezzullo, P. C. (2003). Resisting "national breast cancer awareness month": The rhetoric of counterpublics and their cultural performances. *Quarterly Journal of Speech, 89*(4), 345–365. doi:10.1080/0033563032000160981

Rank, B. (2017, May 12). Why should I pay indeed? [Letter to the editor]. *Telegraph Herald.* Retrieved from http://telegraphherald.com/news/public_announcements/article_824b24ac-3dbf-5390-8cf3-0c4a17b76dbb.html

Ryan, P. [@PRyan]. (2017, February 21). Freedom is the ability to buy what you want to fit what you need. Obamacare is Washington telling you what to buy regardless of your needs [Tweet]. Retrieved from https://twitter.com/pryan/status/834140136082284544?lang=en

Schram, S. F. (2015). *The return of ordinary capitalism: Neoliberalism, precarity, occupy.* New York, NY: Oxford University Press.

Selk, A. (2017, May 15). A congressman said making a man get maternity insurance was "crazy": A woman's reply went viral. *The Washington Post.* Retrieved from https://washingtonpost.com/news/the-fix/wp/2017/05/15/a-congressman-said-making-a-man-get-maternity-insurance-was-crazy-a-womans-reply-went-viral/?utm_term=.a2b3a06d7b86

Springer, S. (2012). Neoliberalism as discourse: Between Foucauldian political economy and Marxian poststructuralism. *Critical Discourse Studies, 9*(2), 133–147. doi:10.1080/17405904.2012.656375

Squires, C. R. (2002). Rethinking the black public sphere: An alternative vocabulary for multiple public spheres. *Communication Theory, 12*(4), 446–468. doi:10.1111/j.1468-2885.2002.tb00278.x

Tend. (2017). *Oxford English Dictionary*. Retrieved from http://oed.com/view/Entry/199029?rskey=jtTbbc&result=1

Turner, R. S. (2007). The "rebirth of liberalism": The origins of neoliberal ideology. *Journal of Political Ideologies, 12*(1), 67–83. doi:10.1080/13569310601095614

Van Horn, R., & Mirowski, P. (2009). The rise of the Chicago school of economics and the birth of neoliberalism. In P. Mirowski & D. Plehwe (Eds.), *The road from Mont Pèlerin: The making of the neoliberal thought collective* (pp. 139–178). Cambridge, MA: Harvard University Press.

Wapshott, N. (2011). *Keynes Hayek: The clash that defined modern economics*. New York, NY: W. W. Norton.

Wingard, J. (2017). Branding citizens: The logic(s) of a few bad apples. In K. H. Nguyen (Ed.), *Rhetoric in neoliberalism* (pp. 135–155). London, United Kingdom: Palgrave Macmillan.

Young, I. M. (2000). *Inclusion and democracy*. New York, NY: Oxford University Press.

PART I

SPOTLIGHTED THEORIES AND PRACTICES OF NETWORKING ARGUMENT

2

SUBSTANCE

An Exploration of the State of Argument in the Post-Fact Era

James F. Klumpp

Turns out I am something of a seer. In 2006, I wrote an essay titled "When Foundations Fail: Argument Without Institutions of Fact." Back then, considerable public discussion focused on how American political values had become so polarized. I argued that in fact the problem was not divergent values. "When argument stops," I observed, "the unbridgeable barrier is more often facts than values" (Klumpp, 2016, p. 52). Well, that essay had a rather winding journey to print, but finally reached e-publication in 2016. By that time, the punditry had migrated my direction. In the face of "fake news," "alternative facts," Fox News vs. MSNBC, and overloaded fact-checkers, facts were the new values.

But the essence of my argument in 2006 has been slower to reach the pundits. Indeed, the division on facts was the symptom, but the analysis showed that the twentieth century public resolved its disputes efficiently by granting authority to societal institutions that had since fallen into disfavor. When questions arose, the academy, the government statistical bureaus, and the media sought and supplied answers to resolve disputes.

The questions left open in my earlier essay were, what do we do once the institutions of fact have lost their authority? And, how do we then resolve disputes? Unfortunately, those questions have neither become moldy nor been answered in the intervening decade. In this essay, I want to contribute what I can to moving the field a step closer to answering them. My argument is that we do not currently have the framework for inquiry that will allow us to manage the quandary the questions present. In this essay, I urge an alternative vocabulary and structure to begin the project that admittedly will take considerable additional effort.

Perspective on the Problem: History and Theory

Let me begin by trying to put the relationship between fact and argument into some perspective. The early draft of my essay lamented the demise of an essential force for effective argument: a source of authoritative facts. But one of my graduate student colleagues, Jade Olson, read the manuscript and observed that I was guilty of overgeneralizing a historical variation. The twentieth century, she argued, may well have been a unique time when institutions of fact were available and dominant. She pointed out that already I had taught her the different ways that citizens had argued about policy and government in the nineteenth century. The tendency for hasty generalization always endangers an inductive inquiry, assuming a historical moment as the norm. I had fallen into the trap.

Of course, I was not the only researcher in argumentation to fall into that trap. My shelf was full of argumentation textbooks from throughout the twentieth century that constructed factual evidence as the beginning point for linear models of what Daniel O'Keefe (1977) called argument₁, or put another way, making an argument. The oldest argumentation text on my shelf, Andrew Fox's 1932 textbook, *Modern Debating*, for example, indicated, "Evidence is derived from three sources, 1) the testimony of 'fact witnesses' […]; 2) the testimony of competent 'authority'; [and] 3) from circumstance, where certain given facts support a fact to be established" (p. 41). Indeed, generations of academic debaters had, as their foundation, researched media and governmental sources for large volumes of evidence reporting facts to cite in support of claims regarding policy.

Some argumentation theorists, however, hinted at the contingency of argument from facts. Richard Weaver (1985), for example, declared, "facts are never dialectically determined" (p. 27), maintaining that the "reasoner reveals his philosophical position by the source of argument that appears most often in his major premise" (p. 55). Weaver differentiated facts into types and then arrayed the types into a hierarchy. The lowest of those types was what he termed "argument from circumstance" (p. 57), which corresponds to notions of material fact. Weaver, the favorite rhetorician of modern conservatism, favored arguments from definition or principle. Weaver's disparagement would, in fact, indict New Deal arguments grounded in factual circumstance

Kenneth Burke seethed because he thought he had discovered Weaver's conclusion first. In organizing the hierarchy of argument, Weaver had plagiarized Burke's (1969) project that identified philosophical positions by the origin of their reasoning in particular pentadic terms, at least in Burke's view. Thus, Burke read Weaver's position as: argument from scene is inferior to argument from purpose. Bernard Brock (1965) picked up the association of philosophies with political positions, but arrayed them across the political spectrum rather than into a hierarchy. His typology associated scenic argument with liberals and arguments from principle or purpose with reactionaries. Indeed, G. Thomas Goodnight described differences between conservative and liberal argument at the first Alta Conference in 1979. So, variations from dominant counsel that reasoning begins exclusively in facts has a longstanding history.

Other theorists have elaborated the predilection toward facts with refined typology. For example, Perelman and Olbrechts-Tyteca (1969), while still holding to the linear model for argument₁ and the idea that argument begins in agreements (p. 65), divided starting points into those concerning the real (e.g., facts, truths, and presumptions), and those concerning the preferable (e.g., values, hierarchies, and loci; p. 66). In addition, of course, they differentiated the universal audience—appeal could be general—from the particular audience who might acknowledge a starting point that other audiences would not consider (pp. 31-33).

All this theory testifies that the normative demand that all reasoning ought to proceed from a set of verifiable and widely accepted facts is not nearly as universal as the punditry—and to be fair, argumentation scholars—pretended. But teasing out the implications of that critique of normativity never quite came to fruition.

A Framework for Inquiry: Argumentative Ecology

The other thing noteworthy about the theoretical territory just reviewed is that it all concerns argument₁. The questions I posed—What do we do once the institutions of fact have lost their authority? How do we then resolve disputes?—instead implicate argument₂. O'Keefe (1977)

conceptualized argument$_2$ as "having an argument" (p. 121), but argumentation scholars should avoid this shorthand and recognize that what is at stake is how societies proceed, dependent upon argumentative exchange, to resolve differences of opinion and coordinate cooperative response to life situations. The questions I ponder and the direction that emerges must expand our gaze to circumscribe our focus on individual arguers within an inquiry into culture.

In 2009, I offered a project in meta-thinking to produce a perspective that might guide such study. I exploited the metaphor of ecology and termed the viewpoint "argumentative ecology." I explained,

> "Argumentative ecology" refers to both a mode of study and the artifact for that study. An argumentative ecology is an interaction of arguers and arguments sited in and producing a community of coordinated, reasoned action [... .] As a mode of study, argumentative ecology promotes study of argument as interconnected and evolving patterns of reason giving and coordination that structure human understanding and action. The study entails both the substance and the structure of arguing in particular human communities.
>
> *(Klumpp, 2009, p. 184)*

The first term in that last pair—"substance"—is the focus of this essay. I want to use the concept to expand our gaze. Let me set aside substance for a moment, however, and recall what I (2009) labeled "An Ecology of Democratic Argument" (p. 189). In democracies, argument is essential to the synthetic work that melds differences into a coherent culture. Thus, we want to understand argument as synthetic rather than analytic (see also Klumpp, 1993). We want to feature its power to negotiate difference into a working cooperation. Doing so compels three observations about democratic culture. First, arguments of great variety richly saturate democratic culture. Certainly, Aristotle's deliberative, forensic, and epideictic genres are present, but they only touch the surface. In republics, the public elects and judges its leaders. Arguments about the character of people are central to ethics and ethos. Facts, connections, relationships, values, principles, and good reasons saturate arguments. Second, the necessity to define the culture and guide its actions compels an intensity and urgency to democratic argument. Identity, conflict, and resolution all map onto the stream of argument. Third, democratic argument produces argumentative resources that persist, evolve, and infuse arguments going forward. Argument is not just in the moment but crosses time. Synthetic arguments exploit the resources we often label "beliefs," "values," "principles," "ethics," or "mores" to transcend time and bring history to bear in a moment.

This last thought prepares us to consider substance. What is it? Kenneth Burke (1969) will help us on that question. He worked etymologically, noting that the term lies in the stā- family, to stand. Sub-stance is thus what stands under (p. 22). Introducing substance to argument suggests that we complicate our traditional horizontal metaphor of linear argument in favor of a vertical metaphor in which we see argument building on a foundation that defines the argumentative culture. With Burke, we talk about argument transforming substance into new commitments to action even as they evolve in argumentative exchange. We are familiar with the notion that arguments entail risk from our maxim that arguers risk themselves in argumentative exchange (Brockriede, 1974, p. 166). But more than the arguer is at risk in an argument; so is the power of substance to generate and resolve dispute. That is, the power of substance has its roots in the culture's acknowledgment of its foundational place. When arguers invoke particular arguments, the argument's power emerges as reinforced or eroded, turning on the success of the argument in guiding the community wisely. This is the power substance brings to argument.

In defining "substance" we should also, of course, turn to another popularizer of that notion in our discipline, Karl Wallace. In his essay, "The Substance of Rhetoric: Good Reasons," Wallace (1963) defined substance by setting up two groups of what he called "correlative terms" (p. 240), indicating that the terms in one group were meaningless without the other. This same concept is what Kenneth Burke would call dialectical definition (1969, p. 33; 1969, pp. 183-89). On the one side, Wallace (1963) placed "substance, matter, material, content, or subject matter" (p. 240). On the other, he placed "form, structure, order, arrangement, organization, shape and figure" (p. 240) to which we might add argument. "There is also lurking," he noted, "the idea of substratum—of that which stands under, of support" (p. 240), thus invoking Burke's notion of substance. Wallace's fundamental argument was that theory "must deal with substance of discourse as well as with structure and style" (p. 240), thus our project.

Taken together, these two figures point to an understanding that argument supports claims by bringing together—synthesizing—substance into claim. The action here is not so much a linear advance—the way most of our thinking about argument was in the twentieth century—but synthetic—transforming substance into support for a claim. What this change highlights is the complex combinations of substance—stated and implicit—called into synthesis in argument$_2$. The magic of argument comes not simply from getting from one fact to another, but from drawing various substance into creating something new: invention through argument.

Rethinking Argument

Let me illustrate the expansiveness of this thinking by rehearsing a recent claim: Universal health insurance realizes the promise of preventive medicine. Inventing an argument to support this claim synthesizes many things. The argument calls upon the value that the society places upon health. It draws from a sense that part of the character of the United States is its compassion for those temporarily requiring the assistance of others. It also draws upon the potency of preventive medical procedures for improving health. And it calls upon a comfort with government assuming responsibility for bringing the society's values to all. An argument synthesizing these various threads into support for a particular government program actually calls upon values, facts, causality, character of the society, and practical concerns about approaches for achieving a just society. The force of the argument will transform the various substance invoked into support for the claim. Even when some of this substance is enthymematic in the articulation, it remains an empowering element.

Perhaps I can illustrate another facet of the problem by taking a point at issue in our public dialogue: the importance or wisdom of immigration. As various claims relate to this issue, arguers will assemble different substance to support each of their positions. Some will bring together evidence on job availability and immigrant pressure, a hierarchy that favors current citizens over new arrivals, nationalism itself with the attendant importance of controlling borders, and even the central role a satisfying job plays in the happiness of citizens. Others will assemble historical accounts of how immigrants have advanced our culture, the pervasiveness of the immigrant experience in forming our national character, and the empirically verified work ethic of immigrants. The foundation of other positions will synthesize other points of fact, value, connection, history, and character.

Of course, arguments are stronger or weaker, more effective or less effective, and more moral or less moral. Arguers invoke ideas about these criteria and their importance in judging arguments. Democratic texture, as well as other aspects of culture, requires hierarchies of argument quality.

I'll offer one final word on thinking synthetically versus analytically about arguments. Thorough critics could work analytically. They could laboriously take the arguments on health care or immigration and form a catalog of different arguments available on the issue. Still, when complete, the task would have provided a list, rather than a conceptualized way of thinking about how the various arguments in that archipelago reinforce or undermine each other. In short, thinking through the synthesis by bringing various substances into conjunction to give an argument force elevates awareness of the complex resources that enable responsible and productive argument.

So finally, return to our time when facts fail to synthesize the argumentative ecology. We are not without substance that can resolve our disputes and shape common approaches to living our lives. Changes in the demands on our argument imply changes in our strategies to synthesize substance into resolution. The "taken for granted" of another day may not qualify as the "taken for granted" for our own time. These are the times that call for expanding understanding of argument's synthetic power and for an expanding appreciation of the greater variety of claims and substance a democracy invokes. Democratic engagement flourishes in a rich soup of argument. If we draw our gaze at substance broadly, expanded awareness fuels the inventive power of argument. From a broader, more complex consciousness of the substance our society uses to understand and guide coordinated response emerges greater creativity to adapt to the world we encounter.

An Agenda

This essay set out to answer two questions: What do we do once institutions of fact have lost their authority? How do we then resolve disputes? I approached the questions by retreating from some of the assumptions built into the questions themselves. Our overly narrow focus on the authorized facts in argument is itself an artifact of a particular time and a particular approach to argument. It is a convenient simplification, but a simplification nonetheless. If we are going to set the simplification aside, I believe that we must have vocabulary and ways of thinking that will allow us to reconceptualize democratic argument's difficulties. I do not mean to dismiss the importance of facts, but grounding that importance properly requires a broader context.

Whether I have succeeded or not, providing this perspective on context has been the goal of this essay. I have built on others, including some of my own earlier work, to try to suggest a different understanding of argument: argument synthesizes substance—subject matter, material values, principles, hierarchies, good reasons, elements of physical and social context, and even Perelman and Olbrechts-Tyteca's (1969) real and the preferable—into support for claims. Argument arrays substance to advance the argumentative ecology's efforts to come to terms with their lives and their times. The assertiveness of argument is a symbolic advancing of risk, adjusting the moment to the past, and adapting the required to the familiar to provide guidance as life in the ecology moves forward.

But having set forth a perspective, argumentation scholars need to consider many refinements to understand the power of argument to enhance our argumentative ecology. Ahead is work with the metaphoric power of new vocabulary—ecology, synthesis, substance—terms that in analogous contexts suggest additional resources to point the way. In the end, the agenda is similar to any agenda of a defined perspective. We need to come to a historical understanding of how past arguments synthesized within our argumentative ecology. We need to come to a historical understanding of how the synthesis of argument in our argumentative ecology has worked in the past, including where it succeeded and failed. We need to come to a pedagogical understanding of how arguers contributing to our moment can achieve the quality of argument that the times require and they desire. We need to come to a critical understanding that allows us to point to failures and praise successes in the sort of corrective to ongoing life that criticism fosters. I invite you to join me in that rich quest.

References

Brock, B. L. (1965). *A definition of four political positions and a description of their rhetorical characteristics* (Unpublished doctoral dissertation). Northwestern University, Evanston, IL.

Brockriede, W. (1974). Rhetorical criticism as argument. *Quarterly Journal of Speech, 60*(2), 165-175. doi: 10.1080/00335637409383222

Burke, K. (1969). *Grammar of motives*. Berkeley, CA: University of California Press.

Burke, K. (1969). *Rhetoric of motives*. Berkeley, CA: University of California Press.

Farrell, T. B. (1976). Knowledge, consensus, and rhetorical theory. *Quarterly Journal of Speech, 62*(1), 1-14. doi: 10.1080/00335637609383313

Fox, A. N. (1932). *Modern debating: A debater's and speaker's guide*. Chicago, IL: Follott.

Goodnight, G. T. (1979). The liberal and the conservative presumptions: On political philosophy and the foundation of public argument. In J. Rhodes & S. Newell (Eds.), *Proceedings of the summer conference on argumentation* (pp. 304-337). Salt Lake City, UT: University of Utah Press.

Klumpp, J. F. (1993). A rapprochement between dramatism and argument. *Argumentation and Advocacy, 29*(4), 148-163. Retrieved from EBSCOhost database.

Klumpp, J. F. (2009). Argumentative ecology [Special issue]. *Argumentation and Advocacy, 45*(4), 183-197. Retrieved from http://tandfonline.com

Klumpp, J. F. (2016). When foundations fail: Argument without institutions of fact. In R. Von Burg (Ed.), *Dialogues in argumentation* (pp. 52-67). Windsor, Ontario: Windsor Studies in Argumentation. doi: 10.22329/wsia.03.2016

McGee, M. C. (1975). In search of "the people": A rhetorical alternative. *Quarterly Journal of Speech, 61*(3), 235-249. doi: 10.1080/00335637509383289

O'Keefe, D. J. (1977). Two concepts of argument. *Journal of the American Forensic Association, 13*(3), 121-128. Retrieved from http://dokeefe.net/pub/OKeefe77JAFA.pdf

Perelman, Ch., & Olbrechts-Tyteca, L. (1969). *The new rhetoric: A treatise on argumentation* (J. Wilkinson & P. Weaver, Trans.). Notre Dame, IN: University of Notre Dame Press.

Wallace, K. R. (1963). The substance of rhetoric: Good reasons. *Quarterly Journal of Speech, 49*(3), 239-250. doi: 10.1080/00335636309382611

Weaver, R. M. (1985). *The ethics of rhetoric*. Davis, CA: Hermagoras Press.

3

IDEOLOGY, ARGUMENT, AND THE POST-TRUTH PANIC

Dana L. Cloud

Our historical moment of rapid global warming, ongoing racism and police murders, mis-ogyny, war, and the most significant economic inequality in U.S. history demands discourse that is accountable to reality. We cannot concede ground to post–truth forces. However, here I expose two wrong ways for responding to the "reality crisis." One is to hunker down in the trenches of massive numbers of facts and hope that analysis of those facts will result in publics engaging in enlightened rational debate. The other is to give up entirely and embrace relativism, or the idea that no foundational reality exists, only the production in discourse of what "counts" as reality.

My argument is a challenge to scholars of argumentation who attempt to hold public discourse to empirical and rationalist standards. Researchers in our field should recognize the limits to rationalism, the reliance on facts, and the valorization of the good argument in pol-itical discourse. Aune (1994) faulted the Left for its love affair with the culture of critical discourse—and he was right in some ways. Speaking truth to power is not that clear-cut. And we avoid some of the affordances of right-wing rhetoric—affect, embodiment, myth, narrative, and spectacle—at our peril. Progressives and the Left are mired in the epistemic when our historical moment demands that we mobilize knowledge as common sense in the public domain.

At the same time, I am not making a relativist or post-dialectical turn in my thinking. In recent work, I advocate a rhetorical realism based on a theory of standpoint and mediation in the work of the Hungarian Marxist Georg Lukács (1968), supplemented by theories of mediation that scholarship on rhetorics of inquiry and science has developed. I argue that the Left has a particular and partisan mediating role—to intervene rhetorically and not just argumentatively (if we make such a distinction) in the space between experience and con-sciousness in ways that reach ordinary people beyond the level of the fact. We should embrace the affordances of affect, embodiment, myth, narrative, and spectacle either as modalities of argument or as supplements to propositional discourse.

Of course, these ideas are not new to those working on visual rhetoric, counterpublics or affective enclaves, for example. And, of course, the Left does not always ignore those means of persuasion. On July 19, 2017, immigrant rights organizers staged an unusual protest in Austin, Texas. Young women dressed in traditional gowns held a *quinceñera* on the Capitol grounds. The women's point was to highlight the contributions of immigrants to Texas culture and economy. The performance insisted on dignity and respect for Mexican culture and for immigrants in the context of severe legislative efforts to restrict immigration and criminalize immigrants living in Texas. Alanna Vagianos (2017) of *The Huffington Post* wrote,

> Organized by the Latinx advocacy group Jolt, the rally was called the "Quinceañera at the Capitol." The event's description on Facebook explained that Jolt chose to use quinceañeras as the theme of the protest because they are an important tradition that "highlight the bonds of family, community, culture and bring people together through celebration."

(para. 4)

In one moment of the protest a movement photographer captured, the women paraded around the rotunda of the Capitol building, at one point appearing one by one under portraits of historic, white, male Texas legislators. This moment employed the tactic that rhetorical scholar Kenneth Burke (1964) called "perspective by incongruity," startling viewers into the recognition of disparities of power that cultivate restrictive and oppressive immigration laws.

This protest employed rhetorical strategies of affect, embodiment, narrative, and spectacle to tremendous effect. In contrast to this event, I explore the limit and ideological function of the post-truth frenzy and the rise of fact-checking as a rhetorical form.

Figure 3.1 Immigrant rights protestors participating in a quinceñera in the Texas Capitol building on July 19, 2017 draw a sharp contrast to the portraits of white male legislatures adorning the walls. (jolttexas, Twitter, 2017)

Of course, our President is a big fat lying liar. But apocalyptic dread of a post-truth era predates his election and administration by more than a decade, if not centuries. *The New York Times* would have us believe, though, that Trump, uniquely, is "trying to create an atmosphere in which reality is irrelevant" (Leonhardt & Thompson, 2017, para. 4). But Trump is not the first or last President to lie to the people (consider President Johnson and the Gulf of Tonkin), and the accusation of "fake news" serves as a standard in every situation of political conflict in our nominally democratic society. So, if the crisis of truth is not of an historic scale, how do we explain the frenzy over facts?

The widespread outcry against the perjurious commander-in-chief constitutes what Hall, Critcher, Jefferson, Clarke, and Roberts (1978) called a "moral panic" (p. 18): "[a situation where] a condition, episode, person or group of persons emerges to become defined as a threat to societal values and interests" (Cohen, 1972, p. 1). Editors, scholars, politicians, clergy, and other experts diagnose a condition or problem and thus position themselves as the credible proposers of remedies—all located within a bounded set of political, economic, and cultural expectations. Discourses surrounding the objects of a moral panic are always ideological. They take a situation and mediate its interpretation and uptake in ways always imbricated with power.

If this rush to facticity is itself ideological, the embrace of mainstream journalism and the implicit support for Trump's major opponents, along with Hillary Clinton and the Democratic Party, are consequential. Such groups ask audiences to accept what they once knew were partial and interested accounts of reality as given fact. The corporate news media, once targets of ideology critique for their framing practices, become authoritative in a way that belies that critique. The cry of "fake news!" implies that audiences had—or ought to have had—some faith in the news before this historical moment as conveying "truth." Readers have taken thirstily to pro-corporate, traditional news sources as if those sources constituted fountains of undistilled, undiluted, clear political truths.

Avid fact-checking sustains and symptomatizes the moral panic. A July 2017 Google search of the term "fact-checking" returns more than 7 million results. And an explosion of efforts to "fact-check" political rhetoric has emerged, starting with those of the *Tampa Bay Times*'s PolitiFact project and the fact-checking blog of Glenn Kessler at *The Washington Post*. Graves, Nyhan, and Reifler (2015) of the American Press Institute documented this surge:

> Though precise figures are hard to come by, the available evidence tells a fairly dramatic story about the growth of fact-checking. One count early this year found 29 branded fact-checking ventures in the U.S., all but five of which were established since 2010 [....] almost every major national newsroom has embraced the genre in some way. The list of outlets that engage in some form of fact-checking includes elite standard-bearers like *The New York Times, The Washington Post,* the Associated Press, and National Public Radio as well as *USA Today,* the three major broadcast networks, CNN, Fox, and MSNBC.
>
> *(p. 1, emphases added)*

Journalists who perform fact-checking investigate a politician's claim and rate it on some sort of "truth-o-meter" scale from "true" or "mostly-true" to "pants on fire!" (referring to the children's rhyme, "liar, liar, pants on fire!"). These noble efforts belie the critical limits of efforts attempting to document myriad falsehoods without taking on the values frames and political perspectives that set the conditions for the productions of "truths." In short, telling the truth—and telling truth from lies—is not a simple task, as both truth and falsehood are complex and multidimensional.

As Marxist theorist Raymond Geuss (2008) argued, falsehood is not only a matter of empirical misrepresentation. I advocate a rhetorical perspective that acknowledges the *mediation* of all truth claims, or in other words, that society filters such claims through perception, interpretation, and explanation of people with varying power and perspectives. Any account of falsehood needs to account for the relationship between truth claims and power. While, as Geuss argued, a category of *epistemic* falsehood exists that refers to simple lies, he noted that ideology—or the pattern of commonsense ideas that frame and inform ideas and behavior—can also be false in a *functional* way, in which plausibly true ideas can function nonetheless in the service of oppressive power. Geuss (2008) argued most controversially that critics of ideology could legitimately fault a claim on the basis of who was making it. In other words, what scholars in argumentation studies often discredit as the "genetic fallacy" (Damer, 2012, p. 99)—the idea that the motivation of an arguer can discredit an otherwise reasonable claim—is not a fallacy in every case.

What appears to a conservative as perversion is the condition of freedom for a transgender person. What appears as the smooth operation of free enterprise to the employer can function as alienation and exploitation for the employee. A manager attempting to mediate the worker's experience to induce cooperation need not deny the work process, pay, or conditions, but her claims should be suspect on the basis of her motivation. The framing of experience in line with what are the employer's motivated interests is genetically false to the interests of the workers. However, mobilizations of affect and experience that exhibit fidelity to those interests also appear. Fact-checking by definition, because it denies the perspectival character of knowledge, meaning, and truth, is not faithful to those interests.

By way of illustration, I will examine a 3200-word article (Kiely, 2016) where *FactCheck.org* took on a critical inspector general's report on presidential candidate Hillary Clinton's use of personal phones for emails in her role as Secretary of State. The article examined in painstaking detail every subcategory of the report's main claim that Clinton was wrong to use her personal email for official business. Describing the fact-checking process, Kiely (2016) examined at great length Clinton's claims that her use of personal email was "allowed by the State Department" (para. 16), "fully complied" (para. 24) with department regulations, and was the same thing as what had been done by her predecessors. An update at the bottom of the article corrects a quotation from a campaign spokesperson:

> Fallon, the Clinton spokesman, said "[the Clinton campaign] agree in retrospect" with the IG finding that "her practice of copying aides on her emails did not end up producing a full record since State's IT systems didn't save everything." But that doesn't mean she didn't take steps to comply.
>
> *(para. 28)*

Like all formal fact-checking attempts, this article relies on the empiricist assumption that measuring public statements against an absolutely certain reality is possible and that producing discourse that corresponds with reality is also possible. The conclusion's equivocality in acknowledging how the process of confirmation and refutation relies upon actors' (the IG report, campaign staffers) statements or representations of reality undermines this assumption. In other words, every attempt to get at the facts of the matter necessarily relies upon mediation and interpretation.

However, the most significant limitation of this instance of fact-checking and of this practice in general is the narrowness of focus. If one were to ask a potential and undecided voter what concerned her about the Clinton email scandal, she might well respond: Is she trustworthy? Did she imperil national security? Did she lie intentionally? Can I trust her to be an ethical com-mander-in-chief? Fact-checking refuses to ask or answer these sorts of questions.

The basic idea is that neutral facts are not just inadequate to establish truth, but they are also ideological. Paradoxically, the "non-frame" claims of fact-checking, or the idea that we have access to unmediated truth, is itself a rhetorical frame (the non-frame frame) that redeems two capitalist institutions: the Democratic Party and the corporate news industry. The hype about the post-truth moment suggests that the commercial media had always been on the side of truth and light. Trump's election and the post-truth panic have thus let the media—and all of the ideological work they have done his-torically—off the hook.

As in the case of *The New York Times*, major papers across the country have painstakingly documented the President's lies. Shortly after the presidential election, *The Washington Post* added the pretentious phrase to its masthead: "Democracy dies in darkness." The origin of the phrase dates back to Bob Woodward's and Carl Bernstein's reporting on Watergate. But what is the implication of this statement today? Is the meaning that *The Washington Post* and all the other corporate media outlets are suddenly the source of democracy itself?

And what about the politicians? On May 2, 2017, *The Huffington Post*'s Paige Lavender (2017) reported:

> Former Secretary of State Hillary Clinton said she's not standing down after her loss to Donald Trump in the 2016 presidential election. "I'm back to being an activist citizen—and part of the resistance," Clinton said during an interview at a Women for Women event in New York Tuesday.
>
> *(para. 2)*

In short, the post-truth panic has redeemed the political establishment as it stood before the 2016 presidential election. Prior to the election, progressives, liberals, and conservatives had significant doubts about the capacity of Clinton to represent the interests of ordinary people —as evidenced by the success of the Sanders' campaign in winning the allegiance of more than 2 million young voters, more than twice as many as either Clinton or Trump during the primary season. The panic over facts repositions Clinton as, in her words, the candidate of the "resistance," not just of the lesser of two evils (Burns, 2017, para. 1).

In addition, the panic propagates a culture of elitism among liberals who believe that the lack of facts among ignorant Americans resulted in Trump's victory. The main aim of fact-checking, like other "lectureporn" (Penney, 2017), is confirming the moral and intellectual superiority of its enlightened practitioners who take pleasure in nodding their heads and laughing about Trump's lies and his base's ignorance.

Toward a Rhetorical Realism

Converts to the post-truth panic ridicule those they consider wrong; they also convince their followers that matters of truth and falsehood are simple. The result is an ideological "non-frame" frame that denies the perspectival character of knowledge and belief, thereby denying the operation of power that circulates as accepted truth. Just as the media and political system deny societal class divisions, the ideology of fact-checking denies that the experience and inter-pretation of reality could also diverge along class lines. In other words, fact-checking is a process that denies its own rhetoricity. The *fact* of fact-checking actually prevents the expansion of crit-ical thinking by implying nothing exists beyond "just the facts." Following Elster's (1985) frame-work of ideological discourses, fact-checking is palliative, as audiences take comfort in thinking that meaningful checks can test the truthfulness of politicians. In this way fact-checking is itself an example of ideological control. It is well intentioned, but in a very real sense, it lies.

Liberals agitated by the crisis of facts perpetuate the ideological faith in the possibility of apolitical neutrality based on objective facts. Penney (2017) explained the elitist implications of liberal investments in "the truth":

> The level of cognitive dissonance here is incredible. There is no such thing as political neutrality. And this ideological contradiction creates a major problem: the fetishization of rationality. The fetishization of rationality means you think reasonableness paves the road to political office and, on an individual level, that anyone who opposes you is an idiot who can't understand reality.
>
> *(para. 11)*

Rationalism is thus an ideological feature—an elitist, narcissistic one—of the Left. At the same time, relativist stances that suggest that no foundational reality exists independent of subjective perceptions are impoverished due to their inability to make moral and political judgments about competing accounts of reality and truth. A "rhetorical realism" embraces the idea that reality exists, even if none of us can know it except through frames of mediation from politicians, activists, pundits, the mass media, and social movement organizations. The necessity of mediation means that we cannot simply put "facts" in front of audiences and expect them to respond in a meaningful political way.

Between rationalism and relativism, rhetorical realism identifies and deploys epistemic resources. It utilizes "scientific" knowledge alongside lived experience, and it mobilizes knowledge in rhetorical modalities in a way to succeed in throwing one's claims over the transom of the epistemic to circulate as common sense. However, a rhetorical realism does not concede all grounds for truth claims to the operations of power or to the universalism of Aune's red republicanism. A rhetorical realism should try to establish the fidelity of a commonsense construct to the interests of those individuals society exploits and oppresses, whose experiences, in reality, are the conditions of possibility for alternative realities and the rhetorics they generate.

The participants in the quinceañera protest danced to the songs "Immigrants (We Get the Job Done)" and "Somos Más Americanos." The activists delivered flowers and flyers describing how the bill affects their communities to legislators who voted in favor of it. In a complex negotiation of traditional gender roles and beauty standards, the women addressed politicians who denied the realities of immigrant life in Texas.

Participant Magdalena Juarez, 17, told a journalist, "If lawmakers want to attack and criminalize us, then we will fight back. We will resist through celebrating our families and our culture" (quoted in Linan, 2017, para. 4). Juarez indicated an implicit rhetorical awareness of the significance of promoting one's cultural experience and knowledge about political oppression in narrative and spectacle. Doing so did not make her truths any less real—it simply made them rhetorical. No amount of fact-checking about immigration, crime, and employment can win the day against punitive legislation, but maybe the rhetorical realism of these young women made a start.

References

Aune, J. A. (1994). *Rhetoric and Marxism*. Boulder, CO: Westview Press.

Burke, K. (1964). *Perspectives by incongruity*. Bloomington, IN: Indiana University Press.

Burns, A. (2017, May 2). Clinton, denouncing Trump, calls herself "part of the resistance. *The New York Times*. Retrieved from https://www.nytimes.com

Cohen, S. (1972). *Folk devils and moral panic*. London, United Kingdom: MacGibbon & Kee.

Damer, T. E. (2012). *Attacking faulty reasoning* (7th ed.). Boston, MA: Wadsworth.

Elster, J. (1985). *Making sense of Marx*. London, United Kingdom: Cambridge University Press.

Geuss, R. (2008). *Philosophy and real politics*. New Brunswick, NJ: Princeton University Press.

Graves, L., Nyhan, B., & Reifler, J. (2015). *The diffusion of fact-checking: Understanding the growth of a journalistic innovation* [White paper]. Retrieved April 22, 2017 from IssueLab: http://www.issuelab.org/

Hall, S., Critcher, C., Jefferson, T., Clarke, J., & Roberts, B. (1978). *Policing the crisis: Mugging, the state, and law and order*. New York, NY: Palgrave.

jolttexas. (2017, July 20). Thanks @time for posting this photo of these brave Latina activists in the Capitol demanding the respect and dignity that our community deserves! [Photograph]. Retrieved from https://www.instagram.com/p/BWxt5FdFxKa/

Kiely, E. (2016, May 27). IG report on Clinton's emails. *FactCheck*. Retrieved from http://www.factcheck.org/2016/05/ig-report-on-clintons-emails/

Lavender, P. (2017, May 2). Hillary Clinton: I am "part of the resistance." *The Huffington Post*. Retrieved from http://www.huffingtonpost.com/entry/hillary-clinton-resistance_us_5908cb4de4b0bb2d0872763d

Leonhardt, D., & Thompson, S. A. (2017, July 21). Trump's lies. *The New York Times*. Retrieved from https://www.nytimes.com/interactive/2017/06/23/opinion/trumps-lies.html

Linan, A. (2017, July 19). Texas teens hold quinceañeara protest of SB 4 at Capitol, walk to lawmaker offices. *Austin American-Statesman*. Retrieved from http://www.statesman.com

Lukács, G. (1968). *History and class consciousness*. Cambridge, MA: The MIT Press.

Penney, E. (2017, June 26). Lectureporn: The vulgar art of liberal narcissism. *Paste*. Retrieved from https://www.pastemagazine.com

Vagianos, A. (2017, July 20). Teen girls protest Texas immigration bill with powerful quinceañera rally. *The Huffington Post*. Retrieved from http://www.huffingtonpost.com/entry/teen-girls-protest-anti-immigration-bill-outside-of-texas-capitol-with-powerful-quincea%C3%B1era-rally_us_5970dbf0e4b062ea5f9075e3

4

A MATERIALIST PERSPECTIVE ON ARGUMENT NETWORKS AS CONTENTIOUS POLITICS

Ronald Walter Greene

Traditionally, a rhetorical perspective on argumentation attends to the "symbolic means (primarily language) by which people try to influence one another's beliefs, values, and actions" (Wenzel, 1990, p. 15). Greene and Hayes (2012) advanced a more materialist orientation for a rhetorical perspective on argumentation, claiming it should be less concerned with symbolic action and attend more to argumentation as "a socially productive, and therefore, contingent, human technology" (p. 191). Rose (1989) described human technologies as "the calculated organization of human forces and capacities, together with other forces—natural, biological, mechanical—and artifacts—machines, weapons—into functioning networks of power" (p. 8). As a human technology, argument is likely always bundled with non-human agents and exists as a way to govern a self and others (Greene, 1998; Greene & Hicks, 2005).

A second consequence of this materialist perspective is that argument, as a human technology, exists as a mode of communicative labor (labor-power, to be more precise) valuable for the production and reproduction of human needs (Greene, 2004; Greene & Hayes, 2012; Greene & Nelson, 2014). An important human need that argumentative labor accounts for is the management of disagreement (Wenzel, 1990). As such, argumentative labor expresses "reasoning-in-interaction" (Lewiński & Mohammed, 2015, p. 291). Rhetorically-based argumentation scholars often approach this reasoning from within the social context of controversy (Olson & Goodnight, 1994). Thus, the claims-making activities participate in a mode of contentious politics. Tarrow (2011) defined contentious politics as "what happens when collective actors join forces in confrontation with elites, authorities, and opponents around their claims or the claims for those they claim to represent" (p. 4).

A third consequence of a materialist perspective is that arguers can register their arguments in different modalities of reasoning and media. As collective action, argumentative labor is embedded within different historical processes, political opportunities, and cultural contexts. To that end, those interested in argumentation should appreciate Michael Gilbert's (1994) multi-modal approach to argumentation. Gilbert extended the modes of argument beyond the logical (with an emphasis on the linguistic and the rational) to the realms of the emotional (the realm of feelings), the visceral (the physical), and the kisceral, a mode of argument he associated with the intuitive and non-sensory (p. 164).

Digital convergence interacts with other social forces bringing about the de-differentiation of modern life. In so doing new hybrid forms of public and private connection come together in mediated spaces of social interaction (Papacharissi, 2010, pp. 161-167). As Pfister (2010) noted, "networked digital media" create "new opportunities" to produce and criticize argumentation "with an unprecedented degree of publicity and interconnectivity" (p. 64). One consequence of the scale and speed of networked interactivity is the constitution of new publics escaping the territorial boundaries of the nation-state. Winkler (2015) emphasized how "circulating constellations of argumentative practices work to constitute groups of strangers who form, and subsequently function as, sub-national or trans-national collectives" (p. 5). However, as Winkler's (2015) research on the circulation of jihadi videos demonstrated, the emergence of new networked publics may be indifferent to the democratic norms often associated with the celebration of multiple publics and/or counter-publics. In contrast, the intensive and extensive effects of new communication technologies suggest that argumentation scholars approach the social dimensions of networked argumentation as an expression of "the network society, characterized by the pre-eminence of social morphology over social action" (Castells, 2010, p. 500). As a social morphology, Castells (2010) meant that a "networking logic substantially modifies the operation and outcomes in processes of production, experience, power, and culture" (p. 500). If so, the media ecology of networked argument may not only work against the norms of deliberative democracy, it may prefer more affective/emotional modes of reasoning (Harsin, 2014). From a materialist perspective, since the communicative labor of argumentation finds itself dispersed across different social processes, argumentation scholars may find added benefit from a focus on argument's role in contentious politics rather than the normative assumptions of public(s) (sphere) theory.

To better account for argument's role in contentious politics, the central claim of this essay is that the "networking logics" of argument should not limit the study of networks to its computational forms and digital technologies of interaction. Argumentation scholars should insist on the different material modalities in which networks of different kinds form and how argument networks confront other networks. For this reason I prefer the concept of "argument networks" to "networked argument." An argument network, I advance, posits that communicative networks increasingly materialize the production, circulation, and reception of arguments. Over thirty years ago, Monge (1987) identified four kinds of social networks: personal, group, organizational, and inter-organizational (p. 241). An argument network may traverse each of these network levels. If a communicative network describes the "patterns of contact that are created by the flow of messages among communicators through time and space" (Monge & Contractor, 2003, p. 3), argument networks focus on the flow and form of claims-making activities among and between different network levels as those networks orient themselves to collective action. In contrast, networked argument, and its big sister "networked rhetoric," describes how digital technologies provide a platform for argumentative practices. To be sure, argument networks and networked arguments inform one another, just as other media technologies have done so in the past. The value of the analytical distinction between argument networks and networked argument is important, nonetheless, because it allows argumentative networks to incorporate different kinds of networks into its contentious politics. Furthermore, it avoids having digital technologies enclose the potential values of argument. For as Goodnight (2012) argued, such a digital capture is extremely dangerous for the critical and participatory dimensions of argument: "The habituating of publics to communication technologies creates network divides, expands institutional surveillance, and saturates life with instruments that secretly measure, control, and feed desire" (p. 265). The digital has a role to play, but this role requires attending to its specific situational variation in how argument networks generate contention and confrontation. A rhetorical perspective on argumentation requires a stitching of digital arguments to the contentious politics of an argument network. This paper will unfold in two parts: First, it will blend insights from network theory and social movement theory to appreciate the conceptual value of an argument network. Second, it will provide a brief description of the organizing of "Indivisible" groups to resist President Trump's political agenda.

Argument Networks

How might argumentation scholars begin to think of an argument network? At a minimum, argument networks make claims to express a disagreement. Since argument networks emphasize disagreement as a mode of contentious politics, they participate in a rhetoric of confrontation (Scott & Smith, 1969). As a mode of interaction, argument networks are bilateral (Ehninger, 1970), assuming the participation of audiences as active interlocutors. In so doing, arguers are potentially both speakers and audiences adapting to one another's moves. Yet, as Lewiński and Mohammed (2015) noted, the bilateral nature of argumentation might be too dialogic (or dyadic) for the present media environment. They advanced the claim that argument networks are polylogues: consisting of "*multiple parties* [...] around *multiple issues* [...] attentive to achieving *multiple* argumentatively-relevant *goals* and to managing *multiple* levels of *addressees*" (p. 295). One might borrow the terminology, if not also the mathematics, of graph theory to map the topography of argument networks as a set of nodes connected by lines (or edges). The multiplicities that make up an argument network suggest the possibility that the nodes of the network might be different depending on whether the analysis begins with the issues, the parties, the goals, or the levels of address, but the claims are likely the edges that connect speakers and audiences as nodes. Moreover, the multiple parties in disagreement gesture to the existence of different lines that may connect to different argument networks drawn into contention/confrontation with one another.

To approach argument networks as contentious and confrontational is to implicate argument networks in networks of power. The Foucauldian inspiration for the materialist perspective informing this paper approaches the network as less centralized and hierarchical and more distributed and dispersed across different domains of governance (Greene, 1998). Yet, for Castells (2010), one of the fault lines of a network society fell between the "space of flows and the space of places" (p. 453). He argued that "the dominant tendency is toward a horizon of networked, ahistorical space of flows, aiming at imposing its logic over scattered, segmented places, increasingly unrelated to each other, less and less able to share cultural codes" (p. 459). For Castells, network power participated in the space of flows and its force registered in its ability to include and exclude the space of places into its space of flows. Moreover, the ways different places integrate into the space of flows constrains and enables the actions of those places to affect the logics embedded in the space of flows. If network power is more than a metaphor, then one should appreciate how different argument networks participate in different networks of power. This requires critics to avoid assuming only one kind of network topography relates to power (centralized, hierarchical) while another (decentralized, distributed) relates to resistance (counter-power). As Galloway and Thacker (2007) commented, "Networked power has learned from history and may use all varieties of authority and organization: centralized, decentralized, distributed, violent, coercive, desiring, liberating, and so on" (p. 18). The point of the materialist perspective is not so much to demystify the power relationships within and among argument networks as much as it is to account for how argument networks distribute claims making activities across human and non-human agencies pulling different kinds of networks together to disrupt different ways of governance. Argument networks have no pre-determined political orientation. For Dingo (2012), to appreciate how arguments networked was to "demonstrate the complex ways that rhetorical appeals reach a diffused yet linked audience while also accounting for how contiguous power relationships add meaning and force to arguments" (p. 18). I would only add that power is not simply contiguous to an argument network but immanent to its form and content. Argument networks are forms of networked power that are stronger or weaker depending on their composition, political opportunities, and their ability to mobilize action to "enable a particular end" (Cox, 2010, p. 123).

Indivisible as an Argument Network

By way of illustration, a group of U.S. congressional staffers uploaded a Google Doc titled "Indivisible" after the election of Donald Trump as the 45th President of the United States (Indivisible Project, 2017). It went viral after one of the authors posted the guide to his Twitter account and it gained the attention of some famous people and different media organizations (Bethea, 2016). The Indivisible Project claims the formation of over 5000 "indivisible groups" to resist the Trump agenda. The Indivisible Project registers as a 501(c)(4) nonprofit organization that can use its operating budget without limit for lobbying purposes and/or to support candidates.

The "Indivisible Guide" (hereafter the Guide) is a useful rhetorical artifact for trying to account for the different elements that make up an argument network. At the most abstract level, its speakers consist of members of local indivisible groups, but it also includes the organizational form of the Indivisible Project and rhetorical actions of each group as a collective actor. Argumentative agency functions as a distributed commodity across the different nodes of its argument network including individuals and groups throughout the United States. The Guide encourages each indivisible group to orient is collective action to target members of Congress (hereafter MoCs) as its primary audience for its contentious claims. It promotes a core set of advocacy tactics targeting different occasions: town halls, local public events, district office visits, and coordinated calls. As to the question of proposed change (effects), its purpose is to stop the Trump agenda.

Though Indivisible uses digital networks to publicize, circulate, organize, educate, and mobilize collective action, it relies on the use of personal, group, organizational, and inter-organizational networks to compose itself as a group. The Guide noted the role of personal networks, including those that are mediated: "If you are reading this, you're probably already part of a local network of people who want to stop the Trump agenda—even if it's just your friends or a group on Facebook" (Indivisible Project, 2017, p. 2). The Guide also suggested the furtherance of group level networks. To the question "Should I Form a Group?," the Guide answered: "There's no need to reinvent the wheel—if an activist group or network is already attempting to do congressional advocacy along these lines, just [join] with them" (p. 12). Argument networks generate and borrow from advocacy networks, issue networks, and policy networks. The common denominator is that "these networks consist of more or less organized actors who in synergy try to achieve a shared political end-result" (Oermen, 2012, p. 3). Personal/social networks and group networks take center stage in the Guide's organizing logics. When forming a group, the Guide encouraged one to "identify a few additional co-founders [...] ideally, these are people who have different social networks from you so that you can maximize your reach" (Indivisible Project, 2017, p. 13). Furthermore, to diversify an indivisible group, the Guide called on people to reach though one's "own networks" to communities most vulnerable to Trump's agenda and to form "relationships with community groups that are already working on protecting the rights of marginalized groups" (p. 15).

As an argument network, any specific Indivisible group exists as a "network local" (Asen, 2017) in two senses. First, advocates target specific MoCs in their own electoral locations (Indivisible Project, 2017). In contrast, the Guide specifically argued against disruptive action outside of an Indivisible group's electoral geography. It is the rhetorical pressure of local constituents that provides strategic leverage by providing the advocates "a place to stand within a system of power" (Cox, 2010, p. 128). Second, since the Guide encouraged local action at specific public settings (e.g., town halls), they generate the appearance of the "network local" in public. The bodies and voices of resistance occupy these public yet local spaces. In this sense, argument networks do different things than generate new forms of private/public sociality. As agents of advocacy, argument networks organize connection to generate confrontation and contention. The public encounter provides a "certain energy to re-direct the momentum of forces at this site" (Cox, 2010, p. 128). The Guide encouraged the use of digital platforms as a means of communication. For example, it mentioned the creation of a Facebook group, a Google group, or Slack Team "in order to coordinate actions" (Invisible Project, 2017, p. 15). It also encouraged groups to consider the use of "secure or encrypted platforms" (p. 15) to limit the audience of the group's internal communication. But, Indivisible groups harness this use and regulation of social connections for the purpose of organizing and mobilizing scenes of public contention.

In the language of network theory, Galloway and Thacker (2007) argued leverage requires an "exploit": "a resonant flaw designed to resist, threaten, and ultimately desert the dominant paradigm" (p. 21). The Guide approached the exploit as the MoCs' need to maintain an image of constituent care: "Constant reelection pressure means that MoCs are enormously sensitive to their image in the district or state, and they will work very hard to avoid signs of public dissent or disapproval" (Indivisible Project, 2017, p. 8). Activating the exploit requires linking indivisible groups to MoCs in light of the electoral geography and election time-tables of Congressional districts and state-wide Senate campaigns. Social movement scholars are well aware of the limits of the "election exploit" (Greene-May, 2011), but the election exploit, in this case, provides an occasion for the strategic maneuverability of an argument network.

Indivisible is more than a networked argument (a Google doc and website) because it builds an argument network by layering different networks into its organizing logic. The communicative labor of building local indivisible groups is then put to the purpose of contentious politics in an effort to block the Trump agenda. Leonhardt (2017) reported some success of the network. Indivisible exploits the link between the local and the national by focusing its claim-making activity at places and occasions where constituents and MoCs meet. Thus, Indivisble illustrates how argument networks materialize the social action of argument as a network of power in resistance to the Trump presidency. Moreover, argument networks are likely to intensify their influence when they escape their digital enclosure so as to organize bodies and voices of confrontation into public space.

References

Asen R. (2017, July). *Disavowing networks, affirming networks: Neoliberalism and its challenge to democratic deliberation.* Paper presented at the Biennial NCA/AFA Summer Conference on Argumentation, Alta, UT.
Bethea, C. (2016, December 16). The crowdsourced guide to fighting Trump's agenda. *The New Yorker.* Retrieved from http://newyorker.com

Castells, M. (2010). *The rise of the network society* (2nd ed.). Oxford, United Kingdom: Wiley-Blackwell.

Cox, J. R. (2010). Beyond frames: Recovering the strategic in climate communication. *Environmental Communication, 4*(1), 122-133. doi: 10.1080/17524030903516555

Dingo, R. (2012). *Networking arguments: Rhetoric, transnational feminism, and public policy writing.* Pittsburgh, PA: University of Pittsburgh Press.

Ehninger, D. (1970). Argument as method: Its nature, its limitation and its uses. *Speech Monographs, 37*(2), 101-110. doi: 10.1080/03637757009375654

Galloway, A. R., & Thacker, E. (2007). *The exploit: A theory of networks.* Minneapolis, MN: University of Minnesota Press.

Gilbert, M. A. (1994). Multi-modal argumentation. *Philosophy of the Social Sciences, 24*(2), 159-177. doi: 10.1177/004839319402400202

Goodnight, G. T. (2012). The personal, technical, and public spheres: A note on 21st century critical communication inquiry [Special issue]. *Argumentation and Advocacy, 48*(4), 258-267. Retrieved from http://tandfonline.com

Greene, R. W. (1998). Another materialist rhetoric. *Critical Studies in Mass Communication, 15*(1), 21-40. doi: 10.1080/15295039809367031

Greene, R. W. (2004). Rhetoric and capitalism: Rhetorical agency as communicative labor. *Philosophy and Rhetoric, 37*(3), 188-206. doi: 10.1353/par.2004.0020

Greene, R. W., & Hayes, H. A. (2012). Rhetorical materialism: The cognitive division of labor and the social dimensions of argument. *Argumentation and Advocacy, 48*(3), 190-193. Retrieved from http://tandfonline.com

Greene, R. W., & Hicks, D. (2005). Lost convictions: Debating both sides and the ethical self- fashioning of liberal citizens. *Cultural Studies, 19*(1), 100-126. doi: 10.1080/09502380500040928

Greene, R. W., & Nelson, S. H. (2014). Struggle for the commons: Communicative labor, control economics, and the rhetorical marketplace. In J. S. Hanan & M. Hayward (Eds.), *Communication and the economy: History, value and agency* (pp. 259-283). New York, NY: Peter Lang.

Greene-May, M. R. (2011). Corruption and empire: Notes on Wisconsin. *Journal of Communication Inquiry, 35*(4), 342-348. doi: 10.1177/0196859911417440

Harsin, J. (2014). Public argument in the new media ecology: Implications of temporality, spatiality, and cognition. *Journal of Argumentation in Context, 3*(1), 7-34. doi: 10.1075/jaic.3.1.02har

Indivisible Project. (2017, March 9). Indivisible: A practical guide for resisting the Trump agenda. Retrieved from file:///Users/test/Downloads/IndivisibleGuide_2017-03-09_v10.pdf

Leonhardt, D. (2017, August 1). The Americans who saved health insurance. *The New York Times.* Retrieved from https://nytimes.com

Lewiński, M., & Mohammed, D. (2015). Tweeting the Arab Spring: Argumentative polylogues in digital media. In C. H. Palczewski (Ed.), *Disturbing argument* (pp. 291-297). New York, NY: Routledge.

Monge, P. R. (1987). The network level of analysis. In C. R. Berger & S. H. Chaffee (Eds.), *Handbook of communication science* (pp. 239-270). Beverly Hills, CA: SAGE.

Monge, P. R., & Contractor, N. S. (2003). *Theories of communication networks.* Oxford, United Kingdom: Oxford University Press.

Oermen, J. (2012). The issue network as a deliberative space: A case study of the Danish asylum issue on the internet. *CEU Political Science Journal, 7*(1), 1-31. Retrieved from http://politicalscience.ceu.edu/2012

Olson, K. M., & Goodnight, G. T. (1994). Entanglements of consumption, cruelty, privacy, and fashion: The social controversy over fur. *Quarterly Journal of Speech, 80*(3), 246-279. doi: 10.1080/00335639409384072

Papacharissi, Z. A. (2010). *A private sphere: Democracy in a digital age.* Cambridge, United Kingdom: Polity Press.

Pfister, D. S. (2010). Introduction to special issue: Public argument/digital media [Special issue]. *Argumentation and Advocacy, 47*(2), 63-66. Retrieved from http://tandfonline.com

Rose, N. (1989). *Governing the soul: The shaping of the private self.* New York, NY: Routledge.

Scott, R. L., & Smith, D. K. (1969). The rhetoric of confrontation. *Quarterly Journal of Speech, 55*(1), 1-8. doi: 10.1080/00335636909382922

Tarrow, S. G. (2011). *Power in movement: Social movements and contentious politics* (3rd ed.). Cambridge, United Kingdom: Cambridge University Press.

Wenzel, J. (1990). Three perspectives on argument: Rhetoric, dialectic, logic. In R. Trapp & J. E. Schuetz (Eds.), *Perspectives on argumentation: Essays in honor of Wayne Brockriede* (pp. 9-16). Prospect Heights, IL: Waveland Press.

Winkler, C. (2015). Challenging communities: A perspective about, from, and by argumentation. In C. H. Palczewski (Ed.), *Disturbing argument* (pp. 4-17). New York, NY: Routledge.

5

MORE DISINGENUOUS CONTROVERSY

Hashtags, Chants, and an Election

John Fritch and Catherine Helen Palczewski

In the 1991 Alta keynote, Goodnight identified how controversy "pushes the limits of the available means of communication" (p. 2) as it generates new arguments and new objections to argumentation processes. Further developing the theory, Olson and Goodnight (1994) defined the concept of "social controversy" as:

> [...] an extended rhetorical engagement that critiques, resituates, and develops communication practices bridging the public and personal spheres. The loci of such controversy include participation in governance, distribution and use of economic resources and opportunities, assumption of personal and collective identities and risks, redress of common grievances, assignments of rights and obligations, and the processes of social justice [...]. Social controversy occupies the pluralistic boundaries of a democracy and flourishes at those sites of struggle where arguers criticize and invent alternatives to established social conventions and sanctioned norms of communication.
>
> *(p. 249)*

Political elections in which issues of race, gender, and class rise to the fore make it possible for campaigns to function as sites of social controversy that bridge the public and personal spheres of argument. However, superficial engagement with questions of collective identity may function as disingenuous controversy when they re-entrench social conventions and participate in norms of communication that constrict, rather than expand, argumentative networks.

Generally, argumentation scholars celebrate the value of controversy, and even Goodnight's critics suggest controversy is a positive force (Phillips, 1999). Yet, in this expanded conception of controversy, Goodnight (1991) warned: "The confections of mass media should not obscure the greater horizon of discursive norms still available to the public sphere" (p. 7). Some argumentative norms are still necessary for arguers to make controversy productive.

Controversy is not always argumentatively productive. Ceccarelli's (2011) astute work on the way arguers manufacture scientific controversy in the public sphere "through the exploitation of balancing norms and the topoi of freedom of speech and freedom of inquiry" also identified "argumentative traps that constrain" respondents (p. 218). For Ceccarelli, a *manufactured controversy* occurs when a deception generates controversy for public consumption, thereby exploiting "political interests [...] to achieve a particular policy objective" (p. 219). The point is not that public sphere deliberation has no place in resolving scientific disputes, but that arguers manufacture some scientific disputes solely for political ends rather than because any real scientific disagreement actually exists.

In previous work introduced at this conference (Fritch, Palczewski, Short, & Farrell, 2005) and published in *Argumentation and Advocacy* (Fritch, Palczewski, Farrell, & Short, 2006), we argued for a conception of *disingenuous controversy* grounded in the legal doctrine of ripeness. Legally, issues are ripe when an "individual has standing to sue, damage has occurred, and the hardship of delay is certain" (Fritch et al., 2006, p. 198). Argumentatively, issues are ripe when they warrant public attention, a clearly identifiable injury exists, and public argument is timely for engaging in the dispute. In the case of the controversy that focused on Ward Churchill's response to September 11, 2001, we argued that rather than being ripe, the controversy was rotten (Fritch et al., 2006).

Argumentation scholars should focus more attention on the dark side of controversy because not all controversies are genuine. Specifically, "a complete understanding of the dynamics of controversy requires attention *both* to controversy's genuine ability to expand discursive space *and* to its artificial deployment so as to divert attention from the claims advanced" (Fritch et al., 2006, p. 193). Given that in Churchill's case, the controversy occurred more than 40 months after the publication of his original essay, the legal concept of ripeness helped explain how critics used controversy to cloud the issues. Others have used the concept of disingenuous controversy to explore the ways global warming (Banning, 2009), whale hunting (Brigham, 2017), and creationism (Kelly & Hoerl, 2012) appear to be the subject of robust argument, even when typical conditions for uncertainty and/or proof are lacking.

Disingenuous controversy is distinct from Ceccarelli's manufactured controversy in terms of both content and effect. While both attend to the generation of controversy for political ends, arguers ignite personal outrage to divert attention from public sphere deliberation in disingenuous controversy, while in manufactured controversy, they publicly magnify technical disputes for political ends. In terms of effect, disingenuous controversy closes off debate for political ends, while manufactured controversy generates debate for political ends.

Under conditions of uncertainty, controversy can open processes of argumentation to expand the argumentative terrain, but disingenuous controversy closes off argumentation's potential to offer guidance in decision making. The concept of networks is relevant here on two levels. First, understanding argument as a network enables one to track how argument norms and topoi can become traps, as Ceccarelli did with manufactured controversy. Second, accounting for the speed of circulation and the spread of arguments in a networked communication environment is necessary to understand how disingenuous controversy can grow quickly and overwhelm argument norms. Here, we consider this temporal dimension through a further development of justiciability as a means of evaluating public argument.

In the legal realm, the doctrine of justiciabilty addresses when "an issue is and is not susceptible of judicial decision" (Borchard, 1936, p. 1), thereby identifying issues that warrant a decision. It includes several aspects: "The court must not be offering an advisory opinion, the plaintiff must have standing, and the issues must be ripe but neither moot nor violative of the political question doctrine" ("Justiciability," n.d.). Here, we expand our previous conception of disingenuous controversy to identify how some controversies fail components of the legal doctrine of justiciability. We use the 2016 campaign to illustrate how issues, despite their ripeness, may not meet other conditions of justiciability. In public argument, justiciability translates into determinations of when an issue is worthy of public debate, deliberation, and decision.

Obviously, the application of legal principles to a political campaign is neither direct nor precise. However, the application can yield understandings regarding the nature of genuine and disingenuous controversy. In addition, the philosophical underpinnings of justiciability goad the articulation of the conditions for productive argument, including the identifiable nature of particular issues or controversies (*standing*), the liveness of particular controversies (*mootness*), and the evolution, development, and focus of issues across time (*similar to issue narrowing by appellate courts*). We turn to justiciability because it is a method the legal system uses to distinguish controversies worthy of the investment of time and attention from those that are not.

In the case of the 2016 presidential campaign, Donald Trump repeatedly violated norms, settled nothing, and invited debate about moot issues rather than about the candidates' various policy positions. He did not manufacture controversy, as room for a robust controversy certainly existed; instead, he offered voters disingenuous controversy. He used the veneer of argument to create the appearance of debate when, instead, confections of social media obscured the discursive norms necessary for argumentation. At its base, the controversy never evolved or grew to a level warranting public decision. Here, our emphasis is not on the Republican nominee's failure to offer coherent and complete arguments. Instead, we explore the broad processes of argumentation that allowed statements to appear as though they were actual arguments that warranted assent.

Tweets, Soundbites, Hashtags, and Chants

The Republican candidate's rhetorical choices in the 2016 presidential campaign mimicked the appearance of genuine controversy, but failed to participate in productive argument. His arguments were disingenuous because they closed off opposition and reinforced existing power structures (despite claims of populism). They foreclosed opposition by clouding rather than illuminating issues and by relying on personal outrage to divert attention. To illustrate the utility of justiciability to identify disingenuous controversies, we focus on three aspects of the legal concept: mootness, standing, and failure to narrow issues. The repeated recurrence of moot issues and lack of standing proliferated issues exacerbated the failure to narrow focus to issues central to the question of who should be president.

Mootness

Mootness holds that when no *live* controversy exists, the courts should not act ("Mootness," 2007). An issue is moot when "actions or policies […] are temporary in nature, […] factual developments after the suit is filed [that] resolve the harm alleged, and […] claims have been settled" (Gutman, 2016b, para. 2). In the legal system, mootness is important as it precludes courts from examining cases where the judge cannot award damages due to already settled claims and where judges and juries do not hear arguments that have no real relevance. Mootness precludes advocates from using arguments designed to clog the system or to distract from the relevant issues at hand.

Scholars of public argument can employ mootness to assist in the determination of whether a controversy is disingenuous. In public argument, mootness also examines whether the argument is live. Analysts can determine mootness by looking to see if the proposed solution resolves the alleged harms or if the alleged harms even exist. In 2016, the Republican presidential campaign employed the slogan "Make America Great Again." The eventual nominee, even before accepting the nomination, appeared to create controversy by challenging whether America is currently great, hearkening back to an Edenic moment of the nation's ascendency in the past, and claiming the ability to return America to its former greatness. The phrase unquestionably motivated supporters. On Twitter, the hashtag #MAGA perhaps served as a sign of defiance against establishment Republican candidates. The candidate adopted the phrase as his own, and his lawyers issued cease and desist letters when other candidates used the phrase (Tumulty, 2017).

However, #MAGA did not produce a vibrant public controversy. A live controversy over U.S. identity never took place; rather, the confection fed supporters in ways that induced them to disregard argumentation norms. First, voters and members of the press failed to examine the candidate for his ability to resolve the harm alleged. As commentators too infrequently noted, the phrase failed to answer key questions about when America was great, what greatness looked like, or how to achieve greatness. In short, the claim was inarticulable. Supporters responded to questions about the meaning of the phrase by advocating (a) the freedom of states to make their own decisions about marijuana laws, (b) reducing tax rates while making the wealthy pay more, (c) reducing regulations, (d) avoiding America's secondary status, (e) returning America to the way it was 30 or more years ago, or (f) by simply shrugging (Brown, Ayoola, & Matza, 2016; "Can Trump Supporters," 2016). In addition, the phrase was ambiguous. Ambiguity can allow for identification to occur (Burke, 1969) and, in this case, it did so with the nominee's supporters; they found what they wished to find in the slogan. However, the ambiguity simultaneously precluded a resolution of the alleged harm. The disagreement between the Republican nominee's supporters over the meaning of the phrase added difficulty, if not impossibility, to the task of determining what actions would make America great again.

The application of mootness to a public argument can demonstrate the lack of legitimate controversy. In this instance, the use of #MAGA prevented the development of argument and prevented the realization of a genuine controversy's benefits. The dispute was not live. No candidate in the primary or general election opposed the greatness of America; the claim had no opposition. The rhetorical and legal efforts to claim the ground of American greatness as exclusively belonging to a particular candidate illustrate the closing off of argumentation rather than the opening up of controversy. The Republican campaign treated the controversy as a moot point—one where only one candidate could appear on the correct side.

Standing

Standing examines if the court is the proper venue for a discussion to take place. The legal system applies three tests to determine standing: an injury in fact, a causal connection between the injury and the alleged act, and the likelihood that a favorable decision will resolve the injury (Gutman, 2016a, para. 2). Courts employ standing to prevent false allegations of damage or false attributions of the cause of the damage.

An example from the final presidential debate illustrates how argumentation scholars can employ standing in studies of public controversy. The debate covered numerous issues: Supreme Court nominees, the Second Amendment, abortion, immigration, and the economy. Yet, the key moment in the debate occurred when Clinton turned to the issue of Russia's involvement while answering a question about WikiLeaks's email release. Clinton suggested that Putin would prefer a puppet as the U.S. president. The Republican candidate responded, speaking over her to say, "No puppet. No puppet. You're the puppet" ("Full Transcript," 2016, 27:51-27:54). Post-debate coverage focused heavily on this interaction between the two candidates (Earl, 2016).

This exchange would fail the justiciability conception of standing. Standing, in public controversy, examines if the opposing parties are discussing a particular issue. Here, the candidates seem to have agreed that Russian interference was deleterious to the United States. However, "no puppet" closed off controversy by failing to satisfactorily answer Clinton's charge and instead focusing on Clinton's use of the word "puppet." The Republican candidate shifted the dispute from the key policy question of Russian interference in the U.S. election to a linguistic game of name-calling instead of using the moment to reinforce discursive norms. Accordingly, post-debate commentary focused more on what the exchange revealed about the candidates' assessments of each other and less on what the candidates thought about policy.

Failure to Narrow Issues

Genuine controversies are productive because they open ground for argument by focusing and developing greater depth of argument. In the 2016 campaign, the Republican candidate and his supporters employed two arguments to attack Clinton that did the opposite. First, at rallies and at the Republican National Convention, speakers and the audience chanted, "Lock her up!" Second, on more than a dozen occasions, the vice-presidential nominee discussed how the presidential nominee possessed "broad-shouldered American strength" (cited in Chait, 2017, para. 3), thus qualifying him to serve as president. Concerns about character and stamina are, indeed, relevant when considering who should lead a nation.

However, these two charges violate notions of justiciability. First, "Lock her up" relied on an ever-evolving litany of charges, including Benghazi (Graham, 2016), use of a private server for email, hacking of the DNC emails, financial management of the Clinton Foundation, Pizzagate, and the death of a DNC worker in Washington (Marcotte, 2016). The result was a constantly shifting line of attack that confused issues. For instance, no hackers seem to have ever hacked Clinton's server, yet the controversy conflated hacking of DNC emails with her own lack of security and elevated fake news such as Pizzagate (Aisch, Huang, & Kang, 2016). Using a simple phrase to insinuate a list of charges is not new. Gorman (2016) wrote that the "lock her up" motto was "the ideological successor of the 'birther' myth perpetuated against Barack Obama" (para. 13). Second, the coy reference to shoulders did not allow focus on questions of gender because the Republican vice-presidential nominee denied that the comments had anything to do with masculinity (Griffiths, 2016). The presidential nominee's repeated comments about "stamina" reinforced this argument, but did not develop it. Although these phrases never, to our knowledge, appeared together, they worked together to paint Clinton as the stereotypical woman: physically weak and emotionally corrupt. Yet, the constant shifts in the arguments, and the refusal to defend them, meant controversy could not focus on the gendered implications of this claim.

Such an approach creates disingenuous controversy. The *whack-a-mole* approach runs afoul of justiciability by failing to identify what issues the arguers contest, so issues are unable to develop across time. As cases move through the courts, judges seldom allow new arguments because of the need to deliberate existing arguments. Unfortunately, the approach of the 2016 Republican campaign was to raise numerous issues, many of which were diversionary and grounded in fake news. Arguably, social media enables such proliferation of disingenuous arguments. In previous elections, the traditional media reporting cycles constrained candidates; a story would break on Monday in a newspaper and a campaign could respond in the Tuesday paper. In the 2016 election, the reliance on social media created a situation in which rumors and lies (and even truths) become widespread even before the candidates could respond. And, as one campaign developed a response, the other propagated another rumor or lie. Thus, attention to questions of justiciability may help keep focus on central controversies rather than disingenuous ones.

Limits of Justiciability

Issues of justiciability in the court setting are all or nothing. No case has partial standing. Although arguments in the legal arena are contingent, decisions are not. In public argument, however, decisions are contingent, creating a challenge for applying justiciability to public controversy. When employing tests for mootness or standing to public argument, critics are not determining if the argument may proceed. Instead, critics are considering the implications for public discourse. Do arguments that lack standing discourage genuine argument? Does an argument that is moot forestall the development of additional arguments?

Argumentation scholars can use tests of justiciability to understand the impact of a claim on future discourse. Our point is not that justiciability is a test for the soundness of an argument: Justiciability is not a fallacy. Rather, justiciabilty is a means of understanding why certain discursive moves—particularly those that take on the appearance of an argument or enthymeme—can thwart genuine controversy in ways that render the controversy disingenuous.

In public argument, justiciability looks at whether an argument is live, addresses particular issues, and is timely. The relevancy of such tests suggests whether disputed issues can narrow and develop depth rather than proliferate to create breadth. Perhaps legally, the most important use of justiciability is to constrain and limit the arguments a court makes. The same is true in public controversy.

Conclusion

In the legal system, justiciability provides standards that help legal arguments become productive. As we employ this concept, we are aware of the criticisms of its legal use. But even critics such as Chemerinsky (1991) argued for reform, rather than abandonment, of the concept. Similarly, scholars should not abandon the concept of controversy. An application of justiciability to public argument (with its attendant standards of ripeness, mootness, and standing) can help critics identify arguments that seek to subvert the benefits of genuine controversy. Disingenuous argument often does this by proliferating (rather than narrowing) issues and by failing to develop depth of argument. Genuine controversy, at its best, elevates public discourse by creating space for new voices and a deeper consideration of the issues.

References

Aisch, G., Huang, J., & Kang, C. (2016, December 10). Dissecting the #Pizzagate conspiracy theories. *The New York Times*. Retrieved from https://nytimes.com

Banning, M. E. (2009). When poststructural theory and contemporary politics collide—The vexed case of global warming. *Communication and Critical/Cultural Studies*, 6(3), 285–304. doi:10.1080/14791420903049736

Borchard, E. (1936). Justiciability. *The University of Chicago Law Review*, 4 (1), Article 1. Retrieved from http://chicagounbound.uchicago.edu/uclrev/vol4/iss1/1

Brigham, M. P. (2017). Chrono-controversy: The Makah's campaign to resume the whale hunt. *Western Journal of Communication*, 81(2), 243–261. doi:10.1080/10570314.2016.1242023

Brown, T. K., Ayoola, T., & Matza, M. (2016, November 9). Election 2016: Trump voters on why they backed him [Interview responses compiled by authors]. *BBC*. Retrieved from http://bbc.com

Burke, K. (1969). *A grammar of motives*. Berkeley, CA: University of California Press.

Can Trump Supporters Describe What They Think Trump Means by "Make America Great Again" and Would It Be Great for All Americans or Just Them? [Question and answers]. (2016). *Quora*. Retrieved from https://quora.com/Can-Trump-supporters-describe-what-they-think-Trump-means-by-Make-America-great-again-and-would-it-be-great-for-all-Americans-or-just-them

Ceccarelli, L. (2011). Manufactured scientific controversy: Science, rhetoric, and public debate. *Rhetoric & Public Affairs*, 14(2), 195–228. doi:10.1353/rap.2010.0222

Chait, J. (2017, August 22). Mike Pence strongly believes Donald Trump's shoulder width guarantees his foreign-policy acumen. *New York Magazine*. Retrieved from http://nymag.com

Chemerinsky, E. (1991). A unified approach to justiciability. *Connecticut Law Review*, 22, 677–701. Retrieved from http://scholarship.law.duke.edu

Earl, J. (2016, October 19). The internet can't get over Donald Trump's response to being called a "puppet" [Video file included]. *CBS News*. Retrieved from http://cbsnews.com

Fritch, J., Palczewski, C. H., Farrell, J., & Short, E. (2006). Disingenuous controversy: Responses to Ward Churchill's 9/11 essay. *Argumentation and Advocacy*, 42(4), 190–205. Retrieved from http://tandfonline.com

Fritch, J., Palczewski, C. H., Short, E., & Farrell, J. (2005). Ripe for controversy: Churchill's 9/11 essay. In P. Riley (Ed.), *Engaging argument* (pp. 348–358). Washington, DC: National Communication Association.

Full Transcript: Third 2016 Presidential Debate [Transcript and video file]. (2016, October 20). *Politico*. Retrieved from http://politico.com

Goodnight, G. T. (1991). Controversy. In D. W. Parson (Ed.), *Argument in controversy: Proceedings of the seventh SCA/AFA conference on argumentation* (pp. 1–13). Annandale, VA: Speech Communication Association.

Gorman, M. (2016, July 20). "Lock her up!" Hillary Clinton and the unofficial slogan of the 2016 Republican National Convention. *Newsweek*. Retrieved from http://newsweek.com

Graham, D. A. (2016, July 20). "Lock her up": How Hillary hatred is unifying Republicans. *The Atlantic*. Retrieved from https://theatlantic.com

Griffiths, B. (2016, September 26). Pence denies "broad shoulders" remark is about Trump's masculinity. *Politico*. Retrieved from http://politico.com/story/2016/09/trump-broad-shoulders-mike-pence-228703

Gutman, J. S. (2016a). 3.1 Standing. *Shriver Center: Federal practice manual for legal aid attorneys*. Retrieved from http://federalpracticemanual.org/chapter3/section1

Gutman, J. S. (2016b). 3.3 Mootness. *Shriver Center: Federal practice manual for legal aid attorneys*. Retrieved from http://federalpracticemanual.org/chapter3/section3

Justiciability. (n.d.). *Legal Information Institute*. Retrieved from https://law.cornell.edu/wex/justiciability

Kelly, C. R., & Hoerl, K. E. (2012). Genesis in hyperreality: Legitimizing disingenuous controversy at the creation museum. *Argumentation and Advocacy*, 48, 123–141. Retrieved from http://tandfonline.com

Marcotte, A. (2016, August 29). The Clinton BS files: "Lock her up" isn't really about emails—the right's been accusing the Clinton's of murder for decades. *Salon*. Retrieved from http://salon.com/2016/08/29/the-clinton-bs-files-lock-her-up-isnt-really-about-emails-the-rights-been-accusing-the-clintons-of-murder-for-decades/

Mootness: An Exploration of the Justiciability Doctrine (Report No. RS22599). (2007, February). *Every-CRSReport.com*. Retrieved from https://everycrsreport.com

Olson, K. M., & Goodnight, G. T. (1994). Entanglements of consumption, cruelty, privacy, and fashion: The social controversy over fur. *Quarterly Journal of Speech, 80*(3), 249–276. doi:10.1080/00335639409384072

Phillips, K. R. (1999). A rhetoric of controversy. *Western Journal of Communication, 63*(4), 488–510. doi:10.1080/10570319909374655

Tumulty, K. (2017, January 18). How Donald Trump came up with "make America great again." *The Washington Post.* Retrieved from https://washingtonpost.com

6

HOW TECHNOLIBERALS ARGUE

Damien Smith Pfister

Technoliberalism, the intensification of neoliberalism through computational technology, is the guiding ideology of Silicon Valley. The arguments of corporate technology leaders like Sergey Brin, Elon Musk, Mark Zuckerberg, and Jeff Bezos, alongside popularizers like Chris Anderson, Kevin Kelly, and Robert Scoble, shape the digital culture of technoliberalism: lionizing individual empowerment through technology; enabling quantification, calculation, and control of more and more granular dimensions of life; and amplifying the centrality of market logics in judgment. However, the consolidation of technoliberalism as a dominant ideology is an achievement of argumentation rather than a natural byproduct of technical evolution. Technoliberalism is the dominant framework of technology development because the "thread ends" (Simonson, 2010, p. 25) of influential industrial leaders effectively focalize widely dispersed cultural assumptions. Though technoliberal assumptions shape how arguments network through the platforms that now influence much communicative interaction, argumentation scholars have paid relatively little attention to the arguments of technoliberals. This essay identifies how technoliberals argue, through strategies of effacement and strategies of code-ification, as a first step in denaturalizing their assumptions and instigating alternative possibilities for contemporary digital culture.

Strategies of Effacement

Technoliberals efface their own arguments *qua* arguments in three ways: by claiming that information (especially in the context of Big Data) trumps the need for argumentation, by relying on "proof of concept" to demonstrate the potency of an idea, and by evincing a faith in emergence as a sign of naturalism. These three strategies of effacement are not new; rather, they are intensifications of early modern attitudes toward rhetoric and argumentation.

Technoliberals believe that information severely attenuates, or even replaces, the role of argumentation by assuming the flow of data will naturally illuminate the obvious judgment. This belief, what I have called "informationism" (Pfister, 2014, pp. 22-23) in previous work, is especially intense in the context of Big Data discourses. The most robust articulation of this belief is *Wired* editor-in-chief Chris Anderson's (2008) provocative claim about the "end of theory":

Out with every theory of human behavior, from linguistics to sociology. Forget taxonomy, ontology, and psychology. Who knows why people do what they do? The point is they do it, and we can track and measure it with unprecedented fidelity. With enough data, the numbers speak for themselves [....] The new availability of huge amounts of data, along with the statistical tools to crunch these numbers, offers a whole new way of understanding the world. Correlation supersedes causation, and science can advance even without coherent models, unified theories, or really any mechanistic explanation at all.

(para. 7, 18)

For Anderson, bigger data is the answer to every question; acquire the right data, and then designers can create systems that nudge citizens into more productive habits. With the current production, tracking, and analysis of so much data, the argument goes, deep patterns of human behavior are now decipherable. Of course, argumentation theory does not even rise to the level of mentionability in Anderson's breathless account of how Big Data mooted theoretical models. Why do you need an account of argumentation theory when you can simply mine Twitter for information about how people argue? The cautionary tale of the chatbot, Tay, suggests why. Microsoft intended Tay, its infamous chatbot released onto Twitter on March 23, 2016, as an experiment in artificial intelligence. Instead, Tay learned from fellow Twitterers how to be an invective spewing racist in just a few hours, disclosing, as a side effect, the often toxic argument culture of Twitter.

The belief that information is the key that unlocks the world, however, effaces the role of argument cultures in shaping flows of communication (Zarefsky, 2009). Moreover, as Hartelius (2018) adroitly observes, scholars ought not conflate measurement with understanding or judgment. The foundation of measurement is inference and representation, both of which are in the wheelhouse of culture and argumentation (Faltesek, 2013). Nonetheless, technoliberals revise Blair's (1822) famous claim about rhetoric providing the "polish" (p. viii) to scientific knowledge by asserting that information *is* knowledge, and rhetoric is needed just to burnish insights derived from the analysis of big data sets.

If, in the networked imaginary, information plays the role that science played in the early modern imaginary, then proof of concept is an updated version of demonstration. Demonstration refers to the belief that improved methods of scientific inquiry would irrefutably prove that which rhetoric had henceforth only been able to argue for probabilistically (Nelson & Megill, 1986, p. 22). As it turns out, we humans are beings that thrive amidst non-demonstrable worlds of contingency and normativity. Nonetheless, technoliberals have reanimated this particular zombie from rhetoric's past by drawing on the assumptions of demonstration's power through the term proof of concept. Thomas Malaby's anthropological study of Linden Labs, the creator of the quasi-virtual reality site *Second Life*, expresses the central role of proof of concept in technoliberal argument. At Linden Labs, certain technical problems confront designers, such as how to represent through code the shade that a light source should throw. "When someone at Linden in 2005 claimed to have created, or to have been planning to create, a proof of concept," Malaby explained, "this was a reliable sign that a difference of opinion had arisen among members of a team working together on a project or between individual employees and their immediate superiors" (2009, p. 62). Malaby made the connection between proof of concept and demonstration explicit: the proof of concept was "a demonstration of a creation [that] stands itself as testament to its viability as a solution to a recognized problem or dilemma" (2009, p. 111). As he noted,

> The notion of a 'proof of concept' stands as a practical (rather than discursive) means by which an argument can be made. The best way to convince people that something can be done, proofs of concept suggest, is simply to do it, if only in a rough and unpolished fashion.
>
> *(Malaby, 2009, p. 117)*

Confining oneself to the realm of the demonstrable is useful for addressing certain technical problems, but it also risks repeating logical positivism's fetishism for empiricism at the expense of ethics. Brian Merchant's account of the secret history of the iPhone underlines this point. Engineers had to nail the proof of concept for the iPhone in order to persuade a skeptical Steve Jobs to jump further into the hardware business. Those same engineers are now ambivalent about the larger cultural consequences of their device (Merchant, 2017a, 2017b). Yet, proof of concept's dominance as an argument strategy yields an engineering culture that believes "if you *can* do it, you *should* do it."

Proof of concept is an insider argument strategy. When products go public, the rhetoric of emergence legitimizes the product as necessary and useful based on the presumed efficacy and ethicality of market logics. Build it, and the commercial market will sort it out. Replicating assumptions associated with early liberalism's marketplace of ideas, technoliberalism assumes that, since internetworked technologies operate on a level playing field, the emergence of certain technologies and habits is natural and ideal. In this networked, technoliberal imaginary, institutions are irrelevant, social divisions are infinitely surmountable, and class distinctions are dissolved. The technoliberal imaginary envisions a world devoid of power, which allows adherents to believe, as Malaby (2009) put it, "The emergent properties of complex interactions enjoy a certain degree of rightness just by virtue of being emergent" (p. 56). The roll out of Google Glass is a case in point. Despite the protests of the developer team who realized that Glass was not ready for the market, Sergey Brin wanted a fast public release so that Google could use their feedback to "iterate and improve the design" (Bilton, 2015, para. 19). Thus, Google designed a "Glass Explorer" program that invited people to apply for the right to buy Glass for $1500. Glass Explorers were glorified beta testers, tasked with identifying the use cases and working out the kinks with the first optical head mounted display. While Glass 1.0 was a commercial failure, Google is now using the data gleaned from user interaction to identify emergent uses and redesign the product for a future form factor. For technoliberals, emergence is a suitable replacement for argumentation—if a particular device, or app, or use of software emerges, then the existence of a market proves the need for, and legitimacy of, a product.

Informationism, proof of concept, and emergence are intensifications of (neo)liberal strategies that assume rhetorical argumentation is but an epiphenomenon irrelevant to the way things really are. The naturalistic fallacy—the assumption that what *is*, *ought* to be—threads through technoliberal discourse: Google's search results, trending topics on Twitter, and the context collapse that Facebook accelerated all figure as natural results of free-flowing information. The experience of argumentation scholars in problematizing the naturalistic fallacy could prove especially useful as we diagnose how the new intellectual formation of technoliberalism reinscribes certain patterns of networked arguments as reflective of the real.

Strategies of Code-ification

Although scholars should explore how technoliberals often efface the role of argumentation through conventional rhetorical forms like speeches, books, and op-eds, we also must focus on how technoliberals argue through code. In the same way that argument scholars like Fleming (1998) turned our attention to how the infrastructures of *built* environments shape argument, *digital* environments constituted through algorithmic code have consequences for argument, too. Strategies of code-ification refer to how, in making certain principles of argument more durable through code, technoliberals have turned modern techniques of argumentation into technologies of argumentation (Peters, 2015). This subtilization of argumentation through code occurs in two ways. At a macro-level of code-ification, the historical traffic between formal logic and computer science claims to encode principles of deduction and induction. At a more micro-level, certain algorithms, like the one that shapes Facebook's newsfeed, code-ify criteria for evaluating evidence.

In the mid-19th century, new developments in formal logic, modeled after the method of proof found in mathematics, set the stage for computational programming. The key figure here was George Boole, who established a logical system that replaced words with variables and syntax with algebraic notation. Boole's key contribution to logic in *Laws of Thought* emphasized the form of human reasoning outside propositional content. His purpose was

> [...] to investigate the fundamental laws of those operations of the mind by which reasoning is performed; to give expression to them in the symbolical language of a Calculus, and upon this foundation to establish the science of Logic and construct its method.
>
> *(Boole, 1854, p. 1)*

Shannon's (1937) master's thesis applied Boolean logic to electrical circuits, making possible the contemporary electrical computing paradigm. Early computers were explicitly deductive machines, but the advent of machine learning "has brought programming closer to the other main branch of logic, inductive logic, which deals with inferring rules from specific instances" (Dixon, 2017, para. 73). That the formal branches of argumentation are integrated into the circuitry of computers is an odd, but significant, common intellectual heritage of computer programming and argumentation studies.

This encode-ing of formal logic into computer programming provides a powerful narrative of self-understanding for technoliberals, who claim to reflect the natural order of reasoning just as Boole was identifying the fundamental laws of thought. Yet, emphasizing how contemporary programming is essentially *trans*ductive shows the limits of deduction and induction as part of the conventional computational imaginary. "Transduction," literally to lead or carry (*-ducere*) across or beyond (*trans-*), refers to "how what has come before lays the ground for what comes after" (Walsh & Boyle, 2017, p. 12). Gilbert Simondon's sense of transduction

> [...] denotes a process—be it physical, biological, mental or social—in which an activity gradually sets itself in motion, propagating within a given domain, by basing this propagation on a structuration carried out in different zones of the domain: each region of the constituted structure serves as a constituting principle for the following one, so much so that a modification progressively extends itself at the same time as this structuring operation.
>
> *(quoted in MacKenzie, 2002, p. 16)*

For Simondon, the process of crystal formation was an apt metaphor for transduction: A germ introduced to a solution activates the processes of crystallization, which is a gradual layering of minerals onto each other, each layer providing parameters for the next.

Transduction emphasizes the co-constructedness of things rather than linear progression from one thing to another. Notably, Simondon developed transduction to counter the dominant mid-twentieth century model of cybernetics precipitated by Shannon's adaptation of Boole's formal logic as a first step in developing information theory. Transduction emphasizes ecologies, not systems; feedforward instead of just feedback; the contingency of variables instead of their fixity; the dialectic of structure and agency instead of just structure or agency. In other words, transduction refers to how every act restructures the conditions of possibility for future acts.

Despite the *mythos* of formal logic that pervades computer programming, contemporary iterative algorithms operate transductively. Faltesek's (2015) explanation of Facebook's news feed captures the quintessential transductivity of social networking sites:

> Facebook is not so much a website but a process for producing a new site with every load. This object is the creation of a call upon hundreds of databases with thousands of read/write commands. Loading Facebook is not like making a copy of a running software program called Facebook, but like making an impression of the relationships currently articulated between the databases. The act of producing the interface leaves a trace. Any particular Facebook page is a creation of that moment and the ways that the algorithmic logic of Facebook reads the relationship between the databases of friends, families, strangers, pictures, and news events to know what should be in that version of the Feed.
>
> *(para. 13)*

Facebook's news feed algorithm is not involved in a simplistic application of a pre-established deductive logic; rather, the algorithm is a flexible tool that transforms as one uses it.

As another example, consider the algorithm that develops "recommended for you" suggestions based on prior Netflix habits. This algorithm integrates certain formal features (e.g., "shows starring Kevin Spacey"), personal rankings and the site's collective rankings of shows, some consideration of "people who liked X also watched Y," and so on. What makes Netflix's recommendation algorithm so powerful is its transductive properties. It "grows" with watching and ranking habits of the individual and collective, modifying itself as it is fed more information. The structure of the algorithm itself changes with the viewing habits of a user: if an individual only watches 4 star shows and above, then the algorithm will learn to privilege highly ranked shows at the expense of formal features like who stars in the show.

The *Napoleon Dynamite* problem shows the variables that feed into the recommendation algorithm are themselves transduced. *Napoleon Dynamite* is a polarizing film, usually garnering either 5 stars or 1 star in a mathematical expression of love it or hate it. The problem is that such a polarized reaction skews the recommendation algorithm. The winner of the million dollar Netflix Prize to improve the recommendation algorithm addressed this problem by adjusting the ranking for *Napoleon Dynamite* based on temporally proximate rankings. If a user 5 starred *Napoleon Dynamite* but 2 starred a number of other recently viewed films, then the "true" rating for *Napoleon Dynamite* would be lowered below 5 stars in order to shape future recommendations (Hallinan & Striphas, 2016). This example shows the degree to which Netflix's recommendation algorithm is always in a state of becoming, reflexively affected by and through the larger ecology of communication. Google's PageRank serves as another illustration, constantly shifting based on linking practices, internet traffic, or Facebook's news feed, which adjusts what is visible based on certain ever-evolving criteria. The ultimate evidence of algorithms as transductive is that, as the title of an *Atlantic* blog post puts it, "Not Even the People Who Write Algorithms Really Know How They Work" because the capacity of machine learning has outstripped programmers' ability to track it (LaFrance, 2015).

The ordering of Facebook's news feed is a good example of the code-ification of argumentation at a more micro-level of a specific algorithm, EdgeRank. Although Facebook's algorithm is proprietary, Facebook's official documents disclose that posts are sorted according to "relevance" in order to facilitate "engagement" (Birkbak & Carlsen, 2016). The criteria for what makes a "relevant" status update happens to coincide with what makes "good" evidence. Facebook's news feed privileges *recent* posts with its emphasis on reverse chronological presentation. The news feed determines *qualification* first by friendship status and second by degree of communicative interaction. EdgeRank's gradual privileging of photos and videos over textual posts might function as a preference for the presumed *clarity* of the imagistic. *Consistency* helps sort the news feed, too; if certain individuals always like baby pictures, then they will see more of them and vice versa. Since EdgeRank assesses a user's social network to populate their feeds with posts from ideological viewpoints with which they already agree, news feeds contain *bias*. Facebook aims to provide *sufficient* posts about a user's social network to maintain ambient intimacy with others. In short, EdgeRank has taken criteria for good evidence—recency, qualification, clarity, consistency, bias, sufficiency—and turned them into variables for sorting status updates.

Clearly, EdgeRank engineers are not paging through argumentation textbooks to help improve their algorithms. EdgeRank essentially sees every post as communicative evidence of one's social network, so it makes sense that engineers might organically generate ways of sorting that evidence which coincides with ways that argumentation scholars have historically evaluated evidence. Yet, this isomorphism between evaluative standards for evidence in argumentation and the metrics that have organically arisen in the EdgeRank algorithm does not extend to *telos*. The *telos* of EdgeRank is to promote user engagement, while the *telos* of evidence in argumentation is to provide grounds for judgment. These two different end goals make a rather substantive difference when considering the role of social networking sites in public deliberation. In acts of public arguing, evaluation of evidence is highly context-dependent: sometimes recency is the best guide to judgment; other times, the qualifications of a particular source are. Argumentation itself could be seen as the original transductive algorithm, reflexive enough to adapt to different deliberative scenarios in order to transform opinions. Interlocutors argue about what makes for the best evidence in a particular situation, and revise criteria for evaluation as public argument unfolds. Edgerank's reflexivity is limited, by contrast, because it always prioritizes relevance in the service of engagement and profit.

These conditions of Facebook's EdgeRank at least partially explain the circulation and consequences of the Pizzagate story, which identified Hillary Clinton as the leader of a child sex ring operating out of a Washington, D.C. pizzeria. The traditional press summarily dismissed Pizzagate as failing to meet evidentiary standards, but the recency and confirmatory bias of the story fueled its circulation on Facebook. Pushers of Pizzagate gamed Facebook's algorithm, but the black box of EdgeRank gives analysts and critics reduced opportunity— compared to public argument—to understand how. Algorithmic ordering, like all arrangement, makes an argument about what individuals should pay attention to, so scrutinizing algorithms gives insights into how implicit technoliberal assumptions ultimately shape networks of argument. Recognizing algorithms as transductive is thus important for two reasons. First, it denaturalizes technoliberal assumptions about how information is arranged. Transductive algorithms are shaping culture, not just reflecting it—which means that they are shaping the flow of arguments across digital communication networks. Second, it raises important questions about accountability that are likely to become more frequent as algorithmic decision-making and more sophisticated artificial intelligence evolves.

How We Argue Back

The conceit of *techno*liberalism suggests the long overdue potential for scholars in argumentation studies to intervene in larger conversations stimulated by software studies and digital culture more broadly. Efforts to address, through technical solutions, the problem of "fake news," for example, are likely to be doomed without a richer appreciation of argumentation, culture, and democratic deliberation. To be effective in intervening in these broader debates, argumentation scholars must engage with how technoliberals argue in order to map their terms, *topoi,* and argument strategies—and we must generate alternatives to the dominant technoliberal understanding of information and communication. Doing so requires avoiding the potential pitfalls of algorithmic formalism (a technocratic exploration of the specifics of computer programming) in favor of connecting the study of algorithms to circulation, influence, and deliberation. Perhaps, if argumentation scholars participate in these larger conversations, the impending algocracy be made more democratic and humane.

References

Anderson, C. (2008, June 23). The end of theory: The data deluge makes the scientific method obsolete. *Wired*. Retrieved from https://wired.com/2008/06/pb-theory/

Bilton, N. (2015, February 4). Why Google Glass broke. *The New York Times*. Retrieved from http://nytimes.com

Birkbak, A., & Carlsen, H. B. (2016). The world of Edgerank: Rhetorical justifications of Facebook's news feed algorithm. *Com1putational Culture: A Journal of Software Studies, 5*. Retrieved from http://computationalculture.net

Blair, H. (1822). *Essays on rhetoric and Belles lettres, abridged from Dr. Blair*. London, United Kingdom: F. C. & J. Rivington.

Boole, G. (1854). *An investigation into the laws of thought: On which are founded on the mathematical theories of logic and probabilities*. New York, NY: Dover.

Dixon, C. (2017, March 20). How Aristotle created the computer. *The Atlantic*. Retrieved from https://theatlantic.com

Faltesek, D. (2013). Big argumentation? *tripleC: Communication, Capitalism, and Critique, 11*(2), 402–411. Retrieve from http://triple-c.at/index.php

Faltesek, D. (2015). Coding the public screen: Connections at the nexus of code, affect, and the stop online piracy act. *Technoculture, 5*. Retrieved from http://tcjournal.org/vol5/faltesek

Fleming, D. (1998). The space of argumentation: Urban design, civic discourse, and the dream of the good city. *Argumentation, 12*(2), 147–166. doi: 10.1023/A:1007735612744

Hallinan, B., & Striphas, T. (2016). Recommended for you: The Netflix prize and the production of algorithmic culture. *New Media & Society, 18*(1), 117–137. doi: 10.1177/1461444814538646

Hartelius, J. (2018). Big data and global knowledge: A protagorean analysis of the United Nations' global pulse. In M. Kennerly & D. Pfister (Eds.), *Ancient Rhetorics & Digital Networks* (pp. 67–86). Tuscaloosa, AL: University of Alabama Press.

LaFrance, A. (2015, September 18). Not even the people who write algorithms really know how they work. *The Atlantic*. Retrieved from https://theatlantic.com

Mackenzie, A. (2002). *Transductions: Bodies and machines at speed*. New York, NY: Continuum.

Malaby, T. (2009). *Making virtual worlds: Linden Lab and second life*. Ithaca, NY: Cornell University Press.

Merchant, B. (2017a). *The one device: The secret history of the iPhone*. New York, NY: Little, Brown, & Co.

Merchant, B. (2017b, June 22). What hath Jobs wrought? [Audio file]. *1A*. Retrieved from http://the1a.org/audio/#/shows/2017-06-22/its-been-10-years-since-everything-changed/111337/@00:00

Nelson, J. S., & Megill, A. (1986). Rhetoric of inquiry: Problems and prospects. *Quarterly Journal of Speech, 72*(1), 20–37.

Peters, J. D. (2015). *The marvelous clouds: Toward a philosophy of elemental media.* Chicago, IL: University of Chicago Press.

Pfister, D. S. (2014). *Networked media, networked rhetorics: Attention and deliberation in the early blogosphere.* University Park, PA: The Pennsylvania State University Press.

Shannon, C. E. (1937). *A symbolic analysis of relay and switching circuits* (Unpublished M.S. thesis). Massachusetts Institute of Technology, Cambridge, MA.

Simonson, P. (2010). *Refiguring mass communication: A history.* Urbana, IL: University of Illinois Press.

Walsh, L., & Boyle, C. (2017). From intervention to invention: Introducing topological techniques. In L. Walsh & C. Boyle (Eds.), *Topologies as techniques for a post-critical rhetoric* (pp. 1–16). New York, NY: Palgrave Macmillan.

Zarefsky, D. (2009). What does an argument culture look like? *Informal Logic, 29*(3), 296–308. doi: 10.22329/il.v29i3.2845

7

NETWORK MATTERS

Black Lives and Blue Lives Advocacy
in On and Offline Settings

Maegan Parker Brooks

In a 2015 broadcast, National Public Radio (NPR) host Martin Kaste (2015) interviewed retired New York Police Department (NYPD) officer, Edward Conlon for a segment entitled, "Is There A 'War On Police'? The Statistics Say No." Kaste introduced Conlon by remarking, "he says when it comes to public opinion, his former colleagues do feel embattled" (para. 31). To which Conlon proclaimed: "It's not even half right that cops are at war with black America, and it's not even half right that there's a war on cops" (para. 34)—and Kaste riffed: "But there does seem to be at least one kind of war going on. It's a war of perceptions" (para. 35).

Enter the study of public argument. The deadly tension between the contemporary movement for black lives and the criminal justice system, synecdochally distilled into the figure of a police officer, utilizes the rhetoric of war. #BlackLivesMatter and #BlueLives-Matter hashtags appear as battle lines drawn, advocates on each side refer to the other as a terrorist organization, and opponents render the idea that one could both support a movement to recognize the humanity of black people and also support the police force nonsensical. Perhaps the nonsensical seems like an ironic opening for argumentation scholars to enter the conflict between communities of color and the criminal justice system, but as Judith Butler (2004) implored:

> If the humanities has a future as cultural criticism, and cultural criticism has a task at the present moment, it is no doubt to return us to the human where we do not expect to find it, in its frailty and at the limits of its capacity to make sense.
>
> *(p. 151)*

Indeed, human frailty and limited sense making abound in online fora, reflecting what Mari Lee Mifsud (in press) described in her chapter "On Network," as the *amphibolic* nature of networks. "In the elaborately woven threads of ancient Greek rhetorics," explained Mifsud, "emerge a complex and striking story-cloth of network, which tells as well of being human." By attending to this "story-cloth of network," Mifsud continued,

> [...] we see the [...] amphibolia, a network of relations that is [...] characterized by turns of ambiguity, throwing one's arms around in embrace, and throwing ideas

and meanings around as to create doubt. Amphibolia is not a simple reversal [...] or a dialectical synthesis [...] Amphibolia acts as a rhetoric of networking relations of, in, and through ambiguity.

(p. 38)

In the amphibolic space that networks enable, furthermore, scholars of argument find what Farrell (1995) referred to both as the "forum [that] helps to stabilize rhetorical practice" (p. 284) and the "appearances [that constitute the] material of public argument" (p. 32).

Networks, online fora woven from amphibolic threads, express the ambiguity, the frailty, and the irrationality of the human condition. In so doing, they offer spaces for argumentation scholars to understand, analyze, and ultimately intervene in the controversies that comprise rhetorical culture. Moreover, argumentation scholars' expertise in the study of spheres of discourse, everyday expressions of public thought, and the processes of ethical life position scholars in the field particularly well to provide lifelines out of the war of perceptions that protestors and police are currently battling. For instance, argumentation scholars could make a crucial intervention by reframing this conflict away from the zero-sum rhetoric of war, with its violent internecine entailments, and toward the rhetoric of network. This essay demonstrates that conceptualizing the conflict that #BlackLivesMatter and #BlueLivesMatter hashtags represent—through the more constructive vocabulary of the metaphor of network—provides a fundamental intervention into antiracist police training programs. Consideration of how threads weave and how nets work as amphibolic spaces enables argumentation scholars to affirm the labor of queer women of color. Explicating the cooptation of this communicative labor by Blue Lives Matter advocates, furthermore, reveals the fragility of frayed threads, which ostensibly loosens the net's gauges and invites argumentation scholars to join antiracist educators in the development of training programs designed to help police interact more productively with communities of color. As these training programs work to make visible and tangible the complexities of institutional racism, reframing the relationship between police and communities of color through the rhetoric of network primes officer receptivity to further antiracist education. A networked conception of the police force also binds officers to the communities they serve, to one another, and to the criminal justice system. Disentangling knotted threads in these relationships, furthermore, belies the "bad apples" defense that blames individual officers for the systemic mistreatment of black lives. Finally, a networked conception permits unraveling and provides a forum for reworking the social fabric.

Making Lives Matter

What began on Facebook in 2013 as Alicia Garza's love letter to black people following the acquittal of George Zimmerman for the murder of Trayvon Martin became a repost with the hashtag #BlackLivesMatter on Patrisse Cullors's wall. The network expanded when Opal Tometi proffered the hashtag as an invitation for friends to share stories about *how* #BlackLivesMatter on their Tumblr and Twitter accounts. #BlackLivesMatter began trending one year later in the wake of Michael Brown's death at the hands of Ferguson, Missouri police officer Darren Wilson. By 2015, the hashtag #BlackLivesMatter had grown into a multifaceted space to celebrate blackness, to organize and perpetuate on-the-ground protest, and to critique not only police violence but also the media's victim-blaming tendencies ("About: Build Power," 2017).

   Just as the idea of making Black lives matter through repetition, circulation, and the constitution of virtual community moved forward within the amphibolic space that social networks provide, #BlueLivesMatter emerged as a self-described pro-police media company organized to defend the force against attacks from the media, politicians, and protestors (OfficerBlue, 2017). Blue Lives Matter propagated a competing world view to counter what Black Lives Matter activists narrate in their "herstory," as efforts to broaden "the conversation around state violence to include all of the ways in which Black people are intentionally left powerless at the hands of the state" (Cullors, 2017, para. 4). Narrating their organization's history, the Blue Lives Matter (OfficerBlue, 2017) webpage claimed, "The officers who founded this organization were motivated by the heroic actions of Officer Darren Wilson [...] and decided to create this organization in the hopes that it could prevent more officers from being hurt" (para. 18). Arguing that Brown had "attacked" Wilson in an "aggravated assault" (para. 7) and that "agitators spread outright lies and distortions of the truth about Officer Wilson and all police officers" (para. 8). Advocates for Blue Lives Matter (OfficerBlue, 2017) insisted that "the media catered to movements such as Black Lives Matter, whose goal was the vilification of law enforcement" (para. 9). What is worse, they claimed that "political leaders pandered to these criminals and helped spread this false narrative, with no thought of the consequences" (para. 13). In the following sentence, Blue Lives Matter advocates implied that the deaths of "NYPD Officer Rafael Ramos and Officer Wenjian Liu"—who "were ambushed and murdered by a fanatic who believed the lies of Black Lives Matter, the media, and politicians" (OfficerBlue, 2017, para. 14)—were a direct consequence of this multilayered offensive against law enforcement.

   Noted antiracist educator Robin DiAngelo (2011) insisted, "The language of violence that many whites use to describe anti-racist endeavors is not without significance" (p. 65). "By employing terms that connote physical abuse," she noted, "whites tap into the classic discourse of people of color (particularly African Americans) as dangerous and violent" (p. 65). Blue Lives Matter advocates' characterizations of Black Lives Matter activism as attacks against police, coupled with Blue Lives Matter's efforts to link such activism with extremist ambush killings of law enforcement officials, perpetuates the very perceptions of blackness that Black Lives Matter activists are struggling to redefine. Such characterization of Black Lives Matter activism by Blue Lives Matter advocates, furthermore, re-centers whiteness by casting the protectors of its institutionalized supremacy, Blue Lives, as endangered. Although an array of evidence suggests that attacks against police are at an all-time low, any instances of fatal confrontations are justifiably frightening (Anderson, 2017). The conspiratorial reasoning that these killings function as manifestations of a collusive plot that protestors, the media, and politicians devise, however, illustrates just "how fragile and ill-equipped most white people are to confront racial tensions" (DiAngelo, 2011, p. 65); such fragility commonly leads to a "projection of this tension onto people of color" (p. 65).

Recasting the Conflict

Blue Lives Matter advocates have recently gone a step beyond projecting the tension that antiracist endeavors engender back onto people of color by coopting civil rights advocates' strategy of enlisting the protection of federal and state governments. In the past year, at least 14 states have introduced "Blue Lives Matter" bills; Kentucky and Louisiana have successfully passed legislation that renders offenses against police felonious hate crimes, adding the profession of law enforcement to the list of protected immutable characteristics such as gender, race, and sexuality. Moreover, the National Fraternal Order of Police is lobbying the United States Congress to pass a similar measure; members of both the House and the Senate have introduced the "Thin Blue Line Act" to strengthen penalties for attacks on law enforcement.

Critics argue that not only is the Blue Lives Matter legislation redundant, since most states already impose harsh sentences for crimes committed against first responders, they insist that such laws are a confusing perversion of hate crimes legislation and threaten to suppress dissent. Kate Miller, advocacy director at the American Civil Liberties Union of Kentucky, claimed that her state's law has already been used to "charge activists against police brutality with hate crimes for protesting" (Anderson, 2017, para. 20). Miller also bemoaned the fact that debate over Kentucky's legislation "failed to encourage deeper con- versations or require preventive measures such as required training for officers to learn how to avoid dangerous encounters and 'de-escalate potentially violent situations'" (quoted in Anderson, 2017, para. 19). As Miller's assessment intimated, Blue Lives Matter advocates effectively reversed the terms of the public conversation that Black Lives Matter advocates initiated. The Blue Lives Matter advocates parlayed this reversal into legislation that could quash Black Lives Matter activism and divert attention away from key policy initiatives, like enhanced police training which Black Lives Matter activists' had previously proposed.

Blue Lives Matter's cooptation of Black Lives Matter's strategic constitution of commu- nity, the perversion of the very terms that define Black Lives Matter's claims to the public's attention, and the re-centering of whiteness through allegations of police endangerment are not just prototypical responses to antiracist endeavors; they also reflect age-old misogynistic tendencies associated with net work. Reflecting on the theme of gender-based exploitation in ancient Greek myths related to weaving, Mifsud (2018) wrote, "To loathe women is to steal their work, to turn it against them, to structure society via political network in such a way as to trap them." By tracing the threads of controversies, students of networked argu- ment can recognize cooptation and work to counteract its racist and misogynistic effects. As Blue Lives Matter advocates coopt the communicative labor of women of color and then use their innovative outreach to silence them, argumentation scholars can affirm the value of this coopted labor by both attributing it and by bringing the arguments "cast [...] into the limen" (Mifsud, 2018) through institutionalized oppression back above the threshold of per- ception for more careful public consideration.

In August 2015, for instance, Black Lives Matter advocates integrated "recommendations from communities, research organizations and the President's [Obama] Task Force on 21st Century Policing" into a ten-point policy initiative designed "to protect and preserve life" ("Solutions," 2017, para. 2). Radley Balko, a leading law enforcement policy journalist, praised Campaign Zero, contending "the ideas here are well-researched, supported with real-world evidence and ought to be seriously considered by policymakers" (quoted in Friedersdorf, 2017, para. 16). At least some policymakers are, in fact, seriously considering Campaign Zero's core tenets. According to the campaign's website, "[Ten] states [...] have enacted legislation addressing three or more Campaign Zero policy categories" ("Campaign Zero," 2017, Take Action section, para. 3) and 32 states have passed legislation focused spe- cifically on enhanced police training. The passage of this legislation is imperative, consider- ing that, on average, "police recruits spend 58 hours learning how to shoot firearms and only 8 hours learning how to de-escalate situations" ("Solutions," 2017, Training section, para. 1). This staggering imbalance, coupled with endemic fragility surrounding antiracist education, bolsters Campaign Zero's contention that "an intensive training regime is needed to help police officers learn the behaviors and skills to interact appropriately with communi- ties of color" ("Solutions," 2017, Training section, para. 1). The growing number of these legally-mandated training programs, moreover, bolsters the contention here that argumentation scholars have both unique perspectives to lend and compelling reasons to engage the conflict between communities of color and the criminal justice system.

Fragile Threads Fray

By re-characterizing the relationship between Black Lives and Blue Lives Matter advocates from warring factions to a framework of more appropriate association, argumentation scholars recover the labor of queer women of color, appreciating how communities pull together and loosen knots of institutionalized repression while also explicating how opponents coopt communicative labor to reify dominant ideologies. Moreover, argumentation scholars could recover Black Lives Matter's movement toward Campaign Zero and recognize the fragility implied in Blue Lives Matter's cooptation. An amphibolic understanding of network directs critical attention toward tenuousness. In this case, apparent claims of police vulnerability and broad-based institutionalized support for their lives convey inconsistent instability. This fragility itself loosens the gauge of the net and calls for reinforcement. As DiAngelo (2011) suggested, "Viewing white anger, defensiveness, silence, and withdrawal in response to issues of race through the framework of White Fragility may help frame the problem as an issue of stamina-building, and thereby guide our interventions accordingly" (p. 67). To build stamina, police officers must train, which is consonant with Campaign Zero's stance and to which argumentation scholars can contribute fundamental insight.

At the most basic level, the hashtag-as-net gathers, documents, and makes visible the very public thoughts that constitute and convey the ideology of white supremacy, which undergirds the institutionally sanctioned practices tightly woven into the publicly projected identity of Blue Lives Matter. If the networked conception of Blue Lives Matter advocacy were to inform police training sessions, this conception could challenge the ubiquitous "bad apple" explanation for police violence against black lives by foregrounding how officers are synechdochally connected to one another and to the criminal justice system. The tangibility of this abstract conception could emerge by reading and discussing threads of Blue Lives Matter social media nets in which participants, using their names and oftentimes mentioning their law enforcement credentials, are caught calling for "the massacre of Black Lives Matter protestors," wherein

> [...] cops and their supporters have proposed denying police services to citizens who publicly support Black Lives Matter [...] called for white Americans to organize as a race against civil rights protests, demanded that police operate exclusively in white neighborhoods, and demonized black victims of lethal police violence as "thugs," "hoodrats," and worse.
>
> *(Blumenthal, 2016, para. 6-7)*

The visibility of this threatening and seemingly institutionally-sanctioned white supremacy, gathered and documented through Blue Lives Matter fora, holds the potential to counteract what many Black Lives Matter activists see as a denial of their lived reality among representatives of the police force. Reframing of the conflict between communities of color and the criminal justice system through the metaphor of weaving and a corollary understanding of interconnection rooted in the figure of synecdoche is a fundamental first step in priming police officers for further anti-racist endeavors.

As Blue Lives Matter advocates' responses to Black Lives Matter activism suggest, police training programs comprised of anti-racist education tenets will meet formidable resistance.

In no small part because, as Butler (2015) explained, "undoing whiteness has to be difficult work" (para. 26). Nevertheless, she instructed:

> It starts [...] with humility, with learning history, with white people learning how the history of racism persists in the everyday vicissitudes of the present, even as some of us may think we are "beyond" such a history [...] It is difficult and ongoing work, calling on an ethical disposition and political solidarity that risks error in the practice of solidarity.
>
> *(Yancy & Butler, 2015, para. 26)*

For police training sessions geared toward improving relationships with communities of color to succeed, these sessions must spark an acknowledgement of whiteness's effects and require a commitment to unraveling this ideology's stranglehold on the criminal justice system. Networked fora contribute to these anti-racist objectives by visually demonstrating how officers connect to one another and to a larger system, by gathering the discourse of their peers so that officers can consider how these words shape the worldviews that direct their split-second judgments, and by providing an iterative space to try again differently. Networks provide iterative spaces to acknowledge the exploitation of queer women of color's communicative labor. This acknowledgment could serve as a starting point for communicating with police force peers about communities of color in recognition of their humanity. Reconceptualizing the fora enabled through network as spaces for resilient democratic iteration provides perceptual safety nets for training in the hopes that stamina with interracial confrontation acquired online might translate into greater offline security for both Black and Blue lives.

References

About: Build Power. (2017). *Black Lives Matter*. Retrieved from http://blacklivesmatter.com/about/

Anderson, M. D. (2017, March 24). Kentucky governor signs redundant "blue lives matter" law. *Rewire*. Retrieved from https://rewire.news

Blumenthal, M. (2016, July 20). Is blue lives matter a racist hate group? *Alternet*. Retrieved from http://alternet.org/grayzone-project/blue-lives-matter-racist-hate-group

Butler, J. (2004). *Precarious life: The powers of mourning and violence*. New York, NY: Verso Press.

Campaign Zero. (2017). *Campaign zero: We can end police violence in America*. Retrieved from https://joincampaignzero.org/

Cullors, P. (2017). Black lives matter: Not a moment, but a movement. *Patrisse Cullors*. Retrieved from http://patrissecullors.com/black-lives-matter/

DiAngelo, R. (2011). White fragility. *International Journal of Critical Pedagogy, 3*(3), 54–70. Retrieved from http://libjournal.uncg.edu/ijcp/article/view/249

Farrell, T. B. (1995). *Norms of rhetorical culture*. New Haven, CT: Yale University Press.

Friedersdorf, C. (2017, April 18). A new exhibit in the case for the black lives matter movement. *The Atlantic*. Retrieved from https://theatlantic.com

Kaste, M. (2015, September 17). Is there a "war on police"? The statistics say no. *National Public Radio*. Retrieved from http://npr.org

Mifsud, M. L. (2018). On network. In M. Kennerly & D. S. Pfister (Eds.), *Ancient rhetorics & digital networks* (pp. 28–46). Tuscaloosa, AL: University of Alabama Press.

OfficerBlue. (2017, May 14). About Blue Lives Matter. *Blue Lives Matter*. Retrieved from https://bluelivesmatter.blue/organization/

Solutions. (2017). *Campaign zero: We can end police violence in America*. Retrieved from https://joincampaignzero.org/solutions/#solutionsoverview

Yancy, G., & Butler, J. (2015, January 12). What's wrong with "all lives matter"? [Interview]. *The New York Times*. Retrieved from http://opinionator.blogs.nytimes.com

8

NETWORKED PUBLIC ARGUMENT AS TERRAIN FOR STATECRAFT

Craig Hayden[1]

What does the rise of networked argumentation mean for the practice of public diplomacy? In 2012, Paul Foldi, a legislative analyst for Senator Richard Lugar, spoke to a conference on the future of U.S. public diplomacy. Foldi described U.S. public diplomacy, not as a kind of formal debate or strategy to induce a specific opinion, but as a means to cultivate "the benefit of the doubt" (quoted in Hayden, 2013, p. 212). His remarks underscored an inevitably uncertain terrain for public diplomacy—the practice by which countries seek to persuade, build relationships, and cultivate understanding among foreign publics. Given the challenges of the abundance of voices online, the use of digital propaganda tools, and the plurality of alternative perspectives, public diplomacy routinely involves a certain amount of contingency, as the efficacy of its argument strategies are never fully predictable.

If argumentation is a way to bridge contingency (i.e., to resolve differences through risk and accept the possibility of change), public diplomacy makes a daily wager on the methods of appeal rooted in the inducements of soft power resources. The assumptions of effect and impact, adjusted through revision and policy, drive public diplomacy. But, is such practice capable of addressing the seemingly daunting context of a networked public argument as the terrain for how states engage each other?

Put simply, the impact of digital communication on influence and politics is unfolding in unpredictable ways for argumentation scholarship and informed practice. In a moment of mediatized political controversy, digital appeals enable politics and leadership through difference and dissensus, exploiting the network structure and the dismantling of publics into a constellation of interests and public sphericules. Advocates engage publics strategically as networks. How these publics reason together based on the emergent norms and practices of communication technology upend the conventions, genres, and ends of public argument. Public argument acts both on and through the morphology of the network.

But the international dimension of this transformation bears further scrutiny, as nation-states leverage the capacity of communication through digital platforms to achieve strategic ends. While nation-states have always relied on information to make decisions, signal intentions, and propagandize foreign publics, active attempts to dominate narratives, shape the discourse of domestic politics, and deploy technologies that leverage the properties of social networks demands critical scrutiny and a revision of assumptions (Miskimmon, O'Loughlin,

& Roselle, 2013). Put differently, scholars and practitioners alike need to describe and understand how states seek to influence through public argument within networks.

Argument has a longstanding association with international relations and the broad contours of statecraft, including classical cases to the controversies over discourses of foreign policy, to the language games and signaling that occurs between states (Crawford, 2002; Milliken, 1999). But the rise of information interventions and interference among nation-states in their respective mediatized "markets for loyalty" (Price, 2014, p. ix) signals the importance of argumentation in statecraft focused on the expected utility of networks. Nation-states are not acting on unitary counterparts, but on allies and adversaries composed of networks and attendant network vulnerabilities.

Of course, the idea of networks and statecraft is not new. Diplomacy operates through networks of contact work. Representation is the messy "'engine room' of international relations" (Jönsson & Hall, 2005, p. 1), where global policy networks and the convening power of diplomatic agency implement policy. The communication work of public diplomacy, likewise, bases its foundation on the belief that networks are the gatekeepers to policy influence. The heightened visibility of states engaged in coordinated argumentation campaigns invites further inquiry into the convergence of argumentation within the context of networked audiences and enabling communication platforms.

To explain, the first section below deals with the adaptation of argument to the network form elevated to significance through digital network platforms. Accordingly, it reviews theoretical observations on the nature of digitally enabled, public argumentation. The second section presents the rise of machine-based public argument—the use of bots and AI to transform the practice of state-based influence and communication efforts. The third section explores how recent government attention to the context for U.S. public diplomacy practice illustrates adaptation to the realities of digital influence and how the "folk theories" of communication underscore the limits of responding to foreign influence.

Characteristics of Networked Argument

The advent of networked argument raises significant issues for argumentation studies in terms of the subject. For example, how does the practice of argument define interlocutors, the location of influence, and the social practices that digital networking platforms sustain? Goodnight (2016), in his elaboration of a "cybersphere," proposed a new context for practices, norms, and genres based in part on a reconstitution of the argument subject through nodes and edges. For him, the ends of argumentation moved away from generative controversy and towards dissensus and identity posturing. Goodnight's portrait reconfigured online audience research in the context of an argument lens. He contended that self-organization online reinforces a fragmented public sphere, where homophily provides the over-arching dynamic for association and exchange.

Participation in online networks closes off avenues to deliberation, reinforces behaviors and associations, and increases vulnerability to crucial online gatekeepers that can exploit ties. Digital networks not only provide enclaves for similar opinions, news flows, or identity formations, but the structure of the social form helps explain their influence. The "cybersphere" illustrates a "pragmatic space" (Goodnight, 2016, p. 87) whereby media consumption practices define and the communication production encourage. Affordances of the technology reinforce rituals of public argument that move argument away from rational-deliberative usage and toward communication that affirms identity, tribe, and information reduction.

The constellation of these argumentation elements signifies a shift toward a performative aspect that reinforces difference, questions dominant framing, and rewards cues that signal community distinction. Simultaneously, it eschews reasonableness grounded in the standards of experience, legal authority, or expert knowledge per se. Users place emphasis on mimetic qualities and affective expression that encourage further attention and sharing. Thus, online networks have destabilized "the expectations that regulate the uses of argument, tests of validity, and best-practices of construction" (Goodnight, 2016, p. 99). The affordances of argumentation's platforms—that is, what the technology platforms invite participants to do—bend toward dissensus and difference.

The media ecology of argumentation carries strong implications for the emergent conventions of argumentation in practice. Harsin (2014) argued that the technological context challenges the process and products of argument by shifting argumentation to circulation and attention. Drivers of influence include how technology impacts the timing and scale of argument propagation. Harsin (2014) maintained that publics are awash in the circulation of arguments that limit the capacity to "reason out a problem" in a collective moment of "continuous partial attention" (p. 15). The downstream consequences of sharing online is an increased reliance on affective cues based on identity positions, cultural knowledge, and shared perspectives derived from network affiliations. Harsin described the distribution of positions online as non-deliberative argumentation, epitomized through the advent of "rumor bombs" (p. 18), that is, chaotic sharable arguments that destabilize conventional argumentation practices and make more traditional processes of agenda-setting and framing obsolete. The materiality of public argument impacts the way that political communication circulates and repackages original content, but likewise, how audiences consume and interpret that content as meaningful. The online environment has transposed media logics onto the norms and practices of political communication (Couldry & Hepp, 2013).

Networked Argument as Tool of Statecraft

The remarkable growth of information politics as tools for statecraft amplifies theoretical claims about the conventions of networked public argument. While online strategies and techniques represent a staple of extremist organizations to recruit fighters and promote their actions, the work of nation-states and their targeted use of automated social media traffic raises the stakes of online argument. Nation-states have increased their targeting of information networks in order to influence, shape, or otherwise "hack" the mechanisms through which a media system sustains a domestic political process of deliberation, persuasion, and cultural affirmation (Powers & Kounalakis, 2017).

Perhaps no act of statecraft is more emblematic of this information targeting than the work of governments to directly manipulate the flow of information through social media networks via computational propaganda. The approach is not simply the work of countries such as Russia, China, or North Korea. "Political campaigns, governments, and regular citizens around the world are employing both people and bots in attempts to artificially shape public life" (Woolley & Howard, 2017, p. 6). Western countries, corporate actors, and citizens are engaging in this use of available social media technology. Social media automated account "bots" provide targeted information diffusion of arguments to particular networks. Bots can post information more than 1000 times a day, relatively free of scrutiny or suspicion. This kind of digital influence campaign relies on algorithms, recommender systems that automate the delivery of targeted messages, and human curation "to purposefully distribute misleading information over social media networks" (Woolley & Howard, 2016, p. 3). Computational propaganda "learns" and mimics human communication to "manipulate public opinion across a diverse range of platforms and device networks" (Woolley

& Howard, 2016, p. 3). At least one research project studying millions of tweets uncovered bots that amplified the reach and significance of human user accounts, as well as the presence of a "black-market for reusable political disinformation bots" (Timberg, 2017, para. 15).

Computational propaganda manifests as false news, creates directed attacks on journalists opposed to government actors, and can work to counter social media efforts or bolster government positions. It may also embody the use of social networks to shape narratives that impact the battle space or theater of operations for deployed military forces. Cyber operations for such forms of strategic communication have incorporated the creation of "official government applications, websites or platforms for disseminating content; using accounts—either real, fake or automated—to interact with users on social media; or creating substantive content such as images, videos or blog posts" (Bradshaw & Howard, 2017, p. 9).

The integration of computational and machine-based communication with purposive human-led efforts to shape news and information flows is widespread. By maintaining multiple accounts across platforms, such efforts monitor user web traffic to gain access to how users frequent other sites. Bots develop content that reflects the characteristics of the user network. The automatically generated, persuasive content "[reflects] your particular psychological frame [to] achieve a particular outcome" (Chessen, 2017a, p. 39). The bots not so much sideline conversation as they simulate in the attempt to propagate the persuasiveness of a narrative by the structure of network associations.

These efforts distort the terrain of public argument online. Artificial accounts bank on their ability to mimic human communication, in order to give the perception of credibility or scale. Bradshaw and Howard (2017) argued that such accounts "flood social media networks with spam, hashtags, and fake news […] amplify marginal voices and ideas by inflating the number of likes, shares and retweets they receive, creating an artificial sense of popularity, momentum or relevance" (p. 11). These accounts create noise in the information system —cultivating credibility while potentially disrupting "civic conversations" (Woolley, 2017, p. 14). Such efforts also present challenges for more traditional international engagement efforts, the promotion of meaningful dialogue, and exchange through public diplomacy.

Lessons Learned for Conducting Public Diplomacy

Countries like the United States seeking to adapt to this mediated context must address their tacit understanding of how messaging cultivates influence. Indeed, U.S. public diplomacy initiatives have evolved away from providing a strictly message-centric, counter-argument strategy. As a 2016 RAND study indicated, a narrowly defined counter-message strategy has failed for a number of reasons (Paul & Matthews, 2016). Countries such as Russia have a vertically integrated, tightly controlled, media distribution system that bots and other coordinated messaging campaigns amplify. What argumentation scholar Damien Pfister (2011) identified—a strategy of "flooding the zone" (p. 142)—anticipated what a coordinated messaging strategy of crowding out alternatives could accomplish. But more importantly, the Russian "firehose of falsehood" (Paul & Matthews, 2016, p. 1) relied on technologically enabled cognitive factors to reject information that threatened identity positions.

In May 2017, the U.S. government released a report highlighting the consequences of such networked, online influence activities for U.S. public diplomacy (Powers & Kounalakis, 2017). The report also questioned logics that underwrite public diplomacy programs and counter-disinformation strategies' tacit notions of influence, by interrogating the "folk theories" (p. 4) and tacit assumptions about media effects, online media usage, and what counts as persuasion

(Powers, 2017). The contributors found that the challenges of online networked argumentation is not simply a function of enclaved publics or competition for attention—but about the tensions between fact-driven strategies and cognitive biases (Chessen, 2017b).

The audiences for public diplomacy argumentation are more than simple products of a "post-truth" contest for media influence. They engage in a continuing process of "epistemic vigilance" (Powers, 2017, p. 2). The influence campaigns target the public by validating their understanding of the world. The increased use of online news sources equates to more, not less, exposure to multiple perspectives. The problem of networked argumentation is not that audiences find themselves in siloes or enclaves; rather, users do not have a motivation to attend to the arguments from differing perspectives and identity positions (Henick & Walsh, 2017).

Campaigns of online argumentation are also not predominately contests for attention (Powers & Kounalakis, 2017). While the viral metaphor offers some insight into the culture of sharing information online, it also infers that messages and arguments gain traction and spread through exposure alone. Network theory suggests possibilities of engagement happen through viral messaging, but such attention metrics derive from corporate promotion and online revenue generation. Public diplomacy's intent to build credibility and engage in deliberative exchange across international publics seems at cross-purposes with the ends of the attention economy online. An engagement strategy that maximizes attention enables quantifiable metrics of output by foreign ministries engaged in strategic international communication, but may fall short of demonstrating substantive influence on enduring opinions and positions that matter to foreign policy (Pamment, 2012).

Finally, the exploitation of digital platforms to manipulate social networks through computational propaganda erodes trust among publics for these platforms. This raises concerns about the credibility of any public diplomacy that relies on media that audiences recognize as already compromised (Chessen, 2017a). Online users may distrust communication technologies that they recognize bots have compromised, thereby calling into question the legitimacy of a networked based strategy. This challenge is not only a problem for governments, but for the technology providers themselves as well—such as Facebook and Twitter.

Recent policy recommendations suggest that public diplomacy, considered as an argument strategy to foster informed and reasoned exchange between publics, should recommit to the promulgation of facts as both a counter-narrative strategy and as a means to address the firehose model of influence. Yet, this approach raises important questions about how to overcome the tensions between quantitative diffusion of arguments and the cognitive and identity-driven factors that reinforce some narratives over others.

Some Preliminary Conclusions

The case of recent government research into the implications of digital networked propaganda illustrates the limitations of existing critical and theoretical treatments of a networked argumentation. This is not to suggest that argumentation as a field does not have important contributions to make. The U.S. government's attention, if anything, should spark further inquiry at the crossroads of practice and study. A number of challenges emerge at this crossroads—where the problems that confront public diplomacy practitioners begin to reflect questions emergent in the interdisciplinary study of online argument practice.

First, the resistance to argument is as big an issue as the ability to grapple with computational interventions and bot campaigns. Identity-based, cognitive biases foreclose opportunities for persuasion, and the very act of argument may activate defenses to resist change (Garrett, Weeks, & Neo, 2016). The networked argument context strengthens the defense of positions despite the force of the better argument. So, while network routes to dissemination improve the "hit rate" of attention, scholars may have to take more seriously the psychological factors that foreclose on internal attitude change.

Second, the challenge posed by the disaggregation of the arguing *subject* complicates our conception of how argument practice establishes credibility and legitimacy. How should we consider these factors when argument interlocutors may include machine-based arguing agents? At the very least, computational argumentation presents an urgent need for argument literacy among discerning digital publics. If the network itself remains the significant locus for how arguments and narratives chain out, should we also consider the network as a subject itself?

Third, networked argumentation challenges some of the conventional insights of argumentation, as well as the tacit logics and assumptions about how to leverage social media to counter state-based disinformation campaigns and extremist recruitment. More rigorous mapping of online argument networks functions as an important tool for uncovering argument communities and clusters. However, the emergent cultural norms of these argument communities necessitate a wider scope of ethnographic attention to argumentation practices that defines such digital public spaces. Computational propaganda highlights critical concerns that the argumentation scholarly community voices—and raises the urgency for continued intervention.

Note

1 The views expressed by the author of this chapter are his own, and do not necessarily reflect those of the U.S. government.

References

Bradshaw, S., & Howard, P. N. (2017, July). *Troops, trolls and troublemakers: A global inventory of organized social media manipulation* (Working Paper No. 2017.12). Oxford, United Kingdom: Oxford Internet Institute, University of Oxford. Retrieved from http://blogs.oii.ox.ac.uk/politicalbots/wp-content/uploads/sites/89/2017/07/Troops-Trolls-and-Troublemakers.pdf

Chessen, M. (2017a, May). Understanding the challenges of artificial intelligence and computational propaganda to public diplomacy. In S. M. Powers & M. Kounalakis (Eds.), *Can public diplomacy survive the Internet? Bots, echo chambers, and disinformation* (pp. 39–47). Washington, DC: U.S. Advisory Commission on Public Diplomacy.

Chessen, M. (2017b, May). Understanding the psychology behind computational propaganda. In S. M. Powers & M. Kounalakis (Eds.), *Can public diplomacy survive the Internet? Bots, echo chambers, and disinformation* (pp. 19–26). Washington, DC: U.S. Advisory Commission on Public Diplomacy.

Couldry, N., & Hepp, A. (2013). Conceptualizing mediatization: Contexts, traditions, arguments. *Communication Theory, 23*(3), 191–202. doi: 10.1111/comt.12019

Crawford, N. C. (2002). *Argument and change in world politics: Ethics, decolonization, and humanitarian intervention.* Cambridge, United Kingdom: Cambridge University Press.

Garrett, R. K., Weeks, B. E., & Neo, R. L. (2016). Driving a wedge between evidence and beliefs: How online ideological news exposure promotes political misperceptions. *Journal of Computer-Mediated Communication, 21*(5), 331–348. doi: 10.1111/jcc4.12164

Goodnight, G. T. (2016). Argumentation and the cybersphere. In R. Von Burg (Ed.), *Dialogues in argumentation* (Vol. 3, pp. 83–104). Windsor, Ontario: University of Windsor.

Harsin, J. (2014). Public argument in the new media ecology: Implications of temporality, spatiality, and cognition. *Journal of Argumentation in Context, 3*(1), 7–34. doi: 10.1075/jaic.3.1.02har

Hayden, C. (2013). Logics of narrative and networks in US public diplomacy: Communication power and US strategic engagement. *Journal of International Communication, 19*(2), 196–218. doi: 10.1080/13216597.2013.775070

Henick, J., & Walsh, R. (2017, May). U.S. 2016 elections: A case study in "inoculating" public opinion against disinformation. In S. M. Powers & M. Kounalakis (Eds.), *Can public diplomacy survive the Internet? Bots, echo chambers, and disinformation* (pp. 65–70). Washington, DC: U.S. Advisory Commission on Public Diplomacy.

Jönsson, C., & Hall, M. (2005). *Essence of diplomacy.* New York, NY: Palgrave Macmillan. doi: 10.1057/9780230511040

Milliken, J. (1999). The study of discourse in international relations: A critique of research and methods. *European Journal of International Relations, 5*(2), 225–254. doi: 10.1177/1354066199005002003

Miskimmon, A., O'Loughlin, B., & Roselle, L. (2013). *Strategic narratives: Communication power and the new world order.* New York, NY: Routledge.

Pamment, J. (2012). What became of the new public diplomacy? Recent developments in British, US and Swedish public diplomacy policy and evaluation methods. *The Hague Journal of Diplomacy, 7*(3), 313–336. doi: 10.1163/187119112X635177

Paul, C., & Matthews, M. (2016). The Russian "firehose of falsehoods" propaganda model: Why it might work and options to counter it. *RAND Corporation.* Retrieved from https://rand.org

Pfister, D. S. (2011). The logos of the blogosphere: Flooding the zone, invention, and attention in the Lott imbroglio. *Argumentation and Advocacy, 47*(3), 141–162.

Powers, S. M. (2017, May). Executive summary. In S. M. Powers & M. Kounalakis (Eds.), *Can public diplomacy survive the Internet? Bots, echo chambers, and disinformation* (pp. 2–5). Washington, DC: U.S. Advisory Commission on Public Diplomacy.

Powers, S. M., & Kounalakis, M. (Eds.). (2017, May). *Can public diplomacy survive the Internet? Bots, echo chambers, and disinformation.* Washington, DC: U.S. Advisory Commission on Public Diplomacy. Retrieved from http://state.gov

Price, M. E. (2014). *Free expression, globalism, and the new strategic communication.* Cambridge, United Kingdom: Cambridge University Press.

Timberg, C. (2017, July 17). Spreading fake news becomes standard practice for governments across the world. *The Washington Post.* Retrieved from https://washingtonpost.com/news/the-switch/wp/2017/07/17/spreading-fake-news-becomes-standard-practice-for-governments-across-the-world/?utm_term=.d6ce12a6550e

Woolley, S. C. (2017, May). Computational propaganda and political bots: An overview. In S. M. Powers & M. Kounalakis (Eds.), Can public diplomacy survive the Internet? Bots, echo chambers, and disinformation (pp. 13–17). Washington, DC: U.S. Advisory Commission on Public Diplomacy.

Woolley, S. C., & Howard, P. N. (2016). Automation, algorithms, and politics│political communication, computational propaganda, and autonomous agents—introduction. *International Journal of Communication, 10,* 4882–4890. Retrieved from http://ijoc.org/index.php/ijoc/article/view/6298

Woolley, S. C., & Howard, P. N. (2017, June). *Computational propaganda worldwide: Executive summary* (Working Paper No. 2017.11). Oxford, United Kingdom: Oxford Internet Institute, University of Oxford.

PART II

STRATEGIC USE OF
DEFINITION IN
NETWORKED ARGUMENT

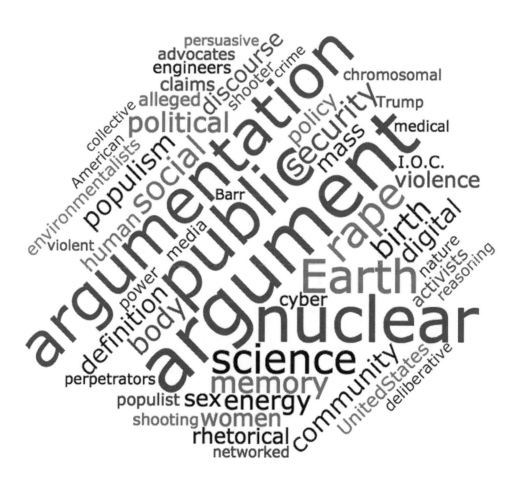

9

IDEOLOGICAL CONSERVATISM VS. FAUX POPULISM IN DONALD TRUMP'S INAUGURAL ADDRESS

David Zarefsky

The inaugural address is a well-recognized genre of presidential discourse. Each president's term has begun with one, although it is not constitutionally required. In the most thorough discussion of its features, Campbell and Jamieson (2008) noted that its chief characteristics were unification of the audience, reaffirmation of traditional values, setting forth the general principles that will guide the new administration, enacting the role of president, and adapting these characteristics to the nature of epideictic (ceremonial) discourse. Some of these features are similar to the British monarch's speech from the throne opening each session of Parliament, in that it sets forth the overall outlook and general program of the government. Although often classified as epideictic addresses, inaugurals also deploy arguments as a key part of their substance. Indeed, Perelman and Olbrechts-Tyteca (1969) objected to separating epideictic and deliberative genres on the grounds that the ways in which a speech celebrates shared values also makes a case for actions of a certain kind, if not for specific legislative measures.

Donald Trump's 2017 Inaugural Address is no exception. It celebrates nationalism, often in contrast to globalism, but it also characterizes problems and proposes a solution; the problems and solution are the speech's argumentative substance. The problems are (a) political elites who have reaped the rewards of the system while ignoring the needs of the people they were meant to serve, (b) widespread "American carnage"[1] epitomized by an alleged rise in crime, and (c) a sense that we are no longer in control of our own future because we are losing industries and jobs to other nations and because we are vulnerable to "radical Islamic terrorism." The solution is his own inauguration, because he embodies the will of the people. As he said, "this moment is your moment." And with his inauguration comes "a total allegiance to the United States of America" that will produce empathy, solidarity, and "a new national pride" that "will stir ourselves, lift our sights and heal our divisions."

Does this network of claims align Trump's address with conservative values (Lee, 2014) as they have evolved since the Second World War? To answer that question, I will consider several aspects of contemporary conservatism.

Conservatism?

Probably the strongest pillar in the conservatism ideology is an assumed antagonism between the people and the government that goes back to Thomas Jefferson (Staloff, 2005).[2] Chief among the defenses of this view is the claim that government threatens liberty. If it is powerful enough to dispense benefits, it is powerful enough to take away freedoms. The unfettered decisions of individual citizens are thought to contain more wisdom than the centralized directions issued by government. Of course, conservatives recognize the need for *some* government—for national defense, for diplomacy, for homeland security, for providing essential services such as police protection, for responding to natural disasters that overwhelm the capacity of private citizens, and for the protection of selected individual rights. But the natural tendency of conservatives is to be suspicious of government, presuming against its expansion (Goodnight, 1980), and to reject the notion that the existence of a public problem is necessarily a warrant for government action.

Trump's Inaugural Address partakes of this ideology—but only to a point. In his opening remarks, he announced that he was "transferring power from Washington, D.C. and giving it back to you, the people." But one is hard pressed to find in the remainder of the speech an example of power being devolved in this way. Nor does one find clarification of who "you, the people" are. Notably, Trump does not discuss government in institutional terms; he is strikingly personal. He said, "For too long, a small group in our nation's capital has reaped the rewards of government while the people have borne the cost." Then he said, "Politicians prospered, but the jobs left and the factories closed. The establishment protected itself but not the citizens of our country." This is not the sound of a conservative ideologue but of a conspiracy theorist. The problem is not government per se but malevolent politicians—the very people, presumably, who were sitting behind him on the inaugural platform.

The definition of "the people" conservatives defend from government, however, is relatively elastic. Jefferson regarded them as yeoman farmers who were under siege from the commercial and mercantile elites. Andrew Jackson enlarged the category to unite the emerging laboring classes with the farmers, in opposition to capitalists, industrialists, and financiers (Cole, 2009). Franklin Roosevelt built the New Deal coalition by uniting labor, minorities, small farmers, Southerners, immigrants, and many intellectuals against the economic elite that, ironically, he himself embodied (Brands, 2008). Trump also alters the definition of the term to include *everyone* except the aforementioned corrupt politicians. On this reading, even the wealthiest corporate leaders are part of "the people," besieged as they are by excessive regulation and taxation imposed by and for the benefit of corrupt politicians.

From the assumed hostility between the people and the government comes a second tenet of modern conservatism: a call to shrink the size of government. But Trump does not make such an appeal. He seems to want not to shrink government but to redirect it. It may remain just as large and as active, but it will serve different masters. He implies, although he does not explicitly state, that government will do something about the problems he classified as "American carnage": poverty in the inner cities, "rusted-out factories," an education system "flush with cash" yet that leaves students "deprived of all knowledge," and "the crime and the gangs and the drugs." The government will act to "protect our borders from the ravages of other countries making our products, stealing our companies and destroying our jobs." And he explicitly committed himself to a major infrastructure program: "We will build new roads and highways and bridges and airports and tunnels and railways all across our wonderful nation." Not only that, but we "will reinforce old alliances and form new ones and unite the civilized world against radical Islamic terrorism." This set of missions, if anything, calls for *more* government. Even though Trump later would call for substantial budget reductions, he does not foreshadow any in his Inaugural Address, not even the promised repeal of the Affordable Care Act. In sum, by this understanding of conservatism, Trump's Inaugural Address is not the argument of a conservative.

Another theme of contemporary conservatism is ambivalence about America's place in the world. Following the Second World War, conservatives drew back from their interwar expressions of overt isolationism, but they remained skeptical about aiding other nations, taking direction from international bodies, and defending a world order. At the same time, convinced that America has whatever power it needs to work its will merely by expressing what it wants, conservatives tend to blame American perfidy for policy disappointments. This was especially true during the Cold War years.[3]

Trump's Inaugural partakes of this ambivalence, but in a novel way. He argued for pulling back commitments not because they threaten American sovereignty but because the United States was getting a bad deal. Far from pledging himself to "pay any price, bear any burden," as President Kennedy (1962) did, Trump alleged, "We've enriched foreign industry at the expense of American industry, subsidized the armies of other countries while allowing for the very sad depletion of our own military." After providing a few more such examples, Trump concluded, "We've made other countries rich while the wealth, strength, and confidence of our country has dissipated over the horizon." But other nations will no longer take such advantage of the United States. Trump is promulgating a new vision—America first: "Every decision on trade, on taxes, on immigration, on foreign affairs will be made to benefit American workers and American families." Strictly speaking, this is not a return to isolationism, since he preserves alliances. But he embraces a decided shift in priorities. America sacrificed to rebuild Europe, knowing or believing that a stable Europe was in America's best long-run interest. Now, Europe is strong again, so Trump will determine American relationships according to whether the United States "wins" on the deal.

If Trump expresses ambivalence, however, it is not the ambivalence of the conservative, because he ultimately does not call on the U.S. to pull back. Rather, the very threat to do so provides leverage to negotiate better agreements, so that the United States will be "winning" again. Furthermore, expressing ambivalence about foreign affairs is not unique to conservatism. Both liberals and conservatives often are enthusiastic, initial supporters of unilateral American military action, but when no option for a quick and easy victory appears, they become frustrated, whether with Korea, Vietnam, Iraq, Afghanistan, or Syria.

A fourth feature of conservatism focuses less on its explicit statement of ideology and more on the nature of its argument. Weaver (1953), who *was* a conservative, suggested another criterion: Look to the method of argument more than to the expressed statement of principles. He wrote that the conservatives argue from definition, from statements about the nature of things, and are not swayed by the transient. They filter perceptions through an interpretive framework guided by principles. In contrast, liberals argue from circumstance, reading empirical conditions dispositive of action. On this standard, Trump is no conservative. His method of argument resembles Weaver's characterization of the liberal. He asserts the existence of conditions that self-evidently warrant actions that he favors. Examples include the conditions grouped under "American carnage," the areas in which we supposedly have "lost" to foreigners, and the loss of middle-class wealth. Recitation of these conditions compels action and Trump promised to provide it.

Judged against these pillars of contemporary conservatism, then, Trump is not a conservative ideologue, but another possibility exists: perhaps, even so, he is a conservative rhetor. Scott (1973) noted that "the conservative voice in radical rhetoric" was a common phenomenon. He described radical departures as if they were restorations, returns to the custom and practice of an earlier day. This practice reflects the belief that audiences are somewhat conservative by nature and will be more inclined to accept drastic changes if they are portrayed not as a bold new argument but as a return to the familiar.

Trump used calls for restoration in his Inaugural Address, but only superficially. Near the beginning he said that he was giving power "back to you, the people"—implying that the people once had power but somehow lost it. Later in the speech, he said, "We will bring back our jobs. We will bring back our borders. We will bring back our wealth. And we will bring back our dreams." The phrase "bring back" clearly implies that the objects of his attention were once here and will be restored. And most notably, the peroration reprises Trump's campaign promises to make America strong, wealthy, proud, safe, and great "again." And a careful reading of the inaugural suggests that despite slogans such as "Make America Great Again," Trump is really not calling for restoration at all. He said as much: "We assembled here today are issuing a new decree…From this day forward, a new vision will govern our land." And later: "We stand at the birth of a new millennium ready to unlock the mysteries of space, to free the earth from the miseries of disease and to harness the energies, industries and technologies of tomorrow." Pledges such as these are offering not restoration but bold new directions.

Populism?

On each of these grounds, Trump's Inaugural Address fails to provide evidence of conservative ideological underpinnings. What then is the underlying rationale of the speech? Trump provides a clue when he promised that, "America will start winning again. Winning like never before." The reason was that "the forgotten men and women of our country came forward by the tens of millions to become part of an historic movement, the likes of which the world has never seen before." He promised that their struggle will succeed because "I will fight for you with every breath in my body, and I will never, ever let you down."

Championing the people in a struggle against a real or imagined elite is the chief characteristic of populism, going back at least to the 1880s in the United States. It is not an ideology but a rhetorical stance that the right or the left of the political spectrum can adopt. As I wrote elsewhere, this stance consists of (a) a claim to represent and speak for the people, (b) identification of an enemy that is undermining the people and enriching itself, (c) the democratization of evidence and disdain for expertise, (d) the normalization of hyperbole, and (e) a predilection for simple, preferably single-factor, causal explanations and a willingness to believe in conspiracies (Zarefsky, 2017). What mainly distinguishes left- from right-wing populist discourse is who is named as the enemy. Left-wing populists see the enemy as an *economic* elite and view the concentration of wealth as inimical to democracy; right-wing populists see the enemy as a *political* elite that undermines the will of the people. Right-wing populists rail against "big government"; left-wing populists want to use big government as a counterweight against the "one percent."

If the alleged enemy is real, then populist rhetoric is genuine. If the elite is only a rhetorical construction, then the argument is more of a faux populism. Trump's Inaugural Address falls into the latter category. Like his predecessors Jefferson and Jackson, Trump effectively redefines who counts as "the people" and who is the alleged elite. In Trump's case, "the people" is "you"— his entire viewing audience—and the elite consists of unnamed politicians located in Washington, D.C. Although some might see Trump as becoming part of Washington as he enacts the presidential role, he is not there yet. He is still part of "we," referring to the incoming administration that is assuming power committed to reverse the record of his predecessor. He is the agent of "you, the people."

As the speech proceeded, however, Trump merged "we" and "you" into an enlarged conception of "we" that includes the new administration as part of the "people." This "we" will bring back our jobs, borders, wealth, and dreams, achieving the promises enumerated in the last part of the address. And this "we" "will no longer accept politicians [the enemy elite] who are all talk and no action, constantly complaining but never doing anything about it."

On this reading, for example, millionaires are not elites, because they, the working class and the victims of "American carnage," all are united against the corrupt political elite. And who makes up this corrupt political elite? If the category is not a null set, it must prominently include the national leaders of both political parties with whom Trump joked and engaged in friendly banter immediately after excoriating them in his inaugural address. This incongruity supports the judgment that the inaugural address appeals to a faux populism rather than the genuine article. Trump's apparent disinterest in a genuine populism would become more evident in the coming weeks as the president announced initiatives that would harm the very elements of the population that he regarded as "the people" responsible for his victory.

Conclusion

Donald Trump's 2017 Inaugural Address, then, is neither genuinely conservative nor genuinely populist. For that matter, it fulfills the letter but not the spirit of the generic expectations of an inaugural address. He reconstitutes "the people" in the image of working-class voters like those of the Midwest who provided his slim margin of victory. He calls overtly for national unity but offers no compromise to achieve it; rather, it is as if he expects supporters of his defeated opponent to capitulate and acquiesce. He does announce general themes but they are not anchored to the programs he will propose. He refers to scriptural authority with the confident promise—not just the hope—that "we will be protected by God," and by the allusion to a passage in Numbers that celebrates the achievement of unity, which he apparently misunderstands as submission to him.

Donald Trump's Inaugural Address does not connect him to the network of conservative ideological argument. It partakes of populist discourse but does not really enact it. If the inaugural fits in any category, it would be the campaign speech, for if anything it attempts to reprise the themes of his campaign. In that respect, the speech seems to be *sui generis* as an inaugural address, and that appears to comport with a president who seems unconstrained by presidential norms or by decorum.

Especially in this polarized time, a temptation exists for scholars to base their analysis of this speech purely on whether they agree with its sentiments, or else to avoid that temptation by engaging in a simple matching of the speech's contents against the generic expectations for inaugural addresses. Argumentation studies offers a different approach: examining the speech's explicit and implicit claims and then scrutinizing the ways those claims, their support, and what the relationship between claims and support reveals about the speech's underlying ideological underpinnings. In the case at hand, to establish a claim that Donald Trump's presidency heralds an era of conservative resurgence, one would need to find other supporting evidence than his inaugural address.

Notes

1 All quotations from Trump's Inaugural Address are taken from "This Moment Is Your Moment," *The New York Times,* January 21, 2017, p. A16. Since they all are on the same page, they are not cited individually in the text.
2 Although today regarded as conservative, Jefferson's anti-government orientation at his time was liberalism.
3 The most obvious example was the controversy surrounding the "loss" of China to the Communists in 1949.

References

Brands, H. W. (2008). *Traitor to his class: The privileged life and radical presidency of Franklin Delano Roosevelt.* New York, NY: Doubleday.

Campbell, K. K., & Jamieson, K. H. (2008). *Presidents creating the presidency: Deeds done in words.* Chicago, IL: University of Chicago Press.

Cole, D. B. (2009). *Vindicating Andrew Jackson: The 1828 election and the rise of the two-party system.* Lawrence, KS: University Press of Kansas.

Goodnight, G. T. (1980). The liberal and the conservative presumption. In J. Rhodes & S. Newell (Ed.), *Proceedings of the summer conference on argumentation, 1979* (pp. 304–337). Falls Church, VA: Speech Communication Association.

Kennedy, J. F. (1962). Inaugural address, January 20, 1961. In *Public papers of the presidents: John F. Kennedy, 1961* (pp. 1–3). Washington, DC: Government Printing Office.

Lee, M. J. (2014). *Creating conservatism: Postwar words that made an American movement.* East Lansing, MI: Michigan State University Press.

Perelman, Ch., & Olbrechts-Tyteca, L. (1958/1969). *The new rhetoric: A treatise on argumentation* (J. Wilkinson & P. Weaver, Trans.). Notre Dame, IN: University of Notre Dame Press.

Scott, R. L. (1973). The conservative voice in radical rhetoric: A common response to division. *Speech Monographs, 40*(2), 123–135. doi:10.1080/03637757309375787

Staloff, D. (2005). *Hamilton, Adams, Jefferson: The politics of Enlightenment and the American founding.* New York, NY: Hill and Wang.

Weaver, R. M. (1953). *The ethics of rhetoric.* Chicago, IL: Henry Regnery.

Zarefsky, D. (2017, July). *The rhetorical stance of populism.* Paper presented at the Conference of the Rhetoric Society of Europe, Norwich, United Kingdom.

10

POPULISTS ARGUE, BUT POPULISM IS NOT AN ARGUMENTATION (AND WHY THE DISTINCTION MATTERS FOR ARGUMENTATION THEORY)

David M. Cheshier

In the realm of populist phenomena, argumentation scholarship has been broadly assimilative, where the work on populism done in other disciplines often pushes back against approaches that primarily treat populists as offering a distinctively structured set of coherent ideas. So-called ideological theories of populism immediately encounter the problem that, on their face, the many available cases of populism globally and historically actually share almost no common ideas. That populism is an "*empty* signifier" (p. 71) is the starting point of Laclau's (2007) work, *On Populist Reason*. Mény and Surel (2002) referred to this as populism's "empty shell" problem (p. 4). Taggart (2000) described populism as having an "empty heart" (p. 4). Both political practice and political theory evidence the problem. Venezuela's Hugo Chavez offered a statist economic program, while Peru's Alberto Fujimori and the American Tea Party defend free market politics. Nineteenth century American populism typically emerged out of the prairie grassroots, while Argentina's Juan Peron and France's Marine Le Pen organized populist fronts around hierarchical top down strategies (Katsambekis, 2016). University of Georgia political scientist Cas Mudde (2004) provoked sharp debate by arguing that populism is a thin ideology, a sort of ideology without ideas, reducible finally to the simple Manichean claim, "It's us against them."

Scholars of argumentation are attentive to all this, of course, but in every case, they seem to find little difficulty in applying the theoretical and methodological apparatus of argumentation studies in reading populism as an argument formation. Wodak (2015) wrote extensively on the relevance of argumentative topoi and associated methods of argument reconstruction as appropriate to populism. Lee (2006) argued for the idea that populism both enacts and is shaped by an "argumentative frame" (p. 362), a position that inspired others to use that terminology (cf. Duffy, 2015; Foster, 2011; Maddux, 2013; Waisanen, 2011).

Wider disciplinary reasons exist for why argumentation scholars are more likely to assimilate populism into the realm of argument than not. The discipline's DNA includes the idea of an ever-expanding "Empire of Argument," starting with the well-justified impulse in Toulmin and Perelman and Olbrechts-Tyteca to take seriously modes of informal argument that philosophy had ignored, and continuing to the present with what has become a central impulse to read an ever-widening range of texts and artifacts through the methods of argumentative reconstruction (cf. Gilbert, 1994). And certainly, populists argue. They engage with recognizable argumentative forms: They make claims and articulate specific policy programs based on argumentative warrants explicit or implicit, and they occasionally debate.

Despite all this, my aim here is to push back against the persistent effort to assimilate populism into argumentation studies, and consider the alternative possibility that reading populism as a deliberative practice erases or elides its true power to convince. Here is a case, I suggest, where the argumentative reconstruction of populism not only leaves unexamined a discursive remainder but, in that remainder, is the main motor force of populism's symbolic efficacy. I do not design my effort to apprehend populism as the potential outside of argument, to disparage it, but to better understand its raw political attractiveness, and in turn, to identify the boundaries of argumentation theory's analytical reach.

Three central tendencies in populist discourse suggest how it falls outside of the realm of public argument. First, populism, even when its key leaders participate in deliberative encounters (public fora, debates, policy and platform negotiations), is finally hostile or indifferent to deliberative practice. The suasory engine of populism is often the impatient appeal to sideline or suspend the deliberative encounter, that is to suspend democracy in the name of reclaiming the unarguable will of the People. Second, even when its discursive moves are contestatory, populism is not the enactment of a dialectic but rather of a monism, where the Manichean gesture of Otherization finally gives way to the instantiation of the charismatic leader or collective. Here I am following Laclau's position and the disagreement it provoked. The populist gesture is neither transcendence nor sublation, but, when realized, the imposition of a singular idealized nation, or put another way, a people without remainder. And third, populism, even when its program outlines an apparently propositional logic, does not convince by reliance on reasoning or argumentative inference, but by a more viscerally embodied and identificatory tribalism.

Populism Is Indifferent to (And Often Hostile To) Deliberation

Wodak (2015), who has undertaken the most extensive discourse analytical work on European populism, noted how populists often "seem to endorse what can be recognized as the 'arrogance of ignorance'; appeals to common-sense and anti-intellectualism mark a return to pre-modernist or pre-Enlightenment thinking" (p. 2). Although some highly contest the consensus view that populism can be antithetical to public argument culture, such a position remains the consensus view (cf. Moffitt, 2016, p. 135).

Populists utilize a wide repertoire of tactics to subvert deliberative norms and practices. Populists often rob the wider culture of the oxygen or attentional bandwidth necessary for reflective argument by provoking scandals. A "predictable dynamic" is thus set into motion which allows "populist parties to set the agenda and distract the media (and the public) from other important" issues (Wodak, 2015, p. 19). New media complicates the situation further. Because social media platforms enable instantaneous response, the consequences can be sharply negative for deliberative interaction, thoughtful engagement, and the possibilities for confirming assertions (Moffitt, 2016, p. 91).

Many discredit the procedures and institutions that mediate public argumentation. As Moffitt (2016) explained:

> Institutional simplification [...] is evident in the way populist actors use crisis to attack and attempt to simplify the existing political system, as it is perceived as being perverted or corrupted. Here, intermediary or unelected bodies that stand between "the people" and their elected representatives are seen as illegitimate, while anything that stands in the way of "solving" the crisis – such as the political opposition or checks and balances – is to be bulldozed over.
>
> *(p. 128)*

Extreme examples illustrate the point. On taking power, Ecuadorean President Rafael Correa closed his country's Congress through illegal means. Ugandan populist president Yoweri Museveni used the pretext of the Uganda Bush War to ban political parties for nineteen years (Moffitt, 2016).

The overall implications for public deliberation can seem substantively grim. Saurette and Gunster (2011) argued that the repertoire of tactics available to populists produce an "epistemological populism" (p. 196) where the glorification of everyday knowledge, the valorization of common sense, and the dismissal of expert or technical knowledge disable or sidestep richer deliberative alternatives. Populists offer unserious policy proposals, not for debate on their merits, but for their pure shock value and the manner with which their sheer audacity galvanizes followers. As Judis (2016) put it when describing the appeal of Trump's "build the wall" demand: The Trump appeal was his "equivalent of 'free silver' or Long's confiscatory tax on the wealthy – incapable of being negotiated, even by the great dealmaker, but just for that reason dramatizing the difference between what the 'silent majority' wanted and what the 'establishment' would condone" (p. 72).

Now, the above summary puts the anti-deliberative case in the strongest possible terms, when the case requires more nuance. Recalling that populism widely varies from case to case means no generalization can capture the actual variation. Judis (2016) noted that in many contexts, the populist goal is to restore deliberation rather than to obliterate it (p. 155). And most important of all, the work that populists do to discredit the work of argumentation is often undertaken precisely because, in context, advocates have deformed deliberative practice, failed to address urgent demands, or corrupted the system into paralysis (cf. Judis, 2016).

Yet, reasons exist to believe that the increasing mediatization of politics will amplify the anti-argumentative impulses of populist politics, given its invariable focus on scandal, celebrity, and narrative dramatization (Axford & Huggins, 1997). The key is less that populists intend to destroy the mechanisms of public argument than that their discourses place no value in the legitimating authority that robust cultures of deliberative interaction provide. We might then understand populism as engaging deliberation when useful, but operationalizing a persuasive effort that does not rely on argumentation in any meaningful way. Perhaps we best understand populists as agnostic or indifferent to or impatient with argument, and much more reliant on appeals that persuade not because they evoke coherent propositional claims, but because they dog whistle to like-minded identity formations or activate particular affective states. As Molyneux and Osborne (2017) reasoned:

> Populism can be hyper-political in terms of enthusiasm, the generation of strong passions and commitments; equally, it can be anti-political in the sense of a refusal of compromise, [and] a resistance to engaging in the give-and-take of politics [...] So

often populism actually seems to bypass politics-as-usual [...] It has an energy that is surplus to the problems in hand, and in spite of the get-things-done ethos it tends to be more often than not about the release of emotion than getting anything done.

(p. 11)

Populism Is a Monism

Populism deploys several strategic maneuvers to achieve a radical unification of the discursive field. Advocates use rhetorics of crisis to achieve utter simplification. As the Trump presidency reveals, nuance is often sacrificed for impact, and while the evocation of crisis can either function as signifying or opening an emancipatory breakthrough, this occurs at the expense of richly textured contestation.

At the same time, populism's central tendency is to reduce "the people" to a unity, an indivisible singularity, and to collapse the representational distance between citizen and leader. The strategic maneuver brings to mind the Hugo Chavez boast that "I am not an individual, I am the people" (quoted in Moffitt, 2016, p. 100) or Donald Trump at a rally last May stating, "the only important thing is the unification of the people – because the other people don't mean anything" (quoted in Muller, 2016, p. 17). In a mediatized age of spectacle, "the people" are indivisible, if only because slogans, icons, and images strip away the complexities of community, ideas, and identity. Such representations escape or evade argumentative logics, since their mechanisms of affiliation are visceral, reducible to stark strategies for style and visualization, and "owe their power to the heart, to evocation of sentiments that may not be necessarily either rationalized or rationalizable" (Taggart, 2000, p. 95).

This conceptual reduction has an institutional parallel. While populists in practice have often entered governing coalitions, their often-expressed goal is to consolidate political party power. Ideological unification generates one rallying cry, invariably centered on the presumed authenticity of the populist leader, and the challenge this presents for deliberative practice is that any disagreement becomes heresy. Debate becomes impossible if adherents can dismiss counterclaims as blasphemy (Muller, 2016).

Even if one refuses Ernesto Laclau's larger conceptualization of populist reason, and the controversy it evokes regarding the nature of charismatic leadership, the wider literature rightly emphasizes the frequent historical reality that a single leader ends up as a stand-in for a unified political Totality. Populist icons infuse their talk with messianism to validate their unifying authority (e.g., Chavez: "Jesus Christ is my commander-in-chief"; Berlusconi: "I am the Jesus Christ of politics"). They seek to embody physical vigor, strength, potency, and health so that the body of the leader metaphorically merges as one with the body of the people.

Populism's Appeal Is Visceral and Affective, Not Propositional

Populism, Laclau (2007) insisted, is a logic whose "minimal unit of analysis would not be the *group*, as a referent, but the socio-political *demand*" (p. 224). This move implies a necessary correspondence between populist discourses and public argumentation, where advocates articulate reason-backed, evidence-warranted demands. But the shift away from the group to the demand, for Laclau, is not an effort to render populism as a propositional logic, but to make clearer his view of populism as affectively driven, the consummating quest for an identificatory wholeness.

The populist literature often argues that the work of populism aims to galvanize affect rather than operate to induce assent by processes of reason-giving. As Molyneux and Osborne (2017) noted,

> Fear is a normal part of political – and other kinds of – existence; but populism makes fear, as it were, prior to reason; it builds makeshift reasons around its fears rather than basing its fears on reason. Populism in this sense is passion draped in *ad hoc* reasoning, rather than the proper impassioned reasoning of politics [...] Populist fear is not always specific as to what its object is. This, paradoxically, gives populism a fundamentalist quality; it is the unknowability of the fear that makes it so unarguable.
>
> *(p. 12)*

Conclusion

The central impulses of populist discourse are demands that are not claims, agonisms that are not properly dialectical, and disagreements that are not controversies. They rely on absent evidence signifying not enthymematic warrant, but simply deliberative absence and the activation of emotion. While argumentative reconstruction yields important insights on populist ways of thinking and reasoning, it, if too narrowly conceived, misses important dimensions of the more critical drivers of political influence, risking a form of methodological misrecognition.

The principal benefits of my position are not the insights it suggests about populism. That is, even if understood as expressing the limitations of an argumentation approach to populism, the wider universe of scholarship certainly corrects for those limits in other ways. Rhetoricians, affect theorists, political theorists, sociologists, and others do not lack for resources to navigate the complex scenes of populist mobilization.

The main implications are thus for argumentation theory, that is, where the basic question to which we finally ought to return is: Why argumentation? The matter is salient, since many of the traditions mentioned here use argumentation's defense of critical rational action as their first point of departure, offering accounts of affect, the visual, the psychoanalytic encounter, and more to urge what they insist is a turn away from the work of deliberative democrats and public argument defenders. A key, then, is to ask: Can we better specify the analytical purchase we gain by thinking of populism as a public argument formation or coherent deliberative practice?

The point, then, is not to prohibit work on populism in the argumentation field. Rather, as scholars apply the techniques of argumentation reconstruction to texts not self-evidently making reasoned claims to their audiences, we must also do more than assume the relevance of our criticism. Three suggestions for how this alternative view might work come to mind.

Scholars of argumentation, and of populism, might *more fully specify the boundary conditions of argument*. The field can strengthen its accounts of deliberation only to the extent that we can more precisely demarcate argument from non-argument, the limit conditions or constitutive prospects of the limit case from what might simply be outside and extraneous, and detail the value of using argumentative reconstruction on objects that otherwise exceed their reach.

We might also *more fully specify our theoretical vocabularies*. Laclau (2007) described his account as explaining populist reason and explicating its logic. But the logic he offered did not finally connect him to the practices of argumentative analysis or reconstruction. Missing is the language of deliberation, fallacy, warranted assent, reconstruction, and the other terms of informal logic. He replaced these items with an analytical toolkit focused on empty signifiers, dislocation, nodal points, and antagonism.

Finally, *argumentation scholars should revisit and clarify the practices of argumentative reconstruction*, given the considerable tendencies in the wider scholarship to see populism as activating an affective and not a rationalized propositional logic. Wodak (2015) read instances of populist appeals through topoi (danger, criminality, history), and in ways that invariably do the work of rationalizing populist claims. Nevertheless, the galvanizing force of populist appeals often do not seem to rest on a deeper propositional logic, but on visceral associations, fear, and slogans that signal identity allegiances (cf. Karaliotas, 2017; Truong, 2017) without any attempt to argue for them.

References

Axford, B., & Huggins, R. (1977). Anti-politics or the triumph of postmodern populism in promotional cultures? *Javnost - The Public: Journal of the European Institute for Communication and Culture, 4*(3), 5–25. doi:10.1080/13183222.1997.11008650

Duffy, D. (2015). States' rights vs. women's rights: The use of the populist argumentative frame in anti-abortion rhetoric. *International Journal of Communication, 9*, 3494-3501. Retrieved from http://ijoc.org

Foster, L. (2011). Populist argumentation in Bruce Springsteen's *The Rising. Argumentation and Advocacy, 48*(2), 61–80. Retrieved from http://www.tandfonline.com

Gilbert, M. A. (1994). Multi-modal argumentation. *Philosophy of the Social Sciences, 24*(2), 159–177. doi:10.1177/004839319402400202

Judis, J. B. (2016). *The populist explosion: How the great recession transformed American and European politics.* New York, NY: Columbia Global Reports.

Karaliotas, L. (2017). Staging equality in Greek squares: Hybrid spaces of political subjectification. *International Journal of Urban and Regional Research, 41*(1), 54–69. doi:10.1111/1468-2427.12385

Katsambekis, G. (2016). The populist surge in post-democratic times: Theoretical and political challenges. *The Political Quarterly, 88*(2), 202–210. doi:10.1111/1467-923X.12317

Laclau, E. (2007). *On populist reason* (Reprint ed.). New York, NY: Verso.

Lee, M. J. (2006). The populist chameleon: The People's Party, Huey Long, George Wallace, and the populist argumentative frame. *Quarterly Journal of Speech, 92*(4), 355–378. doi:10.1080/00335630601080385

Maddux, M. (2013). Fundamentalist fool or populist paragon? William Jennings Bryan and the campaign against evolutionary theory. *Rhetoric & Public Affairs, 16*(3), 489–520. doi:10.1353/rap.2013.0026

Mény, Y., & Surel, Y. (2002). The constitutive ambiguity of populism. In Y. Meny & Y. Surel (Eds.), *Democracies and the populist challenge* (pp. 1–21). London, United Kingdom: Palgrave Macmillan.

Moffitt, B. (2016). *The global rise of populism: Performance, political style, and representation.* Stanford, CA: Stanford University Press.

Molyneux, M., & Osborne, T. (2017). Populism: A deflationary view. *Economy and Society, 46*(1), 1–19. doi:10.1080/03085147.2017.1308059

Mudde, C. (2004). The populist zeitgeist. *Government and Opposition: An International Journal of Comparative Politics, 39*(4), 541–563. doi:10.1111/j.1477-7053.2004.00135.x

Muller, J.M. (2016). *What is populism?* Philadelphia, PA: University of Pennsylvania Press.

Saurette, P., & Gunster, S. (2011). Ears wide shut: Epistemological populism, argutainment and Canadian conservative talk radio. *Canadian Journal of Political Science, 44*(1), 195–218. Retrieved from http://www.jstor.org/stable/41300521

Taggart, P. (2000). *Populism.* Maidenhead, United Kingdom: Open University Press.

Truong, F. (2017). Total rioting: From metaphysics to politics. *Sociological Review, 65*(4), 563–577. doi:10.1111/1467-954X.12436

Waisanen, D. (2011). Argument ecologies in social media: Populist reason in Facebook immigration pages. In R. C. Rowland (Ed.), *Reasoned argument and social change* (pp. 715–722). Washington, DC: National Communication Association.

Wodak, R. (2015). *The politics of fear: What right-wing populist discourses mean.* Thousand Oaks, CA: SAGE.

11

CONTRASTING IDEOLOGICAL NETWORKS

Ronald Reagan and Donald Trump

Robert C. Rowland

Ronald Reagan's small government perspective dominated conservatism for decades. Nicholas Lemann (2016a) wrote of Reagan's influence that his views became "for at least a generation, an unassailably dominant set of positions in national politics" (para. 27), giving "his name [...] a talismanic quality" (para. 1). Accordingly, historian Sean Wilentz (2008) labeled both his book and the last three decades the "Age of Reagan."

Political commentators have viewed Donald Trump as either a continuation of Reaganism or a sharp break from it. For example, Jeet Heer (2015) claimed, "Donald Trump is the new Reagan" (para. 1) and former Reagan speech-writer, Patrick Buchanan (2017) added, "they have much in common" (para. 2). Others disagreed vehemently with this judgment. Notably, Michael Gerson (2017) argued that "Trump's inaugural speech is a funeral oration at the death of Reaganism" (para. 9), and Dana Milbank (2016) labeled Trump's nomination as "the de-Reaganization of the Republican Party."

The appropriate way to compare the views of Reagan and Trump is to consider their underlying symbolic perspectives. In *Shared Land/Conflicting Identity*, David Frank and I (2002) argued that coherent symbolic systems contain an ideological worldview describing the world as it is and as it could be, a narrative (usually mythic) justifying that worldview, and a set of value principles defining the good and ill. The key point is that in certain cases critics can identify the symbolic essence of a political movement by isolating the ideological terms, narrative elements, and value commitments evident in the symbolic practice of a campaign or movement. This constellation of elements functions as the defining symbolic network, capable of comparison with other networks. The absence of a coherent symbolic practice also can be revealing. Movements in which the symbolic perspective is not coherent may succeed for a time because of circumstance, pragmatic adaptation, or the charisma of leaders such as Bill Clinton, but they are unlikely to have the ongoing influence of a more coherent movement, such as Reaganism. This insight led then Senator Barack Obama to observe, "Ronald Reagan changed the trajectory of America in a way that [...] Bill Clinton did not" (quoted in Balz & Johnson, 2009, p. 160). In this case, the definition of the world evident in the symbolic practice of Donald Trump is both revealing and frightening.

Reagan's Symbolic Network

A full development of the symbolic network evident in the rhetorical practice of Ronald Reagan is beyond the scope of this essay. Fortunately, previous research has identified that network in both his domestic and Soviet policy rhetoric (Goodnight, 1986; Ivie, 1984; Jones & Rowland, 2015; Lewis, 1987; Rowland & Jones, 2010; Rowland & Jones, 2016; Rowland & Jones, in press; Schiappa, 1989; Smith, C. A., 1987; Smith, C. R., 2017). In what follows, I draw on this work, which is based on decades of analysis of Reagan's rhetoric and argument, to sketch Reagan's symbolic network. My focus is on the domestic sphere because Trump collapses domestic and foreign challenges together in his treatment of the state of the nation.

The ideological structure of Reagan's symbolic network was obvious in his First Inaugural Address, when he said, "in this present crisis, government is not the solution to our problem; government is the problem" (Reagan, 1981, para. 9). In the remainder of the first inaugural, which, according to the Heritage Foundation (n.d.), functioned as a statement of "first principles" for conservatism, Reagan called for reductions in the size of government, tax cuts, less regulation, and shifting power back to the states—policies that he consistently supported over the next eight years. At the same time, unlike many conservatives who opposed government based on core principles (Tanenhaus, 2008), Reagan's approach was more pragmatic. Reagan was not opposed to government philosophically, a position quite evident in the enormous arms build-up he supported, but because he thought less government would raise economic growth and achieve other objectives. Five paragraphs after his famous indictment of government, Reagan (1981) explained:

> Now, so there will be no misunderstanding, it's not my intention to do away with government. It is rather to make it work—work with us, not over us; to stand by our side, not ride on our back. Government can and must provide opportunity, not smother it; foster productivity, not stifle it.
>
> *(para. 14)*

Reagan used the rhetorical style of liberalism (Jones & Rowland, 2015) in service of a pragmatic conservatism that had little in common with anti-government conservatives bent on "starving the beast" (Editorial Board, 2007).

The narrative and the value terms in Reagan's symbolic system were consonant with ideological principles. Reagan's dominant narrative was an individualistic variant of the American Dream (Rowland & Jones, 2007), in which America was a place of infinite possibility. Ordinary people could achieve greatness through hard work as long as government got out of the way and focused on national defense and other essential services. Reagan's individualistic variant of the American Dream was an enactment of American Exceptionalism. The nation would forever experience peace and prosperity as long as America remained committed to the "first principles" (Reagan, 1989, para. 17) that had founded the "shining city upon a hill" (Reagan, 1989, para. 33). The value terms that dominated Reagan's rhetoric—freedom, progress, optimism, opportunity, patriotism, and related terms—were evident in the heroic narrative and ideological statements. Notably, values and ideas defined American identity, not ethnicity or nationalism. In the conclusion of the farewell address, Reagan (1989) described the "shining city" as "teeming with people of all kinds living in harmony and peace" (para. 34) and added that the dream was "open to anyone with the will and the heart to get here" (para. 34). Reagan's policies often favored the rich and disadvantaged people of color, but his rhetoric defined American identity based on ideas that transcended personal identity.

Dystopian Populism, the Strong "Man," and Magical Thinking

Like Reagan, Trump's symbolic network is broadly consistent across his rhetoric. In describing Trump's discourse, I focus on the most important single works from his campaign and his presidency: the nomination acceptance address at the Republican Convention and his inaugural address (Trump, 2016; Trump, 2017).[1] The *New York Times*'s reporters Patrick Healy and Jonathan Martin (2016) commented that the convention speech was a "vehement appeal to Americans who feel that their country is spiraling out of control and yearn for a leader who will take aggressive, even extreme, actions to protect them" (p. A1). They added that the speech included "dark imagery and an almost angry tone" (p. A1), a description that fit Trump's campaign as a whole. Similarly, their colleague Mark Landler (2017) observed the speech was "uncompromising in tone and entirely in keeping with his insurgent campaign" (p. A1). These speeches in concentrated form contain the symbolic pattern evident in the tweets, interviews, and rallies that dominated his campaign and that continue to dominate his presidency.

Elements of traditional conservative ideology emerge in Trump's (2016) rhetoric including support for "law and order" (para. 96), but the dominant message is nationalist populism with almost no policy analysis or supporting evidence. Unlike Reagan's well-developed ideology, Trump's ideological vision is derivative of and merges with his narrative of a nation under siege. In the 2016 convention address, he said the nation faced "a moment of crisis" (para. 5) and then claimed that a "rollback of criminal enforcement" (para. 16) has led to an enormous crime wave. He blamed illegal immigrants for much of this crime and stated that Hispanic and Black Americans were living in awful conditions. In foreign policy, the nation has endured one "humiliation after another [producing …] death, destruction, terrorism and weakness" (para. 36, 53). Trump's dystopian vision bore little resemblance to the actual status of the nation and, instead, targeted white working–class voters (especially men) who had lost economic ground and felt threatened by cultural change, as people of color and women achieved a modicum of economic and political power (Linnett, 2016).

In contrast with Reagan who identified real problems and laid out a coherent ideology for confronting them, Trump simply blamed special interests who had "rigged our political and economic system" (Linnett, 2016, para. 66). In response, Trump claimed that he would be the "voice" (para. 75) for "the forgotten men and women of our country" (para. 74). Other than calling for a wall and other means to block immigration, Trump provided almost no policy analysis in the convention speech. Rather, he claimed that the power of his leadership by itself would produce "millions of new jobs and trillions in new wealth" (para. 64). Rather than explaining the policies that would produce this economic miracle, he said, "nobody knows the system better than me, which is why I alone can fix it" (para. 84). Reagan made a case for small-government conservatism as a means of enacting the American Dream. Trump's vision was of the "strongman" who, through the force of his leadership, would produce astounding results. Nicholas Lemann (2016b) was clearly right when he noted that Trump's "strongman" persona "struck a chord" with many voters (p. 35). In Trump's (2016) statements such as "I'm going to make our country rich again" (para. 146), the absence of ideological argument and the presence of grandiose magical thinking were evident.

Unlike Reagan who defended values consonant with his fundamentally optimistic vision, Trump appealed to the baser emotions, notably fear of the "other," including immigrants, Islamic terrorists, and, by implication in his discussion of crime, people of color (Associated Press, 2016). As *The New York Times* writer, Amanda Taub (2017) noted, Trump's "pitch to voters both created the sense of threat and promised a defense: a winning, political strategy for the age of identity politics" (p. A10). His appeal to fear often morphed into hate. Trump rallies commonly included moments when the crowd chanted "lock her [Secretary Clinton] up" or cheered mean-spirited attacks on the press. For the presidential candidate, the dominant emotion was clearly an expression of ego. Imagining Reagan (or any other significant figure in American political history) bragging that he "alone" could solve the nation's problems appear beyond the pale.

A similar pattern was evident in the inaugural address. After an uncharacteristically gracious opening in which he thanked President Obama and others, Trump again presented a "dystopian" (Friedman, 2017, p. A25) vision of a nation in crisis. The President (Trump, 2017) described "mothers and children trapped in poverty in our inner cities; rusted-out factors scattered like tombstones across the landscape of our nation" (para. 24) and a host of other problems that he collectively referenced as "American carnage" (para. 25). Once again, he used no ideological argument. Rather, he simplified his positions as defined by "two simple rules: Buy American and Hire American" (para. 46). Later in the same speech, he summarized his approach as "total allegiance to the United States of America" (para. 50), a slogan that implicitly accused President Obama and others of lacking that allegiance.

As in the convention speech, the narrative elements of the inaugural were dominant, subsuming the ideology. In Trump's (2017) vision of "American carnage," ordinary people were the "forgotten men and women of our country" (para. 18), victimized by "a small group in our nation's Capital" (para. 7) who have "reaped the rewards of government while the people have borne the cost" (para. 7). For Trump, the greedy elites had failed to "protect our borders from the ravages of other countries making our products, stealing our companies, and destroying our jobs" (para. 40). Nor had they protected the people from "crime and gangs and drugs" (p. 24), defended the "nation's borders" (para. 30) from illegal immigrants, or countered "Radical Islamic Terrorism" (para. 49). Once again, the "other" threatened the nation. As in the convention speech, the solution was simply Trump as "strongman." Again, the magical thinking was evident. Trump claimed, "America will start winning again, winning like never before" (para. 42) and added "We will bring back our jobs. We will bring back our borders. We will bring back our wealth. And we will bring back our dreams" (para. 43). He rejected a politics that was "all talk and no action" (para. 59), claiming ironically that "the time for empty talk is over" (para. 60). The irony was that in policy terms, the inaugural was entirely empty, devoid of serious argument.

Although the value and emotional content of the inaugural address was more muted than that of the convention speech, the same dynamic was present. In his description of "American carnage," Trump (2017) appealed to the fears of the white working class of losing dominance in society, telling his supporters "you will never be ignored again" (para. 69). Trump did appeal to unity when he noted, "whether we are black or brown or white, we all bleed the same red blood of patriots" (para. 66), but his narrative vision of a scared, angry nation under siege dominated the speech.

In the convention speech and the inaugural, a dystopian narrative in which elites allowed the "other" to destroy the economy, commit crimes, and undermine security through terrorism dominated Trump's symbolic network. The solution was not based in ideology, but in a vision of the "strongman" who could magically save the nation. The base values were consonant with the narrative. The contrast with Reagan's optimistic small-government ideology and vision of an American Dream "open to anyone with the will and the heart to get here" (Reagan, 1989, para. 34) is striking.

Conclusion

The description of Trump's symbolic system is immensely disquieting. It speaks to the alienation and anger of a sizable portion of the American electorate. As conservative columnist David Brooks (2017) noted, Trump drew on a sense of alienation that "breeds a distrust that corrodes any collective effort … [and creates] … a hysterical public conversation" (p. A25) based on a desire to "smash the system … [without a] … positive agenda" (p. A25). Trump's rhetorical practice identified immigrants, adherents of Islam, liberal elites, and implicitly Hispanic and Black Americans as a threat to the nation. His slogan, "Make America Great Again," expressed a longing for a time not only of strong economic growth, but a time when white men dominated the nation. Trump rallies often were angry affairs in which audiences booed the press and other elites, and threatened protesters. The anger evident in the chant "Lock her up," a chant that Republican delegates loudly cheered at their national convention, is a sign of political dysfunction. In 1980 and 2008, Reagan and Obama led political revolutions that were fundamentally optimistic. The Trump campaign evoked very different emotions—anger and fear—and for the candidate a sense of vanity and entitlement.

A number of commentators have noted Trump's ties to the Alt Right and similarities between his campaign and far right groups of the past and present. Chip Berlet (2015) observed that "the examples of Trump's fascist-sounding rhetoric are numerous" (para. 5), and Paul Krugman (2016) added, "it takes willful blindness not to see the parallels between the rise of fascism and our current political nightmare" (p. A21). Given the strong resistance facing Trump, Krugman's fears may seem overstated, but a group of "democracy experts" nevertheless recently estimated "an 11 percent chance of democratic breakdown within four years" (Miller, 2017, para. 4) and identified "the greatest threat […] in anti-democratic rhetoric, especially by the president" (Miller, 2017, para. 15).

This sketch of Trump's symbolic network is also revealing for what it says about the status of public deliberation. Trump barely made policy arguments and still more rarely cited evidence for his grandiose claims. Both at the time and in retrospective analyses, academics have critiqued strongly the ideological system that Reagan presented, but no one disputes that he presented a coherent argument for small-government conservatism. Trump is no Reagan. His appeal is not based in reasoned argument or the coherence of his ideological system, but in magical thinking, or put another way, the view that the celebrity strongman could simply wave his wand and strong wage growth and other accomplishments would somehow appear. Argument scholars must recognize that the success of Trump's non-argument provides strong evidence of the limited power of reasoned discourse in the contemporary public sphere.

Notes

1 This essay cites all quotations from Trump's two speeches using date and paragraph numbers only.

References

The Associated Press. (2016, July 22). Critics: Trump convention speech signals shift to coded race language. *Chicago Tribune*. Retrieved from http://chicagotribune.com

Balz, D., & Johnson, H. (2009). *The battle for America 2008: The story of an extraordinary election.* New York, NY: Viking.

Berlet, C. (2015, December 12). "Trumping" democracy: Right-wing populism, fascism, and the case for action. *Political Research Associates*. Retrieved from http://politicalresearch.org

Brooks, D. (2017, May 23). The alienated mind. *The New York Times*, p. A25.

Buchanan, P. J. (2017, January 17). Is Trump the new Reagan? *The American Conservative*. Retrieved from http://theamericanconservative.com

The Editorial Board. (2007, November 8). Does "starving the beast" work? [Editorial]. *The New York Times*. Retrieved from https://theboard.blogs.nytimes.com

Friedman, T. L. (2017, May 24). Road trip through rusting and rising America. *The New York Times*, p. A25.

Gerson, M. (2017, January 21). Trump's funeral oration at the death of Reaganism. *The Washington Post*. Retrieved from https://washingtonpost.com

Goodnight, G. T. (1986). Ronald Reagan's re-formulation of the rhetoric of war: Analysis of the "zero option," "evil empire," and "star wars" addresses. *Quarterly Journal of Speech, 72*(4), 390–414. doi:10.1080/00335638609383784

Healy, P., & Martin, J. (2016, July 22). His tone dark, Donald Trump takes G.O.P. mantle. *The New York Times*, p. A1.

Heer, J. (2015, December 31). Donald Trump is the new Reagan. *New Republic*. Retrieved from https://newrepublic.com

Heritage Foundation. (n.d.). Reagan's First Inaugural: "Government is not the solution to our problem; government is the problem." Retrieved from https://thf_media.s3.amazonaws.com/2011/pdf/FP_PS36.pdf

Ivie, R. L. (1984). Speaking "common sense" about the Soviet threat: Reagan's rhetorical stance. *Western Journal of Speech Communication, 48*(1), 39–50. doi:10.1080/10570318409374140

Jones, J. M., & Rowland, R. C. (2015). Redefining the proper role of government: Ultimate definition in Reagan's First Inaugural. *Rhetoric & Public Affairs, 18*(4), 691–718. doi:10.14321/rhetpublaffa.18.4.0691

Krugman, P. (2016, December 19). How republics end. *The New York Times*, p. A21.

Landler, M. (2017, January 21). A broadside for Washington. *The New York Times*, pp. A1, A15.

Lemann, N. (2016a, March 10). Reagan: The triumph of tone. *The New York Review of Books*, pp. 8, 10.

Lemann, N. (2016b, November 10). On the election—III. *The New York Review of Books*, pp. 34–35.

Lewis, W. F. (1987). Telling America's story: Narrative form and the Reagan presidency. *Quarterly Journal of Speech, 73*(3), 280–302. doi:10.1080/00335638709383809

Linnett, R. (2016, December 31). What the "godfather of populism" thinks of Donald Trump. *Politico*. Retrieved from http://politico.com/magazine/story/2016/12/populist-trump-fred-harris-demagogue-politics-214536

Milbank, D. (2016, October 5). The de-Reaganization of the Republican party. *The Washington Post*. Retrieved from https://washingtonpost.com

Miller, M. K. (2017, May 23). A new expert survey finds warning signs for the state of American democracy. *The Washington Post*. Retrieved from https://washingtonpost.com

Reagan, R. (1981, January 20). Inaugural address. Retrieved from http://reagan.utexas.edu/archives/speeches/1981/12081a.htm

Reagan, R. (1989, January 11). Farewell address to the nation. Retrieved from https://reaganlibrary.archives.gov/archives/speeches/1989/011189i.htm

Rowland, R. C., & Frank, D. A. (2002). *Shared land/conflicting identity: Trajectories of Israeli and Palestinian symbol use*. East Lansing, MI: Michigan State University Press.

Rowland, R. C., & Jones, J. M. (2007). Recasting the American dream and American politics: Barack Obama's keynote address to the 2004 Democratic national convention. *Quarterly Journal of Speech, 93*(4), 425–448. doi:10.1080/00335630701593675

Rowland, R. C., & Jones, J. M. (2010). *Reagan at Westminster: Foreshadowing the end of the Cold War*. College Station, TX: Texas A&M University Press.

Rowland, R. C., & Jones, J. M. (2016). Reagan's strategy for the Cold War and the evil empire address. *Rhetoric & Public Affairs, 19*(3), 427-464. Retrieved from https://muse.jhu.edu/article/638219

Rowland, R. C., & Jones, J. M. (in press). Reagan's farewell address: Redefining the American dream. *Rhetoric & Public Affairs*.

Schiappa, E. (1989). The rhetoric of nukespeak. *Communication Monographs, 56*(3), 253-272. doi:10.1080/03637758909390263

Smith, C. A. (1987). Mistereagan's neighborhood: Rhetoric and national unity. *Southern Speech Communication Journal, 52*(3), 219-239. doi:10.1080/10417948709372692

Smith, C. R. (2017). Ronald Reagan's rhetorical re-invention of conservatism. *Quarterly Journal of Speech*, *103*(1-2), 33-65. doi:10.1080/00335630.2016.1231415

Tanenhaus, S. (2008, November 6). A once-united G.O.P. emerges, in identity crisis. *The New York Times*, pp. 1, 9.

Taub, A. (2017, April 13). Partisanship as a tribal identity: Voting against one's economic interests. *The New York Times*, p. A10.

Trump, D. J. (2016, July 22). Transcript: Donald Trump at the G.O.P. convention. *The New York Times*. Retrieved from https://nytimes.com

Trump, D. J. (2017, January 20). The inaugural address: Remarks of President Donald J. Trump – as prepared for delivery. *The White House*. Retrieved from https://whitehouse.gov/inaugural-address

Wilentz, S. (2008). *The age of Reagan, A history: 1974-2008*. New York, NY: Harper.

12

THE CYBER IMPERATIVE

Ligatures as Ordering Devices

Ilon Lauer

Over the past year, the public dialogue regarding internet security has developed a more urgent tone. In testimony before the U.S. Senate in March, Caleb Barlow, Vice-President at IBM, reported that cyber criminals had stolen over two billion records in the past year (cited in Promises and Perils, 2017). In 2016, computer crime victimized nearly 600 million people (Licalzi, 2017). Based on United Nations' estimates, the annual cost of internet crime around the globe is more than 445 billion dollars (Barlow, 2017). Politicians, pundits, and industry representatives with increasing frequency are demanding a national digital security policy suited to the needs of the networked society. Accordingly, they have generated an increasingly voluminous set of legislative hearings, executive commissions, and academic reports advocating a national solution to the problem.

The corpus of governmental discourse on cybersecurity fits within the purview of "public argument-driven security studies" (Mitchell, 2002, p. 58), or research that communication and political science scholars primarily conduct focusing on the material and discursive conditions of security. Communication scholars have contributed to such research by documenting the ways security discourse corrodes deliberative decision-making processes. Dunmire's (2005) study of the temporal language framing National Security Strategy concluded that "political actors and institutions constrain the ways the future can be imagined, articulated, and realized" (p. 482). Similarly, Macmillan (2011) singled out communication as "one of the main vectors of this hierarchical structure of authority and control" (p. 358). Nissenbaum (2005) identified cyber-security discourse as an underexplored domain of security discourse and has encouraged scholars to draw from the approaches and insights of security studies. Nevertheless, despite Nissembaum's (2004) observation that "established institutions of cyberspace have enlisted the power of conceptual schema in their quest for order and control" (p. 213), scholars have paid little attention to cyber-security discourse. In fact, "surprisingly little explicit discussion [has occurred] within Security Studies of what hyphenating 'security' with 'cyber' might imply" (Hansen & Nissenbaum, 2009, p. 1156).

The implications of this hyphenation process are apparent in instances of public deliberation addressing cyber-security, and accordingly, I analyze how hyphenation creates argumentative texture. Using Vico's (1996) notion of ligature (i.e., a word or set of words connecting senses to things) as a heuristic for understanding the connective processes that render arrangement rational, I detail how *cyber* securitizes discourse. By itself, the word "cyber" is an unremarkable, abstract noun designating internet-related things, but in public argumentation, it prefigures the terms it modifies and links them to a highly securitized argumentative field. More than seemingly similar terms such as *network, web,* and *digital,* the cyber prefix binds its modified terms to pre-existing fields of argumentation. Insinuating established assumptions about security, power, and control, the cyber prefix guides and even distorts deliberation. To demonstrate how cyber secures deliberative ligatures binding the digital citizenry to the regulatory demands of the network society, I first define ligature and explain how it orders argumentative conditions. Then, I follow arrangement patterns evident in testimony from recent House Hearings and a draft report of the Commission on Enhancing National Cybersecurity (2016) concerning the cyber threat. These texts demonstrate how the cyber ligature guides argument by embedding militarized and neoliberal assumptions into public deliberation about computer security.

Connection and Subordination

Argument scholars have described an argument's skeletal structure as the fundamental ideas that form an argument (e.g., Zulick, 1997). I extend this metaphor by speculating about the verbal equivalents to the tendons, tissue, and cartilage that bind a skeleton together. A ligature, in its most basic sense, is a connection; in argumentation, a ligature is a conceptual or symbolic connection linking arguments, argument fields, and their constituent parts. A ligature renders topics relevant, engenders reasoning by similitude, and facilitates the repurposing of prior reasoning processes. Ligatures often work conceptually and implicitly, but may be explicitly present when particular words or other elements of symbolic action mark them.

Tracking these implicit and explicit linkages gives argument scholars insight into the ways arrangement patterns emerge and operate. Stormer (2004) recommended that scholars view arrangement, or taxis, "as a critical problem" and ponder relevant questions such as, "how are the order of discourse and the order of things formed, and what are their possible relationships" (p. 262). I agree and add that analysis of public argumentation reveals the type of words and phrases that produce order and establish conceptual relationships. In argumentation, words and phrases contribute to arrangement by building connections and rendering relationships more visible. Even basic arrangement patterns can influence both perceptions of causality and understanding of the underlying relationships between things. More complex ordering processes can exert tremendous argumentative force when they subordinate related concepts.

One way connections subordinate concepts involves a process Perelman and Olbrechts-Tyteca (1969) called "hypotaxis" (p. 158). Perelman and Olbrechts-Tyteca described the process of hypotactic argument as one in which the joining of two terms limits one, creates an exception, and establishes different fields within a hierarchy. They noted that qualification initiates this subordination process and explained how "depending on the subordination we are establishing, we shall speak of 'pious sorrow' or 'sorrowing piety'" (p. 157). Because adjectives, participles, and prefixes modify concepts, they can prime these concepts for an argumentative assumption or conclusion. In other words, parts of speech function as ligatures that connect broader concepts to particular orientations, limitations, and qualifications which, in turn, can secure adherence to particular claims or premises. The combination of the qualification with some sort of concession may appear to advance a concession, but in fact, when positioned well "show the degree of importance attached to what is conceded" (p. 157). Hypotaxis can extend beyond the subordination of specific concepts and assists with argument configuration as it "establishes precise relations between elements of discourse" (p. 157). Far from being an ancillary figure, Perelman and Olbrechts-Tyteca (1969) argued, "The hypotactic construction is the argumentative construction par excellence" (p. 158). They even theorized that the hypotactic construction alters the perception and understanding of specific arguments. They identify three persuasive effects of hypotaxis: "Hypotaxis creates frameworks [and] constitutes the adoption of a position. It controls the reader, forces him [*sic*] to see particular relationships, restricts the interpretations he [*sic*] may consider, and takes its inspiration from well-constructed legal reasoning" (p. 158). So, as ligatures create connections between ideas, they order conceptual relations, creating or adjusting hierarchies that influence arguments. Analysis of arguments associated with the cyber-ligature will illustrate the ways the term creates hypotactic relationships and demonstrates the ligature's persuasive force.

The Accelerating Cyber Imperative

When the cyber prefix links conceptually dense policy terms (e.g., security or attack) to the digital domain, it subordinates the digital to a pre-existing discursive structure, a subordination process that enables hypotaxis. As it prefigures security (e.g., cyber-security), the cyber term appears to concede that it is a subspecies of security, but recalling Perelman and Olbrecht's observation, such a concession specifies digital security and underscores its broad significance as a critical element of the nation's security. The cyber ligature influences public argument by prefiguring sites of digital exchange as domains of hostility, risk, and vulnerability that require protection.

Recent testimony presented by then acting Department of Homeland Security Secretary John Kelly utilized the cyber prefix to introduce seven distinct compounds into the public debate on internet security: terrorists, threats, networks, attacks, security, partnerships, and space. These compounds establish boundaries that strongly determine what is acceptable in this debate. Consider the distinctly different sense conveyed by alternate compounds of these words, such as hyphenated linkage to the word "digital" (e.g., digital-terrorism or digital-threat). Similarly, imaginary terms like cyber-citizenry or cyber-deliberation do not refer to anything tangible. The cyber compound uniquely combines with these seven terms to mark contested and hostile boundaries around an abstract, decentered, and imaginary space.

The trope of a persistent threat presents malicious cyber-activity as a continuous and intensifying consequence of connectivity, and it demarcates digital space as a targeted and vulnerable place. Along with deictic temporal markers stressing the threat's immediacy, descriptions of a quickening tempo and accelerating risk give salience to perceived vulnerabilities by demonstrating the increasing likelihood of future and more virulent attacks. The persistent threat trope, evident in every recent cyber security hearing, links digital connectivity to risk. For instance, Global Vice President of the East West Institute Bruce McConnell (Borderless Battle, 2017b) characterized the cyber landscape as "a dynamic risk environment, augmented by our electronic connectedness and interdependence" (p. 5). Similarly, Director of the Center for Cyber and Homeland Security at the George Washington University Frank J. Cilluffo (Borderless Battle, 2017a) predicted that the accelerating threat tempo will continue to gain momentum as the emergent Internet of Things fosters "an exponential growth in connectivity that runs parallel to a growth in the digital attack surface" (p. 9). Thematically, equating connectivity with vulnerability presents digital activity as a vector of insecurity. Moreover, presenting threats and attacks as inevitable events rearranges vulnerability from being a consequence of connectivity to a cause for response. Enunciations of the persistent threat trope reinforce demands for a more visible cyber security presence by establishing a framework that replaces consideration of whether to do something with an imperative to do something and ultimately channels this imperative into demands to develop and deploy cyber-weaponry.

As part of a larger arrangement pattern, the persistent threat trope creates a link to neoliberal and militaristic discourses to engender reasoning by similitude. As the cyber ligature renders the digital domain familiar, understandable, and workable, it amplifies appeals to modernize the nation's cyber-defense arsenal and to cultivate appropriate relationships with tech companies. In the Senate appropriation testimony outlining the Department of Homeland Security's 2018 budget priorities, Secretary Kelly (FY 2018 DHS Budget, 2017) identified a "real, pervasive, and ongoing series of attacks on public and private infrastructure and networks" (p. 5) as evidence of a growing threat. He used similar language in a speech at the George Washington University, declaring that the homeland was "under constant attack by a wide range of adversaries with an even wider range of capabilities" (DHS, 2017, Illustrating the Threat: Cyber section, para. 1). Kelly characterized the DHS as a plodding bureaucracy, likening its approach to cyber-warfare to a military that "send[s] troops to take Fallujah armed with muskets and powdered wigs" (DHS, 2017, New Approach to Cyber section, para. 2). He depicted the DHS as an agency armed with the digital equivalent of flint-lock rifles and he advocated the cultivation of public and private partnerships to help the DHS modernize its offensive and defensive cyber-arsenal: "By integrating [industry's] cutting-edge, commercially-available technology with our interagency partner's unique capabilities, we can aggressively defend our federal networks against the endless stream of cyber-attacks. No more muskets; our federal cybersecurity needs heavy artillery" (DHS, 2017, Cyber Partnerships section, para. 2-3). Kelly's militarized language provokes the question: What is the digital equivalent to military preparedness?

In policy reports detailing the full scope of a cyber-security mobilization, the cyber prefix insinuates a broad range of military assumptions. To encourage prioritization of cyber capabilities in governmental policy, the December 2016 Presidential Commission Report on Internet Security (RIS) stated that "cybersecurity must be made a national security priority equal to counterterrorism and protection of the homeland" (Commission on Enhancing, 2016, p. 39). From overt demands for "enlisting the capabilities of the National Guard" (p. 34) to calls for "a nationwide network of cybersecurity boot camps" (p. 34), the RIS urged an unprecedented cyber-conscription effort. It recommended firmly ensconcing the internet security profession within the broader national security apparatus. Securing a sufficient cadre of professionals capable of meeting the nation's cybersecurity needs depended upon a "national surge that increases the workforce" (p. 33) and training programs that "enable preparedness for cybersecurity careers in high school" (p. 35). To establish new tech procurement policies, the report advised technical procurement policies modeled after those followed in the defense industry: "Possible models are DoD's Defense Innovation Unit – Experimental (DIUx) and the R&D and rapid acquisition programs of the Defense Advanced Research Projects Agency (DARPA), the Intelligence Advanced Research Projects Activity (IARPA), and the Air Force's Rapid Capabilities Office (RCO)" (p. 41). In carving out cyber-security as a distinct component of the nation's security, the cyber-ligature associates the persistent threat trope with detailed description of a national mobilization effort.

Producing the Digital Citizen

In addition to embedding digital policy with military assumptions, the compound cyber-security also functions as a ligature, adding qualification to certain terms (e.g., behavior and awareness). Such qualification elevates the digital consumer above the digital person. The RIS urged action within the first 100 days of the new Administration, broadly orienting cybersecurity around market-sustaining goals. The RIS prioritized the internet as an engine of "social change and economic prosperity" (Commission on Enhancing, 2016, p. 1) and seeks to balance a "commitment to cybersecurity" with a "commitment to innovation," "account-ability and responsibility" (p. 1) and of course, "security and privacy" (p. 16). Its emphasis on balance drew attention to a range of competing interests within the internet's "marketplace and in public sector" (p. 3). These appeals reveal the rhetorical assumptions currently guiding federal cyber-policy and were evident at the outset; the opening reiteration of the executive directive authorizing the committee to assess the "state of our nation's cybersecurity" linked such an assessment to actions that helped in "securing the digital economy" (p. 1) The report defined digital users as vulnerable consumers, not as engaged citizens, and its six categories of action-items—four to sustain the digital economy and one to protect digital consumers—pri-oritized securing the digital economy as the ultimate public good.

Labeling internet users as consumers occludes their civic identity. Just as a biopolitical state engages in population-regulating activities as a mode of governance, the RIS ideal-ized governance that promotes and regulates digital consumption. The report depicted the consumer as an unsure and unaware individual dependent upon sovereign regulatory power for the maintenance of digital life. For instance, it recommended a "Consumer's Bill of Rights and Responsibilities for the Digital Age" (p. 31) to coincide with a "national cybersecurity awareness campaign in 2017" (Commission on Enhancing, 2016, p. 31) that could help consumers understand what information the government is and is not protecting. A crude and imprecise analogue to a citizen's constitutional guar-antees, the RIS advocated a broad pronouncement of the digital consumer's rights and responsibilities. The report's goal was to

> [...] simplify consumer education on their rights: provide insights on what technol-ogy vendors and providers are legally allowed to do with consumer information; clarify privacy protections; articulate responsibilities of all citizens that participate in the digital economy, and identify the security attributes of products and services.
>
> *(Commission on Enhancing, 2016, p. 31)*

The Consumer Bill of Rights remains undrafted, but the RIS's two-dimensional caricature of the digital person as a dependent consumer points to a collection of troubling normative assumptions concerning digital life. Moreover, the approach leaves little room for more pluralistic visions of internet users as autonomous deliberative agents.

The report also promoted digital hygiene practices as a way for consumers to help protect the nation. Connecting the nation's computer security with individual activity, the report advocated attention to the need to use secure advices because engaging in such practices to help "all users who rely on the internet" (Commission on Enhancing, 2016, p. 29) This language binds consumers to other users (presumably other consumers) and governing agents. It promotes security by default because "most consumers are unsure about how to protect their data and personal information" (p. 29). The explicit purpose of the RIS is to change consumers' *"cybersecurity behavior"* (p. 29). At the same time the RIS makes the nation's computer security an individual's responsibility; it argues that easing regulatory standards could induce companies to take part in cyber-security activities.

Using language emphasizing partnerships, which the RIS defined as "collaboration between the public and private sector" (Commission on Enhancing, 2016, p. 2), the report insinuates a neoliberal agenda into the digital security domain. Partnerships imply equal risk and shared decision-making, but the actual shape these partnerships aim to take is a securing of the digital domain as a market for commercial transactions. The RIS seeks a broad easing of regulations constraining companies. One short-term action recommendation is the immediate shielding of companies from public disclosure and public responsibility. Administered through DHS and the critical infrastructure information protections, the report called for companies to participate in information sharing without fear of public obligations and without having to comply with FOIA requests, discovery, "regulatory enforcement," and "evidence in regulatory rule-making processes" (Commission on Enhancing, 2016, p. 15). The neoliberal strain of cyber-security discourse presents security companies as guardians of digital liberties and seeks to relieve them of their civil obligations in exchange for greater commitment to this guardianship.

Conclusion

This paper has traced how discourse embeds neoliberal assumptions that militarize digital space and regulate internet consumption. The prefix "cyber," alone or functioning as a modifier as in "cyber-security" adds argumentative texture by fostering subordination and facilitating hypotactic argument. The semantics of the term prefix denote these argumentative operations; one morpheme, *fix*, derives etymologically from the word for figure (infinitive *fingere*), and the other one *pre-* designates its syntactic and semantic precedence. Specifically, by connecting securitized terms (defense, security, war) to the digital domain, the cyber prefix prefigures the layout and order of public argumentation concerning internet security. As the term cyber demonstrates, prefixes can be dynamic and potent terms when mobilized in an argumentative setting.

Argument scholars contribute to scholarly understanding of securitization by revealing the implicit assumptions, institutional practices, and material conditions informing deliberation concerning cyber-security. Additional scrutiny of emergent discursive fields, like cyber security, should include analysis of ligatures, including the way they link topics together and create hierarchies between concepts. In addition to such synchronic analysis of the cyber ligature, diachronic analysis of the ligature has the potential to enrich scholarly understanding of the development of argumentation and argument fields over time. Tracking ligatures is a useful way to reveal arrangement patterns, determine connections between different argument fields, and understand the assumptions operating in public argumentation. The syntactic linking that prefixes or hyphenation produce is one example of a ligature, but more forms of ligature remain for argumentation scholars to discover and analyze.

References

A Borderless Battle: Defending Against Cyber Threats: Hearing before the Committee on Homeland Security, House of Representatives, 115th Cong. 8 (2017a) (Testimony of Frank J. Cilluffo). Retrieved from https://hsdl.org/?abstract&did=800990

A Borderless Battle: Defending Against Cyber Threats: Hearing before the Committee on Homeland Security, House of Representatives, 115th Cong. 1 (2017b) (Written statement of Bruce W. McConnell). Retrieved from https://hsdl.org/?abstract&did=800990

Commission on Enhancing National Cybersecurity. (2016). *Report on securing and growing the digital economy.* Retrieved from https://nist.gov

Department of Homeland Security. (2017, April 18). Home and away: DHS and the threats to America, remarks delivered by Secretary Kelly at George Washington University Center for Cyber and Homeland Security. Retrieved from https://dhs.gov

Dunmire, P. L. (2005). Preempting the future: Rhetoric and ideology of the future in political discourse. *Discourse & Society, 16*(4), 481–513. doi: 10.1177/0957926505053052

The FY 2018 Department of Homeland Security Budget: Hearing before the Committee on Appropriations and Subcommittee on Homeland Security, House of Representatives, 115th Cong. 1 (2017) (Testimony of John F. Kelly). Retrieved from http://docs.house.gov/meetings/AP/AP15/20170524/106005/HHRG-115-AP15-Wstate-KellyJ-20170524.pdf

Hansen, L., & Nissenbaum, H. (2014). Digital disaster, cyber security, and the Copenhagen school. *International Studies Quarterly*, *53*(4), 1155-1175. doi: 10.1111/j.1468-2478.2009.00572.x

Licalzi, C. (2017). Computer crimes. *American Criminal Law Review*, *54*(4), 1025-1072. Retrieved from HeinOnline database.

Macmillan, A. (2011). Empire, biopolitics, and communication. *Journal of Communication Inquiry*, *35*(4), 356-361. doi: 10.1177/0196859911415678

Mitchell, G. R. (2002). Public argument-driven security studies. *Argumentation and Advocacy*, *39*(1), 57-71. Retrieved from http://tandfonline.com

Nissenbaum, H. (2004). Hackers and the contested ontology of cyberspace. *New Media & Society*, *6*(2), 195-217. doi: 10.1177/1461444804041445

Nissenbaum, H. (2005). Where computer security meets national security. *Ethics and Information Technology*, *7*(2), 61-73. doi: 10.1007/s10676-005-4582-3

Perelman, Ch., & Olbrechts-Tyteca, L. (1969). *The new rhetoric: A treatise on argumentation* (J. Wilkinson & P. Weaver, Trans.). Notre Dame, IL: Notre Dame University Press.

The Promises and Perils of Emerging Technologies for Cybersecurity: Hearing before the Committee on Commerce, Science and Transportation, Senate, 115th Cong. 3 (2017) (Testimony of Caleb Barlow). Retrieved from https://commerce.senate.gov

Stormer, N. (1984). Articulation: A working paper on rhetoric and *taxis*. *Quarterly Journal of Speech*, *90*(3), 257-284. doi: 10.1080/0033563042000255516

Vico, G. (1996). *The art of rhetoric (Institutiones Oratoriae, 1711-1741)* (G. A. Pinton & A. W. Shippee, Trans. & Eds.). Amsterdam, The Netherlands: Rodopi.

Zulick, M. (1997). Generative rhetoric and public argument: A classical approach. *Argumentation and Advocacy*, *33*(3), 109-120.

13

THE AGENTIC EARTH TOPOS

Figuring a Violent Earth at the End of the Anthropocene

Joshua P. Ewalt

Early in Coole and Frost's (2010) volume, *New Materialisms: Ontology, Agency, and Politics*, the editors provided a justification for theorizing ontologies where matter itself, as it exists at multiple scales and in multiple forms, features a vital agency. In doing so, they included a phrase that appears somewhat perplexing given the stated purpose of the volume. "Our existence," they explained, "depends from one moment to the next on myriad micro-organisms and diverse higher species, on our own hazily understood bodily and cellular reactions and on *pitiless* [emphasis added] cosmic motions" (p. 1). In a volume whose chapters concern the way agency extends to the materiality of the world, the notion that the writers render the cosmic motions of the universe incapable of pity appears curious. Why, if matter is capable of agency and physiological processes and complex systems have capacities as actors in assemblages (as Coole and Frost argued), did the authors so quickly deny cosmic motions this relational capacity? And why, if the universe and one of its planets gave rise to the human being (i.e., an entity that undoubtedly has the capacity for pity), would the authors not readily extend that same ability to the cosmos?

Coole and Frost's statement fits within a broader cultural argument that conceptualizes an antagonistic relationship between macro material forms (the Earth, galaxies, universe) and humans, positing on the part of those macro material forms a preference for violent agencies over argumentative inducement and rhetorical responsiveness. As Colebrook (2014) argued, these cultural products stage violent encounters between human beings and the larger material world

> [...] just when the historical actuality of life's end is becoming apparent, though not witnessed, it is possible to note a shift of genre away from human-to-human adversity to, at least initially, something like a war between humans and the cosmos.
>
> *(p. 188)*

Against a backdrop of human extinction and a transition out of the Anthropocene, cultural texts characterize macro-level material systems as exhibiting a lack of concern for human efforts to establish peace and ensure survival. This remains true despite the fact that such material forms are not necessarily denied the prerequisites for rhetorical action, including agency, creativity, and the ability to strategize.

Here, I focus on popular and academic texts that imagine a violent Earth and present responsive rhetorical practice as the limit of the Earth's agentic capacities. This limit then structures the authors' arguments about climate change and human responsibility as the Earth transitions out of the Anthropocene. If, as Crosswhite (2013) maintained, the activities of responding, caring, showing concern for another's context and perspective, undergoing the experience of transcendence in an effort to move others, and disclosing an experience of one's own suffering are all *rhetorical* habits, then the texts I study present the Earth as incapable of implementing such behaviors. Instead, the Earth, posited first in a subject-object relationship with human beings, represents a thinking, planning, and feeling body, but one that nonetheless prefers more brute violent agencies to deal with human action. The Earth will enact more forceful means for removing humans in order to transition into a new geological epoch. As I demonstrate here, this discursive figuration of a violent, agentic Earth then becomes employed as part of public argument about the significance—or, more appropriately, insignificance—of climate change legislation.

I begin by mapping some key moments in the popular conception of a violent Earth that seek retribution for human irresponsibility, staging a war between human beings and the agentic Earth. I then turn to an example of how this discursive configuration becomes mobilized against climate change policy by focusing on an essay Nobel Prize winning physicist Robert Laughlin authored for *The American Scholar,* as well as some of its circulation and networked uptake in online news outlets. Finally, I argue that an alternative imagination of a *rhetorical* Earth, whose efforts to maintain its livelihood unfold as much through argumentative inducement as brute force, involves avoiding the subject-object split. The earth argues through multiple components, including human representation, and on multiple time-scales, both geological and human.

Imagining a Violent, Agentic Earth

The Happening, 20th Century Fox's 2008 science fiction film, opened with a strange phenomenon related to broader issues of the Anthropocene. Set in urban parks at the movie's beginning, human beings started killing themselves by jumping off buildings or stabbing their necks with sharp objects. As more and more people repeated the suicidal acts and the news spread, the audience learned of a mysterious air-borne toxin that made people kill themselves. Although characters initially rushed to blame the incident on human terrorists, the real culprit became apparent early in the movie: Plants, not humans, were responsible for releasing chemical compounds that threaten the human species. Moreover, the plants were adjusting, adapting, and communicating with each other to target human beings. As the central protagonists, Elliott and Alma Moore and three children, fled the plants' deadly emissions, they passed a billboard for a new suburb. The developer's slogan—"You Deserve This!"—served as a commentary on the larger film. The same impulse that made humans believe they deserved a new house also made them deserving of the plants' punishment. Elliott and Alma miraculously survived and embraced each other as they celebrated their pregnancy at the end of the film. The couple, it turned out, learned nothing from the event.

Director M. Night Shyamalan's *The Happening* presents just one instance of a larger deployment of violent conceptions of an agentic Earth. George Carlin's HBO special "Jammin' in New York," which first appeared in 1992 but found a lasting home on the internet, offered such an argument in the closing section. After saying that he was tired of Earth Day and white liberals "trying to make the world safe and clean for their Volvos,"

Carlin (1992) suggested efforts to "save the planet" are part of an arrogant tendency to meddle with nature. He imagined an Earth capable of ousting humans:

> Besides there's nothing wrong with the planet. The planet is fine. The people are f****d. The people are f****d. Compared to the people, the planet is doing great. The planet has been here for four and a half billion years, alright, four and a half billion [...] the planet has been through a lot worse than us for a long time [...] the planet isn't going anywhere. We are [...] the planet will be here and we'll be long gone, just another failed mutation, just another closed-end biological mistake, an evolutionary cul-de-sac...the planet will shake us off like a bad case of fleas [...] I mean to be fair the planet probably sees us as a mild threat, something to be dealt with. And I'm sure the planet will defend itself in the manner of a large organism. Like a bee hive or an ant colony can muster a defense, I'm sure the planet will think of something.
>
> *(Carlin, 1992, 52:01)*

This personifies the planet, imagining the Earth strategizing about how to get rid of human beings and choosing viruses, particularly AIDS, to do so. Earth, in Carlin's (1992) account, has the capacity to withstand violence, to struggle, to defend itself and think, and to attack, but not engage in rhetorical deliberations with humans or to take their concern for "saving the planet" as a sign of goodwill or as an opening to intra-organismic communication.

Public reception of the Gaia hypothesis further evidenced this discursive construction of a violent Earth. Lovelock's *Gaia: A New Look at Life on Earth* (1979) offered the central tenets of the Gaia hypothesis, or "the model, in which the Earth's living matter, air, oceans, and land surface form a complex system which can be seen as a single organism and which has the capacity to keep our planet a fit place for life" (p. vii). Although Lovelock (1979) denied that the Earth was a sentient being, he nonetheless presented the case that the Earth was a living entity, a complex organism that regulated itself and decreased the likelihood of its entropy. For some members of the public, *Gaia* offered a terrifying reality of an Earth that could oust humans at will, particularly if humans threatened its existence. On August 1, 1989, John Brock (1989), responding to an op-ed published in *The New York Times,* argued that the Gaia hypothesis was dangerous:

> The Gaia hypothesis allows us to believe that the Earth, *when pushed by man, has the ability to push back with some strength* and attempt to right itself. The *alternative is terrifying,* but the truth is we really have no idea *how strong the Earth is!*
>
> *(para. 7, emphases added)*

The following month William K. Stevens (1989) published another article in *The New York Times* that sought to further explain the Gaia hypothesis and its uptake in the scientific world:

> The Earth is neither as fragile as some environmentalists would have it nor as forgiving as some people, who have taken the Gaia hypothesis to mean that the environment will adjust to pollution and disruption by humans, would like to believe. It will adjust [...] but the adjustment may well be disastrous for Homo sapiens.
>
> *(para. 9)*

A common picture of Earth emerges in these examples: The Earth is alive, but along with that condition emerges fear of the Earth's capacity for violence. These examples suggest that the Earth will use its agentic capacities to rid itself of humans and that violent encounters will be the basis for that action. To further illustrate the consequences of the agentic Earth *topos* deployed in a violent mode, I turn to an example that illustrates how conceptions of a violent and resilient agentic Earth operating in the face of human violence can inform arguments against climate change legislation.

Conceiving an Un-Rhetorical Earth: Laughlin's "What the Earth Knows"

In June 2010, Robert Laughlin published an essay entitled "What the Earth Knows" in the summer issue of *The American Scholar*. Laughlin (2010) argued that to deliberate about climate change, a person must begin by thinking in terms of geological time. In doing so, citizens would recognize that, time and again, the Earth has experienced suffering and has healed itself: "The Earth has suffered mass volcanic explosions, floods, meteor impacts, mountain formation, and all manner of other abuses greater than anything people could inflict, and it's still here. It's a survivor" (para. 4). For Laughlin, thinking in terms of geological time contained implications for energy policy in the contemporary context of climate change. While well-intentioned policies might allow human beings to feel better, they maintain little ability to impact the Earth because the Earth lacks responsiveness to such human efforts. Laughlin (2010) explained:

> Energy procurement is a matter of engineering and keeping the lights on under circumstances that are likely to get more difficult as time progresses. Climate change, by contrast, is a matter of geological time, something that the Earth routinely does on its own *without asking anyone's permission or explaining itself.* The Earth doesn't include the potentially catastrophic effects on civilization *in its planning.*
>
> *(para. 28, emphases added)*

Laughlin's essay circulated widely in online networks as it became the topic of blogs, forum reposts, and newspaper and magazine columns published in outlets ranging from *The Globe and Mail* to *MarketWatch* and *Newsweek* (Farrell, 2010; Reynolds, 2010; Will, 2010).

Laughlin's (2010) essay shares common arguments with the instances of popular discourse mentioned earlier. Laughlin presented the Earth as a resilient body that has survived many abuses and violent events. He suggested the Earth exhibits significant recovery and strength; if it wanted to, it could remove us. His essay, however, also contributes an additional dimension to this discourse: It explicitly denied that the Earth has the rhetorical capacities for transcendence, for caring, for including other perspectives in its decision-making, or for moving others through inducement. For Laughlin,

> The Earth *doesn't care* about any of these governments or their legislation. It *doesn't care* whether you turn off your air conditioner, refrigerator, and television set [....] Far from being responsible for damaging the Earth's climate, civilization might not be able to forestall any of *these terrible changes once the Earth has decided to make them.*
>
> *(para. 4, 26, emphases added)*

His essay characterized the Earth as decidedly incapable of rhetoric. In the context of systemic changes, the Earth remains uncaring; it will not ask for permission or bother explaining itself.

Laughlin's (2010) argument, however, featured a contradiction. Although he argued that the Earth would not include the potentially catastrophic effects on human civilization in its planning and decision-making, and thus it would decide *on its own* whether to shift the climate, he did not deny that the Earth had the faculty to plan, strategize, or make decisions. Indeed, he titled the essay, "What the Earth Knows." For him, the Earth simply refused to employ those cognitive capacities in the context of rhetorical practice. In other words, Laughlin granted the Earth the prerequisites for rhetoric, but not rhetorical capacities. Rhetoric formed the limits of Laughlin's discursive imagination of the agentic Earth, and this constitutive limit also existed in discourse predating Laughlin's essay. Carlin, for instance, personified the Earth, imagining the planet thinking of viruses and retaliation strategies; *The Happening* suggested plants communicate across species, with trees encouraging grasses to release the toxin. Earthly faculties for communication, strategy, and decision-making exist, but violence nonetheless becomes the preferred method for dealing with human beings and their behaviors.

Ultimately, this presentation of a non-rhetorical Earth helped Laughlin invent arguments against climate change policy. While humans enact legislation and remain worried about the health of the Earth, Laughlin (2010) insisted,

> This concern isn't reciprocated. On the scales of time relevant to itself, the Earth doesn't care about any of these governments or their legislation [....] It doesn't notice when you turn down your thermostat and drive a hybrid car. These actions simply spread the pain over a few centuries, the bat of an eyelash as far as the Earth is concerned.
>
> *(para. 4)*

One reason for the failure to communicate remains temporal in nature. The Earth's agency— its capacity for adaptation—occurs over the long (relatively speaking) temporality of geology beginning with the Earth's formation 4.5 billion years ago, while human agency inhabits a far different, and much more recent, temporality. What happens in human time has little ability to impact the Earth in geological time. This led authors who subsequently drew upon Laughlin's essay to make and repeat arguments against interfering with the natural, nonhuman-caused processes of climate change. In an article citing Laughlin's piece, Reynolds (2010), for example, paraphrased Laughlin, writing, "For planet Earth [...] the crisis of climate change, if crisis it be, will be a walk in the park" (para. 2). Will (2010), similarly citing Laughlin, titled his article, "Earth Doesn't Care What Is Done to It." And Farrell (2010), in *MarketWatch*, wrote, "Forget Going Green" because the "Earth doesn't care" (para. 1). Subsequent articles explicitly repeated the terms of Laughlin's unrhetorical Earth.

Transcending the Subject-Object Split

The texts analyzed here echo new materialist thinking in some ways. Carlin's (1992) argument that humans were an evolutionary cul-de-sac resonates with Coole and Frost's (2010) contemporary insistence that,

> The human species, and the qualities of self-reflection, self-awareness, and rationality traditionally used to distinguish it from the rest of nature, may now seem little more than contingent and provisional forms or processes within a broader evolutionary or cosmic productivity.
>
> *(p. 20)*

Other texts also rhetorically deploy the Gaia argument. As Howard (1998) showed, online communities present the invention of the internet as a step in which "the self-consciousness of Gaia will manifest. The entire planet will gain sentience through the aggregate of networked thoughts and thus become a single self-aware organism" (p. 63). However, Coole and Frost, as well as Howard, both argued that a relation of immanence defines humans' relationship to the rest of the Earth. The Techno-Gaians, for instance, maintained that Gaia reaches self-consciousness through the efforts of humans, namely their ability to develop networked, digital minds.

For the arguments of this essay to function, they must reproduce a subject-object split. A rhetor must assume that a fundamental difference exists between the agencies of the Earth (operating on geological time) and the rhetorical work of human beings, despite the fact that earthly substances compose human bodies in their entirety. To suggest that "saving the planet" and enacting climate change legislation are useless activities, the arguers must assume that human representational and policy-generating practices are not two of the ways the Earth tries to correct its temperatures during the Anthropocene. Collapsing the subject-object split, and thus the relation of exteriority, permits a different argument: namely that the Earth's agency operates on multiple time scales, and it is precisely through modes of human representation that the Earth enacts one of its multi-temporal efforts at self-management. In this sense, something like *The Happening* appears more as a warning, and Laughlin's essay becomes one part of the Earth's deliberations about how to best handle temperature changes. While engaging in violence, rhetorical Gaia would also be a deliberative body, one that thinks and acts on multiple time scales and through multiple modes, each responding to each other. In that sense, to be a part of the living thought of the Earth is to be a part of the making of a contingent future, one made in both human and geologic time, with both belonging to the Earth.

References

Brock, J. (1989, August 1). Let's not count on the Earth to heal itself. *The New York Times*. Retrieved from http://nytimes.com

Carlin, G. (Writer), & Urbisci, R. (Director). (1992). *George Carlin: Jammin' in New York* [Documentary]. United States: Cable Stuff Productions.

Colebrook, C. (2014). *Death of the posthuman: Essays on extinction, vol. 1.* Ann Arbor, MI: Open Humanities Press.

Coole, D., & Frost, S. (2010). Introducing the new materialisms. In D. Coole & S. Frost (Eds.), *New materialisms: Ontology, agency, and politics* (pp. 1–46). Durham, NC: Duke University Press.

Crosswhite, J. (2013). *Deep rhetoric: Philosophy, reason, violence, justice, wisdom.* Chicago, IL: University of Chicago Press.

Farrell, P. B. (2010, September 7). Forget going green – Earth doesn't care. *MarketWatch*. Retrieved from http://marketwatch.com

Howard, R. G. (1998). Researching folk rhetoric: The case of apocalyptic Techno-Gaianism on the world-wide web. *Folklore Forum, 29*(2), 53–73. Retrieved from http://hdl.handle.net/2022/2274

Laughlin, R. B. (2010, June 1). What the Earth knows. *The American Scholar*. Retrieved from https://theamericanscholar.org

Lovelock, J. E. (1979). *Gaia: A new look at life on Earth.* Oxford, United Kingdom: Oxford University Press.

Reynolds, N. (2010, July 19). Please remain calm: The Earth will heal itself. *The Globe and Mail.* Retrieved from https://theglobeandmail.com

Shyamalan, M. N. (Director). (2008). *The happening* [Motion picture]. United States: Twentieth Century Fox Film Corporation.

Stevens, W. K. (1989, August 29). Evolving theory views Earth as a living organism. *The New York Times.* Retrieved from http://nytimes.com/

Will, G. F. (2010, September 12). George Will: The Earth doesn't care what is done to it. *Newsweek.* Retrieved from http://newsweek.com/george-will-Earth-doesnt-care-what-done-it-71901

14

WHAT MAKES A WOMAN A WOMAN?

The I.O.C.'s Deliberation over Sex in International Sport

Jaclyn Nolan

The fear of so-called "gender imposters" who spoil the corporeal purity of female sporting contests have long haunted international athletics. From sport-specific organizations to the powerful International Olympic Committee (I.O.C.), administrators have grappled over how to legislate questions of gender and sex identity in elite athletics. For the better part of the mid-to-late-twentieth century, sports organizations employed various measures to police female sporting bodies. In 1968, the I.O.C. and affiliate organizations implemented the policy of chromosomal examination to ensure that the women participating in female events were, as one official worried years earlier, "normal feminine girls and not monstrosities" (Brundage, 1936, p. 1).

This essay examines the I.O.C.'s rationale for the introduction of compulsory chromosomal examination to women competing in the Olympics and other international contests, as well as the vigorous debate the policy prompted. Despite the chromosomal examination's shortcomings as a measure of sex determination, its inability to catch male infiltrators in women's events, and a great deal of protest among the I.O.C. membership and the public, the process reigned supreme in international sport until 1992. Scholars can best describe policy deliberation over how to police female sex in the history of international sport as competing arguments across what Goodnight (2012) called personal, technical, and public spheres of argumentation. Moreover, the chromosomal examination's intersection with public controversy (Goodnight, 2005) concerning the science of bodies (Hauser, 1999), and particularly the science of sex (Fausto-Sterling, 2000), compels scholars in argumentation studies to consider the contours of this debate.

The I.O.C.'s chromosomal examination named the body as the locus of argument, which in turn served as evidence for the committee's claim that "one is born a man or a woman and one remains of that sex" (Berlioux, 1967, p. 1). The approach is consistent with Palczewski's (2011) observation that "the body not only can serve as data as it enacts proof of the claim advanced, but it also can be the site of argument itself" (p. 384). This case study also reveals the patriarchal standpoint that informed chromosomal examination and the rhetorical gap that existed between the I.O.C.'s purported rationale and their chosen method. Even as the body's chromosomal makeup enacted the claim of biological womanhood based on the I.O.C.'s chosen scientific protocols, the policy could not guarantee the enforcement of Western gender norms or arrive at the proposition that female sex and gender were mutually reinforcing ideas. Thus, although the I.O.C.'s measure sought to arrive at a clear-cut definition of the female sex, the examination process was more productive as an instigator of debate than a non-controversial understanding of the female sex. Indeed, it set in motion an endless array of strategies and a conversation that continues to enliven the world of sport today.

A Brief History of Chromosomes in International Sport

The implementation of sex/gender tests fell to the I.O.C.'s newly created Medical Commission. In 1968, the commission faced a variety of issues about sex itself, even beyond the longstanding historical precedent whereby "scientists defined some bodies as better and more deserving of rights than others" (Fausto-Sterling, 2000, p. 39). Clearly, then, the "critical policy decisions" confronted by the I.O.C. "needed to be based on highly technical scientific and medical knowledge" (Wrynn, 2004, p. 211). Despite these challenges the head of the I.O.C. appointed Belgian aristocrat Prince Alexandre de Mérode to lead the nascent Medical Commission beginning in 1967. De Mérode gained favor within the I.O.C. after he presented a report to the organization on doping that "borrowed heavily from a paper that Belgian doctor Albert Dirix" had written (Pieper, 2016, p. 58). Along with a committee composed of a physical education teacher, two professors, and a handful of medical doctors of varying backgrounds, the commission sought to establish a policy that could effectively weed out corporeal criminality. De Mérode told the *Los Angeles Times*, "We are trying to help the world [....] we think that under our present regulations it is difficult if not impossible for cheating—on the feminine side or doping—to succeed" (quoted in "Swimmers Won't Take," 1968, p. E10).

The Medical Commission decided to rely on the Barr body exam procedure. They considered the test a decidedly modern move and, ultimately, a more evolved way of examining the bodies of those hoping to qualify as women for the purposes of competition. Efficient, reliable, and inexpensive, the procedure helped the I.O.C. "to dissuade the 'hybrids' from competing in the Games" through "a process designed to affirm totally the diagnosis of sex" (Thiebault, 1968, p. 4). The exam called for officials to simply swab an athlete's mouth and examine the sample under a microscope for Barr bodies—and thus evidence of sex chromatin. In a 1968 report prepared for the Medical Commission, Dr. Jacques Thiebault concluded, "The presence of chromatinian corpuscles is exclusive to the female sex and will be evident whenever there are two chromosome X, as the cell of a normal man does not have them" (p. 4). Importantly, "although various chromosomal constitutions illustrate the fallacy of a clear chromosomally delineated definition of sex" (Pieper, 2016, p. 66), the Medical Commission nevertheless believed that the Barr body exam could weed out the presence of such "hybrids" (Thiebault, 1968, p. 4).

The I.O.C.'s Rationale for Chromosomal Testing

The I.O.C. considered their chromosomal policy the application of a non-controversial sex standard. Or, put another way, they understood their policy intervention as harnessing a-rhetorical, non-discursive resources in order to maintain sport as a binary-driven enterprise. Their official correspondence revealed several arguments in favor of universal sex testing for female competitors. Each of these arguments articulated the body as the province of progressive politics, an entity warranting protection, and a cavity of economic convenience.

First, I.O.C. officials claimed their motivation to implement chromosomal testing was consistent with the tenets of the women's liberation movement. Dr. Eduardo Hay, the gynecologist in charge of testing at the 1968 Mexico Summer Olympics, emphasized that the I.O.C. policy embraced a feminist point-of-view because it constituted a mechanism for realizing "equality" in sport. This purpose was in lockstep with a larger societal trend in which "women [were] demanding equality of position, responsibility and salary" (Hay, 1974, pp. 119-120). The proliferation of feminist politics suggested that the I.O.C. should logically pursue the Barr body exam, as women were "seek[ing], demand[ing] and obtain[ing] equal rights in all aspects of life" (Hay, n.d., p. 1). Suturing "equal rights" to the business of the Medical Commission, Hay (1974) raised the issue that "women [were] fighting against all discrimination" (p. 120). The chromosomal examination brought the fight to sport by enabling female athletes to "still cling to their gifts of beauty, grace and maternity as endowments exclusive to them" (Hay, 1974, p. 120). The I.O.C.'s co-optation of the women's movement vision of equity masked the commission's view that such equality was born of a certain kind of womanhood and gender performance.

In addition to bringing women's equality to sport, the I.O.C. argued for the implementation of chromosomal examination because it acted as a form of protection for female competitors: protection from themselves and one another. The Barr body exam was a mechanism for moral protection in sport precisely because it could reveal medical truths: the sex of competitors' bodies. The Medical Commission considered themselves helpmates in this endeavor. Their intervention, wrote Dr. Jacques Thiebault (1968), "must spring from the desire to help, not to harm" (p. 2). The doctor's ethical obligation was to "help" female athletes learn of their hybridity. "Above all other things – even the Olympic Games – we should place our duty as physicians and, should we come across such hybrid creatures, prescribe medical treatment if possible, or at least help them accept their fate" (Thiebault, 1968, p. 2). Geared "towards effectively helping the poor girl as much morally as medically" (Thiebault, 1968, p. 6), the I.O.C. stressed that the Barr body exam disclosed medical certainties that were otherwise unknowable to competitors and equally revelatory for the function of drama-free (binary) competition. Besides saving athletes from themselves, chromosomal examinations were moralizing because they offered "real women" protection from competitors who failed to qualify as women under official test guidelines. Whether to secure self-protection or a defense from a "mannish" competitor, the I.O.C. naturalized their introduction of scientific measures to sport through claims of bodily security.

The third position advanced in favor of chromosomal examination was an economic one. The Medical Commission claimed the Barr body test was practically desirable because it possessed a simplicity that other methods lacked, and at a fraction of the cost. In his 1968 report, Dr. Jacques Thiebault detailed that the Barr body test was the epitome of "discretion" and "efficiency" (p. 15). After its second usage at the 1968 Mexico City Summer Olympic Games, the Medical Commission praised its economical output by the numbers: "The cost of each examination was 50 pesos (Mexican Currency), being 4.00 dollars U.S." (International Olympic Committee, 1968, p. 4). In general, the I.O.C. celebrated the Barr body exam for the "ease of performance at low cost" (Hay, n.d., p. 3). Not only could the exam definitively weed out imposters, it could do so in a way that was not financially burdensome.

While the I.O.C. celebrated the Barr body test as a modern, even feminist, advance, its pretenses were hardly progressive. Despite cloaking the policy in the discursive resources of liberal feminism, the commission's argument only appeared in step with feminist politics. In her history of sex testing, Pieper (2016) cited "the rise of the women's liberation movement in many Western countries, and its focus on equality" (p. 96) as the impetus for objections to the policy, not affirmation. The usage of chromosomal examination—a policy that an all-male commission handed down and that the male dominant system of health care and science/medicine informed—speaks to the fact that the I.O.C.'s policy was hardly the kind of equality that feminists championed in the late 1960s and 1970s. Indeed, the women's liberation movement "eschewed the epistemic authority of the male medical establishment" (Poirot, 2014, pp. 64-65). The I.O.C.'s examination was functional precisely because of the desires of the "gentlemen's club." With the Barr body test, the group defined women's bodies through the policies (and politics) of the Medical Commission first and foremost.

The equality benchmark that drove the I.O.C.'s policy also came at a cost to some would-be competitors. The commission granted "equality" to some, but not all athletes who wished to qualify as women. Berlioux (1967) referred to an athlete who failed to qualify as "the 'unfortunate' girl" (p. 2). The "unfortunate girl" included a feared imposter of deliberate and unknown variants. She quite literally embodied the cost of the I.O.C.'s mission to calibrate its organization to the progressivism of the 1960s. Berlioux (1967) argued that equality in the main required an initial sacrifice. If sport was to be "indispensable to woman's advance towards equality," then "this charlatanry" of "the 'unfortunate' girl" (p. 2) required policy prevention. In other words, the I.O.C. had to deny these performances as live possibilities well before an event occurred.

Finally, the paternalistic underpinning to the I.O.C.'s rationale for chromosomal sex tests once again erected a barrier that has long haunted women. In the case of chromosomal testing, the policy enabled a patriarchal form of power that disallowed women from claiming authorship and ownership over their own bodies. The I.O.C. conveyed that women were ignorant about the so-called truths located in their bodies and that gender fraud was, most of the time, an unknowingly committed "crime." The addition of laboratory science to international sport helped to widen the gap between womanhood and corporeal knowledge, especially as the advent of human karyotyping was still rather novel when the I.O.C. introduced the Barr body test to international athletics. As Richardson (2013) commented in her history of the human genome, "by the 1960s, human sex chromosome errors and other chromosomal anomalies had become potent symbols of the sensational new genetics" (p. 78). The paternalism of the policy was also evident in its perpetuation of the stereotype of the vulnerable woman in need of protection. The I.O.C.'s reasoning conveyed that if women were really women, they could prove it by acquiescing to the committee's bodily oversight. The lack of compliance with the policy accordingly served as strong proof of embodiment that exceeded the parameters of the Barr body exam.

Reaction to the Barr Body Exam

The struggle over the I.O.C.'s vision of the body as reducible to chromatin investigation was particularly evident in the dissenting opinions of various doctors who wrote to the organization. In 1972, six Danish doctors attached their signatures to a lengthy "Memorandum" which charged the I.O.C. with "making its own definition of sex" (Sehested et al., 1972, p. 1). In the view of the six signatories, defining sex was always a rhetorical pursuit because "no medical or legal definition of sex exists in man [*sic*]" (p. 1). The issue was not that the I.O.C. possessed a "natural attitude toward definition" (West, 2011, p. 175), but that their chosen definition rang hollow "for scientific as well as for medical and ethical reasons" (Sehested et al., 1972, p. 1). The doctors argued the Barr body exam constituted "a coarse way of getting information about the chromosomal sex, as it gives information about the number of X chromosomes only, and no information about the somatic or psychosocial sex" (Sehested et al., 1972, p. 6). The result was bodily integrity for some, but not all, because "a number of women would be excluded from the Olympics and other international sports games for no acceptable reason" (Sehested et al., 1972, p. 6). Although the position of the Danish detractors did make its way to de Mérode's desk, he "reasoned that 'practical' issues raised by the IOC outweighed the professors' 'scientific side'" (Pieper, 2016, p. 83). The objection raised in the Danish "Memorandum" highlights an argument that eventually resonated over time, and more immediately evidences that the I.O.C. privileged political expediency over reasoned argument.

Well into the 1980s, a range of doctors and scientists publicly registered their sentiments against chromosomal sex tests. A particularly strong form of dissent came from the discoverer of the Barr body himself. In a June 2, 1987 letter, Dr. Murray L. Barr wrote Roger Jackson, the President of the Canadian Olympic Committee, concerning the attachment of his namesake to the I.O.C.'s procedure. Barr (1987) claimed the policy served the political needs of international sport, but failed to meet the standards of those who populated the technical sphere. As proof, he noted several "scientists and clinicians known to me" who all "agree that buccal smear testing in the area of athletics is totally inappropriate" (p. 1). In 1987, Barr's stance on the matter was "old news." In the pages of *The Lancet*, Barr (1956) had warned that "the presence or absence of sex chromatin [...] is a minor detail in the femaleness or maleness of the whole person" (p. 47). Over thirty years later, he pleaded once more, imploring officials to cease the use of the Barr body exam as a singular measure of female sex: "Its use in this way has been an embarrassment to me and I request that it be stopped" (p. 1). The I.O.C. waited five more years and, in 1992, turned to hormone-based tests to verify biological proof of womanhood.

Conclusion

Barr's letter to sporting officials, as well as the broader technical expertise of the day regarding chromosomes and sport, invites questions for argumentation scholars. If the exam was not scientifically accurate as Barr himself suggested years prior to the implementation of sex testing, then why did such examinations succeed on their merits in 1968, and why did they endure for so many years in the international sporting scene? The I.O.C.'s approach to sex —through its own particular definition—illustrates that a preference for policing womanhood in favor of gender norms and organizational management subordinated reasonable competing arguments concerning the nature of sex. The I.O.C.'s use of gender/sex tests evidences argumentation that shifted from the technical sphere to the public sphere, and the politics that enabled this movement. Although the Medical Commission sought to base the tests on the science of bodies, and Barr's ideas in particular, the science of sex also helped them to discipline the corporeal. The I.O.C. cloaked their rationale in the language of the feminist movement, but a closer inspection reveals that their reasons reproduced a regressive political agenda that limited gender performance and the autonomy of women's bodies. The I.O.C.'s cultural preoccupations poached on the technical sphere to adjudicate the body in sport.

The biological dimorphism that gave purchase to sport's chromosomal examination was not inconsequential. Separating sex into two distinct female and male categories both derided alternative hypotheses about sex based in science and medicine, as well as undercut transgressive gender performances in international sport. Under the guise of science and medicine, sport's entanglement with chromosomal testing illustrates that women in the history of international sport were a distinctly rhetorical pursuit.

References

Barr, M. L. (1956). Cytological tests of sex [Letter to the editor]. *Lancet, 267*(6906), 47. doi: 10.1016/S0140-6736(56)91883-9

Barr, M. L. (1987, July 2). [Letter to Roger Jackson]. IOC Medical Commission Papers, 1983-1987 (Series B-ID04-MEDIC/036, Folder SD2). Archives of the International Olympic Committee, Olympic Studies Centre, Lausanne, Switzerland.

Berlioux, M. (1967). Feminity*. *Olympic Review, 3*, 1-2. Retrieved from http://library.la84.org/OlympicInformationCenter/OlympicReview/1967/ore03/ore03c.pdf

Brundage, A. (1936, June 23). [Letter to Count Baillet-Latour]. IOC Medical Commission Papers, 1936-1982 (Series B-ID04-MEDIC/035, Folder SD4). Archives of the International Olympic Committee, Olympic Studies Centre, Lausanne, Switzerland.

Fausto-Sterling, A. (2000). *Sexing the body: Gender politics and the construction of sexuality*. New York, NY: Basic Books.

Goodnight, G. T. (2012). The personal, technical, and public spheres of argument: A speculative inquiry into the art of public deliberation [Special issue]. *Argumentation and Advocacy, 48*(4), 198-210. Retrieved from http://tandfonline.com

Goodnight, G. T. (2005). Science and technology controversy: A rational for inquiry. *Argumentation and Advocacy, 42*(1), 26-29. Retrieved from http://tandfonline.com

Hauser, G. A. (1999). Incongruous bodies: Arguments for personal sufficiency and public insufficiency. *Argumentation and Advocacy, 36*(1), 1-8. Retrieved from EBSCOhost database.

Hay, E. (n.d.). *Femininity controls in the Olympic Games*. IOC Medical Commission Papers, 1974-1988 (Series B-IEO4-MEDIC/O37, Folder SD2). Archives of the International Olympic Committee, Olympic Studies Centre, Lausanne, Switzerland.

Hay, E. (1974). Femininity tests at the Olympic Games. *Olympic Review, 76-77*, 119-124. Retrieved from http://library.la84.org/OlympicInformationCenter/OlympicReview/1974/ore76/ore76m.pdf

International Olympic Committee. (1968, September-October). *General report on the work of the Medical Commission of the International Olympic Committee during the Games of the XIXth Olympiad*. Archives of the International Olympic Committee, Olympic Studies Centre, Lausanne, Switzerland.

Palczewski, C. H. (2011). When body argument becomes militant argument. In R. C. Rowland (Ed.), *Reasoned argument and social change* (pp. 379-386). Washington, DC: National Communication Association.

Pieper, L. (2016). *Sex testing: Gender policing in women's sports*. Urbana, IL: University of Illinois Press.

Poirot, K. (2014). *A question of sex: Feminism, rhetoric, and differences that matter*. Amherst, MA: University of Massachusetts Press.

Richardson, S. S. (2013). *Sex itself: The search for male and female in the human genome*. Chicago, IL: University of Chicago Press. doi: 10.7208/chicago/9780226084718.001.0001

Sehested, N. A., Strömgren, E., Nielsen, J., Ingerslev, M., Bruun Petersen, G., & Therkelsen, A. J. (1972, February 3). *A memorandum on the use of sex chromatin investigation of competitors in women's divisions of the Olympic Games*. IOC Medical Commission Papers, 1936-1982 (Series B-ID04-MEDIC/035, Folder SD2). Archives of the International Olympic Committee, Olympic Studies Centre, Lausanne, Switzerland.

Swimmers Won't Take Sex Tests. (1968, October 10). *Los Angeles Times*, p. E10.

Thiebault, J. (1968). *Report made by Doctor Thiebault to the Medical Commission of the International Olympic Committee on the Grenoble Games*. Medicine at the 1968 Winter Games in Grenoble Papers, 1968 (Series CIO JO-1968W-MEDIC, Folder SD3). Archives of the International Olympic Committee, Olympic Studies Centre, Lausanne, Switzerland.

West, I. (2011). What's the matter with Kansas and New York City? Definitional ruptures and the politics of sex. *Argumentation and Advocacy, 47*(3), 163-177. Retrieved from http://tandfonline.com

Wrynn, A. (2004). The human factor: Science, medicine and the International Olympic Committee, 1900-70. *Sport in Society: Cultures, Commerce, Media, Politics, 7*(2), 211-231. doi: 10.1080/1461098042000222270

* The original article title contains this typo.

15

THE DISCURSIVE CONSTRUCTION OF THE ANTI-NUCLEAR ACTIVIST

Ian Summers, Alley Agee, Monica Renae Scott, and Danielle Endres

Scholars have identified that social movements direct rhetoric at multiple audiences, both internal (e.g., Chávez, 2011; Lake, 1983) and external (e.g., DeLuca & Peeples, 2002; Schwarze, 2006); examined how institutional powers can suppress, control, or appropriate protest arguments (e.g., Husting, 2006); and considered the ways in which activist discourses permeate and contour the public sphere (e.g., Palczewski & Harr-Lagin, 2017; Pezzullo, 2003). Yet, researchers in social movements have not conducted a sustained examination of argumentation about social movements within oppositional spheres, that is, groups with antagonistic views of the movement. In this paper, we study how members of oppositional groups develop argumentative resources that characterize the social movement activists they oppose. Specifically, we examine how pro-nuclear advocates talk among themselves about anti-nuclear and environmental activists. While scholars have analyzed the public arguments of establishment oppositional groups that characterize the members of a movement (e.g., Black, 2002), we seek to shift focus to the internal and semi-private contexts in which members of an oppositional group discursively construct a social movement and its members. This is critical because activists frequently fashion their arguments based on what they think their opposition believes, rather than understand how adversarial audiences interpret their claims.

We define oppositional groups as collectives that include members who could function as part of the establishment, a competing social movement/counterpublic, or other types of advocacy organizations. Through fieldwork with nuclear scientists and engineers—the oppositional group in this case—we document and analyze the ways that they characterize anti-nuclear activism and activists. In so doing, our paper addresses two critical questions. First, how do members of oppositional groups internally discuss and construct the activists who campaign against their positions and ideologies? Second, how do members of oppositional groups strategically construct activists in reference to existing frames of argumentation within the group's discursive community?

We contend that nuclear scientists and engineers use strategic maneuvering, which van Eemeren and Houtlosser (2002) defined as "a systemic integration of rhetorical considerations in an [argumentative] framework" (quoted in Zarefsky, 2006, p. 400) to characterize environmentalists and anti-nuclear activists (hereafter "antis") in ways that reinforce dominant rhetorical and argu-mentative norms within their discursive community. Rather than simply dismiss or ignore envir-onmentalists and "antis," nuclear scientists and engineers characterize activists in ways that reinforce technoscientific reasoning (Goodnight, 2005), downplay risks of nuclear technologies, and call into question activist claims about the danger of nuclear technologies. This strategic argu-mentation also allows nuclear scientists and engineers to blame their industry's troubles on activists and effectively elides the economic, environmental, and technological hurdles facing the expansion of nuclear energy in the United States.

To illustrate, we first demonstrate how strategic maneuvering in the internal rhetoric of scien-tists upholds a particular set of beliefs about science and technology, or what George Marcus called "technoscientific imaginary" (Marcus, 1994, p. 3). Then, we highlight three ways nuclear scientists and engineers discursively characterize activists via strategic maneuvering. Finally, we conclude with implications for social movement studies, rhetoric of science, and future collaborations between environmentalists and scientists.

Strategic maneuvering, internal rhetoric, and technoscientific reasoning

The efficacy of arguments oftentimes hinges on the terms of the debate and how both inter-locutors and the audience commonly understand them. Hence, Zarefsky (2006) explained that the effectiveness of strategic maneuvering works through persuasive definition, or "a non-neutral characterization that conveys a positive or negative attitude about something in the course of naming it. The name is [...] an implicit argument [....and] the definition is put forward as if it was uncontroversial" (p. 404). Under this form of rhetorical argument, the user of the persuasive definition attempts to make it the foundation of the debate. If they are successful, they can effectively rebut challenges to the strategic maneuvering by showing that their opponent's arguments weaken the values in question. As Zarefsky (2006) noted, "what matters is how strongly the *audience* is committed to the [definition]" (p. 407); however, Zarefsky's formulation is predicated on the assumption that the audience's "impli-cit commitments to specific rules of critical discussion" (p. 408) are usually unknown.

Previous research has examined how the persuasion of *external* audiences works through strategic maneuvering (e.g., Bricker, 2014); however, our research looks at the way groups invent and deploy strategic maneuvering *internally* among members of a community. In par-ticular, we expand on internal rhetoric of science research (e.g., Ceccarelli, 2001; Endres, Cozen, O'Byrne, Feldpausch-Parker, & Peterson, 2016) by revealing how scientists and engineers construct arguments in conversations among themselves. Our fieldwork provides a unique insight into how enclosed communities discuss among themselves the arguments of their opponents and refashion them in a way that reifies their existing logical norms. This project demonstrates how nuclear scientists and engineers in their persuasive definition of environmentalists and "antis" uphold technoscientific reasoning. Specifically, by strategically maneuvering nuclear power as a clean energy source regardless of public health concerns, persuasive definitions reify a technoscientific imaginary (Jasanoff & Kim, 2009; Marcus, 1994) that presumes that technological advancements will adequately address any future potential problems stemming from nuclear power.

Analysis

We gained access to the internal argumentation of nuclear scientists and engineers through rhetorical fieldwork (Endres, Hess, Senda-Cook, & Middleton, 2016) at six separate national conferences for a prominent international nuclear science and engineering society from 2014 to 2017. We collected audio transcripts of conference sessions, field notes, and ethnographic and semi-structured interviews with participants at the conferences. For the purposes of our study, we only examined the discourse of nuclear science and engineering professionals who preferably had an MA or PhD level of education in the field. In total, we transcribed 46 different panel sessions, 24 interviews, and 111 field notes. Using the Socio-Political Evaluation of Energy Deployment (SPEED) framework for assessing the social aspects of energy technology development (Stephens, Peterson, & Wilson, 2014), we coded each sentence to identify how scientists and engineers invoked cultural, environmental, economic, political/legal, and technical functions of nuclear energy in their internal discourse. In total, we coded 10,471 lines of data.

For this paper we focus specifically on how nuclear professionals characterized environmentalists and "antis." Even though activists were never present at the nuclear professional conferences, they constituted an unprompted topic of formal and informal discourse. Out of the entire data set, 226 sentences (2.16%) mentioned an environmentalist or anti-nuclear activist. Although this figure represents a low percentage of the total, our analysis focuses on internal discourse at a scientific conference where most of the discourse was technical in nature (e.g., discussing research results). This discourse about environmentalists and "antis," while not widespread, offers a unique opportunity to examine how nuclear scientists and engineers talk among themselves about their perceived opponents. Within these characterizations of environmentalists and "antis," only 12 instances occurred where nuclear scientists viewed environmentalists favorably. Yet, interestingly, 1,111 sentences from our fieldwork (10.62%) expressed nuclear energy's positive relationship to the environment. This suggests that while nuclear scientists and engineers argue that nuclear energy is a pro-environmental technology (see also American Nuclear Society, 2015), they characterize environmentalists and "antis" negatively. Building from these initial coding results, we closely analyzed the texts for argumentative themes within the rhetorical characterization of environmentalists and anti-nuclear activists.

Overall, members of the nuclear science community acknowledge the long and complicated history of nuclear technologies in the United States, including the 1979 accident at Three Mile Island, the environmental and health consequences of the development of nuclear weapons, and the difficulty for publics to separate nuclear energy from nuclear weapons. Multiple nuclear scientists and engineers cite each of these as reasons for why activists opposed nuclear energy expansion and many local communities distrusted nuclear scientists. Despite this history, scientists persuasively define nuclear as a clean energy. For example, a Department of Energy nuclear official declared in a speech delivered on June 17, 2014, "nuclear energy is already an important part of clean energy solutions here in the United States." Speakers assert these definitions as non-controversial and cast a positive framework toward this energy technology. Yet, with a few notable exceptions of environmentalists who have recently embraced nuclear energy (Cozen, 2015), activists largely contest this persuasive definition of nuclear technology. This disputation causes a tension between nuclear scientists' perceptions of nuclear energy as pro-environmental and environmentalists and "antis" perceptions of nuclear energy as damaging for the environment. As such, the nuclear scientist community cannot ignore or dismiss activists, but instead must view them a potential ally. As a nuclear engineer noted in a business meeting on November 8, 2015, "Environmentalists are one of the most prized third-party advocates that we can have." Hence, while many nuclear scientists and engineers openly chafe at environmentalists and "antis," they simultaneously want to win over their support for nuclear power.

To rectify the aforementioned tension, nuclear scientists construct an internal strategic maneuver where activists' opposition argumentatively validates the scientific supremacy of nuclear. Instead of directing their rebuttals to a public audience, nuclear professionals do so internally within their accepted argumentative framework. Since nuclear scientists and engineers already commit to the conception of nuclear as "clean," the persuasive definition serves as the basis for argumentative invention. Nuclear professionals use three central argumentative themes that denigrate environmentalists to strategically situate nuclear as a clean energy source: "antis" are ignorant of science, they forward disingenuous arguments, and they are an outsized group.

First, nuclear scientists assert repeatedly that environmentalists and "antis" are either too ignorant or dogmatic to understand the nature of nuclear science. This argument, in turn, reinforces technoscientific norms that the supremacy of nuclear science outweighs any of its potential concerns. In other words, those who oppose the strategic definition of nuclear as a clean energy source simply cannot—or will not—accept the scientific reasoning that purportedly proves the overblown nature of concerns over radiation, leaks, or accidents. For example, one prominent nuclear scientist and former environmental activist lamented in an interview on May 12, 2016, "the environmental movement has become a religion—they have deviated from looking at things scientifically." This contention was recurrent across the texts in the study's sample: Environmentalists and "antis" are simply blind to the truth that nuclear energy is not a public health and environmental risk. In this characterization, the supposed "neutrality" of nuclear as a clean energy source holds because of its foundation in scientific reasoning, whereas non-scientific dogma or ignorance fuels the opposition.

Likewise, this argumentative theme illustrates the circular reasoning of a persuasive definition among an internal audience. Scientists hail environmental activists who support nuclear energy as examples of those who have "seen the light" once they understand the science, thereby warranting the superiority of technoscientific reasoning. One nuclear scientist remarked in a June 17, 2014 interview, "If you look in England, you'll see that quite a few of the environment groups have already embraced nuclear because they saw what coal from Wales has done to their country." In this observation, the ability to look at a situation objectively persuaded activists of the superiority of nuclear energy. The implicit argument is that the benefits of eliminating coal outweigh other concerns, thereby reifying technoscientific reasoning that holds nuclear energy as a clean, carbon-free technology. The small number of environmentalists who accept this persuasive definition therefore function as proof of its validity.

Second, the nuclear community accuses "antis" of intentionally being disingenuous, exaggerating claims, or lying outright. The premise is that "antis" are fully aware about the "truth" of nuclear energy and its benefits, but instead promulgate falsehoods to advance ulterior agendas. The former environmentalist highlighted this tactic in an interview on May 12, 2016:

> The Department of Energy people certainly make mistakes, but they don't lie overtly the way the environmental movement lies explicitly [...] I'm a little bit at a loss to know why, except for some kind of political advantage…I really don't understand what it is they [environmentalists] want.

Nuclear scientists and engineers never explicitly advance the underlying assertion that nuclear energy is something that environmental activists *should* want. Instead, such a claim underpins the scientist's apparent befuddlement at what environmentalists desire. In so doing, the scientist employs the rhetorical argument that their opponent's position actually undermines environmentalists' stated goals of promoting carbon-free and sustainable energy. The only way to logically resolve this conundrum is to accuse "antis" of knowingly lying for political gain rather than advocating for environmental protection.

Moreover, the nuclear scientists and engineers place the motivations of environmental groups in question. Within the persuasive definition of nuclear as a "clean" energy, they characterize environmentalist critiques as invalid and nuclear scientists as caring more about clean energy than environmentalists and "antis." One university professor reflected this notion in an interview on June 24, 2015 when he opined, "I think these [environmentalists] who are pushing this [anti-nuclear stance] are less interested in climate solutions than they are radical social change." Thus, those who challenge the persuasive definition are simply using the environmental movement to forward radical ends and lack the legitimacy to arbitrate which energy sources are truly "clean." Additionally, the scientist forwards an implicit, technoscientific assumption that climate change should be the primary concern when evaluating nuclear energy, thereby negating any other risks concerning the technology, such as accidents and radiation exposure.

Third, nuclear scientists and engineers portray "antis" as an outsized but vocal group. Within this line of reasoning, activists do not represent the general public's actual views on nuclear energy; instead, they deploy sophisticated communication campaigns to sway laypeople, media, and politicians against nuclear. This contention utilizes the logical fallacy of mass appeal to reinforce the validity of technoscientific reasoning. Nuclear scientists reaffirm their persuasive definition through the assertion that broader audiences share their beliefs and not those of environmentalists. As one nuclear science graduate student said in a February 19, 2015 interview, "I don't think there's a huge problem, aside from these very loud people, who make others perceive that everyone doesn't like nuclear, when really it's actually not that bad." Here, the nuclear professional portrays the wider public as actual adherents to the argument that nuclear is a clean energy. This argumentative move offers external validation of the nuclear community's stance through highlighting that "antis" are only a vocal minority when the silent majority supports nuclear energy.

Yet, this strategic move poses a potential contradiction. Although nuclear scientists characterize the broader public as viewing nuclear energy as clean energy, policies curtailing the expansion of nuclear energy continue to emerge. Nuclear scientists and engineers resolve this tension, however, by asserting that nuclear activists hold outsized influence on policy and compensate for their small numbers through their level of coordination and sophistication. For instance, one French nuclear scientist noted in a panel session on November 9, 2015, "What we're going up against are really powerful [anti-nuclear] international campaigns that have been going on for years." Within this frame public challenges to the nuclear science community's persuasive definition are not because of any inherent flaws in the community's argument. Instead, the nuclear scientists and engineers shift the blame to their opponents and the structural disadvantages of using scientific reasoning. One nuclear professional illustrated this argumentative move in a panel on June 16, 2016: "I think that the science-based [message is] more carefully deliberated and some of the activists' messages can be sort of glib and thrown out there, so maybe it's just the nature of the beast." Overall, within this persuasive definition, nuclear scientists and engineers never question the technoscientific soundness of nuclear energy as clean and pro-environmental, but instead seek to characterize activists as irrational, deceitful, and outsized. Implicitly, this approach allows the nuclear science community to maintain the environmental benefits of nuclear energy while denigrating the argumentative practices of "antis." In a sense, then, the persuasive definition seeks to redefine environmentalism from the perspective of nuclear scientists and engineers.

Implications

Our research expands on social movement and counterpublic scholarship by turning attention to examine how a group that sees itself in opposition to a social movement internally invents arguments about that social movement. Our findings are useful for understanding how these groups' definitions of activists can have broader implications for the argumentative constraints that social movements face. Furthermore, our unique focus on examining the *in situ* rhetorical and argumentation practices of scientists and engineers as they talk among themselves furthers the study of the internal rhetoric of science by shifting focus away from the finished products of science (e.g., journal articles) to the messy and complicated everyday discursive practices of an evolving scientific community. Our findings not only reveal how scientists and engineers talk among themselves but also how they engage in both technical and prudential forms of reasoning (Goodnight, 2005). Finally, our analysis offers a practical implication for the future possibility of collaboration between nuclear scientists and engineers and environmentalists and anti-nuclear activists. Simply put, successful efforts to win over activists will necessitate discarding the current argumentative frames that reinforce technoscientific reasoning, as evidenced in the recent documentary *Pandora's Promise* that highlights the conversion stories of four prominent environmentalists who came to see the light of nuclear science (Cozen, 2015). Instead, nuclear scientists and engineers must employ frames that genuinely address environmentalist and anti-nuclear concerns.

References

American Nuclear Society. (2015). *UN climate change conference (COP 21) Paris 2015*. Retrieved from http://ans.org/pi/ps/docs/ps44-other.pdf

Black, J. E. (2002). SLAPPS and social activism: The wonderland v. Grey2K case. *Free Speech Yearbook*, *40*(1), 70-82. doi:10.1080/08997225.2002.10556284

Bricker, B. J. (2014). Feigning environmentalism: Antienvironmental organizations, strategic naming, and definitional argument. *Western Journal of Communication*, *78*(5), 636-652. doi:10.1080/10570314.2013.835065

Ceccarelli, L. (2001). Rhetorical criticism and the rhetoric of science. *Western Journal of Communication*, *65*(3), 314-329. doi:10.1080/10570310109374708

Chávez, K. R. (2011). Counter-public enclaves and understanding the function of rhetoric in social movement coalition-building. *Communication Quarterly*, *59*(1), 1-18. doi:10.1080/01463373.2010.541333

Cozen, B. (2015). *Mediating energy: Rhetoric and the future of energy resources* (Doctoral dissertation). Retrieved from the University of Utah J. Williard Marriott Library database: https://databases.tools.lib.utah.edu/

DeLuca, K. M., & Peeples, J. (2002). From public sphere to public screen: Democracy, activism, and the "violence" of Seattle. *Critical Studies in Media Communication*, *19*(2), 125-151. doi:10.1080/07393180216559

Endres, D., Cozen, B., O'Byrne, M., Feldpausch-Parker, A. M., & Peterson, T. R. (2016). Putting the U in carbon capture and storage: Rhetorical boundary negotiation within the CCS/CCUS scientific community. *Journal of Applied Communication Research*, *44*(4), 362-380. doi:10.1080/00909882.2016.1225160

Endres, D., Hess, A., Senda-Cook, S., & Middleton, M. K. (2016). *In situ* rhetoric: Intersections between qualitative inquiry, fieldwork, and rhetoric. *Cultural Studies: Critical Methodologies*, *16*(6), 511-524. doi:10.1177/1532708616655820

Goodnight, G. T. (2005). Science and technology controversy: A rationale for inquiry. *Argumentation and Advocacy*, *42*(1), 26-29. Retrieved from http://tandfonline.com

Husting, G. (2006). Neutralizing protest: The construction of war, chaos, and national identity through US television news on abortion-related protest, 1991. *Communication and Critical/Cultural Studies, 3*(2), 162-180. doi:10.1080/14791420600633089

Jasanoff, S., & Kim, S.-H. (2009). Containing the atom: Sociotechnical imaginaries and nuclear power in the United States and South Korea. *Minerva, 47*(2), 119–146.

Lake, R. A. (1983). Enacting red power: The gonsummatory* function in Native American protest rhetoric. *Quarterly Journal of Speech, 69*(2), 127–142. doi:10.1080/00335638309383642

Marcus, G. E. (1994). *Technoscientific imaginaries: Conversations, profiles, and memoirs.* Chicago, IL: University of Chicago Press.

Palczewski, C. H., & Harr-Lagin, K. (2017). Pledge-a-picketer, power, protest, and publicity: Explaining protest when the state/establishment is not the opposition. In C. R. Foust, A. Pason, & K. Z. Rogness (Eds.), *What democracy looks like: The rhetoric of social movements and counterpublics* (pp. 129–151). Tuscaloosa, AL: University Alabama Press.

Pezzullo, P. C. (2003). Resisting "national breast cancer awareness month": The rhetoric of counterpublics and their cultural performances. *Quarterly Journal of Speech, 89*(4), 345-365. doi:10.1080/0033563032000160981

Stephens, J. C., Peterson, T. R., & Wilson, E. J. (2014). Socio-political evaluation of energy deployment (SPEED): A framework applied to smart grid. *UCLA Law Review, 61*, 1930–2068. Retrieved from https://uclalawreview.org/pdf/61-6-7.pdf

Schwarze, S. (2006). Environmental melodrama. *Quarterly Journal of Speech, 92*(3), 239–261. doi:10.1080/00335630600938609

van Eemeren, F. H., & Houtlosser, P. (2002). Strategic maneuvering: Maintaining a delicate balance. In F. H. van Eemeren & P. Houtlosser (Eds.), *Dialectic and rhetoric: The warp and woof of argumentation analysis* (pp. 131–159). Dordrecht, The Netherlands: Kluwer Academic.

Zarefsky, D. (2006). Strategic maneuvering through persuasive definitions: Implications for dialectic and rhetoric. *Argumentation, 20*(4), 399–416. doi:10.1007/s10503-007-9030-6

* The title, as it appears in search engines, contains this typo. The correct term is *consummatory.*

16

THE VISIBLE AND THE INVISIBLE

Arguing about Threats to Loyalty in the Internet Age

Adam Blood and Ronald Lee

During times of national crisis, political anxiety generates suspicion about citizen loyalty. Whether Socrates' execution in the wake of the Peloponnesian War, Cicero's death at the hands of Mark Antony, or the Red Scare that gripped the United States during the Cold War, accusations and defenses concerning individuals' attachment to the state have functioned as recurring features of political practice.

In the post-9/11 world, what Talbott (2002) called the Age of Terror has ratcheted up anxiety over attachment to the state. In this essay, we think about this anxiety through the complexity of loyalty argumentation. First, we examine loyalty as a civic virtue. Second, we demonstrate that sign reasoning advances disloyalty claims through the rhetorical *topos* of the visible and the invisible. Third, we argue that the rise of the lone-wolf terrorist has made invisible signs increasingly salient. Finally, we contend that invisibility is a key premise in justifying aggressive counterterrorism policies as a defensible exception to liberal democratic norms.

The Nature of Loyalty as a Civic Virtue

The U.S. Constitution establishes citizens as rights holders, but the efficient functioning of political community requires virtuous civic actors. Rights are principles or entitlements; virtues are preferential qualities of persons (Pincoffs, 1986). In times of crisis, these different moral forms may spark incendiary political discourses. Among the flammable elements, loyalty is dry kindling because its virtuous status rests on problematic, contingent relationships that inevitably clash with rights-based limits on sovereign authority.

Scholars often conceive the concept of loyalty as a public obligation, a moral virtue with a dispositional attachment to some end apart from the self (Pincoffs, 1986). Definitions of loyalty employ synonyms such as "devotion" (Cochran, 1982, pp. 25-28), "attitude" (Doob, 1964, pp. 4-9), and "identification" (Grodzins, 1956, p. 21; Schaar, 1957, pp. 2-7). In political terms, loyal Americans possess the requisite sentiment toward their country. The presence of this sentiment is important because it motivates acts in support of the government and leads citizens to willingly sacrifice for the common good.

Because loyalty is not a term describing an event's occurrence, like treason, establishing its presence relies on findings based on identifying acts that are signs of the disposition. "In argument from sign," Walton (1996) wrote, "the conditional says if *A* is true, in a certain type of situation, then you can *normally* expect *B* to be true too (subject to exceptions)" (p. 70).

The difficulty is that signs of disloyalty are more or less visible. This is an understandable characteristic in the context of a liberal polity, where constitutional rights assure domains of privacy. To say that a sign is visible is to identify a symptom of a disposition that is in the public domain—resides in public records or is readily visible in public spaces. The state has long justified security restrictions based on visible signs. From the Alien and Sedition Acts of 1798 to Franklin Roosevelt's Executive Order establishing the internment camps in 1942 to Donald Trump's travel ban on immigrants from certain Muslim countries, group characteristics have served as visible signs justifying repressive political acts.

The argument that a sign is invisible suggests that a disposition is ensconced in the private/personal domain. In the McCarthy era, for instance, rooting out "concealed communists" (Lichtman, 2004, p. 25) was at the center of the witch-hunt. The accused were neither official members of the party nor vocal sympathizers for the cause. Thus, the putative signs of disloyalty were either hidden from view or interpretable as ordinary behavior. The signs of chronic disease constitute a useful analogy. Some debilitating conditions are readily visible —coughing, physical deformity, shaking, etc.—and others are fairly, easily hidden. "When a condition is invisible, as with diabetes, it may be possible to conceal the signs from others, and pass for healthy" (Joachim & Acorn, 2000, p. 245). This does not mean that no signs of well-controlled diabetes exist—taking medication, blood test results, etc.—but such indicators may effectively hide behind walls of privacy (legally through HIPPA laws and physically by concealment) that they are practically invisible.

In the Age of Terror, the signs of disloyalty are increasingly *invisible*. Terrorism crosses borders and thus belies the metrics of identity. As Engle (2004) wrote, "The enemy could reside anywhere, even within the United States [...] the war against terrorism requires [a] turn inward to rout out the enemy" (p. 59). Because U.S. counterterrorism efforts quite successfully detect foreign plots and degrade the capabilities of international terrorist networks, the greatest security risk increasingly is the domestic, self-radicalized lone wolf (Bates, 2012; Fort Hood Attack, 2009, p. 20; Weimann, 2012).

The concepts of individual privacy and agency are in tension with the expectation of security from lone wolf terrorist attacks. Brian Jenkins of the Rand Corporation argued, "authorities are going to confront [...] the actions of individuals which, in a free society, are always going to be hard to predict and prevent" (Fort Hood Attack, 2009, p. 22). "We do not have," he observed, "an X-ray for a man's soul" (p. 21). The visible symptomology, which is a precursor to other types of violence, is frequently absent before terrorist acts. Because terrorists plan attacks with intentionality and rationality as justified defensive undertakings, the "traditional violence risk factors—history of such behavior, psychiatric disorder, or drug abuse—are somewhat useless in predicting the risk of lone terrorist acts" (Meloy, 2016, p. 1). The remaining signs are largely ideological and "it is not illegal to believe [...] inherently exclusionary and violent" ideas (Fort Hood Attack, 2009, p. 17). Markers of disloyalty are perhaps in some cases visible to the intimate associates of the potential perpetrator, but "lone wolves are solitary actors, whose intentions are hard to discern since they usually avoid contact with others" (Bakker & de Graaf, 2011, p. 46).

To illustrate the increasing prevalence of the invisible, we analyze the Fort Hood and the Charleston, South Carolina shootings. Nidal Malik Hasan, the Fort Hood shooter, conformed to the metrics of visibility and invisibility. He was ethnically visible as a man of Palestinian descent and was raised as a Muslim with a distinctly Middle Eastern name. He was invisible as a U.S. citizen, graduated from Virginia Tech, joined the army, received medical training, and took a position at Fort Hood as an on-base psychiatrist. As General John Keane testified, "The 10,000 Muslims in the military [...] are not seen as Muslims but as soldiers, sailors, airmen, and marines" (Fort Hood Attack, 2009, p. 7). The military intentionally assimilates soldiers into the Army culture so markers of ethnic and religious identity become largely invisible. The story that frequently arose in popular discourse and media narratives was the amount of online activity that led to his self-radicalization (Carter & Carter, 2012).

Dylann Roof, the assailant in the Mother Emmanuel AME Church shooting, was also largely invisible. His self-radicalization is a chilling story of the invisible forces at work in the process of turning a seemingly ordinary citizen into a violent threat (Norris, 2017). Richard Cohen of the Southern Poverty Law Center testified, "Dylann Roof [...] represents the new face of domestic terrorism: the extremist who acts alone after being radicalized and inspired on-line by an extremist ideology." He argued that Roof's invisibility was aided by his failure to become "a [member of] a racist hate group" (The Rise of Radicalization, 2015, p. 20).

Invisibility and the Argument for the Terrorism *Exception*

A major theme in contemporary politics is that the threat of terrorist violence presents an exceptional demand for increased security. Agamben (2005) referenced counterterrorism policies in his analysis on the phenomenon of the exception, which he defined as "the original structure in which law encompasses living beings by means of its own suspension" (p. 3). Agamben was describing a structural relationship between juridical order and sovereign authority, which manifests in bio-political usurpations into the lives of individuals, and in some cases, removal of their constitutional protections. In the context of counterterrorism, where "there are many restrictions on individual rights that may be necessary and tolerable on an emergency basis" (Brooks, 2004, p. 737), the common limitations on sovereign authority, such as geographical and temporal boundaries and the distinction between acts of crime and war, stretch beyond their limiting capacity. Thus, the inability to know fully the invisible disposition of the individual creates an epistemological gap that serves as a rationalization for violence as it justifies governmental intrusion into the lives of ordinary citizens. Put simply, the presence of a threat that is largely invisible to the state creates a discourse of suspicion that implies a necessity of surveillance, unlawful search and seizure, and in the most harrowing circumstances, the use of proactive force and detention. Add the ambiguities of the self-radicalized lone wolf and the pretenses for justifying a permanent state of exception become increasingly persuasive.

These exception arguments appear in a set of elite discourses—FBI reports, think-tank papers, law review articles, testimony by national security experts at Congressional hearings, scholarly treatises—all intersecting through cross-citation and arriving at a growing consensus about the limits of counterterrorism in a democratic society. The Constitution's protection of civil liberties prevents the unchecked cyber surveillance required to guard effectively against lone-wolf terrorists. Understood in this way, a familiar liberal-democratic story of rights emerges. Thus, the conventional account of the Red Scare portrays Joseph McCarthy as an enemy of the Bill of Rights. In some sense, this is correct, but more fundamentally these security-liberty conundrums are dramas about the nature of loyalty. This is what the counterterrorism interlocutors implicitly understand. The move from disrupting a terrorist network to detecting a self-radicalized lone wolf is the move from the outside to the inside, the external act to the internal thought. Put another way, it is the move to investigate and interrogate the character of the citizen.

The exception is the point at which argumentation over rights and virtues diverge. Rights are limits on the sovereign's visible actions; virtues are the citizens' invisible dispositions. Behavioral scientists have identified the lone wolf's key pathway to violence as ideological "fixation" (e.g., Meloy, 2016, p. 2). The terms "ideology" and "virtue" have the same is-ought jumping property because they both have a teleological premise. They move from beliefs to dispositions to right action. So, an ideological fixation is a focus on a set of political beliefs that create attitudes toward justifying violent acts.

Thus, when policymakers acknowledge this dimension of the lone-wolf terrorist, two moves are available. The first is to recognize the lone-wolf threat as the price of liberal democracy. Because the United States has been highly successful at integrating immigrants into the larger national narrative and has been effective at degrading terrorist networks, the lone wolf has become the dominant threat to security (Hamm & Spaaij, 2017). The potential damage from lone wolves is considerably smaller in magnitude than organized terrorist attacks. Therefore, if the United States has already mitigated the greater threat, maintaining the prevailing Constitutional limits on intelligence services and law enforcement is the wise course.

The alternative is to argue that terrorism and the self-radicalized, lone wolf justify an *exception* to democratic norms. The relevant scholarship on exception rhetoric demonstrates that the Western ideal of individual rights is in greatest peril when people in power construct the threat to security as extraordinary. Since 9/11, Neal (2010) argued, "The category of the 'exceptional' has been invoked to legitimize and mobilize an array of violent and illiberal practices" (p. 2). Out of this evocation of the exceptional, an "argument has emerged about the proper relationship between liberty and security" (p. 1). The "liberal subject [is] a historical achievement [which] is taken as a central principle of Western politics, yet the liberal subject, bearing freedom and rights, is thrown into contestation in the liberal/security debate" (p. 2).

During the McCarthy era, the red hunters assaulted the First Amendment by focusing not on treasonous acts, but on patterns of speech and association. Who were the suspects' friends? What political meetings did they attend? What did they read and write? Members of the public might think of this network of contact and expression as external signs of ideological thought. In many cases these signs were fleeting explorations like joining a socialist lawyer's guild as a young law student (Fred Fisher) or being invited to a gathering where an American Communist Party official was a guest (Lillian Hellman). Yet the sense of the external was still considerably greater than it is in the digital age. The tight analogy between thinking and Googling goes to the heart of liberal individualism.

To put this differently, when civic participants begin to think with the logic of loyalty, then the whole specter of the witch-hunt becomes reasonable. Those signs of disposition—association, reading material, Internet search history, religious affiliations—become the bread crumbs left on the counterterrorism trail. These signs are often hidden, opened to inspection only through highly intrusive surveillance. Even observed, the determination of what constitutes a disloyal sign is an ideological judgment. As a cautionary tale, think about the evidence J. Edgar Hoover took as signs that Martin Luther King Jr. was not only a communist sympathizer but also a Soviet agent (Cooper, 2008, pp. 521-525).

Conclusion

Identifying the tension between liberal democratic norms and security precautions is hardly a revelation. George Orwell (1950) painted an unforgettable portrait of state-created technology capable of making signs of thought crime visible. Like Oceania and the political philosophy of Ingsoc, the post-9/11 world of lone-wolf terrorism relies on increasingly robust systems of surveillance to make visible those signs of disloyalty. Such systems, Foucault (1977) wrote of Bentham's Panopticon, create "a state of conscious and permanent visibility that assure the automatic functioning of power" (p. 201). The terror threat makes the fault lines in the liberal democratic consensus more obvious.

What should interest argumentation scholars is the logic of loyalty that underwrites this political condition. The rhetorical pathology that often accompanies loyalty dramas is a product of the inherent vulnerability of virtue discourse. Requiring a particular disposition of citizens is deeply problematic. Wolff (1968) analyzed this difficulty in the nonsensical notion of the loyalty oath (pp. 72-73). Individuals might reasonably swear to not engage in future acts of treason, but dispositions, especially those related to character, are not obviously acts of will. In the liberal tradition, the concept of property encompasses both ownership of real property and the personal possession of thought and conscience (Peters, 1989).

As the shape of the security threat evolves, the difficulty in reasoning from sign to disposition justifies broader and more open-ended exceptions to liberal democratic norms. So, this should draw attention to assessing the advisability of thinking through the logic of loyalty and to contemplating alternative discourses. We end by offering four points for consideration.

First, regimes create systems of socialization—schools, civic rituals, cultural norms—that encourage the development of a loyal attachment to the state. These efforts perhaps should include "disseminating counter narratives" that are "a crucial ingredient" in the "delegitimisation of perpetrators […] and the falsification of their ideologies" (Bakker & de Graaf, 2011, p. 47). Second, the state could turn its focus to the occurrence of criminal acts rather than the presence of civic virtues. Under normal conditions, law enforcement operates in just this way. An ancient maxim of the Anglo-American law holds that "the imagination of the mind to do wrong, without an act done, is not punishable" (*Hales v. Petit*, cited in Goldstein, 1959, p. 405). Third, counterterrorist officials, who focus on preventing criminal acts, have tools available that stand at least some distance away from the logic of loyalty. Certainly, conspiracy laws can be problematic on grounds not dissimilar from the concerns this essay articulates, but legislatures can craft statutes that require the presence of an overt act of agreement among the conspirators and at least one overt act in furtherance of the criminal enterprise (buying weapons, etc.; Abbate, 1974). Finally, the lone wolf, although acting outside of a conspiracy, does engage in preparatory acts. Lone wolves have typically relied on firearms (Bakker & de Graaf, 2011, p. 48). Second Amendment fundamentalists aside, advocating a case for stricter gun control is an important alternative discourse, which occurs without the exceptions required for the implementation of present counterterrorism strategies.

References

Abbate, F. J. (1974). The conspiracy doctrine: A critique. *Philosophy & Public Affairs*, 3(3), 295-311. Retrieved from http://jstor.org/stable/2264982

Agamben, G. (2005). *State of exception* (K. Attell, Trans.). Chicago, IL: University of Chicago Press.

Bakker, E., & de Graaf, B. (2011). Preventing lone wolf terrorism: Some CT approaches addressed. *Perspectives on Terrorism*, 5(5-6), 43-50. Retrieved from http://terrorismanalysts.com/pt/index.php/pot

Bates, R. A. (2012). Dancing with wolves: Today's lone wolf terrorists. *Journal of Public and Professional Sociology, 4*(1), 1-14. Retrieved from http://digitalcommons.kennesaw.edu/jpps

Brooks, R. E. (2004). War everywhere: Rights, national security law, and the law of armed conflict in the age of terror. *University of Pennsylvania Law Review, 153*(2), 675-761.

Carter, J. G., & Carter, D. L. (2012). Law enforcement intelligence: Implications for self-radicalized terrorism. *Police Practice and Research 13*(2), 138-154. doi: 10.1080/15614263.2011.596685

Cochran, C. E. (1982). *Character, community, and politics.* University, AL: University of Alabama Press.

Cooper, F. R. (2008). Surveillance and identity performance: Some thoughts inspired by Martin Luther King. *New York University Review of Law and Social Change, 32*(4), 517-541.

Doob, L. W. (1964). *Patriotism and nationalism: Their psychological foundations.* New Haven, CT: Yale University Press.

Engle, K. (2004). Constructing good aliens and good citizens: Legitimizing the war on terrorism. *University of Colorado Law Review, 75*(1), 59-114. Retrieved from HeinOnline database.

The Fort Hood Attack: A Preliminary Assessment: Hearing before the Committee on Homeland Security and Governmental Affairs, Senate, 111th Cong. 1 (2009).

Foucault, M. (1977). *Discipline and punish: The birth of the prison* (A. Sheridan, Trans.). New York, NY: Random House.

Hamm, M. S., & Spaaij, R. (2017). *The age of lone wolf terrorism.* New York, NY: Columbia University Press.

Goldstein, A. S. (1959). Conspiracy to defraud the United States. *Yale Law Journal, 68*(3), 405-463.

Grodzins, M. (1956). *The loyal and the disloyal: Social boundaries of patriotism and treason.* Chicago, IL: University of Chicago Press.

Joachim, G., & Acorn, S. (2000). Stigma of visible and invisible chronic conditions. *Journal of Advanced Nursing, 32*(1), 243-248. doi: 10.1046/j.1365-2648.2000.01466.x

Lichtman, R. L. (2004). Louis Budenz, the FBI, and the "list of 400 concealed communists": An extended tale of McCarthy-era informing. *American Communism History, 3*(1), 25-54. doi: 10.1080/1474389042000215947

Meloy, J. R. (2016, April). Identifying warning behaviors of the individual terrorist. *FBI Law Enforcement Bulletin,* 1-6. Retrieved from EBSCOhost Legal Collection database.

Neal, A. W. (2010). *Exceptionalism and the politics of counter-terrorism: Liberty, security and the war on terror.* London, United Kingdom: Routledge.

Norris, J. J. (2017). Why Dylann Roof is a terrorist under federal law, and why it matters. *Harvard Journal on Legislation, 54*(1), 501-541.

Orwell, G. (1950). *1984.* New York, NY: Signet Classics.

Peters, J. D. (1989). John Locke, the individual, and the origin of communication. *Quarterly Journal of Speech, 75*(4), 387-399. doi: 10.1080/00335638909383886

Pincoffs, E. L. (1986). *Quandaries and virtues. Against reductionism in ethics.* Lawrence, KS: University Press of Kansas.

The Rise of Radicalization: Is the U.S. Government Failing to Counter International and Domestic Terrorism? Hearing before the Committee on Homeland Security, House of Representatives, 114th Cong. 1 (2015).

Schaar, J. H. (1957). *Loyalty in America.* Berkeley, CA: University of California Press.

Talbott, S. (2001). *The age of terror: America and the world after September 11.* New York, NY: Council on Foreign Relations.

Walton, D. N. (1996). *Argumentation schemes for presumptive reasoning.* Mahwah, NJ: Lawrence Erlbaum.

Weimann, G. (2012). Lone wolves in cyberspace. *Journal of Terrorism Research, 3*(2), 75-90. doi: 10.15664/jtr.405

Wolff, R. P. (1968). *The poverty of liberalism.* Boston, MA: Beacon.

17

WHEN DO PERPETRATORS COUNT

A Longitudinal Analysis of News Definitions of Deceased Mass Shooters

Dakota Park-Ozee and Jason Jordan

A study by researchers at the Harvard School of Public Health and Northeastern University (Cohen, Azrael, & Miller, 2014) and a joint report by Texas State University and the Federal Bureau of Investigation (Blair & Schweit, 2014) have independently confirmed the rise in mass shootings in the United States (Follman, 2014) with a distinct upturn in the second decade of the twenty-first century. In response, scholars (e.g., Towers, Gomez-Lievano, Khan, Mubayi, & Castillo-Chavez, 2015), media organizations (e.g., Wemple, 2015), and public officials (e.g., Pearce, 2015) have begun to examine the potential ramifications of the extensive media coverage dedicated to mass shooters. Previous studies have focused exclusively on school shootings across multi-year periods (Muschert & Carr, 2006) and the lifespan of coverage of a single shooting incident (Chyi & McCombs, 2004). The 1999 shooting at Columbine High School occurred as part of a string of shootings in U.S. schools and received more media coverage than almost any other similar incident in that period (Muschert & Carr, 2006), marking a shift in the coverage of these events.

Despite increased media attention, the argumentative dimensions of how the media defines the alleged perpetrators of gun violence remains unexamined. Filling this research gap is important because the arguments embodied in media representations of mass shootings and their alleged perpetrators sets the context for subsequent public arguments about these and related issues, such as gun control and mental health care. To remedy this oversight and to expand the scope of earlier studies, this essay analyzes news broadcasts of mass shooter gun violence of three major networks from 1990 to the present. Our study seeks to answer two questions. First, how do news broadcasts account for the death of alleged mass shooters? Second, how do broadcasts characterize the factors influencing the actions of alleged perpetrators? In answering both questions, we focus on definitional and associational argumentative schemas. Our results elucidate how the media makes claims about the persistence of gun violence within the United States and the sorts of individuals who perpetuate such acts. While each story focuses on one incidence of gun violence, together the stories form a diachronic network of related rhetorical claims.

Defining the American Gun Debate

A growing body of contemporary research examines the relationship between guns and American culture. Extant rhetorical analyses of American gun cultures illuminate the mythic status of firearms as a symbol of nostalgic ideals of western expansionism (Ott, Aoki, & Dickinson, 2011; Rushing, 1983), the role of guns as ideographs tied to values such as democracy or liberty (Moore, 1994), and the imbrication of gun-bearing subjects with racialized and gendered identities (Lunceford, 2015). Similarly, recent studies in the field of argumentation examine the strategic framing of broad democratic values and American ideals in political debates surrounding firearm policies (Duerringer & Justus, 2016; Eckstein & Partlow Lefevre, 2016; Harpine, 2016). While these efforts explicate common argumentative strategies appearing in public debates about the Second Amendment of the United States Constitution, our analysis goes further, focusing on a different element of the public discourse of the American gun violence epidemic. Specifically we address how the media defines the alleged perpetrators of mass shootings as agents of violence.

Definitions carry normative and ethical implications tied to networks of rhetorically induced social knowledge (Schiappa, 2003). Such narrowing via definition is important because naming an event lays the groundwork for how we understand and react to that event (Zarefsky, 2004). Definitions function argumentatively and persuasively through valenced characterizations, which imply an audience should hold a non-neutral perception of the defined (Zarefsky, 2006). By utilizing associative techniques to establish and appeal to the reality that definitions create (Perelman & Olbrechts-Tyteca, 1973), argument by association furthers the positive or negative evaluation of a subject. This study adds to previous analyses of public debates surrounding firearms in the United States by addressing how the media accounts for the death of alleged mass shooters and the ways in which broadcasts characterize the factors influencing the actions of alleged perpetrators.

Method

This study identified trends in news coverage of alleged perpetrators in mass shooting incidents between January 1990 and May 2017 to serve as a point of comparison between coverage before and after the Columbine-related shift in attention to incidents of mass gun violence. Further, the rise in mass shooting events in the second decade of the twenty-first century—as well as one author's place of residence in Orlando during the 2016 shooting at Pulse nightclub—compelled the extension of the study's coverage through the most recent calendar year (Follman, 2014; "Mass Shootings Becoming," 2014; Zambelich & Hurt, 2016). We included all evening news broadcasts from the three major networks—ABC, CBS, and NBC. While recent declines in television news viewing mean Americans are now less dependent on evening network broadcasts (Bennett & Iyengar, 2008), these networks still hold significant sway (Callaghan & Schnell, 2001; Coe, 2011; Groeling & Baum, 2009). To identify the relevant texts, we searched for the phrase "mass shooting" in both the Vanderbilt Television Archives and full transcripts of LexisNexis stories to ensure completeness of the sample. After identifying all relevant news stories, we excluded those not pertaining to a specific incident of mass gun violence, as the study focused on broadcasts reporting singular shooting events. After exclusions, our search returned a dataset of 143 news broadcasts: ABC (n=37); CBS (n=48); and NBC (n=58).

After establishing the final census of broadcasts, we used the data set to determine the total number of unique mass shooting incidents the broadcasts covered. We identified features discussed in the broadcasts—date of the shooting, names of perpetrators, shooting location, etc.—to group those stories discussing the same incident. The transcripts represented 39 mass shooting incidents that 48 persons perpetrated across 20 states and the District of Columbia. After identifying discrete shootings, the authors compiled a database detailing the common name for each event—e.g., Sandy Hook—the date, location, and perpetrator(s). We also used the transcripts to determine whether the alleged perpetrator died during or because of the shooting incident, the total number of injuries and deaths the shooting caused, and the inclusion/exclusion of the shooter. In instances in which the transcripts of the included broadcast news stories did not present this information, we utilized contemporary local news coverage to ascertain the outcomes of the incident.

We performed a content analysis of the full story transcripts to identify the implicit associational and definitional arguments the evening news broadcasts employed in discussing mass shooting incidents. To identify the definitional and associational arguments the media used to include or exclude alleged perpetrators from broader communities, we examined the total body count ("body count"), the mention of the death of the shooter ("death of shooter"), and the inclusion or exclusion of the shooter from these enumerations ("shooter inclusion"). We used these codes to answer our first research question: how do news broadcasts account for the death of alleged mass shooters?

To isolate definitional arguments related to the characterization of factors leading to alleged perpetrators' actions, we coded for labels related to the shooter. The categories of these labels included loner and other isolating terminologies like "lone wolf" ("loner") and labels conveying mental incompetence or irrationality ("irrational"). Such labels define alleged perpetrators as extra-societal or unhealthy actors. As an indication of definitional and associational arguments implying positive or negative valence, the coding scheme categorized external factors linked to the alleged perpetrators actions. These included discussions of mental illness in the context of the incident ("mental illness") and mention of socio-cultural factors, such as bullying, gang violence, or domestic altercations ("social problems"). Such descriptors both defined speculative shooter motivations and associate alleged perpetrators with violent groups or exigencies. These codes were utilized to answer our second research question: how do broadcasts characterize the factors influencing the actions of alleged perpetrators?

Two coders—the authors—trained on the codebook using mass shooting transcripts employing alternative event labels to preserve the census for final coding. We used a pilot sample of 15% of the census to ascertain reliability, with an additional sample added for those variables not attaining reliability in the pilot study. The final inter-coder reliability for all variables using Krippendorf's alpha was above 0.80: body count (1), death of shooter (1), shooter inclusion (0.88), loner (0.81), irrational (0.88), mental illness (1), and social problems (0.83). We completed all data computations using StataIC 13 software. To answer our first research question, we calculated the frequency with which the "body count," "death of shooter," and "shooter inclusion" codes appeared in the sample. To determine how often a shooter appeared in body counts relative to how often they died due to the incident, we compared the frequency of the "shooter inclusion" variable to the frequency with which "death of shooter" variable. To determine the potential significance of any covariance between these two variables, we created a correlation matrix whose coefficients indicate the strength of association between the variables. To answer our second question, we calculated the frequency with which the codes for shooter labels and characterizations occurred in the sample.

Results and Analysis

Less than 7% of broadcast stories using the "mass shooting" label occurred before 2000. Nearly 85% of stories using this label occurred between 2009 and 2017. However, 13% of the actual, discrete incidents occurred in the first period and 74% occurred in the second. The 78 percentage point differential in mass shooting news stories across the two time periods far exceeds the simultaneous 61 percentage point increase in actual shootings.

Media stories report the deaths of alleged mass shooters without necessarily counting the alleged perpetrator among the enumeration of the dead. The vast majority (80%) of news broadcast stories dedicated to a specific mass shooting incident enumerate the casualty counts for those incidents. And of those, only 43% mention the death of the alleged perpetrator(s) and only 16% of broadcasts include dead perpetrators within their counts of casualties related to the incident. Together, the broadcast stories account for a little over one third (38%) of perpetrators among the cumulative enumeration of the deceased. Corroborating this finding is the non-predictive correlation of dead shooter mentions and shooter inclusion in the enumeration of counts of the dead. With a weak to moderate correlation coefficient of 0.43, the acknowledged death of a shooter is not a significant predictor of the likelihood the perpetrator will be associated with the body count of the deceased.

The media tends to define shooters as independent and unpredictable agents of violence. Discussion of mental illness occurs in nearly one quarter (22%) of the mass shooter stories, as do labels identifying shooters as irrational or mentally unstable. The media stories define the shooter as a lone wolf or extra-societal actor in 15% of cases and as issues or problems in the shooter's social setting as relevant factors in 37% of broadcasts.

Discussion

By analyzing the census of broadcast stories using the label "mass shooter" between 1990 and 2017, this study reveals several argumentative trends in the news coverage. First, the media has sharply increased the number of stories it dedicates to covering mass shooting incidents in the United States. Second, broadcast news often excludes deceased perpetrators from counts of the dead in "mass shootings" stories, thereby dissociating the shooters from both the attacked populace and the broader community needing protection from similar future events. Finally, the broadcast media tends to focus on individual mental health problems or broader systemic societal ills to explain the shooters' behaviors.

The lack of predictive correlation between the death of a shooter and their appearance in the counts of the victims of violence illustrates the existence of a discursive process that major news outlets consistently perform when reporting on mass shooting events in the United States. While the media often deems the death of an alleged perpetrator as a reportable fact in stories of incidents of mass gun violence, major news outlets do not tend to deem these deaths as loss that fits within the same category of bereavement as other casualties at the scene. Accordingly, the media removes perpetrators from belonging to the decent, productive community that law enforcement and civil society protect. After all, to consider mass shooters as "one of us" would associate these events with other products of the same good life that has come under attack and society must now defend. Thus, our findings seem to display an empirical example of alleged perpetrators being discursively redefined from grieve-able casualties into *Homo Sacer*, or forms of being that are outside of the good life we must protect and securitize (Agamben, 1998). Furthermore, this trend offers an example of the precarious subjectivities under cultural neoliberalism (Butler & Athanasiou, 2013). Bodies—both living and deceased—that are productive or offer evidence of the goodness of the normative values of our society are precious, while those that raise questions of what our culture produces—both in material and cultural terms—require removal from the broader body politic. Thus, the three news networks dissociate perpetrators into externalized threats that oppose those who enjoy the good life, while simultaneously eschewing the alternative possibility that the shooters constitute products of the communities, institutions, and policies benefiting the public.

Similarly, the two-pronged process of removing deceased perpetrators from the counts of grieve-able mass shooting tragedies and repeatedly associating the violent acts with isolation or anomalous, unhealthy behaviors offers a better understanding of the argumentative grounds of public and political debates about gun violence in the United States. Paradoxically, the strategy defines extrinsic social ills (e.g., mental health, domestic violence, and gang related crime), as well as policies of gun control and accessibility, outside of the realm of subsequent public argumentation. The invocation of these extrinsic, systemic societal problems defines these events as the consequence of issues unrelated to firearm policies in the United States. However, the discounting of the alleged perpetrator(s) as fully accountable, grieve-able members of the society experiencing those extrinsic societal problems renders the behavior of such individuals unpredictable and uncontrollable. Thus, the cumulative consequence of these trends in the media's network of arguments position both advocates and potential political actors as terminally ineffectual. Thus, the nexus question of public argumentation on gun violence remains stymied at the level of defining what the issue(s) of causality and significance should be within such a debate, creating seemingly intractable grounds of argument when considering solutions to gun violence.

Conclusion

The frequency and devastation of mass shooting events remains a disheartening fact of life in the United States. Our findings indicate that efficacious public deliberation focused on gun violence will require researchers across many disciplines, political actors of varying ideological positions, and communities of all sorts to confront the argumentative context the mass media has set. The unwillingness of news agencies and their audiences to account for deceased perpetrators of mass gun violence as grieve-able subjects that are products of the very communities where they enact their acts of violence plays a notable role in the intractability of ongoing political and public debates about gun violence in the United States.

References

Agamben, G. (1998). *Homo sacer: Sovereign power and bare life* (D. Heller-Roazen, Trans.). Stanford, CA: Stanford University Press.

Bennett, W. L., & Iyengar, S. (2008). A new era of minimal effects? The changing foundations of political communication. *Journal of Communication, 58*(4), 707–731. doi: 10.1111/j.1460-2466.2008.00410.x

Blair, J. P., & Schweit, K. W. (2014). *A study of active shooter incidents in the United States between 2000 and 2013.* Washington, DC: Texas State University, Federal Bureau of Investigation, and U.S. Department of Justice. Retrieved from https://fbi.gov

Butler, J., & Athanasiou, A. (2013). *Dispossession: The performative in the political.* Cambridge, United Kingdom: Polity Press.

Callaghan, K., & Schnell, F. (2001). Assessing the democratic debate: How the news media frame elite policy discourse. *Political Communication, 18*(2), 183–213. doi: 10.1080/105846001750322970

Chyi, H. I., & McCombs, M. (2004). Media salience and the process of framing: Coverage of the Columbine school shootings. *Journalism & Mass Communication Quarterly, 81*(1), 22-35. doi: 10.1177/107769900408100103

Coe, K. (2011). George W. Bush, television news, and rationales for the Iraq War. *Journal of Broadcasting & Electronic Media, 55*(3), 307–324. doi: 10.1080/08838151.2011.597467

Cohen, A. P., Azrael, D., & Miller, M. (2014, October 15). Rate of mass shootings has tripled since 2011, Harvard research shows. *Mother Jones.* Retrieved from http://motherjones.com

Duerringer, C. M., & Justus, Z. S. (2016). Tropes in the rhetoric of gun rights: A pragma-dialectic analysis. *Argumentation and Advocacy, 52*(3), 181–199. Retrieved from http://tandfonline.com

Eckstein, J., & Partlow Lefevre, S. T. (2016). Since Sandy Hook: Strategic maneuvering in the gun control debate. *Western Journal of Communication, 81*(2), 1–18. doi: 10.1080/10570314.2016.1244703

Follman, M. (2014, October 21). Yes, mass shootings are occurring more often. *Mother Jones.* Retrieved from http://motherjones.com

Groeling, T., & Baum, M. A. (2009). Journalists' incentives and media coverage of elite foreign policy evaluations. *Conflict Management and Peace Science, 26*(5), 437–470. doi: 10.1177/0738894209104551

Harpine, W. D. (2016). The illusion of tradition: Spurious quotations and the gun control debate. *Argumentation and Advocacy, 52*(3), 151–165. Retrieved from http://tandfonline.com

Lunceford, B. (2015). Armed victims: The ego function of second amendment rhetoric. *Rhetoric & Public Affairs, 18*(2), 333–345. Retrieved from ProjectMUSE database.

Mass Shootings Becoming More Frequent. (2014, October 15). *Harvard T.H. Chan School of Public Health.* Retrieved from https://hsph.harvard.edu

Moore, M. P. (1994). Life, liberty, and the handgun: The function of synecdoche in the Brady Bill debate. *Communication Quarterly, 42*(4), 434–447. doi: 10.1080/01463379409369948

Muschert, G. W., & Carr, D. (2006). Media salience and frame changing across events: Coverage of nine school shootings, 1997–2001. *Journalism & Mass Communication Quarterly, 83*(4), 747–766. doi: 10.1177/107769900608300402

Ott, B. L., Aoki, E., & Dickinson, G. (2011). Ways of (not) seeing guns: Presence and absence at the Cody firearms museum. *Communication and Critical/Cultural Studies, 8*(3), 215–239. doi: 10.1080/14791420.2011.594068

Pearce, M. (2015, October 3). "Don't say his name": Oregon community wants to make shooter anonymous. *Los Angeles Times.* Retrieved from http://latimes.com

Perelman, Ch., & Olbrechts-Tyteca, L. (1973). *The new rhetoric: A treatise on argumentation.* Notre Dame, IL: University of Notre Dame Press.

Rushing, J. H. (1983). The rhetoric of the American western myth. *Communication Monographs, 50*(1), 14–32. doi: 10.1080/03637758309390151

Schiappa, E. (2003). *Defining reality: Definitions and the politics of meaning.* Carbondale, IL: Southern Illinois University Press.

Towers, S., Gomez-Lievano, A., Khan, M., Mubayi, A., & Castillo-Chavez, C. (2015). Contagion in mass killings and school shootings. *Plos One, 10*(7): e0117259. doi: 10.1371/journal.pone.0117259

Wemple, E. (2015, December 8). CNN's Anderson Cooper, too, has baffling shooter-naming policies. *The Washington Post.* Retrieved from https://washingtonpost.com

Zambelich, A. & Hurt, A. (2016, June 26). 3 hours in Orlando: Piecing together an attack and its aftermath. *NPR.* Retrieved from http://npr.org

Zarefsky, D. (2004). Presidential rhetoric and the power of definition. *Presidential Studies Quarterly, 34*(3), 607–619. Retrieved from http://jstor.org/stable/27552615

Zarefsky, D. (2006). Strategic maneuvering through persuasive definitions: Implications for dialectic and rhetoric. *Argumentation, 20*(4), 399–416. doi: 10.1007/s10503-007-9030-6

18

DEFINING "BIRTH RAPE"

Networked Argument Resources for Mothers' Advocacy

Beth L. Boser

Birth advocates have long sought recognition and justice for women mistreated within the professional medical establishment during childbirth. Many believe that the health care industry has inappropriately medicalized childbirth to the detriment of women's autonomy. Birth, advocates hold, is not an illness, but rather a natural function of the body; thus, many routine medical interventions during birth are unnecessary. Instead, interventions serve the efficient and financially-driven functioning of the hospital, rather than the mother's and child's needs. Further, they disempower women and, at times, lead to worse outcomes (e.g., Davis-Floyd, 1992). Yet, the overwhelming hegemony of the hospital birth leaves mothers with little recourse. Even innovations like in-hospital birth centers—available to those who can pay for a modicum of "choice"—are subject to medical schedules, conventions, and interventions. Moreover, by discursively situating the "healthy baby" (e.g., Reed, 2010, para. 1) outcome as preeminent, any actions the doctors or other medical professionals take in the service of this result appear justified. In birth contexts, argumentative resources for resistance are scarce.

The term "birth rape" emerged within the last fifteen years to promote justice for women abused at the hands of medical professionals and illustrate the severity of some such abuses. According to some mothers and advocates, experiences of having medical professionals non-consensually penetrate and otherwise act upon the woman in childbirth amount to rape. A range of online contexts debated this interpretation, constituting a clear example of digitally networked argument. Of course, argumentation theorists have long noted the networked nature of argument. Perelman and Olbrechts-Tyteca (2008) painted the context of argument as one in which a host of discursive elements interact in complex ways. Numerous elements may be "integral parts of one and the same discourse […] which together constitute a single argument" (p. 187). In the present example, advocates networked personal experiences to build an argument about the nature and severity of birth violations.

Use of the term birth rape inspired backlash. In opposition to those who describe the term as a fitting explanation of traumatic and violating birthing experiences were skeptics who claimed the term as misleading and offensive. Indeed, the argument network that grew up around the term centered more on debating the term itself than on the event the term purported to describe. This essay examines networked arguments for and against the term birth rape, for the purpose of understanding the significance of the term as one strategy within the larger context of childbirth advocacy. It posits that understanding the argumentative dynamics of such debates is important for at least two reasons. First, although prior scholarship has identified birth as a key site for inquiry (e.g., Owens, 2009), argumentation scholars have devoted very little attention to birth advocacy. Thus, a more well-rounded understanding of the discursive contexts of reproductive justice will better position scholars and activists to support diverse women. Second, consideration of why birth rape most prominently spurred debate over the term itself, rather than childbirth injustices, may prove useful to both advocates and argumentation scholars interested in other topics undergoing similar types of public debates.

Although birth rape continues to emerge in the occasional feminist or birth-related blog (e.g., Backup9270, 2016), its use has not spread beyond a relatively small number of individuals within the birth activism community. Therefore, as an argumentative strategy intended to raise awareness and empower women, the term appears inadequate. I argue that analyzing the term as a form of associational and definitional argument best explains such inadequacy. Specifically, the term paired previously unassociated ideas for purposes of creating new meaning, and explanations of the term offered a new definition of a particular situation. Advocates used associational and definitional strategies to build an ontological argument for the reality of women's experiences by redefining a situation. At the same time, opponent responses indicate—overtly and implicitly—the constraints upon such strategies. I explain these claims in the following steps: first, I provide grounding for the argumentative nature of novel terms like birth rape; second, I describe the specific ways in which advocates argue for birth rape as a descriptor for their experiences; third, I consider resistant responses to the term; and, finally, I speculate explanations for the argumentative impasse that characterizes the networked debate overall.

Novel Terms as Argument

The term birth rape illustrates Burke's (1969) point that, in a name, one can posit a world of meaning. Strategic uses of unexpected or shocking language to describe phenomena argue powerfully for particular interpretations and responses. Moreover, pairing two previously unrelated terms cultivates new meanings through inductive association, thereby structuring a new reality in relation to an experience. Perelman and Olbrechts-Tyteca's (2008) associational argument explains the argumentative dynamics of such a strategy. Such arguments are products of "schemes which bring separate elements together and allow us to establish a unity among them, which aims either at organizing them or at evaluating them, positively or negatively, by means of one another" (Perelman & Olbrechts-Tyteca, 2008, p. 190). Advocates engage in argument by example and analogy to invite interlocutors to re-evaluate knowledge of both birth and rape.

Zarefsky's (1998) work on definitional argument establishes the usefulness of such practices in the present context, as he explains ways in which terms argue for a particular definition of "a situation or frame of reference" (p. 5). Advocates craft terms to intentionally argue for a particular way of understanding something, or to argue for the legitimacy of an experience. Zarefsky (2006) stated that persuasive definitions convey attitudes about things through naming; moreover, such definitions or names provide implicit arguments about how the thing should be viewed. The use of terms in this way is persuasive because, for example, they "facilitate visualization" (Zarefsky, 2006, p. 405) and "provide anchors for analogies" (p. 406). Both functions are important here, as advocates illustrate their experiences for interlocutors and imbue those experiences with meaning through comparison with more familiar phenomena.

Defining Birth Rape

Defining rape is no simple undertaking. In the United States, definitions of the crime vary across statutes at the state and national level, and to an even greater extent, among the public. Until five years ago, the FBI's definition of the crime—for purposes of reporting—was the unchanged-since-1927 "carnal knowledge of a female, forcibly and against her will" (U.S. Department of Justice, 2012, para. 7). Such a definition implies that rape comprises sexual desire, a violent attack, and that (only) men can rape (only) women. Use of this definition at the federal level proved problematic, as a range of crimes the public widely understood as rape did not fall within its scope. In 2012, the Justice Department updated the definition to be "more inclusive [and] better [reflect] state criminal codes" (para. 1). Thus, the FBI's current definition is "the penetration, no matter how slight, of the vagina or anus with any body part or object, or oral penetration by a sex organ of another person, without the consent of the victim" (U.S. Department of Justice, 2012, para. 1). Despite the broadened nature of such a definition, no consensus on the meaning of the crime exists. Researchers note that many women whose experiences fit definitions of rape may not self-define their experiences as such (Koelsch, 2014). Furthermore, definitional problems relating to rape manifest in all sorts of past and present public controversies centering on spousal rape, acquaintance rape, and rape culture, among others.

Advocates seeking to define the experience of birth rape connect their personal traumatic birthing experiences to established understandings of rape in relation to interwoven actions, power dynamics, and contexts. Personal birth stories provide the evidence for a series of arguments by analogy. For example, women describe widespread non-consensual penetration (Reed, 2010). One recalled, "the doctors gave me an episiotomy without telling me [...] or asking my consent. I asked what they were doing and why it was necessary and got no answer. I screamed at them to stop" ("Natasha's Story," 2012, para. 9). Advocates claim that doctors frequently perform episiotomies to quicken labor for the convenience of the doctor and the institution; hence, surgical scissors become a weapon of intimidation and abuse. Another described a midwife "ramm[ing] a hand up into [a woman's] vagina to manually dilate her cervix" (para. 5) because the midwife was "tired of how long [the woman's labor] was taking" (quoted in Reed, 2008, para. 8). For advocates, non-consensual penetration equals rape.

Adding a layer to the analogy, others report the physical or medicinal taking of their capacity to act or consent. Some recalled the medical professional's use of forcible restraint (Reed, 2008), which likens birth rape to the physical overpowerment common to traditional rape definitions. Others reported that deceptive professionals drugged them against their will. One woman remembered a doctor telling her that her baby needed more oxygen. Instead of having oxygen provided as she anticipated, the breathing mask delivered a drug that caused her to lose consciousness—and hence, all awareness of the medical procedures done to her—until she awoke in recovery (Luehrs, 2012). Another advocate—a midwife—

described witnessing labor-accelerating drugs, like Pitocin and Cytotec, inserted into women's vaginas using injections or gauze, without their knowledge ("Navelgazing Midwife," 2004). Such drugs make bodies behave in ways beyond personal control, much like Rohypnol in more broadly acknowledged contexts of rape. Examples like these analogize actions medical personnel take upon birthing women with those of rapists.

The power dynamic that facilitates such acting-upon is an important layer of the birth rape definition. For example, one writer stated that birth rape describes situations wherein those providing care pressure or even force women to submit to procedures. In doing so, powerful medical professionals are able to manipulate or coerce vulnerable women into compliance (Zimmerman, 2010). Advocates argue that in instances of birth rape, the doctor/patient power dynamic is equivalent to perpetrator/victim.

Advocates go beyond defining the specific actions and power dynamics of birth rape to compare contexts and motivations. Just as the notion that a husband, partner, or acquaintance cannot rape a woman needed eradication, so too does the notion that a doctor cannot rape (Lights, 2013; Reed, 2010). Reflecting current understandings of rape that separate it from the "carnal," writers indicated that medical personnel exert control over powerless women just as readily in hospitals as others do in more common contexts of sexual assault (Reed, 2010). By defining the situation of birth rape in these ways, advocates argue the legitimacy of both the term and their experiences by crafting multi-level analogies. According to Perelman and Olbrechts-Tyteca (2008), "The effect of an analogy is to bring the terms [...] closer together, which leads to an interaction" (p. 378). The birth rape analogy encourages readers to consider the ways in which elements of rape network with elements of birth. Such analogies position birth rape as the next progressive step toward justice for rape survivors.

Furthermore, the newly-defined situation warrants reordering of the established birth hierarchy. Advocates resist the notion that the only outcome of concern is the healthy baby. One writer claimed that women who experience birth rape find others "dismissive of their feelings, sure that they should instead try to focus on how grateful they are that their babies are safe and well" (Lights, 2013, para. 15). Numerous writers have repeated this notion, some of whom point to the guilt they felt upon being exhorted to "'get over it' and be grateful" (para. 4) for a healthy baby ("Natasha's Story," 2012). Here, advocates imply connections to victim-blaming. They argue for expanding conceptions of what matters during birth, believing women, and stopping the dismissal of experiences as exaggerations or petty concerns. These strategies, together, invite a reordering of meanings surrounding birth and rape. For advocates, definitional claims simply, "furnish the real, true meaning of the concept[s]" at hand (Perelman & Olbrechts-Tyteca, 2008, p. 444).

Resisting Birth Rape

Claims of birth rape spurred strong resistance, including refusals to even acknowledge the existence of such experiences. Oppositional voices drew distinctions between traumatic birth experiences and rape, grounding their justifications in affect- and motive-related assumptions. For example, one opponent claimed that the feelings of despair, rage, and violation women experienced after a traumatic birth were not the same as those experienced after rape (Faulkner, 2012). Another claimed the motives of a rapist were not the same as the motives of a doctor (Marcotte, 2010). Still another maintained that violating birth experiences cannot be rape because they are not sexual (Beyerstein, 2010). Opponent responses indicate a belief that the overall analogous argument advocates make is weak. In short, opponents feel that the differences between the concepts at hand are greater than the similarities. Yet, in claiming such a belief, opponents do not specifically address the arguments and evidence that advocates present. They do not demonstrate or explain the differences between the concepts; they simply state them as if self-evident. Opponents appear to ground their claims in outmoded understandings of rape (i.e., that it must be sexual, that it must include a particular sort of violent perpetrator, and that a woman must be a particular kind of victim). Despite changing societal understandings of rape, these claims indicate that many do not easily jettison such engrained definitions. Obsolete definitions appear to hold so much presumptive weight that opponents do not even feel the need to explain themselves. Women who experienced birth rape are simply not the same as real rape victims, and use of the term is wrong simply because it is.

Opponents also argue that the term diminishes the experiences of actual sexual assault survivors (Shoot, 2010), which suggests that the designation of rape survivor is a constituting factor of identity. This particular resistant claim hints at one reason why women who have experienced violations during birth seek to claim the term for themselves: The identity of survivor connotes empowerment. Yet, hesitancy to extend the term to women who experienced somewhat different, albeit related, forms of abuse indicates the tenuousness of such an empowerment, and the persistent cultural anxiety surrounding rape definitions.

Conclusion

The networked debate over birth rape hints at some limitations and constraints upon the argument strategies employed. First, the fact that opponents do not address the claims of advocates highlights the trouble with using analogies. According to Perelman and Olbrechts-Tyteca (2008),

> Analogy is an unstable means of argument. For the person who rejects the conclusions will tend to assert that "there is not even an analogy," and will minimalize the value of the statement by reducing it to a vague comparison or merely verbal resemblance. On the other hand, the person invoking an analogy will almost invariably endeavor to assert that it is more than just a simple analogy. The analogy is thus stuck between two disavowals—disavowal by its opponents and disavowal by its supporters.
>
> *(p. 393)*

This double-disavowal is evident in the present case. For advocates, birth rape is not a mere figurative analogy; birth rape is literally rape. For opponents, the purported analogy is so incongruous that it requires rejection outright.

Second, the emphasis on arguing about the term itself—as opposed to the events it describes—suggests trouble with associations. Perelman and Olbrechts-Tyteca (2008) presented a conundrum. They stated, "What is given before argumentation can seem more firmly established than what results from it alone: should separate elements be tied together, or should they be presented as already forming a whole?" (p. 191). Advocates set the stage by providing overt explanations and justifications for the term, whereas Perelman and Olbrechts-Tyteca suggested that by overtly arguing for an association, advocates are implying the separateness of the elements and thereby undermining their own claims. Zarefsky (2006) seemed to agree, stating that a name or definition should be "an implicit argument [...] put forward as if it was uncontroversial" (p. 404). Here, the highly incongruous nature of the term presumably leads advocates to believe that arguments of and about the term must be overtly made, as opposed to simply "'smuggled in' through the use of the definition itself" (Zarefsky, 2006, p. 404).

Finally, resistance to birth rape and the impasse evidenced in the nature of opposing claims indicates trouble with the term itself. Although advocates want to locate birth rape among other crimes like spousal rape or acquaintance rape, these terms are not of the same kind. The latter terms designate a perpetrator—an agent. Other terms like marital rape or date rape designate a context—a scene. Although it is possible to read birth as a scene, the experience is likely an event—an act—which causes confusion. The other terms offer explanatory context by defining a different person or a different place where rape occurs. Birth rape does not do either of these clearly, and makes the event seem as if the child being born determines the nature of the violation. This obscures focus on the relevant associations relating to consent, control and power. Alternatively, physician rape or obstetrical rape might encourage opponents to consider the ways in which abuse occurs in the context of a medical institution at the hands of a medical professional.

References

Backup9270. (2016, March 1). Birth discussion: Birth rape [Discussion forum]. *Baby Center, L.L.C.* Retrieved from https://community.babycenter.com/post/a61701355/birth-discussion-birth-rape

Beyerstein, L. (2010, September 10). "Birth rape" rhetoric is ugly, misleading. *Big Think*. Retrieved from http://bigthink.com/focal-point/birth-rape-rhetoric-is-ugly-misleading

Burke, K. (1969). *Grammar of motives*. Berkeley, CA: University of California Press.

Davis-Floyd, R. E. (1992). *Birth as an American rite of passage*. Berkeley, CA: University of California Press.

Faulkner, J. (2012, May 17). It's not birth rape; It's birth trauma. *FitPregnancy*. Retrieved from http://fitpregnancy.com/labor-delivery/ask-labor-nurse/its-not-birth-rape-its-birth-trauma

Koelsch, L. E. (2014). Sexual discourses and the absence of agency. *Women & Language*, *37*(2), 11–29.

Lights, Z. (2013, January 19). It's time to start recognising birth rape. *The Huffington Post*. Retrieved from http://huffingtonpost.co.uk/zion-lights/birth-rape_b_2155384.html

Luehrs, D. (2012, April 24). VBAC denied, horrid experience [Blog post]. *Babycenter*. Retrieved from http://community.babycenter.com/post/a26519895/vbac_denied_horrid_experience

Marcotte, A. (2010, September 8). Bad birth experiences aren't rape. *Slate*. Retrieved from http://slate.com/blogs/xx_factor/2010/09/08/birth_rape_is_a_misleading_term.html

Natasha's Story. (2012, March 9). Birth/rape [Blog post]. Retrieved from http://birthraped.wordpress.com/2012/03/09/natashas-story/

Navelgazing Midwife Blog. (2004, July 7). Birth – rape and otherwise. *Navelgazing Midwife*. Retrieved from http://navelgazingmidwife.squarespace.com/navelgazing-midwife-blog/2004/7/8/birth-rape-and-otherwise.html

Owens, K. H. (2009). Confronting rhetorical disability: A critical analysis of women's birth plans. *Written Communication*, *26*(3), 247–272. doi: 10.1177/0741088308329217

Perelman, Ch., & Olbrechts-Tyteca, L. (2008). *The new rhetoric: A treatise on argumentation*. Notre Dame, IL: University of Notre Dame Press.

Reed, A. (2008, March 7). Not a happy birthday. *The F-Word: Contemporary UK Feminism*. Retrieved from http://thefword.org.uk/features/2008/03/not_a_happy_bir

Reed, A. (2010, September 30). "It's not RAPE rape." *The F-Word: Contemporary UK Feminism*. Retrieved from http://thefword.org.uk/features/2010/09/its_not_rape_ra

Shoot, B. (2010, September 10). When giving birth is a traumatic violation, is it rape? *Change.org*. Retrieved from http://web.archive.org/web/20100916005323/http://womensrights.change.org/blog/view/when_giving_birth_is_a_traumatic_violation_is_it_rape

The United States Department of Justice, Office of Public Affairs. (2012, January 6). *Attorney General Eric Holder announces revisions to the uniform crime report's definition of rape* (Press Release No. 12-018). Retrieved from https://justice.gov/opa/pr/attorney-general-eric-holder-announces-revisions-uniform-crime-report-s-definition-rape

Zarefsky, D. (1998). Definitions. In J. F. Klumpp (Ed.), *Argument in a time of change: Definitions, frameworks, and critiques* (pp. 1–11). Annandale, VA: National Communication Association.

Zarefsky, D. (2006). Strategic maneuvering through persuasive definitions: Implications for dialectic and rhetoric. *Argumentation, 20*(4), 399–416. doi: 10.1007/s10503-007-9030-6

Zimmerman, J. (2010, November 29). What feminists should know about birth rape. *Birth Activist.* Retrieved from https://web.archive.org/web/20101203024626/http://birthactivist.com/2010/11/what-feminists-should-know-about-birth-rape/

19

WHEN THEY FOUND HER

Networked Argument and
Contested Memory

Sarah T. Partlow Lefevre

On January 17, 2013, a dramatic shootout with police ended the life of Boede Paul, a 25-year-old father and suspected murderer (Journal Staff, 2013). Eleven days earlier, police had received a missing person report on Paul's ex-girlfriend, Angelea Schultz (O'Donnell, 2013a). While she was missing, most people in the community became aware of the case through the print and digital iterations of the local paper, Facebook discussions, and word of mouth. Community members searched for her. Police discovered her abandoned vehicle. Relatives took care of her small children. In the end, Paul confessed to her murder and orchestrated a standoff with police. Paul, who was in his truck with a cell phone and multiple guns during the standoff, called and confessed to killing Angelea to both his and the Schultz's family members. He constructed the event as an accident, a blackout crime of passion. After confessing to the authorities, he provided the location where police later found her body and other gruesome items, such as a baseball bat, bloody clothes, and heavy construction equipment used to bury the body 10-12 feet underground (O'Donnell, 2013b).

The murder and the ensuing shootout with police rocked the small Idaho cities of Pocatello and Chubbuck. The intimacy of the community complicated the evolving public memory of the event. Pocatello and Chubbuck are adjacent communities where connections abound among the residents, including many who personally knew the Schultz and Paul families. As the events unfolded, members of the public discussed every detail. When the local newspaper announced that police had found Shultz's body, community members engaged in arguments via Facebook. Participants in such arguments constructed and contested understandings of the nature and function of memories of the event.

Social memory and collective memory come into conflict as community members debated how people should understand Schultz's and Paul's deaths. Questions hinged on the distinction between social and collective memory, including the components of the crime and how the small community should understand and discuss that crime. Tension between the social and collective interpretations reflected the needs of different populations. Family and friends tended to support social memories of events that functioned as epideictic rhetoric, due to its characteristic heavy reliance on emotion in an effort to heal family and friends. In contrast, the community at large favored a collective memory approach that tended toward a more deliberative and forensic approach, focusing on legalistic, fact-based interpretations that categorized the murderer as a social anomaly.

Networked Argument and Contested Memory

A growing body of literature has begun to address the topic of contested memory. Phillips's (2004) collection, *Framing Public Memory*, featured a variety of scholars examining the framing of public memory in different contexts. Phillips introduced the volume by foregrounding the inherently contested nature of public memory and its resulting rhetorical fluidity, features that made it "open to context, revision, and rejection" (p. 2). Deeply persuasive and constitutive of social epistemologies, public memories involve rhetorical struggle over the "dynamic relations of authority over public memories" (p. 5). In the same volume, Casey (2004) recognized that debating private traumas "made public" involves both social and collective memory. For Casey, social memories involved the remembrances of those affiliated by kinship or geographical proximity; collective memory, by contrast, focused on "the circumstance in which different persons, not necessarily known to each other at all, nevertheless recall the same event" (p. 23).

Further complicating conceptions of public memory is the emerging role of the online environment. In Pfister's (2014) book, *Networked Media, Networked Rhetorics*, he argued that public deliberation through communication about societal events "requires a combination of formal and informal sites" (p. 37) that include virtual venues, such as Facebook. As part of a larger structural transformation that would "surely rearrange social categories, relationships, and imaginaries in ways that are barely perceptible now" (p. 48), these venues form "public spheres" in which "the shape of public life is thematized, problematized, revised, and enacted" (p. 37). Pfister outlined three mechanisms of networked argument including: (a) flooding the zone, that is the blogosphere's tendency to saturate "public discourse by working the controversy from every conceivable angle" (p. 6); (b) ambient intimacy which incorporates emotion into networked argument in a "constant cycling of affect into public life" (p. 6); and, (c) shallow quotation, a mechanism to "transfer highly technical scientific claims into public spheres of argumentation" (p. 6). Each of these aspects shape Pfister's networked rhetorical imaginary and function to construct and perpetuate the features of networked social life.

Moreover, networked contestation of social and public memory is articulated in a special issue of *Argumentation and Advocacy*, where scholars explored "how new forms of mediation alter the norms and conduct of argumentation" (Pfister, 2010, p. 64). Hartelius (2010), for example, noted that online memorializing creates public memories that help shape group identity. In networked spaces, individuals deliberate about the meanings of events, identities, and future actions. Such spaces serve as a "mode of mediated deliberation" whereby "publically knowable subjects" have their "private traumas" exposed to the community (Hartelius, 2010, pp. 69–70). Individuals directly connected or tangentially involved with such events (e.g., crimes, natural disasters, and other unplanned events) affix meaning to the events within the arc of experiences in the public sphere. Smith and McDonald (2010) demonstrated the contestation by showing how conservative blogs worked to dispute and change a public memorial that was "a controversial display of public memory" (p. 135). While Smith and McDonald studied disputed public memories about a physical memorial site, this study extends their analysis to a uniquely networked public memorial in a quotidian online sphere, namely a Facebook comments section.

In this case study, the community deliberated about the meaning of a crime and to what degree the details of the crime should become publically knowable.[1] The study builds on the Casey's (2004) conception of social and collective memory by exploring how the concepts functioned within a contested networked deliberation. In this case, networked argumentation aided social meaning-making as social and collective memory collided, producing a multifaceted, contested public memory. Within the community, differential approaches for discussing the dead grounded in Aristotle's (trans. 1991) deliberative and epidictic frameworks worked for different segments of the audience. The general public, representing a call for collective memory, preferred a more deliberative and forensic approach to make sense of the horrific event. Conversely, family members and friends preferred a social or private memory that relied heavily on the epideictic approach. The study also extends Pfister's (2014) concept of shallow quotation from the technical to the private sphere of social memory.

Social and Collective Memories of a Crime

Social memory perspectives expressed on the local Facebook argued for family privacy to allow grieving. The social memory posts included: calls for privacy, grieving for the loss, defining the event as a tragic accident, quotations of family members, challenges to media and fact based accounts, blaming the victim, and arguing Paul's actions were redemptive.

Various commenters humanized Paul's violence by reminding the audience of Paul's family, including the variety of his own familial roles of father and son. Based on these foundational relationships, Steggell called for privacy, "His family is hurting to! [*sic*] They […] don't need everyone talking about their son PUBLICLY!!" (Steggell, para. 48). Posts relied on public appeals by family members to support calls for ceasing public deliberation. Thiecke quoted Schultz's brother suggesting he did not want to hear the community denigrating Paul as the father of his sister's son (paras. 53-54). Bucher wrote, "Let the family grieve in peace" (para. 62). These comments situated the event as a private—not a public—loss, and requested privacy for the families and friends of the dead to grieve.

Social memory perspectives also questioned the validity of particular arguers on Facebook. Suggesting that the media and those who depended upon it lacked access to undisclosed information, these individuals claimed that many who posted lacked the "real story." Smith wrote, "DO NOT judge. I knew both of these young people and what happened was an accident. Neither was meant to die" (para. 23). Similarly, Waddoups argued, "The ones judging are the ones that don't know ether [*sic*] family and don't know all of the story […] you have no right to judge" (paras. 73, 76). Waddoups argued facts were partial because the police had not released full information (para. 81). Use of the term "accident," combined with appeals to unknown information, implied that Schultz was somehow responsible for her own death. Later reports confirmed that Paul called both families during the police standoff and claimed it was an accident (Bryce, 2013, p. A16), including Maria Whorton, Schultz's mother, and said, "he and Angelea had gotten into an argument and she had attacked him with the bat" (p. A16).

Finally, social memory commenters created a redemptive narrative to reconcile Paul's brutal actions. Hansen cited Paul's confession and his help in locating the body as evidence of Paul's chance for redemption, "I'm just thankful that Boede told us the truth! Before Boede [Paul] came into the picture we had no lead on where Angelea was at all […] Heck it's a blessing he confessed!" (para. 93). Additionally, Cleverly used the idea that Paul committed "suicide by cop" to suggest he was "appalled by his own behavior" (para. 131) and redeemed himself by forcing the cops to execute him. The redemptive narrative suggested that he "wasn't aiming for the police" (Bouribon, quoted in Frederick, para. 133) during the shootout. In the eyes of those arguing for a social memory, Paul redeemed himself by confessing, identifying the location of Schultz's body, and sacrificing himself. Such acts added credibility to the view that the murder constituted a crime of passion that Paul was incapable of processing.

Quotations from the family Facebook walls evidenced the redemptive narrative by placing family members as experts with special knowledge and the sole ability to judge. Despite their failure to meet Pfister's (2014) characteristic notion of "technical, scientific claims" (p. 6) as the basis of shallow quotations, the posts depicting the family's sentiments nevertheless accessed elided, complex, publically inaccessible social memories. As a result, the families' quotations cultivated a "shallow argument pool" resulting in "slanted, superficial conversation" including calls to cease public argument and leave factual information in the social rather than collective memory (Pfister, 2014, p. 59). For example, Lisa Frederick posted a comment attributed to "Leah's brother [...] Jordan Boriboun" (ISJ, 2013, para. 133):

> Yes my sister was the victim and I love her and miss her [...] But Boede Paul [...] was also a great father, i had spoke to him just before he passed [...] so please [...] Never speak bad about anybody, especially them. They wouldn't want that. [*sic*]
>
> *(para. 133)*

Comments invoked the feelings of the family or imagined themselves in the place of Paul's parents. These examples located family and friends as experts on Paul's character and grouped Paul and Schultz as a couple who were together in the afterlife. Not posted by the family members themselves, the comments functioned as evidentiary support for calls to cease public discussion and shift the matter from collective memory to social memory. Rejecting deliberative and forensic modes, commenters focused on grieving, and rehabilitating Paul's character.

The second approach, collective memory, functioned in a more deliberative and forensic mode, attempting to exact imagined social justice and to restore a sense of normalcy to the community. Collective memory appeals included: arguing that the event was public which gave rights to the whole community to deliberate, viewing the police and the media as legitimate sources of information, preferring facts, determining Paul's guilt, and expressing a desire for punishment.

Collective memory commenters disputed characterizations of the murder as outside the realm of public judgment. Neal said, "You can't stop people from talking [...] over a public forum" (para. 48). Others argued that the community had the right to understand and that collective talk was appropriate. Jensen wrote, "Situations like this [...] effect the WHOLE community. People will come on these boards/comments and vent as a means of dealing with the situation" (para. 83). Welker suggested that collective memory of the situation could give individuals an opportunity to reflect and learn, "Killing is wrong. Physical abuse [...] is WRONG [...] know that it's okay to seek help [...] Michael Lane Sparks just plead guilty to killing his ex in the same manner. That's 2 deaths in our community" (para. 85). Walker asserted the community's right to discuss to shape the collective memory of the situation as one of partner violence. She justified discussion, highlighted a trend, and cited another example of a similar violent act.

Collective memory commenters also emphasized reliance on facts. Davis said, "The police released FACTS, and that is what the ISJ has given us" (para. 79). Swenson cautioned against the emergent double standard revealed when Paul's name emerged in the public sphere. She recalled responses before Paul confessed, "When the story about 'A missing girl' hit the news [...] everyone's thoughts were 'poor Leah,' 'we must find the horrible person that did this' 'whoever did this deserves to be punished,'" (para. 106). When Paul emerged as the killer, Swenson noted, many in the community explained or justified his actions. She argued that, "It doesn't matter WHO commits the crime [...] He made the decision to do what he did. There is no justifying it. Period [...] He brutally killed a girl [...] He's a murderer" (para. 106). Challenging the double standard and the use of terms such as crime and murderer brutally suggested a need to apply fact-based justice to Paul's memory.

Collective memory commenters argued that prompting the police to kill him allowed Paul to evade legal punishment. Steggell wrote, "He took the cowards [sic] way out" (para. 94). Ratliff–Edwards argued firmly for Paul's guilt. She wrote, "He admitted to it. He showed law enforcement where he buried her body [...] His judgement had he lived would have been a lot worse in a court of law! [sic] (para. 102). Collective memory commenters determined guilt and imagined Paul's punishment in a court of law as they sought to restore a sense of normalcy in the community.

Conclusion

Both the social and collective approaches functioned for parts of the community and demonstrated the dynamic tension between public and private memories. Social memory approaches lessened the impact on friends and family, while collective memory approaches asserted the community's right to deliberate and impose legal punishment for murder. Both approaches allowed their constituents to heal. To reckon with the loss, deal with grief, and return to the community, friends and family needed to believe Paul was a good person who did a bad thing. However, the broader public promoted community healing by examining Paul's guilt to imagining a legal punishment and closure for the crime.

This case study adds to the study of contested memory in networked argument by enhancing understanding of contested memory in a close community. While conflict between social and collective approaches is inevitable, the form that each approach takes enhances critical understandings of their functions for different audiences. The reliance on epideictic discourse to facilitate social memory highlights the potentially regressive nature of privileging the needs of family and friends in the wake of a public crime. The tendency to elide the perpetrator's responsibility for his actions while rehearsing redemptive narratives leaves both the victim and the community without appropriate representation. Conversely, accepting the collective memory approach and its forensic function may restore a sense of normalcy to the community, but raise questions as the use of shallow quotations in a nontechnical context constitutes a complex domain of knowledge that is inaccessible the broader community.

Note

1 All quoted Facebook comments in this analysis respond to one initial story post; the cited paragraph numbers refer to the posts in sequence.

References

Aristotle. (1991). *On rhetoric: A theory of civic discourse* (G. A. Kennedy, Trans.). New York, NY: Oxford University Press.

Casey, E. S. (2004). Public memory in place and time. In K. R. Phillips (Ed.), *Framing public memory* (2nd ed., pp. 17–44). Tuscaloosa, AL: University of Alabama Press.

Bryce, D. (2013, February 10). Family tries to cope after daughter's murder. *Idaho State Journal (Pocatello, ID)*. Retrieved from http://idahostatejournal.com/members/family-tries-to-cope-after-daughter-s-murder/article_2d37302a-7362-11e2-a8ac-001a4bcf887a.html

Hartelius, E. J. (2010). "Leave a message of hope or tribute": Digital memorializing as public deliberation. *Argumentation and Advocacy*, *47*(2), 67–85. http://tandfonline.com

Idaho State Journal. (2013, January 18). Here's everything we know so far [Facebook status update]. Retrieved from https://facebook.com/idahostatejournal/posts/10151261177854862

Journal Staff. (2013, January 1). Hail of bullets ends standoff; Boede Paul killed in shootout with area officers. *Idaho State Journal (Pocatello, ID)*, pp. A1, A5.

O'Donnell, M. H. (2013a, January 9). Hunt for missing mom; Deputies find car, but no sign of 23-year-old. *Idaho State Journal (Pocatello, ID)*, pp. A1, A5.

O'Donnell, M. H. (2013b, January 19). Mom's body found; Murder victim, bloody baseball bat located at Fort Hall work site. *Idaho State Journal (Pocatello, ID)*, pp. A1, A5.

Pfister, D. S. (2010). Introduction to the special issue: Public argument/digital media. *Argumentation and Advocacy*, *47*(2), 63–66.

Pfister, D. S. (2014). *Networked media, networked rhetorics*. University Park, PA: Pennsylvania State University Press.

Phillips, K. R. (2004). Introduction. In K. R. Phillips (Ed.), *Framing public memory* (pp. 1–14). Tuscaloosa, AL: University of Alabama Press.

Smith, C. M., & McDonald, K. M. (2010). The Arizona 9/11 Memorial: A case study in public dissent and argumentation through blogs [Special issue]. *Argumentation and Advocacy*, *47*(2), 123–139. Retrieved from http://tandfonline.com

PART III

STRATEGIC USE OF ASSOCIATION AND DISSOCIATION IN NETWORKED ARGUMENT

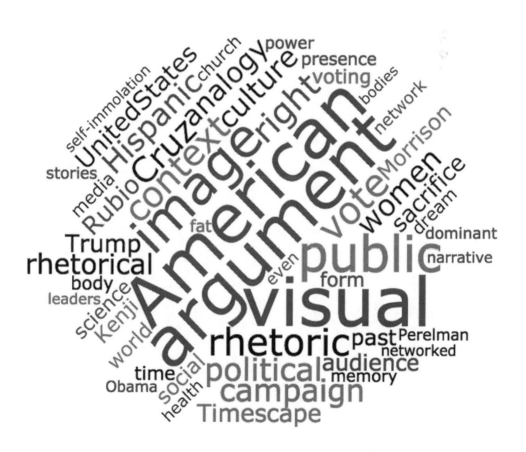

20

READING FREAKS

Trump in an Analogical Hermeneutic Network

Angela G. Ray and Robert Elliot Mills

Contemporary commentators find it challenging to interpret Donald Trump's campaign and ensuing presidency, especially those features that seem so discordant with presidencies past. Journalists, comedians, and protesters frequently rely on the literal analogy: Trump is like P. T. Barnum, Adolf Hitler, Idi Amin, or Silvio Berlusconi. Scholars of the U.S. presidency, wary of analogy's imprecision, prefer other approaches, from genre analysis to close reading. Yet such perspectives appear unable to capture fully the novelties of Trump's political career or the characteristics of his discourse. Trump's rhetoric defies our long-standing assumptions about the institutional voice of the presidency and the unity of the individual and the office (Campbell & Jamieson, 2008). Donald Trump is a persona and a personality and a character, specific and individual, and his speech as president and his embodiment of the presidency are not reducible to the institution. His attitude toward the office is desirous, aspirational, abnormal, antagonistic, and partial; his rhetoric is regularly hyperbolic, contradictory, and vulgar. If historical precedents of the office or expectations for presidential speech and behavior guide our analyses of Trump too strictly, we risk normalizing a presidency that is anything but normal.

Therefore, we propose a reading strategy that recognizes the potential of analogical reasoning to produce useful structures of knowledge. We take seriously the impulse to seek explanations via analogy that is often seen in popular media, and we appreciate the promise of the question: What is this like? At the same time, we recognize the peril of relying on apparent correspondences as a basis for understanding. Hence, we generate an approach to reading Trump that utilizes difference as well as similarity and situates the central figure not only within binaries but also within an analogical network. After a brief discussion of the concept of analogy, we proffer a reading of Trump as campaigner and as president via two analogies. We first compare the discourses of Trump the campaigner and Barnum the showman, particularly as they used freakishness to gain popularity. Then, drawing on the scholarship of Cameroonian political theorist Achille Mbembe, we investigate analogies between the presidential Trump and the figural postcolonial autocrat. In generating a hermeneutic network that is transhistorical, transgeographic, and transpolitical, we show the productive potentials of analogical reasoning to illuminate features of Trumpian rhetoric that more familiar approaches miss.

In Defense of the Analogy

Scholars have long noted the ubiquity of analogical classification, and many remain skeptical of its utility. Since analogy "expresses the *similarity* of *different* things" (Burbidge, 1990, p. 4), it is logically weak (Walton, Reed, & Macagno, 2008). Researchers show that analogies are a perilous basis for decision-making, especially when elites use them in moments of crisis (e.g., Noon, 2004; Stuckey, 1992). Yet Perelman and Olbrechts-Tyteca (1969) noted analogy's power to "facilitate the development and extension of thought" (p. 385), and Zarefsky (2006) called it "a particularly potent form of rhetorical argument" (p. 406). Despite its logical precarity, analogy can be "imaginatively engaging and profoundly influential" (Ray, 2012, p. 98).

Although analogies seem a slender reed upon which a rhetorical critic might lean, we agree with philosopher John Burbidge (1990) that arguments from analogy can be productive and illuminating. For instance, Ray (2012) argued that, in the 1870s, Frederick Douglass's study of the 16th-century Dutch prince William of Orange allowed him to reimagine the characteristics of Abraham Lincoln's leadership. The key to the analytic utility of this analogy, according to Ray, was that Douglass "openly test[ed] the quality of the analogy" (p. 106), retaining historical particularity and noting difference as well as likeness. Likewise, here we emphasize juxtapositions to explain Trump's uniqueness and show his correspondence to social, cultural, and political phenomena across time and space.

Analogizing Trump and Barnum

Throughout the 2016 campaign, comparisons were rife between Trump and the 19th-century showman and entrepreneur Phineas Taylor Barnum. Journalists focused on the two men's tendency for spectacle, exaggeration, and deception, summarizing shared biographical attributes. Samantha Schmidt (2017) of *The Washington Post,* for example, highlighted their abstinence from alcohol, opulent lifestyles, and outsized egos. She linked Barnum's use of newspaper advertising to Trump's dependence on Twitter as a quick, inexpensive way to attract attention. Political aspirations buttressed the comparison: Although Barnum failed in a congressional bid, he served as a mayor and Connecticut state legislator.

Scrutinizing the Barnum-Trump analogy less biographically and more rhetorically opens further interpretive possibilities. Two examples will suffice as illustrations. First, the formal features of exaggeration and amplification in Barnum's discourse clarify the oft-repeated claim that Trump's supporters take him "seriously, but not literally" (Zito, 2016, para. 21). In the 1830s Barnum, a master of hyperbole, exhibited an enslaved woman, Joice Heth, claiming that she was 161 years old and the former nurse of George Washington; a typical ad called her "the greatest curiosity in the world, and the most interesting, particularly to Americans" (Barnum, 1855, p. 57). Such language recurred, as ads for Barnum's American Museum as well as the later circus described exhibits as celebrated, world-renowned, and the greatest, biggest, smallest, or best wonders of the world. He applied similar language to himself, writing that "I have been a public benefactor, to an extent seldom paralleled" (Barnum, 1855, p. 158). Barnum's exaggerations are formally similar to Trump's—"loser!" "greatest," "the least racist person that you have ever met"—and these analogical linkages ground a broader claim of classification (see Walton et al., 2008). Both men supply a rhetoric of commercial advertising, in which embellishment is common and audiences can find amusement in hyperbole and also in the credulity of others.

A second analogical link focuses on audiences, and especially a perception of normality among a comparatively narrow public, although one characterized as "the" public. Barnum notoriously built his antebellum empire on the exhibition of "freaks"—both human and animal, from Heth to a rhinoceros labeled a unicorn. The freakish was the physically excessive: the very small, the very large, the ancient, the young, the very black, the very white. Often, as historian James Cook (2005) noted, these figures "resisted final categorization" (p. 156). William Cammell, a man likely afflicted with vitiligo, appeared black and white and hence racially confusing; Josephine Clofullia, the Swiss Bearded Lady, ambiguously represented female and male; and Chang and Eng Bunker, the original Siamese twins, challenged assumptions of the separate self. Even so, Tom Thumb's wedding, Chang and Eng's carriage rides, or an albino child's violin playing all represented normalcy amid freakishness. These activities emulated conventional gentility and yet appeared as its grotesque double.

Grotesquerie, however, is in the eye of the beholder. Barnum's exhibitions, and the press reports about them, aggressively reinforced the normalcy of the spectator. A lithograph from the early 1860s makes this point clearly (Cook, 2005, p. 175). It depicts the What Is It?, a creature posited as the missing link between man and monkey; at the museum, a short African American man performed this role. Depicting well-dressed white spectators scrutinizing a black figure represented as primitive in posture and attire, the lithograph asserts the white, well-to-do body as a higher order of being and shows the white gaze—and hence white assessment—as itself unthreatened. At the same time that Barnum's exhibitions could satisfy spectators' curiosity about difference and make the "wonders" of the world available for scrutiny, they reassured prosperous white patrons that they were civilized, in control, and vastly different from the freaks.

Donald Trump's rhetorical representations of the freakish vary from Barnum's, although a comparison with Barnum's exhibitions of human beings might illuminate Trump's possession of the Miss Universe Pageant. Trump claimed ownership over contestants' bodies, noting that he could invade the women's dressing rooms: "I'm the owner of the pageant and therefore I'm inspecting it," he said (quoted in Kertscher, 2016, para. 19). If we generalize Barnum's and Trump's rhetoric to broader cultural traits, then we can understand Trump's notorious behaviors—denigrating people who differ from him by sex, race, sexuality, ability, national origin, religion, or other characteristics—not as juvenile vulgarities but rather as part of a dehumanizing ideological system in which the bodies of others are accessible and available for viewing, assessment, and exploitation. In such a system, difference is a predicate for judgment: Those who are unlike the speaker become freaks, and those like the speaker find assurance that they are normal.

If a transhistorical analogy can illuminate Trump the campaigner as well as a longer arc of cultural resources upon which Trump's rhetoric draws, a transgeographic and transpolitical analogy can elucidate his approaches to governance. Whereas a comparison with Barnum helps to explain Trump's rhetorical construction of others as freaks, comparisons with the figure of the postcolonial autocrat illumine others' freakish renderings of him.

Analogizing Trump and the Postcolonial Autocrat

South African comedian Trevor Noah, the host of Comedy Central's *Daily Show*, popularized the analogy of Trump to postcolonial autocrats. The analogy hinges on the aesthetics, styles, and rhetorics of authority common to these figures. Murphy (2008) argued that in a postmodern world where the traditional pillars of authority—religion and reason—have given way to the contingencies of language as the primary mode of meaning-making, leaders must engage in a "performance of legitimacy" (p. 35) to generate authority. What was once an assumed, inherent quality of the presidential office has become a rhetorical burden. Whereas appeals for authority in a liberal democracy are primarily claims to the rightness of a leader's actions, comparison across other political forms reveals considerable variation.

Authority in the postcolony, according to Mbembe (2001), takes the form of a fetish, of "an object that aspires to be made sacred" (p. 111). Mbembe argued that postcolonial regimes construct a rhetorical universe in which citizens revere political power. "Signs, vocabulary, and narratives," he said, "are officially invested with a surplus of meanings that are not negotiable and that one is officially forbidden to depart from or challenge" (p. 103). The ruling autocrat, embodying the fetish, becomes "an object that feeds on applause, flattery, lies" (p. 111). Authority in the postcolony is thus not a means to achieve effective governance; rather, authority is itself the prize, because authority alone is the substance of the fetish.

Trump's attitude toward presidential power, as exhibited through his words and actions, shares significant similarities with the postcolonial autocratic fetish. For example, in the postcolony, Mbembe (2001) argued, the state and the public interact primarily through pretense. On his first day in office, Trump directed then-Press Secretary Sean Spicer to present the administration's first official fiction: The crowd at the inauguration was the largest in history. This demonstrably false claim set the tone for how his administration would handle the truth.

Further, in a performance analogous to the fetish, Trump believed that assuming the presidential office would improve his public image, almost magically conferring adulation, respect, and loyalty. "You know, when I won, I said 'Well the one good thing is now I'll get good press.' And it got worse" (Trump, 2017, para. 70). It keeps getting worse: "Look at the way I've been treated lately [...] especially by the media," Trump said in May 2017. "No politician in history—and I say this with great surety—has been treated worse or more unfairly" (White House, 2017, para. 34). In a Barnumesque mode, popularity, publicity, and public image command the president's attention. When media reports stray from his preferred narrative, Trump does not merely correct the record. Instead, he attacks the media's character, branding them "hateful," "dishonest," and "fake news." Although the magic of the ruler's office can operate with impunity in the postcolony, liberal democratic institutions in the United States, like the fourth estate, attenuate the fetish's power. But does attenuation constitute meaningful political resistance?

Mbembe (2001) rejected the binary between resistance and support in the postcolony. Instead, he said, the ruled craft a convivial relationship with their rulers because they must live together. The language of power in the postcolony is intimately connected to the body of the autocrat, and laughing at vulgar and grotesque representations of that body is a common form of conviviality. "Hence," Mbembe wrote, "the image of, say, the president's anus is not of something out of this world—although, to everyone's amusement, the official line may treat it as such; instead, people see it as it really is, capable of defecating like any commoner's" (p. 108). The obverse of adulation, vulgar depiction is a recurrent form in discourse by and about Trump as well.

Trump's body and its attempts to articulate power are a subject of considerable public fascination: his aggressive handshake, his compulsive rearrangement of items on conference tables, or his shoving his way past Montenegro's prime minister at a NATO summit (Bruni, 2017). Artists have also made his body freakish. In August 2016, five grotesque statues depicting Trump's obese, pale, and veiny nude body, titled *The Emperor Has No Balls* appeared in cities across the United States. Like the statues, artist Illma Gore's portrait of a nude Trump draws attention to his pouting lips and small penis. In March 2016 Trump himself reassured the audience of a Republican primary debate about his size: "I guarantee you there's no problem. I guarantee" (Krieg, 2016, para. 2). By vulgarizing his body, these artists—and the man himself—make it possible to laugh at the fetish of power, which is one strategy of living intimately with the fact of Trump's presidency.

Although vulgarity may function as critique, it is not a mode of resistance. "Taking over the signs and language of officialdom," Mbembe (2001) wrote, "produces a situation of disempowerment (*impouvoir*) for both ruled and rulers" (p. 111). Alec Baldwin, whose caricature of Trump on *Saturday Night Live* drew the president's ire on Twitter, remarked on the disempowerment of his own vulgar representations: "The maliciousness of this White House has people worried. That's why I'm not going to do it much longer—the impersonation. I don't know how much more people can take it" (quoted in Williams, 2017, para. 9). Baldwin's comment acknowledged the existence of an irreducible material base to political power that ridicule could not erode. Although freakish representations of Trump may disrupt his embodiment of the presidential fetish—that is, because they prevent him from enjoying the popularity he apparently desires—they will not stop his policy agenda. Other institutions of political power are the loci for that task: the courts, the legislature, and the independent executive. These checks and balances mark a crucial difference between liberal democracies and postcolonial autocracies.

Conclusion

In a technological illustration of the disunity of the current presidency, Donald Trump broadcasts from two Twitter accounts: @therealDonaldTrump and @POTUS. Such disunity deserves scholarly scrutiny, and analogical networks can supply important interpretive frameworks for such inquiries. Although analogies assert similarity not identity, juxtapositions illuminate features of individual performance and historical context. Furthermore, placing Trump not only within analogical binaries but also within an analogical network reveals dynamic interplay among attributes and pinpoints the limits of comparisons. Trump's exaggerated statements display a Barnumesque showmanship, but he is not only a showman. Indeed, neither was Barnum: As a Connecticut state legislator in 1879, Barnum supported a law criminalizing the use of birth control that stood for 86 years. The analogy to the autocrat who expects unquestioning obedience to his dictates highlights the material effects of political power even further.

Neither analogy quite fits the case. We are arguing that analogies are useful for cultural comprehension, not prediction. Although the use of historical analogies often asserts teleology (see Zarefsky, 2010), this function is flawed. If Barnum and Trump are alike, and Barnum was unable to achieve national political office, then surely Trump cannot win the presidency. Time has shown the error of that reasoning. Similarly, noting commonalities between Trump's behavior and that of the postcolonial autocrat does not mean that the United States is on the verge of an autocracy. The two analogies, however, do offer "templates for thinking about the present" (Zarefsky, 2010, p. 574). These networks of intelligibility do not provide easy answers. Although quick claims of similarity often have persuasive effect, a more substantive and productive use of the analogy is to promote careful thought and imaginative engagement, investigate differences as well as similarities, and recognize signs of danger.

References

Barnum, P. T. (1855). *The autobiography of P. T. Barnum* (2nd ed.). London, United Kingdom: Ward and Lock.

Bruni, F. (2017, May 26). The awkward body language of Donald Trump. *The New York Times.* Retrieved from https://nytimes.com

Burbidge, J. W. (1990). *Within reason: A guide to non-deductive reasoning.* Peterborough, Ontario: Broadview Press.

Campbell, K. K., & Jamieson, K. H. (2008). *Presidents creating the presidency: Deeds done in words.* Chicago, IL: University of Chicago Press.

Cook, J. W. (Ed.). (2005). *The colossal P. T. Barnum reader: Nothing else like it in the universe.* Urbana, IL: University of Illinois Press.

The Daily Show with Trevor Noah. (2015, October 3). Donald Trump—America's African president: The Daily Show [Video file]. Retrieved from https://youtube.com

Kertscher, T. (2016, October 18). The allegations about Donald Trump and Miss Teen USA contestants. *Politifact.* Retrieved from http://politifact.com

Krieg, G. (2016, March 4). Donald Trump defends size of his penis. *CNN.* Retrieved from http://cnn.com

Mbembe, A. (2001). *On the postcolony* (A. M. Berrett, J. Roitman, M. Last, & S. Rendall, Trans.). Berkeley, CA: University of California Press.

Murphy, J. M. (2008). Power and authority in a postmodern presidency. In J. A. Aune & M. J. Medhurst (Eds.), *The prospect of presidential rhetoric* (pp. 28–45). College Station, TX: Texas A&M University Press.

Noon, D. H. (2004). Operation enduring analogy: World War II, the war on terror, and the uses of historical memory. *Rhetoric & Public Affairs, 7*(3), 339–366. doi: 10.1353/rap.2005.0015

Perelman, Ch., & Olbrechts-Tyteca, L. (1969). *The new rhetoric: A treatise on argumentation* (J. Wilkinson & P. Weaver, Trans.). Notre Dame, IN: University of Notre Dame Press.

Ray, A. G. (2012). Making history by analogy: Frederick Douglass remembers William the Silent. In F. H. van Eemeren & B. Garssen (Eds.), *Exploring argumentative contexts* (pp. 97–114). Amsterdam, The Netherlands: John Benjamins.

Schmidt, S. (2017, January 17). Why people keep comparing Donald Trump to P. T. Barnum, of circus fame. *The Washington Post.* Retrieved from https://washingtonpost.com

Stuckey, M. (1992). Remembering the future: Rhetorical echoes of World War II and Vietnam in George Bush's public speech on the Gulf War. *Communication Studies, 43*(4), 246–256. doi: 10.1080/10510979209368376

Trump, D. (2017, April 23). Transcript of AP interview with Trump [Interviewed by J. Pace]. Retrieved from https://apnews.com

Walton, D., Reed, C., & Macagno, F. (2008). *Argumentation schemes.* Cambridge, United Kingdom: Cambridge University Press.

The White House, Office of the Press Secretary. (2017, May 17). Remarks by President Trump at United States Coast Guard Academy commencement ceremony. Retrieved from https://whitehouse.gov

Williams, J. (2017, March 29). Becoming Donald Trump: How Alec Baldwin perfected his SNL impression. *Newsweek.* Retrieved from http://newsweek.com

Zarefsky, D. (2006). Strategic maneuvering through persuasive definitions: Implications for dialectic and rhetoric. *Argumentation, 20*(4), 399–416. doi: 10.1007/s10503-007-9030-6

Zarefsky, D. (2010). Obama's Lincoln: Uses of the argument from historical analogy. In D. S. Gouran (Ed.), *The functions of argument and social context* (pp. 572–578). Washington, DC: National Communication Association.

Zito, S. (2016, September 23). Taking Trump seriously, not literally. *The Atlantic.* Retrieved from https://theatlantic.com

21

PETITIONING A MORMON GOD

Analogical Argument as a Means of Revelation in the Ordain Women Movement

Brian Heslop

Analogizing, drawing comparisons between two things or identifying one thing in terms of another, is a form of arguing. Analogies explain the unfamiliar by way of the familiar, and in so doing, make assertions about the truth. As Perelman (1982) deduced, "In criticizing a thesis illustrated by an analogy, we must either adapt the analogy so that it corresponds better to our own conceptions, or replace it by another, thought to be more adequate" (p. 119). Analogies, therefore, often appear in the midst—or even at the center—of controversy. Perelman (1982) explained that analogies invite conflict because agonists can disagree about the adequacy of a *phoros* (or what is familiar) used to render the identity of a *theme* (what is unfamiliar).

While analogical arguments appear in oral or written speech (e.g., "that would be like..."), in side-by-side images on social media, or even in labs that test drugs on animals before testing humans, this essay explores an untapped site of analogical argument: divine revelation. Beyond an examination of how analogy puts words to God's ineffable realm, this essay looks at how lay Mormons seeking doctrinal and policy changes utilize *revelatory analogy* (or the use of analogy to name or claim divine truths) as a form of argument.

To counter the long-established practice of excluding women from priesthood ordination, Ordain Women (OW) activists, comprised mostly of devoted Mormon women, have sought to inspire church leaders toward a revelatory decree that would change the ordination policy to give women access to the administrative and spiritual duties within priesthood offices. Given their subordinate status as lay members, as well as the gender constraints of women in the church, their analogical strategy invoked a vision meaningful to prophetic leaders that places women together with performances of priesthood authority. In other words, they wanted to redefine and bring to light the wholly unrealized Mormon meaning of womanhood, envisioning how the physical and spiritual capacities of women are similar to those of men. Some key efforts they have used to enact this revelatory analogy include displaying photographs of women performing priesthood ordinances, describing vivid scenes of women fulfilling priesthood responsibilities, and walking with men to a conference exclusive to priesthood holders.

This essay examines how OW activists have petitioned the prophet and apostles in The Church of Jesus Christ of Latter-day Saints (hereafter the LDS or Mormon Church) to appeal to a Higher Power to validate, by revelation, their analogical comparison—namely, that the abilities of women in the church are comparable to those of men, and subsequently, women should have the same responsibilities. Specifically, I argue that the visual renderings of their analogies are more than just a fitting form of argument OW activists adopted because, as my findings will demonstrate, the function of argument by visual analogy parallels that of revelation in Mormonism. In short, analogy's deductive function to discover (or *reveal*) parallels revelation's visual capabilities as envisioned (or *seen*) truths. Thus, OW's visual construction of the analogies appealed to practices of prophetic divination, inviting prophets to envision Mormon women in a new light.

Visions and Visual Analogies

Scholars have afforded the visual dimension of argumentation much attention (e.g., see Alcolea-Banegas, 2009; Hahner, 2013; Pineda & Sowards, 2007; Richardson & Wodak, 2009), but the OW case invites examination of a unique, unobserved "medium" or site of visual argument—visions. The LDS Church forms its policies by way of revelation and such divine communications unfold through a variety of spiritual modes, including visions. Within the Mormon canopy, visions provide a "visual link" (Bergin, n.d., para. 3) to divine information distinct from other revelatory forms, and descriptions of their mechanics often accompany the content they produce. Mormon prophets adopt the language of ancient scripture as "eyes being opened" (e.g., see Doctrine and Covenants 101:1, 136:32, 138:11, 29) to describe them. In one vision, Church founder Joseph Smith wrote that "the Lord touched the eyes of our understandings and they were opened [....] And we beheld the glory of the Son, on the right hand of the Father" (Doctrine and Covenants 76:19-20).

Continuing revelation is a distinguishing theological characteristic of Mormonism that separates it from most Christian faiths. Modern-day prophets that Mormons regard as "revelators" (Davies & Madsen, n.d., para. 6) transcend biblical authority as they embody the "living word" (Davies & Madsen, n.d., para. 12). Yet, even while prophets maintain an authority to discern God's will, Joseph Smith explained, paradoxically, that "God hath not revealed anything to Joseph, but what He will make known unto the Twelve, and even the least Saint may know all things as fast as he is able to bear them" (The Church, 2011, para. 37). Thus, although Mormonism's God selects key representatives who impart His will, paradoxically, any member can access and discern heavenly law using the same means. This "inexplicable contradiction," for both leader and congregant to know God's mind, observed historian Richard Bushman (2007), is a "conundrum [that] lies at the heart of Joseph Smith's Mormonism" (p. 175).

While OW activists' call for reform could have rejected the role of prophets in establishing doctrine and criticized the revelatory conventions that led to gender inequality, they chose instead to petition prophets by way of these revelatory conventions. "I believe and I sustain the leaders of the church," said OW founder Kate Kelly. "That's why we're going through the church leadership structure. That's why 'the ask' of Ordain Women has been to prayerfully consider the ordination of women because we acknowledge that that's how revelation occurs, that the prophet leads the church" (quoted in Fabrizio, 2014, 40:13). But that revelation would require a planted "seed" of inspiration to prod the current prophet just as Joseph Smith's wife Emma had prodded him in the past, leading to the revelation of the dietary regimen synonymous with Mormon identity (Fabrizio, 2014, 41:32). Thus, OW's objective has been "to help open up people's imaginations, open up modern Mormon women and modern Mormon men to the idea of what it could look like" (quoted in Fabrizio, 2013, 19:59).

Photographs and Thought Exercises

The analogical actions that OW took came in several forms. First were photographed scenes of ordinances and rites on the organization's website, *OrdainWomen.org*. One image portrayed a group of women encircling an individual with their hands on the person's head and imparting a blessing. Another photo presented a young girl passing a tray of water, or Holy Communion, to congregants. Another displayed a woman standing in a pool of water, ready to baptize a convert. Mormons are familiar with these scenes and recognize them as sacred ordinances, but depicting *women* performing the ordinances is, for most Mormons, shocking. Far removed from the Latter-day Saint mind is the idea of women engaging in priesthood duties. The sacredness of these practices comes from a belief in their divine implementation and a piety to the patriarchal tradition that maintains them. Contradicting those conventional revelations and traditions in any degree would, as a consequence, be confusing and upsetting. As Brigham Young University Idaho historian Andrea Radke-Moss explained, "you are so culturally taught that that's not what women do [....] When you have the image of a priesthood blessing that's taking place, it's not done with women involved" (quoted in Fabrizio, 2013, 18:55).

Along with the photographs, a central part of the OW's website are six "conversations" that enable supporters to instigate cultural and social change. These manuals contain "thought exercises" that invite readers to envision scenarios highlighting the inequality between men and women and to open new possibilities for experiencing the church. One question asked, "What would happen if there were no men at church?" The answer: "There would be no bishop on the stand to lead the meeting, and no bishopric to fill in for the bishop. No priests to bless the sacrament [....] Church would likely need to be cancelled that day." Reversing the scenario, the exercise concluded that the church meeting "could carry on as scheduled without women [....] Everything could run as usual" (Ordain Women, 2014a, Thought Exercise 1: Sacrament Meeting section, para. 2, 4).

Some of the thought exercises consist of detailed hypotheticals that vividly place the reader, for example, at a church meeting with women fulfilling priesthood roles.

> Picture a typical future Sacrament meeting when women are ordained [....] The bishop is a woman, surrounded by her two counselors, one male and one female, all in their Sunday best [....] As you look to your left, you notice your ward's youth, both the Young Men and the Young Women, sitting in the first two rows by the sacrament table, ready and willing to pass the sacrament.
>
> *(Ordain Women, 2014b, Thought Exercises: Sacrament*
> *Meetings and Official Declaration 3 section, para. 1-2)*

The website invites leaders and members to open themselves to the possibility for new revelation, and it creates an opportunity to engage in the revelatory process within Mormonism. The images and thought exercises on the OW website add to the construction of the analogy in-process: that imagining women fulfilling male-typical duties constitutes the true role of women.

Entering Male Spaces

As a part of the worldwide semiannual conference of the church, the Priesthood Session invites all males over the age of twelve to attend the session and listen to talks by General

Authorities—including the prophet—concerning priesthood duties and responsibilities. This meeting is broadcast to LDS chapels across the world from the Conference Center in Temple Square in Salt Lake City, the location where all the sessions of Conference take place. To enter, one must have a free ticket distributed through a congregation's local leader.

On October 5, 2013, a group of 200 supporters of OW walked toward Temple Square. After church leaders had denied the women entrance beforehand during their official requests for tickets, they walked alongside men young and old on their way to get standby tickets. "What we hope to do," Kelly explained, "is to go into the session, to listen to the prophet, to participate and demonstrate to our leaders not only are we ready to participate in the priesthood session, but that we wish to be ordained to the priesthood" (quoted in Green, 2013, para. 6).

Once inside Temple Square, the line of activists halted as church spokesperson Ruth Todd "met amicably" (Higginbottom, 2013, A Walk in the Park section, para. 2) with OW organizers. "We were expecting you" (quoted in A Walk in the Park section, para. 3), Todd said, and then politely declined entrance to the Conference Center. Later, the church released a statement in response to the "protest," positing that "millions of women in this church do not share the views of this small group who organized today's protest, and most church members would see such efforts as divisive" (Associated Press, 2013, para. 19). However, the Church added that these women "are our sisters and we want them to be among us, and hope they will find peace and joy we all seek in the gospel of Jesus Christ" (para. 19).

Notwithstanding the rejection, the march on Temple Square constituted the same aim as the OW's website—to visually prepare members and leaders to accept the analogous relationship between women and men's capacities in the church. Walking alongside men toward the Priesthood Session and requesting tickets, women activists' rhetorical performance displayed different genders participating in the church in similar ways.

The site of women amongst thousands of men was striking and meaningful in both positive and negative ways for viewers. The *Salt Lake Tribune* described the scene as "a powerful image, just as the Ordain Women group intended" (Moulton, 2013, para. 1). Some saw the analogical argument as defiant and aggressive. LDS blogger Kathryn Skaggs wrote, "I really believe that what God is trying to do with each of us is make us equal to him, versus what the world wants to do which is to make men and women the same" (quoted in Higginbottom, 2013, A Walk in the Park section, para. 11). Furthermore, she posited, "It's not their job to push revelation" (quoted in A Walk in the Park section, para. 9). The statement foreshadowed a resistance that would continue the next year, when OW would march a second time at Temple Square. For many members, and especially leaders, the analogical push would be too much to bear. On Monday, June 23, 2014, Kate Kelly was excommunicated (Stack & McFall, 2015, para. 6).

Responding to the Analogy

Despite public affairs statements to the contrary, the OW's visual analogy clearly affected church leaders. One of the most notable responses to the OW movement was a sermon from M. Russell Ballard (2013), a member of the Quorum of the Twelve Apostles. Ballard's talk, "Let Us Think Straight," spoke of the "foundational truths about the separate roles of men and women" (Number 2 section, para. 21), claiming that "our Church doctrine places women equal to and yet different from men" (Number 3 section, para. 1). Without mentioning the OW organization specifically, Ballard directed his remarks to the OW's constructed analogy, making efforts to challenge it directly. Delineating the divinely appointed roles for women and men, he stated, "The responsibilities and divine gifts of men and women differ in their nature but not in their importance or influence" (Number 3 section, para. 1). Speaking of the co-dependent relationship inherent between the two genders, he described the genders as "[having] different gifts, different strengths, and different points of view and inclinations" (Number 3 section, para. 5). He specified those roles, saying, "It takes a man and a woman to create a family, and it takes men and women to carry out the work of the Lord in the Church. A husband and wife righteously working together complete each other" (Number 3 section, para. 5).

Ballard's remarks engage the analogy also at a revelatory level in that he is an apostle, or a church member sustained as a prophet, seer, and revelator. His response, however, was a revelatory style distinct from OW in its authoritative base—simply *proclaiming* truth and lacking evidence that classical rhetoric typically depends upon in persuasion. Ballard backed his power to issue a revelatory decree through past prophets' statements on women's separateness from priesthood, a move that reinforced God's longstanding authority and will on the issue.

Ultimately, the OW activists and the church's response represent two opposing revelations in conflict: one that is a lay-constructed vision dependent upon visual analogy for persuasive aims, and the other a traditional authoritative decree not needing to persuade anyone. "Let Us Think Straight," then, was an explanatory injunction for differences in roles between genders, but also, as evident in the title, it implied an unbalanced rationality of the feminine mind—a tactic used to dismiss women's arguments for centuries. Even within the prophetic tradition, as Pernot (2006) explained, the historical account of masculine and feminine divination techniques recognizes "an opposition between the wise rhetoric of masculine prophets and the crazed voices of inspired women" (p. 239).

Conclusion

The goal of this project was to understand how activists in the OW controversy utilized analogies as a resource for empowering women in the LDS Church. This case illustrates that visual analogies maintain useful argumentative capacities in religious communities, particularly to Mormons who abide in and respond to the rhetoric and practice of prophecy. The concept of revelatory analogy serves as the means that those who interact with the church can envision, reveal, and deduce an analogy's theme in the process of making an analogical argument. Because this kind of revelation is visually-driven, it focuses on the visual work of the analogy—how its visual elements work together to reason and claim spiritual truth. While revelatory analogies may seem to have constrained applications to Mormonism or other religious communities, I encourage further research that ventures into the civic arena. Given the well-established research on the civil religious dimension of American culture, future analyses could explore how citizens of the state have utilized revelatory analogies, especially in seeking change under the authority of the nation's "prophet"—the president.

The OW case illustrates that analogies can begin to level the power dimensions at play when lay citizens and powerful officials argue. LDS General Authorities could have ignored women advocates petitioning for a more capacious role in the church, but chose to engage in the analogical enthymemes, thus creating a space for deliberation between invested agonists. Resistance on either end is not a failed outcome, for it allows advocates to find new pathways to communicate and argue a given position, expanding the boundaries through which interlocutors discuss the issue (Mendelson, 1997).

References

Alcolea-Banegas, J. (2009). Visual arguments in film. *Argumentation*, *23*(2), 259–275. doi:10.1007/s10503-008-9124-9

The Associated Press. (2013, October 5). Mormon women's group shut out of all-male meeting. *USA Today*. Retrieved from http://usatoday.com

Ballard, M. R. (2013, August 20). Let us think straight. *BYU Speeches*. Retrieved from https://speeches.byu.edu

Bergin, A. E. (n.d.). Visions. In *Encyclopedia of Mormonism*. Brigham Young University, UT: Harold B. Lee Library. Retrieved from http://eom.byu.edu

Bushman, R. L. (2007). *Joseph Smith: Rough stone rolling*. New York, NY: Vintage Books.

The Church of Jesus Christ of Latter-day Saints. (2011). Chapter 22: Gaining knowledge of eternal truths. *Teachings of the presidents of the church: Joseph Smith* (pp. 261–270). Retrieved from https://lds.org

Davies, W. D., & Madsen, T. G. (n.d.). Scriptures. In *Encyclopedia of Mormonism*. Brigham Young University, UT: Harold B. Lee Library. Retrieved from http://eom.byu.edu

Fabrizio, D. (2013, April 10). Mormon women and the priesthood [Podcast]. *RadioWest*. Retrieved from http://radiowest.kuer.org/post/mormon-women-and-the-priesthood

Fabrizio, D. (2014, June 15). Facing excommunication [Podcast]. *RadioWest*. Retrieved from http://radiowest.kuer.org/post/facing-excommunication

Green, M. (2013, October 5). Women asking to attend priesthood session of LDS general conference denied. *Fox 13 News*. Retrieved from http://fox13now.com/2013/10/05/women-who-want-to-attend-priesthood-session-of-lds-general-conference-rally-for-that-right/

Hahner, L. (2013). The riot kiss: Framing memes as visual argument. *Argumentation and Advocacy*, *49*(3), 151–166. Retrieved from http://tandfonline.com

Higginbottom, J. (2013, October 9). Mormon women march for entry into priesthood. *Al Jazeera America*. Retrieved from http://america.aljazeera.com/articles/2013/10/9/mormon-women-marchforentryintopriesthood.html

Mendelson, M. (1997). Everything must be argued: Rhetorical theory and pedagogical practice in Cicero's "de oratore." *Journal of Education*, *179*(1), 15–47. Retrieved from http://jstor.org/stable/42743882

Moulton, K. (2013, October 18). Mormon women shut out of all-male priesthood meeting. *The Salt Lake Tribune*. Retrieved from http://archive.sltrib.com

Ordain Women. (2014a). *See the symptoms: Conversation one*. Retrieved from http://ordainwomen.org/wp-content/uploads/2014/07/OW1SeeTheSymptoms_FINAL_July.pdf

Ordain Women. (2014b). *Visualize our potential! Conversation five*. Retrieved from http://ordainwomen.org/wp-content/uploads/2014/07/OW5VisualizeOurPotential_July.pdf

Perelman, Ch. (1982). *The realm of rhetoric*. Notre Dame, IN: University of Notre Dame Press.

Pernot, L. (2006). The rhetoric of religion. *Rhetorica: A Journal of the History of Rhetoric*, *24*(3), 235–254. doi:10.1525/rh.2006.24.3.235

Pineda, R. D., & Sowards, S. K. (2007). Flag waving as visual argument: 2006 immigration demonstrations and cultural citizenship [Special issue]. *Argumentation and Advocacy*, *43*(3–4), 164–174. Retrieved from http://tandfonline.com

Richardson, J. E., & Wodak, R. (2009). The impact of visual racism: Visual arguments in political leaflets of Austrian and British far-right parties. *Controversia*, *6*(2), 45–77.

Stack, P. F., & McFall, M. (2015, July 21). Kate Kelly out as leader of Mormon group Ordain Women. *The Salt Lake Tribune*. Retrieved from http://archive.sltrib.com/article.php?id=2694608&itype=CMSID

22

EXTINGUISHED DISSENT

Norman Morrison's Self-immolation as Argument by Sacrifice

Meredith Neville-Shepard

On November 2, 1965, thirty-year old Quaker Norman Morrison set himself on fire outside of Robert McNamara's Pentagon office window. Even more shocking, Morrison had his baby, Emily, with him. Bystander accounts conflict on whether he put her down prior to lighting himself or dropped her after beginning to burn (Hendrickson, 1996). Ultimately, Emily suffered no injuries, but Morrison died before reaching the hospital. Morrison's wife, Anne, and his other two children were unaware of his actions until receiving a phone call from a *Newsweek* reporter (Welsh, 2008). Even though Morrison left no public manifesto, Anne knew the cause that prompted Morrison to commit self-immolation. She wrote a statement for the press asserting that Morrison had "given his life" in order "to express his concern over the great loss of life and human suffering caused by the war in Vietnam [....] He felt that all citizens must speak their true convictions about our country's actions" (Welsh, 2008, p. 6). Throughout this essay, I analyze Morrison's self-immolation as a form of embodied argument.

Rhetorical scholars are continually pushing disciplinary boundaries to expand conceptions of what counts as argument. Scholars like DeLuca (1999) have presented compelling cases that "the non-linguistic can argue" (p. 12), with the body, in particular, gaining recognition as "a pivotal resource for the crucial practice of public argumentation" (p. 10). As Palczewski (2011) pointed out, body argument is not limited to the body itself or the image of a body, but includes "the site of contest over the meaning and status of the body" (p. 383). Here, I follow Palczewski's conceptualization of body argument by examining how the American public constructed meaning out of Morrison's bodily sacrifice. Although evidence indicates that Morrison hoped that his body would function as a rhetorical resource for the anti-war movement, the primary frame for his action was that of a futile suicide, not a worthwhile sacrifice. As Watts (2011) described, "*Sacrifice* is a value-laden term whose meaning is determined by [the] stories" we tell (p. 16). Examining the stories about Morrison helps to account for how his body was set apart from the network of self-immolated bodies (e.g., those of Buddhist monks in Vietnam) whose images had penetrated the consciousness of the American public. Furthermore, Morrison's case illuminates the pliability of ethical standards concerning legitimate violence, standards adjustable based on the identity of the actor and/or the setting of the act.

Argumentation scholars can productively read Morrison's action as an argument by sacrifice. According to Perelman and Olbrechts-Tyteca (1969), "One of the most frequently used of the arguments by comparison is that which is based on the sacrifice which one is willing to make in order to achieve a certain result" (p. 248). Because an argument by comparison is quasi-logical, "the term of reference has no fixed value, but interacts constantly with the other elements" (p. 250). This conception of sacrificial argument as a quasi-logical comparison provides a useful framework for analyzing public narratives about Morrison. Here, I argue that the public reframed Morrison's comparative terms in a way that nullified his action as a sacrifice. In other words, I extend Perelman and Olbrechts-Tyteca's notion of a "useless sacrifice" (p. 251) by illustrating how some attempted to depoliticize Morrison's self-immolation and, in the process, tried to erase the sacrificial nature of his protest. To begin, I review some of the existing rhetorical scholarship on self-immolation. Next, I provide a reading of Morrison's act as an argument by sacrifice. This reading sets the stage for the analysis that follows, in which I examine major themes from the media's coverage of Morrison in order to illuminate how the media framed his comparative terms out of proportion. Finally, I conclude with a discussion of implications concerning sacrificial argument and a glance at how many individuals suffering in Vietnam weighed Morrison's comparative terms differently than much of the American public.

The Rhetoric of Self-Immolation

The field of argumentation studies has made great strides in expanding the traditional view of argument as a wholly discursive practice. Numerous scholars have explored how non-linguistic mediums, such as bodies in pain, can function rhetorically. Self-immolation in particular has received recent attention as a rhetorical form. For example, in her examination of the famous 1963 photograph of Thich Quang Duc committing self-immolation, Yang (2011) contended, "Self-immolation is a powerful rhetorical act that utilizes self-inflicted violence as a means of performing a visual embodiment of violence done by an 'other'" (p. 2). Following the lead of Hariman and Lucaites (2003), Yang (2011) concluded that the picture of Duc was "one of the defining images of the Vietnam War" (p. 2). Similarly, in an analysis of Chun Tae-il's death in 1970, Cho (2016) argued that self-immolation "is a form of public embodiment for those who have been marginalized and excluded from political participation" (p. 22). In an essay concerning Tibetan resistance rhetoric, Hartnett (2013) explained that politically powerless actors may employ extreme protest measures when denied access to more traditional communicative forms. Tibetans, he suggested, resorted to self-immolation as a form of "embodied testimony to the horror of living in occupied Tibet" (p. 301).

Although many are familiar with a few historic cases of self-immolation, more tend to ignore or remain silent about such acts. With estimates of incident numbers ranging from 800 to 3,000 since 1963, communities lack even a clear notion of the extent of the phenomenon (Biggs, 2005). Thus, the cases of self-immolators ignored, forgotten, or largely erased from public memory emerge as crucial sites of exploration. Morrison's case is of particular interest given his privilege as a white American male, who technically had many other protest options at his disposal. His act represents a significant divergence from many self-immolators, who, as summarized above, resorted to self-immolation due to a lack of rhetorical resources. In what follows, I build upon existing literature by using a framework of self-immolation as a quasi-logical comparative argument by sacrifice.

Self-immolation as Argument by Sacrifice

Morrison's self-immolation functions as an argument by sacrificial comparison in which he attempted to connect death in Vietnam with death in America. According to Perelman and Olbrechts-Tyteca (1969), an argument by comparison is one in which "several objects are considered in order to evaluate them through their relations to each other" (p. 242). Specifically, Morrison's protest called upon Americans to link their feelings over the death of an American in America to the deaths of those abroad. Thus, Morrison's death itself was one of his comparative terms. At a memorial service, a friend contextualized Morrison's comparison: "In a society where it is normal for human beings to drop bombs on human targets [...] Morrison was not normal. He said, 'Let it stop'" (quoted in Hendrickson, 1996, p. 224). Although Morrison's act was "not normal," his death had the potential to be understood in the scene of current events. Morrison, who was a staunch activist against the war, was seeking an adequate way to communicate his anguish over death in Vietnam, an issue he had been struggling over how to address "for weeks, even months" prior to his self-immolation (quoted in Welsh, 2008, p. 36).

Morrison's baby Emily, who was with him when he lit the match, served as another point of comparison. A friend of Morrison wrote, "Emily [is] symbolic of Vietnamese children. [Morrison likely hoped that] the Americans who felt revulsion at the idea she was endangered would look & [*sic*] feel differently at the news accounts of children napalmed in Vietnam" (quoted in Hendrickson, 1996, p. 211). As an adult, Emily herself noted the significance of her presence: "I feel Norman was intrinsically asking the question, How would you feel if this child were burned too? [....] perhaps he wanted us to question this horrifying possibility" (quoted in Welsh, 2008, p. 162). Furthermore, in a letter to his wife Anne delivered after his death, Morrison wrote, "I shall not plan to go without my child, as Abraham did. Know that I love thee but must act for the children of the Priest's village" (quoted in Welsh, 2008, p. 36). As a pacifist, Morrison's leap to violence was surprising. Although he ultimately did not sacrifice Emily, his initial recorded impulse suggests that Morrison viewed the suffering of those in Vietnam great enough to warrant such a sacrifice. Perelman and Olbrechts-Tyteca (1969) described this type of comparison as being rooted in "*loci* of order" in which the "superiority of the cause" appears to justify "the effects" (p. 93).

Due to its quasi-logical nature, the terms employed in an argument by sacrifice are in a constant state of negotiation. As Perelman and Olbrechts-Tyteca (1969) explained, "To measure something by sacrifice presupposes that there are constant elements placed in a quasi-logical framework, elements which are in fact subject to variation" (p. 250). Morrison's choice of self-immolation compounded the potential for variation by making his comparative terms less concrete, and thus more open to a broader interpretation. Furthermore, one of the confounding aspects of self-immolation as a deliberative form is that the act almost always results in death. In perhaps what is an ultimate declaration of agency over one's body, self-immolators surrender their agency as rhetorical actors. Unlike other rhetors who can refute counter-arguments or attempt to clarify their messages after the fact, a self-immolator depends upon the negotiated definitions of others. For Morrison, others chose to largely suppress his intended message.

American Rejection of Morrison's Sacrifice

Based on the various responses to Morrison, Perelman and Olbrechts-Tyteca (1969) might have categorized his action as a useless sacrifice, which they defined as "either unnecessary, because the circumstances do not require it, or ineffectual, because it would not really achieve the desired result" (p. 251). However, Morrison's detractors took this notion a step further. By reframing his terms and deeming his act useless, Morrison's critics characterized his death as being sacrificially vacant. In particular, many deemed Morrison's self-immolation as inappropriate and sinful (especially within American democratic society) and as the action of a madman.

One risk of argument by sacrifice is that if audiences see the offering as too great, backlash can result toward the rhetor (Pereleman & Olbrecht-Tyteca, 1969). Morrison certainly received harsh criticism for his methods. Some argued that democratic societies did not warrant such a tactic given the other forms of protest available. For example, in a *Washington Post* article ("Torch Suicides," 1965), the author reported, "The [nine] clergymen were unanimous in objecting to suicide, their remarks ranging from mere disapproval to strong condemnation" (p. B3). Reverend Birdwell was perhaps the harshest by describing the act as "utter despair or utter arrogance, or both. It is morally as indefensible as murder" (quoted in "Torch Suicides," 1965, p. B3). In a *Nashua Telegraph* piece ("To What Effective End," 1965), an editorialist also shared his disapproval: "The role of the living is to take part in the action [....] To choose death [....] is pathetic" (p. 4). Phil Newsom (1965), a United Press International Foreign News Analyst, commented, "Even death on a Vietnamese battlefield would seem to have been easier and to greater purpose" (p. 6). Newsom had sarcastically stumbled on the thread that strings together most American critiques of Morrison—the dichotomy between the inappropriateness of violence in Western, democratic countries versus its appropriate deployment in non-Western countries. Furthermore, these excerpts showed a rejection of Morrison's act as a sacrifice, reframing his self-immolation as "suicide" and "murder." Perelman and Olbrechts-Tyteca (1969) described critical responses to sacrifice as reactions to disproportionate comparative terms. However, in Morrison's case, such criticisms (which focused on his method rather than his message) also served their own argumentative purpose. Specifically, as ad hominem attacks on Morrison's credibility, they functioned to distract from the issue at hand and provided Americans a justification for ignoring Morrison's message regarding violence in Vietnam. Labeling Morrison's act as "futile" is self-fulfilling, since insisting on its futility (rather than revaluating foreign policy) begets its futility.

Another way many tried to invalidate Morrison's sacrifice was by labeling him psychologically unstable. Perelman and Olbrechts-Tyteca (1969) noted, "A grave objection can always be made to the argument by sacrifice" (p. 250) by questioning the rhetor's psychological motivations. Reporter Frank White (1965) wrote of Morrison, "Regardless of how he felt about the war, few Americans will disagree that for a man to commit suicide means he is mentally ill" (p. 2). In his article, "Suicide by Fire: Martyr or Madman," Glass (1965) compared Morrison's act to non-political suicides by fire such as that of Patricia Conway, who killed herself out of depression after losing her three-month-old baby. Glass further diminished Morrison's sacrifice by quoting a psychiatrist, Dr. Davis, who argued that "psychotic individual[s] will not respond to pain in the way you or I do" (quoted in Glass, 1965, p. 7A). By labeling Morrison insane, his critics de-politicized his action. Additionally, by stating that Morrison would not feel the same pain as a sane person, his detractors downplayed his physical suffering, thus lessening the intensity and sacrificial nature of his self-immolation. Unfortunately, because he died, Morrison could not prove his sanity or reframe the conversation.

One way to account for this characterization of Morrison may be the contextual factor of the public's lack of knowledge concerning America's involvement in Vietnam in 1965 due to governmental misdirection. For example, in a response to an attack on the Saigon embassy, President

Johnson spoke to the press on April Fool's Day telling them that "no far-reaching strategy [was] being suggested or promulgated" (Kendrick, 1974, p. 197). Government secrecy meant the public had little way to predict the number of people who would ultimately die in the war. In fact, not until the number of American troops climbed to nearly 400,000 in 1967 did the war really displace "all other political issues [...] in the concern of the public" (Viorst, 1979, p. 383). Thus, to most, Morrison's act was extremist. However, as noted in his wife's press statement, Morrison was attempting to draw attention to "human suffering caused by the war in Vietnam," not just the loss of American life. Therefore, if the described context serves as a rationale for the rejection of Morrison's sacrifice, then it reveals a prioritization of American life over others. By acknowledging the oppressive conditions in South Vietnam, many Americans were able to make sense of the self-immolations of Buddhist monks on Vietnamese soil (Halberstam, 1963). Yet, for an American to sacrifice himself on U.S. soil was untenable. Further, many could not comprehend risking an American baby's life to draw attention to the plight of foreign children.

Conclusion

This essay expands upon the literature concerning self-immolation as a form of embodied argument by analyzing the dominant themes that arose about Norman Morrison following his 1965 protest. Utilizing the framework that Perelman and Olbrechts-Tyteca (1969) provided, I illustrated how Morrison's act could have served as an argument by sacrifice but was, instead, reframed by many who, perhaps because they lacked any personal costs, were not ready to critically evaluate American foreign policy in Vietnam. My analysis extends Perelman and Olbrechts-Tyteca's idea of argument by sacrifice by illustrating that if comparative terms are deemed disproportionate, counter-narratives may develop to delegitimize the rhetor, potentially expunging the offering of the sacrifice. Thus, the public may not only deem the sacrifice "useless" but also non-existent. In this case, if Morrison's critics had evaluated the lives of those suffering in Vietnam as being worthy of great sacrifice, perhaps they would have been more sympathetic to his message. Instead, their characterizations stifled the deliberative potential of his body.

One of the most distressful implications of this analysis is the degree to which many Americans seemed to place a lower value on foreign lives than on American lives. Ultimately, as Perelman and Olbrechts-Tyteca (1969) pointed out, "In argumentation by sacrifice, the sacrifice is a measure of the value attributed to the thing for which the sacrifice is made" (p. 248). Perhaps unsurprisingly, Morrison's sacrifice moved many Vietnamese. Two days after his death, a North Vietnamese press agency wrote: "The noble self-immolation of Norman R. Morrison symbolizes the earnest aspirations of American youth and people who do not want to shed their blood for the interests of the United States warmongers" ("North Vietnamese Praise," 1965, p. 5). The North Vietnamese people honored Morrison's act by releasing a postage stamp of his face, marking a street in his name, and commissioning a famous poet to write a work titled "Emily, My Child." Following a visit to North Vietnam, British reporter James Cameron (1965) also noted the jubilant atmosphere:

> The immolation of Norman Morrison [...] was so electrifying to the Vietnamese that even now, weeks after his death, they are having public demonstrations in his honor [...] It is the case that Norman Morrison has gone into Vietnamese mythology. They consider that his gesture marks the total watershed of United States opinion. "Now, at last, the Americans will understand."
>
> *(p. 16)*

Of course, most Americans certainly did *not* understand.

References

Biggs, M. (2005). Dying without killing: Self-immolations, 1963–2002. In D. Gambetta (Ed.), *Making sense of suicide missions* (173–208). Oxford, United Kingdom: Oxford University Press.

Cameron, J. (1965, December 11). From Hanoi: Premier says "let U.S. go and the war is over." *The New York Times*, p. 16. Retrieved from http://newspapers.com

Cho, Y. C. (2016). The art of self-concretization as a necropolitical embodiment: The self-immolation of Chun Tae-il. *Quarterly Journal of Speech, 102*(1), 21–40. doi:10.1080/00335630.2015.1136073

DeLuca, K. (1999). Unruly arguments: The body rhetoric of Earth First!, ACT UP, and Queer Nation. *Argumentation and Advocacy, 36*(1), 9–21. Retrieved from ResearchGate.

Glass, I. (1965, December 5). Suicide by fire: Martyr or madman? *The Miami News*, p. 7A. Retrieved from http://newspapers.com

Halberstam, D. (1963, August 14). Another Buddhist immolates himself. *The New York Times*, p. 1. Retrieved from ProQuest Historical Newspapers, *The New York Times*.

Hariman, R., & Lucaites, J. L. (2003). Public identity and collective memory in U.S. iconic photography: The image of "accidental napalm." *Critical Studies in Media Communication, 20*(1), 35–66. doi:10.1080/0739318032000067074

Hartnett, S. J. (2013). "Tibet is burning:" Competing rhetorics of liberation, occupation, resistance, and paralysis on the roof of the world. *Quarterly Journal of Speech, 99*(3), 283–316. doi:10.1080/00335630.2013.806819

Hendrickson, P. (1996). *The living and the dead: Robert McNamara and five lives of a lost war.* New York, NY: Alfred A. Knopf.

Kendrick, A. (1974). *The wound within: America in the Vietnam years, 1945–1974.* Boston, MA: Little, Brown.

McNamara, R. S. (1995). *In retrospect: The tragedy and lessons of Vietnam.* New York, NY: Vintage Books.

Newsom, P. (1965, December 1). Red China misled over protests. *The Daily Times*, p. 6.

North Vietnamese Praise. (1965, November 4). *The New York Times*, p. 5. Retrieved from http://newspapers.com

Palczewski, C. H. (2011). When body argument becomes militant argument. In R. C. Rowland (Ed.), *Reasoned argument and social change* (pp. 379–386). Washington, DC: National Communication Association.

Perelman, Ch., & Olbrechts-Tyteca, L. (1969). *The new rhetoric: A treatise on argumentation.* Notre Dame, IN: University of Notre Dame Press.

To What Effective End ? (1965, November 10). *Nashua Telegraph*, p. 4. Retrieved from http://newspapers.com

Torch Suicides: Sinful at Worst, Futile at Best. (1965, November 15). *The Washington Post*, p. B3. Retrieved from ProQuest Historical Newspapers, *The Washington Post* (1877–1994).

Viorst, M. (1979). *Fire in the streets: America in the 1960's.* New York, NY: Simon & Schuster.

Watts, J. (2011). The rhetoric of sacrifice. In C. A. Eberhart (Ed.), *Ritual and metaphor: Sacrifice in the Bible* (pp. 3–16). Atlanta, GA: Society of Biblical Literature.

Welsh, A. M. (2008). *Held in the light: Norman Morrison's sacrifice for peace and his family's journey of healing.* Maryknoll, NY: Orbis Books.

White, F. W. (1965, November 9). The Hoosier day: Congressional jaunts. *The Call-Leader*, p. 2. Retrieved fromhttp://newspapers.com

Yang, M. M. (2011). Still burning: Self-immolation as photographic protest. *Quarterly Journal of Speech, 97*(1), 1–25. doi:10.1080/00335630.2010.536565

23

TIMESCAPE 9/11

Networked Memories

Jeremy David Johnson

Embodied experiences, networked mediation and remediation, and thorough argumentative processes constitute public memory. Memorials and museums provide arguments as to what and how individuals should remember. Electronic forms of memorialization have spurred insightful scholarly research seeking to characterize the argumentative dynamics of networked memory (e.g., Hartelius, 2010; Hess, 2007; Smith & McDonald, 2010). But as Gruber (2014) illustrated, embodied exhibition can productively incorporate digital memorials. Smith and McDonald (2010), for example, analyzed the interplay of blogs and the Arizona 9/11 Memorial, highlighting the internetworked natures of public deliberation and public memory. Indeed, the events of September 11, 2001 have provided ground for creating novel memory practices, such as *The September 11 Digital Archive*, "a comprehensive online effort to document public involvement in commemorating the tragedy of 11 September, 2001" (Haskins, 2007, p. 402).

Perhaps fitting, then, is that the foundation of the National September 11 Memorial and Museum (NSMM) is a physical-digital hybrid model of memorialization. One of NSMM's specific exhibits, *Timescape*, features networks as the primary mode for remembering the events of 9/11. Built on the design of Mark Hansen, Ben Rubin, and Jer Thorp, *Timescape* is an electronic display of news stories pertaining to 9/11. A plaque explaining the exhibit reads, "*Timescape* uses a computer algorithm that searches a continually growing database of millions of news articles for combinations of key terms that frequently appear with references to 9/11, September 11th, September 11, 2001, the World Trade Center attacks, and the like" (Hansen, Rubin, & Thorp, 2014). *Timescape* generates an ever-evolving network map, connecting items in groups of three, such as "Afghanistan/Pakistan/Osama bin Laden." The exhibit then displays news stories describing those events. Alice Greenwald, director of the 9/11 museum, heralded *Timescape* as a complete escape from human subjectivity, insisting that "there's a kind of objectivity to that that [*sic*] you don't have in a more subjective, organized, curated environment" (Shahani, 2014, para. 12). In Greenwald's statement and in the structure of the exhibit, the argumentative force of objectivity emerges from mapping the network.

Timescape, I argue, centers the network as a medium for argument. Instead of leveraging networks to make an argument, *the network itself becomes the argument*. As Rickert (2013) revealed, "Networks are not a structural epiphenomenon but an ontological way of being-in-relation-and-movement and hence come to have descriptive power for everything that is" (Rickert, 2013, p. 102). Galloway and Thacker (2007) added, "The idea of connectivity is so highly privileged today that it is becoming more and more difficult to locate places or objects that don't, in some way, fit into a networking rubric" (p. 26). The argumentative force of the network is one of being, crafting a notion of reality predicated on connecting and moving nodes. That is to say, audiences understand the networked as real. The connection to public memory, then, is an argument of incorporating a purportedly real past into collective recall. In the remainder of this essay, I consider how *Timescape* stitches together its network of news stories to leverage arguments about the events following September 11. By analyzing *Timescape's* network maps in the exhibit's ecological context, I contend that the argumentative force of the network is paramount in understanding contemporary public memory practices.

An Embodied, Ecological Argument

The weight of the argument is only possible in the embodied ecology of NSMM. Over the last few decades, "argumentation theory has reinvigorated the study of argumentation and advocacy in verbal, visual, embodied, and multimodal forms" (Groarke, Palczewski, & Godden, 2016, p. 217). To that end, I will linger on the multimodal ecology of the NSMM. I visited the museum with an admittedly pre-determined mindset—that memorials, monuments, and museums are profoundly rhetorical. I stepped into Ground Zero as a rhetorical critic. Despite my confirmation bias, I could not help but feel I was taking part in a communal, rhetorical ritual. The memorial's massive scale is, without a doubt, meant to convey the magnitude of the losses of September 11, 2001. As soon as I crossed West Street, the memorial implicitly asked me to contemplate those lives and the destruction caused when the towers fell. In this way *Timescape* is not understandable outside of its context, its meaning wrapped up in the twisted metal and crumbling concrete burrowed beneath the Manhattan soil.

The NSMM is "meaningful as one of the constitutive elements of a larger landscape" (Dickinson, Ott, & Aoki, 2006, p. 41). It offers "a constitutive rhetoric that offers visitors an identity through which they perceive not only the museum exhibits but also the larger world outside the museum" (Lynch, 2013, p. 6). Entering the memorial grounds, one confronts two large memorial fountains shining prominently. One World Trade Center looms over the reflecting pools, giving a ghostly presence to the heights that these towers once reached. The pools flow downward into a smaller square hole, the bottom of which is unseeable. In the face of One World Trade Center (and in contrast to what once was), the reflecting pools serve as reminders of the depths from which New Yorkers and other U.S. citizens rose after September 11. Brushed bronze squares surround an enormous waterfall in place of each tower that once stood there. Almost 3,000 names appear etched into the bronze, some adorned with white flowers visitors placed in memory of loved ones who perished. One sign implores, "Please be reminded that the 9/11 Memorial is a place of remembrance and quiet reflection." Meshed with the sounds of the waterfalls are screeches, car horns, and the rumble of construction vehicles, the memorial is a reminder that this tranquility exists in the cacophony of New York City. The memorial is as much a part of New York as it is an American experience.

After waiting in line and proceeding through security similar to a TSA checkpoint, the museum funnels visitors into its main body. The ground floor includes entry and exit points, with a large ceiling and open glass windows. The second floor sports a café and a small theater. Museumgoers plunge from the brightness of the outside world into an incomplete, but unmistakable, darkness. At the bottom of the stairs are desks for coat checks and information. The entryway next funnels visitors into a small hallway with electronic images displayed on pillars via projector. Audio interviews play back reflections of victims' friends, families, and others the events of September 11 affected, with some of their images displayed on the columns. Continued descent through the darkness might produce, as it did in me, a visceral response; to those who remember the events of 9/11, the dark decline is but a small reminder of the terror of that day. This museum "'teaches' experientially," taking the visitor down a path that is "dark, crowded, and confusing" (Blair, 2001, p. 286). The entranceway communicates visually and spatially the fear, anxiety, and despair of September 11 as visitors shuffle toward the center of the museum.

When the darkness suddenly gives way to an enormous and bright underground chamber, a balcony allows visitors to view a significant portion of the base floor, with benches, bits of wreckage, and the reinforced concrete walls that once rested on the outside of one of the World Trade Center towers. Upon the tremendous concrete wall positioned quite a distance away (perhaps 300 feet) glows a projected electronic display. Three dark screens project upon the wall with white text, giving life to *Timescape* among the cold, gray concrete. *Timescape* asks viewers to accept the projected reality of its network maps, amid the chilling reality of the remains of the World Trade Center.

Network as Objective Force

New forms and modes of argumentation have spurred new research into argumentation and digital culture; "the emergence, perpetuation, and success of arguments in public discourse are indeed changing in the new media environment" (Smith & McDonald, 2010, p. 137). Digital forms of communication have become pervasive, with people "[living] in a reality that is not merely visually permeated—it is visually mediated" (Groarke et al., 2016, p. 233). Memorials like the NSMM are sensory experiences, with visual elements and spatial arrangements functioning as much of the argumentative content. Memorials make arguments about history and public memory through embodied procedures tied to extant knowledge and memories.

Timescape's visual product is relatively simple. The projectors display timelines in light text on dark backgrounds. The algorithm selects three words related to September 11, groups news articles by those terms, and limits its display to around ten articles at a time. As *Timescape* shifts between groupings, word clouds emerge. The live network map reinforces that "networks are only networks when they are 'live,' when they are enacted, embodied, or rendered operational" (Galloway & Thacker, 2007, p. 62). The algorithm continually traces relationships among news articles based on key terms. Selected terms almost always appear related at first glance. As a result, the timeline presents a neat and tidy chronology of how the terms map together.

Timescape's rhetorical act is stitching together news articles, which reflect the writers' attitudes and subject positions. The words clustered together evidence a common goal in post-9/11 reporting: to assign blame. In my visit, nearly every story on the timeline focused on foreign actors, often pegged as extremists or terrorists. For example, "Khalid Sheikh Mohammed," "Zacarias Moussaoui," and "Captured" grouped together with news stories such as "Suspected Sept. 11 mastermind was uncle of 1993 World Trade Center plotter" and "Pakistan arrests six terror suspects, including planner of Sept. 11 and USS Cole bombing." In another example, the algorithm grouped "Malaysia," "Indonesia," and "Philippines" with entries concerning "Muslim extremists" and "Islamic terrorists." The related terms are often familiar clusters of events from the post-9/11 world, allowing visitors to recall their personal experiences and to discover more specific connections among the stories displayed.

Digital imagery represents the network, constantly changing and forging new connections. Building on the dynamics of visual culture, *Timescape* renders events into data points and filters the data into coherent connections. Referencing visual culture broadly, Chun (2016) explained, "if earlier visual indexicality guaranteed authenticity (a photograph was real because it indexed something out there), now 'real time' does so, for 'real time' points elsewhere: to 'real-world' events, to the user's captured actions" (p. 75). Networks "render time into space—they spatialize the temporal" (Chun, 2016, p. 50). *Timescape's* portrayal of events—though not perfectly indexical to "real time"—provides access to an unfolding series of relationships. "What is real is what unfolds in 'real time'" (Chun, 2016, p. 75), meaning that *Timescape* leverages the visual force of reality.

The argument *Timescape* advances—that visitors can understand reality through the algorithmic lens of the network—nonetheless emerges from human data points. *Timescape* surveys human-authored, news articles. These English-language stories, likely only usable through copyright agreements with institutions such as *Lexis Nexis*, signal journalists' concerns of blame and agency, with no more claim to an objective past than any individual human. The stories reflect journalistic biases and tendencies, particularly in their attempts to assign blame. The stories may also reflect government priorities, particularly since the Bush administration used the press to cover its post-9/11 policies (John, Domke, Coe, & Graham, 2007). Conversely, they do not necessarily reflect the memories of victims or average citizens. As an amalgamation of journalistic voices, the exhibit highlights a narrow slice of socially constructed history—a history still being written today.

At its core, *Timescape* is narrativizing data, creating a story out of millions of news articles. But even the exhibit's creators are indecisive regarding how this narrative functions. Designer Jake Barton claimed in one interview: "This piece isn't necessarily trying to write a historic narrative. What it's trying to do is chart the impact of 9/11 on our world in a variety of places" (quoted in Shahani, 2014, para. 6). At the same time, he also proclaimed that the challenge in creating the display was "to make things graspable and to tell an engaging, meaningful story" (quoted in Ferro, 2014, para. 5). Certain narratives have rhetorical power, particularly when they define a people's past. The visual narratives of *Timescape* join individual data points with collective relations to render a networked reality of public memory, in ways that Chun (2016) described as encapsulating "neoliberal collectivity" (p. 39) and replacing "postmodern relativism with data analytics" (p. 40).

Timescape stands as a potentially powerful memory device. Like Haskins' (2007) analysis of vernacular archives, the exhibit "collapses the assumed distinction between modern 'archival' memory and traditional 'lived' memory by combining the function of storage and ordering on the one hand, and of presence and interactivity on the other" (p. 401). By providing interactivity, many electronic memory archives make audiences part of the memory-making process. Intriguingly, however, *Timescape* subverts Haskins' "hegemonic official memory" (p. 403) in a different way. Rather than moving toward a vernacular model of remembrance—a project surely possible through interaction and participation even in the confines of the museum—the exhibit defers to the authority of the algorithm. This is a peculiar compromise in that curators maintain control of the exhibit, but they are not exclusively responsible for its content. *Timescape* bolsters its claims to objectivity by moving from human to algorithm, resting power in the mathematical operations of a machine. The algorithm can map the network, represent reality, and establish a "real" past for audiences to remember.

Timescape serves a vital rhetorical function in making sense of a complex and ever-changing world of politics, culture, and current events. On the plaque explaining the exhibit reads an intriguing thought: *Timescape* displays "a galaxy of associated terms radiating out from that one event [9/11]" (Hansen et al., 2014). The use of "galaxy" could be coincidental, but the term has powerful connotations. Much like the seeming entropy of the cosmos, networks of human events seem chaotic—at least until a constant arrives to create order and make sense of the universe. For the designers of *Timescape*, the events of September 11 represent the center of that universe, the myths surrounding that event give shape to the world after 9/11, and *Timescape* provides order. The map "alters our sense of spatial structure by transforming space into digital information, and, in turn, by making digital information public imagery" (Rice, 2012, p. 16). *Timescape's* every line of code writes the networked human memory and displays, in every node, the public world unfurling through it.

Conclusion

Timescape offers a conception of memory based on "real" events of the past. The exhibit does so "objectively," by using an algorithm to map networks onto human events. It links its mapping to a galaxy, an extra-human spatialization of memory. Its "code is *logos*" (Chun, 2016, p. 70), reasoning via algorithmic filtering. The network, so conceptualized, carries the force of truth; it is through the medium of the network, itself remediated by digital displays, that an argument about the past forms. In short, the memorial connects things, renders such connections objectively real, and thus, presents a real past that audiences should remember.

As part of the NSSM, *Timescape* is a fascinating artifact. The museum provides an affective experience perhaps not possible without visiting its physical location. *Timescape* has brought the electronic interface to this embodied ecology, fulfilling Ulmer's (2005) call for joining electracy and collective identity (p. xxi). Operating within a limited database and network, *Timescape* puts memory in extra-human scale. Part of the larger NSMM environment, *Timescape* reflects our tendency to call upon technology to fill gaps in human subjectivity. Given that electronic forms of memorialization only seem to be growing, exhibits like *Timescape* may well be the way of the future. If such trends continue, argumentation scholars would do well to investigate, scrutinize, and interrogate the use of algorithms and other networked memorial practices.

Networked memory is not new, but the potential power embodied in the algorithmic network maps of *Timescape* is extraordinary, highlighting the need to understand argumentation and rhetoric as networked practices. As Rickert (2013) explained, "If networks are not just a technological infrastructure but also a fundamental organizational dynamic tied to being itself, then we must see rhetoric as a networked practice, even if this has not been clear to us before" (p. 102). *Timescape* etches new nodes into memory by networking visitors with the physical space of the museum and with its digital galaxy of events. It asserts this networked argument in both algorithmic bits and bytes and in the ballast of the fallen World Trade Center, tying together humans, machines, and the rubble of our past.

References

Blair, C. (2001). Reflections on criticism and bodies: Parables from public places. *Western Journal of Communication, 65*(3), 271–294. doi:10.1080/10570310109374706

Chun, W. H. K. (2016). *Updating to remain the same: Habitual new media.* Cambridge, MA: The MIT Press.

Dickinson, G., Ott, B. L., & Aoki, E. (2006). Spaces of remembering and forgetting: The reverent eye/I at the Plains Indian Museum. *Communication and Critical/Cultural Studies, 3*(1), 27–47. doi:10.1080/14791420500505619

Ferro, S. (2014, May 14). New museum uses algorithms to visualize how 9/11 still shapes the world. *Fastco Design*. Retrieved from http://fastcodesign.com/3030603/new-museum-uses-algorithms-to-visualize-how-9-11-still-shapes-the-world

Galloway, A. R., & Thacker, E. (2007). *The exploit: A theory of networks*. Minneapolis, MN: University of Minnesota Press.

Groarke, L., Palczewski, C. H., & Godden, D. (2016). Navigating the visual turn in argument [Special issue]. *Argumentation and Advocacy*, *52*(4), 217–235. Retrieved from http://tandfonline.com

Gruber, D. R. (2014). The (digital) majesty of all under heaven: Affective constitutive rhetoric at the Hong Kong Museum of History's multi-media exhibition of terracotta warriors. *Rhetoric Society Quarterly*, *44*(2), 148-167. doi:10.1080/02773945.2014.888462

Hansen, M., Rubin, B., & Thorp, J. (2014). *Timescape* [Visualization]. New York, NY: National September 11 Memorial Museum.

Hartelius, E. J. (2010). "Leave a message of hope or tribute": Digital memorializing as public deliberation. *Argumentation and Advocacy*, *47*(2), 67-85. Retrieved from http://tandfonline.com

Haskins, E. (2007). Between archive and participation: Public memory in a digital age. *Rhetoric Society Quarterly*, *37*(4), 401-422. doi:10.1080/02773940601086794

Hess, A. (2007). In digital remembrance: Vernacular memory and the rhetorical construction of web memorials. *Media, Culture & Society*, *29*(5), 812–830. doi:10.1177/0163443707080539

John, S. L., Domke, D., Coe, K., & Graham, E. S. (2007). Going public, crisis after crisis: The Bush Administration and the press from September 11 to Saddam. *Rhetoric & Public Affairs*, *10*(2), 195-220. doi:10.1353/rap.2007.0039

Lynch, J. (2013). "Prepare to believe": The Creation Museum as embodied conversion narrative. *Rhetoric & Public Affairs*, *16*(1), 1-28. doi:10.14321/rhetpublaffa.16.1.0001

Rice, J. (2012). *Digital Detroit: Rhetoric and space in the age of the network*. Carbondale, IL: Southern Illinois University Press.

Rickert, T. J. (2013). *Ambient rhetoric: the attunements of rhetorical being*. Pittsburgh, PA: University of Pittsburgh Press.

Shahani, A. (2014, June 30). An algorithm is a curator at the Sept. 11 Museum. *NPR*. Retrieved from http://npr.org

Smith, C. M., & McDonald, K. M. (2010). The Arizona 9/11 Memorial: A case study in public dissent and argumentation through blogs [Special issue]. *Argumentation and Advocacy*, *47*(2), 123-139. Retrieved from http://tandfonline.com

Ulmer, G. L. (2005). *Electronic monuments*. Minneapolis, MN: University of Minnesota Press.

24

ANALOGY AND ARGUMENT IN THE RHETORIC OF SCIENCE

Jay Frank

The very idea of a rhetoric of science seems contradictory. Scientists rarely train in rhetoric, and few of them would claim Gorgias or Isocrates as a part of their intellectual lineage. Even Aristotle (trans. 2007) reminded readers, "We debate about things that seem capable of admitting two possibilities" (1357a2-3) rather than the cold exactness of science. On what grounds, then, can argumentation scholars constitute a rhetoric of science (hereafter RS)? Such a question is cause for considerable anxiety. Indeed, scholars from Plato to Gaonkar considered rhetoric's epistemic value a source of consternation. Gaonkar (1997) particularly suggested that RS is made possible through a "globalization" (p. 31) of rhetoric itself—that is, through a "hermeneutic" (p. 25) redeployment of rhetoric's ancient pedagogical vocabulary.

But contemporary literature in RS is quite different than what Gaonkar encountered some decades ago. The former is no longer so easily reducible to a hermeneutic metadiscourse, since its practical activities are now every bit as pedagogical as they are critical (Ceccarelli, 2011). They are just as much about the *production* of science as they are about its *interpretation* (Herndl, 2017). Perhaps the most remarkable feature of this transformation, however, is that contemporary scholars of RS have kept rhetoric's hermeneutic tradition alive at the same time as they have shifted its cultural and political implications. Drawing on the work of scholars in science and technology studies and, in particular, the methodological implications of Collins and Evans's (2002) seminal essay, "The Third Wave of Science Studies," Herndl (2017) suggested that scholars of RS have begun to redeploy their interpretive insights "upstream" (p. 3) of scientific production. The result is a new wave of engaged RS scholarship wherein rhetoric demonstrates its epistemic value by playing a direct role in the production of scientific knowledge and in the processes of scientific discovery.

RS has thus ostensibly outgrown its former anxieties. It has learned to cope with Gaonkar's critique, to rehabilitate its hermeneutic project, and put it to good use. Nevertheless, the latter remains something of a "sore subject" (Ceccarelli, 2014, p. 2). Leah Ceccarelli (2014), for example, worried that the embedded nature of contemporary RS scholarship—which often puts scholars of rhetoric in scientific settings they have long considered "hostile territory"—

has led its practitioners to downplay their reliance on the ancient vocabulary (and, subsequently, to put in jeopardy their distinction from other "embedded" experts). But scholars of RS are still prone to identify themselves as rhetoricians. Likewise, they are still prone to identify their methods as rhetorical, even when that means modifying or, perhaps, silently deploying the hermeneutic powers of rhetoric's ancient vocabulary. What distinguishes the latest iteration of rhetoric's cultural deployment—that is, the latest manifestation of RS—from its predecessors is thus something greater than an idea of rhetoric. Indeed, the difference may have more to do with the scientific contexts that deploy rhetoric and its uses.

A necessary supplement to Gaonkar's now famous account of the nature of rhetoric in RS is therefore an account of the ways that RS organizes and is organized around a set of ideas about science. This paper offers the beginnings of such an account, and it does so in two ways. First, it outlines the shape and direction of RS's break from what Gaonkar might have called a colonial analogy for the relationship between rhetoric and science. In doing so, it argues that the primary difference between RS's contemporary idea of science and its predecessors is that scholars of rhetoric have begun to describe science in terms of its differences from public life. Second, this paper outlines how a particular line of thinking borrowed from the discipline of argumentation studies facilitates such descriptions. In particular, it demonstrates how G. Thomas Goodnight's (2012) landmark essay, first published in 1982, on the personal, technical, and public spheres of argument makes possible a new analogy for the relationship between rhetoric and science. Last, it suggests that this new analogy enjoins contemporary scholars of RS to think through a politics of difference rather than through a politics of assimilation, and subsequently to reconceive of rhetoric in RS (and, by extension, the turn toward "engagement") through a network metaphor that likens RS itself to what Damien Pfister (2014) called a "translation station" (p. 136).

The Polis and the Colony

The beginnings of the idea of science in RS were already implicit in Gaonkar's work. Indeed, he wrote that science became susceptible to rhetorical (re)description only once rhetoric underwent a series of transformations. A first step in that series was the translation of the *rhetorica docens*—the theoretical vocabulary present in the handbooks of ancient Athens and Rome. But rhetoric's ancient vocabulary was also closely linked to a specific "realm of appearances"—to a "'public sphere' as the Greeks understood it" (Gaonkar, 1997, p. 30). The theoretical globalization of rhetoric in RS thus required an analogy wherein a given scientific community resembled a Greek (or Roman) polis, namely, the appearance of rhetoric.

Gaonkar (1997) worried that the *rhetorica docens* was stretched dangerously "thin" (p. 33) by that analogy. "Between precept and performance," he wrote, "there is talent and practice, the regimen of the body" (pp. 33–34). In order to make the analogy work, then, the *rhetorica utens*—both the living practice of rhetoric and the privileged relationship it maintained with the *rhetorica docens* of the ancient world—needed forgetting. In order to notice that scientists "do rhetoric," in other words, scholars of RS had to ignore that scientists are rarely masters of the art. But once they took this step, scholars of RS began to see scientific discourse more or less like they saw public discourse, with the result that they believed they could seamlessly apply the tools of analysis for the latter to the former (Ceccarelli, 2001).

Yet, as Ceccarelli (2001) wrote, a difference exists between the potential and actual applications of rhetoric's interpretive vocabulary to scientific discourse. A second step in the transformation of rhetoric in RS is thus the actual application of the analogy between the polis and the scientific community. Gaonkar (1997) subsequently worried, "In order to disclose its presence" (p. 36) in places where it is hardly *practiced* (let alone recognized), rhetoric must carry out that application through a "politics of recognition" (p. 36). But just what is a politics of recognition? Or, rather, who are its key figures? What positions do they occupy? And what are the stakes of their interaction? On these questions Gaonkar said a great deal in a few precious words. "The very idea" of RS, he wrote, "suggests that we are now turning our attention to the furthest outpost in rhetoric's quest for universal hegemony. Thus, we might here observe the perils and possibilities of globalization under conditions of determined resistance" (p. 36). Gaonkar was undoubtedly referring (at least) to rhetoric's theoretical globalization. Given his care in documenting rhetoric's transformation into an interpretive discourse designed to make science lose "all of its recalcitrance and become transparent" (Gaonkar, 1997, p. 25), he clearly thought that science offers up forms of resistance.

Yet Gaonkar's insight here is that the cultural practice of scientists (and not just the "recalcitrance" of science itself) resists the interpretive capacities of RS. To notice the "double transformation" of rhetoric in RS is therefore to notice the double meaning of the word "globalization" in Gaonkar's account. One view focuses on devising a system of interpretation. The other is something else entirely, that is, "to dismantle the entire scientific culture by showing that it is in fact a self-deluded copy" (McGuire & Melia, 1989, p. 90) of an ancient rhetorical culture. McGuire and Melia (1989) wrote, "This is like describing native magic as bad science, or the clearing between grass huts in terms of the playing fields of Eton—imperialistic and to some extent impertinent" (p. 90). They added that RS performs (or at least mimics) the broader cultural practices associated with Western colonization by conducting the "original sin of anthropology" (p. 90). Here, Gaonkar's (1997) use of the word "hegemony" (p. 36) and his description of science as a remote "outpost" (p. 36) are of particular significance: What characterizes rhetoric in RS is not simply its emergence as a "hermeneutic metadiscourse" (p. 25), but also its deployment of a colonial analogy that prepares scholars of rhetoric to enter foreign communities and engage in translation processes that subordinate the political life of those communities to the rhetorical tradition.

But RS is changing. A key feature of this change—and, moreover, the ways that it has resulted in the redeployment of rhetoric's ancient vocabulary as *both* a hermeneutic and a pedagogical tool—is the idea that scientific communities are distinct from rhetorical (less specialized and more broadly "public") communities. As a result, drawing analogies with their communicative practices is not easy. And with such a distinction in mind, new questions arise: How do scientists and lay citizens interact, and what are the stakes of their interaction? What role does rhetoric play in mediating, facilitating, or even judging these interactions, and what are the stakes of *its* involvement? To better answer these questions, scholars of rhetoric are spending less and less time making the "hard case" (Ceccarelli, 2001, p. 315) that science itself is rhetorical. They are, instead, growing more concerned with the nature of citizen participation in scientific processes (Druschke, 2013; Endres, 2009) or with the role of science in legal and political settings (Ceccarelli, 2011; Crick & Gabriel, 2010; Keränen, 2005; Paliewicz, 2012; Paroske, 2009; Von Burg, 2017). And they are also beginning to understand both themselves and scientists (Besel, 2011; Pfister, 2014) as intermediaries in a vast communicative network that links two spheres of argument, and subsequently, demands interdisciplinary practices that reconfigure the production of scientific knowledge itself around the inclusion of rhetorical practices (Ceccarelli, 2011; Wilson & Herndl, 2007).

175

Networked Metaphor and the Politics of Difference

RS did not come by its recent emphasis on the difference between rhetorical and scientific communities haphazardly. Indeed, it emphasizes the different "forms of reason" (Goodnight, 2012, p. 202) that distinguish scientific and rhetorical communities, as well as the political implications of those forms. Goodnight's (2012) account of argument spheres and their relations thus deeply informs the contemporary idea of science in RS. For Goodnight (2012), persuasive and deliberative processes did not take place across a uniform social terrain, but rather in, across, and between a variety of distinct channels. "In the democratic tradition," he wrote, "we can categorize these channels as the personal, the technical, and the public spheres. 'Sphere' denotes branches of activity—the grounds upon which arguments are built and the authority to which arguers appeal" (p. 200).

Technical spheres of argument were, according to Goodnight (2012), most often organized around certain forms of expertise. Expertise, in turn, came with a set of "formal expectations of scholarly argument (footnotes, titles, organization, documentation, and so forth)," and the judgment of "referees" that shared the expertise of a given debate's participants (p. 202). A public sphere of argument, by contrast, is greater in scope than its technical counterpart. It does not limit its inclusion to experts. Insofar as it "must encompass its sub-sets," Goodnight explained that "the forms of reason" in a public sphere of argument must be "more common than the specialized demands of a particular professional community" (p. 202). What is remarkable about this argument is that it affords both rhetoric and science the cultural imagery they have built for themselves: Science can function as a discourse of a specialized subculture, while rhetoric can function as the discourse of a mass culture (and perhaps even a general or "governing" hermeneutic).

At the same time, Goodnight (2012) refused to rely on the similarities between public and technical spheres of argument (or, alternatively, between rhetoric and science) to describe the ways that they influenced each other. He worried, for example, that the technical sphere of argument was increasingly dominating state governance. For him, the result of an ever more technical form of deliberation was the gradual disappearance of the public sphere of argument from democracy. Indeed, he wrote,

> Issues of significant public consequence, what should present live possibilities for argumentation and public choice, disappear into the government technocracy or private hands [....] Questions of public significance themselves become increasingly difficult to recognize, much less address, because of the intricate rules, procedures, and terminologies of the specialized forums.
>
> *(p. 206)*

Goodnight largely built his concept of an argument sphere, then, on his analysis of the political relationship between expert and lay cultures. As a result, his conception relied on an assumption about the nature and value of democratic deliberation—specifically, that the latter should be more broadly accessible than the deliberative processes of specialized technical communities. Contemporary RS likewise has no interest in the cultural colonization of science. As a means of analyzing the relations between argument spheres, RS values a politics of difference (and, in turn, the cultural distinction between public and scientific forums) rather than a politics of assimilation.

This distinction has renewed the anxiety over RS's relevance. Indeed, if Gaonkar's RS found its place through a double process of globalization (all the while revealing its anxieties about its epistemic value), the "engaged" RS that Goodnight's spheres of argument inform resides between two worlds. Ceccarelli (2014) summed this concern nicely:

> Jamie L. Vernon, a scientist who served as my fellow respondent to the papers on collaborative research, told us that he finds our work valuable because he believes that we (a bunch of scholars of the humanities) are fulfilling the call of the National Academy of Science for work on the *science* of science communication.
>
> *(p. 2)*

This problem becomes more complicated insofar as the affinity between government and technical expertise constantly intertwines scientific and public deliberations as "public scientific controversies" (Crick & Gabriel, 2010, p. 203). Communicative norms that do not perfectly resemble either a scientific community or a deliberative democracy often characterize these public scientific controversies. Moreover, the rise of mass media (particularly the internet) has resulted in the proliferation of deliberative forums not easily categorized as either "technical" or "public" spheres of argument, as new communicative technologies emphasize soundbites or "shallow quotations" (Pfister, 2014, p. 136). RS thus faces what Pfister called a "deliberative trap" (p. 136) that works through the difference between public and technical spheres of argument at the same time as social factors intertwine and distort them. Indeed, scientists often struggle to clearly communicate the political implications of their findings. And even when scientists are clear, the differences between the public and technical spheres of argument create difficulties. Ceccarelli (2011), moreover, suggested that the interactions between the public and technical spheres of argument are not reducible to a gap in expertise. Differences in communicative norms often allow arguers to distort scientific discourse as it moves in and through the public sphere. The result becomes difficulties in resolving public problems linked to scientific knowledge.

Contemporary scholars of RS thus demonstrate their ideas of science by contributing to scientific discourse in political (rather than merely epistemic) ways. Often this means providing training or assistance to scientists and stakeholders as they navigate the interaction between public and technical spheres of argument. My point is that a *discursive* shift accompanies this practical shift. RS has begun to imagine science as a culture in need of translators. It has, in turn, begun to imagine *scientists* as those translators. Further still, it imagines their translations to be particularly ineffective in an increasingly networked society. RS's newfound focus on "participation," then, accompanies a particular discursive representation of scientific culture.

References

Aristotle. (2007). *On rhetoric: A theory of civic discourse* (G. A. Kennedy, Trans.) (2nd ed.). Oxford, United Kingdom: Oxford University Press.

Besel, R. D. (2011). Opening the "black box" of climate change science: Actor-network theory and rhetorical practice in scientific controversies. *Southern Communication Journal, 76*(2), 120–136. doi:10.1080/10417941003642403

Ceccarelli, L. (2001). Rhetorical criticism and the rhetoric of science. *Western Journal of Communication, 65*(3), 314–329. doi:10.1080/10570310109374708

Ceccarelli, L. (2011). Manufactured scientific controversy: Science, rhetoric, and public debate. *Rhetoric and Public Affairs, 14*(2), 195–228. doi:10.1353/rap.2010.0222

Ceccarelli, L. (2014). Where's the rhetoric? Broader impacts in collaborative research. *Poroi, 10* (1):Article 12. doi:10.13008/2151-2957.1182

Collins, H. M., & Evans, R. (2002). The third wave of scientific studies: Studies of expertise and experience. *Social Studies of Science, 32*(2), 235–296. doi:10.1177/0306312702032002003

Crick, N., & Gabriel, J. (2010). The conduit between lifeworld and system: Habermas and the rhetoric of public scientific controversies. *Rhetoric Society Quarterly, 40*(3), 201–223. doi:10.1080/02773941003614464

Druschke, C. G. (2013). Watershed as common-place: Communicating for conservation at the watershed scale. *Environmental Communication, 7*(1), 80–96. doi:10.1080/17524032.2012.749295

Endres, D. (2009). Science and public participation: An analysis of public scientific argument in the Yucca Mountain controversy. *Environmental Communication, 3*(1), 49–75. doi:10.1080/17524030802704369

Gaonkar, D. P. (1997). The idea of rhetoric in the rhetoric of science. In A. G. Gross & W. M. Keith (Eds.), *Rhetorical hermeneutics: Invention and interpretation in the age of science* (pp. 25–85). Albany, NY: SUNY Press.

Goodnight, G. T. (2012). The personal, technical, and public spheres of argument: A speculative inquiry into the art of public deliberation [Special issue]. *Argumentation and Advocacy, 48*(4), 198–210. Retrieved from http://tandfonline.com

Herndl, C. G. (2017). Introduction to the symposium on engaged rhetoric of science, technology, engineering, and medicine. *Poroi, 12* (2):Article 2. doi:10.13008/2151-2957.1259

Keränen, L. (2005). Mapping misconduct: Demarcating legitimate science from "fraud" in the B-06 lumpectomy controversy. *Argumentation and Advocacy, 42*(2), 94–113. Retrieved from http://tandfonline.com

McGuire, J. E., & Melia, T. (1989). Some cautionary strictures on the writing of the rhetoric of science. *Rhetorica: A Journal of the History of Rhetoric, 7*(1), 87–99. doi:10.1525/rh.1989.7.1.87

Paliewicz, N. S. (2012). Global warming and the interaction between the public and technical spheres of argument: When standards for expertise really matter [Special issue]. *Argumentation and Advocacy, 48*(4), 231–242. Retrieved from http://tandfonline.com

Paroske, M. (2009). Deliberating international science policy controversies: Uncertainty and AIDS in South Africa. *Quarterly Journal of Speech, 95*(2), 148–170. doi:10.1080/00335630902842053

Pfister, D. S. (2014). *Networked media, networked rhetorics: Attention and deliberation in the early blogosphere.* University Park, PA: The Pennsylvania State University Press

Von Burg, R. (2017). The Supreme Court cleans the air: Legal and scientific standards for argument in *Massachusetts v. EPA. Argumentation and Advocacy, 53*(1), 41–58. doi:10.1080/00028533.2016.1272898

Wilson, G., & Herndl, C. G. (2007). Boundary objects as rhetorical exigence: Knowledge mapping and interdisciplinary cooperation at the Los Alamos National Laboratory. *Journal of Business and Technical Communication, 21*(2), 129–154. doi:10.1177/1050651906297164

25

SPECIFICATION, DISSOCIATION, AND VOTING RIGHTS IN THE UNITED STATES

James Jasinski

In a review of voting rights litigation in the mid-1990s, Averill (1995) noted, "In the generations since our nation's birth, courts and legislative bodies have labored to define the right to vote and divine what that right requires in the treatment of the individual citizen" (p. 1949). I draw attention to this passage not for its uniqueness, but because it nicely adumbrates a commonplace narrative about voting rights in the United States. Numerous scholars have chronicled the gradual, highly contentious expansion and the occasional contraction of voting rights (e.g., Keyssar, 2009; Waldman, 2016). But these sweeping chronicles, and the myriad monographs devoted to specific cases on which they draw, rarely examined the specific argumentative dynamics that define and divine the right to vote, as Averill suggested. This paper represents an initial effort to unpack those dynamics.

The next section briefly explains the concept of specification that, while prominent in contemporary bioethics, emerged in the context of the late twentieth-century revival of Aristotelian ethics. Consistent with this literature, I argue that the right to vote is not so much defined as it is specified and, consistent with the Aristotelian roots of the concept, the specification process exists in and emerges through the deliberative practices in particular legal cases. The third section will examine specific cases that specify the right to vote, illustrating the way deliberative specification of the right frequently arises through dissociative argument. Dissociation, I hope to show, is critical to one important line of legal cases that specify the right to vote.

Before proceeding, I need to digress briefly on textual sources. The phrase "the right to vote" does not appear in the unamended Constitution. Article I, Section 2 stipulated that "the House of Representatives shall be composed of Members chosen every second Year by the People of the several States," but then delegated to the States the task of identifying what qualifications electors need to possess in order to exercise the franchise. A few court cases emphasize, and hence specify, what it means for representatives to be "chosen ... by the People," but the unamended text does little to secure the franchise.

The precise phrase "the right to vote" enters our constitutional conversation via the Fourteenth Amendment, but in a somewhat indirect way. Section 2 of that amendment mandates that "when the right to vote at any election [...] is denied to any of the male inhabitants of such State [...] or in any way abridged [...] the basis of representation" (U.S. Const. amend. XIV) in that state's delegation to the U.S. House shall be reduced in proportion to the number of male citizens denied the right to vote. The prohibition on denying or abridging the right to vote would be repeated in the Fifteenth (black make), Nineteenth (women's suffrage), and the Twenty-Sixth Amendments (voting rights begin at eighteen years of age), thereby introducing the question: How is the right to vote abridged? Additionally, the Fourteenth Amendment's first section guaranteed to each citizen "the equal protection of the laws." As it emerges in the context of a particular legal case, deliberative specification of the right to vote weaves these constitutional provisions together while, in at least some cases, also utilizing provisions from the federal Voting Rights Act (e.g., the language of "standard, practice, or procedure" as well as the "effects test" inscribed in the 1982 Amendments).

Noting the fundamentally dialogic character of deliberative specification in the context of voting rights reinforces the distinction between specification and such neighboring practices as clarification and interpretation. Judicial deliberation on the right to vote is more than a narrow form of constitutional interpretation; legal advocates specify the nature of the right as they imbricate constitutional text, legal doctrine, prior precedents, and (sometimes) federal statutes with specific local conditions, histories, and practices.

Specification

Specification has emerged as a key concept in contemporary bioethics (e.g., Beauchamp & Childress, 2013), thanks largely to Henry Richardson's influential 1990 essay "Specifying Norms as a Way to Resolve Concrete Ethical Problems." While Richardson's essay merits attention, I want to focus instead on one of its principal sources. In note 41, Richardson directed his readers' attention to David Wiggins' "Deliberation and Practical Reason," indicating that his approach to specification was "much influenced" (Richardson, 1990, p. 297) by it. In this widely reprinted essay, Wiggins sought to clarify certain aspects of Aristotle's theory of *phronesis* or practical reason.

In a key passage in the *Nicomachean Ethics*, Aristotle (trans. 2011) wrote: "We deliberate not about ends but about things conducive to the ends" (1112b12–13). As Wiggins noted, many commentators use this passage to reconstruct "a restricted and technical notion of deliberation" (1975–1976, p. 29) centered on discovering the best *means* to predetermined *ends*. Insisting on the autonomy of practical reason (cf. Garver, 2004), Wiggins contested this "technocratic" reading by rejecting the assumption "that reason has nothing to do with the ends of human life, its only sphere being the efficient realization of specific goals in whose determination or modification argument plays no substantive part" (1975–1976, p. 36). As an alternative, Wiggins introduced the idea of deliberative specification, explaining that we should understand Aristotle as claiming that people "may seek by deliberation to make more specific and more practically determinate that generalized *telos* [end or goal]" (1975–1976, p. 36) that organizes domains of human practice (common practices Aristotle discussed include medicine and navigation). "Deliberation," Wiggins maintained, "is still *zetesis*, a search, but it is not primarily a search for means. It is a search for the best specification [....] of the end" (1975–1976, p. 38).

Deliberative specification of the right to vote has produced two competing traditions in American jurisprudence. Justice Clarence Thomas's concurring opinion in *Holder v. Hall* (1994) represents the tradition of minimalist specification. Specifically glossing the VRA's language of standards, practices, or procedures, Justice Thomas maintained in *Holder v. Hall* (1994):

> The general terms in the section are most naturally understood, therefore, to refer to any methods for conducting a part of the voting process that might similarly be used to interfere with a citizen's ability to cast his [*sic*] vote, and they are undoubtedly intended to ensure that the entire voting process—a process that begins with registration and includes the casting of a ballot and having the ballot counted—is covered by the Act.
>
> *(pp. 917-918)*

In this passage (and throughout the opinion), Justice Thomas specified that the VRA-protected right to vote encompassed "the entire voting process" (*Holder v. Hall*, 1994, p. 924): registration, casting a ballot, and having the ballot counted. Elsewhere in the opinion, Justice Thomas acknowledged that polling locations and hours of operation were part of the "process" and thus covered by the VRA. Citing the authority of the second Justice Harlan, Justice Thomas insisted that "an 'effective' vote is merely one that has been cast and fairly counted" (*Holder v. Hall*, 1994, p. 919). The next section of this paper will trace the emergence of a more robust alternative to Justice Thomas's specification of an "effective vote" and, in so doing, demonstrate that dissociative argument is essential to this tradition's development.

Dissociation, Specification, and the Right to Vote

Threats to the right to vote occur in two primary ways: forms of vote denial and/or suppression (i.e., from poll taxes and literacy tests to voter ID laws) and various ways that communities have rendered an individual or group's vote impotent or ineffective. My focus is on the latter threat and the use of dissociative specification to combat it. Dissociation is crucial in this specification process because, as critics of these court decisions have maintained, the voting practices in question did not disenfranchise anyone or deny anyone the ability to cast a ballot. Therefore, critics have asked, how can a practice that does not actually deny someone the right to vote somehow violate a person's right to vote? Dissociative argument is the key to resolving this apparent paradox.[1]

Dissociative specification has been pivotal in three interrelated clusters of cases: the first cluster consists of the now largely completed challenges to the problem of malapportionment; the second cluster consists of the ongoing challenges to the problem of minority vote dilution; and the third cluster consists of the newly revitalized challenge to the asserted problem of partisan gerrymandering. The remainder of the paper focuses on the first cluster with a few observations on the latter two.

Explicit congressional efforts to protect citizens' right to vote appeared in the various Reconstruction-era Enforcement Acts, as the judicial efforts to specify the nature of that right arose in cases brought under those acts. In *United States v. Mosley* (1915), the Supreme Court reversed a district court decision that had dismissed a federal indictment against Oklahoma election officials who discarded ballot boxes into a nearby river. Writing for the majority, Justice Oliver Wendell Holmes argued that the indictment was valid because Congress possessed the authority to criminalize the defendant's behavior. In a widely cited passage, Holmes wrote:

> It is not open to question that this statute is constitutional, and constitutionally extends some protection at least to the right to vote for Members of Congress

[....] We regard it as equally unquestionable that the right to have one's vote counted is as open to protection by Congress as the right to put a ballot in a box.

(United States v. Mosley, 1915, p. 386)

Voting minimalists, such as Justice Thomas, have no difficulty endorsing Holmes' position, but other justices will employ dissociation to expand on it.

In *U.S. v. Saylor et al.* (1944), federal prosecutors indicted Harlan County, Kentucky election officials for ballot box stuffing, maintaining that such behavior jeopardized Kentucky citizens'

[...] right and privilege to express by their votes their choice of a candidate for Senator and their right to have their expressions of choice given full value and effect by not having their votes impaired, lessened, diminished, diluted and destroyed by fictitious ballots fraudulently cast and counted.

(p. 386)

The majority opinion drew on Justice Holmes' comment that the right to vote involved more than putting a "ballot in a box" (p. 387) to support the conviction. Justice William O. Douglas dissented on federalism grounds (believing that Congress had repealed "the much despised 'reconstruction' legislation"), but explicitly endorsed the idea that bribery and ballot box stuffing "dilutes my vote" (p. 392).

Justice Douglas echoed Holmes' language and extended his *Saylor* dissent by developing a dissociative argument more clearly in his dissent in *South v. Peters* (1950), a case involving a challenge to Georgia's "county unit" voting system. In that dissent, he insisted:

There is more to the right to vote than the right to mark a piece of paper and drop it in a box or the right to pull a lever in a voting booth. The right to vote includes the right to have the ballot counted [....] It also includes the right to have the vote counted at full value without dilution or discount [....] That federally protected right suffers substantial dilution in this case. The favored group has full voting strength. The groups not in favor have their votes discounted.

(p. 279)

Justice Douglas reiterated the connection between ballot box stuffing and vote dilution a page later: "The interference with the political processes of the state is no greater here [Georgia's county unit system] than it is when ballot boxes are stuffed or other tampering with the votes occurs" (*South v. Peters*, 1950, p. 280). Recalling the Court's position in *Nixon v. Herndon* (invalidating the white democratic primary in Texas), he insisted "that where there is voting there be equality" (*South v. Peters*, 1950, pp. 280-281). For Justice Douglas, given the way Georgia's "county unit" system operated, a vote in Fulton or DeKalb County was not equal to that cast in Georgia's smallest counties and was, therefore, a "diluted vote." And a diluted vote was, Douglas implied, not really a vote; it was only the appearance of a vote.

Justice Hugo Black joined Douglas's *Saylor* and *South v. Peters* dissents, indicating his support for the claim that the right to vote involves something more than placing a ballot in a box. Justice Black dissented from the Court's plurality opinion in *Colegrove v. Green* (1946), which held that malapportionment cases were nonjusticiable. In *Colegrove*, Illinois citizens challenged the constitutionality of the state's congressional districts given their significant disparities in size (and the fact that the Illinois legislature had not engaged in reapportionment since 1901). Justice Black's dissent cited all the cases that Justice Douglas cited in his dissents (and Douglas joined Black's *Colegrove* dissent), but he framed his dissociative argument in different terms. Justice Back did not focus on diluted votes. Instead, he specified that the various constitutional provisions on voting had an "obvious" purpose: "to make the votes of the citizens of the several States equally effective in the selection of members of Congress" (*Colegrove v. Green*, 1946, p. 570). Over a dozen times in his dissent, Justice Black maintained that the Constitution mandated that citizens be able to cast "effective" votes and that challenges to voting systems must evaluate the "effectiveness" of votes cast within it. He concluded his dissent by insisting that the Constitution requires voting practices that provide "all the people an equally effective voice in electing their representatives" (p. 574).

Perelman and Olbrechts-Tyteca (1969) recommended attending to the dissociative function of adjectival and adverbial modifiers. Such modifiers generate "condensed dissociations" (Jasinski, 2001, p. 179) because the modifier's presence cues readers and/or listeners to consider how the modifier's dissociative antithesis impacts the concept being modified. As Zarefsky, Miller-Tutzauer, and Tutzauer's (1984) analysis of Reagan's "truly needy" dissociation illustrates, the presence of the adverb "truly" cues readers and/or listeners to consider the possibility that some only *apparently* needy people are currently receiving federal assistance. Comparing and contrasting Black's and Douglas's dissents illustrates how advocates promoting a similar objective can, in at least some cases, draw upon either of the fundamental terms—"appearance" or "reality"—in fashioning a dissociative argument. Black's use of "effective" is aspirational; he was specifying the direction in which the nation must move in order to actualize the right to vote. The term "effective" implicitly aligns with "reality" as it urges readers to accept the proposition that only "effective" votes should be considered "real" votes. Diminished effectiveness, Black implied, transformed a completed ballot into an only "apparent" vote.

Like Black, Douglas believed the court should specify the equal protection clause in a way that guaranteed voting equality, but his dissociative argument foregrounded the "appearance" end of the dissociative spectrum. Douglas's dissociation did not specify a desired *telos* towards which the nation should aspire; his dissociation identified a flawed understanding of voting that must be abandoned. The terms "diluted" or "discounted" align with "appearance" and urge readers to accept the proposition that "diluted" votes should not be considered "real" votes; they are functionally equivalent to the ballots soaking in a ballot box floating down the river. Black and Douglas both employed dissociation to resolve the apparent paradox noted earlier: while not the same as disenfranchisement, diluted or ineffective votes are nonetheless antithetical to our constitutional (and statutory) commitment to robust voting rights. Despite the fact that practices such as county unit voting and significant legislative district malapportionment (at both the state and federal level) do not deny a person the right to cast a ballot, they were, Black and Douglas insisted, unconstitutional abridgments of a citizen's right to vote. Despite practices such as county unit voting and significant legislative district malapportionment (at both state and federal levels) do not deny a person the right to cast a ballot, they were, Black and Douglas insisted, unconstitutional abridgments of a citizen's right to vote.

Conclusion

Justice Black and Justice Douglas's dissociative logic would eventually prevail. Douglas wrote the majority opinion in *Gray v. Sanders* (1963) that declared Georgia's county unit system unconstitutional, and Black authored the majority opinion in *Wesberry v. Sanders* (1964) that invalidated, on constitutional grounds, Georgia's congressional apportionment system. Chief Justice Earl Warren would use Douglas's "one person, one vote" formulation in *Reynolds v. Sims* (1964) to encapsulate the newly specified constitutional standard for creating legislative districts. Equally sized legislative districts would ensure effective, undiluted votes.

Dissociative argument continues to play an important role in how advocates specify the right to vote. As African Americans began registering and voting in greater numbers, cities, counties, and states (mainly in the South) began adopting new electoral practices, "at large" voting systems being one of the most common (see Davidson, 1984). In cases such as *Allen v. State Board of Elections* (1969), the Court first recognized that Congress reaffirmed Justice Black's "effectiveness" criteria in the VRA, specifying that voting encompasses "all action necessary to make a vote effective" (pp. 545-546) and then extended Justice Douglas's position that "the right to vote can be affected by a dilution of voting power, as well as by an absolute prohibition" (p. 569) to strike down a Mississippi county's shift to at-large elections for country supervisors.

In the Supreme Court's next term (beginning October 2017), the judges will hear *Gill v. Whitford*. In this case, a three-judge district court panel ruled in November 2016 that the Wisconsin legislature violated the equal protection clause through excessive partisan gerrymandering. One of Whitford's attorneys, Nicholas Stephanopoulos, proposed a standard, endorsed by a majority of the three-judge district panel, for determining when districting practices create an excessive and unconstitutional number of "wasted votes." The concept of a "wasted vote" is a new phase in the dissociative specification of the right to vote; Stephanopoulos and McGhee's (2015) "efficiency gap" standard provided the criteria for distinguishing real from apparent/wasted votes creating an even more elaborate dissociation (see Jasinski, 2001).

Note

1 While this analysis focuses on dissociation, the essay is not trying to imply that the form of argument is the only important one found in the trajectory of cases discussed here. Consistent with Wiggins' interest in *phronesis*, dissociation plays a central role in a broader process of practical reasoning that stands in opposition to forms of formalist or technical modes of legal arguing/reasoning.

References

Allen v. State Board of Elections, 393 U.S. 544 (1969)

Aristotle. (2011). *Nicomachean ethics* (R. C. Bartlett & S. D. Collins, Trans.). Chicago, IL: University of Chicago Press.

Averill, M. P. (1995). *Holder v. Hall*: Sizing up vote dilution in the 1990s. *North Carolina Law Review*, *73*(5), 1949-1984. Retrieved from http://scholarship.law.unc.edu/.

Beauchamp, T. L., & Childress, J. F. (2013). *Principles of biomedical ethics* (7th ed.). Oxford, United Kingdom: Oxford University Press.

Colegrove v. Green, 328 U.S. 549 (1946)

Davidson, C. (Ed.). (1984). *Minority vote dilution*. Washington, DC: Howard University Press.

Garver, E. (2004). *For the sake of argument: Practical reasoning, character, and the ethics of belief*. Chicago, IL: University of Chicago Press.

Gray v. Sanders, 372 U.S. 368 (1963)

Holder v. Hall, 512 U.S. 874 (1994)

Jasinski, J. (2001). *Sourcebook on rhetoric: Key concepts in contemporary rhetorical studies*. Thousand Oaks, CA: SAGE.

Keyssar, A. (2009). *The right to vote: The contested history of democracy in the United States* (Rev. ed.). New York, NY: Basic Books.

Perelman, Ch., & Olbrechts-Tyteca, L. (1969). *The new rhetoric: A treatise on argumentation* (J. Wilkinson & P. Weaver, Trans.). Notre Dame, IN: University of Notre Dame Press.

Reynolds v. Sims, 377 U.S. 533 (1964)

Richardson, H. S. (1990). Specifying norms as a way to resolve concrete ethical problems. *Philosophy & Public Affairs*, *19*(4), 279–310. Retrieved from http://jstor.org/stable/2265316.

South v. Peters, 339 U.S. 276 (1950)

Stephanopoulos, N. O., & McGhee, E. M. (2015). Partisan gerrymandering and the efficiency gap. *University of Chicago Law Review*, *82*, 831–900. Retrieved from https://lawreview.uchicago.edu.

United States v. Mosley, 238 U.S. 383 (1915)

United States v. Saylor et. al., 322 U.S. 385 (1944)

Waldman, M. (2016). *The fight to vote*. New York, NY: Simon & Schuster.

Wesberry v. Sanders, 376 U.S. 1 (1964)

Wiggins, D. (1975–1976). Deliberation and practical reason. *Proceedings of the Aristotelian Society, New Series*, *76*, 29–51. Retrieved from http://jstor.org/stable/4544879.

Zarefsky, D., Miller-Tutzauer, C., & Tutzauer, F. (1984). Reagan's safety net for the truly needy: The rhetorical uses of definition. *Central States Speech Journal*, *35*(2), 113–119. doi:10.1080/10510978409368171

26

HISPANIC POLITICIANS ON THE RISE

Argumentation Strategies of Ted Cruz and Marco Rubio

Ann E. Burnette and Wayne L. Kraemer

Rapid demographic changes within the United States mean that the country will soon have a majority-minority population. American Hispanics are becoming a critical political population because of this shift. According to the May 2016 Annual Latino Public Affairs Forum, "Latinos represent the fastest growing population in the United States, increasing 43% between 2000 and 2010, and they are the leading edge of a demographic change transforming the U.S. into a 'majority minority' country" (Bell, 2016, p. 1). Scholars of political rhetoric have studied the argumentative strategies that non-Hispanic political rhetors have used historically to gain support from Hispanic voters (Connaughton, 2004; Connaughton & Jarvis, 2004a, 2004b). In contrast, this study examines how Hispanic politicians reach out to Hispanic and non-Hispanic audiences with their political arguments.

This essay analyzes the argumentative strategies of two prominent Hispanic politicians: Republicans Ted Cruz of Texas and Marco Rubio of Florida. Cruz represents a state that is already majority-minority and Rubio represents a state that soon will become so. Both politicians made high profile, national debuts as prominent speakers for their party during the 2012 presidential campaign, and both have parlayed that success into national political recognition. *USA Today* described Cruz and Rubio as "among the most eloquent conservatives on Capitol Hill" (King, 2015, para. 6). Both ran strong campaigns in the 2016 Republican presidential primary race and have returned to the Senate in the wake of the 2016 election outcome.

Ted Cruz addressed the 2012 Republican National Convention on Tuesday, August 28, while Marco Rubio spoke on Thursday, August 30, immediately before Republican presidential nominee Mitt Romney. During the 2016 presidential election cycle, Cruz was the first Republican to announce that he was entering the 2016 presidential race with a Twitter video message on March 22, 2015. He followed with a formal announcement speech the next day at Liberty University in Lynchburg, Virginia. Cruz won 11 states during the 2016 Republican primary and finished second behind eventual nominee Donald Trump. Cruz suspended his campaign on May 2, 2016. Rubio announced that he was running for president on April 13, 2015, in Miami, Florida. Rubio was the third Republican to join the Republican presidential primary and finished fourth after Trump, Cruz, and Ohio Governor John Kasich. Rubio suspended his campaign on March 15, 2016.

In both their 2012 convention addresses and their 2015 announcement addresses, Cruz and Rubio sought to create identification by using personal narratives that outlined their vision of the American dream and by invoking Hispanic culture. To illustrate, we first outline the potential political influence of the Hispanic voter in the United States. Second, we examine how narratives in particular provide opportunities for identification in political rhetoric. Then we analyse the 2012 Republican National Convention speeches and the 2015 presidential announcement speeches of Cruz and Rubio. We chose these speeches because both speakers began to develop their identification appeals in 2012 and continued elaborating upon them in 2015. In this way, we could evaluate the creation and maintenance of their identity as national political candidates. In each case, we examine two aspects of the speakers' political rhetoric: their narratives of the American dream and their invocation of Hispanic culture. Cruz and Rubio used these two aspects in an effort to identify with both Hispanic and non-Hispanic voters. Finally, we consider implications of Cruz and Rubio's identification strategies for the field of argumentation studies.

The Rise of the Hispanic Voter

Hispanic political candidates, like all political candidates, must persuade many kinds of voters to win elections and serve diverse constituencies. Stuckey (2000) argued that during political campaigns, candidates must try to create "a political coalition large enough [and] diverse enough" (p. 453) to win office and govern. The Annual Latino Public Affairs Forum observed that "Latinos are the fastest growing ethnic group among eligible voters in the United States" (p. 3), with an estimated 27.3 million Latinos eligible to vote in the 2016 elections, which translates into 11.3% of the U.S. electorate (Bell, 2016). The dramatic increase of Hispanic voters potentially gives Hispanic politicians a ready constituency; it also means that non-Hispanic politicians must now consider strategies for garnering Hispanic support. Both Hispanic and non-Hispanic politicians must also contend with the reality that Hispanic voters have diverse experiences and viewpoints that means they do not vote as a bloc. Nevertheless, according to Connaughton and Jarvis (2004a), analysts have often hailed Latino voters as a "'sleeping giant' in politics" (p. 464) because of "their numbers, their relative youth and their location in 10 key electoral states" (p. 464).

Both the Democratic and Republican Party covet the support of such a significant population. The Republican Party, however, faces a steeper challenge. Bell (2016) noted, "a large part of the Republican Party's struggle with Latino voters is rooted in the party's relationship to its base—primarily white, working-class, and older voters in the South, Midwest, and West" (p. 8). Connaughton and Jarvis (2004a) provided a root cause for the tension by characterizing Republicans as more likely to identify strongly with the value of individualism than with ethnic identity. Republicans, however, must maintain the support of this base "while at the same time adapting to demographic changes that will make the United States a truly multiracial, multiethnic nation over the next several decades" (Bell, 2016, p. 8). While the party must broaden its electoral base, it must simultaneously take care not to alienate current non-Hispanic voters who identify as Republican. Cruz and Rubio are politicians who potentially can address these two needs by articulating Republican principles and expanding the Republican base to include more Hispanic voters.

Identification and Narrative

Both Cruz and Rubio relied on various strategies of identification to draw in Hispanic voters to support their electoral pursuits. Identification is "central to understanding the dynamics of American politics" (Connaughton, 2004, p. 132) as politicians often try to build connections between themselves and their audiences using experiences, values, or self-images. Speakers may try to articulate these connections overtly in their argumentative claims or they may try to invoke this sense of connection implicitly through particular forms of address, use of pronouns, or choices of examples.

One way of achieving identification is through narrative. Fisher (1984) claimed that people do not reason and persuade within a "rational world paradigm" (p. 4) characterized by formal argumentation, rationality, and claims of technical expertise. Instead, he outlined a "narrative paradigm" (pp. 7-8) in which people make and judge arguments according to "good reasons" (p. 7) and standards of narrative probability and fidelity (Fisher, 1984). Fisher (1987) argued that narrative relies on Burke's idea of "identification rather than [...] demonstration" (p. 18). Burke (1969) described identification as the basis of persuasion and contended that rhetors persuade only if they can align their "language by speech, gesture, tonality, order, image, attitude, [or] idea" (p. 55) with the audience. For Fisher, people judge narratives based on the degree to which they can identify with the narratives.

Through the use of narrative and identification, Cruz and Rubio worked to position themselves as reflecting not only the Hispanic community, but also American society at large. One narrative that American political rhetors commonly use is the American dream, which stresses political freedoms, an egalitarian economic and political system based on mer-itocracy, and the expectation that immigrants can improve their lot for themselves and their descendants. Rowland and Jones (2011) argued, "The heroes present in such stories are not larger than life but thoroughly ordinary men and women who do extraordinary things in the society" (p. 132). This reliance on the ordinary hero is especially important in what Rowland and Jones (2007) claimed was the conservative interpretation of the American dream. Conservative politicians like Cruz and Rubio maintained that individuals can be suc-cessful regardless of their circumstances because "enactment of personal values ensures fulfil-ment of the American dream" (Rowland & Jones, 2007, p. 432).

Cruz and Rubio's American Dream

In his 2012 convention speech, Ted Cruz explicitly evoked the narrative of the American dream. He began by saying, "I want to tell you a love story [...] of freedom" (TexasGOP-Vote, 2012, para. 7) that included the Founding Fathers, the "greatest generation" (para. 10) of World War II, Martin Luther King, Ronald Reagan, and, finally "each and every one of you" (para. 15). He established the obstacles to freedom that his father had to overcome by relaying when his father was "imprisoned and tortured in Cuba, [and] beaten nearly to death" (para. 9). Cruz described his parents, after relocating to the United States, as having achieved the American dream: "My parents worked together to start a small business, to provide for their family and to chart their own future" (para. 22). Cruz cast his parents' experience as the quintessential American experience.

During his 2015 announcement speech, Cruz again shared a series of stories about how prominent Americans throughout history, including his parents, had lived the American dream (Cruz, 2015). Cruz also extended the narrative by including himself in the experience. He recounted growing up, "being raised in Houston, hearing stories from his dad about prison and torture in Cuba, hearing stories about how fragile liberty is, [and] beginning to study the United States Constitution" (para. 30). He used argument by association to link his family's stories together by saying, "These are all of our stories. These are who we are as Americans" (para. 34). While the experience of Cruz's father was specific to Cuban immigrants of that generation, Cruz treated his father's biography as one of many examples of the American dream. Cruz thus invited Hispanic and non-Hispanic voters to view this immigrant experience as a viable American dream narrative.

Marco Rubio also used the American dream narrative featuring the experiences of his family to identify with his audience. In his convention speech, Rubio (2012) described his parents' immigration to the United States and how they achieved the American dream: "They never made it big [...] And yet they were successful. Because just a few decades removed from hopelessness, they made possible for us all the things that had been impossible for them" (para. 46). In both his convention and announcement speeches, Rubio used his father as a representative hero. Rubio told the story of his father who worked for many years as a banquet bartender. He reflected that his father "stood behind a bar in the back of the room all those years, so one day I could stand behind a podium in the front of the room" (Rubio, 2012, para. 51; Washington Post Staff, 2015). Rubio (2012) stressed the accessibility of the American dream for everyone, arguing, "That's not just my story. That's your story. That's our story" (para. 54). He argued that the story of Cuban immigrants was "part of the larger story of the American miracle" (Washington Post Staff, 2015, para. 7). For Rubio, his family illustrated the American dream "where even the son of a bartender and a maid" (para. 59) could succeed. Rubio emphasized the ordinary nature of the characters of the American dream narrative to establish identification with every member of the audience.

Cruz and Rubio's Invocation of Hispanic Culture

In addition to using identification with the American dream to reach voters, Ted Cruz explicitly targeted Hispanic listeners during his 2012 convention speech. Noting that his father was at the convention, Cruz said, "When he came to America, él no tenía nada, pero tenía corazón. He had nothing, but he had heart. A heart for freedom" (TexasGOPVote, 2012, para. 9). Cruz also addressed Hispanic voters openly, arguing that President Obama was "try[ing] to divide America," and "tell[ing] Hispanics that we're not welcome here" (para. 13). His own vision, he insisted, was more inclusive.

While Cruz was making these explicit overtures to Hispanic voters, however, he was careful to convey the position of Hispanic Americans within the larger American narrative. He associated the cause of Hispanic voters with causes the broader Republican party could embrace: "Two thirds of all new jobs come from small business, and 2.3 million Hispanics own small businesses" (TexasGOPVote, 2012, para. 25). Further, when recalling his father's immigrant experience, Cruz said he was grateful that no one told his father, "and by the way, don't bother learning English. That would have been the most destructive thing anyone could have done" (TexasGOPVote, 2012, para. 21). Cruz insisted that Hispanic voters could fit within the community fabric of America through allegiance to the conservative belief that individual effort would also serve as their key to success.

During his 2015 announcement speech, Cruz again traced his father's experience as a Cuban immigrant to the United States, but he did not explicitly reference Hispanic culture. Nor did he speak any Spanish while giving the speech. He also did not talk about the plight of Hispanic Americans under Barack Obama. Instead, Cruz treated his family's stories as exemplars of the typical American narrative. By normalizing the Hispanic experience, Cruz transformed Hispanic experiences into ones more organically American.

Like Cruz, Rubio used similar language strategies to convey stories about his father at the 2012 Republican National Convention and his 2015 announcement speech. He recalled, "My Dad used to tell us: 'En este pais, ustedes van a poder lograr todas las cosas que nosotros no pudimos.' 'In this country, you will be able to accomplish all the things we never could'" (Rubio, 2012, para. 48). Rubio's use of a Spanish phrase with its English translation invited both Spanish-speaking and English-speaking audience members to identify with his personal story, as well as with the broader American dream narrative.

Rather than taking extensive time to articulate Hispanic identity and how it fit into the larger American society, both Cruz and Rubio instead invoked Hispanic identities by infrequently speaking in Spanish or quoting the Spanish remarks of their family members. Such an approach is an efficient way to self-identify as Hispanic and invite identification with other Hispanic citizens, while not excluding non-Hispanic voters.

Conclusion

Ted Cruz and Marco Rubio are Hispanic politicians who needed to attract non-Hispanic as well as Hispanic voters to win political campaigns. Each used similar identification strategies in their speeches to accomplish that goal. Both told personal stories that connected to the American dream. Cruz and Rubio spoke Spanish in their speeches to signal their Hispanic identity, but made the Spanish phrases understandable to non-Spanish-speaking audience members by using only short Spanish phrases and by translating them into English for the wider audience.

Both Cruz and Rubio described the American dream in terms that were consistent with Rowland and Jones' (2007) observation that politically conservative American dream narratives feature ordinary individuals able to overcome their circumstances through their own effort. Cruz (2015) described his father as "a teenage boy, not much younger than many of you here today" (para. 12). Rubio (2012; Washington Post Staff, 2015) recounted how the Rubio family moved symbolically from the back of the ballroom (his father serving as bartender) to the podium in the front of the room (Rubio himself speaking to an audience). In these versions of the American dream, all people who work hard and believe in the dream can participate in the dream, no matter how humble their circumstances. Moreover, Cruz and Rubio's personal narratives took place against the backdrop of communist Cuba and its oppression.

Finally, both Cruz and Rubio presented themselves as beneficiaries of the American dream because of the struggles of previous generations. Personally, they did not have to experience the hardships of the previous generation, yet, they could still identify with those difficulties in ways that targeted young and old audiences alike. Stuckey (2005) argued that political rhetors want to connect with voters on a personal level and that voters want to see themselves "reflected" (p. 654) in their politicians. Cruz and Rubio's stories of personal success are consistent with a newer generation of American Hispanics who are younger, better educated, more fluent in English, and more likely to be native born (Bell, 2016).

The identification strategies Cruz and Rubio used are not unique to Hispanic politicians. All politicians want to create identification with potential voters, including Hispanic voters. Many use narratives of the American Dream; some non-Hispanic politicians use implicit strategies (e.g., speaking Spanish). Cruz and Rubio, however, illustrated how Hispanic politicians can celebrate their own experiences and the experiences of other Hispanic Americans and make their personal stories an organic part of the American Dream.

References

Bell, A. T. (2016, May). *The role of the Latino vote in the 2016 elections* (Center for Latin American & Latino Studies Working Paper No. 13). doi:10.2139/ssrn.2778173

Burke, K. (1969). *A rhetoric of motives*. Berkeley, CA: University of California Press.

Connaughton, S. L. (2004). Multiple identification targets in examining partisan identification: A case study of Texas Latinos. *The Howard Journal of Communication, 15*(3), 131–145. doi:10.1080/10646170490483610

Connaughton, S. L., & Jarvis, S. E. (2004a). Apolitical politics: GOP efforts to foster identification from Latinos, 1984-2000. *Communication Studies, 55*(3), 464–480. doi:10.1080/10510970409388632

Connaughton, S. L., & Jarvis, S. E. (2004b). Invitations for partisan identification: Attempts to court Latino voters through televised Latino-oriented political advertisements, 1984-2000. *Journal of Communication, 54*(1), 38-54. doi:10.1111/j.1460-2466.2004.tb02612.x

Cruz, T. (2015, March 23). Transcript: Ted Cruz's speech at Liberty University. *The Washington Post*. Retrieved from https://washingtonpost.com

Fisher, W. R. (1984). Narration as a human communication paradigm: The case of public moral argument. *Communication Monographs, 51*(1), 1–22. doi:10.1080/03637758409390180

Fisher, W. R. (1987). *Human communication as narration: Toward a philosophy of reason, value, and action*. Columbia, SC: University of South Carolina Press.

King, L. (2015, December 10). Marco Rubio, Ted Cruz battle to become Trump alternative. *USA Today*. Retrieved from http://usatoday.com

Rowland, R. C., & Jones, J. M. (2007). Recasting the American Dream and American politics: Barack Obama's keynote address to the 2004 Democratic National Convention. *Quarterly Journal of Speech, 93* (4), 425–448. doi:10.1080/00335630701593675

Rowland, R. C., & Jones, J. M. (2011). One dream: Barack Obama, race, and the American Dream. *Rhetoric & Public Affairs, 14*(1), 125–154. doi:10.1353/rap.2011.0007

Rubio, M. (2012, August 30). Transcript: Florida Sen. Marco Rubio's convention speech. *National Public Radio*. Retrieved from http://npr.org

Stuckey, M. E. (2000). The presidency and political leadership. *Rhetoric & Public Affairs, 3*(3), 452–454. Retrieved from http://jstor.org/stable/41940247

Stuckey, M. E. (2005). One nation (pretty darn) divisible: National identity in the 2004 conventions [Special issue]. *Rhetoric & Public Affairs, 8*(4), 639-656. Retrieved from http://jstor.org/stable/41940018

TexasGOPVote. (2012, August 29). Video and transcript of Ted Cruz speech at 2012 Republican National Convention. Retrieved from http://texasgopvote.com

Washington Post Staff. (2015, April 13). Full text of Marco Rubio's 2016 presidential campaign announcement. *The Washington Post*. Retrieved from https:/washingtonpost.com

27

ESCAPING THE "BROKEN MIDDLE"

Establishing Argumentative Presence within Association and Disassociation

Aaron Dicker

For Perelman and Olbrechts-Tyteca, the primary loci of argumentation follows a delicate balance between association, or bringing separate items together, and dissociation, or separating a unified group. Their seminal work *The New Rhetoric: A Treatise on Argumentation* (1969) explained,

> Psychologically and logically, all association implies dissociation, and conversely: the same form which unites various elements into a well-organized whole dissociates them from the neutral background from which it separates them. The two techniques are complementary and are always at work at the same time; but the argumentation through which a datum is modified can stress the association or the dissociation which it is promoting without making explicit the complementary aspect which will result from the desired transformation. At times these two aspects are present together in the consciousness of the speaker, who may wonder to which one it is better to draw attention.
>
> *(p. 190)*

This dichotomous yet fluid schema provides the categorization of all types of argumentation, as even speakers can consciously decide between associating and disassociating their arguments. Arguments by association and disassociation are mutually exclusive and discuss only the structure of the argument, not the argument's reception.

The decision of a speaker to pick either associative arguments or dissociative arguments is easily applicable when a speaker faces an audience; however, Perelman and Olbrechts-Tyteca spent their careers discussing ways to present arguments to the universal audience consisting of multiple particular audiences simultaneously. Speakers attempt to increase argumentative presence, or an argument's staying power in the audience, by operating within this dichotomy (Perelman, 1982). Speakers make conscious decisions regarding which argument to present, as their choice associates with one part of the universal audience (thereby strengthening argumentative presence), while simultaneously dissociating another part of the audience (thereby weakening the same argument's presence). This essay explains the process in which speakers attempt to gain the most argumentative presence when making arguments from both association and disassociation. Specifically, this essay investigates those caught in-between particular audiences, hereafter the "broken middle," and their attempts to establish argumentative presence in order to define this phantasmagoric position of both association and disassociation.

First, I outline this argumentative conundrum by identifying its situation and the attend-ant, embedded risks to argumentative presence. Second, I use a specific moment in Ameri-can history to demonstrate how one group attempted to escape the broken middle. Last, I present directions that future scholarship could use to investigate this new perspective on Perelman and Olbrechts-Tyteca's work.

The Broken Middle

In most circumstances, making arguments from a middle position (i.e., caught between two groups) to a bigger audience carries little chance of losing large amounts of argumentative presence. A sports fan arguing that their team qualifies as "the greatest" risks decreasing pres-ence with audience members who root for his or her rival, but the majority of the audience will still engage with the associative argument. Historically, policymakers have often attempted to bring together multiple stakeholders under the position of common ground when proposing large-scale change. In contrast, the broken middle refers to instances where the risk of alienation is imminent from arguments of both association and disassociation. The broken middle often appears when a subordinate group attempts to sway members of the dominate group in society, specifically when that group serves as an associated opposite (e.g., the U.S. native born children of illegal immigrants, Japanese Americans during World War II, etc.). Presenting arguments is the only choice to increase argumentative presence; silence does not advance the claim. Where does compromise exist in this situation in regards to argumentation? How can a person compromise without losing argumentative presence?

Speakers caught in the broken middle face three hindrances to increasing argumentative presence with the universal audience. Imagine a two-set Venn diagram with one set as LGBTQA+ rights advocates and the other as fundamentalist religious lawmakers. First, the overlapping neutral ground is small based upon minimal agreement on fundamental aspects of the structure of reality. Further, key categorical differences restrict the neutral ground for argument to expand the boundaries of the center set. Second, this constricted neutral ground robs the speaker from utilizing the most effective arguments to sway either set of particular audiences. Using the core religious text as evidence may strengthen argumentative presence with the fundamentalist lawmakers but risks alienating large numbers from the other set. This often leads speakers to propose compromised arguments, leaving both groups unhappy. Third, speakers remain conflicted between representation and contradiction regarding goal fulfillment. If the speaker strays too far from the original goals of the argu-mentative position, they risk mispresenting either group within the universal audience, lead-ing to credibility loss.

Silence for those in the broken middle perpetuates real world consequences. Instead, speakers embrace one of two less than perfect actions. In the first action, speakers entrenched in their original position refuse to compromise argumentative presence with the core, subordinated constituency. While faithful to the original position, speakers lose argu-mentative presence with the dominate group and face longer periods of stagnation. In the second action, the speaker tries to expand the middle ground by moving one group closer to the other by shifting the argumentative ground of one particular audience. The process of shifting argumentative ground involves three steps: choose a new area of targeted ground, make changes in the targeted constituents by shifting argumentative schemes, and present the new rhetorical formations using arguments by association. While this process appears similar to compromise on the surface, shifting argumentative ground does not sacrifice the speakers' identity to either affiliation within the larger universal audience.

Speakers in the broken middle gain stronger argumentative presence with the universal audience when moving between arguments by association and disassociation in ways that shift ground to form a larger middle. Some groups have successfully shifted argumentative ground to escape the broken middle. The following section illustrates an example of a successful attempt by a group to escape the broken middle by shifting argumentative ground.

American Jews in the Broken Middle

After enduring ideological persecution, anti-Semitism, and the Shoah, Zionists succeeded in establishing the first modern Jewish homeland in 1947. Jews have settled throughout the world in diaspora, but as early Zionists began returning to Mandated Palestine, anti-Semitic violence forced thousands to flee their homes and become refugees in the 1930s and 1940s (Roumani, 2003). The 1950s brought laws that discriminated against Jews in almost every major Arab and non-Arab Muslim country, causing hundreds of thousands of Jews to flee these nations (Trigano, 2010), reducing their presence in the MENA region by ninety percent in just two decades (Zamkanei, 2016).

Anti-Semitism worldwide embraced Israel as a scapegoat, a place to expel their unwanted Jews (Negrine, 2013). The ominous fear of expulsion loomed over American Jews who knew all too well of the growing American anti-Semitism and remembered when American ports turned away boats filled with Jewish refugees, condemning them to Nazi Holocaust (Medoff, 2003). Even though Jews had lived in the United States since the 1650s, the politics of the time provided little reassurance to millions who feared that the American government might renounce their citizenship and force them to leave for citizenship in Israel (Shub, 1951). Anti-Semitism has a long and detailed history in both the United States (Obama, 2016) and worldwide (Kahler, 1939; Mendes, 2003). Hate groups, such as the Ku Klux Klan and unpatriotic communists in an era of demagoguery during the Cold War targeted violence against American Jews labeled as strangers, even in their country of birth (Alper & Olson, 2011; Dushkin, 1959). Even with predominant American Jews of the era openly campaigning against communism (Marcus, 1956), the 1950 public espionage trail of Ethel and Julius Rosenberg solidified society's connection between American Jews and communism (Windmueller, 2009, p. 63).

American Jews thus became entrenched in the broken middle. They were American citizens. Yet, other groups questioned American Jews' patriotism as many non-Jewish Americans believed their true allegiance was with Israel (Friesel, 1988). American Jewish leaders began the long process of shifting the argumentative ground of American Judaism toward a more secular position more closely in line with mainstream society. This occurred through changing the rhetoric of American Jewish society, both religiously and culturally, by accepting more mainstream understandings of the U.S. government, language, and culture. In the 1950s, the Reform Movement established itself as the predominant Jewish movement in the United States and began actively incorporating pro-democracy/anti-communist rhetoric into services and prayer books (Aberbach, 2006). Synagogues embraced the public call for religion to defeat communism, thereby separated Jewish citizens from communism theologically and culturally (Greenberg, 1968). These moves worked to shift the argumentative ground of American Jews, create a larger middle, and enable stronger argumentative presence for arguments by association to the American universal audience.

The next step was to convey this new version of American Judaism to the mainstream. In the bestseller *What is a Jew?*, Rabbi Morris Kertzer (1996) introduced secular audiences to a version of American Judaism that specifically incorporated American values such as freedom, justice, and democracy. Influential Jewish speakers gave orations to large secular crowds about the importance of Jews supporting America and Israel's fight against the communists (Lilienthal, 1950; Weller, 1953). American Jews' most important rhetorical move for escaping the broken middle during the Red Scare was the reinvention of the phrase "Judeo-Christian" that sociologists popularized in the 1950s (Mart, 2004). The label functioned as a direct associative argument that implied a Christianity rooted in Jewish religious text and values. It also helped catalyze the rise of Christian Zionism into mainstream popular culture, scholarship, and politics. Soon, high-profile ministers such as Billy Graham in the 1950s and Jerry Falwell in the 1970s began preaching the importance of regular church attendance and the need to support Israel. By the mid-1960s, television evangelical Pat Robertson made Christian Zionism a fundamental aspect of *The 700 Club*. Throughout the early Cold War era, a Judeo-Christian version of Zionism emerged in American religious culture and actively worked to help reconceive Jews as patriots.

Toward Argumentation Scholarship

A focus on American Judaism during the Cold War highlights how a speaker or group can escape the dichotomous relationship between association and disassociation or the burden of the broken middle ground. A key contributing factor to the success of this example is the timing of the group's shift in argumentative ground. While anti-Semitism seeped into everyday interactions, the public did not have daily-televised reminders of the Jewish communist. These cooling periods provided the *kairos* necessary for Jewish leaders to orate influential speeches and policymakers to change the government's stance toward Israel. Future scholarship into the broken middle should consider how the 24-hour news cycle removes the public's ability to cool down. Although anti-Semitism continues rising in the United States and globally, treatment of Muslim Americans has rapidly deteriorated since the turn of the twenty-first century. Islamophobia has curtailed American Muslims' civil rights (Peña, 2009), decreased their power as a democratic voting block (Ahmad, 2007), and decreased their overall quality of life (Ghaffar & Çiftçi, 2010). In the present day, American Muslims, and to a larger degree the subset of foreign-born American Muslims, exist in the broken middle.

References

Aberbach, D. (2006). Nationalism, reform Judaism and the Hebrew prayer book. *Nations and Nationalism, 12*(1), 139–159. doi:10.1111/j.1469-8129.2005.00234.x

Ahmad, M. (2007). Muslims and contestations of religio-political space in America. *Policy Perspectives 6* (1), 47–62. Retrieved from http://jstor.org/stable/42909224

Alper, B. A., & Olson, D. V. A. (2011). Do Jews feel like outsiders in America? The impact of anti-Semitism, friendships, and religious geography. *Journal of Scientific Study of Religion, 50*(4), 822–830. doi:10.1111/j.1468-5906.2011.01599.x

Dushkin, A. M. (1959). Israel's need to understand American Judaism. *The Reconstructionist*, *25*(7), 10–14. Retrieved from http://rrc.edu/

Friesel, E. (1988). American Zionism and American Jewry: An ideological and communal encounter. *American Jewish Archives*, *40*, 5–23. Retrieved from http://americanjewisharchives.org/publications/journal/PDF/1988_40_01_00_friesel.pdf

Ghaffar, A., & Çiftçi, A. (2010). Religiosity and self-esteem of Muslim immigrants to the United States: The moderating role of perceived discrimination. *The International Journal for the Psychology of Religion*, *20*(1), 14–25. doi:10.1080/10508610903418038

Kahler, E. (1939). Forms and features of anti-Judaism. *Social Research*, *6*(4), 455–488. Retrieved from http://jstor.org/stable/40981692

Kertzer, M. N., & Hoffman, L. A. (1996). *What is a Jew?* (Rev. ed.). New York, NY: Touchstone.

Lilienthal, A. M. (1950, April 15). The state of Israel and the state of the Jew. *Vital Speeches of the Day*, *16*(13), 406–409.

Marcus, A. J. (1956). What religion can do to defeat communism: Rendering aid and comfort to the enemy is treason. *Vital Speeches of the Day*, *22*(18), 561–566.

Mart, M. (2004). The "Christianization" of Israel and Jews in 1950s America. *Religion and American Culture: A Journal of Interpretation*, *14*(1), 109–147. doi:10.1525/rac.2004.14.1.109

Medoff, R. (2003). America, the Holocaust, and the abandonment of the Jews. *Journal of Ecumenical Studies*, *40*(4), 350-369. Retrieved from EBSCOhost database.

Mendes, P. (2003). The Melbourne Jewish left, communism and the Cold War. Responses to Stalinist anti-Semitism and the Rosenberg spy trial. *Australian Journal of Politics & History*, *49*(4), 501–516. doi:10.1111/j.1467-8497.2003.00311.x

Negrine, R. (2013). "Are Jews who fled Arab lands to Israel refugees, too?" (*New York Times*, 2003): The representation of Jewish migration from "Arab lands" in Anglo-American newspapers, 1949–1957. *Media History*, *19*(4), 450–463. doi:10.1080/13688804.2013.844895

Peña, A. (2009). American Muslims' civil liberties and the challenge to effectively avert xenophobia. *The Muslim World*, *99*(1), 202–220. doi:10.1111/j.1478-1913.2009.01261.x

Perelman, Ch. (1982). *The realm of rhetoric* (W. Kluback, Trans.). Notre Dame, IN: University of Notre Dame Press.

Perelman, Ch., & Olbrechts-Tyteca, L. (1969). *The new rhetoric: A treatise on argumentation* (J. Wilkinson & P. Weaver, Trans.). Notre Dame, IN: University of Notre Dame Press.

Roumani, M. M. (2003). The silent refugees: Jews from Arab countries. *Mediterranean Quarterly*, *14*(3), 41–77. doi:10.1215/10474552-14-3-41

Shub, L. (1951). Zionism and the American Jewish scene. *The Reconstructionist*, *17*(4), 21–27. Retrieved from http://rrc.edu/

Trigano, S. (2010, November 4). The expulsion of the Jews from Muslim countries, 1920–1970: A history of ongoing cruelty and discrimination. *Jerusalem Center for Public Affairs*. Retrieved from http://jcpa.org

Weller, G. A. (1953, May 15). Our future in the Middle East: Significance of the Anti-Zionist drive of the Soviets. *Vital Speeches of the Day*, *19*(15), 458–463.

Windmueller, S. (2009). Jews in the psyche of America. *Jewish Political Studies Review*, *21* (3/4),57–73. Retrieved from https://jcpa.org

Zamkanei, S. (2016). The politics of defining Jews from Arab countries. *Israel Studies*, *21*(2), 1–26. doi:10.2979/israelstudies.21.2.01

28

CHALLENGES OF NETWORKED CIRCULATION WITHIN ADVOCACY CAMPAIGNS

Ruth J. Beerman

Advocacy campaigns frequently draw on social media such as Facebook, Twitter, Instagram, and Pinterest to promote their idea or issue. Social media allows circulation of such ideas with ease, particularly with the use of visual images such as memes, posters, and photographs. It also creates a system of interactions between the various platforms and the intended audience. This system of interactions is one way to understand networked argument, whereby digital content creates a chain of arguments. Rhetorical scholars have examined circulation of images, from Olson's (2009) idea of re-circulation to Edwards and Winkler's (1997) representative form and visual ideograph. However, most scholars limit that analysis of visual circulation of images to one side of a social controversy, rather than examining the logic of networked interactions between competing campaigns' visual rhetorics.

This essay asks the question, can the visual strategy of circulation serve as a way to dissociate meaning, critique a dominant ideology, and create a new framework? It uses a case study of two interacting campaigns: a state of Georgia anti-childhood obesity campaign and an alternative health advocacy campaign titled "I Stand Against Weight Bullying." I argue that the networked argument of circulation makes the use of arguments by disassociation more difficult between the two competing campaigns. Further, I maintain that an over-reliance on the visual argumentative strategy of mirroring/matching and the visual enthymeme may explain the alternative health campaign's failure to reach its desired goal of challenging dominant ideologies of fatness and obesity.

Visual Argument and Fatness Ideology

Rhetorical scholars have focused on how visual displays create meaning. In particular, visual discourses both about and of bodies create bodily meanings (DeLuca, 1999; Jordan, 2004; Palczewski, 2005; Prelli, 2006). Rather than bodies serving as simple, ancillary material for the argument, bodies function as the core site of argument, with interactions between rhetoric and culture causing certain bodies to matter.

For example, the meanings of fatness depend upon cultural and rhetorical processes. Farrell (2011) argued that fatness is not neutral as the concept developed during the nineteenth, twentieth, and twenty-first centuries. The idea of fatness functions as visible stigma, which becomes crystalized through material bodies. Images of bodies also help to reflect "each person's experience of society" (Douglas, 1996, p. xxxvi). As the public typically sees fat bodies as grotesque, those same bodies become socially undesirable (Ross & Moorti, 2005). Rhetorics of fatness and obesity in U.S. culture draw heavily on medicalized discourses, as well as control and constraint in that they draw upon notions that individuals should be able to simply not be fat (Farrell, 2011). For example, Thomson (2007) noted that many 21st century advertisements against fatness and obesity use a form of "spectacular decapitation" (para. 1). Rather than including a full body photograph, the images begin at the neck and end mid-thigh, centering the attention on an overwhelming belly. The dominant fatness ideology revolves around the idea that fatness exists as a problem society must solve, whether through social and/or health stigmatized motivations.

Strategies for Campaigns

Social advocacy campaigns have always utilized a variety of argumentation strategies. Networked argument, however, requires an understanding of the logic of interactions between two or more opposing sides of a controversy. Lange (1993) argued that the campaigns will often use mirror and/or matching strategies. Mirroring involves "communicative behavior that duplicates the other party's tactic by presenting antithetical, polar or 'mirror image' information" (p. 245); matching refers to "communicative behavior that copies or repeats the other party's strategy" (p. 245). Although Lange focused on text-based discourses, his theory has potential applicability for understanding how visual networked argument could function.

The concept of mirroring works well with the concept of dissociation. According to Perelman and Olbrechts-Tyetca (1969), dissociation functions to reduce or resolve a tension between two concepts, a process of breaking connecting links between elements. For them, the most common form of dissociation was the appearance/reality pairing, where although something appears to be true or real, it is not. A mirrored image, when using dissociation, breaks connections, offering a way to critique ideology.

This breaking of connections and challenging ideology presumes that the audience can follow the logic between or among argument(s). If the arguer implies the logic of the interaction by providing premises while eliding the conclusion, the networked argument utilizes an enthymeme that might weaken the potential critique of dominant ideologies. Young (2015), for example, argued that Caster Semenya's use of visual markers of femininity foreclosed challenging dominant understandings of gender and sex binaries. Indeed, dominant cultural ideologies often function as a primary way for audiences to complete implied arguments. Palczewski (2005) noted that visual arguments of public controversy help make ideology concrete rather than abstract. Thus, dominant ideologies undercut differing, possible interpretations, particularly in a visual context. To illustrate, I will examine the Strong4Life and I Stand Against Weight Bullying campaigns.

Background of the Two Campaigns

As part of social efforts aimed at reducing the problem of obesity, the state of Georgia in 2011 began an anti-childhood obesity health campaign entitled Strong4Life. The campaign circulated a series of print and billboard advertisements with the stated goal of preventing childhood obesity. The campaign also utilized social media, including a website, Facebook page, Twitter account, and a YouTube channel, to circulate their advocacy. During 2011 and early 2012, Strong4Life's most prominent visual poster featured a black and white photograph of a young White girl, her arms crossed over her chest, and her lips turned down in a frown. At the bottom of the image, the campaign producers superimposed the following statement over the girl's belly: "Warning. It's hard to be a little girl when you're not. Stop childhood obesity. strong4life.com" (Lohr, 2012, photo ad inset). The word "Warning" appeared in red capital letters to draw attention and frame the issue in line with the title of the broader advertising campaign, "Stop Sugarcoating It, Georgia" (Lohr, 2012, para. 1). The video warning focused on the loss of childhood which reinforced the campaign print ads' message: "Being fat takes the fun out of being a kid" (Salahi, 2012, para. 1).

The "Stop Sugarcoating It, Georgia" advertising image, along with other print advertisements and "stop childhood obesity" YouTube videos, drew criticism from news media and fat activists for its framing of children and/or fatness as a problem (Campos, 2012; DePatie, 2012; "I stand against," 2012b; Jonassen, 2012). As part of a response to the campaign, Marilyn Wann, one of the most prominent and visible figures in the fat activism community, decided to create a counter visual narrative. Wann helped create the fat positive visual campaign titled "I Stand Against Weight Bullying" (hereafter I Stand). The I Stand campaign functioned as a direct "response to Georgia's misguided and harmful Strong4Life campaign against childhood obesity" ("I Stand Against," 2012a, para. 1).

Wann began the campaign by creating and circulating her own personal image, which became known as a STANDard and as the template for future images. To be part of the collection, individuals used Wann's template and submitted their own images advocating for a stance, particularly against bullying and hatred of fat children. On the Tumblr site, I Stand approved and posted 333 images. Of those 333 images, Wann's STANDard became the most circulated image, including appearances on Tumblr, Facebook, Twitter, Pinterest, blogs, and newspapers (Beerman, 2015). Although a direct response to the Stop Sugarcoating It campaign, Wann's STANDard failed to reference that image, provide a side by side comparison of the images, or include a hyperlink to any articles about Georgia's campaign. Instead, the I Stand image was located on an individual, separate Tumblr site. Subsequent circulations of Wann's image online also often did not include the Strong4Life image.

Given the nature of the template and the amount of circulation, I focus my analysis on Wann's STANDard as a reiterated, representative form in the campaign. Wann's STANDard drew specifically from the Strong4Life Stop Sugarcoating it, Georgia campaign by using the little girl from their campaign as its inspiration. As Wann detailed in her explanation of why she decided to create the counter campaign:

> I was very angry when I saw one particular image used in the Georgia hate campaign [...] It shows a fat girl (an actor!) in a striped shirt, with this slogan over her belly: "It's hard to be a little girl when you're not." This is not a health message, it's a hate message [....] I want to show the world that it's not okay to shame fat children or to give them dangerous, discriminatory health advice.
>
> *(quoted in Margaret, 2012, para. 2)*

Thus, this image and the I Stand campaign responded to dominant rhetorics of obesity, including stigmatization and medicalization. However, as the next section will reveal, the combination of the ideological context and I Stand's argumentative approaches undercut its ability to meets its goals.

Mirror/Matching Strategies, Dissociation, and Enthymemes

Wann's STANDard engaged in mirroring/matching and dissociation strategies in an effort to undermine the dominant ideology about fatness. It utilized a clear mirror and matching strategy by mimicking the verbal and visual elements of the Strong4Life campaign. The matching strategy is evident in the ways Wann's image mimicked Strong4Life's photograph through a single subject (Wann herself), a black and white photograph, a similar pose (arms crossed at the chest), a similar placement of text, and a message to stop something. The message of the STANDard, however, also relied on a mirrored reversal of the Strong4Life message. The key differences included Wann's facial expression, the message, and its color. Smiling at the viewer, Wann's statement read: "I stand against harming fat children. Hate ≠ health. Stop weight bigotry. Health At Every Size®" ("I Stand Against," 2012a). To contrast the red lettering of "Warning," the words "I stand" and "stop weight bigotry" appeared in pink.

By matching and mirroring the visual and verbal structure of the Strong4Life image, the I Stand image accepted the medical frame. The I Stand campaign attempted to counter the argument of obesity discourse within the same medical frame by expanding the notion of health, particularly with its accompanying slogan of "health at every size" (hereafter HAES). HAES rejects weight loss and instead focuses on self-acceptance, size diversity, and engaging in health practices (Burgard, 2009). Rather than working to counter the ideologically-entrenched, medicalized obesity framework, the I Stand approach served to reactivate it.

Even while it accepted the medical framing, I Stand also dissociated meanings of health by focusing on breaking stigma and separating hate from health. In Wann's STANDard, the sentence, "Hate ≠ health," created dissociation; hate, through its association with fat shame or stigma, could not associate with health. Health here functioned both in relationship to a material reality of bodies, as well as an idea of fatness. The "does not equal" sign visually challenged the association between the Georgia campaign (a health campaign) and benefits to individuals' health. Wann's description of why she chose to mirror the specific little girl demonstrated her understanding of Georgia's campaign as a hate, not health, campaign. Thus, Wann's STANDard and her subsequent discourse challenged the framing of the Strong4Life campaign.

However, I Stand's mirror and matching strategies, as well as the dissociative strategies, presumes that the audience already has prior understandings of the controversy or knowledge of the campaigns. For this health dissociation to be successful, the audience needed to understand: Why does Wann stand "against harming fat children"? Why is there a need to break the association between hatred and health? The I Stand campaign presumes that the viewer holds an awareness of Georgia's campaign, of how fat shaming harms people, and/or how fat stigma is a form of weight bigotry. If the viewer does not bring that knowledge with them, the dissociation is likely to fail, as the viewer cannot connect the networked circulation between the two campaigns.

Society's dominant ideology showcases fat bodies as problems that make challenges difficult. Relying on the dominant ideology, the Strong4Life image used a photograph of a sad girl, with the phrase "It's hard to be a little girl when you're not." This image argued the problem of fatness for children by showing how being fat creates sadness and strips away childhood. The STANDard, in contrast, relies on enthymemes to challenge the dominant ideology. Missing elements includes the agent committing the bullying, where the bullying occurred, and the resulting harms fat children experience. Additionally, the STANDard's slogan HAES did not fit with dominant understandings of health and fitness, creating another possible argumentative gap. HAES promoted the acceptance of various body types by assuming all bodies were good bodies and by arguing that one could simultaneously experience healthy and fat lives. Within the broader context of dominant media portrayals showcasing fat bodies as aesthetic and health problems, a viewer reading Wann's body within the dominant norms of fatness would likely read the HAES message with skepticism.

Thus, when matching the positioning of the girl in her own image, Wann attempted to visually dissociate the causal linkage between fatness and illness/death and to create a new appearance/reality pairing whereby the reality of the fat body is not death. However, the campaign's visuals of material bodies explicitly tied to the negative ideology of fatness, where centuries of fat stigma in the United States have utilized images of fat bodies to convey shame. Wann's material body within the photograph, however, fails to challenge the fatness ideology and Strong4Life. The I Stand image counters medicalized narratives of fatness as a problem by using verbal dissociation, but failed to provide the HAES context, the specifics of the Georgia campaign, and weight bigotry to complete a visual dissociation. Thus, the overall image of the STANDard relied too much on the viewer to provide key contextual information, which then failed to fully dissociate the verbal and visual elements of Strong4Life's campaign. Consequently, these failures, along with the strategy of mirroring/matching, recast the image within the dominant context and dominant ideology.

Conclusion

I Stand's mirroring strategy presumed that viewers would have familiarity with the Strong4Life advertisement and could thus understand the visual meaning of Wann's image. In so doing, the I Stand image lacked the visual reference to the Strong4Life's image to complete I Stand's health enthymeme. Wann's I Stand image drew on networked argument by directly interacting with the other campaign; however, the lack of a direct side-by-side comparison or other specific context concerning the anti-obesity campaign undermined her argument, particularly within the entrenched nature of fatness as a problem ideology.

Wann's STANDard strategy focused on disrupting the dominant fatness ideology, arguing against the weight bigotry of the Georgia campaign, and used a visual and social media campaign to do so. This case study demonstrates that a visual logic of interaction can exist between competing advocacy campaigns. However, such networked argument can be a problem for those challenging the status quo if the strategies draw too heavily on mirroring/matching while also wanting to dissociate dominant or entrenched ideologies. Rather than use a networked argument, social movements and advocates working against a dominant ideology may need to change the ideological framework and create an opposing image, not a mirrored one, in certain contexts.

References

Beerman, R. J. (2015). *Containing fatness: Bodies, motherhood, and civic identity in contemporary U.S. culture* (Doctoral dissertation). Available from ProQuest Dissertations and Theses database. (UMI No. 3708808)

Burgard, D. (2009). What is "health at every size"? In E. Rothblum & S. Solovay (Eds.), *The fat studies reader* (pp. 41–53). New York, NY: New York University Press.

Campos, P. (2012, January 4). Anti-obesity ads won't work by telling fat kids to stop being fat. *The Daily Beast.* Retrieved from http://thedailybeast.com

DeLuca, K. M. (1999). Unruly arguments: The body rhetoric of Earth First!, ACT UP, and Queer Nation. *Argumentation and Advocacy, 36*(1), 9–21. Retrieved from ResearchGate database.

DePatie, J. (2012, February 7). The HAES files: A tale of two billboards [Blog post]. *Health At Every Size® Blog.* Retrieved from http://healthateverysizeblog.org/

Douglas, M. (1996). *Natural symbols* (2nd ed.). New York, NY: Routledge.

Edwards, J. L., & Winkler, C. K. (1997). Representative form and the visual ideograph: The Iwo Jima image in editorial cartoons. *Quarterly Journal of Speech, 83*(3), 289–310. doi: 10.1080/00335639709384187

Farrell, A. E. (2011). *Fat shame: Stigma and the fat body in American culture.* New York, NY: New York University Press.

I Stand Against Weight Bullying. (2012a, January 22). I stand against harming fat children. Hate ≠ health. Stop weight bigotry. Health At Every Size® [Digital photograph]. *Tumblr.* Retrieved from http://istandagainstweightbullying.tumblr.com/post/16321487655

I stand against weight bullying. (2012b, February 24). Wannt* your STANDard on a bus shelter in Atlanta? As part of Ragen Chastain's billboard project? I'm especially looking for children and people who represent all types of diversity! To participate, your photo needs [Facebook status update]. Retrieved from https://facebook.com/IStandAgainstWeightBullying/posts/196683173765232

Jonassen, J. (2012, March 27). Activist counters fat shaming ads with body positive billboard [Interview transcript with R. Chastain]. *Adios Barbie.* Retrieved from http://adiosbarbie.com

Jordan, J. W. (2004). The rhetorical limits of the "plastic body." *Quarterly Journal of Speech, 90*(3), 327–358. doi: 10.1080/0033563042000255543

Lange, J. I. (1993). The logic of competing information campaigns: Conflict over old growth and the spotted owl. *Communication Monographs, 60*(3), 239–257. doi: 10.1080/03637759309376311

Lohr, K. (2012, January 9). Controversy swirls around harsh anti-obesity ads. *National Public Radio.* Retrieved from http://npr.org

Margaret. (2012, February 28). "I STAND…" campaign takes creative aim at Georgia's anti-obesity ads [Blog post]. Retrieved from http://dietsinreview.com/diet_column/02/i-stand-campaign-takes-creative-aim-at-georgias-anti-obesity-ads/

Olson, L. C. (2009). Pictorial representations of British America resisting rape: Rhetorical re-circulation of a print series portraying the Boston Port Bill of 1774. *Rhetoric & Public Affairs, 12*(1), 1–36. doi: 10.1353/rap.0.0090

Palczewski, C. H. (2005). The male Madonna and the feminine Uncle Sam: Visual argument, icons, and ideographs in 1909 anti-woman suffrage postcards. *Quarterly Journal of Speech, 91*(4), 365–394. doi: 10.1080/00335630500488325

Perelman, Ch., & Olbrechts-Tyetca, L. (1969). *The new rhetoric: A treatise on argumentation* (J. Wilkinson & P. Weaver, Trans.). Notre Dame, IN: University of Notre Dame Press.

Prelli, L. J. (Ed.). (2006). *Rhetorics of display.* Columbia, SC: University of South Carolina Press.

Ross, K., & Moorti, S. (2005). Commentary and criticism: Is fat still a feminist issue? Gender and the plus size body. *Feminist Media Studies, 5*(1), 83–104. doi: 10.1080/14680770500058231

Salahi, L. (2012, January 2). "Stop sugarcoating" child obesity ads draw controversy. *ABC News.* Retrieved from http://abcnews.go.com

Thomson, D. (2007, November). *Spectacular decapitations: The body politics of shaming fat with personal responsibility.* Paper presented at the meeting of National Communication Association Conference, Chicago, IL.

Young, S. L. (2015). Running like a man, sitting like a girl: Visual enthymeme and the case of Caster Semenya. *Women's Studies in Communication, 38*(3), 331–350. doi: 10.1080/07491409.2015.1046623

---

* The original Facebook post contains this spelling, which plays on Wann's last name.

29

ACCUMULATING AFFECT AND VISUAL ARGUMENT

The Case of the 2015 Japanese Hostage Crisis

Naoki Kambe

In the last few decades, scholars in argumentation studies have participated in the debate on whether visual images function as argument (e.g., Birdsell & Groarke, 1996; Finnegan, 2001; Gibbons, 2007; Hahner, 2013). During this period, *Argumentation and Advocacy* published several special issues devoted to visual argument. In the first one, Birdsell and Groarke (1996) argued that questions of contexts were critical in developing a theory of visual argument because contexts involve "a wide range of cultural assumptions, situational cues, time-sensitive information, and/or knowledge of a specific interlocutor" (p. 5). To elaborate, they discussed three kinds of context: immediate visual context, immediate verbal context, and visual culture (Birdsell & Groarke, 1996). Although the first two contexts remain operative as posited two decades ago, social media has altered the third element to a great extent. Indeed, we need to consider some unique characteristics of online networks or spreadable media in a digital age that leads to widespread media circulation (Jenkins, Ford, & Green, 2013).

In this paper, I briefly review the three kinds of context and attempt to extend the third one by attending to participants' visibility and affective capacities that become salient in the participatory visual culture. After presenting some unique characteristics of this visual culture, I apply them to evaluate the global dissemination of the "I am Kenji" movement in the 2015 Japanese hostage crisis in which individuals posted online self-portraits with signs of "I am Kenji," calling for the safety of Kenji Goto, a freelance journalist that the Islamic State of Iraq and Syria (ISIS) had taken captive.

Birdsell and Groarke's Three Kinds of Context

Birdsell and Groarke's (1996) first type of context was the immediate visual context or how an image is related to other images. This type of context is significant for visual argument because "it incorporates a progression of images which allows to recognize a single frame as part of an overarching argument" (p. 6). Viewers can readily identify immediate visual context in film where the sequences of frames matter as they construct an overarching argument.

As the second kind of context, Birdsell and Groarke discussed an immediate verbal context or how an image relates to its accompanying verbal texts. This context is important for visual argument because verbal texts "can establish a context of meaning into which images can enter with a high degree of specificity while achieving a meaning different from the words alone" (p. 6). For example, captions and other verbal messages presented alongside images play a significant role in constructing visual arguments.

Finally, the third kind of context is visual culture. Birdsell and Groarke regarded this context as a set of "cultural conventions of vision [...] include what it means to see, or to represent seeing, as well as changes in the meaning of particular elements of visual vocabulary" (p. 7). This context is different from the other two kinds because it influences the visual meaning production indirectly; it provides the general master narrative whose design becomes the basis for more specific visual images and verbal messages.

Visibility and Affective Capacities in Participatory Visual Culture

In the last two decades, a number of argumentation scholars have attended to Birdsell and Groarke's three kinds of context and proved that they remain relevant in analyzing visual argument (e.g., Gibbons, 2006; Smith, 2006). Although I agree that the immediate visual and verbal contexts remain operative as Birdsell and Groarke described, visual culture has changed dramatically along with the emergence of social networking sites. One significant change is a shift from viewing culture to participatory culture. For example, in social networking sites such as YouTube, Twitter, and Facebook, users create and exchange content on sites that provide some degree of social connection (e.g., Shifman, 2014). This change has influenced the circulation of media content, including visual images, resulting in Birdsell and Groarke's conception of visual culture no longer functioning as adequate for assessing several characteristics of participatory visual culture. In particular, I will attend to two elements that stimulate the circulation of media content and change our understanding of context to a great extent: visibility and affective capacities.

First, the shift from viewing culture to a participatory visual culture has brought a new visibility. As boyd, Ito, and Jenkins (2016) articulated, individuals now easily see their participation in action in social networking sites. Indeed, this "new visibility increases the impact of participatory practices, expanding their reach and scope, and accelerating their circulation" (p. 185). This visibility allows individuals to see their connection or relationality with other participants, and in turn has changed our vision in the participatory visual culture. Jenkins (2014) emphasized that the existence of viewers' relatability, or their manner of engagement, changes our vision because it "orient[s] the interfacing between viewer and image [and] provide[s] implicit instructions in how to view" (pp. 446–447).

The existence of viewers' relatability in the participatory visual culture is a key for visual argument. It connects the manners of engagement to either affective capacities or capacities to affect and be affected (Deleuze, 1998). Unlike the visual culture in the 1990s that was influenced by a one-way flow media such as television, social networks are user-oriented communities bound by affective social relations between users (e.g., Pybus, 2015). Without these social relations, social networks do not exist. As affective capacities stimulate the widespread media circulation on social network sites, attending to these capacities helps us understand not only how to interpret a visual image but how it will "forward arguments" (Birdsell & Groarke, 1996, p. 6).

Social networks such as Twitter and Facebook have a huge impact on the transmission and accumulation of affect. How do affects circulate with/through a visual image? Using Facebook as an example, Pybus (2015) explained that adding one's photograph to one's profile makes adds personal visibility and generates varying numbers of posts from other users. Through this process, the act of uploading one's photograph becomes a personal archive of feelings or "an exploration of cultural texts as repositories of feelings and emotions" (Cvetkovich, 2003, p. 7; see also Pybus, 2015). In social networking sites, an affective meaning of the photograph transmits to another context and, in turn, affects accumulate in networked publics.

Having briefly reviewed Birdsell and Groarke's three kinds of context and extended the concept of visual culture to social networks, I now apply this new conception to a global dissemination of the "I am Kenji" movement during the 2015 Japanese hostage crisis. To do so, I will attend to the ways in which immediate visual and verbal contexts connect to the above-mentioned characteristics of participatory visual culture. In particular, I ask the following questions: What were the manners of engagement in this movement that allowed participants to interface with visual images? Did an argument frame exist that reflected immediate visual contexts? What, if any, verbal messages provided a high degree of specificity to understand a visual image? How did these contexts reveal affective capacities?

Immediate Visual Context: Face as Argument Frame

On January 20, 2015, ISIS posted online a video showing a masked man with a knife, standing between Kenji Goto and Haruna Yukawa, two Japanese civilian hostages. The member of the ISIS militia, known as Jihadi John, threatened to kill the two civilians unless the Japanese government paid a $200,000,000 ransom within days. Soon after ISIS released the video, online discourses emerged and circulated rapidly via social networking sites such as Facebook and Twitter. One of them was the global dissemination of the "I am Kenji" movement through Facebook asking people to post self-portraits with a sign "I am Kenji," imploring, "let's show that we're united, and tell that it's unjust to kill innocent citizens and it's meaningless to turn entire nation against you" (Nettikkara, 2015, para. 2). Viewers posted about a thousand photos with over 16,000 likes in few days and with over 45,000 likes in two weeks, including international responses from Canada, South Korea, India, Yemen and Mexico (e.g., Nettikkara, 2015).

The "I am Kenji" movement is indeed an example of visual argument that reflected the three visual contexts. Argument frames can provide an immediate visual context because they reflect a cultural pattern and help form, interpret, and/or evaluate an argument (Gibbons, 2007). The Facebook site asked people to post self-portraits with most of the images appearing as only *faces* with a sign of "I am Kenji." This facial self-portrait is the visual argument frame of the "I am Kenji" movement, helping to identify how people engage with the movement and its immediate visual context. Although Birdsell and Groarke (1996) saw a progression of images in one textual form such as in film, I also regard a series of only facial self-portraits uploaded through Facebook as a progression of images. The media spread as participants' visibility and their connection with other participants stimulated social networking sites. What made these separate images a composite visual argument was a common visual frame that those people shared.

Furthermore, the framed faces became an essential element of immediate visual context and a platform to transmit one's affect and to bind participants' connection or relationality to each other. Angel and Gibbs (2006) argued that the face is a key interface for transmitting affect because it is an essential element to mediate inner and outer forms of expression. For this reason, Deleuze and Guattari (1987) saw the face as a machine: "Concrete faces [...] are endangered by an *abstract machine of faciality (visagéité)*, which produces them at the same time as it gives the signifier its white wall and subjectivity" (p. 168). The abstract machine of faciality is one of the characteristics present in the argumentative frame of the "I am Kenji" movement. Interestingly, many of the movement's faces did not express emotion explicitly. Indeed, some faces were somewhat impassive. However, even in those photographs, affect was not absent. Rather, in the "I am Kenji" movement, the face became a machinic assemblage of signs or visual argument frame which transmitted and accumulated affect when a series of facial self-portraits turned into a progression of images constructing an overarching argument.

Immediate Verbal Context: "I am Kenji" As Metaphor

Besides the frame of face or immediate visual context, the immediate verbal context of the "I am Kenji" movement needs examination. Here I argue that the sign "I am Kenji" worked as a metaphor which helped interpreters determine the meaning of these words accompanying the faces and transmitting participants' archives of feelings. As Birdsell and Groarke (1996) noted, an implicit verbal backdrop like the traditional enthymeme plays a key role in visual argument. One argumentative function of a metaphor is its work as an enthymeme, inviting the audience to participate in the argument by filling in the associative blanks (e.g., Cooper, 1989). Similarly, visual images' interaction with a metaphor encourages an audience to fill in missing premises to construct a visual argument. In addition, metaphor plays an important role to transmit affect as its Greek origin "*metaphora*" means "transport" or "carry over" (Salovaara, 2015, p. 110). In the participatory visual culture, metaphor functions as a vehicle to transport or carry over one's affect which connects and brings people together.

Salovaara (2015) regarded a three-word slogan *Je suis Charlie* (I am Charlie) as a metaphor functioning to transmit affect. After the terrorist attack on January 7, 2015, *Je suis Charlie* functioned as a slogan showing solidarity with *Charlie Hebdo*, the Paris newspaper publisher which was the target of the attack. Salovaara (2015) discussed three functions of *Je suis Charlie* as a metaphor: (a) it organized news feeds, opinions, affects, and participatory events in social networks; (b) it showed one's identification with supporters of the victims of the *Charlie Hebdo* attack, which became a symbol of the freedom of expression; and (c) it turned an individual statement into a more general or universal value claim. Similarly, the metaphor "I am Kenji" accompanying facial self-portraits transmitted emotions such as hope, anger, and sadness through social networking sites, communicated the identification of a sender or a supporter of the movement, and stated a more general or universal value claim such as world peace. One college student who posted his face with "I am Kenji" said in an interview with *Asahi Shimbun* (January 28, 2015): "I know I am powerless but I hope that our collective call for the release of Kenji would reach the ISIS" (Saito & Tainaka, 2015, para. 2, author's translation). Another user wrote: "Let's prove to the world that Muslims are innocent of the ISIS actions. I'm Muslim, I'm Arab, and I'm Kenji" (Nettikkara, 2015, para. 5).

A series of archived feelings associated with events prior to 2015 also appeared to influence the *Je suis Charlie* and "I am Kenji" movements. Some individuals, for example, might include John F. Kennedy's speech *Ich bin ein Berliner* (I am a Berliner) delivered in West Berlin in 1963, which expressed his solidarity with individuals trapped behind the Berlin wall. Others might recall the "I am Trayvon Martin" movement in 2012, which showed people's solidarity with a 17-year-old African American high school student killed in Sanford, Florida. Those events and metaphors with the same structure functioned as an archive of feelings. Although each one's meaning and transmitted affect were different, the accumulation of the posts as an archive of feelings influenced the global dissemination of the "I am Kenji" movement.

The frame of face with the metaphor "I am Kenji" encouraged the audience to fill in his or her solidarity with Kenji and other participants and became a vehicle to transport users' affect in ways that connected and brought people together. In turn, the global dissemination of the "I am Kenji" movement became a visual argument in the participatory visual culture. As Robert Campbell, an American professor of Japanese literature at the University of Tokyo, uploaded his face with a sign "I am Kenji" and said in an interview: "It's a small act that we can all do...[and] you feel connected to other people" (Variyar, 2015, para. 9). Indeed, the participants of this movement connected through the frame of face and the metaphor "I am Kenji" in ways that archived argumentative affect.

Conclusion

This essay reviewed Birdsell and Groarke's three kinds of context argued two decades ago and extended one of them via two key elements of participatory culture: visibility and affective capacities. Applied to visual arguments globally disseminated in the "I am Kenji" movement, the face frame as the immediate visual context, and the metaphor of "I am Kenji" as the immediate verbal context helped create the conditions for accumulating affect and its potential as visual argument in the participatory visual culture.

In the most recent special issue of *Argumentation and Advocacy* devoted to visual argument, Groarke, Palczewski, and Godden (2016) ended their introductory article by saying that technological developments have made visuals a critical element of communication. In the same issue, Brunner and DeLuca (2016) discussed affective capacities of visual images in social media. Although these recent works have shown development in theorizing a visual argument in the digital age, I argue that the three kinds of context still play a key role in visual argument. In closing their article, Birdsell and Groarke (1996) suggested:

> Coupled with respect for existing interdisciplinary literature on the visual, such an emphasis promises a much better account of verbal and visual argument which can better understand the complexities of both visual images and ordinary argument as they are so often intertwined in our increasingly visual media.
>
> *(p. 10)*

Although more than twenty years have passed since the publication of Birdsell and Groarke's article, their suggestion still matters in debates on visual argument in the digital age. Indeed, respect for several concepts in argumentation theory, such as argument frame and metaphor, underscore the value of retaining the perspective.

References

Angel, M., & Gibbs, A. (2006). Media, affect and the face: Biomediation and the political scene. *Southern Review, 38*, 24–39.

Birdsell, D., & Groarke, L. (1996). Toward a theory of visual argument. *Argumentation and Advocacy, 33*, 1–10. Retrieved from https://public.wsu.edu/~ericsson/birdandgroar.pdf

boyd, d., Ito, M., & Jenkins, H. (2016). Reimagining participatory culture. In H. Jenkins, M. Ito, & d. boyd (Eds.). *Participatory culture in a networked era: A conversation on youth, learning, commerce, and politics* (pp. 180–189). Cambridge, United Kingdom: Polity Press.

Brunner, E. A., & DeLuca, K. M. (2016). The argumentative force of image networks: Greenpeace's panmediated global detox campaign [Special issue]. *Argumentation and Advocacy*, *52*(4), 281–299. Retrieved from http://tandfonline.com

Cooper, M. (1989). *Analyzing public discourse*. Prospect Heights, IL: Waveland Press.

Cvetkovich, A. (2003). *An archive of feelings: Trauma, sexuality, and lesbian public cultures*. Durham, NC: Duke University Press.

Deleuze, G. (1970/1988). *Spinoza: Practical philosophy* (R. Hurley, Trans.). San Francisco, CA: City Light Books.

Deleuze, G., & Guattari, F. (1987). *A thousand plateaus: Capitalism and schizophrenia* (B. Massumi, Trans.). Minneapolis, MN: University of Minnesota Press.

Finnegan, C. A. (2001). The naturalistic enthymeme and visual argument: Photographic representation in the "skull controversy." *Argumentation and Advocacy*, *37*(3), 133–149.

Gibbons, M. (2007). Seeing the mind in the matter: Functional brain imaging as framed visual argument [Special issue]. *Argumentation and Advocacy*, *43*(3–4), 175–188. Retrieved from http://tandfonline.com

Groarke, L., Palczewski, C. H., & Godden, D. (2016). Navigating the visual turn in argument [Special issue]. *Argumentation and Advocacy*, *52*(4), 217–235. Retrieved from http://tandfonline.com

Hahner, L. A. (2013). The riot kiss: Framing memes as visual argument. *Argumentation and Advocacy*, *49*(3), 151–166. Retrieved from http://tandfonline.com

Jenkins, E. S. (2014). The modes of visual rhetoric: Circulating memes as expressions. *Quarterly Journal of Speech*, *100*(4), 442–466. doi: 10.1080/00335630.2014.989258

Jenkins, H., Ford, S., & Green, J. (2013). *Spreadable media: Creating value and meaning in a networked culture*. New York, NY: New York University Press.

Nettikkara, S. (2015, January 26). #IamKenji: Fighting Islamic State with a hashtag. *BBC Trending*. Retrieved from http://bbc.com

Pybus, J. (2015). Accumulating affect: Social networks and their archive of feeling. In K. Hillis, S. Paasonen, & M. Petit (Eds.). *Networked affects* (pp. 235-250). Cambridge, MA: The MIT Press.

Saito, Y., & Tainaka, M. (2015, January 28). Inori todoke: I am Kenji 2000 mai kosu [Pray: "I am Kenji" over 2000 photographs]. *Asahi Shimbun*, evening edition, p. 11. Retrieved from http://database.asahi.com

Salovaara, I. (2015). #Je suis Charlie: Networks, affects and distributed agency of media assemblage. *Conjunctions: Transdisciplinary Journal of Cultural Participation*, *2*(1), 102–115. doi: 10.7146/tjcp.v2i1.22272

Shifman, L. (2014). *Memes in digital culture*. Cambridge, MA: The MIT Press.

Smith, V. J. (2007). Aristotle's classical enthymeme and the visual argumentation of the twenty-first century [Special issue]. *Argumentation and Advocacy*, *43*(3–4), 114–123. Retrieved from http://tandfonline.com

Variyar, M. (2015, January 28). Japan says "I am Kenji," even as the hostage has only "hours" to live. *International Business Times*. Retrieved from http://ibtimes.co.in

30

ANALYZING PUBLIC DIPLOMACY FOR JAPAN-U.S. RECONCILIATION

Hiroko Okuda

Compared to the historic worlds of power politics, politics in globally-linked, communication networks may become much more about whose story shapes or reshapes the course of events (Arquila & Ronfeldt, 1999). With the almost instant accessibility that digital communications provide, national leaders have begun seeking to accommodate their messages to the all-embracing differences that characterize intercultural exchanges. Nations engage in strategic public diplomacy, i.e., the international manifestation of information management by organizations, institutions, or other entities to achieve particular goals, maximize desired impacts, and minimize undesired effects (Manheim, 1994; Nye, 2008). In the increasingly globalized world, strategic communication now functions in what Nye (2008) called "a contest of competitive credibility" (p. 100).

The focus on *strategic* public diplomacy fits easily within the pragma-dialectical theory of argumentation, where individuals trying to resolve a difference of opinion need to maneuver strategically in order to reconcile their pursuit of rhetorical aims with a dialectical standard of reasonableness (van Eemeren & Grootendorst, 2004). For example, viewing commemorative speeches as argumentation practices, Suzuki and van Eemeren (2004) demonstrated how Emperor Akihito and Queen Beatrix resolved a source of conflict between their two nations to the satisfaction of both concerned parties. Viewed through a lens of public diplomacy in argumentative discourse, this paper explores how Prime Minister Shinzo Abe and President Barack Obama used public arguments at a World War II memorial site both to reassure opponents at home worried about the possibility of diplomacy by apology and to appeal to the people of the other country that their once enemy had transformed into a lasting friend.

As the two leaders engage in commemorative rhetoric, rhetorical agency arises as an issue of key concern. Even though rhetorical agency easily divides into the *official* and the *vernacular*, popular forms of memorialization easily confound the dichotomous relationship between the two. By considering their memorial speeches as argumentative discourse, what follows will uncover the ways Abe and Obama attempted to reconcile their countries' differing views of historical issues by looking to the past for inspiration and identity.

To begin, I will examine the "rhetorical situation" (Bitzer, 1968, p. 1) of Abe's first visit to the U.S. naval base at Pearl Harbor, followed by an exploration of the speeches by Abe and Obama at the U.S.S. Arizona Memorial on December 27, 2016 (in Japanese time, December 28). An analysis of their rhetorical acts will help explain how they each faced, and then muted, their country's challenge to overcoming "the animosity of conflict to become enduring partners and allies" (LaFranchi, 2016, para. 11).

Rhetorical Constraints

On December 8, 2016, Chief Cabinet Secretary Yoshihide Suga announced that Prime Minister Abe would visit Pearl Harbor, the site of Japan's attack on the United States 75 years ago. As a nationalist, Abe had spoken about Japan's need to move beyond its history to play a greater role in world peace and security. Hence, the audiences could view his U.S. visit as one in a series of efforts by Japan to come to terms with its past without engaging in direct apologies (Okuda, 2005). U.S. Press Secretary Josh Earnest carefully choreographed Abe's plans for the Pearl Harbor visit to "showcase the power of reconciliation that has turned former adversaries into the closest of allies, united by common interests and shared values" (Fifield, 2016b, para. 7). Framed within the exchange of visits that Obama initiated, Abe's trip to Pearl Harbor indeed marked "the alpha and omega of World War II in the Pacific" (LaFranchi, 2016, para. 10). Recognizing the potential for protests from Japan's nationalist conservatives for Abe's travel plans, the *Japan News* editorial ("Editorial," 2016) cautioned that, "Abe should make the visit of his own volition, not in return for Obama's visit to Hiroshima" (para. 10).

Given his nationalist leaning, Abe arguably was not the most likely Japanese leader to embrace the United States (Sakurai, 2016). But just as "symbolism ha[d] been a key part of the Obama presidency" (para. 8), Abe also appropriated "the historic site for political purposes" (para. 13) to "create positive momentum as he enter[ed] an unpredictable relationship with Trump" (Jeff Kingston, quoted in Smith & McCurry, 2016, para. 19). For friendly bilateral relations, Abe determined to consider "the need for a partner in defending against a rising China" (Rich, 2016, para. 12) to steer Japan closer to the United States. The demise of the global Cold War structure had profound implications for Japan because it brought renewed attention to World War II and Japan's postwar responsibilities for its wartime atrocities in the harsh spotlight of Asian pressure and international criticism.

Furthermore, Abe's visit took place during a U.S. presidential transition that threatened new instability in Asian international relations. It raised questions about the role of the United States as a balancer in the region (Fifield, 2016a). Abe was the first and only foreign leader who, shortly after the election, went to meet with President-elect Donald J. Trump who, in turn, promised to reset the U.S. priorities in the Pacific. The Abe/Trump pre-emptive effort blurred the lines between business and politics, appearing odd to the rest of the world (Eichenwald, 2016). The Obama administration responded, expressing the "one-president-at-a-time" criticism that prompted Abe to overlook his core right-wing constituency and visit Pearl Harbor (Marcus, 2016, p. A15; Rich & Harris, 2016, p. A15). In hindsight, the visit turned him into the last world leader who had a formal meeting with Obama during his presidency. Facing a nationalistic surge at home and abroad, both Abe and Obama made political use of the commemoration at Pearl Harbor to heighten the inclusive, shared experiences of danger, death, and destruction that would evoke a strong need for the two national leaders to offer healing and comfort to the publics.

Strategic Maneuvering in Public Diplomacy

The celebration at the USS Arizona Memorial encouraged the heads of state of the United States and Japan to adopt a eulogistic perspective to memorialize the dead, as each leader recalled wartime deeds and reflected on the causes of the two countries' war efforts. There, the commemorative speeches offered a new beginning for Japan and the United States to promote reconciliation, eschew the backward-looking view on addressing past wrongs, and focus on the forward-looking promotion of peace.

Both speeches corresponded well with the classical epideictic rhetorical form. The audience primarily functioned as onlookers witnessing the celebration. Both Abe and Obama employed the traditional strategies of examples and amplification to praise the individuals. By personalizing wartime history, they also embedded memories of past injustice within a context of shared history that was agreeable to both countries. Abe provided explicit detail that recalled the horror of the sinking of the Arizona:

> And every one of those servicemen had a mother and a father anxious about his safety. Many had wives and girlfriends they loved, and many must have had children they would have loved watch [*sic*] grow up. All of that was brought to an end.
>
> *(The White House, 2016, para. 4)*

Obama incorporated detailed examples and figurative analogies that presented "that morning" as a drama of Americans in conflict.

> We honor Americans like Jim Downing—a gunner's mate first class on the West Virginia [....] We remember Americans like Harry Pang—a fireman from Honolulu who, in the face of withering fire [....] We salute Americans like Chief Petty Officer John Finn, who manned a .50-caliber machine gun for more than two hours and was wounded more than 20 times, earning him our nation's highest military decoration, the Medal of Honor.
>
> *(The White House, 2016, para. 26-29)*

Here, the sequenced parallelism of "We…Americans like" added emphasis, order, and climax to the idea of "the heroism that shone here 75 years ago" (The White House, 2016, para. 23). These image management strategies highlighted and personified the victimization that encouraged audiences in the two countries to develop a shared commitment to grieving those who had lost their lives and loved ones.

Attempting neither to hold the Japanese and American people accountable for their past actions nor to direct the course of future events, Abe focused instead on appreciating the importance of being "here at Pearl Harbor" (The White House, 2016, para. 1) where a war had commenced. After focusing on a memorial resting place for those who died there, he used an analogy, thanking the United States and the world for helping Japan, a "nation in burnt-out ruins" (para. 11), to recover and develop "a free and democratic country that values the rule of law" (para. 7) in the years after World War II. He shifted the focus from "that 'Pearl Harbor'" to "now," and then demonstrated his appreciation for the "leadership of the United States" (para. 12). He argued, "Ours is an alliance of hope that will lead us to the future. What has binded us together is the hope of reconciliation made possible through the spirit, the tolerance" (para. 15-16). By shifting primacy from past wrongs to future peace, the prime minister redefined the site of memory at Pearl Harbor as "a symbol of reconciliation" for "Japanese children and […] people all around the world" (para. 18).

Obama's speech also featured a forward-looking perspective. The U.S. President described "the power of reconciliation and the alliance between the American and Japanese peoples" (The White House, 2016, para. 20). While commenting on the courageous acts of "the Greatest Generation [who] did not seek war, but [...] refused to shrink from it" (para. 31), Obama gave primacy to a vision of the future rather than to a reflection on the painful past, and then consecrated "Pearl Harbor" as a remembrance of "what is possible between nations and between peoples" (para. 36)—"The most bitter of adversaries can become the strongest of allies" (para. 36). By using the Japanese phrase "otagai no tame ni—'with and for each other'" (para. 37) to enhance "the spirit of friendship" (para. 41), Obama moved both countries toward a process of critical reflection that afforded the opportunity to address fundamental values and beliefs that made collective political action "to chart our own futures" (para. 40).

Both Abe and Obama sought to reinforce society's existing values and promote civic cohesion. In spite of facing different political cultures that highlighted different priorities, together they created a positive context for paying homage to "those we lost, and we give thanks for all that our two nations have won—together, as friends" (The White House, 2016, para. 42). Whereas Obama restated that "the fruits of peace always outweigh the plunder of war" (para. 36), Abe reiterated that Japan "must never repeat the horrors of war again. This is the solemn vow we, the people of Japan, have taken" (para. 7). Through serious consideration of "the horrors of war" (para. 7) and "the anguish of war" (para. 37), both leaders encouraged the Japanese and the American people to accept "the sacrifice[s] made here [...] to seek the divine spark that is common to all humanity" (para. 37) and to resist "the urge to turn inward [and] to demonize those who are different" (para. 37). In "increasing adherence to the values it lauds" (Perelman & Olbrechts-Tyteca, 1969, p. 50), the commemorative rhetoric arguably confirmed the close ties between Japan and the United States and prioritized a prosperous future over past grievances.

Conclusion and Consequences

Shinzo Abe's visit to Pearl Harbor offered a good way for the two countries to come to terms with their intertwined history and onetime adversarial past. On the memorial occasion, the epideictic form of speech allowed Abe and Obama to console elderly survivors as well as the souls of the dead in both countries. In a move perhaps unsatisfying to some, both leaders offered minimal reference to the conflict that caused great suffering to both nations in an effort to avoid politically charged world views. Another strategy was to shift the imaginative focus from national pride to individuals with personal narratives. For acknowledging the sensitive history of war remembrance, the focus on individual experience helped both leaders embrace the other side. Overall, focusing specifically on the human dimensions of the deceased and the relationship between the deceased and the living, the complementary gesture of remembrance functioned to address the wrenching issues not just to the populations of their own countries, but to those living in countries around the world.

Just as Obama was in Hiroshima to remember, but not to apologize, so the prime minister did not offer any apology for Japan's surprise attack on the United States but did offer his condolences to the families of the 2,403 Americans who died on December 7, 1941 (in Japanese time, December 8). Most American and Japanese media covered the event positively, evaluating Abe's strategy of embracing the vanquished and the victor in "remembrance and reconciliation" (Jackson, 2016, para. 1). As the White House's senior director Daniel Kritenbrink expected, Abe's historic step was "a powerful demonstration of how the two countries can overcome a very painful history to become the closest of allies and friends" (Nakamura & Lyte, 2016, para. 6). For regional cooperation, the two national leaders took a more proactive stance to call for a clear interest in ensuring that the peace and prosperity of Asia, so vital to its future.

Over the past seven decades, in fact, widespread regional recognition of the need for reconciliation and a final resolution to the historical issues has proliferated, both for the sake of justice and to remove a major obstacle to regional cooperation. In terms of distance to the time and the events mentioned in their speeches, Abe and Obama proposed a collective rather than an individual, personal recognition of the historical past, and thereby integrated the two nations into the inclusive *we* who have come to a reconciled view of history. In this regard, the reciprocal visits have the potential to lay the foundation for mutual understanding and historical reconciliation.

For the first time after 75 years, Japan and the United States redefined Pearl Harbor and Hiroshima as sites of tolerance and reconciliation that gave meaning to the past as a moment of personal grief, while moving towards the group level to the extent that one's identity closely links with one's sense of place, community, and culture. Memory work for an individual or community helps reconstitute one's identity in the present, that is, questions about what happened in the past touch upon the most sensitive issues of national identity, and even national myths that play a powerful role to this day.

Here, the rhetoric of reconciliation promoted an introspective effort to be receptive to a more balanced historical view by offering a shared vision for nations that transcended victimhood and exclusive notions of national identity. Sustaining a reconciled view of the past, however, will not be easy.

By commemorating Pearl Harbor and Hiroshima, the two leaders opened and closed the last war between their countries—without making concessions. They presented their own actions in the best possible light to convey the key message that war is a tragedy for everyone, with neither side emerging unscathed. Although Trump (2016) tweeted about Obama's avoidance of "the sneak attack on Pearl Harbor" while he visited Hiroshima, the general sense of outrage among the U.S. public about a *sneaky* attack dissipated over time (Nakamura & Lyte, 2016; Smith & McCurry, 2016). In Japan, the public was aware of the importance of the symbolic visit to Pearl Harbor at a time of uncertainty in the Japan-U.S. alliance, thus resulting in the rise of Prime Minister Abe's approval ratings (Smith & McCurry, 2016). By reframing historical reconciliation into a process of integrating different views of the past, the Prime Minister and the President together embraced a reluctance to fully confront the complexity of past actions and any blame of the other for their historical actions. In so doing, the joint efforts for reconciliation may set a precedent for dissolving past animosities and have trust and cooperation replace them moving forward.

References

Arquila, J., & Ronfeldt, D. (1999). *The emergence of noopolitik: Toward an American information strategy*. Santa Monica, CA: RAND. Retrieved from https://rand.org

Beale, W. H. (1978). Rhetorical performative discourse: A new theory of epideictic. *Philosophy & Rhetoric, 11*(4), 221–246. Retrieved from http://jstor.org/stable/40237084

Bitzer, L. F. (1968). The rhetorical situation. *Philosophy & Rhetoric, 1*(1), 1–14. Retrieved from http://jstor.org/stable/40236733

Editorial: Abe's Pearl Harbor Visit Should Be a Final Stage for Japan-U.S. Reconciliation [Editorial]. (2016, December 8). *The Japan News*, p. 4.

Eichenwald, K. (2016, December 23). How Donald Trump's business ties are already jeopardizing U.S. interests. *Newsweek*. Retrieved from http://newsweek.com

Fifield, A. (2016a, November 27). For military-weary Okinawa, Trump offers hope of reducing base burdens. *The Washington Post*, p. A18.

Fifield, A. (2016b, December 6). Japanese leader to visit Pearl Harbor. *The Washington Post*, p. A10.

Jackson, D. (2016, December 27). Japanese leader to visit Pearl Harbor with Obama: Able makes first formal trip by Japanese PM to American sacred place. *USA Today*, p. 3A.

LaFranchi, H. (2016, December 27). At heart of Obama-Abe Pearl Harbor meeting: The power of reconciliation. *The Christian Science Monitor*. Retrieved from https://csmonitor.com/USA/Foreign-Policy/2016/1227/At-center-of-Obama-Abe-Pearl-Harbor-meeting-the-power-of-reconciliation

Manheim, J. B. (1994). *Strategic public diplomacy & American foreign policy: The evolution of influence*. New York, NY: Oxford University Press.

Marcus, R. (2016, December 29). Only one president at a time, right? *The Washington Post*, p. A15.

Nakamura, D., & Lyte, B. (2016, December 27). Obama aims to ease tensions with Pearl Harbor event. *The Washington Post*, p. A3.

Nye, J. S., Jr. (2008). Public diplomacy and soft power. *The Annals of the American Academy of Political and Social Science*, *616*(1), 94–109. doi: 10.1177/0002716207311699

Okuda, H. (2005). Murayama's political challenge to Japan's public apology. *International & Intercultural Communication Annual*, *28*, 14–42. Retrieved from EBSCOhost database.

Perelman, Ch., & Olbrechts-Tyteca, L. (1969). *The new rhetoric: A treatise on argumentation*. Notre Dame: University of Notre Dame Press.

Rich, M. (2016, December 28). Obama's departure puts Japan's alliance with the United States at a crossroad. *The New York Times*, p. A9.

Rich, M., & Harris, G. (2016, December 25). In Pearl Harbor visit, a symbol of reconciliation in Japan. *The New York Times*, p. A15.

Sakurai, J. (2016, December 21). Shinzo Abe's act of peace at Pearl Harbor masks a hawkish intent. *The Financial Times*. Retrieved from https://ft.com/

Smith, D., & McCurry, J. (2016, December 26). "Alliance of hope": US and Japan leaders meet for historic Pearl Harbor first. *The Guardian*. Retrieved from https://theguardian.com

Suzuki, T., & van Eemeren, F. H. (2004). This painful chapter. *Argumentation and Advocacy*, *41*(2), 102–111. Retrieved from http://tandfonline.com

Trump, D. J. [@realDonaldTrump]. (2016, May 28). Does President Obama ever discuss the sneak attack on Pearl Harbor while he's in Japan? Thousands of American lives lost. #MDW [Tweet]. Retrieved from https://twitter.com/realdonaldtrump/status/736672123012427776?lang=en

van Eemeren, F. H., & Grootendorst, R. (2004). *A systematic theory of argumentation: The pragma-dialectical approach*. Cambridge, United Kingdom: Cambridge University Press.

The White House, Office of the Press Secretary. (2016). *Remarks by President Obama and Prime Minister Abe of Japan at Pearl Harbor* [Press release]. Retrieved from https://whitehouse.gov/the-press-office/2016/12/28/remarks-president-obama-and-prime-minister-abe-japan-pearl-harbor

Williams, W. (2016, December 28). Prime Minister Abe promises peace at the site of Pearl Harbor attack. *The Christian Science Monitor*. Retrieved from https://csmonitor.com

PART IV

STRATEGIC USE OF AUTHORITY IN NETWORKED ARGUMENTS

31

CHALLENGING A CULTURE OF SECRECY

Investigating the Emergence of Antenarrative Storytelling in Community Responses to the Hanford Nuclear Reservation

R. Brandon Anderson

The Hanford Nuclear Reservation produced plutonium for many of the approximately 70,000 nuclear warheads the United States manufactured for the American nuclear program (Gerber, 1992). Because of a culture of cold war secrecy surrounding the nuclear program, public awareness of nuclear risks was not widespread until the expansion of nuclear power programs during the late 1980s (Kinsella & Mullen, 2007). Findlay and Hevly (2011) asserted that while going about the business of containing communism, the Hanford Site (and the U.S. Government) was spreading millions of curies of radioactive iodine into the Columbia River, the air, and soil of the Columbia Basin. Kinsella and Mullen (2007) found that citizens surrounding the nuclear plant had suspected the adverse health impact of the plant. However, the personal experience and testimony of those living in close proximity to the facilities failed to contradict the Department of Energy's (DOE) assertions that the nuclear facilities were safe to humans (Kinsella & Mullen, 2007). Nevertheless, farmers of this region began taking note of the unusual happenings around them.

In the spring of 1986, a small, citizen-led environmental group in southeastern Washington made a substantial breakthrough. The Hanford Education Action League (H.E.A.L.) filed a legally enforceable request under the Freedom of Information Act that prompted the release of 19,000 pages of concealed governmental documents (Schneider, 1990). The documents revealed that between 1944 and 1972, the Hanford Nuclear Reservation, known for producing weapons-grade plutonium, released roughly 740,000 curies of radioactive iodine into the air. The reports also documented the release of "an estimated 3 million curries of radioactive material into the Columbia [River]" (Tizon, 2005, para. 29) that undoubtedly distributed the radiation throughout the region.

Kinsella (2004) noted that multiple forms of public expertise were necessary in order to breach the system of security and silence surrounding the Hanford Nuclear Reservation.

Kinsella contended that the confluence of technical competencies, public expertise, and local knowledge facilitated a stakeholder conglomeration that was instrumental to challenging governmental power structures. Kinsella and Mullen (2007) clarified that a group of "downwinders" deployed local knowledge in order to infuse their lived experience into traditional scientific and governmental rationalizations.

To review, years before H.E.A.L filed the Freedom of Information Act, the farmers across the river from the nuclear facility began questioning their relationship with the atomic industry. By compiling anecdotal evidence, the downwinder group generated a source of local data that proved useful in their localized sense-making project. Klein, Moon, and Hoffman (2006) contended that sense-making is a retrospective process that has the potential to clarify the past as individuals' "test and improve" (p. 72) explanations for the peculiarities in their lives. In essence, by engaging in this sense-making process, this group of farmers enacted a local knowledge that served as a popular epidemiology. Brown (1997) suggested that popular epidemiology has the potential to mobilize citizens around the goal of identifying and ameliorating environmental stressors and local illness patterns. Accordingly, in 1983, Juanita Andrewjeski began constructing a map that revealed a pattern of illness experienced throughout her Columbia Basin community.

In order to comprehend the ways in which acts of counter-mapping function argumentatively, I interrogate the manufacturing of local knowledge that occurred among a vocal group of farmers living and working downwind from the nuclear facility. In exploring the production of knowledge amongst this group, I analyze the ways in which Andrewjeski's illness map cultivated a consciousness of local expertise. I argue that the map functioned rhetorically to create a space in which the lived experiences of the farmer–citizens could function on par with scientific expertise. As Andrewjeski's concerns made their way into the popular consciousness, the farmer-citizens became an integral part of the network searching for answers from the federal nuclear industry. This essay works to bridge previous works on the rhetoric of mapping with the concept of argumentative good reasons in narrative construction.

With the remainder of this essay, I first explore the rhetoric of mapping. Second, I describe the emergence of the farmer expertise. Then, I analyze the emergency zone map before finally providing some considerations of the ways in which this group produced localized expertise through antenarrative production.

Rhetoric of Mapping

Maps are more than static representations of the past. Hartnett (1998) posited that the functional nature of maps—to allow a user to say with confidence that "this is here" or "that is there" (p. 287)—has its foundation in the belief that maps exist as impartial presentations of space and place. From this basic assumption, maps are visual arguments that foretell ways to experience space and place. However, the act of map construction is a rhetorical process. Mapmakers adopt strategic conclusions regarding what to place, omit, simplify, and even classify. These symbolic decisions behind map production embody persuasive purposes. De Certeau (1985) suggested that the mapping process opens a space for dialectical engagement when he argued, "the map joins, in effect, what *is* to what *could be*. The art of observing is combined with the art of inventing" (p.17). The opening of dialectical space grants the map user the capability to interact with an environment in such a way that the space/place becomes reawakened time and again. Maps harbor multiple levels of possible meanings, which allow the creative user to construct and deconstruct, regardless of the author's intention. Hartnett (1998) suggested that map users have the ability to "'dance' their way to spontaneous creations of new meaning" (p. 286). Thus, every time a user employs a map, the individual opens a new "space of possibility" (De Certeau 1988, p. 100). The mapping of space/place is a living enterprise of new interpretations and landscapes.

Exploiting the rhetorical nature of mapping, Barney (2014) suggested that rhetoricians can—and should—situate cartography as a complex rhetorical practice vital to the discourses of American power. In offering the map user the possibility of recreating the space/place experiences, maps are vulnerable to what Crampton and Krygier (2006) described as a "people's cartography" (p. 18). These deliberate acts of counter-mapping allow individuals to reinterpret state-owned maps in order to challenge dominant power structures. The impact of these subversive mapping exploits are so significant that Hayes (2016) introduced the concept of "rhetorical cartography" as a means of surveying the "apparatus of power and the technologies of governance at work in the social, political, and legal processes of mapping" (p. 56). Accentuating the relationship between rhetoric and cartography allows for examinations of how resistive modes of subjectivity disrupt and remake technologies of governance (Hayes, 2016). The map at the heart of this analysis exemplifies the subversive act of counter-mapping, as the group of farmer-citizens utilized the illness map to disrupt the prevailing narrative of safety and culture of secrecy surrounding nuclear production.

The Emerging Farmer Expertise

In 1983, Juanita Andrewjeski began keeping track of the series of unnatural occurrences surrounding her homestead. Andrewjeski and her husband, Leon, farmed just downwind from the Hanford Nuclear Reservation. Throughout their rural community, farmers initially began diagnosing abnormalities among their livestock. In my conversation with Juanita, she reminisced about the moment she realized that something was amiss. Andrewjeski told of an experience she had butchering chickens. She noted, "As we butchered the hens, I noticed that all of the reproductive organs were dried up like old leather" (personal communication, June 2014). She said that the internal organs of the chickens surprised her and got her thinking about her own physical ailments.

The Andrewjeskis were not alone. As the farmers observed abnormalities with their livestock throughout their community, they began openly discussing their own health conditions. Tom Bailie, the most vocal (and sensational) of the Columbia Basin farmers, told of the ways in which his own health issues piqued his concern. In an interview with the *Washington Post*, Bailie vocalized his suspicions,

> I was born a year after my stillborn brother. I struggled to breathe through under-developed lungs, and suffered to overcome numerous birth defects. I underwent multiple surgeries, endured paralysis, endured thyroid medication, a stint in an iron lung, loss of hair, sores all over my body, fevers, dizziness, poor hearing, asthma, teeth rotting out and, at age 18, a diagnosis of sterility.
>
> *(Harden, 1996, para. 55)*

Bailie directly attributed the list of ailments to living across from the nuclear facilities. While he could not provide any evidence of direct causation, his personal narrative was suggestive of the experiences of others in the region.

Individual anecdotes eventually developed into longer deliberations between the farmers as they began to suspect the nuclear facilities across the river. In an interview with the *Inlander* magazine, Andrewjeski reminisced about her mounting apprehension, "It seemed like every man we knew was having heart problems." She continued, "We knew something was wrong, real wrong, because they were young men" (Coats, 1990, para. 2). As fears continued to develop, Andrewjeski and other farmers began hypothesizing about the causes of their illnesses; she described the conclusion they drew to the *Chicago Tribune,* "Now we have to think that maybe the radiation in the dirt they plowed and leveled and farmed got them" (Coats, 1990, para. 4). Even as the anecdotal evidence mounted and the stories got louder, the federal government remained adamant about the lack of a causal linkage (Schneider, 1990).

As the sharing of individual stories began sparking some progress, multiple actors challenged the farmers' utilization of lived experience as evidence. Andrewjeski noted that officials sloughed off her early concerns about the cardiac cases of her husband and others by pointing out the lack of any scientific evidence linking radiation to heart problems (personal communication, June 2014). In addition to the federal government's doubts, the farmers' neighbors also attempted to stifle the health concerns related to the nuclear plant. Bailie told the *Washington Post* that he "was threatened by his fellow farmers, who feared his alarms might damage the export market for their foodstuffs, and had his loans foreclosed by a local banker who told him it was a warning to stop undermining the community" (Walker, 1993, para. 4). Community members often dismissed Bailie, Andrewjeski, and others who were asking difficult questions as "complainers" (Fries, 2003, para. 7).

The small group of concerned farmers struggled to engage the federal nuclear industry in their search for answers because they did not retain the "right" form of evidence for their discussions. The scientific expertise that federal agencies offered led to the regular dismissal of the farmers' simple anecdotal evidence.

Mapping Illness

Following continued dismissals situated in the scientific expertise of the government's doctors (Schneider, 1990), Andrewjeski began plotting illnesses on an emergency zone map. By itself, the map did not offer much information. Looking at the map, users saw two sections of land that the Columbia River divided. To the west of the river were the nuclear facilities. To the east resided a stretch of land that a hypothetical accident at the production facilities could impact. However, the map included no indicators of houses, businesses, or any other signs of habitation. It simply displayed labeled roads that residents could ostensibly use in case of a nuclear emergency. The map appeared as a blank canvas and its limited information symbolically removed farmers from any possible risk.

Accompanying the emergency plan zone map was a letter from the county disclosing the distribution of special emergency broadcast radios that would "automatically alert [residents] and their families in case of an emergency at the Hanford site" ("Benton Franklin Counties," 1983, para. 1). The letter assured residents that the county was protecting the safety of those within a specific proximity of the nuclear site. Distributed in August 1983, the letter told residents that, "federal law requires that these radios be given to all homes within 10 miles of an operating nuclear plant so that residents are provided with an early warning in the unlikely event of an emergency" ("Benton Franklin Counties," 1983, para. 2). The letter implored community members to feel comforted by actions of local governmental agencies. The letter continued:

The radios are just one part of the counties' overall emergency preparedness program. We will also be handing out a brochure that explains the counties' on-going program to assure the safety of people working and living near the nuclear facilities on the Hanford site.

("Benton Franklin Counties," 1983, para. 3)

The letter from the county attempted to shift any discussion of safety to a forward-looking worldview that strategically dismissed any signs of sickness. The text of the letter encouraged readers to rest assured that everything occurring across the river was safe and secure; they had no reason to worry. Simultaneously, however, the letter overlooked and downplayed the voices and concerns of the rural farmers.

However, Andrewjeski's additions to the map told a far more morbid tale. Clusters of red circles signified heart attacks, while blue crosses denoted cases of cancer. Accompanying the map were several pieces of notebook paper containing the name of every farmer who owned and moved to a plot of land across the river from the nuclear site. Out of 50 neighbors living just beyond the Hanford perimeter, 20 of the men either had died of heart attacks or undergone cardiac surgery before their 50th birthdays. By 1989, Andrewjeski's map signified 47 heart attacks and 33 cases of cancer within the stretch of farmland the emergency plan map showed. The crosses and circles that filled the small map represented the bodies of individuals who no longer could speak for themselves. The symbolism of the circles and crosses retained the power to shift the argumentative landscape available to the farmers by rearticulating personal testimony as a thought-provoking network of illness. No longer were farmers' incidents of sickness isolated; instead, they were part of a pattern of death and disease that demanded attention.

Prospective Sense-making and Local Expertise

As concerns about the nuclear facility mounted, H.E.A.L. formally invited Andrewjeski to join their ranks as they collectively began pressuring the U.S. Department of Energy for further information. With her map, Andrewjeski rearticulated her lived experiences and granted her community access into the popular consciousness by making the invisible visible. The map served as the ground truth of a clear collection of human beings going about their daily lives living in dangerous conditions. By presenting real data about the real experiences of those living across the river, the narrative of "controlled" nuclear production could not persist. Andrewjeski's act of counter-mapping engaged a form of prospective sense-making (future oriented) grounded in what Boje (2011) called "antenarrative storytelling" (p. 1). Andrewjeski's map eventually granted credence to the concerns of the farmers by showing that a system of networked individuals can facilitate change through their lived experiences. Even with continued pushback, the farmer-citizens group understood that their stories and experiences were significant. Antenarrative storytelling effectively re-contextualized the dominant nuclear narrative about safety and, as individuals participated in this narrative production, each farmer's experience played a vital role in the creation of a network of local expertise.

Andrewjeski's map altered the discussion about safety and health by expropriating the governmental agency's emergency map. As the accompanying letter reflected, those living in proximity to the nuclear facilities existed in a world that deemed nuclear production "safe." However, each additional circle and cross on the emergency map integrated individuals' illnesses into the new story about nuclear safety. Boje (2011) contended that stories are always developing. The developing stories—antenarratives—serve as "bets on the future," bridging past narratives that are stuck in place with emergent living stories (p. 1). In this way, antenarratives are self-organizing frontiers wherein fragments cling to other fragments, eventually forming complex new patterns (Boje, 2011). The illness map aided antenarrative production because it bridged the static narrative of nuclear safety with the developing narrative fragments of illness that those living across the river supplied. Evident from this analysis is that antenarrative construction required something to initiate the narrative transformation. Separately, the lived experiences and sicknesses of the farmers were isolated and disparate. However, the map carved out a rhetorical space in which the community of farmers could share their personal expertise of living in the shadow of the nuclear facilities as a collective. These farmer-citizens eventually became localized nodes of expertise that were integral to telling the whole story of the U.S. nuclear industry.

References

Barney, T. (2014). Diagnosing the third world: The "map doctor" and the spatialized discourses of disease and development in the Cold War. *Quarterly Journal of Speech, 100*(1), 1–30. doi: 10.1080/00335630.2014.887215

Benton Franklin Counties Department of Emergency Management. (1983). *Emergency zone plan map* [Map and letters]. Personal collection of Juanita Andrewjeski.

Boje, D. M. (2011). *Storytelling and the future of organizations: An antenarrative handbook*. New York, NY: Routledge.

Brown, P. (1997). Popular epidemiology revisited. *Current Sociology, 45*(3), 137–156. doi: 10.1177/001139297045003008

Coats, J. (1990, July 23). Victims used "death map" to connect cancers, plant. *The Chicago Tribune*. Retrieved from http://articles.chicagotribune.com

Crampton, J. W., & Krygier, J. (2006). An introduction to critical cartography. *ACME: International E-Journal for Critical Geographies, 4*(1), 11–33. Retrieved from https://acme-journal.org

De Certeau, M. (1985). Pay attention: To make art (T. DiPiero, Trans.). In H. Meyer & N. Harrison (Eds.), *The lagoon* (pp. 17–23). Ithaca, NY: Cornell University. Retrieved from http://theharrisonstudio.net/wp-content/uploads/2011/03/payattention.pdf

De Certeau, M. (1988). *The writing of history* (T. Conley, Trans.). New York, NY: Columbia University Press.

Findlay, J. M., & Hevly, B. W. (2011). *Atomic frontier days: Hanford and the American West*. Seattle, WA: University of Washington Press.

Fries, J. H. (2003, December 4). Fallout. *Inlander*. Retrieved from https://inlander.com/spokane/fallout/Content?oid=2175513

Gerber, M. S. (1992). *On the home front: The Cold War legacy of the Hanford nuclear site*. Lincoln, NE: University of Nebraska Press.

Harden, B. (1996, May 5). Nuclear reactions. *The Washington Post*. Retrieved from https://washingtonpost.com

Hartnett, S. (1998). Michel de Certeau's critical historiography and the rhetoric of maps. *Philosophy and Rhetoric, 31*(4), 283–302. Retrieved from http://jstor.org/stable/40238008

Hayes, H. A. (2016). *Violent subjects and rhetorical cartography in the age of the terror wars*. London, United Kingdom: Palgrave Macmillan.

Kinsella, W. (2004). Public expertise: A foundation for citizen participation in energy and environmental decisions. In S. P. Depoe, J. W. Delicath, & M.-F. A. Elsenbeer (Eds.), *Communication and public participation in environmental decision making* (pp. 83–98). New York, NY: State University of New York Press.

Kinsella, W. J., & Mullen, J. (2007). Becoming Hanford downwinders: Producing community and challenging discursive containment. In B. C. Taylor, W. J. Kinsella, S. P. Depoe, & M. S. Metzler (Eds.), *Nuclear legacies: Communication, controversy, and the U.S. nuclear weapons complex* (pp. 73–108). Lanham, MD: Lexington Books.

Klein, G., Moon, B., & Hoffman, R. R. (2006). Making sense of sense-making 1: Alternative perspectives. *IEEE Intelligent Systems, 21*(4), 70–73. doi: 10.1109/MIS.2006.75

Schneider, K. (1990, July 12). U.S. admits peril of 40's emissions at A-bomb plant. *The New York Times.* Retrieved from http://nytimes.com/

Tizon, T. A. (2005, May 15). Neighbors of Hanford nuclear reservation await a verdict. *The Seattle Times.* Retrieved from http://seattletimes.com

Walker, M. (1993, December 12). Racing toward destruction: The nuclear weapons industry worked feverishly during the Cold War in the belief that its dangerous experiments would save the free world.: ATOMIC HARVEST: Hanford and the lethal toll of America's nuclear arsenal, by Michael D'Antonio [Book review]. *The Los Angeles Times.* Retrieved from http://articles.latimes.com/1993-12-12/books/bk-874_1_nuclear-weapons-nuclear-test-site-nuclear-battlefield/2

32

THE VISUAL DEPICTION OF STATEHOOD IN DAESH'S *DABIQ* MAGAZINE AND *AL-NABA'* NEWSLETTER

Kareem El Damanhoury

Visual images serve as key sources of networked arguments. Images can argue (Birdsell & Groarke, 1996; Rodriguez & Dimitrova, 2011), counter-argue (Palczewski, 2002), have the power to authenticate and prove claims (Barthes, 1981), imply a relative proximity to the truth (Messaris & Abraham, 2001), and activate deep structures of belief (Hariman & Lucaites, 2007). An image can serve as "an ideal carrier of a direct and often emotional message [...] without language or other barriers" (Kovács, 2015, p. 65). Images circulating in the context of established states have the capacity to bolster citizenship and create identity by serving as representation forms that help define the boundaries of U.S. culture (Edwards & Winkler, 1997) and by "reproducing ideology, communicating social knowledge, shaping collective memory, [and] modeling citizenship" (Hariman & Lucaites, 2007, p. 9) in the United States. For groups that lack the status of established states, images can serve as imaginative stimuli for "a political state of being" (Azoulay, 2015, p. 3).

One non-state group that has recently relied heavily on a visual imaginary is ISIS (hereafter Daesh). Daesh has disseminated visual propaganda in multiple-language publications to expand its reach to a wider range of audience groups. Up until August 2016, Daesh produced several publications targeting specific audience groups, including *Dabiq* magazine for English-speaking audiences, *Dar al-Islam* for French-speaking audiences, and *Istok* for Russian-speaking audiences. Since then, Daesh has condensed its publications to one monthly magazine, *Rumiyah*, distributed in 10 different languages. Although the use of common imagery and infographics across *Rumiyah*'s multilingual versions might seem like a "one-size-fits-all" strategy, one key audience group is missing: Arab speakers. Daesh targets Arabic-speaking audiences through *al-Naba'*, a weekly online and reportedly offline newsletter distributed in the group's claimed territories. Hence, Daesh has segmented its local and global networks, targeting the former with *al-Naba'* and the latter with *Rumiyah*.

To date, previous studies have not sufficiently analyzed the segmentation strategies of Daesh's visual campaign. This early research has primarily focused on a media product targeting one language. A number of researchers, for example, examined *Dabiq* images, pointing to the magazine's glossiness (Furedi, 2015), tracing the originality of the images vis-à-vis mainstream news sources (The Carter Center, 2017), exploring the about-to-die visual trope (Winkler, Damanhoury, Dicker, & Lemieux, 2016), and breaking down the images by visual frames, purpose and/or narrative themes (Damanhoury, 2016; Fahmy, 2016; "NATO Strategic Communications," 2016). One study examined how the infographics in *al-Naba'* newsletters utilize arguments from authority (Winkler, Damanhoury, & Lemieux, 2018). Studies that examined Daesh's propaganda via Twitter grouped different forms of media output in their analyses, including videos, photo reports, and/or audio productions, breaking them down according to media type and narrative frames (Milton, 2016; Winter, 2015a, 2015b; Zelin, 2015). Although studies have compared the use of Cold War interpretive journalism tenets of the United States and Daesh (Zelizer, 2016) images in *Dabiq* and *Rumiyah* (Wignell, Tan, O'Halloran, & Lange, 2017), and visual representations between al-Qaeda and Daesh's propaganda (Kovács, 2015), further comparative work of Daesh's many different platforms and networks is needed.

This study will expand on previous work by comparing how Daesh utilizes visual argument to justify its state status in communication with its local Arabic-speaking and global English-speaking networks. Three coders examined 1965 images: 1474 images in all 15 issues of *Dabiq* online magazines issued from June 2014 to July 2016, and 491 images in the first 26 available online issues of *al-Naba'* newsletter issued from December 2015 to June 2016. After coding for state-related content elements (e.g., visual depictions of social services, law enforcement activities, maps, economic activities, natural landscapes/cityscapes, pledges of allegiance, official propaganda promotion/distribution, and a mixed option for images depicting more than one visual statehood element), the coders identified 307 statehood images in *Dabiq* and 117 in *al-Naba'*. The overall inter-coder reliability was 0.93 using Cohen's Kappa.

This essay will report on the results of the quantitative and qualitative analysis of the statehood images in the two publications. After identifying international norms for statehood as frameworks for evaluating Daesh's visual arguments, this essay will analyze and compare the relationship between visuals and statehood in *Dabiq* and *al-Naba'* within the context of those global frameworks. As the analysis will show, Daesh's reliance on international norms differs in its visual arguments for different target audiences.

International Norms of Statehood

On December 26, 1933, the United States and 19 Latin American countries met in Uruguay. They approved four criteria for statehood: "a) a permanent population; b) a defined territory; c) government; and d) capacity to enter into relations with the other states" ("Convention on Rights and Duties," 1969, para. 1, Article 1). The convention concluded that an entity meeting the four criteria had the right to "legislate upon its interests, administer its services, and to define the jurisdiction and competence of its courts" (para. 1, Article 3) even if no other state recognized it. Subsequently, the adopted standards of the Montevideo Convention became the conventional benchmarks for identifying statehood (Grant, 1998).

Daesh has arguably met all four criteria for statehood, despite its lack of recognition by other global nation-states (Kilcullen, 2015). As of 2015, the areas under Daesh's control in Iraq and Syria had a pre-war population of between 2.8 million and 5.3 million people (Berman & Shapiro, 2015). Despite its shrinking territories, the Iraqi army reported that Daesh controlled about seven percent of Iraq's territory as of March 31, 2017 ("ISIL Now

Controls," 2017), as well as territory in Syria. Daesh controlled and practiced forms of governance over territories in Iraq and Syria, such as the establishment of *shari'a* courts, providing service provisions, and overseeing markets and economic activities (Al-Tamimi, 2015; Zelin, 2016). In addition, Kilcullen (2015) argued that Daesh exhibited the capacity to enter into relations with other states by exporting oil through Turkey, selling antiquities internationally, and being "accused of receiving state funding from Saudi Arabia and Qatar" (p. 62).

But do these four criteria of the Montevideo Convention form the foundation of Daesh's visual arguments in *Dabiq* and *al-Naba*? Below, I will argue that the two publications rely on the criteria of statehood, but they do so in distinct ways: global utopian vs. a local, realistic approach.

Dabiq Magazine's Visual Depiction of Statehood

Statehood images constitute a prevalent visual strategy in *Dabiq*. Approximately 21 percent of the images appearing in all issues of the online magazine display statehood activity. Averaging 20 statehood images per issue, Daesh promotes its self-proclaimed state predominantly in Iraq and Syria as a so-called utopian Islamic caliphate that is pristine, geographically established, economically sufficient, and media savvy, with established social services and an infrastructure for implementing *shari'a* law.

Daesh's depiction of statehood relies on each of the Montevideo Convention's four criteria of statehood. First, the images of law enforcement, social services, economic activities, and state propaganda promote the *topos* of a functioning government. *Dabiq* photo editors visually emphasize law enforcement as the most important component of its so-called state. About one-third of statehood images show law enforcement activities, such as arrests, public executions, punishments for civil crimes (e.g., stoning to death for committing adultery, throwing homosexuals off the top of buildings, and cutting off the hands of thieves); "Islamic Police" checkpoints; and threat-prevention activities (e.g., enforcing religious norms by confiscating and burning drugs, cigarettes, and alcohol). *Dabiq* images highlight social services as the second most emphasized statehood activity. Almost one quarter of the statehood images show services operating within Daesh controlled territories, such as healthcare, education, *zakat* (tidings) to the poor and needy, and building of infrastructure (e.g., electricity cables, installing street lights, and paving roads). About half of social service images relate to healthcare. They display health workers aiding civilians after the regime's airstrikes in Raqqa, eldercare homes in the Ninawa province, and hospitals in both Syria and Iraq. The third most frequent category of statehood images features the Daesh government's public information apparatus. Fourteen percent of the *Dabiq* statehood images advertise Daesh's English-language propaganda materials: *Dabiq* magazine, Islamic State Report (ISR) newsletters, news of the caliphate hashtags, al-Bayan radio, and the al-Hayat Media Center's video series, for example. Five percent of the statehood images depict economic activities in Daesh's claimed territories to establish the economic vibrancy and sustainability of the state. Over half of economic-related images display Daesh's new gold dinar to announce the return of the Islamic caliphate's currency of Andalusia.

Second, images of maps and natural landscapes deploy another line of argument for statehood established at Montevideo: the physical geographic territory of the Daesh state. More than one in every ten of the statehood images visualizes natural scenery in Daesh territories to establish the "Islamic State" as a pristine landscape with expansive possibilities. A borderless map on the cover page of *Dabiq's* first issue visualizing Daesh's notion of a caliphate reinforces the potential for expansion wherein Muslims refuse to accept secular and/or Western notions of statehood, geographical boundaries, and border control regulations.

The remaining images highlight both the Montevideo Convention criteria of a permanent population and the capacity to enter into relations with other groups and tribes. About seven percent of state images showcase Daesh's expanding population and relationships with tribes and distant militant groups. The pledging allegiance (*bay'ah*) images depict different tribes, Kurdish villagers, members of the Iraqi government, members of other factions in Iraq and Syria, and militant groups in other locations pledging life-long allegiance to Daesh leader Abu Bakr al-Baghdadi—all of which argues for Daesh's strong relationship with its allied groups. The scene of these images expands beyond Daesh strongholds in Iraq and Syria to Libya, Algeria, Pakistan, Afghanistan, Somalia, and Nigeria, thus signifying a permanently expanding population.

Together, the statehood images in *Dabiq* employ the four topoi for statehood. The images portray a functioning government ruling over a defined territory where a permanent population resides and is capable of entering into lasting relationships with other group and tribes.

Al-Naba' Newsletter's Visual Depiction of Statehood

Statehood images also constitute a prevalent visual strategy in *al-Naba'* newsletter for its Arabic-speaking audience. Almost one quarter of the images display statehood activities including maps of controlled/disputed territories, promotion of state propaganda, social services, law enforcement, and pledges of allegiance. Averaging 4.5 statehood images per issue, Daesh promotes a self-proclaimed state quite different from the one depicted in its English-language publication. Daesh's promotion of its statehood in *al-Naba'* imagery evokes the Montevideo Convention's topoi of state government, but does so in a more limited way than *Dabiq*.

Al-Naba' narrows the scope of the visual argument to a functioning government. Only nine percent of the newsletter's statehood images visualize executions of reported spies and local enemies, and none display any other law enforcement activities (i.e., threat-prevention or the punishments for civil crimes). Additionally, the wide variety of social services imagery in *Dabiq*—educational facilities, elder homes, hospitals, and building infrastructure—do not appear in *al-Naba'*. While 12 percent of *al-Naba'* statehood images highlight social services, most focus on paying *zakat* (tidings). The Daesh state pictured in *al-Naba'* neither appears economically vibrant nor sustainable, with only one image showing a market. Nonetheless, *al-Naba'* photo editors extensively highlight the public information apparatus, with almost one-third of statehood images advertising Arabic-language propaganda materials, including al-Himma Library publications (e.g., posters and flyers) and provincial video banners. If viewers accept the visual argument of *al-Naba'*, they can rely on Daesh as a reliable information source, but the group's capacity to achieve other government functions remains more elusive in the imaginary.

Al-Naba' images also recurrently feature the statehood topos of physical territory, but, again they do so in a way that differs from *Dabiq*. With greater emphasis than *Dabiq*, over one-third of statehood images in *al-Naba'* visualize mapped territory of Daesh's claimed lands and sites of military operations. The large display of maps depicts Daesh as a powerful militant group capable of controlling land and fighting simultaneously on multiple fronts. However, unlike the *Dabiq* imagery, *al-Naba'* does not romanticize Daesh's controlled physical territory; instead, it avoids shots of pristine, natural landscapes altogether.

Finally, *al-Naba'* imagery generally avoids visual arguments for permanent populations or relationships with other states, tribes, and other members of the population. Only two images in *al-Naba'* depict pledges of allegiance by groups of militants in the Philippines and Khurasan, leaving the lasting population status of the state in doubt. No images of tribes, villagers, and civilians pledging their allegiance to al-Baghdadi appear in *al-Naba'*.

Together, the newsletter portrays an aspiring militant group that extensively promotes its public information apparatus, constantly fights for control over physical territory, and occasionally enters into relations with distant militants. Less clear is whether the state can provide social services and maintain control over a permanent population.

A Segmented Visual Campaign

The analysis of statehood depictions in Daesh's *Dabiq* and *al-Naba'* publications highlights the importance of argumentative context in Daesh's propaganda and finds that the group uses a segmented visual campaign of statehood with differential visual arguments to target different audience groups. Although violent and militaristic imagery is frequent in Daesh's English and Arabic-language publications, the group constantly balances such imagery with statehood depictions. Targeting an Arab audience in a region mostly ravaged by conflict, the group uses *al-Naba'* to shed light on its capability and persistence to win over other warring factions, and hence presents a localized, militaristic insurgency that is fighting off Arab states—Iraq, Syria, Libya, Yemen, Egypt, Algeria, Tunisia, Saudi Arabia, and Somalia—and other militant groups. *Al-Naba'* imagery foregrounds Daesh's claimed and contested territories in maps and its public information apparatus in promotional propaganda material. By doing so, Daesh adopts a less utopian, more realistic approach when targeting a local Arab audience who are closer in proximity to the group's heartland. Nonetheless, Daesh's local, realistic approach, is arguably more consistent and aligned with actual conditions on the ground, and thus falls short of the four criteria for statehood.

Whereas *al-Naba's* visual argument may convince or force some people living in that context to join the group or at least passively accept its presence, the newsletter is less likely to attract a distant English-speaking Muslim audience. Targeting a global audience that does not live in or around Daesh-claimed territories, the group romanticizes life in its lands and depicts an all-encompassing, fully functional Islamic Caliphate that supersedes nation states, implements *shari'a* law, engages in a global conflict, and emphasizes the individual agency by calling on Muslims to join voluntarily. *Dabiq* imagery foregrounds the group's capability to maintain law and order, provides a wide range of social services, and highlights the beauty of the territory. Hence, *Dabiq's* visual argument globalizes the conflict and presents a viable alternative to living in the West by incentivizing *hijra* (immigration) in search of a self-fulfilling life under the banner of a newly declared utopian caliphate. Taken together, this comparative study helps explain how Daesh deploys segmented, cross-cultural visual arguments. Future studies should further examine the group's visual arguments in its most recent multi-lingual publication *Rumiyah*.

References

Al-Tamimi, A. J. (2015, January 27). Archive of Islamic State administrative documents [Blog post]. Retrieved from http://aymennjawad.org

Azoulay, A. (2015). *Civil imagination: A political ontology of photography* (L. Bethlehem, Trans.). London, United Kingdom: Verso Books.

Barthes, R. (1981). *Camera Lucida: Reflections on photography* (R. Howard, Trans.). New York, NY: Hill and Wang.

Berman, E., & Shapiro, J. N. (2015, November 29). Why ISIL will fail on its own. *Politico Magazine*. Retrieved from http://politico.com

Birdsell, D. S., & Groarke, L. (1996). Toward a theory of visual argument. *Argumentation and Advocacy*, *33*(1), 1–10.

The Carter Center. (2017). *Overview of Daesh's online recruitment propaganda magazine, Dabiq December 2015*. Retrieved from http://cartercenter.org

Convention on Rights and Duties of States (Inter-American); December 26, 1933. (1969). *The Avalon Project*. Retrieved from http://avalon.law.yale.edu/20th_century/intam03.asp

Damanhoury, K. El. (2016, July 26). The Daesh state: The myth turns into a reality. *Center for Global Communication Studies*. Retrieved from http://global.asc.upenn.edu

Edwards, J. L., & Winkler, C. K. (1997). Representative form and the visual ideograph: The Iwo Jima image in editorial cartoons. *Quarterly Journal of Speech*, *83*(3), 289–310. doi: 10.1080/00335639709384187

Fahmy, S. (2016, February 7). What ISIS wants you to see. *Ahramonline*. Retrieved from http://english.ahram.org.eg/NewsPrint/186884.aspx

Furedi, F. (2015, July 25). Islamic State propaganda buys into western culture of victimhood [Blog post]. Retrieved from http://frankfuredi.com

Grant, T. D. (1998). Defining statehood: The Montevideo Convention and its discontents. *Columbia Journal of Transnational Law*, *37*(403), 403–457.

Hariman, R., & Lucaites, J. (2007). *No caption needed: Iconic photographs, public culture, and liberal democracy*. Chicago, IL: University of Chicago Press.

ISIL Now Controls "Less Than 7 Percent of Iraq." (2017, April 12). *Al-Jazeera*. Retrieved from http://aljazeera.com

Kilcullen, D. (2015). *Quarterly essay (58) blood year: Terror and the Islamic State*. Melbourne, Australia: Black.

Kovács, A. (2015). The "new jihadists" and the visual turn from al-Qa'ida to ISIL/ISIS/Da'ish. *Biztpol Affairs*, *2*(3), 47–70. Retrieved from http://epa.oszk.hu/02400/02475/00004/pdf/EPA02475_Biztpol Affairs_2014_03_047–070.pdf

Messaris, P., & Abraham, L. (2001). The role of images in framing news stories. In S. D. Reese, O. H. Gandy, & A. E. Grant (Eds.), *Framing public life: Perspectives on media and our understanding of the social world* (pp. 215–226). Mahwah, NJ: Lawrence Erlbaum.

Milton, D. (2016, October). *Communication breakdown: Unraveling the Islamic State's media efforts*. Retrieved from https://ctc.usma.edu

NATO Strategic Communications Centre of Excellence. (2016, January). *Daesh information campaign and its influence: Results of the study*. Retrieved from http://difesa.it/SMD_/CASD/IM/IASD/65sessioneor dinaria/Documents/DaeshInformationCampaignanditsInfluence.pdf

Palczewski, C. H. (2002). Argument in an off key: Playing with the productive limits of argument. In G. T. Goodnight (Ed.), *Arguing communication and culture* (pp. 1–23). Washington, DC: National Communication Association.

Rodriguez, L., & Dimitrova, D. V. (2011). The levels of visual framing. *Journal of Visual Literacy*, *30*(1), 48–65. doi: 10.1080/23796529.2011.11674684

Wignell, P., Tan, S., O'Halloran, K. L., & Lange, R. (2017). A mixed methods empirical examination of changes in emphasis and style in the extremist magazines Dabiq and Rumiyah. *Perspectives on Terrorism*, *11*(2). Retrieved from http://terrorismanalysts.com

Winkler, C. K., Damanhoury, K. El, Dicker, A., & Lemieux, A. F. (2016). The medium is terrorism: Transformation of the about to die trope in Dabiq. *Journal of Terrorism and Political Violence*. doi:10.1080/09546553.2016.1211526

Winkler, C. K., Damanhoury, K. El, & Lemieux, A. (2018). Validating extremism: Strategic use of authority appeals in al-Naba' infographics. *Journal of Argumentation in Context*, 7, 33–71.

Winter, C. (2015a, July). *The virtual "caliphate": Understanding Islamic State's propaganda strategy*. Retrieved from http://quilliamfoundation.org

Winter, C. (2015b, October). *Documenting the virtual "caliphate."* Retrieved from http://quilliamfounda tion.org

Zelin, A. Y. (2015). Picture or it didn't happen : A snapshot of the Islamic State's official media output. *Perspectives on Terrorism*, *9*(4). Retrieved from http://terrorismanalysts.com

Zelin, A. Y. (2016). *The Islamic State's territorial methodology* (Research Notes No. 29). Retrieved from the Washington Institute for Near East Policy website: http://washingtoninstitute.org

Zelizer, B. (2016). Journalism's deep memory : Cold War mindedness and coverage of Islamic State. *International Journal of Communication*, *10*, 6060–6089. Retrieved from http://ijoc.org

33

NETWORKED ARGUMENTATION VIA COLLECTIVE RHETORICS AT THE WOMEN'S MARCH ON THE UTAH STATE CAPITOL AND THE WOMEN'S MARCH ON WASHINGTON

Alley Agee, Dakota Park-Ozee, and Allison Blumling

The January 21, 2017 Women's March, held in Washington, D.C. after the presidential inauguration was the largest protest event in United States history (Chenoweth & Pressman, 2017). Thousands of sister marches occurred across the globe to stand in solidarity with the Washington protesters. This study focuses on one such sister march held in Salt Lake City, Utah. While the D.C. march and nearly all other marches occurred on January 21, 2017, Utah organizers elected to hold their march on January 23, 2017 in alignment with the first day of the Utah legislative session. As such, the Utah march holds a unique position in the argumentative network of the Women's March by maintaining global ties while creating a resistive moment in which locality remained essential. These interactions of the global with the local are vital to continued study of resistive movements because such movements are "positioned as sites where dispersed publics form collective sentiments [...] in a globalized world" (Hutchins & Lester, 2015, p. 340). Thus, these local sites operate as a nexus point for global political deliberation.

Through a participatory and critical ethnography, we explore how the collective rhetoric functioned to mobilize a networked argument at the Utah Women's March. We explain through a three-step process: first, we examine the formation of the network; second, we show how the argument of the network solidifies through interactions of the individual arguments within a broader, collective ideology; and third, we analyze how the collective mobilizes. Participants of the march utilized (a) a call and response format as a validation of experiences and consciousness raising that form the collective (Campbell, 2002; Carlson,

1992); (b) protest signs, chants, and songs to solidify the networked argument (Wildermuth, Davis, Frederick, & Bolton, 2014); and (c) a "place in protest" (Endres, Senda-Cook, & Cozen, 2014, p. 123) or the physical takeover of the Utah State Capitol to collectively envision what politics, resistance, and the place of women in these two realms should look like to mobilize the collective. Together, such envisioning constructed a collective argument that networked thousands of voices and bodies and challenged how argument functions in protest rhetoric.

Collective Rhetorics in Protest Argument

Scholars studying argumentation in protests and social movements have largely focused on single speakers (Simons, 1982), single events (Delicath & Deluca, 2003; Dubriwny, 2005), historical developments of movements (Grant, 2011), or how disparate acts of protest unify around a single issue (Jakes, 2013; Sobnosky, 2013). McGee (1980), however, argued social movements are the creation of meaning surrounding an issue, rather than a collection of associated events. The Women's March presents an interesting dilemma for the study of argumentation in protest as it represents a single event within a network of protests across time and place, serving a multiplicity of concerns related to women, rather than one flagship issue. Study of the Women's March, then, or any other networked argumentative phenomenon, requires scholars to combine theoretical approaches and apply them to a multiplicity of voices, events, issues, or contexts. Collective rhetoric is one such approach that allows scholars to capture the meaning of a networked social movement.

Collective rhetoric is rooted in literature of protest rhetoric. Simons (1982), a social movement scholar, originally coined the term "collective rhetoric" to explain the phenomenon of social movement leadership or a single speaker speaking on behalf of a collective. Scholars have since re-conceptualized the term to focus on the role of multiple rhetors (Bessette, 2013; Dubriwny, 2005). Models of collective rhetoric re-envision single-speaker models of argumentation, focusing, instead, on the role of multiple, networked voices coming together to achieve persuasive ends. Scholars have studied the use of narrative and anecdotes to share experiences (Bessette, 2013; Dubriwny, 2005), the use of those narratives and anecdotes to inspire identification and disrupt hegemonic narratives (Bacon, 2012; Drüeke & Zobl, 2016), and the articulation of combined experiences as support for the political or counter hegemonic arguments the collective supports (Dubriwny, 2005; Sobnosky, 2013). Utilizing collective rhetoric in these ways has the potential to inspire collective action, transform participant experiences, and allow participants to connect those experiences to broader political issues (Clark, 2016; Durham, 1999). To date, however, how collective rhetorics and argumentation interact within protest settings where participants have already connected their experiences to broader political issues remains underexplored in argumentation scholarship.

This study helps fill that gap by examining in situ rhetoric via rhetorical field methods and participatory critical rhetoric (Endres, Hess, Senda-Cook, & Middleton, 2016). This approach gives researchers "an insider perspective on the lived advocacy of individuals and organizations that struggle to persuade in public for changes in policy, social life, or other issues that affect them" (Hess, 2011, p. 128). We assert that such methods should extend to argumentation studies. Indeed, we believe the best way to understand how publics construct collective arguments and connect them to broader argumentative networks and patterns requires participatory engagement in those argumentative spheres. By focusing on the lived experiences of individuals and the way argument happens via experience and participation, we affirm feminist methodological commitments that privilege individual narratives, participation and experience, and critical engagement with what counts as evidence (Campbell, 1973; Durham, 1999, 2004; Frye, 1990).

The study examines the Women's March on the Utah State Capitol, which started at 2:00 PM and ended at approximately 4:00 PM. Protesters gathered at a park a few blocks south of the capitol building and marched a little over a quarter-mile to arrive at the capitol. While the march itself did not cover a great distance, it involved walking entirely uphill in blizzard conditions. Upon arriving at the top of the hill, protestors spread out onto the capitol lawn and filled the rotunda, stairs, upper levels, and balconies of the capitol building. The Utah Highway Patrol estimated the presence of over 6,000 protesters inside the building with more marchers outside in the snow (Wood, 2017). Some estimates of attendance went as high as 10,000 (Lang, 2017), making it among the largest protests in Utah state history.

We collected data via participant observation at the march itself. The primary data collected included over fifteen pages of field notes, twenty-five minutes of video, eighty-five minutes of audio recordings, nine hundred and thirty-five photographs, and a handout containing the protest song lyrics participants sung in the rotunda that video and audio recordings confirmed. The researchers coded the data set using Charmaz's (2005) constant comparative method consisting of a two-level analysis process, while also recognizing that data collection and analysis happen simultaneously (Charmaz, 2005; Durham, 2004; Senda-Cook, 2013).

Results and Discussion

Collective rhetoric in the 2017 Utah State Women's March functioned in three ways: formation of the network through vocal engagement, solidification of the argument, and mobilization of the collective. First, as marchers began to fill the capitol building, a protest facilitator formed the collective by reading out individual protest signs from the crowd and the crowd subsequently chanting that sign's message over and over until the facilitator read another sign. Dubriwny (2005) argued, "the collective participation of individuals in the creation of an always-transforming text [...] shapes the meaning of the messages through inclusion of many voices and the often diverse stories that such voices repeatedly tell" (p. 399). Indeed, by encouraging active participation of the protesters in a way that unified their voices into one, the facilitator emphasized the collectivity of the protesters through the diverse and polysemic arguments written on the signs. The facilitator amplified individual arguments within the collective, thus making them part of the fight for the network of protesters. These arguments ranged from "love not hate makes America great" to "keep your laws off our bodies." Furthermore, the formation of the collective occurred through the validation of the experiences of the participants, a strategy previously documented as persuasive (Bacon, 2012; Bessette, 2013; Campbell, 1973). The call and response acts as a form of consciousness raising, allowing participants to validate their experiences and realize "the personal is political" (Campbell, 1973, p.82), and can also facilitate the creation of the collective rhetoric or argument.

Second, we argue the combination of protest signs, chants, and songs solidified the argument of the collective by allowing participants to integrate their individual voices and experiences into the broader local and global collective argument network. Local protesters drew inspiration or copied signs from the Women's March on Washington. These signs connected and reinforced the arguments protesters made at both protests, thereby solidifying the arguments of the newly formed global network in ways similar to how previously marginalized groups have attempted to draw attention to overlooked hegemonic norms (Dubriwny, 2005; Sobnosky, 2013). The Utah march and its networked association with the global Women's Marches solidified three key arguments: the physical power and presence of the female body, the necessity of the collective in the fight for women's rights, and the need for resistive momentum to carry beyond the protest.

Signs utilizing aggressive arguments related to the female body embodied female strength. The pervasive presence of signage incorporating the language of pussies and "grabbing back" in conjunction with those utilizing imagery of uteri, ovaries, and breasts featured the unique strength of the female body. Signs telling Utah Gary Governor Herbert to "suck my left one" and Republicans to "stop screwing us" further emphasized the centrality of the female body. The collective rhetoric of the marchers argued embodied, powerful women were ready to fight.

The necessity of the collective as a key element related to the solidification of the argument emerged from the protest song that followed the call and response and individual speech section of the rally. French protest songs dating back to the German Occupation of France in World War II have demonstrated the role of folk songs in reinforcing identities central to broad political dissent and protest (Jakes, 2013). Similarly, the protesters' Utah State Women's March song further solidifies the identity of the collective and its core argument by simultaneously drawing on repeated imagery of physical struggle and repeating language of togetherness. By presenting monumental struggles (e.g., fighting and climbing) that women have overcome and a willingness to overcome these struggles together, the song reinforced the strength of united female bodies within an imagined new political order.

Finally, the physical presence of protesters in the Utah State Capitol mobilized the networked, collective argument by utilizing what Endres, Senda-Cook, and Cozen (2014) called a "*place in protest*, [that is] a heuristic that describes how […] places/spaces are sites of contestation, or protest, wherein the practiced norms are constantly being challenged or reinforced" (p. 123). However, places in protest do not only include the physical presence of protesters; they also relate to metaphorical allusions to space. The Utah marchers took over the seat of state government on the first day of the legislative session, making it one of the only Women's Marches not to occur on January 21st. The presence of the protesters in the Capitol offered an alternative political ideal that included the female body/voice in politics. Protesters highlighted this theme with chants of "welcome to your first day, we are here to stay," but also asserted the message through their embodied presence in the legislative space. The Utah marchers caused so much chaos that they forced the legislators to end the day early, an outcome speakers acknowledged at the event. Additionally, the emphasis on the local makes the overall argument of the protest more achievable. The protesters collectively enacted that unified individuals could make significant changes (including the shutdown of the assembly) in the face of political adversity. The specification of locality in protest signs (e.g., "I am a feminist and your constituent and I vote") makes arguments centered on occupation of the local governments.

By highlighting the local network through place, protestors tightened and strengthened their network of political resistance. However, the rally still connected the local to the global. Despite the alternative date, the Women's March on the Utah State Capitol still shared a name with the global network of Women's March protests and invoked shared arguments of unity with the national and global networks of women.

Thus, collective protest utilizes place/space to both mobilize the network and empower their political action. A song that thousands of protesters sung at the conclusion of the rally exemplifies the power of place/space in networked political action by referencing struggles and walking through struggles together. At the final moment of the protest, the song reminded protesters that place/space could function as a tool of political engagement embodied in collective defiance.

Conclusion

While the Women's March is undeniably a singular event, the larger goal of the collective action is to reinforce collective consciousness around women's issues at large. The march helps create the meaning that is the movement. McGee (1975) proposed a conception of "the people" as a process rather than a phenomenon. We agree with this framing but reject the notion of the process itself. While McGee framed audience formation around the rhetoric produced by a single speaker, the integration of theories of collective rhetoric into the study of argumentation in movement reveals the ways in which audiences envision and create themselves. In doing so, audiences both create and embody the argument of their movement.

Models of rhetoric that envision a single-speaker, single argument, single event, or single issue fail to address the various situations in which rhetoric and argument function in networked or collective spaces. Protest is one such space. The case study presented here pushes back against these narrow conceptions to position protest arguments enacted and embodied by both individuals and groups as part of a globalized network of resistance. The tenets of formation, solidification, and mobilization explicated here provide a model for argumentative scholars to study the creation of these networks both by examining localized sites of resistance and exploring the ways these local instances connect to form broader social movements.

References

Bacon, J. (2012). Until death do us part: Lesbian rhetorics of relational divorce. *Women's Studies in Communication, 35*(2), 158–177. doi: 10.1080/07491409.2012.724523

Bessette, J. (2013). An archive of anecdotes: Raising lesbian consciousness after the Daughters of Bilitis. *Rhetoric Society Quarterly, 43*(1), 22–45. doi: 10.1080/02773945.2012.740131

Campbell, K. K. (1973). The rhetoric of women's liberation: An oxymoron. *Quarterly Journal of Speech, 59*(1), 74–86. doi: 10.1080/00335637309383155

Campbell, K. K. (2002). Consciousness-raising: Linking theory, criticism, and practice. *Rhetoric Society Quarterly, 32*(1), 45–64. doi: 10.1080/02773940209391220

Carlson, A. (1992). Creative casuistry and feminist consciousness: The rhetoric of moral reform. *Quarterly Journal of Speech, 78*(1), 16–32. doi: 10.1080/00335639209383979

Charmaz, K. (2005). Grounded theory in the 21st century. In N. K. Denzin & Y. S. Lincoln (Eds.), *The Sage handbook of qualitative research* (3rd ed., pp. 507–535). Thousand Oaks, CA: SAGE.

Chenoweth, E., & Pressman, J. (2017, February 7). This is what we learned by counting the women's marches. *The Washington Post.* Retrieved from https://washingtonpost.com/news/monkey-cage/wp/2017/02/07/this-is-what-we-learned-by-counting-the-womens-marches/

Clark, R. (2016). "Hope in a hashtag": The discursive activism of #WhyIStayed. *Feminist Media Studies, 16*(5), 788–804. doi: 10.1080/14680777.2016.1138235

Delicath, J. W., & DeLuca, K. M. (2003). Image events, the public sphere, and argumentative practice: The case of radical environmental groups. *Argumentation, 17*(3), 315–333. doi: 10.1023/A:1025179019397

Drüeke, R., & Zobl, E. (2016). Online feminist protest against sexism: The German-language hashtag #aufschrei. *Feminist Media Studies, 16*(1), 35–54. doi: 10.1080/14680777.2015.1093071

Dubriwny, T. N. (2005). Consciousness-raising as collective rhetoric: The articulation of experience in the Redstockings' abortion speak-out of 1969. *Quarterly Journal of Speech*, *91*(4), 395–422. doi: 10.1080/00335630500488275

Durham, M. G. (1999). Articulating adolescent girls' resistance to patriarchal discourse in popular media. *Women's Studies in Communication*, *22*(2), 210–229. doi: 10.1080/07491409.1999.10162421

Durham, M. G. (2004). Constructing the "new ethnicities": Media, sexuality, and diaspora identity in the lives of South Asian immigrant girls. *Critical Studies in Media Communication*, *21*(2), 140–161. doi: 10.1080/07393180410001688047

Endres, D., Hess, A., Senda-Cook, S., & Middleton, M. K. (2016). In situ rhetoric: Intersections between qualitative inquiry, fieldwork, and rhetoric. *Cultural Studies ↔ Critical Methodologies*, *16*(6), 511–524. doi: 10.1177/1532708616655820

Endres, D., & Senda-Cook, S. (2011). Location matters: The rhetoric of place in protest. *Quarterly Journal of Speech*, *97*(3), 257–282. doi: 10.1080/00335630.2011.585167

Endres, D., Senda-Cook, S., & Cozen, B. (2014). Not just a place to park your car: Park(ing) as spatial argument. *Argumentation and Advocacy*, *50*(3), 121–140. Retrieved from http://tandfonline.com

Frye, M. (1990). The possibility of feminist theory. In D. L. Rhode (Ed.), *Theoretical perspectives on sexual difference* (pp. 174–184). New Haven, CT: Yale University Press.

Grant, K. (2011). British suffragettes and the Russian method of hunger strike. *Comparative Studies in Society and History*, *53*(1), 113–143. doi: 10.1017/S0010417510000642

Hess, A. (2011). Critical-rhetorical ethnography: Rethinking the place and process of rhetoric. *Communication Studies*, *62*(2), 127–152. doi: 10.1080/10510974.2011.529750

Hutchins, B., & Lester, L. (2015). Theorizing the enactment of mediatized environmental conflict. *The International Communication Gazette*, *77*(4), 337–358. doi: 10.1177/1748048514568765

Jakes, K. (2013). La France en chantant: The rhetorical construction of French identity in songs of the resistance movement. *Quarterly Journal of Speech*, *99*(3), 317–340. doi: 10.1080/00335630.2013.806817

Lang, N. (2017, January 24). The women's march makes its way to Mormon country: Utah protesters take up the resistance against Trump. *Salon*. Retrieved from http://salon.com/2017/01/24/a-womens-march-in-the-heart-of-mormon-country-meet-the-utah-protesters-leading-the-resistance-against-trump/

McGee, M. C. (1975). In search of "the people": A rhetorical alternative. *Quarterly Journal of Speech*, *61*(3), 235–249. doi: 10.1080/00335637509383289

McGee, M. C. (1980). "Social movement": Phenomenon or meaning? *Central States Speech Journal*, *31*(4), 233–244. doi: 10.1080/10510978009368063

Senda-Cook, S. (2013). Materializing tensions: How maps and trails mediate nature. *Environmental Communication*, *7*(3), 355–371. doi: 10.1080/17524032.2013.792854

Simons, H. W. (1982). Genres, rules, and collective rhetorics: Applying the requirements-problems-strategies approach. *Communication Quarterly*, *30*(3), 181–188. doi: 10.1080/01463378209369441

Sobnosky, M. J. (2013). Experience, testimony, and the women's health movement. *Women's Studies in Communication*, *36*(3), 217–242. doi: 10.1080/07491409.2013.835667

Wildermuth, S., Davis, C. B., Frederick, E., & Bolton, J. (2014). Sign, sign, everywhere a sign: An analysis of the argument, target and content of protest signs displayed during the Wisconsin budget repair bill/act 10 protests of 2011. *American Communication Journal*, *16*(1), 15–35.

Wood, B. (2017, January 25). "We raised our voices here": Massive women's march headlines Utah legislature's opening day. *The Salt Lake Tribune*. Retrieved from http://sltrib.com/home/4853488-155/womens-march-on-utah-capitol-will

34

CLIMATE CHANGE ARGUMENTATION

Subnational Networks, Interest Convergence, and Multiple Publics

William Mosley-Jensen

This essay seeks to unravel tensions between John Dewey's conception of the "public" and its relationship to state formation. Transnational argument networks are forming to supplant oppositional government structures in ways that demonstrate that publics can form and function autonomously, as the case of climate change advocacy networks transcending national boundaries and state authority illustrates. Of additional interest to scholars is the impact this phenomenon has on theories seeking a remedy to neoliberalism. By contesting the long-held presupposition that states arise and respond to publics (and that scholarly analyses should direct their inquiry towards those interactions), this essay challenges existing conceptions of political progress. Responding to the challenge of neoliberalism requires recognizing the potential for extra-institutional coordination, a "public" that doesn't appeal to a governing institution, but only to other like-minded individuals.

Dewey's Conception of Publics

Dewey's (2016) *The Public and Its Problems* provided a widely applicable, foundational theory for the formation of a "public." Dewey was grappling with the rapidity of change in the United States in the early 20th century and sought to process how technological development and informational expansion complicated the ability of groups to coalesce and organize. He combined a philosophical approach to state formation with a sharp-eyed analysis of how groups come together to create collectivities. He argued that individuals identify externalities others impose upon them and "those indirectly and seriously affected for good or for evil form a group distinctive enough to require recognition and a name" (p. 65). He settled on the name "The Public" (p. 65).

Dewey (2016) theorized the origin of the state as an effect of publics coalescing to demand institutional action. A particular public could function effectively or ineffectively, however, with its efficacy tied to its political institution's responsiveness to the group's appeals. He argued that the "public is organized and made effective by means of representatives who […]

care for its especial interests by methods intended to regulate the conjoint action of individuals and groups" (p. 65). Thus, Dewey theorized the causal explanation for the conception of the state as having its basis in public appeals. In short, the public and the state remain intertwined in a mutually reinforcing relationship. The stronger the need for publics becomes, the more power the publics provide to the states that govern them. For Dewey (2016), a "public articulated and operating through representative officers is the state, there is no state without a government, but also there is none without the public" (p. 82).

Historical conceptions of sovereignty offer a similar analysis to Dewey's notion that the state arises from publics. In 1978, Quentin Skinner, a leading political historian at Cambridge, described the emergence of the concept of "the state" in early 16th century writings as the establishment and sustainment of political authority. By the mid-1500s, French humanists had incorporated the concept into their lexicon, theorizing the state as an institution beholden to the people. Jean Bodin distinguished "the powers of the State from those of its rulers, for he speaks of 'magistrates and officers' as having a duty 'to command, judge and provide for the government of the state'" (quoted in Skinner, 1978, p. 356). Furthermore, the foundation of political theory regarding the role of the state suggests that its province is to secure the common good, an enduring principle that served as the basis for much of modern political theory (Skinner, 1978).

Given the age of Dewey's original writings dating back to 1927, a possible objection to Dewey's conception of a public is that it misses the complexity of contemporary publics due to his focus on technological change at the dawn of the 20th century (Warner, 2002). Noting this objection to Dewey's public, Asen (2003) argued for an understanding of the concept that incorporated two important characteristics: multiplicity and permeability. He maintained that Dewey preserved multiplicity as a value by adhering to a complex, nuanced approach to the analysis of a public as one amongst many, not as a singular homogenous. Additionally, Dewey created the possibility for a permeable public by insisting that these publics are not necessarily cut off from each other, but have porous boundaries facilitating the exchange of individuals and arguments.

Here, I will argue that the existence of transnational networks of argumentation in the contemporary period represent a public consistent with many of Dewey's principles, but the same networks challenge his conception of the state. Specifically, the instantiation of these networks as multiple and permeable across national borders calls into question the basis for understanding the constitution of national political authority. Citizens around the globe are witnessing a reconfiguration of sovereign authority, crafted along the lines of argumentative networks. Rather than appealing to a central authority to impose a solution, these networks have instead, begun to craft extra-institutional frameworks for addressing common problems, making the case for the creation of a public without the concordant creation of a governing institution.

Transnational Networks of Argumentation

Kern and Bulkeley (2009) introduced the concept of transnational municipal networks (TMS) to demarcate current trends in the increasingly globalized world. They offered three defining characteristics of TMNs:

> First, member cities are autonomous and free to join or leave. Second, because they appear to be non-hierarchical, horizontal and polycentric, such networks are often characterized as a form of self-governance. Third, decisions taken within the network are directly implemented by its members.
>
> *(pp. 309-310)*

237

Transnational municipal networks have existed at various points in history, but nation-states tend to subsume them. A useful illustration is Fink's (2011) description of the Hanseatic League, that is, a network of mutually beneficial arrangements between Northern German cities influential in politics and trade for over 500 years from the mid-12th century to the mid-17th century. The League coordinated mercantile activity and established a series of rules and regulations that members adhered to on a voluntary basis. The political authority of the league, known as *Kontore*, maintained a contract between the associations, which in the early stages superseded the sovereign power of the national identity of the cities. Although the *Kontore* persisted for nearly 500 years, it ultimately fell under the authority of the governing nation-states, in part because the members failed to make a strong case for the relevance of the League.

Transnational municipal networks (Bansard, Pattberg, & Widerberg, 2016) have sought to incorporate the feedback of citizens and local stakeholders in their decision-making (Yang & Zagorowski, 2017). These networks operate to maximize the cross-fertilization of knowledge in interdisciplinary and global multi-scalar frameworks, creating uniquely productive modes of argumentative engagement. While such networks have an over-arching interest in preserving a livable world through adaptation and mitigation, they are not without areas of disagreements (Herrschel & Newman, 2017). Differing cultural and economic priorities impact the capacity of subnational and transnational entities to come to agreement on a wide variety of issues. Given that transnational networks cannot appeal to a higher authority, what explains their motivation to craft voluntary policies that could negatively impact their economic development? The answer lies in the theory of "interest convergence" defined as "relative congruence in either the outcomes desired by stakeholder groups or about the means used to realize those outcomes" (Fryxell, 1990, p. 50).

Transnational Networks and Climate Change

On June 1, 2017, President Donald Trump announced his intention to withdraw the United States from the historic Paris climate agreement (Busby, 2017). While the terms of the agreement do not allow for a unilateral withdrawal until November 2020, the U.S. announcement has spurred a number of reactions, including increased involvement by subnational groups around climate action (Comstock, 2017). These efforts have accelerated participation in existing transnational forums with common interests, such as the C40 Cities Climate Leadership Group and the Global Covenant of Mayors. While the constitution of these networks confirms Dewey's hypothesis regarding *how* publics arise, their character disconfirms the postulated relationship between publics and state apparatuses, suggesting that transnational argumentation networks need not involve formal governance arrangements.

The C40 Cities Climate Leadership Group and the Global Covenant of Mayors represent a forum for transnational argumentation on climate, with attendant goals for cities to reach on climate change initiatives. Both are large and impactful networks. Launched in 2005 with 18 participating cities, the C40 Cities Climate Leadership Group now has more than 80 cities involved, representing over 600 million people (Paes & Bloomberg, 2016) and organizing around 25% of global GDP (Bansard et al., 2016). The Global Covenant of Mayors includes over 7,000 cities, with more than 680 million people represented (Global Covenant of Mayors, 2017). Together, the two networks represent multiple city publics with permeable boundaries that form many and diverse coalitions (some related to climate change and some not). Current C40 board president Michael Bloomberg is the former

Mayor of New York City and has led a push for the global network to press forward with the goals outlined in the Paris Accord, despite the intransigence on the part of the U.S. executive branch (Watts, 2017).

Bloomberg's advocacy constitutes a significant linkage between existing transnational networks concerned with climate change and U.S. based groups. On June 5th, 2017, Bloomberg announced the creation of "America's Pledge" with a letter to United Nations Secretary-General António Guterres & Executive Secretary of the UN Framework Convention on Climate Change Patricia Espinosa. In the letter, Bloomberg outlined the efforts of U.S. cities to meet the America's obligations under the Paris agreement, noting that the "bulk of the decisions which drive U.S. climate action in the aggregate are made by cities, states, businesses, and civil society" ("About America's Pledge," 2017, Letter section, para. 3). In addition, he argued that the federal government's inaction was regrettable, but not insurmountable. He noted that subnational actors would be able to quantify their aggregate actions, "which will constitute 'America's Pledge' to the world" ("About America's Pledge," 2017, Letter section, para. 5) and will "fulfill our responsibility to help lead the world in reducing emissions" ("About America's Pledge," 2017, Letter section, para. 5).

On January 1, 2017, the Global Covenant of Mayors emerged through a merger of two groups: the Compact of Mayors, an organization Michael Bloomberg founded in his capacity as United Nations Special Envoy for Cities and Climate Change, and the Covenant of Mayors, a consortium the European Commission created in 2008 to foster the implementation of the EU's 2020 Climate and Energy Package (Gesing, 2017). The Global Covenant of Mayors sought to combine the grassroots approach of the Compact of Mayors with the elite focus of the European Commission's Covenant. The Global Covenant of Mayors included a formal mechanism for creating compliance with city-led climate change mitigation efforts. Each joining city signed a compact obligating them to create a Greenhouse Gas Emissions (GHG) inventory, engage in a climate vulnerability assessment, and produce a climate action plan to achieve specific GHG reduction targets (Gesing, 2017).

Subnational climate actions such as the C40 Climate Leadership Group and the Global Covenant of Mayors are what Bansard et al. (2017) referred to as "transnational municipal networks" (p. 230). The stakeholder groups in this case are the cities in question and their residents, while "the means" refers to the creation of transnational, voluntary mechanisms for addressing emissions of greenhouse gases. Despite the failure of many of the most powerful governing bodies to impact the problem, the recognition of the scale of the problem of climate change, and the necessity for action, has galvanized transnational networks.

The development of transnational argumentation networks on climate change demonstrates that while Dewey's theory of the public remains salient, it also undermines his theory of the state. Dewey (2016) drew on classical understandings of sovereignty to argue that the rise of publics necessitates the emergence of governing structures. The current case study of climate change finds that the relationship between the two is rather more contingent than necessary, and the future of governance structures may function as the subject of debate.

Concluding Thoughts: Transnational Networks and Neoliberalism

Contemporary scholarly investigations have focused on how "publics" can challenge or undermine neoliberalism (Asen, 2017; Biesecker & Trapani, 2014), a real and pressing concern given the potential havoc that unregulated corporations and industries pose to democracy, the environment, and the realization of a more equal world. The theoretical insight of this essay challenges this scholarship, however, as the relationship between publics, the state, and political progress is not as unidirectional as previous scholarship has argued. While some accounts are hopeful about the possibility of public formation(s) to challenge neoliberal structures of governing (Asen, 2017), others argue for the abandonment of public organizing in the face of neoliberal capture (Biesecker & Trapani, 2014). In each case, previous work has adhered to Dewey's belief that publics arise to appeal to institutions. Unfortunately, this model assumes that sovereign collectives control the possibility of political progress by serving as gatekeepers of change. Moving beyond this understanding of state-centric politics, however, is a vital ingredient in challenging a neoliberal configuration of power, as only a complex and nuanced theory of how publics coalesce to create a negotiated "public good" grapples with the contemporary reality of institutional intransigence.

Recent public sphere scholarship fails to grasp the role that extra-institutional forces must play in undermining neoliberal frameworks. In *Neoliberalism, the Public Sphere, and a Public Good*, for example, Asen (2017) identified the danger that neoliberalism poses for the future of public education and argued that hope lies in activism pushing back against the Republican- controlled Wisconsin government's proposed privatization of schooling. For Asen, neoliberalism is dangerous because it "upholds a market populated by atomistic individuals as a singular and universal sphere of activity" (p. 330). Analyzing the impact that this atomization has on the capacity for public formation led Asen (2017) to conclude that neoliberalism "obfuscates the means for redressing inequality and mobilizing diversity by weakening relations among people and devaluing coordinated action" (p. 331). For Asen (2017), the solution to this problem rests in examples of networked publics that coordinate and resist efforts to further atomize the public. The significant example that Asen used to illustrate his point was Governor Scott Walker and the legislative assembly's attempt to undermine public education in Wisconsin. Unfortunately, these activist groups have ultimately failed to sway state institutions to change direction on school voucher funding, a key mechanism to privatize education. In fact, the most recent Wisconsin budget expanded funding for vouchers (Sommerhauser, 2017). This case demonstrates the incompleteness of Asen's analysis, which emphasized the outsized role that state institutions play in configuring publics and sustaining their engagement, rather than recognizing the emergence and potential of transnational networks. When faced with an intransigent institution, publics can move laterally and create alternative frameworks for achieving their desired ends. Sometimes the best hope for political progress is not to try and persuade the government to change its mind, but rather to create the desired future through coordinated extra-institutional action.

Another example of leading scholarship that fails to adequately grapple with the reality of contemporary public organizing comes from a post-structuralist perspective. Biesecker and Trapani (2014) shared Asen's concern regarding the power of neoliberalism to undermine the formation of coordinated publics, but disagreed about the appropriate remedy. In *Escaping the Voice of the Mass/ter: Late Neoliberalism, Object-Voice, and the Prospects for a Radical Democratic Future*, they argued, "In late neoliberalism the so-called good or prudent personal choice is the very mode of belonging to a community" (Biesecker & Trapani, 2014, p. 27), indicting the idea that public formation could serve any end other than to reinforce the "calculating mentalit[y]" (p. 27) that lies at the heart of neoliberal governance. Biesecker and Trapani proposed that the only way out of this deadlock was to engage in polemics where a political agent rejects the subtending logic of neoliberalism, "boldly declaring and embodying something other" (2014, p. 31). For them, the purpose of this polemic was to break the stranglehold that neoliberalism had on individual subjectivity and facilitate a way out of an otherwise inevitable return to neoliberal logics and practices. The mode of polemics that they defend is only necessary if the neoliberal governing institutions are fixed and immoveable. Fortunately, neoliberal capture of community efforts is hardly inevitable, as significant climate action by transnational groups demonstrates. For example, Michael Bloomberg's work in the Global Covenant of Mayors supports the idea that there are other pathways forward for individuals and groups to challenge neoliberalism writ large, undermining Biesecker and Trapani's core claim. Future scholarly engagements with public formation and institutional progress must take note of the possibility that external, community-driven networks represent a potent site for political progress and change. If scholars remain wedded to an antiquated notion of public(s) interaction with government as the source of political progress, we will likely trail innovative groups that have found new modes of creating the futures they wish to inhabit.

References

About America's Pledge. (2017). *Bloomberg Philanthropies*. Retrieved from https://americaspledgeoncli mate.com/about/

Asen, R. (2003). The multiple Mr. Dewey: Multiple publics and permeable borders in John Dewey's theory of the public sphere [Special issue]. *Argumentation and Advocacy, 39*(3), 174–188. http://tandfon line.com

Asen, R. (2017) Neoliberalism, the public sphere, and a public good. *Quarterly Journal of Speech, 103*(4), 329–349. doi: 10.1080/00335630.2017.1360507

Bansard, J. S., Pattberg, P. H., & Widerberg, O. (2016). Cities to the rescue? Assessing the performance of transnational municipal networks in global climate governance. *International Environmental Agreements: Politics, Law and Economics, 17*(2), 229–246. doi: 10.1007/s10784-016-9318-9

Biesecker, B. A., & Trapani, W. (2014). Escaping the voice of the mass/ter: Late neoliberalism, object-voice, and the prospects for a radical democratic future. *Advances in the History of Rhetoric, 17*(1), 25–33. doi: 10.1080/15362426.2014.886926

Busby, J. (2017, June 1). Trump says goodbye to the Paris climate agreement. Here's what that means. *The Washington Post*. Retrieved from https://washingtonpost.com

Comstock, A. (2017, June 13). U.S. cities and states want to implement the Paris climate accord goals. It's not that simple. *The Washington Post*. Retrieved from https://washingtonpost.com

Dewey, J. (1927). *The public and its problems*. New York, NY: Holt.

Dewey, J. (2016). *The public and its problems: An essay in political inquiry* [E-reader version]. Athens, OH: Ohio University Press.

Fink, A. (2011). Under what conditions may social contracts arise? Evidence from the Hanseatic League. *Constitutional Political Economy, 22*(2), 173–190. doi: 10.1007/s10602-010-9099-z

Fryxell, G. E. (1990). The interaction of interest divergence and facility of strategy operationalization as determinants of business-unit culture. *International Journal of Value-Based Management, 3*(1), 43–64. doi: 10.1007/BF01560523

Gesing, F. (2017). The new global covenant of mayors for climate & energy and the politics of municipal climate data. *ZenTra Working Paper in Transnational Studies No. 71*. Retrieved from https://ssrn.com/ abstract=2984761

Global Covenant of Mayors for Climate & Energy. (2017, November). *Raising global climate ambition: Aggregate impact of the Global Covenant of Mayors for Climate & Energy* [Research report]. Retrieved from http://globalcovenantofmayors.org/wp-content/uploads/2017/11/GCoM_COP23Aggregation_Bro chure-FINAL.pdf

Herrschel, T., & Newman, P. (2017). *Cities as international actors*. London, United Kingdom: Palgrave Macmillan.

Kern, K., & Bulkeley, H. (2009). Cities, Europeanization and multi-level governance: Governing climate change through transnational municipal networks. *Journal of Common Market Studies, 47*(2), 309–332.

Paes, E., & Bloomberg, M. R. (2016, July). C40 cities climate leadership group: 10 years of results. Retrieved from http://c40-production-images.s3.amazonaws.com/fact_sheets/images/ 11_C40_on_its_10-year_anniversary_reOct2016.original.pdf?1475504972

Skinner, Q. (1978). *The foundations of modern political thought*. Cambridge, United Kingdom: Cambridge University Press. doi: 10.1017/CBO9780511817892.012

Sommerhauser, M. (2017, September 19). A quick primer on what's in the 2017-19 Wisconsin state budget. *Wisconsin State Journal*. Retrieved from: http://host.madison.com/wsj

Warner, M. (2002). Publics and counterpublics. *Public Culture 14*(1), 49-90. doi: 10.1215/08992363-14-1-49

Watts, M. (2017, December 6). Presidents may get it wrong but mayors can still save the planet. *Euronews*. Retrieved from http://euronews.com

Yang, Z., & Zagorowski, P. M. (2017). Climate variability, opposition group formation and conflict onset. In V. G. Duffy (Ed.), *Advances in applied digital human modeling and simulation* (pp. 181-193). Cham, Switzerland: Springer International.

35

NETWORKING, CIRCULATION, AND PUBLICITY OF CLIMATE CHANGE DISCOURSES AND ARGUMENTS

An Examination of Leonardo Dicaprio's Climate Change Advocacy

Andrew J. Hart

Climate change remains one of the foremost issues today as temperatures continue to rise and political, economic, and environmental impacts begin to take shape. The Intergovernmental Panel on Climate Change (2014) linked climate change to sea level rise, more severe weather events (e.g., more powerful hurricanes and more extreme droughts), increased stress on ecosystems, species extinctions, increased risks of international conflicts through human migration and degradation of resources, and risks to economic growth. Despite a scientific consensus on anthropogenic climate change, current efforts to combat it in the United States are insufficient. With scant discussion of climate change in the 2016 presidential election, Leonardo DiCaprio filled the void through the release of his 2016 documentary *Before the Flood* weeks before the election. The release date, designed as a calculated move intended to influence the outcome of the election, sought to mobilize voters to elect politicians who would take action on climate change.

While the effort ultimately failed to swing the election, DiCaprio's documentary represents an important study in how argument functions in celebrity climate activism. Attention is one of the scarcest and perhaps most crucial resources in politics today, with few issues, peoples, or groups commanding the public's attention in the competitive attention economy. Celebrity activism can gain and maintain our attention through various performances and forms of "enviro-tainment" (Thrall et al., 2008; Goodman, 2018). Celebrities operate as critical mediators of public affairs between citizens and the environment, function as witnesses of the consequences of failing to address climate change, and act as muses for how to save the planet. Celebrity activists may also revitalize public deliberation over climate change because they can connect the more formal spaces of climate science, policy, and politics to the spaces of everyday Western culture (Boykoff, Goodman, & Littler, 2010).

In analyzing how arguments function in celebrity activism, I provide three arguments. First, I contend that DiCaprio's celebrity status and activism garnered attention, sparked public deliberations, and expanded the audience base for engaging climate change arguments. Second, I examine how DiCaprio's documentary networked disparate communities, experts, and arguments from across the globe and from diverse public and technical spheres. Finally, I evaluate how the documentary utilized what Doyle, Farrell, and Goodman (2018) call an "after data" mode in which DiCaprio witnessed the effects of climate change first hand and worked to persuade the audience to engage in public deliberation through appeals to their affective and emotional registers. The essay will extend Doyle et al.'s conclusion that *Before the Flood* operates within an after data mode by moving beyond their focus on witnessing suffering to examine other affective/emotional appeals within *Before the Flood*, such as hope.

In the last two sections, I use Al Gore's documentary *An Inconvenient Truth* (David & Guggenheim, 2006) as a comparison to *Before the Flood*. These films, the two most known and most viewed climate change documentaries, utilize dramatically different argumentative and persuasive strategies. Although both DiCaprio and Gore are celebrities, they speak from different positions of authority: Gore operates as a celebrity politician who speaks with authority from political and policymaking experience, but DiCaprio operates as a political celebrity whose authority comes from his fame as an actor. The comparison demonstrates the differences in how arguments can function in celebrity activism.

Celebrity Culture in Argument

Celebrity activism in public affairs is not inherently democratizing or distracting, but is instead situationally and contingently produced. Celebrity activism that functions as a democratizing force increases public participation, opens spaces in the public sphere for discussions and political action, and raises sustained attention. Boykoff and Goodman (2009) argued that celebrities have been able to leverage their privileged position to "raise public and policy attention to various social, political, economic, cultural and environmental issues" (p. 396). Celebrities capitalize on their status in society to draw media and cultural attention to issues like climate change and "to bring it within the popular cultural sphere, as well as utilizing their fan bases to mobilize engagement and action via social media" (Doyle et al., 2018, p. 2). Celebrity participation also functions to draw in other people and supporters to a cause, which expands the boundaries of the conflict by "expanding both the audience and the number of legitimate actors in a political conflict" (Meyer & Gamson, 1995, p. 185).

Celebrity activism can also entail risks for the causes that they support. While celebrities do, at times, become distractions, I focus here on how they displace more expert voices. Despite their influence, celebrities are not experts or authorities in environmental or scientific enterprises in any traditional sense. The boundary blurs between who counts as authorized to speak and who counts as an expert given that new actors populate the climate science-policy public interactions (Boykoff et al., 2010). Boykoff and Goodman (2009) noted, "These newly 'authorized' speakers and 'experts' might open up spaces in the public sphere and the science/policy nexus through 'celebritization' effects" (p. 395). Because celebrities are not climate experts, they can displace expert voices because "the privileged voices of celebrity actors have gained greater influence in the framing of climate science-policy/practice discourses" (Boykoff & Goodman, 2009, p. 404).

Attention, Public Deliberation, and Audiences

In the highly competitive attention economy, DiCaprio's celebrity status drew attention to climate change as *Before the Flood* emerged as one of the most watched documentaries of all time. As Hickman (2016) noted, "In terms of box-office draw alone, Before the Flood [*sic*] is the most significant film about climate change since Al Gore's An Inconvenient Truth [*sic*]" (para. 4). Less than three weeks after the release on the National Geographic Channel and for free on numerous streaming platforms, Calvario (2016) noted,

> [The documentary] reached more than 60 million people worldwide and surpassed a record-setting one billion minutes viewed across linear, digital, streaming and social platforms—making it arguably one of the most watched documentaries in history and the most watched NatGeo film ever.
>
> *(para. 1)*

Before the Flood raised attention, but more importantly, the documentary spurred public deliberation about climate change as it was trending on Facebook, Twitter, and YouTube and continued to spark what Gerard (2016) considered "passionate conversations across many platforms" (para. 5) well after its release. These continued conversations worked to prevent *climate silence*, which Doyle et al. (2018) argued occurs when "there are not enough public, media or even personal discussions about the severity and impacts of climate change" (p. 23). Instead, DiCaprio functioned as one of several "emotional climate celebrities [...] working to maintain climate change as a topic worthy of continued urgent and critical public discussion" (p. 23). This increased engagement on social media indicates that *Before the Flood* succeeded in reaching and energizing young people on the issue of climate change —the audience climate change was most likely to affect and one of the key target audiences of the film (Stevens, 2016). However, the most important audience DiCaprio accessed "might actually not be the general public but rather other elites and those in power in order to make affective connections and get them to work for more and better climate policy" (Doyle et al., 2018, p. 23). Because of his celebrity status and position as United Nations Ambassador of Peace for Climate Change, DiCaprio accessed powerful audiences capable of enacting change.

Networking Expertise

Before the Flood, in some senses, is an extension of Gore's documentary *An Inconvenient Truth,* as both DiCaprio and Gore relied upon their celebrity status to attract viewers and utilized argument by authority for credibility. However, one of the biggest differences between these two films is where the authority/expertise resided. For Gore, authority rested in himself, as viewers only heard his voice. *An Inconvenient Truth* included no neutral voiceover or expert interviews; only Gore's narration brought together data and multiple arguments to try to persuade the audience that, in turn, positioned the documentary to rely solely on Gore's authority for credibility. Thus, many opponents, rather than having to address the substance of the arguments, discredited the film through *ad hominem* attacks because attacking Gore's authority would destabilize the documentary's entire line of arguments (Aaltonen, 2014).

For DiCaprio, expertise rested in the people he interviewed rather than himself. He was not a self-proclaimed expert, which he explicitly acknowledged by stating, "the truth is, the more I've learned about this issue and everything that contributes to the problem, the more I realize how much I don't know. How much I don't know about this issue" (DiCaprio & Stevens, 2016,

11:52). Those interviewed in the film were not just climate scientists but experts from across multiple sectors in the technical sphere, ranging from politics to science to economics to religion to business leaders. DiCaprio focused the interviews on their specific field of expertise and wove together those interviews to create a coherent narrative about anthropogenic climate change. In China, DiCaprio interviewed Ma Jun, the Founding Director of the Institute of Public and Environmental Affairs, about the health effects of emissions. He went to the Pacific Islands to interview the President of Kiribati, Anote Tong, about the effects of sea level rise and the plan for dealing with the islands disappearing underwater. These diverse experts shielded DiCaprio's advocacy from character assassination through *ad hominem* attacks against DiCaprio alone. Instead of attacking one person, opponents would have to attack the dispersed network of experts from diverse fields to make the tactics effective. By interviewing these experts, DiCaprio used the authority of others to bolster his argument and to forge a coherent and resilient argument about anthropogenic climate change.

DiCaprio's interviews with experts from religious, political, and economic fields cut across various group affiliations within the audience to broaden the persuasive appeal of his arguments. Many observers frame climate change as a partisan issue of Republicans against Democrats, but DiCaprio interviewed members of both parties in an attempt to transcend partisanship. DiCaprio interviewed both Gregory Mankiw, the head economist for President George W. Bush and a staunch conservative, and Phillip Levine, the Democratic mayor of Miami, to show that climate change was not a partisan issue. As Levine noted during his interview, "The ocean is not Republican and it's not Democrat, all it knows how to do is rise" (DiCaprio & Stevens, 2016, 22:40). To appeal to those with strong religious affiliations, DiCaprio interviewed Pope Francis. To appeal to those with strong economic concerns, DiCaprio interviewed Mankiw and Elon Musk. These interviews with experts outside the sciences helped inoculate the issue from a smear campaign against science because climate change is not just a scientific issue; it is also an economic, political, and religious issue.

Rather than displace more expert voices, DiCaprio functioned as a guide for the audience to meet and to hear these experts. Instead of creating another climate change documentary that orbited "around a heroic expert who has devoted his or her vocational life to a cause" (Stevens, 2016, para. 10), DiCaprio maintained a focus on experts while using his charisma and celebrity to make these expert witnesses accessible and relevant to a wide audience. Rather than serve as a distraction, DiCaprio played a crucial role in making climate change accessible and culturally meaningful to audiences outside of political and scientific discourses.

Affect as Argument: After Data Mode

More than simply an amalgamation of expert voices, DiCaprio's documentary was also distinctive from Gore's due to its use of an after data mode of documentary filmmaking. Gore's documentary used the latest data, information, and knowledge about climate change to establish the threat it posed to the earth in an attempt "to educate and convince the public in minute Power Point detail about the rise in CO2 emitted by humans and the corresponding rise in global average temperatures" (Doyle et al., 2018, p. 19). Gore raised attention to the issue and acted as a public pedagogue "who could speak about the science of climate change and vouch for its 'reality'" (Doyle et al., 2018, p. 20). Instead of utilizing interviews, Gore reported on information from other people with scientific authority. He spoke of the impacts to people, but did not talk to them or show these effects. While this documentary "put climate change on the map in a great way" (Stevens, 2016, para. 6), this data and education-driven form of documentary has limitations because it lacks the personal and emotive registers to access different and potentially more powerful forms of persuasion.

In striking contrast to the Gore film, *Before the Flood* provided the viewer with an entirely different experience by using an after data mode. Instead of dry accounts of the latest scientific knowledge about climate change, *Before the Flood* documented DiCaprio's journey to witness the impacts of climate change around the world. By going to these places personally, interviewing experts, and witnessing the ongoing impacts of climate change first hand, the audience could not easily dismiss the reality of climate change. This after data mode showed a "change in both the format—from tell to show/witness—and also timbre—from knowledge and exhortations for action to affective and emotional appeals to audiences and the public" (Doyle et al., 2018, p. 18). Instead of relying on numbers and science, this new mode focused on affective and emotional appeals to persuade the audience of the necessity of urgent action on climate change by using "stories of personal and/or literal journeys upon the climate landscape and those of climate-related impacts" (p. 19). Much like how celebrities have borne witness to suffering by visiting places of poverty, DiCaprio did so by bearing witness to the suffering of climate change through visiting places affected by climate change (Doyle et al., 2018). He went to the Pacific Islands and witnessed the islands disappearing underwater. He went to India and witnessed the devastation to local farmers when there is half a year's rainfall in five hours. He went to Miami where sunny day flooding had forced the city to fund a - 400 million dollar infrastructure project to keep the streets above water perhaps for 40 or 50 years. By viewing these impacts, the audience witnessed the effects of climate change at the level of the everyday in DiCaprio's documentary, an experience quite different from the more distant and logic-driven climate change documentaries of the past.

While I agree with the conclusion Doyle et al. (2018) offered that *Before the Flood* represented a critical shift in celebrity climate activism by taking the audience on a journey to witness suffering, they failed to account for the other critical affective appeal in *Before the Flood*—hope. *Before the Flood* shifted to hope of a better future by presenting viable policy options to prevent catastrophic climate change supported through interviews with economists and business leaders Mankıw, Musk, and Johan Rockstrom. Perhaps the greatest show of hope came not from those advocating for specific policies, but from interviews with astronaut Piers Sellers and Pope Francis, both of whom expressed sincere hope and faith in humanity's ability to find a solution. By taking the audience along for this journey, viewers arguably felt the shift from pessimism, from witnessing suffering, to hope for the future and faith in humanity.

Conclusion

DiCaprio's documentary represents an important look into how arguments function in celebrity activism. His celebrity status garnered attention and provoked public deliberations about climate change. Perhaps more importantly, *Before the Flood* achieved what researchers and practitioners have increasingly called for in climate change media: more "*localized*, *emotional/affective*, and *participatory* modes of communication that more clearly link to, as well as challenge, people's existing social values and identity in order to make climate change understood and felt at the level of the everyday" (Doyle et al., 2018, p. 14). By interviewing these experts from diverse fields from across the globe, DiCaprio cut across multiple group identities within the audience to appeal to and to challenge the audience's diverse social values and networked those expert voices to form a coherent and resilient argument about climate change. By visiting different places personally, DiCaprio witnessed the ongoing and localized impacts of climate change and the human face of suffering for the audience. For the United States, the Miami segment showed that the impacts of climate change were not a distant or future problem. Fortunately, hope continues to exist for a better future.

References

Aaltonen, J. (2014). Claims of hope and disasters: Rhetoric expression in three climate change documentaries. *Studies in Documentary Film, 8*(1), 61–75. doi:10.1080/17503280.2014.900947

Boykoff, M. T., & Goodman, M. K. (2009). Conspicuous redemption? Reflections on the promises and perils of the "celebritization" of climate change. *Geoforum, 40*(3), 395–406, doi:10.1016/j.geoforum.2008.04.006

Boykoff, M., Goodman, M., & Littler, J. (2010). "Charismatic megafauna": The growing power of celebrities and pop culture in climate change campaigns (Paper No. 28). London, United Kingdom: King's College.

Calvario, L. (2016, November 16). "Before the flood": Leonardo DiCaprio's climate change doc gets record 60 million views. *Indie Wire*. Retrieved from http://indiewire.com/2016/11/before-the-flood-climate-change-documentary-record-60-million-views-1201747088/

David, L. (Producer), & Guggenheim, D. (Director). (2006). *An inconvenient truth* [Motion Picture]. United States: Paramount.

DiCaprio, L. (Producer), & Stevens, F. (Director). (2016). *Before the flood* [Documentary]. United States: National Geographic Films.

Doyle, J., Farrell, N., & Goodman, M. (2018). Celebrities and climate change: History, politics and the promise of emotional witness. In M. Nisbet (Ed.), *The Oxford encyclopedia of climate change communication*. Oxford, United Kingdom: Oxford University Press.

Gerard, J. (2016, November 3). Leonardo DiCaprio's "before the flood" sampled by 30M+ worldwide for National Geographic. *Deadline*. Retrieved from http://deadline.com/2016/11/before-the-flood-ratings-leonardo-dicaprio-national-geographic-1201847781/

Goodman, M. (2018). Environmental celebrity. In N. Castree, M. Hulme, & J. Proctor (Eds.), *The companion to environmental studies*. London, United Kingdom: Routledge.

Hickman, L. (2016, November 20). Review: 7 key scenes in Leonardo DiCaprio's climate film before the flood. *Carbon Brief*. Retrieved from https://carbonbrief.org/7-key-scences-leonardo-dicaprio-climate-film-before-the-flood

Intergovernmental Panel on Climate Change: Summary for Policymakers. (2014). In C. B. Field, V. R. Barros, D. J. Dokken, K. J. Mach, M. D. Mastrandrea, T. E. Bilir, … L. L. White (Eds.), *Climate change 2014: Impacts, adaptation, and vulnerability. Part A: Global and sectoral aspects. Contribution of working group II to the fifth assessment report of the intergovernmental panel on climate change* (pp. 1–32). Cambridge, United Kingdom: Cambridge University Press.

Meyer, D. S., & Gamson, J. (1995). The challenge of cultural elites: Celebrities and social movements. *Sociological Inquiry, 65*(2), 181–206. doi:10.1111/j.1475-682X.1995.tb00412.x

Stevens, F. (2016, October 22). The new "inconvenient truth": Leonardo DiCaprio's new documentary wants to challenge climate change skeptics [Interviewed by E. G'Sell]. *Salon*. Retrieved from https://salon.com/2016/10/22/the-new-inconvenient-truth-leonardo-dicaprios-new-documentary-wants-to-challenge-climate-change-skeptics/

Thrall, A. T., Lollio-Fakhreddine, L., Berent, J., Donnelly, L., Herrin, W., Paquette, Z.,… Wyatt, A. (2008). Star power: Celebrity advocacy and the evolution of the public sphere. *The International Journal of Press/Politics, 13*(4), 362–385. doi:10.1177/1940161208319098

36

ARGUMENTS FOR WOMEN'S BANKS AND THE POSSIBILITIES AND LIMITS OF CORPORATE STRUCTURAL MIMESIS AS PRIVATE-PUBLIC ARGUMENT NETWORKS

David B. Hingstman

"Apparently, it takes a superhero to advocate for the rights of women. At least that's the message some people received when earlier Friday the United Nations appointed Wonder Woman as Honorary Ambassador for the Empowerment of Women and Girls"
— Erik Alexander. *CNN*, 2016

In the conclusion to the Gettysburg Address, President Lincoln called upon those living in this nation committed to human equality to dedicate themselves to a new birth of freedom and ensure that "government of the people, by the people, and for the people, shall not perish from the earth" (Lincoln, 2008). Craig R. Smith (2000) has argued that Daniel Webster's *Second Reply to Hayne* may have influenced the construction of this final phrase, since Webster characterizes the federal government as "made for the people, made by the people, and answerable to the people" (p. 7).

Even a cursory review of U.S. political history would justify the conclusion that the nation systematically denied equality, freedom, and participation in government to women well into the twentieth century, and in many ways, the leadership has yet to redeem the Gettysburg commitments. The right to vote did not guarantee that the halls of government would hear women's voices. If women lacked the resources to participate fully, such as traveling to petition for grievances and running for political office, the government could manage, rather than heed, their demands. Finding the necessary resources would be nearly impossible without accessing income or loans, which unequal employment opportunities and credit discrimination limited. Thus, government would have to ensure progress in all of the domains of political economy if the nation was to answer Lincoln's call. But the traditional dichotomy between private and public spheres of activity seemed to place many of the sources of discrimination and oppression outside the reach of organized political opposition.

Scholars in communication and the humanities more generally have thoroughly documented how feminist activists and critics have created and deployed arguments that challenge the legitimacy of the private-public dichotomy. They have examined and advocated for alternative communication practices, such as consciousness-raising and invitational rhetorics that have emancipatory potential for feminist counterpublics (e.g., Campbell, 1973, 1999; Foss & Griffin, 1995). The well-known slogans "the personal is political" and "the private is political" summarize diverse strategies of argument that undermine the private-public dichotomy by connecting individual experiences with social structures and institutional practices. These strategies have opened many areas of concern to political analysis and discussion (Warner, 2014). But, as Carol Hanisch observed in a 2006 revisiting of her famous essay that helped to popularize the slogans, risks of misappropriation attendant to such arguments abound—"These ideas have been revised or ripped off or even stood on their head and used against their original, radical intent" (para. 16).

Contemporary U.S. banking institutions are particularly compatible with neoliberal logics because people in the private economic sector, in large part, own and operate them. Nevertheless, government agencies still charter, capitalize, and heavily regulate them. As the 2008 economic crisis attests, federal control of the currency is the ultimate guarantor of the ability of banks to operate. The neoliberal arguments that legitimate the structure and functions of the U.S. banking system claim that governments and private corporations can work together to promote economic growth, employment, and efficiency in capitalization while also fine-tuning supervision and risk assessment to avoid fraudulent or unsafe lending practices. At the same time, government and private activities mold citizen subjects into responsible suppliers and consumers of credit by creating opportunities for them to set up and manage financial instruments and obligations, as well as enforcing formal and informal sanctions upon their actions. Banks, then, are neoliberal private-public hybrid institutions that, like other financial businesses, network diverse reasons and interests of participants into consensus-building norms and practices that, on the whole, expand the availability of credit and debt, but also undermine other desired outcomes through their very operation (Goodnight, Hingstman, & Green, 2015).

Advocates for women's rights fought for measures that would end credit discrimination on the basis of gender. Bowdish (2010) described the movement as a "three-pronged approach" (p. ii) that included organizing publicity about the problems, lobbying for legislation, and participating in institution building that could circumvent the barriers to lending. In terms of discourse practices, the movement sought to raise consciousness, threaten recalcitrant lenders with regulation and lawsuits, and demonstrate through collective action that women were trustworthy managers and consumers of credit and debt responsibly. This essay will focus on the second and third prongs, which in this case lead to regulatory legislation, the Equal Credit Opportunity Act ("ECOA") of 1974 as amended in 1976, and the founding of "women's banks" at roughly the same time. It will argue that, in the spirit of "the personal is the political," the combination of approaches seemed compelling because it worked both inside and outside of the movement. It would be a counterpublic realization of Lincoln and Webster's institutional criteria for self-governance—the banks would be made for, made by, and made accountable to, women. What the analysis will suggest is that, as actually implemented and publicized over time in the neoliberal networked consensus about banking, the combination of the ECOA and "women's banks" worked against the concept's emancipatory intent.

Made of the People and for the People: How Big Data Presumptions Made the ECOA and Women's Banks Work at Cross-Purposes for Equality and Freedom

In the public debate surrounding the consideration of state statutes on credit access and then the federal bill that became the ECOA, opponents put much stock in the claim that no solid proof existed to prove that banks discriminated against women in the provision of credit due to the absence of disaggregated quantitative data on the reasons for refusal of commercial or private loans. Terms attempted to curb credit discrimination did exist in federal laws, such as the Truth in Lending and Consumer Credit Protection Acts. But the successful application and enforcement of these laws depended on findings grounded in quantitative data.

Why did the federal government consider the ability to find quantitative data that either confirmed or refuted the claims about gender discrimination so difficult? One motive lay in the consensus of the major credit agencies prior to the ECOA that they should treat married people as an economic unit for collecting data on their financial activities. Since most women in the United States were married at that time (Roberts, 2007), their credit histories depended on their marital relationship, tethering them to the choices and actions of their partners. But the credit agencies considered such risks acceptable because the approach reduced their cost of gathering, aggregating, and analyzing personal financial data. If women's financial standing generally improved upon marriage, then a "rational"—not "invidious"—form of discrimination required spousal permission (Bowdish, 2010, p. 87).

Another motive was that legislators were loath to challenge directly the autonomy of private banking institutions that enabled them to hold their loan acceptance and rejection information as a trade secret. The assumption was that the quality of assessment procedures at individual banks made all the difference between competitive success or failure. Moreover, the banks argued that they would be conducting "bad business" ("irrational" in free market terms) to discriminate against potential borrowers who could and would repay their debts, so they could attribute any differences in lending rates to historical statistics on the probability of default (Bowdish, 2010). The reaction of most state legislators in such situations was to pass laws that simply stated the unacceptability of gender as the sole basis for denying credit without providing any alternative lending assessment procedures. This situation mirrors the problems of the Fair Credit Reporting Act of 1970, did not root out errors in reported credit scores even as it promoted transparency (Cassady & Mierzwinski, 2004).

What was at stake in the ECOA debate, then, was whether the law justifiably could shift the presumptions that labeled the banking industry's reliance upon marital status in loan decision-making procedures "rational" rather than "invidious." This exigency was similar to the one facing advocates attempting to challenge discriminatory practices under the Equal Protection clause or to demand the ratification of the Equal Rights Amendment to the U.S. Constitution during the same period. Should, as Stearns (2012) asked, the test for enforceable, unlawful discrimination be the sheer absence of business justification (rational basis) or the failure to refute anecdotal evidence of discriminatory intent or effect (strict scrutiny)?

Testimony in the hearings on the ECOA uncovered a great deal of qualitative, anecdotal evidence of credit discrimination. The denial of claims included situations where women could not get credit in their own names even when their income was sufficient to meet standard guidelines, or when lenders would discount income statements over doubts about commitments to continued employment or eventual debt repayment. In some instances, lending institutions had required women to sign affidavits that they would not bear children during the term of the loan, or husbands to cosign loan agreements (Bowdish, 2010). At a point in the history of feminist movements when activists and scholars valorized narratives of personal experience as a principal emancipatory practice (Hanisch, 2006), those who engaged in the collection and dissemination of those narratives claimed both authenticity from these voices in petitioning for redress and the moral high ground of continuing the struggle for civil rights (Bowdish, 2010).

The process of congressional passage illustrates how neoliberal governance reaches consensus when qualitative grievance narratives clash with the quantitative presumptions in favor of private corporate activities. First, distinct differences appear in framing and attitude between the initiating (epideictic) and finalizing (deliberative) phases for the bill between the two houses of Congress. The personal passion of Senator Brock and his legislative assistant Emily Card, helped to promote the issue and draft the Senate version of the legislation, which passed overwhelmingly with little debate. The Senate version foregrounded the condemnation of invidious credit discrimination on the basis of "race, color, religion, national origin, sex or marital status, or age," but backgrounded any significant discussion of implementation. The House Banking and Currency Subcommittee, on the other hand, sought a "balance" between equity and efficiency. Their bill stated its purpose as enhancing economic stabilization and competition and promoting the informed use of credit, thus implicitly accepting the argument of the banks that credit discrimination on the basis of gender must be economically "irrational" and not systemic (Bowdish, 2010, pp. 93-96). If curtailing certain kinds of inquiries might increase loan default rates, such as marital status in community property states, then banks could make exceptions. Eventually, the women's groups supporting the House bill asked the committee to remove all identity categories other than "sex or marital status" from the bill because they believed that only the gender-based qualitative evidence could sustain its passage. This move alienated civil rights advocates at a time when the campaign to ratify the Equal Rights Amendment was beginning to flounder, and forced amendments to the ECOA to reinscribe the other categories a year later (Bowdish, 2010).

Second, the congressional committees deferred rationalization of the conflicting data sources to administrative agencies, but the Federal Reserve under Regulation B turned out no more capable of generating a replacement for the big data assumptions of the banking system than Congress did. No solid data existed because of the assumption that married people should function as an economic unit had been the basis for the data collection efforts of credit institutions.

Thus, in advocating for the ECOA, the representatives of the aggrieved parties took the position that reliance on storytelling and qualitative indications of the problem was merely a temporary expedient. The advocates never attempted to defend the position that access to credit should be a right for all, rather than a privilege the credit agencies could dole out as they saw fit. Perhaps some of the advocates even believed that women's banks, which catered to women for both personal and business loans, would provide the needed data because of their specialized focus. But the story did not end up quite that way.

Answerable to the People: Entrepreneurial Wonder Women Financiers Undermine Gendered Economic Solidarity

Conservative women's groups opposed the imaginary of obtrusive bureaucratic interference with the operation of free market credit institutions. Their vision was that banks could simultaneously cater to the specific credit needs and tutoring of aspiring women entrepreneurs, staff themselves primarily with women who had experience with and understanding of the general banking industry, and generate more profits than the industry as a whole. This super-heroic vision was ultimately betrayed in each aspect:

> With the exception of a few specific credit unions, the women's banks began in earnest in July 1975 with the establishment of FWB-NY. Of all the women's financial institutions, FWB-NY operated under the most public scrutiny. Even at its opening on October 16, 1975, the *New York Times* was quick to point out the difficulties First Women's New York encountered in raising capital, but it tempered that statement by blaming the weakened stock market and the general unpopularity of bank stocks at the time because of a bad credit market in the mid 1970s.
>
> *(Bowdish, 2010, p. 141)*

A total of 10 women's banks appeared between 1975 and 1979. Almost all of these banks either failed or had male-led banking leadership take them over by the end of the 1980 with their emphasis on marketing primarily to women abandoned. What argumentative problems related to the neoliberal banking model undermined the success of these banks in dealing with credit access problems faced by women? First, the rhetorical confidence in the appeal to microtargeting did not account for the gendered expectations of the sources of capital. The early strategy was to tap prominent women in Hollywood and in the business community to make initial capital contributions, but those contributions functioned as seed money only. Later, the women's banks sought ongoing capitalization from the very banking community they were trying to embarrass, and the capital was not forthcoming, ostensibly because of competitiveness stemming from banking deregulation in the 1980s.

Second, the banks were unable to find sufficient numbers of experienced and educated women to provide the leadership to meet the elevated expectations of the bank founders. When the women placed in leadership went through the painful process of trial and error for making lending decisions to new client categories, the banks blamed them for the capital losses that the educational process entailed. By the late 1980s and early 1990s, the general financial sector was luring women's bank executives away to administrative jobs or the banks forced them to resign in favor of male leadership.

Third, acceding to performance benchmarks requiring women's banks to do better than male-run banking institutions eventually undermined the very reason for having women's banks in the first place. Pressure to attract more male customers to the women's bank services emerged. In spite of periodic advertising blitzes and comparison to "farmers and workers' banks" that had grown to national scale, the bank managements could not overcome prejudices against identification of male entrepreneurs with a "woman's bank." At the same time, large competitors like Chase established educational programs that mirrored the operations of the women's banks, but without the feminist consciousness-raising attitudes and experiences of women managers.

Only an enclaved public strategy justifying short-term sacrifices of profitability in the name of gender solidarity could have challenged the neoliberal free market narrative. The fact that the women's banks relied heavily on government incentive deposits from the Treasury during the early stages could have mobilized the antidiscrimination rationale in favor of solidarity. Perhaps such steps would not have been rhetorically possible until the rise of Third Wave Feminism in the 1990s, but the celebration of personal consumption might have continued to hinder an effective resistance to neoliberalism.

David B. Hingstman

When It Comes to Banking and Credit, Networked Women Need to Be Nastier

The record of the ECOA and women's banks in failing to eliminate some of the most annoying aspects of neoliberal deference to the data collecting and interpreting practices of the U.S. banking system suggests that a different argumentative strategy might have made a difference. First, arguing that equal access to credit should be a right, rather than a privilege, would have focused the ECOA debate on the gendered assumptions about married people, rather than on the question of whether credit agencies should have autonomy as long as no substantial data proved they had discriminated against women. And this broader antidiscrimination focus beyond women's interests alone might have discouraged some advocates from taking the expedient of dropping coalitional efforts among other groups by claiming that, "only women can prove discrimination in credit access." Second, arguing that the women who were operating the "women's banks" deserved evaluative standards based on their ability to achieve solidarity rather than "superhero" criterions, such as those suggested by those who had been excluding them from management in the past, might have allowed that movement to develop in different directions. The relative conservatism of the founders need not make them insensitive to the gendered implications of their decision to take a short-term risk for long-term goals.

The growth of the economy over the period between 1982 and 2008 masked the continuing problems of discrimination, as even traditional banks began to recognize that more women were participating in the workforce and beginning to break the "glass ceiling" in executive corporate positions as well. Those banks were eager to extend credit to women who fit this profile. Perhaps instructive will be whether the Great Recession's longer-lasting legacy is to spur new arguments about remaining issues of credit access and banking management.

References

Alexander, E. (2016, October 24). Wonder Woman named UN ambassador in controversial move. *CNN*. Retrieved from http://cnn.com/2016/10/21/health/wonder-woman-un-ambassador-trnd

Bowdish, L. A. (2010). *Invidious distinctions: Credit discrimination against women, 1960s-present* (Doctoral dissertation). Retrieved from The Ohio State University, OhioLINK Electronic Theses & Dissertations Center website: http://etd.ohiolink.edu

Campbell, K. K. (1973). The rhetoric of women's liberation: An oxymoron. *Quarterly Journal of Speech*, *59*(1), 74–86. doi:10.1080/00335637309383155

Campbell, K. K. (1999). "The rhetoric of women's liberation: An oxymoron" revisited. *Communication Studies*, *50*(2), 138–142. doi:10.1080/10510979909388480

Cassady, A., & Mierzwinski, E. (2004, June). *Mistakes do happen: A look at errors in consumer credit reports*. Washington, DC: National Association of State Public Interest Research Groups.

Foss, S. K., & Griffin, C. L. (1995). Beyond persuasion: A proposal for an invitational rhetoric. *Communication Monographs*, *62*(1), 2–18. doi:10.1080/03637759509376345

Goodnight, G. T., Hingstman, D., & Green, S. (2015). The student debt bubble: Neoliberalism, the university, and income inequality. *Journal of Cultural Economy*, *8*(1), 75–100. doi:10.1080/17530350.2014.947307

Hanisch, C. (2006, January). The personal is the political: The women's liberation movement classic with a new explanatory introduction. Retrieved from http://carolhanisch.org/CHwritings/PIP.html

Lincoln, A. (2008). Gettysburg Address. *Yale Law School Lillian Goldman Law Library: The Avalon Project*. Retrieved from http://avalon.law.yale.edu/19th_century/gettyb.asp

Roberts, S. (2007, January 16). 51% of women are now living without spouse. *The New York Times*. Retrieved from http://nytimes.com

Smith, C. R. (2000). Criticism of political rhetoric and disciplinary integrity. *American Communication Journal, 4*(1).

Stearns, M. L. (2012, November). *Scrutinizing tiers*. Paper presented at the Northwestern University School of Law Constitutional Law Symposium. Retrieved from http://imbs.uci.edu/files/scrutini zing_tiers_feb_20_2014_final_send_0.pdf

Warner, M. (2014). Public/private. In C. R. Stimpson & G. Herdt (Eds.), *Critical terms for the study of gender* (pp. 358–392). Chicago, IL: University of Chicago Press.

37

ADMINISTRATIVE ARGUMENTS AND NETWORK GOVERNANCE

The Case of Women's Health

Zornitsa Keremidchieva

For some time now, a persistent trend toward the "disarticulation of the state" (Frederickson, 1999, p. 702) has emerged as the complexities of social and public problems spill beyond traditional lines of jurisdiction and control (Frederickson, 1999). Characteristic of this trend is the rise of network governance—a regime where public policy making and implementation appear through, alongside, in the absence of, despite, or even against state regulation (Jordan, Wurzel, & Zito, 2005; Rhodes, 1996; Skelcher, 2005). Capturing this transition from government to governance, Salamon (2002) noted:

> Instead of the centralized hierarchical agencies delivering standardized services that is caricatured in much of the current reform literature and most of our political rhetoric, what exists in most spheres of policy is a dense mosaic of policy tools, many of them placing public agencies in complex, interdependent relationship with a host of third-party partners.
>
> *(p. 3)*

Network governance has frayed the political process to the point that scholars now call for the development of post-liberal democratic theory (Bogason & Musso, 2006; Sørensen & Torfing, 2005).

Yet, argumentation studies' conception of political argument appears to remain beholden to a liberal notion of the democratic public sphere as a "public forum" where arguments "handle disagreements transcending private and technical disputes" and which "inevitably limits participation to representative spokespersons" (Goodnight, 1982/2012, p. 202). This formulation privileges overt forms of argumentation, orients decision making toward established institutions, and delimits social identities through the logics of representation. Each of these presumptions breaks down in network governance. For their part, argumentation scholars have kept apace by calling out the emergent character of the identities that politics bring forth (Biesecker, 1989), their assemblages into argumentative contexts (Greene & Hayes, 2012), and their affective circulation well beyond any single occasion (Chaput,

2010). The field has ways to go, however, in capturing the particular modes of deliberation and advocacy where market, government, and civil society actors come together to form the webs and establish the legitimacy of network governance.

This essay attempts to identify some of the unique characteristics of argumentation in network governance and, in doing so, to consider what becomes of the polity, of knowledge, and of political action in this new regime (Hajer, 2003). Specifically, I highlight how arguments now flow through networks of intersecting and interlocking genres and textual artifacts that collectively constitute administrative rhetoric: "the official language of laws governing reorganizations, many public statements about it, and the obligatory terminology of reports" (March & Olson, 1983, p. 283). In such intertextual webs, the etymology of administration as an organizing process of giving or dispensing, simultaneously aiding and controlling, ordering and managing, directing and serving comes in full force. I find that in women's health, as in other sectors, administrative arguments perform their ordering function mainly through the practice of documentation, which infuses networks with certain durability, simultaneously producing and delimiting their complexity, and most importantly, constituting the centers and peripheries of social action. Without being fully vested or even indicative of enforcement power, administrative arguments in network governance arrange the circulation of discourse in a way that effectively slows down and channels the political process, thus generating a perception of stability that may offset the precarity and emergent character of social identities. Put simply, I argue that social identities appear as a key product of network governance and tracing their emergence requires attention to the multi-modality and materiality of administrative claims.

Administrative Rhetoric

With all the excitement that the technological proliferation of deliberative practices has created, we might be overlooking a powerful rhetorical form that is hiding in plain sight. Administrative claims have a bad reputation in a tradition of argumentation studies rooted in liberal and republican models of democracy (Habermas, 1994). Viewed as the idiom of modern bureaucratic institutions, argumentation scholars have defined administrative rhetoric as little more than "an undemocratic response to protest" (Windt, 1982, p. 249). Generally lumped together with other forms of technical or technocratic discourse along a contested continuum between experts and non-experts, institutional and lay speakers, the field often faults administrative arguments for serving as a barrier to participation in debates over various public issues (Farrell & Goodnight, 1981).

Despite the apparent diminution of the traditional institutions of government, however, administrative arguments appear only to be proliferating and doing so fast. Hood and Jackson (1991) catalogued and evaluated the acceptance and resilience of a large volume of claims that have defined the practice of public administration since World War II, demonstrating their tendency to cluster into doctrines of organizational thinking and practice in ways not too different from those constituting scientific paradigms. These claims appear to be also just as powerful and flexible, as the interaction between the scientism of the field of public policy studies and the techno-scientific transformation of the social sphere fuels them (Asdal, Moser, & Brenna, 2007). The ever-intensifying flurry of actionable documents—scientific and administrative reports, certificates of identity, grant applications, memoranda, etc.—create an archive of modern knowledge that, as some suggest, is characterized by "a persistent endeavor reflexively to seek further knowledge about itself" (Riles, 2006, p. 6).

Thus administrative rhetoric is more than the sum of public service managers, elected officials, and rank bureaucrats' claims. Rather, it is an aggregating concept that aims to capture the organizing features of what Lynn, Heinrich, and Hill (2000) called the "logic of governance": the means of structuring and managing the public sector and other collective activity. Three features of Lynn et al.'s (2000) logic of governance merit note: (a) the "configurational nature of governance" (p. 236), which refers to the interplay between distinct, but nonetheless endogenous, processes in constituting the networked character of a governance regime; (b) the invariably political character of governance as resources and interests often fuel both competition and cooperation; and (c) the constant interplay of formal and informal authority and judgment. Administrative arguments make the unfolding of the logic of network governance possible by coordinating the who, the how, and the what of socio-political organization (Hood & Jackson, 1991). In doing so, they constitute the field of politics as acts of "'heterogeneous engineering' in which bits and pieces from the social, the technical, the conceptual, and the textual fit together, and so convert (or 'translate') into a set of equally heterogeneous [social and political] products" (Law, 1992, p. 381). In the case that I examine next, women's health, and by extension women, emerge as this kind of a heterogeneous product that illustrates the material role of administrative arguments in organizing social identities in network governance.

Administrative Argument and the Network Governance of Women's Health

What is women's health and is it governable? The career of the concept illustrates the role of administrative arguments in ordering socio-political reality. Borne out of an epistemological dispute, women's health is now a complex network of agencies, technologies, practices, and regulatory frameworks that surpass the nation state. As a governing regime, women's health dates back at least to the 1980s, when feminist movements in the United States were facing growing backlash. The 1973 decision in *Roe v. Wade* galvanized antiabortion organizations that sought strong "protections" for women of "childbearing potential" in biomedical research, which soon resulted in FDA guidelines barring menstruating women from participating in early testing of drug therapies (Johnson & Fee, 1994/1999). In 1981, a research article (Kinney, Trautmann, Gold, Vesell, & Zelis, 1981) documented the scientific cost to women's underrepresentation in new drug trials, but received little public attention. However, as news coverage of public health crises such as the inappropriate administration of diethylstilbestrol (DES) to pregnant women began to appear, women's advocacy groups such as the Boston Women's Health Collective and the National Women's Health Network created alliances with sympathetic legislators, many of whom were members of the Congressional Caucus for Women's issues (Keremidchieva, 2012). Together, they sought ways to ensure that women would receive due attention in research related to reproductive issues, as well as other ailments such as breast cancer and osteoporosis which were of particular importance to women. Following their efforts, the National Institutes of Health (NIH) in 1986 created a new policy that promised that from 1987 onward, scientists would include women in study populations (Hillstrom, 2012).

The creation of a semi-regulatory administrative framework, however, would hardly be the end of the story for how women's health became a governing regime in its own right. Instead the framework brought into view the importance of administrative arguments in organizing the diverse practices surrounding the concept of women's health and, soon after, the identity category of woman. In 1990, Associate Director of the National Public Health

Issues Human Resources Division Mark V. Nadel wrote a report on the status of women's health studies that created much uproar. The report made clear that despite a general will and widespread support in the scientific community to include women, the NIH were failing at implementing their own policy (Nadel, 1990). A U.S. General Accounting Office audit followed. Notably, in his statement before the House Subcommittee on Housing and Consumer Interest and the House Select Committee on Aging, Nadel attributed the NIH's failure to a series of textual and intertextual disconnects between the heterogeneous groups needing to come together to encode women's health into the routine practices of biomedical research.

Specifically, Nadel noted that the agency first announced the policy in October 1986, but did not publish the actual guidance for implementation until July 1989. Neither the actors within the NIH nor the larger research community understood the new policy on women, as the agency had not revised the grant application booklet to provide proper instructions. Inconsistencies also appeared in the printed guidelines for the reviewers of grant applications. While the Division of Research Grants was apparently instructing reviewers not to consider the inclusion of women as "a factor of scientific merit" (Nadel, 1990, p. ii), the National Heart, Lung, and Blood Institute and the Alcohol, Drug Abuse, and Mental Health Administration and another public health service agency claimed the opposite. As NIH's policy on women appeared only to apply to extramural research, the scope of the institutional network's policies pertaining to women's health was precarious. Furthermore, no findable written instructions were present to encourage researchers to analyze study results by gender. Finally, no readily accessible sources of data existed on the demographics of NIH study populations that would have allowed secondary gender-differentiated analyses of research findings.

The mundaneness of such omissions and their "corrections" ten years later (United States General Accounting Office, 2000, p. 34) should not distract from their material, political significance. For all practical purposes, if not for the routinized administrative arrangement of interactions between techniques of observation, textualization, and recognition, women's health would be unthinkable, illustrating Law's (1992) point that "what counts as a person is an *effect generated by a network of heterogeneous, interacting, materials*" (p. 383). Women's health in this sense is not really located in women's bodies, as "social agents are never located in bodies and bodies alone" (p. 384); rather, it emerges through "a patterned network of heterogeneous relations, or an effect produced by such a network" (p. 384). Women's heath became governable when women's bodies were "converted into a complex network of processes, and a set of human, technical and pharmaceutical interventions" (p. 384). Series of administrative routines and inscriptions made women scrutable by laying them neatly on page after page.

In this sense, the textual protocols NIH developed are important for the way they encourage other practices of textualization, as scientists record, analyze, and present their findings, thus forming the networks of women's health. Hence argumentation scholars should not delimit their conceptions of administrative arguments to the statements of government agencies. Instead, they should more broadly consider the presence of organizing guidelines for routine practices of knowledge. Textual inscriptions and documentation— whether administrative, scientific, or other—emerge as techniques of organization that produce social identities.

The precise definition of these identities will likely remain in flux. Some might imagine that such indeterminacy invites the creation of formal and external regulatory controls of biomedical practice. Indeed, such calls have appeared. Observers and advocates have noted that women's erasure in biomedical scholarship persists. For example, the Institute of Medicine's 2012 report suggested the need for a "'culture shift within science' [to] occur to make the changes necessary to fully incorporate the study of sex and gender in health research" (quoted in Mazure & Jones, 2015, p. 13). To bring forth such a cultural shift, the institute invoked an image of hierarchical control, calling for various recommendations to result in requirements for research, "coupled with rewards for following mandated guidelines" (Mazure & Jones, 2015, p. 13). Other scientists have argued, on the contrary, that "public policy documents on gender and health mostly rely on categorical understandings of gender that are now inadequate" (Connell, 2011, p. 1675).

Administrative arguments in no way resolve this tension between inducement and control. They play a role, however, in the distinctive processes of consolidation and ordering that Law (1992) attributed to networks. In network governance, administrative arguments *matter* only partially for their content or form, but more so for (a) their appearance and re-appearance in print or other physical platforms, allowing them to persist over time; (b) their re-appearance through citations and re-prints across institutional distance; (c) the novel relations they create when disparate actors come in contact with common materials, thus creating a perception of central and peripheral responsibility; and (d) the relatively strategic calculability of their scope of ordering. They matter, in other words, for the ways they delimit the character of the polity, of knowledge, and of political action. At the nexus of ever flexible arrangements constituting women's health and status, but also in other domains emanating from the intersection of scientific, government, commercial, or lay discourses, administrative arguments arrange the flow of governance the way traffic signs and systems arrange the flows of human movement. They affect the speed, direction, and tempo of movement, they demarcate permissible from impermissible turns and connections, and they serve as both reminders of and assurances against the precarity and conditionality of bodies and knowledge, thus inviting continuous engagement with the politics of identity. The challenge of analyzing and harnessing administrative rhetoric, then, might involve developing ways to encounter such identities while resisting the impulse of control.

References

Asdal, K., Moser, I., & Brenna, B. (Eds.). (2007). *Technoscience: The politics of interventions*. Norway, The Netherlands: Oslo Academic Press.

Biesecker, B. A. (1989). Rethinking the rhetorical situation from within the thematic of *"différance."* *Philosophy & Rhetoric, 22*(2), 110–130. Retrieved from http://jstor.org/stable/40237580

Bogason, P., & Musso, J. A. (2006). The democratic prospects of network governance. *The American Review of Public Administration, 36*(1), 3–18. doi:10.1177/0275074005282581

Chaput, C. (2010). Rhetorical circulation in late capitalism: Neoliberalism and the overdetermination of affective energy. *Philosophy & Rhetoric, 43*(1), 1–25. doi:10.5325/philrhet.43.1.0001

Connell, R. (2011). Gender, health and theory. Conceptualizing the issue, in local and world perspective. *Social Science & Medicine, 74*(11), 1675–1683. doi:10.1016/j.socscimed.2011.06.006

Farrell, T. B., & Goodnight, G. T. (1981). Accidental rhetoric: The root metaphors of Three Mile Island. *Communication Monographs, 48*(4), 271–300. doi:10.1080/03637758109376063

Frederickson, H. G. (1999). The repositioning of American public administration. *PS: Political Science and Politics, 32*(4), 701–711. doi:10.2307/420159

Goodnight, G. T. (2012). The personal, technical, and public spheres of argument: A speculative inquiry into the art of public deliberation [Special issue]. *Argumentation and Advocacy, 48*(4), 198–210. Retrieved from http://tandfonline.com

Greene, R. W., & Hayes, H. A. (2012). Rhetorical materialism: The cognitive division of labor and the social dimensions of argument. *Argumentation and Advocacy, 48*(3), 190–193. Retrieved from http://tandfonline.com

Habermas, J. (1994). Three normative models of democracy. *Constellations, 1*(1), 1–10. doi:10.1111/j.1467-8675.1994.tb00001.x

Hajer, M. (2003). Policy without polity? Policy analysis and the institutional void. *Policy Sciences, 36*(2), 175–195. doi:10.1023/A:1024834510939

Hillstrom, K. (2012). *U.S. health policy and politics: A documentary history* (Rev. ed.). Washington, DC: CQ Press.

Hood, C., & Jackson, M. (1991). *Administrative argument*. Brookfield, VT: Dartmouth.

Johnson, T., & Fee, E. (1999). Women's participation in clinical research: From protectionism to access. In A. C. Mastroianni, R. Faden, & D. Federman (Eds.), *Women and health research: Ethical and legal issues of including women in clinical studies, volume 2, workshop and commissioned papers* (pp. 1–10). Washington, DC: National Academies Press. doi:10.17226/2343

Jordan, A., Wurzel, R. K. W., & Zito, A. (2005). The rise of "new" policy instruments in comparative perspective: Has governance eclipsed government? *Political Studies, 53*(3), 477–496. doi:10.1111/j.1467-9248.2005.00540.x

Keremidchieva, Z. (2012). Legislative reform, the congressional caucus for women's issues and the crisis of women's political representation. *Women & Language, 35*(1), 13–38.

Kinney, E. L., Trautmann, J., Gold, J. A., Vesell, E. S., & Zelis, R. (1981). Underrepresentation of women in new drug trials: Ramifications and remedies. *Annals of Internal Medicine, 95*(4), 495–499. doi:10.7326/0003-4819-95-4-495

Law, J. (1992). Notes on the theory of the actor-network: Ordering, strategy, and heterogeneity. *Systems Practice, 5*(4), 379–393. doi:10.1007/BF01059830

Lynn, L. E., Jr., Heinrich, C. J., & Hill, C. J. (2000). Studying governance and public management: Challenges and prospects. *Journal of Public Administration Research and Theory, 10*(2), 233–262. doi:10.1093/oxfordjournals.jpart.a024269

March, J. G., & Olson, J. P. (1983). Organizing political life: What administrative reorganization tells us about government. *The American Political Science Review, 77*(2), 281–296. doi:10.2307/1958916

Mazure, C. M., & Jones, D. P. (2015). Twenty years and still counting: Including women as participants and studying sex and gender in biomedical research. *BMC Women's Health, 15*(94). doi:10.1186/s12905-015-0251-9

Nadel, M. V. (1990, July). *Statement on problems in implementing the national institutes of health policy on women in study populations before the Subcommittee on Housing and Consumer Interest, Select Committee on Aging, and House of Representatives* (Report No. GAO-T-HRD-90-50). Retrieved from http://gao.gov/assets/110/103418.pdf

Rhodes, R. A. W. (1996). The new governance: Governing without government. *Political Studies, 44*, 652–667. doi:10.1111/j.1467-9248.1996.tb01747.x

Riles, A. (Ed.). (2006). *Documents: Artifacts of modern knowledge*. Ann Arbor, MI: The University of Michigan Press.

Salamon, L. M. (Ed.). (2002). *The tools of government: A guide to the new governance*. New York, NY: Oxford University Press.

Skelcher, C. (2005). Jurisdictional integrity, polycentrism, and the design of democratic governance. *Governance: An International Journal of Policy, Administration, and Institutions, 18*(1), 89–110. doi:10.1111/j.1468-0491.2004.00267.x

Sørensen, E., & Torfing, J. (2005). Network governance and post-liberal democracy. *Administrative Theory & Praxis, 27*(2), 197–237. Retrieved from http://jstor.org/stable/25610725

United States General Accounting Office. (2000, May). *Women's health: NIH has increased its efforts to include women in research* (Report No. GAO/HEHS-00-96). Retrieved from http://gao.gov/new.items/he00096.pdf

Windt, T. O., Jr. (1982). Administrative rhetoric: An undemocratic response to protest. *Communication Quarterly, 30*(3), 245–250. doi:10.1080/01463378209369456

38

NETWORKS OF VIOLENCE

Converging Representations of the Eric Garner Lynching

Samuel P. Perry

Officer Daniel Pantaleo killed Eric Garner. A grand jury issued a no bill on criminal charges, although the City of New York rendered a $5 million civil judgment to Garner's family. The video of Gardner's death showed Pantaleo with his forearm across Garner's neck. The video aired repeatedly on major news networks. Garner gasped, fell to the ground, and pled with Pantaleo as he repeated 11 times, "I can't breathe!" In the background, a supervising officer told Pantaleo to "let up" (Baker, Goodman, & Mueller, 2015, para. 20). Subsequent protests invoked Garner's pleas and used the hashtag #ICantBreathe. While news coverage brought attention to the case, the repeated showing of the video created serious ethical problems. Coverage restaged the spectacle created on the street, created a digital archive for viewers to return to ad infinitum, and participated within a network of arguments descended from the era of spectacle lynching. In both the aftermath of lynchings and in the wake of Garner's death, the fundamental question is: *How* should communities kill black people? Not *whether* they should kill black people.

News coverage of Garner's death recycled arguments used to justify the aggressive and deadly policing of black bodies and repeated patterns of circulation and consumption associated with lynching photographs. In other words, current day coverage of police violence against African Americans, of which the Garner case is an exemplar, animate the topoi historically present in lynching photography and news accounts of lynching. Aristotle (trans. 2006) argued that *topoi* or lines of argument related to topics could be general or specific, and that the metaphorical starting locations of given arguments generate standard arguments or premises. Black bodies provide a starting point for standardized arguments about (in)justice in the United States, and lynched black bodies have long been topoi for these arguments. Single bodies as *topos* are particular starting points for more generalized arguments concerning or eliding race.

Eric Garner's body became a *topos* from which arguments justifying lynching proceeded. This essay examines news coverage of the killing of Garner by considering "the contingency of the rhetorical encounter by teasing out the complex relationships between the visual and its audience" (Hahner, 2015, p. 608). The contingency in this situation is the convergence of viewing practices and arguments onto particular black bodies both historically and contemporaneously. Black bodies have typically been a point of argumentative convergence in American political discourse. Winkler (2011) argued that bodies in videos can serve as points of convergence and that "convergence need not be explicit; inferences warranted by visual images can implicitly contribute to convergence for knowledgeable audiences" (pp. 738-739). Audiences create a relationship to multimedia representations of violence based on the composition of those representations and culturally established practices of media consumption. The lurid images of suffering and dead bodies in lynching spectacles provided topoi to rehearse the standard arguments used to justify lynching.

Context and Historical Framing

Historically, white perpetrators of violence against people of color have rarely, if ever, faced punishment or incarceration. Even if the act of violence was a public spectacle with perpetrators in plain view, coroners' inquests often read "at the hands of persons unknown" (Dray, 2003, p. ix). Practices of looking at violence against black bodies reified culturally normative networks of white supremacy. Smith (2004) argued, "In turn-of-the-century photographs of lynchings, black death clearly functions as a spectacle for a white audience" (p. 118). The systemic, or networked, practice of consuming images of violence against black bodies still operates and has its roots in the viewing practices associated with lynching. The voyeurism surrounding Eric Garner's death followed the established viewing practices and patterns of circulation associated with written accounts of spectacle lynching and lynching photographs.

The network that secreted lynching photographs and lurid press accounts informs the contemporary viewing of violence against black bodies. According to Goldsby (2006), representations of racial violence circulated surreptitiously through "secretion," and "the secretion of lynching photographs codified what was emerging at the turn of the century as the civil right to look at and interpret the world in ways that perfected racism's hierarchies of privilege" (p. 249). People casually consumed disturbing representations of violence against black people. Walter White, head of the NAACP during the height of the anti-lynching movement in the 1920s and 1930s lamented, "An uncomfortably large percentage of American citizens can read in their newspapers of the slow roasting alive of a human being in Mississippi, and turn promptly and with little thought, to the comic strip or sporting page" (quoted in Hale, 1998, p. 204).

Black bodies often provide a genitive point for reframing brutality as a means of maintaining law and order. For example, a lynch mob in Stuttgart, Arkansas in 1916, feeling falsely accused of excessive cruelty to its victim, felt compelled to send a letter to their local newspaper explaining that the execution had been "humane," further explaining, "We must withhold our names and be to sign ourselves: Yours for the proper and unfailing enforcement of the law, 'THE COMMITTEE'" (Ginzburgh, 1996, pp. 108-109). Though lynching was extralegal, law enforcement was often complicit and to that end lynching was considered an expression of the "community's will" (Dray, 2003, p. ix). Violence against black bodies has often been conflated with keeping law and order.

Black bodies have also often been a *topos* for arguments that justify violence to protect white femininity and structures of white patriarchy. Perceived threat versus the actual probability of harm to individuals or established racial hierarchies justified lynching. The de facto justification offered for lynching was sexual assault of a white woman by a black man. Most often lynching victims were engaged in wage disputes, accused of some petty crime, perceived to have slighted a white person, or did nothing at all. In an early comprehensive sociological study of lynching and its causes, Cash (1991) argued, "The chance [of sexual assault] was much less, for instance, than the chance that she [a white woman] would be struck by lightning" (p. 115). Historically, violence against black people became more frequent and gruesome in lynching spectacles, even as the premises undergirding the practice of lynching were shown to be myths.

Perhaps most insidious, images of black bodies and violence against them often serve as genitive points for entertainment. H. L. Mencken demeaned Southerners' lack of culture and sophistication by indicting lynching as something that replaced "the merry-go-round, the theater, the symphony orchestra, and other diversions available to large communities" (quoted in Wood, 2009, p. 5). Even Mencken, an opponent of lynching, invited equivocation, and newspaper coverage of lynching often provided salacious play-by-play (Ginzburgh, 1994). As one Southern Methodist bishop at the turn of the last century mused,

> Now-a-days, it seems the killing of Negroes is not so extraordinary an occurrence as to need explanation; it has become so common that it no longer surprises. We read of such things as we read of fires that burn a cabin or a town.
>
> *(Litwack, 1998, p. 293)*

As Hale (1998) argued, "The amusement, the cultural power of spectacle lynchings, lay not in the assignment of cause and blame, the tallying of rights and wrongs, but in the [rights of] looking" (p. 221). Mirzoeff (2003) maintained that circulation of lynching photography "created still another more shadowy, even hooded, archive of race, housed on mantelpieces and in desk drawers across the United States from Minnesota and Illinois to the deep South" (p. 123). After the initial spectacle, lynching photographs moved into the "hooded archive," a space where white people's right to look at black suffering was unquestioned, where one selectively viewed and shared images of racial violence to reassure themselves and like-minded people that racial hierarchies remained indexed and could be affirmed through the repeated viewing of a singular event.

Representations of lynching assumed black bodies were always already dead. As a *topos*, the dead black body was a standard point from which discussion of whiteness began. As a particular type of *topos*, lynching photographs became "folk pornography" (Hall, 1979, p. 150). Lynching created space for the convergence of arguments concerned with how to look at a black man dying in the street—people knew how to look at Eric Garner's body long before he died. The initial spectacle of Garner's death—the public altercation with police and the internet broadcast of it—was followed by intense media coverage that used Garner's body as a starting point for well-established arguments.

The Lynching of Eric Garner

Mainstream media news coverage regularly features the repeated broadcast of videos, images, and accounts of unarmed black people dying in altercations with police, police shootings of black men, black bodies in police custody, or black corpses killed at the hands of self-appointed vigilantes who often go unpunished. In both content and circulation, coverage of the Garner case mirrored content reporting on the killing of Oscar Grant, Tamir Rice, Freddie Gray, Walter Scott, Sandra Bland, and a depressingly long list of others. The videos featured the moments before their deaths and moments of their deaths. Of the deaths of Philando Castile and Alton Sterling, President Obama lamented, "We have seen tragedies like this too many times [....] These are not isolated incidents. They're symptomatic of a broader set of racial disparities that exist in our criminal justice system" (The White House, 2016, para. 3-4). These disparities are not new but stretch back into networks of representations that used lynching to structure and reify white supremacy. Black bodies that constitute the killed American citizens mentioned above function as *topoi* to rehearse racist arguments and draw from the argumentative well of lynching.

Historical networks of representing lynching moved largely unquestioned into new media platforms and journalistic practices where "the lines that formerly separated participants, reporters, and networked publics have grown dim and elastic" (Russell, 2013, p. 905). Lynching, lynch mobs, and the argumentative justifications for lynching moved into networked publics with fewer established boundaries between perpetrators and observers. The killing of Eric Garner in New York on July 17, 2014 and representation of that event are exemplary of black bodies as *topoi* operating in today's media networks, and they illustrate the blurred lines in networks of representation between observers and perpetrators.

People who were not punished but who claimed to uphold law and order killed an unarmed Garner for selling loose untaxed cigarettes. Although Officer Pantaleo initiated the conflict, he claimed he had been in danger when Garner resisted arrest. While Garner may not have been compliant with the officer's orders, he did not show signs of initiating a fight (Voorhees, 2014). In the Garner case, Pantaleo perceived a threat in a situation where risk was not present until police confronted Garner for a crime that posed no immediate danger to the public. Reasonably, viewers might infer that Garner's size and race had something to do with Pantaleo's actions. They certainly played into the defense of Pantaleo's actions. As Klein (2014) argued, "the legend of the giant negro" (para. 3) subsumed the discussion of Garner's death, just as it had in Michael Brown's death and as it regularly did in turn of the century news coverage that sensationalized lynching. What Pantaleo perceived was a threat to an established order of policing.

That order of policing often uses black bodies to maintain its cultural and argumentative dominance. As such, discussions of Garner's death often turned into a referendum on whether or not his execution was carried out properly. One police press conference discussed everything from the legality of the chokehold to whether or not people protesting Garner's death respected police. Despite the coroner's ruling that Garner died of asphyxiation, Pat Lynch, the president of the Patrolman's Benevolent Association, said, "It was not a chokehold [...] I have never seen a document that was more political" (quoted in Speri, 2014, para. 13). Sidestepping the question of whether or not Garner deserved to die for selling loose cigarettes, the conversation turned toward a discussion of whether the methods used to kill Garner were appropriate. The assumption was that Garner's death was inevitable, and the discussion devolves into whether the police appropriately killed him with an arm instead of a firearm or a rope.

Most news coverage included a video loop and dissection of every moment of Pantaleo choking Garner. News outlets ranging from CNN to Breitbart featured pieces and invited guests to discuss whether or not the chokehold was necessary or legal. CNN ran a story online titled "Was a New York police officer's chokehold on Eric Garner necessary?" that featured New York Police Commissioner William Bratten arguing the police force had no local prohibitions on chokeholds and as a counterpoint Spike Lee condemning the actions of the NYPD (Botelho, 2014). Such commentary provided legitimacy to the denial of due process. One analyst argued, "At a certain point, they've got to touch him [...] That's just the way it goes. And when you resist arrest—physically resist—bad things can happen" (Botelho, 2014, para. 30). Breitbart approached the matter by putting the term chokehold in quotation marks and providing apologia that asserted "[Pantaleo] was applying a submission hold" (Shapiro, 2014, para. 13). The dissection of the replay of Garner's death resembled an official review of a play in a sporting event. Providing the sort of commentary one might when discerning whether a wide receiver planted two feet inbounds before leaving the field of play when discussing the killing of one human being by another seems particularly callous, but it follows a pattern of utilizing black bodies as *topoi* that stretches back to the practice of spectacle lynching as Walter White, H. L. Mencken, and others have attempted to explain it.

The callousness extended even after Garner died. Officers handcuffed Garner's breathless body; medical personnel rendered no aid even when paramedics arrived (Baker et al., 2016). Officers on the scene and the gathered crowd looked on as life left Garner's body. Millions of onlookers peered at the video on their computers, phones, and televisions. The corpse remained. Even now, the online *Time* coverage of Garner's death includes a video at the head of the page, a sidebar media player tracks with the viewer's scrolling up and down the page, and both show Garner's struggle on a loop (Sanburn, 2014). The images of Garner's death literally follow the viewer, even years after the removal of his body from the street. Similarly, lynching spectacles often included leaving the body hanging from the scaffolding or a tree for sometimes days and lynching photographs indexed "strange fruit" in perpetuity. The media have secreted the representations of this lynching into the hooded archive like so many before them.

Conclusion

As shared texts that constitute networked publics vary greatly and the nature of those publics change as the array of media that transmit texts evolves, some arguments circulating through networks remain remarkably static. The live and mediated consumption of racial violence has remained eerily similar even as newspapers and photographs have given way to digital multimedia platforms. Paying particular attention to how coverage of the killing of black people in the present day resembles the coverage of and reactions to lynching provides a means of "sight[ing] the public" (Finnegan & Kang, 2004, p. 379). The circulations of representations of racial violence tell us something about race relations in any historical period. As Finnegan and Kang (2004) argued, "Embracing as it does movement and flow, circulation might be an analytic term that can free us from the impulse to freeze-frame all types of discourse, not just images" (p. 396). Here circulation refers to the ways in which images and discourse circulate together. Representations of racial violence travel through different mediums, across audiences, and span time periods. Mainstream media coverage of the police killings of black people in questionable circumstances dominates our media consumption practices. The bodies of people of color, especially when they are victims of violence, are topoi, and they are used to rehearse, animate, and amplify arguments that maintain networks of white supremacy.

References

Aristotle. (2006). *On rhetoric: A theory of civic discourse* (G. A. Kennedy, Trans., 2nd ed.). New York, NY: Oxford University Press.

Baker, A., Goodman, J. D., & Mueller, B. (2015, June 13). Beyond the chokehold: The path to Eric Garner's death. *The New York Times*. Retrieved from http://nytimes.com

Botelho, G. (2014, December 18). Was the chokehold on Eric Garner necessary? *CNN*. Retrieved from http://cnn.com

Cash, W. J. (with Wyatt-Brown, B.). (1991). *The mind of the South* (Vintage Books ed.). New York, NY: Vintage Books.

Dray, P. (2003). *At the hands of persons unknown: The lynching of Black America* (Reprint ed.). New York, NY: Modern Library.

Finnegan, C. A., & Kang, J. (2004). "Sighting" the public: Iconoclasm and public sphere theory. *Quarterly Journal of Speech*, *90*(4), 377–402. doi:10.1080/0033563042000302153

Ginzburg, R. (1996). *100 years of lynchings* (Reprint ed.). Baltimore, MD: Black Classic Press.

Goldsby, J. (2006). *A spectacular secret: Lynching in American life and literature*. Chicago, IL: University of Chicago Press.

Hahner, L. A. (2015). "It's always more complicated than that": Bruce Gronbeck on visual method. *Rhetoric & Public Affairs, 18*(3), 607–618.

Hale, G. E. (1998). *Making whiteness: The culture of segregation in the South, 1890–1940*. New York, NY: Vintage Books.

Hall, J. D. (1979). *Revolt against chivalry: Jessie Daniel Ames and the women's campaign against lynching*. New York, NY: Columbia University.

Klein, E. (2014, December 5). Watch Jon Stewart's face when "martial arts student" Sean Hannity discussed Eric Garner. *Vox*. Retrieved http://vox.com/xpress/2014/12/5/7339327/jon-stewart-sean-hannity

Litwack, L. (1998). *Trouble in mind: Black Southerners in the Age of Jim Crow*. New York, NY: Vintage Books.

Mirzoeff, N. (2003). The shadow and the substance: Race, photography, and the index. In C. Fusco & B. Wallis (Eds), *Only skin deep: Changing visions of the American self* (pp. 129–14). New York, NY: Abrams.

Russell, A. (2013). Innovation in hybrid spaces: 2011 UN Climate Summit and the expanding journalism landscape. *Journalism, 14*(7), 904–920. doi:10.1177/1464884913477311

Sanburn, J. (2014, July 23). Behind the video of Eric Garner's deadly confrontation with police [Video file]. *Time*. Retrieved from http://time.com

Shapiro, B. (2014, December 3). The actual facts of the Eric Garner case. *Breitbart News*. Retrieved from http://breitbart.com

Smith, S. M. (2004). *Photography on the color line: W. E. B. Du Bois, race, and visual culture*. Durham, NC: Duke University Press Books.

Speri, A. (2014, August 6). A chokehold didn't kill Eric Garner, your disrespect for the NYPD did. *Vice News*. Retrieved from https://news.vice.com/article/a-chokehold-didnt-kill-eric-garner-your-disrespect-for-the-nypd-did

Voorhees, J. (2014, December 3). Of course it happened again. *Slate*. Retrieved http://slate.com/articles/news_and_politics/politics/2014/12/daniel_pantaleo_not_indicted_why_the_nypd_officer_wasn_t_indicted_in_the.html

The White House, Office of the Press Secretary. (2016, July 7). *Statement by the President. Warsaw Marriott Warsaw, Poland* [Press release]. Retrieved from https://obamawhitehouse.archives.gov

Wood, A. L. (2009). *Lynching and spectacle: Witnessing racial violence in America, 1890–1940*. Chapel Hill, NC: University of North Carolina Press.

39

PERFORMING HEGEMONIC MASCULINITY

Trump's Framing of U.S. Foreign Policy

Heidi Hamilton

Since taking office in January 2017, President Trump's foreign policy rhetoric has only increased the pugnacious tone he evidenced during the campaign. From his first calls with the Mexican President and the Australian Prime Minister early in his term through this summer's events in London and the Persian Gulf, Trump has consistently performed a hegemonic masculinity in his foreign policy discourse. He does not limit this performance strategy to offline rhetoric, however. His tweets, both about his own actions and others' responses to his actions, provide seemingly endless reiterations and repetitions of his foreign policy discursive performance. Analyzing his use of argument by definition to illustrate how his tweets framed a gendered political reality, this essay examines how, in the synergistic play between online and offline networks, Trump's gendered performance functions as an action that produces the character of a hyper-masculine President Trump. Not only does Trump's performance define his own persona, it also frames the state as a masculine subject, reclaiming a hegemonic form of American leadership.

While scholars have applied Butler's (1990) theory of performance to an individual's discursive acts, understanding a nation's performances has received less attention. This essay, building upon Wadley's (2010) suggestion that security discourse constitutes both a gendered leader and gendered state, offers a case study illustrating how the practice occurs and the need to expand the scope of analysis of performative discourse. This essay thus indicates that the reiterated performances of hegemonic masculinity not only assert dominance but also may combine with potentially dangerous forms of nationalism (i.e., "America First") that could destabilize international norms.

Argument by Definition and Hegemonic Masculinity

To begin, numerous scholars have posited that definitions are themselves arguments. Schiappa (1993) commented, "Even uncontroversial definitions function as *claims* about how part of the world should be conceptualized" (p. 404). Arguments *by* definition, however, function differently than arguments *about* definition or arguments *from* definition. Zarefsky (1998) explained that rather than an understanding of argument as claims and support, arguments by definition occur when definitions "are simply proclaimed as if they were indisputable facts" (p. 5). Instead of an "explicit claim," the persuader provides definitions within the context of their statements as if they "were natural and uncontroversial rather than chosen and contestable" (Zarefsky, 2004, p. 612). Additionally, Cox (1981) suggested the importance of defining because it frames how we view the situation. In analyzing Trump's rhetoric, this essay utilizes the four types of argument by definition that Zarefsky (1998) outlined to evaluate Trump's performance of hegemonic masculinity.

Looking at Trump's rhetoric through the lens of argument by definition is particularly useful because of his rhetorical style. Offline, he often speaks in declarative statements. Online, his tweets amplify this characteristic through their confinement to 140 characters. In both contexts, although especially in his Twitter usage, Trump offers "claims" as if they were facts. Examining Trump's use of argument by definition may be particularly illuminating given that argument by definition may say more about the user than the argument. Minielli (2010) claimed that "while argument *from* definition has as its primary locus the definition itself" (para. 3), the locus shifts "to the definition's *user*" (para. 3) in argument by definition. McGee (1999) argued that advocates often use argument by definition to frame the argument in favor of the user. Minielli's (2010) concern, then, is the user's ability to "garner significant power and control" (para. 3).

This analysis thus provides a lens for seeing how Trump frames both himself and the global situation. Zarefsky (2004) argued that through defining, presidents may have the capacity to frame how citizens see events and actions. Drury (2014) added that presidents have the ability to construct "political reality" through "defining the threats to the nation, identifying friends and foes, and articulating a vision of the nation's role in global affairs" (p. 88). Drawing upon the work of Judith Butler, Wadley (2010) went further, claiming that nation-states "[reify] themselves through performances of security" (p. 40). These performances make visible the gendered nature of states as actors. Butler (1988) argued that gender is not stable but constituted through a "*stylized repetition of acts*" (p. 519). For Butler (1990), gendered performance occurs within the constraints of cultural norms, but it may also challenge those cultural norms. Wadley (2010) subsequently pointed out that the "action *produces* the actor" (p. 47). For him, advocates can constitute the state and the state's leader as masculine through security discourse. Wadley's chief concern was hegemonic masculinity, which subordinates other forms of masculinity and constitutes the state as more powerful than others. In fact, hegemonic masculinity positions a particular form of masculinity as dominant over *all* women and men who do not meet this form (Carrigan, Connell, & Lee, 1985). Scholars have also defined hegemonic masculinity through a set of characteristics. Connell (1990) connected the concept to toughness and competitiveness. In his study of baseball player Nolan Ryan, Trujillo (1991) outlined five characteristic qualities: physical force and control, occupational achievement, familial patriarchy, frontiersmanship, and heterosexuality. In sum, Hanke (1990) claimed that it "refers to the social ascendency of a particular version or model of masculinity that […] defines 'what it means to be a man'" (p. 232).

Trump's Defining of Foreign Policy

In commenting on foreign policy, Trump frequently utilizes argument by definition to characterize U.S. actions and global events in ways that perpetuate his worldview. First, argument by definition can work through association with other terms (Zarefsky, 2004) or by applying connotative meanings associated with one term to a new denotative referent (Zarefsky, 1998). In several cases, Trump associated terms through analogies and metaphors. For example, in discussions of North Korea, he (2017c) tweeted, "they have been 'playing' the

United States for years." Use of the word "playing" evokes the analogy of a game, carrying the connotation of being less serious in appearances. Trump disapproves of North Korea's actions, as he began his tweet with "North Korea is behaving very badly" (2017c) before disparaging their behavior. Announcing the U.S. withdrawal from the Paris Accord, Trump (2017e) tweeted that he needed "to give America a level playing field." Here, he used the sports metaphor to suggest that the Paris Accord disadvantaged the United States. While the metaphor would seem to suggest equality between nations, he followed the statement with "#AmericaFirst," which further expands the definition of what "level" means to elevate the United States' position. Trump also defined the fight against terrorism through association of connotative meanings to a new referent. In a Reuters interview, Trump discussed the defeat of ISIS by stating, "I have to say, there is an end. And it has to be humiliation" (Adler, Holland, & Mason, 2017, para. 10). He defined the end as more than just no longer fighting; he expanded the meaning to include more negative connotations associated with humiliation. In doing so, he suggested that satisfaction would not come to the U.S. with defeat. The defeat must also be demeaning.

Trump also utilizes a second form of argument by definition: dissociation. Disassociation separates links between terms (Zarefsky, 1998) whereby "a definition is used to reduce the denotation of a concept, by splitting the previous meaning of the term into two concepts" (Walton & Macagno, 2009, p. 83). Thus, the new meaning of the term will carry a new connotation. While Trump's use of this form occurs less frequently, he does use it to delineate some of his actions from others. In tweeting about his travel ban, for example, he (2017h) remarked, "we are EXTREME VETTING people coming into the U.S. in order to help keep our country safe. The courts are slow and political!" In this way, he equated extreme vetting with being safe, as opposed to the delays commonly associated with court processes. Similarly, after the London terror attacks, Trump (2017g) tweeted, "We must stop being politically correct and get down to the business of security for our people. If we don't get smart it will only get worse." In this instance, political correctness served as the negative value, divided from being smart and preferable.

Zarefsky's (1998) third form of argument by definition appears frequently in Trump's rhetoric. Here, Trump draws upon ambiguity to define the situation, often connecting to condensation symbols "which designate no clear referent but 'condense' a host of different meanings and connotations" (Zarefsky, 2004, pp. 612–613). Repeatedly, Trump has referred to the nuclear accord with Iran as "the worst deal." While worst is not good, what makes something "the worst" allows ambiguity. He further defined what made it the "worst" in an interview with Bill O'Reilly, continuing that the United States "lost respect because [the world] can't believe anybody could be so stupid as to make a deal like that" (Trump, 2017a). In this way, Trump indicated that the disrespect for the United States made something the worst, implying the need for the United States to be more highly regarded. In another instance, as Trump was ready to embark on his first official trip abroad, he (2017d) tweeted, "will be strongly protecting American interests." Here, the context defined the ambiguity of "strongly protecting." While protecting might generally connect to military or security, he defined his meetings with foreign leaders as a way for him to protect. Once again asserting his own role, he ended, "That's what I like to do!" (2017d). In a tweet responding to Senator John McCain's criticism of a Navy Seal raid in Yemen, Trump (2017b) stated, "Ryan died on a winning mission (according to General Mattis), not a 'failure.'" Trump defined the mission as a "winning" one, and thus successful, but no clear reference to what qualified as winning was apparent. While viewers might know about materials gained, he made no direct connection to winning a battle or taking out terrorists as implied by "winning." Lastly, Trump twice referred intentionally to terrorists as "losers" after the London terror attack. In his speech at NATO headquarters, he stated,

All people who cherish life must unite in finding, exposing, and removing these killers and extremists—and, yes, losers. They are losers. Wherever they exist in our societies, we must drive them out and never, ever let them back in.

(The White House, 2017, para. 5)

"Losers" is an ambiguous term that can mean different things to different people. Are terrorists losers because they are killers (and thus, the derogatory, "he's such a loser") or are they losers because they will lose this war against us? The multiple connotations allowed Trump to define terrorists in opposition to the United States and other members of NATO which, in turn, made the United States and its allies all winners.

Finally, Trump's rhetoric draws upon frame-shifting to define situations. Here, argument by definition frames a situation previously viewed differently (Zarefsky, 1998, 2004). Early examples were when Trump hung up on the Australian prime minister and had a tense call with the Mexican president. Referring to these two calls, Trump stated,

When you hear about the tough calls I'm having, don't worry about it, just don't worry about it [....] They're tough. We have to be tough.... We're taken advantage of by every nation in the world, virtually. It's not going to happen anymore.

(quoted in "Mr. Trump's Random Insult Diplomacy," 2017, para. 7)

Trump reframed the term "tough." Rather than the calls being tough on him, he defined himself as being tough on those who would take advantage of the United States. In a widely circulated tweet, Trump (2017f) criticized the London mayor after the terror attacks, quoting the foreign official's words out of context: "At least 7 dead and 48 wounded in terror attack and Mayor of London says there is 'no reason to be alarmed!'" In this tweet, Trump shifted the reference from not being alarmed to suggesting a warrant for alarm. He disparaged the mayor of London publicly as he made this shift, thus implicitly asserting his own, more qualified, authority on the situation. A final example of frame-shifting appeared throughout Trump's speech on the U.S. withdrawal from the Paris Accord. Specifically, he remarked, "No responsible leader can put the workers and the people of their country at this debilitating and tremendous disadvantage" (Sitrin, 2017, para. 25). The Paris Accord suggests that countries need to be responsible for their contributions to the global environment. Trump shifted the notion of responsibility away from a global environmental or global community focus to one concentrated on the people of the United States. Later, he stated, "They [foreign capitals and global activists] don't put America first. I do. And I always will" (Sitrin, 2017, para. 27). In the process, he reiterated the shift of frame from a focus on the global to one on the United States through his assertions of American primacy and his leadership.

Performing Hegemonic Masculinity

While the above examples are individual instances of defining, they cumulatively frame the place of the United States in the world. Through Trump's use of argument by definition, the credibility of his actions and the importance of U.S. dominance become apparent. Trump's utilization of the concept allows him to control the discursive performance, placing it within cultural norms of hegemonic masculinity. When he declared facts as if they were obvious and indisputable, he framed the situation in ways that reasserted the hegemonic masculinity of the state and his being. Trump's use of argument by definition repeatedly evokes competitiveness. He called out others who were unfair (e.g., North Korea) and asserted the need for U.S. gains (e.g., through the withdrawal from the Paris Accord). The competitive tone was blatant when he proclaimed, "America first." Others are "the worst," which warranted his decision to hang up the phone. Competitiveness was fully on display when Trump called for not just the defeat but the humiliation of ISIS. In several instances, he tied competitiveness directly to physical force. Presumably, humiliation would come through military force. Winning missions (again a competitive reference) occurred through the physical force of special operations forces and driving out the "losers." Repeatedly, Trump's framing of events positioned the United States as dominant over others.

Trump also constitutes his own hegemonic masculinity through definition. As he insisted the United States was dominant over others, his security discourse constitutes his own persona as a masculine subject. Through definition, he proposes to demonstrate his superior leadership. Trump also performs his own hegemonic masculinity as he asserted his specific actions. He knew more about combating terrorism than the London mayor immediately confronted with a violent attack, thus signaling occupational achievement, and in a move indicative of familial patriarchy (of the national family, in this case), he claimed to be "strongly protecting" Americans as he met with foreign leaders and placed America first as he withdrew from the Paris Accord. Trump even invoked the qualities of the frontiersman as he got "tough," as well as when he pointed out how his travel ban would result in security rather than a bogged down court process. Each boast not only asserted his leadership but drew upon frame-shifting, ambiguities, and other means of defining to place himself as knowing more and acting better than others. The repeated performances of Trump's discourse on Twitter constitute the gendered masculine state as actor, asserting a dominant form of masculinity that subordinates others.

Implications

While some national and international audiences certainly contest Trump's performances, others accept them. As he continues to reify conceptions of U.S. dominance and his own superiority through performances of argument by definition, the related concern becomes how such a stance positions the United States vis-à-vis others. Wadley (2010) warned that successful performances that conform to hegemonic masculinity produce a "unitary" actor "who can claim legitimacy over those 'internal' to it" and "who is hierarchically dominant to certain other international actors" (p. 50). The greater concern is not just that Trump's performance successfully conforms to cultural norms of hegemonic masculinity to assert dominance, but that by elevating (and isolating) himself as the dominant actor, he embraces a particularly destructive form of American nationalism that threatens international norms and relations.

References

Adler, S. J., Holland, S., & Mason, J. (2017, April 27). Exclusive: Trump says 'major, major' conflict with North Korea possible, but seeks diplomacy. *Reuters*. Retrieved from http://reuters.com

Butler, J. (1988). Performative acts and gender constitution: An essay in phenomenology and feminist theory. *Theatre Journal, 40*(4), 519–531. doi:10.2307/3207893

Butler, J. (1990). *Gender trouble: Feminism and the subversion of identity.* New York, NY: Routledge.

Carrigan, T., Connell, B., & Lee, J. (1985). Toward a new sociology of masculinity. *Theory and Society, 14*(5), 551–604. Retrieved from http://jstor.org/stable/657315

Connell, R. W. (1990). An iron man: The body and some contradictions of hegemonic masculinity. In M. A. Messner & D. F. Sabo (Eds.), *Sport, men and the gender order: Critical feminist perspectives* (pp. 83–95). Champaign, IL: Human Kinetics Books.

Cox, J. R. (1981). Argument and the "definition of the situation." *Central States Speech Journal, 32*(3), 197–205. doi:10.1080/10510978109368095

Drury, S. A. M. (2014). Defining national security as peace through strength: Ronald Reagan's visionary rhetoric of renewal in the 1980 presidential campaign. *Argumentation and Advocacy*, *51*(2), 87–102. Retrieved from http://tandfonline.com

Hanke, R. (1990). Hegemonic masculinity in *thirty something*. *Critical Studies in Mass Communication*, *7*(3), 231–248. doi:10.1080/15295039009360176

McGee, B. R. (1999). The argument from definition revisited: Race and definition in the progressive era. *Argumentation and Advocacy*, *35*(4), 141–158.

Minielli, M. C. (2010). "Crisis" and argument by definition in the modern American presidency. In F. H. van Eemeren, B. Garssen, D. Godden, & G. Mitchell (Eds.), *International Society for the Study of Argumentation Proceedings 2010*. Retrieved http://rozenbergquarterly.com

Mr. Trump's Random Insult Diplomacy [Editorial]. (2017, February 5). *The New York Times*, p. SR8.

Schiappa, E. (1993). Arguing about definitions. *Argumentation*, *7*(4), 403–417. doi:10.1007/BF00711058

Sitrin, C. (2017, June 1). Trump is withdrawing the US from the Paris climate agreement. Read the full transcript. *Vox*. Retrieved from https://vox.com

Trujillo, N. (1991). Hegemonic masculinity on the mound: Media representations of Nolan Ryan and American sports culture. *Critical Studies in Mass Communication*, *8*(3), 290–308. doi:10.1080/15295039109366799

Trump, D. J. (2017a, February 6). Interview with President Trump. Interview by B. O'Reilly. *The O'Reilly Factor* [Television Broadcast]. Washington, DC: Fox News. Retrieved from http://foxnews.com/transcript/2017/02/07/bill-oreilly-exclusive-interview-with-president-trump.html

Trump, D. J. [@realDonaldTrump]. (2017b, February 9). ..Ryan* died on a winning mission (according to General Mattis), not a "failure." Time for the U.S. to get smart and start winning again! [Tweet]. Retrieved from https://twitter.com/realDonaldTrump/status/829689436279603206

Trump, D. J. [@realDonaldTrump]. (2017c, March 17). North Korea is behaving very badly. They have been "playing" the United States for years. China has done little to help! [Tweet]. Retrieved from https://twitter.com/realDonaldTrump/status/842724011234791424

Trump, D. J. [@realDonaldTrump]. (2017d, May 19). Getting ready for my big foreign trip. Will be strongly protecting American interests - that's what I like to do! [Tweet]. Retrieved from https://twitter.com/realDonaldTrump/status/865573793531478017

Trump, D. J. [@realDonaldTrump]. (2017e, June 1). My job as President is to do everything within my power to give America a level playing field. #AmericaFirst [Tweet]. Retrieved from https://twitter.com/realDonaldTrump/status/870412262900740096

Trump, D. J. [@realDonaldTrump]. (2017f, June 4). At least 7 dead and 48 wounded in terror attack and Mayor of London says there is "no reason to be alarmed!" [Tweet]. Retrieved from https://twitter.com/realDonaldTrump/status/871328428963901440

Trump, D. J. [@realDonaldTrump]. (2017g, June 4). We must stop being politically correct and get down to the business of security for our people. If we don't get smart it will only get worse [Tweet]. Retrieved from https://twitter.com/realDonaldTrump/status/871325606901895168

Trump, D. J. [@realDonaldTrump]. (2017h, June 5). In any event we are EXTREME VETTING people coming into the U.S. in order to help keep our country safe. The courts are slow and political! [Tweet]. Retrieved from https://twitter.com/realDonaldTrump/status/871679061847879682

Wadley, J. D. (2010). Gendering the state: Performativity and protection in international security. In L. Sjoberg (Ed.), *Gender and international security: Feminist perspectives* (pp. 38–58). New York, NY: Routledge.

Walton, D., & Macagno, F. (2009). Reasoning from classifications and definitions. *Argumentation*, *23*(1), 81–107. doi:10.1007/s10503-008-9110-2

The White House, Office of the Press Secretary. (2017, May 25). *Remarks by President Trump at NATO unveiling of the article 5 and Berlin wall memorials - Brussels, Belgium*. Retrieved from https://whitehouse.gov

Zarefsky, D. (1998). Definitions. In J. F. Klumpp (Ed.), *Argument in a time of change: Definitions, frameworks, and critiques* (pp. 1–11). Annandale, VA: National Communication Association.

Zarefsky, D. (2004). Presidential rhetoric and the power of definition. *Presidential Studies Quarterly*, *34*(3), 607–619. Retrieved from http://jstor.org/stable/27552615

* The tweet, as originally written, contains this typo.

40

ARGUMENT AND THE FOUNDATIONS OF SOCIAL NETWORKS

Affective Argument and Popular American History

Michael Janas

These are dark times for argument studies. Frustrations with the failure of evidence and logic to advance epistemological claims, theorists have increasingly turned to affective theories for explanation. Moral Foundations Theory (Graham, Haidt, & Nosek, 2009), Cultural Cognition Thesis (Kahan et al., 2012), and Motivated Cognition (Nyhan & Reifler, 2010) pose argument as a frustratingly impossible task that has greater social than epistemological significance. The apex of this movement appears in Mercier and Sperber's (2011) Argumentative Theory of Reasoning that placed argument as an evolutionary adaptation, positing that argument was not so much a function of making better decisions or having better beliefs as it was a social phenomenon where truth and accuracy were strategies of social prestige and effective social networks.

Here I am interested in affective argument in the context of studies of the past. History, as a discipline, is frustratingly conservative. Despite the vibrant flow of innovative academic research, new ideas are exceptionally slow to move from academic work into popular variants that fill commercial bookstores. In fact, the history industry tends to be so conservative that it is one of the few fields where professional historians directly compete and largely lose out to less-resourced, but better-networked, amateur competitors.

The site for this study is an especially important American historian, David Barton, who is part of a long line of politically-active American historians. While he has made the most of his reputation as an unapologetic advocate for conservative causes, he has also become one of America's most influential historians. Christian conservatives have been especially complimentary. Political broadcaster and presidential candidate Mike Huckabee, noted that everyone should be "forced at gunpoint" to listen to Barton's history and has called him America's greatest historian (Rodda, 2011). Television commentator Glenn Beck designated him the "most important man in America" (Beck, 2010, para. 11).

My claim is that American conservatives' vision of an exceptional American history finds support in methods of Christian evangelical hermeneutics. While social science standards have largely disciplined academic history, the long tradition of religiously-inspired American history provides a stylized method of interpretation and respite for the evangelical social network seeking to escape the paradox of constantly evolving notions of the past. I will consider two distinguishing aspects of Barton's histories that perform as affective grounds for argumentative claims. First, I will examine how his vision of history claims reactive ground by actively rejecting scientific approaches to history. Second, I will examine how the evangelical interpretive habits of *solo scriptura* encourage his network of consumers to adopt a flat reading of American history as universal principles that insulate interpretations from academic criticisms and move historical debates onto theological ground. Rather than viewing such academic silos as frustratingly impossible argumentative situations, I want to position argumentative networks as communities of reason rooted in distinct and accessible traditions of argumentation.

David Barton's Historical World

David Barton holds only a degree in Christian Education from Oral Roberts University. Yet, he has also published more than twenty books, many of which have appeared on bestseller lists. A key element of his project is that he physically possesses the world's largest collection of Revolutionary War-era documents that he keeps in a warehouse-sized safe in a desert in the southwestern United States.

Unfortunately, David Barton is not a good historian. Barton's 1991 book, *The Myth of Separation*, was popular with Christian evangelicals, but professional historians received it poorly, calling it "pseudoscholarship" (Specter, 1995, p. 582) "laced with exaggerations, half-truths and misstatements of fact" (Byrd, 2012, para. 2) and "schlock history written by religious propagandists" (Lilla, 2005, para. 2). When historians demonstrated that he had fabricated many of his quotations, Barton (1996) withdrew the book, re-edited it, and republished it under the title *Original Intent: The Courts, the Constitution & Religion*. However, even the revised work became a lightning rod for historical debunkers, with the People for the American Way and author Chris Rodda dedicating entire books to debunking it. This antipathy between professional historians and Barton came to a head in late 2012 when publishers withdrew his book, *The Jefferson Lies,* after several Christian historians complained that Barton had poorly researched the book and that he was wrong about Jefferson (Epps, 2012). One poll declared it the least credible book of the year (Schuessler, 2012).

Despite the criticism, Barton's star continued to rise. Even his withdrawn book on Jefferson occupied a top spot on *The New York Times* best-seller list and was briefly the highest rated *Amazon.com* book on Jefferson. Christian conservatives, in particular, complimented the book. Most powerfully, Glenn Beck tapped Barton for the inaugural lecture of Beck University—which attracted more than 300,000 subscribers.

How can a book that a Jefferson historian referred to as "a steady stream of distortions, misrepresentations, spurious claims, overstatements, over-simplifications, and wrenching of material out of context" (Jenkinson, 2012, para. 14) become a best-seller? While blaming an uninformed market or lamenting that people are incapable or disinterested in judgments may be tempting, such broadsides would misunderstand the phenomena that Barton represents. Here, I will discuss four features of the work that help explain its appeal to a networked community of conservatives. Each of these communal habits of reading advantage Barton's version of history over academic history. In fact, the antimony between what people feel and the offerings of academic historians explains a good bit of Barton's appeal.

To begin, Barton seized upon a paradox prevalent in the historical community to reject the evolutionary orientation of modern academic history. On the one hand, very few U.S. professional historians even existed before the 20th century. Most historians were hobbyists and many found inspiration in religion. For example, the first comprehensive history of the United States, George Bancroft's nine-volume product, overtly credited a Christian God for America's development. On the other hand, more recent and professional historians rejected their hobbyist predecessors and their traditional stories in line with the cultural changes of the post-World War II world. Today, historians tend to view modern histories as more reliable because increasingly holistic and less parochial judgments are likely to offer a more nuanced and accurate portrayal of the past. Barton entered into the fray, by noting, "generally, when dealing with early America, we have found that biographies and history works written before 1900 tend to present the most honest view. Those older books typically have not been infected with our modern agendas" ("Issues/Articles," n.d., Book Accuracy & Revisionism section, para. 4). He concluded, "the more modern the book, the more it has been infected with the five modern historical malpractices of Deconstructionism, Poststructuralism, Minimalism, Modernism, and Academic Collectivism" ("Issues/Articles," n.d., Book Accuracy & Revisionism section, para. 4).

Certainly, a logic exists to the claim that contemporaneous documents are more accurate. However, the act of historical interpretation typically involves more than the collection of documents that collapses historians and the act of writing history into a single act. In this conflation, Barton takes academic history as his motivation. As early as his *Original Intent*, Barton focused as much on the inadequacy of previous historical accounts as on the history itself, claiming that they were little more than revisionism that he identified as misrepresentation, lying, confusing fiction with fact, and psychologizing the founders to dispute their stated motives. His ultimate claim is that his history is superior because it cites a greater number of primary documents and fewer secondary documents.

To illustrate his critique, Barton highlighted a single book, *The Search for Christian America*, that three award winning historians (two from Notre Dame and one Wake Forest University) produced and that a religious publishing house (Good News Publishers) published. Noll, Hatch, and Marsden's (1983) book focused on America as a Christian nation and advanced claims that "the facts of history show that America does not deserve to be considered uniquely, distinctly or even predominantly Christian" (p. 17) and that "the idea of a 'Christian nation' is a very ambiguous concept which is usually harmful to effective Christian action in society" (p. 17). Barton's (1996) claim was not so much that the three authors were wrong as that their methodology was aberrant. He noted that the bibliography constitutes the "most glaring evidence of their revisionist approach" (p. 322), where 80 percent of their sources "postdate 1950!" (p. 322). He then dedicated nearly a page to demonstrating that his sources evenly distribute over the course of American history. He ended the chapter with the observation that with "the combined efforts of revisionist leaders in both the judicial and academic spheres of influence, legal protections for public religious expressions and public morality have been nearly destroyed" (p. 324). Barton's affinity for old texts results in his rejection of modern history as anything more than revisionism.

Barton's Reflection of Christianity's Sola Scriptura

One of the essential principles of the evangelical Christian faith is that faith alone can save adherents. This faith is informed *sola scriptura* that holds that adherents can only receive revelation of God's grace through the careful personal study of original scripture, which serves as a clear, self-authenticating, singular source of Christian doctrine (Mathison, 2007). In the words of 19th century evangelist Charles Beecher, one is to look to "the Bible, the whole Bible, and nothing but the Bible" (quoted in Hatch, 1989, p. 182).

Similar to the paradox of academic history, evangelical Christians believe that primary documents are more authentic, meaning that a focus on them opens adherents to an even deeper interpretation than would be available by other means. Barton noted,

> If [a document] was printed or written during or shortly after the time period it addresses, then there is a much higher likelihood that it will be based on what are considered primary sources—the most reliable wellspring of accurate historical information.
>
> *("Issues/Articles," n.d., Book Accuracy & Revisionism section, para. 1)*

Several implications emerge from this doctrine for the evangelical habit of Scriptural interpretation. First, the delineation of a finite text is exceedingly important, as it serves as the primary means that texts gain authority and legitimacy. What is included within the canon is the central problematic of *sola scriptura*. Additionally, to hold the status of Scripture, the text must be closed to outside influence. As such, the text is an object that must be open to literal interpretation, embracing a systematic bias against ironic or contextual interpretations, because the text cannot establish these perspectives itself so that it can speak with a unified and coherent voice.

This is a comfortable move for Barton's audience, as evangelical Christians tend to not view specific contexts as salient to the revelation of God's will (Noll, 2004). The removal of context "flattens" the text (since God's will is universal and consistent). For Barton, such flattening encourages believers to find meaning in a universal context. For example, a plan by Congress to pay off one printing bill by purchasing some left-over Bibles becomes a plan by the Congress to buy Bibles for everyone, thereby illustrating that distributing Bibles is a governmental priority. A larger meaning subsumes the specific goal of a particular situation.

Flat readings start with the assumption that the Bible speaks consistently and frequently on any issue (Noll, 2004). Consequently, adherents can find evidence for any claim in any part of the scripture and most claims have plenty of textual support available. Conversely, the assumption that a text could say more, or speak by saying nothing is transgressive—a reading of what is not there would stand without evidence (Good, 1965/1981; Sharp, 2009).

A stylistic element associated with flattening involves the Christian habit of prooftexting—which generally takes the form of a list of abbreviated citations proffered as support for a proposition. Critics often note that Barton uses an unusual number of citations in his work. As one detractor wrote, "for years, Barton has made a point of incessantly telling his audiences how many footnotes his books have [....] His followers are completely convinced that a lot of footnotes mean a book must be true" ("But He's Got," n.d., para. 6). The purpose of the footnotes, like prooftexting, is not to demonstrate a position more strongly. Instead, the footnotes simply demonstrate the ubiquity of a universal principle.

However, prooftexting is more performative than argumentative. Most members generally know the propositions of faith, and the abbreviated citations give little information to establish the strength of the claim. Instead, the practice establishes the authority of the speaker as a person of great knowledge, or signals the strength or universality of a claim without getting into too much detail. Paradoxically, controversial claims are likely to receive a longer list of prooftexts than would less controversial claims.

Among Evangelical Christians, prooftexting is common, but controversial. The practice finds its roots in the presentation of the scriptures themselves, particularly in the works of Paul that often reference other books of the Bible and in the Judaic tradition of religious argumentation. For any faith rooted in *sola scriptura*, the ability to locate explicit authority in pieces of text is essential. Similarly, a legitimate historical interpretation should find support in copious lists of authority.

Critics also argue that the practice of prooftexting is a variety of contextomy, where followers disaggregate the claims of the Bible, remove them from their context, and deploy them only as ends require. This process of removing quotations from their context and redeployment for quantitative effect undermines the ability to read the text with subtlety or to prioritize more general themes over aberrant ones (McGlone, 2005). In the worst case, readers lose the ability to communicate with scripture at all which undermines the basic tenet of *sola scriptura*. Here, Barton removes quotations from their context to deploy them only as evidence for universal principles.

Conclusion

By the contemporary standards of academic historians, David Barton is inadequate. He eschews the community of historians and indicts their methods. Where academic historians see improvement, he sees revision. Where they see cooperation, he sees "Academic Collectivism" ("Issues/Articles," n.d., WallBuilders and Unconfirmed Questions section, para. 5). However, what appears as an aberrant and contrarian approach to the facts has roots in a common hermeneutic network. Barton does not lack reason, as his academic critics claim. His reasons simply derive from an alternative interpretive frame unique to social networks his audience shares. Barton's framework relies on four basic beliefs: (a) consistency is more believable than innovation; (b) the founders were a coherent community; (c) the founders spoke to universal themes rather than specific contexts; and (d) the founders spoke only with intention.

By the end of the 19th century, historians adopted a professional voice that no longer required them to rely upon selling popular books. Instead, they embraced a method that rejected the comfortable presupposing frameworks and traditions of their predecessors. In their place, historians have enjoyed an active and creative period of historical interpretation, focused, more often than not, on forgotten histories (Wood, 1995). Professional historians have worked to demythologize the inherited, taken-for-grantedness of American history (Appleby, 1993).

However, the established historical narratives did not simply disappear. Instead, they continue to find an appreciative audience. The history of the United States as a Christian nation fulfilling God's design has found support among conservative evangelical Christians (Diamond, 1995). Barton has harnessed this tradition and desire to create his own history market. What is interesting is not just that Barton's history is comforting, but that it finds support in a unified and established method of interpretation. Barton's books do not create new history and do not reveal unknown information. Instead, they draw from a historical common rooted within an established and finite American canon. They apply the techniques of Scriptural interpretation to this canon to find recurring support for a set of Biblically-inspired, universal principles.

This resistance to change and embrace of familiar traditions, however, is not a sign of irrationality. Instead, it has its roots in long-traditions of interpretation. The traditional are unlikely to cede easily to new forms of argument. Instead, the better strategies lie with engaging them from within their own framework.

References

Appleby, J. (1993). A different kind of independence: The postwar restructuring of the historical study of early America. *The William and Mary Quarterly, 50*(2), 245–267. Retrieved from http://jstor.org/stable/2947073

Barton, D. (2008). *Original intent: The courts, the constitution, & religion* (5th ed.). Aledo, TX: WallBuilders.

Barton, D. (2012). *The Jefferson lies: Exposing the myths you've always believed about Thomas Jefferson*. Nashville, TN: Thomas Nelson.

Beck, G. (2010, July 5). "Glenn Beck": Founders' Friday: Women of the American Revolution [Transcript]. *Fox News*. Retrieved from http://foxnews.com

But He's Got Lots of Footnotes! (n.d.). *Debunking David Barton's Jefferson (and other) lies*. Retrieved from http://debunkingbarton.com/but-hes-got-lots-of-footnotes.html

Byrd, D. (2012, May 10). New book questions Barton's scholarship. *Baptist Joint Committee for Religious Liberty*. Retrieved from https://bjconline.org/new-book-questions-bartons-scholarship/

Diamond, S. (1995, February). Dominion theology: The truth about the Christian right's bid for power. *Online Archive of Political Research Associates*. Retrieved from http://publiceye.org/diamond/sd_domin.html

Epps, G. (2012, August 10). Genuine Christian scholars smack down on unruly colleague. *The Atlantic*. Retrieved from https://theatlantic.com

Good, E. M. (1965/1981). *Irony in the Old Testament* (2nd ed.). Sheffield, United Kingdom: Sheffield Academic Press.

Graham, J., Haidt, J., & Nosek, B. A. (2009). Liberals and conservatives rely on different sets of moral foundations. *Journal of Personality and Social Psychology, 96*(5), 1029–1046. doi:10.1037/a0015141

Hatch, N. O. (1989). *The democratization of American Christianity*. New Haven, CT: Yale University Press.

Issues/Articles: Frequently Asked Questions. (n.d.). *WallBuilders*. Retrieved from http://wallbuilders.ccsites.com/LIBissuesArticles.asp?id=100766

Jenkinson, C. S. (2012, June 3). David Barton: The Jefferson lies. *The Thomas Jefferson Hour*. Retrieved from http://jeffersonhour.com/blog/jeffersonlies

Kahan, D. M., Peters, E., Wittlin, M., Slovic, P., Ouellette, L. L., Braman, D., & Mandel, G. (2012). The polarizing impact of science literacy and numeracy on perceived climate change risks. *Nature Climate Change, 2*, 732–735. doi:10.1038/nclimate1547

Lilla, M. (2005, May 15). Church meets state. *The New York Times*. Retrieved from http://nytimes.com

Mathison, K. A. (2007). Solo scriptura: The difference a vowel makes. *Modern Reformation, 16*(2), 25–29. Retrieved from http://bible-researcher.com/mathison.pdf

McGlone, M. S. (2005). Quoted out of context: Contextomy and its consequences. *Journal of Communication, 55*(2), 330–346. doi:10.1111/j.1460-2466.2005.tb02675.x

Mercier, H., & Sperber, D. (2011). Why do humans reason? Arguments for an argumentative theory. *Behavioral and Brain Sciences, 34*(2), 57–111. doi:10.1017/S0140525X10000968

Noll, M. A. (2004). *Between faith and criticism: Evangelicals, scholarship, and the Bible in America*. Vancouver, Canada: Regent College.

Noll, M. A., Hatch, N. O., & Marsden, G. M. (1983). *The search for Christian America*. Wheaton, IL: Crossway Books.

Nyhan, B., & Reifler, J. (2010). When corrections fail: The persistence of political misperceptions. *Political Behavior, 32*(2), 303–330. doi:10.1007/s11109-010-9112-2

Rodda, C. (2011, May 25). No, Mr. Beck, our Constitution is not based on the book of Deuteronomy. *The Huffington Post*. Retrieved from http://huffingtonpost.com/chris-rodda/no-mr-beck-our-constituti_b_637451.html

Schuessler, J. (2012, July 16). And the worst book of history is… *The New York Times*. Retrieved from https://artsbeat.blogs.nytimes.com/2012/07/16/and-the-worst-book-of-history-is/

Sharp, C. J. (2009). *Irony and meaning in the Hebrew Bible*. Bloomington, IN: Indiana University Press.

Specter, A. (1995). Defending the wall: Maintaining church/state separation in America. *Harvard Journal of Law & Public Policy, 18*(2), 575–590.

Wood, G. S. (1995). A century of writing early American history: Then and now compared; Or how Henry Adams got it wrong. *The American Historical Review, 100*(3), 678–696. Retrieved from http://jstor.org/stable/2168600

41

DATA CANNOT SPEAK FOR THEMSELVES

Unreasonable Claims within the Big Social Data Community

Candice L. Lanius

Big social data scholars collect data from information-communication technologies and online social spaces before mining it for insights into human social behavior. Whether relying on data from Twitter or GPS coordinates from cell phones, big data analysts transform social data into evidence to support claims about the world, such as predicting flu outbreaks, describing the personality of a city, or building smart recommendation engines for individual users. Big social data is now pervasive in business, education, and government. Yet, efforts to make sense of what big data analysts are doing remain illusory. The vast majority of engineering research on big social data focuses on the technical values of efficiency and precision. The fields of rhetorical studies and communication studies, however, have begun to produce useful discussions regarding the ideology of the term "big data," such as Hartelius's (2018) Protagorean analysis of the United Nation's aspirations in creating the Global Pulse program or Faltesek's (2013) exploration of the aesthetics of big data visualization. In cultural studies, many are attentive to the politics of big data, including Kitchin's (2014) refutation of the end of theory and boyd and Crawford's (2012) introduction of six critical questions to consider when studying big data. While this scholarship is valuable for providing a macro look at the philosophical ramifications of big data, it does not consider how to address those ramifications. This paper introduces a method to study big data analysts as they work on individual projects, reveal new forms of reasoning, and deny their own rhetorical agency.

The Toulmin Model and Big Social Data

To study something as multifaceted as big social data requires imagination in rhetorical methods, yet definitions help provide a footing. The "big" indicates streams of data records so vast and quick that the human mind cannot process or conceptualize their passing, requiring some form of computation to both store and sort the records. In an effort to seize the conventional authority from qualitative researchers to answer society's oldest questions, social points towards both the source of the social media data records and also the goals of big social data projects. Rhetorical and argumentation scholarship has long focused on sociality and deliberation before modern technology bound "big" and "data" together. While I use data in this context to indicate digital records, the term originates from the Latin for "thing given" and provides another foothold for rhetorical analysis. For a thing to serve as evidence, someone must select and refine it, and that process requires human interpretation.

So what are big social data analysts doing? Many analysts deny that they are doing anything. They claim that their individual decisions and ideas play no role in the final outcome; instead, they describe their research as performing a rote process that has a foregone conclusion. In 2016, I began studying the Association for Computing Machinery and the Institute of Electronics and Electrical Engineers *International Conference on Advances in Social Networks Analysis and Mining*. To understand their activities, I used a survey and participant observation at the ASONAM conference, in addition to analyzing the conference proceedings. The ASONAM community is an interdisciplinary mixture of researchers from mathematics, computer science, and other engineering fields with a wide range of prior research experience and training whose views are not monolithic. That said, approximately 40% of the analysts I surveyed expressed a shared idea that data speak for themselves. The idea that data speak usually appeared in response to my probes about interpretation. For example, in the survey I asked, "How did you decide what research question(s) to ask for this project?" One respondent wrote, "It started with an interesting dataset, and we let the dataset inspire the questions." When asked how they explained any patterns found, another analyst wrote, their conclusions were "based on the data." During my field observations at the ASONAM 2016 conference, I noticed that most panels began with the same underlying premise: They described latent behavioral, social, or psychological processes within the dataset that awaited discovery. The "latency" premise enabled them to deploy different tools without concern for the moving target that is human social behavior. If the final results were latent, innate relationships that researchers could discover within the data, then the analyst's primary task became designing an efficient and reliable tool without concern for *if* and *how* the tool's design would change the final results.

As a rhetorician, I did not take the data's eloquence for granted. My position required a method to address how big social data analysts create arguments. Untangling the web of interpretations embedded in big data results requires a systematic analysis of the "subjective" components the analyst is traditionally not attentive to throughout their research process. Subjective components include moments where flexibility in interpretation exists: rather than having an "objective," right answer often sought in hard sciences, a recognition of the subjective components admits the possibility of a range of appropriate answers (Creswell, 2009). To uncover the interpretive moments embedded in the ASONAM conference proceedings, I turned to Toulmin's (1958) *The Uses of Arguments* for both his argumentation framework and analogy to the discipline of jurisprudence. For Toulmin, logical arguments were not the purely mathematical formalisms philosophers and logicians used. Instead, he uncovered how arguments functioned in practice (a procedural approach). Thus, the ASONAM conference proceedings served as text for the analysts' research process as they were appropriate for application of Toulmin's model to reveal relationships between parts of an argument.

Toulmin's (1958) basic argumentation model includes six elements: data, warrants, claims, ground, backing, and qualifiers. Claims are the statements a rhetor wants the audience to accept, and warrants are what links data and the ground to a claim, or put another way, why the data or ground support the claim. The grounds, which often overlap with the data, are the basis for using a specific type of data, that is, the "truth" or definitions where most arguments begin. Toulmin used questions to explain the roles of these different aspects within an argument. For data, he asked, "What have you got to go on?" While describing the warrant, he asked, "How do you get there?" (p. 90). The backing is additional support for an argument that may respond to different types of criticisms or interrogations of the argument. Toulmin asked, "but does not that warrant in its turn rest on something else?" and "but why do you think that?" (pp. 95–96). These additional "assurances" are the backing necessary to support the argument. Finally, qualifiers are what Toulmin described as force. Qualifiers condition when the claim is acceptable or provide the strength of belief in its veracity.

The constituent parts of Toulmin's (1958) argumentation framework were present in the research designs the data analysts employed, and by using the Toulmin method, my conclusion became clear: The data cannot speak for themselves. Rather, data analysts make interpretive decisions that not only change the stylistic components of their research, they invent and control the substance of their final results. First, the analyst must select, "clean," and pre-process the data, that is, the social media records, appropriate to their research goals. Once the analyst cleans the data records, the records become data in the Toulmin model. Next is the warrant, or the process of reasoning and inference individuals enact upon the data to reveal insights (or, in Toulmin's terms, the claim). In Toulmin's conversational examples, arguers often left their warrants unstated, but in big social data analysis, analysts hard code the warrant into the analytical tools used to construct the results (or claim). The computational technique required to get from the data to the claim is also available for scrutiny. Underlying Toulmin's basic structure of data—warrant—claim is the backing for why the warrant is acceptable as a major premise. Part of the backing for big social data projects involves the research goals. For clarity, I describe this as the *validity backing*. The research goals are the inspiration for the hypotheses and research questions and therefore serve as a foundation for why the analyst seeks the knowledge and answers with their argument. The other type of backing involves what analysts can achieve with available technology, or what I describe as *viability backing*. For big social data projects to emerge as sound research, the analyst must provide justification that their project works both as a technologically feasible project and as a type of knowledge. Due to page limits for the ASONAM conference proceedings, the essays typically understated or assumed the backing, that is, premises the scholars took for granted to do their work. In those cases, scholars only made available the backing if pushed for it during peer review or if solicited during scholarly presentations of the work at the ASONAM conference. Qualifiers in a big social data context are similar to the forms Toulmin analyzed in his study of common arguments. In short, analysts provided varying degrees of assurance for their work through reliability quotients or by claims of slight improvement over baseline models.

Example Case from the ASONAM Conference

To demonstrate the value of Toulmin's model for performing an analysis of analysts working in big social data, I now turn to an article from the ASONAM 2015 conference proceedings. Phan, Dou, Piniewski, and Kil (2015), in their article titled "Social Restricted Boltzmann Machine: Human Behavior Prediction in Health Social Networks," set out to prove that online social relationships influence whether a user will pursue a healthy lifestyle. To test their peer pressure hypothesis, the researchers collected data from a health and wellness application called *YesiWell* over an eleven-week period. The analysts, concerned about the increasing rate of unhealthy weight and obesity in society, reported the existence of "few scientific and quantitative studies to elucidate how social relationships and personal factors may contribute to macro-level human behaviors" (Phan et al., 2015, p. 424). Their research, charted in Figure 41.1, used a deep learning model to search for any patterns in a spectrum of thirty features collected from a cohort of 254 application users. To justify their use of the deep learning model, they argued from the principle of *homophily* (love of the same), that is, users' social behavior would indicate a shared conviction about wellness activities. In other words, healthy people interact with other healthy people, and unhealthy users interact with other unhealthy users. Because the deep learning model disguises some operations from the analysts, they also reasoned from signs that the model indicated significant features for future prediction.

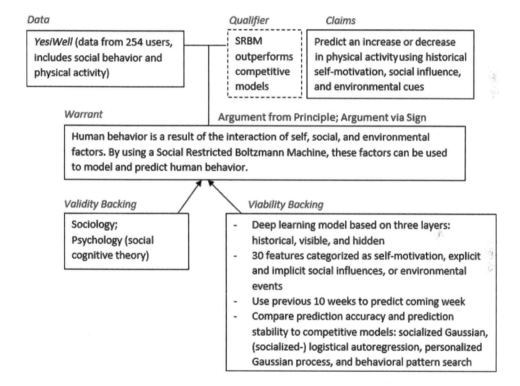

Figure 41.1 Toulmin Chart for Phan, Dou, Piniewski, and Kil's (2015) Research

To establish the validity backing for their modelling activities, Phan et al. (2015) began by discussing existing research into social influences and health behaviors. The analysts wrote that human behavior works as the "outcome of interacting determinants such as *self-motivation*, *social influences*, and *environmental events*. This observation is rooted in sociology and psychology" (p. 424). By establishing validity backing grounded in observational disciplines, the team argued that a deep learning model based on the "interacting determinants" available from the application data would be useful in predicting future behavior. An issue emerges, however, from a closer examination of the previous literature the authors used to support the validity backing. The analysts cited

Christakis and Fowler (2007) who studied the spread of obesity in a large, physical social network over a 32-year period. Therefore the peer pressure hypothesis evolved from research performed outside of digital networks and over a much larger time scale (i.e., the observed changes took three decades to occur, not a matter of weeks). This dilation of time and removal from the original context call into question the validity of the justification for the analysts' predictions. The homophily principle that served as the foundation for their warrant has major problems due to a poor connection to the validity backing.

Next, Phan et al. (2015) showed how their model works algorithmically to understand influences on the user's health behavior. They expected one of the layers embedded in their deep learning model to capture "self-motivation" and "hidden social influences." Because these two concepts constitute ephemeral categories of behavior, the analysts used correlations between "historical and current characteristics" to "capture" (p. 424) the hidden factors. The *YesiWell* data included daily physical activities, social activities, biomarkers, and biometric measures. The researchers used thirty determinants built into three modelling layers to predict future behavior, with one "hidden" layer. While hidden variables have a technical meaning in the research method (e.g., the deep learning method constructs and updates the relationship between input and output variables without the analyst's direct input), the "hidden" layer took on interpretive importance for the analysts. They wrote: "It is *hard to exactly define* [emphasis added] the implicit social influences. Fortunately, the dynamic of neural networks offers us a great solution *to capture the flexibility* [emphasis added] of implicit social influences" (p. 427). While the argument that the authors were observing something mathematically appears reasonable, their method does not support an interpretation for what causes implicit social influences. Nevertheless, they claimed to know the causes, concluding that "individuals tend to be influenced to perform similar behaviors as their friends (*homophily principle*)" (p. 427).

The homophily principle became both an inspirational theory and a holistic explanation: a one-size-fits-all for interpreting the outputs of their deep learning model. The deployment of the homophily principle freed Phan et al. (2015) to focus the majority of their time on comparing their model to "competitive methods" (p. 429). They concluded that their method was superior and outperformed other models on accuracy and stability, two metrics that provide a strong viability backing for their warrant.

The weak connection between the peer pressure hypothesis and list of determinants that produced the model shows why the analysts' decisions and interpretations matter. With a different backing (e.g., if one assumed biology determines healthy behavior), the results would be starkly different, as the warrant used to produce the claim from the available data would also be different. With a large quantity of social data, the risk of *apophenia* (finding false patterns) is very high.

Conclusion

By charting big social data projects as arguments, I reveal moments of interpretation currently hidden behind the guise of objective technology solutions increasingly used to automate decision-making. The application of Toulmin to analytical technologies raises important questions about rhetorical agency and the types of arguments used to justify these complex systems.

Despite the role of big social data analysts in constructing arguments that serve as the foundational assumptions of their findings, the ASONAM community wrongly rejects the analysts' own agency. Agency has a dual meaning for the ability to act and also to take responsibility for that action. To reconcile the non-human actor's agency in new computational settings, Miller (2007) proposed agency as a property of the situation and not a feature of objects. In this way, each actant in the situation takes actions and has varying degrees of responsibility for the outcome. In the big social data research community, researchers are attributing both ability and responsibility to the tools being used and the data under query. If the data (technology) speaks, then whatever the analyst claims as a result is one step removed from scrutiny. The presumption that the data contains obvious meanings disguises the analyst's agency.

The deferral of scrutiny becomes a problem because warrants are not just connecting data to a claim as a justificatory case; instead, the technology has embedded warrants that enact the analysts' worldview upon the data that they are marshalling as evidence. So how can we evaluate the warrants and backing used in big social data analysis? Academic disciplines tend to formulate qualities that they use to evaluate their research community. Professors teach these qualities to students and use the standards in peer review. Currently, the evaluation standards of the ASONAM community focus on engineering principles of efficiency, scalability, and reusability of the technology. However, these principles are not enough. Because big social data analysts are also making knowledge claims about the world, they should include the disciplinary standards of behavioral scientists surrounding rigor, reliability, and validity. Because big data discourse contains a variety of field-dependent logics, different genres for presenting research, and disparate criteria for evaluating a project's appropriateness, big social data projects need to better understand rhetorical flexibility and argument's role within it. The most direct route for changing a discipline's academic culture is to include scholars from other disciplines. An argumentation scholar working alongside a data analyst may initially be frustrated by the lack of common ground, but the results would be vastly superior in quality. The benefits of direct engagement with big social data analysts flow both ways. Argumentation scholars could, and should, be at the leading edge of technological developments, understanding how those developments shape our shared reality while helping guide research inquiries towards a more promising future.

Big social data researchers are writing persuasive documents responding to situational exigencies. Rather than creating evaluation criteria that rely on hard lines of "right" and "wrong," rhetorical consideration facilitates the transcendence and reconciliation of competing disciplinary perspectives (Burke, 1945/1969). A rhetorical analysis reveals opportunities for improving the results in the research design and research practices. Big social data analysis is here to stay, but the field must recognize that data cannot and does not speak for themselves. As analysts give voice to their projects, those projects can function both as powerful technologies and sound sources of knowledge, but only if they evaluate and discard the roots of their unreasonable claims.

References

boyd, d. m., & Crawford, K. (2012). Critical questions for big data: Provocations for a cultural, technological, and scholarly phenomenon. *Information, Communication & Society, 15*(5), 662–679. doi:10.1080/1369118X.2012.678878

Burke, K. (1969). *A grammar of motives*. Berkeley, CA: University of California Press.

Christakis, N. A., & Fowler, J. H. (2007). The spread of obesity in a large social network over 32 Years [Special article]. *The New England Journal of Medicine, 357*(4), 370–379. doi:10.1056/NEJMsa066082

Creswell, J. W. (2009). *Research design: Qualitative, quantitative, and mixed method approaches* (3rd ed.). Thousand Oaks, CA: SAGE.

Faltesek, D. (2013). Big argumentation? *tripleC*, *11*(2), 402–411. Retrieved from https://www.triple-c. at/index.php/tripleC/article/view/464

Hartelius, E. J. (2018). Big data and global knowledge: A protagorean analysis of the United Nation's global pulse. In M. Kennerly & D. S. Pfister (Eds.), *Ancient rhetorics + digital networks* (pp. 67–86). Tuscaloosa, AL: University of Alabama Press.

Kitchin, R. (2014). *The data revolution: Big data, open data, data infrastructures and their consequences.* Thousand Oaks, CA: SAGE.

Miller, C. R. (2007). What can automation tell us about agency? *Rhetoric Society Quarterly*, *37*(2), 137–157. doi:10.1080/02773940601021197

Phan, N. H., Dou, D., Piniewski, B., & Kil, D. (2015, August 25–28). Social restricted Boltzmann machine: Human behavior prediction in health social networks. In J. Pei, F. Silvestri, & J. Tang (Eds.), *Proceedings of the 2015 IEEE/ACM international conference on advances in social networks analysis and mining* (pp. 424–431). New York, NY: Association for Computing Machinery.

Toulmin, S. E. (1958). *The uses of argument.* Cambridge, United Kingdom: Cambridge University Press.

42

SCIENTIFIC ARGUMENT NETWORKS AND THE POLYTECHTONIC ART OF RHETORIC

L. Paul Strait

Scientific argumentation convenes within networks, consists of networks, and constitutes networks. These argument networks develop through the craft of rhetoric, because the "processes of knowing are processes of making and doing" (McKeon, 1975, p. 730). McKeon (1987) described rhetoric as an "architectonic productive art" that "relates form to matter, instrumentality to product, presentation to content, agent to audience, [and] intention to reason" (p. 24). As "an architectonic art relating and directing arts, sciences, and actions by principles" (McKeon, 1981, p. 431), rhetoric organizes institutions and integrates fields of knowledge. I follow Goodnight's (2014) suggestion that in late modernity, a period "characterized by digital material exchange, networks of assembly, and global circulations" (p. 9), the rhetoric of inquiry is not architectonic but "polytechtonic" (p. 2).

This essay adumbrates a network theory of scientific argumentation and polytechtonic rhetoric. Such a theory can help to explain how scientific fields maintain stable identities as they dynamically produce knowledge. I first outline the basic elements of the theory. I then draw on Luhmann's analysis of social systems to consider two critical features of a scientific argument network: reflexivity and autopoiesis. Finally, I take up the question of how a scientific argument network develops and changes. Against the sharp breaks that paradigm shifts imply, I contend that polytechtonic rhetorical maneuvering throughout complex, dynamically self-assembling multi-level networks of argument guides the continuous development and iterative evolutionary process of scientific fields.

Basic Theoretical Elements

Networks link together objects in complex patterns of nodes and edges that can be dynamic and robust without necessarily following a hierarchical substructure (Barrat, Barthélemy, & Vespignani, 2008). Richly differentiated argument networks employ many connective elements: warrants link claims and grounds, controversies link interlocutors and evidence, and institutions link technical arguments and publics. Argument networks feature reflexivity, the "systematic processes of exploration of the prior commitments framing knowledge" (Wynne, 1993, p. 321). Warrants themselves can function as the subject of claims and evidence, the validity of every link and node tested, and entire substructures of the argument network called into question. Interlocutors also serve as auditors, appraising the value of their own arguments and those of their peers. Argumentative claims secure legitimacy when interlocutors link together into a topological sub-structure of consensus. Similarly, the substructure of dissensus serves to highlight problem areas that require new inventional strategies.

In the context of modern institutions, which anchor system to lifeworld, architectonic rhetoric undergirds the intersubjectivity of communities of inquiry while enabling objective judgments and collective action. It foregrounds deliberation in which interlocutors construct possible worlds and stable principles through debates of fact, policy, and value. An etymological metaphor supports the idea that a scientific field is like a building under construction: The Greek word for knowledge, *epistēmē*, combines the verb *histēmi*, meaning "to make to stand," and the prefix *epi-*, meaning "upon." Given appropriate *topoi,* or rhetorical places, the art of rhetoric makes a constellation of signifiers stand upon one another. By linking them together within an internally referential persuasive epistemic system and thereby endowing its argument network with an architectonic communicative structure, rhetoric assembles and maintains a scientific field.

For mature scientific fields built on a high degree of theoretical consensus, or what Kuhn (1962) referred to as "normal science," the architectural metaphor is very helpful. However, a neat structural conception of knowledge fails adequately to represent fields in which fundamental theoretical orienting questions are the subject of dissensus. This inadequacy is particularly apparent for interdisciplinary inquiries, where different kinds of expertise need to come into conversation with one another. This need corresponds with the shift from early modernity's concern for "the *stability and uniformity* of Science" to a late modern need to "protect *diversity and adaptability*" (Toulmin, 1990, p. 183). Interdisciplinarity can introduce incompatible elements into the broader network. If they resemble buildings at all, the builders would appear to be working from very different blueprints constructing the many late modern fields of knowledge.

Consider the field of psychiatry, which sits at a nexus between biological, psychological, social, medical, regulatory, and public interests. Technical psychiatric discourse occurs within a network that has "no center, [...] no privileged locus of growth, [...] and no stable patterns of interconnection among its elements" (Bogue, 2007, p. 127). Writing six years before the revolutionary *DSM-III* was published, two psychiatrists compared their field to the Tower of Babel. They wrote,

> Our psychiatric situation is perhaps even more chaotic than that of the legendary tower, for in that famous example of failed communication, each person was presumably speaking one language consistently, although not the same language as his fellow towerbuilders. What we have in psychiatry is worse: Each person uses a hodgepodge of bits and pieces of ideas, theories, notions, and ideologies, in order to engage in a supposedly common enterprise with others similarly confused.
>
> *(Siegler & Osmond, 1974, p. 11)*

Though the field has developed quite a bit over the last 40 years, the description is still apt today. A theory of polytechtonic argument can help to make sense of the ongoing controversies in psychiatric theory and nosology.

The concept of an argument network that polytechtonic rhetoric structures is more expansive than theory, model, argument field (Toulmin, 2003), or paradigm (Kuhn, 1962), but is less extensive than episteme (Foucault, 1994). Paradigm shifts occur within networks of argument. The concept of fields of argument lacks the reflexivity needed to explain the development of logical types themselves or the way that arguments from converging fields interact. Toulmin's insight that arguments are embedded in larger systems, however, is essential to understanding how dynamically developing social, textual, and rhetorical relations constrain arguments, interlocutors, and the horizons of consensus and dissensus. My approach breaks with Toulmin, who positions fields of argument in hierarchy, and with Foucault, who sees epistemic structures as assemblages of control. Instead, I locate scientific discourse within a hybrid network of arguments with material outcomes that require justification within a larger supply chain of knowledge, technology, capital, and consumer products. The course of development this network takes depends in large part on how it embeds within other argument networks associated with cognate fields, institutional logics, and public advocacy.

Networked Social Systems

An argument network is autopoetic and self-referential. Autopoiesis means a process of self-production. A self-referential communication system is a relational network because meaning is a distinctive property of communication and a communication system must be reflexive to produce meaningful knowledge. But an argument network is less mechanistic than Luhmann's (1995) communication system, and it can account for suasive forms unrelated to its substantive content. Luhmann understood communicative action as a network phenomenon, but his sociological instincts led him to see the social at the expense of the individual subject. He described communication as an emergent reality, "a kind of self-excitation that inundates the system with meaning" (p. 171). Further, where Luhmann dissociated social systems from their materiality (Poli, 2010), an argument network is irreducibly material, discursively enacting material relations and signifying an underlying reality it rhetorically invests with meaning (Law, 2009).

The basic problem guiding Luhmann's inquiry concerned the reproductive dynamics of social systems. In this context, reproduction referred to temporal continuity, that is, a system's ability to maintain a continuous and stable identity over time despite changes in and turnover among its members. Pareto (1935) suggested that a system's reproduction is a consequence of the reproduction of its members. Following Durkheim (1951), Parsons (1951) rejected this solution, arguing against the reduction of sociological phenomena to aggregated individual phenomena. Instead, a social system reproduces through the replication of its characteristic patterns of action, including social roles available to its members, as well as "implementations of perspective points, interests, values, and—more generally, of meanings" (Poli, 2010, p. 2). These patterns of action, which represent both topological and functional properties of a network, appear as sub-graphs of "recurring, significant patterns of interconnections" (Milo et al., 2002, p. 824) called network motifs.

Networks generate their own network motifs. Luhmann borrowed the self-production concept of autopoiesis from biologists Maturana and Varela (1980), who argued that a living cell is an autopoietic machine.

> [It serves as] a network of processes of production (transformation and destruction) of components [...] which: (i) through their interactions and transformations continuously regenerate and realize the network of processes (relations) that produced them; and (ii) constitute it [...] as a concrete unity in space in which they (the components) exist by specifying the topological domain of its realization as such a network.
>
> *(p. 79)*

Like a living system, a social system manufactures what it needs for reproduction. Social systems reproduce through a self-referential process by which they "define their specific mode of operation or determine their identity by reflection to be able to regulate which internal meaning-units enable the self-reproduction of the system and thus are repeatedly to be reproduced" (p. 34). A system's reflexive self-production mediates its contact with its environment. Meta-arguments about argument invention, evaluation, and norms of rhetorical practice unfold within the system itself. This process does not imply isolation, however. Examining the links between argument networks may help resolve the demarcation problem in the philosophy of science. Though a full treatment of the problem is beyond the scope of this essay, scientific fields may differ from pseudoscientific ones in both the quality and quantity of network interconnections with other fields.

Autopoietic reproduction of a system does not mean that the same actions repeat continuously. Rather, reproduction depends on "production out of what has been produced" (Luhmann, 1995, p. 169). So, for autopoietic systems, this means that the system does not end in its actual activities. Rather, its actions, whether by intention or not, have inventional argumentative value. The process of reproduction generates new ideas and practices, introducing change into the social system. But reflexivity places important constraints on the scope of possible change and variation, because a system of meaning can only refer to itself and so must adhere to the types of elements that constitute it.

Constraints also exist on a scientific argument system's ability to resist change. The internal logic of scientific fields demands that they vary as they develop inductively over time according to the rhythms of consensus and dissensus formation. Argument networks contain a temporal dimension. Scientists assemble knowledge diachronically, as new findings and inventions iteratively update and supplement old knowledge. The rhetorical economy of science features "temporalized complexity," undergoing "constant disintegration" (Luhmann, 1995, p. 48). As various network elements pass away, new ones must constantly be produced on the basis of the configuration of elements at any given moment. Argument networks are thus sustained over time through a process of "reflexive production, that is, production out of products" (Luhmann, 1995, p. 49).

Dynamic stability in argument networks therefore involves a change in elements (i.e., symbols, warrants, evidence, *topoi*, etc.) over time. To successfully reproduce, network structures must permit network actors/interlocutors to re-purpose terms, methods, and suasive strategies operative in one case to another, whether univocally, equivocally, analogically, and/or hybridized with other elements of the network. Often this entails retaining the form but not the content of past persuasive appeals (e.g., physicians since Hippocrates have continued to use the case report genre to announce the unexpected). But do scientific argument networks usually develop via sudden revolutionary shifts between incommensurate paradigms featuring non-overlapping field-dependent warrants, or through gradual evolutionary ontogenesis regulated by field-invariant reasoning?

Polytechtonic (R)evolution

Like Luhmann, Toulmin and Goodfield (1965) found parallels between social and biological systems, particularly regarding their evolutionary paths. They took to heart the Darwinian insight that changes of great functional significance are very often the by-products of processes with unrelated manifest goals. Evolutionary success did not require conformation to some teleological historical trajectory, but rather depended on kairotic fitness to the immediate situation that one's environment posed. Just as with organisms, the key to understanding institutional history lies "in recognizing not its single-directedness, but rather its multiple opportunism" (p. 235). In other words, the history of ideas is more a polytechtonic flow than architectonic assembly line (Strait, 2014). The rhetorical productivity of any given form or configuration in some future network context remains undetermined, as does whether such a context, and not a different one, will present itself.

Toulmin's criticism of Kuhn, who posited incompatible paradigms competing with one another for hegemony, built on his theory of field-dependence and field-invariance. If, outside of normal science, two paradigms are truly incommensurate, then they have no basis on which to compete. Interlocutors only may compare conflicting claims that are part of the same argument field. Just as absolutism over-estimates the degree to which warrants are field-invariant, Kuhnian relativism overestimated the degree to which warrants are field-dependent. Elements of both were always at work in any body of discourse. Although analysts would not expect the same "standards of argument relevant in a court of law" to apply when "judging a paper in the *Proceedings of the Royal Society*" (Toulmin, 2003, p. 15), they would expect them to share common logical features and to contain some similar kinds of strategic argumentative maneuvering. Both continuous and discontinuous flows mediate knowledge production and recension. New findings, ideas, and symbols from the "intellectual ecology" of a discipline make their way into the emergent deliberative network as the culling of "entrenched concepts" creates epistemic space, all of which occurs within "forums of competition" in response to forces of symbolic supply and contingent demand (Toulmin, 1972, p. 140).

Polytechtonic argument networks largely comport with Toulmin's account of evolutionary development, although clearly sometimes the forces of consensus and dissensus fail to balance, leading autopoietic systems to fissure. But even in these cases, network flows prevent total loss and prohibit absolute novelty. Argument networks are cultural systems, ordered networks of "interacting symbols [with] patterns of interworking meanings [....that] transform sentiment into significance and so make it socially available" (Geertz, 1964, pp. 56–57). Rhetorical tropes stitch together the cognitive, affective, and normative levels of culture, permitting both continuous and discontinuous semiotic and material circulation. Concepts, symbols, and discursive forms may wander around between fields like "nomads" (p. 159), or even go into exile from the cognitive lifeworld altogether, biding their time in the affective or moral realms (Noyes, 2004). For example, marketers of dietary supplements redeploy medieval tropes of humoral balance predicated on popular anxieties about deficiency and excess as well as counter-industrial values prioritizing the "natural" (Healy, 1997). The "rhizomatic multiplicities" (Deleuze & Guattari, 1987, p. 370) of argument networks reflect the polytechtonic nature of the late modern world. Tropological resonances between scientists, marketers, and the popular imaginary create bridges between network levels, providing an avenue for the return of the repressed. Consider the notion of monoamine imbalance in the etiology of mood disorders, which, while literally inaccurate, helped sell billions of antidepressants and, perhaps counterintuitively, animated a therapeutically productive neuropsychiatric research program (Castrén, 2005).

The rhetorical motives undergirding network replication and differentiation are identification and division (Burke, 1984). Argumentation networks facilitate scientific progress by creating continuity and discontinuity at the right points, connecting or distinguishing old ideas and new, integrating or disentangling separate findings, increasing or reducing theoretical complexity, and embedding or dis-embedding different fields and subfields. Consequently, revolutions and ruptures occur periodically throughout scientific history, but the genres, terminologies, tropes, and *topoi* of the past survive even the most radical of reconstructions, for, as Descartes (1998) eloquently noted, "In tearing down an old house, one usually saves the wreckage for use in building a new one" (pp. 16–17).

L. Paul Strait

References

Barrat, A., Barthélemy, M., & Vespignani, A. (2008). *Dynamical processes on complex networks*. Cambridge, United Kingdom: Cambridge University Press.

Bogue, R. (2007). *Deleuze's way: Essays in transverse ethics and aesthetics*. Burlington, VT: Ashgate.

Burke, K. (1984). *Permanence and change: An anatomy of purpose*. Berkeley, CA: University of California Press.

Castrén, E. (2005). Is mood chemistry? *Nature Reviews Neuroscience, 6*(3), 241–246. doi:10.1038/nrn1629

Deleuze, G., & Guattari, F. (1987). *A thousand plateaus: Capitalism and schizophrenia* (B. Massumi, Trans.). Minneapolis, MN: University of Minnesota Press.

Descartes, R. (1998). *Discourse on method* (D. A. Cress, Trans., 4th ed.). Indianapolis, IN: Hackett.

Durkheim, É. (1951). *Suicide: A study in sociology* (J. A. Spaulding & G. Simpson, Trans.). New York, NY: Free Press.

Foucault, M. (1994). *The order of things: An archaeology of the human sciences*. New York, NY: Vintage Books.

Geertz, C. (1964). Ideology as a cultural system. In D. E. Apter (Ed.), *Ideology and discontent* (pp. 47–76). New York, NY: The Free Press of Glencoe.

Goodnight, G. T. (2014). From architectonics to polytechtonics: Rhetoric, communication, and information. *Poroi, 10* (1), Article 4. doi:10.13008/2151-2957.1185

Healy, D. (1997). *The antidepressant era*. Cambridge, MA: Harvard University Press.

Kuhn, T. S. (1962). *The structure of scientific revolutions*. Chicago, IL: University of Chicago Press.

Law, J. (2008). Actor network theory and material semiotics. In B. S. Turner (Ed.), *The new Blackwell companion to social theory* (pp. 141–158). Malden, MA: Wiley-Blackwell.

Luhmann, N. (1995). *Social systems: Writing science* (J. Bednarz & D. Baecker, Trans.). Stanford, CA: Stanford University Press.

Maturana, H. R., & Varela, F. J. (1980). *Autopoiesis and cognition: The realization of the living*. Hingham, MA: Kluwer.

McKeon, R. (1975). Arts of invention and arts of memory: Creation and criticism. *Critical Inquiry, 1*(4), 723–739. doi:10.1086/447812

McKeon, R. (1981). Philosophy as an agent of civilization. *Philosophy and Phenomenological Research, 41*(4), 419–436. doi:10.2307/2107249

McKeon, R. (with Backman, M.). (1987). The uses of rhetoric in a technological age: Architectonic productive arts. In M. Backman (Ed.), *Rhetoric: Essays in invention and discovery* (pp. 1–24). Woodbridge, CT: Ox Bow Press.

Milo, R., Shen-Orr, S., Itzkovitz, S., Kashtan, N., Chklovskii, D., & Alon, U. (2002). Network motifs: Simple building blocks of complex networks. *Science, 298*(5594), 824–827. doi:10.1126/science.298.5594.824

Noyes, J. K. (2004). Nomadism, nomadology, postcolonialism: By way of introduction. *Interventions: International Journal of Postcolonial Studies, 6*(2), 159–168. doi:10.1080/1369801042000238300

Pareto, V. (1935). *The mind and society [Trattato di sociologia generale]—Vol. 3: Theory of derivations* (A. Bongiorno & A. Livingston, Trans.; A. Livingston, Ed.). London, United Kingdom: Jonathan Cape.

Parsons, T. (1951). *The social system*. Glencoe, IL: Free Press.

Poli, R. (2010). The complexity of self-reference: A critical evaluation of Luhmann's theory of social systems. *Journal of Sociocybernetics, 8*(1/2),1–23. Retrieved from https://unizar.es/sociocybernetics/Journal/journal_1_2_2010_l.pdf

Siegler, M., & Osmond, H. (1974). *Models of madness, models of medicine*. New York, NY: Macmillan.

Strait, L. P. (2014). *Deliberating the science of madness: DSM-5 and the polytechtonic rhetorical economy of psychiatric nosology* (Doctoral dissertation). Retrieved from the USC Digital Library database website: http://digitallibrary.usc.edu/cdm/

Toulmin, S. E. (1972). *Human understanding: The collective use and evolution of concepts*. Princeton, NJ: Princeton University Press.

Toulmin, S. E. (1990). *Cosmopolis: The hidden agenda of modernity*. Chicago, IL: University of Chicago Press.

Toulmin, S. E. (2003). *The uses of argument*. Cambridge, United Kingdom: Cambridge University Press.

Toulmin, S. E., & Goodfield, J. (1965). *The discovery of time*. Chicago, IL: University of Chicago Press.

Wynne, B. (1993). Public uptake of science: A case for institutional reflexivity. *Public Understanding of Science, 2*(4), 321–337. doi:10.1088/0963-6625/2/4/003

PART V

ARGUMENT CIRCULATION IN ONLINE NETWORKS

43

ARGUMENTS OF A NEW VIRTUAL RELIGION

How Athenism "Clicks" New Members and Reimagines the Mind-Body Dualism

Emma Frances Bloomfield

People are increasingly using new technologies to explore and experiment with their religious identity ("Religion and Electronic Media," 2014). While traditional religions invite physical participation in rituals that build communities based on shared locations, online religious networks are often more diffuse. The internet enables connections with people around the world, but makes difficult the performance of physical rituals common to faith communities. Virtual religious adherents have had to reimagine the relationship between the physical and virtual world and negotiate ideas of presence, community, and membership. Previous studies of online religion have noted how physical rituals translate into virtual spaces, "such as e-prayer and virtual pilgrimages" (Campbell, 2005, p. 311), and how people attempt to replicate offline rituals in online gatherings (O'Leary, 1996). Other studies have examined how technologies complement and "support traditional religious practices" (Campbell, 2012, p. 66). Less attention has been paid to how the internet can be a site for organic religious emergence. Instead of examining what faith looks like when it moves online, I analyze a religion, Athenism, which began online and sustains membership solely through digital networks. Without an offline foundation, Athenism must make strategic use of arguments to gain members and convince others of its philosophies. In considering online faith networks, the role that technology plays in mediating contemporary religious identities and affording certain argumentation strategies takes on added importance.

Athenism is a virtual faith named after Athene, the online handle of founder Bachir Boumaaza. Members perform the faith through mental adherence to its tenets and connecting with practicing members around the world. Instead of following a deity, Athenism worships logic, science, and empiricism. The faith's key texts are YouTube videos, which outline a four-step conversion process to achieve enlightenment labeled the "click" (AtheneWins, 2016a, 15:52). The process of clicking shifts followers' thinking into purely logical decision-making. Athenism argues that the collective acceptance and implementation of logic can create an ideal society. Athenism walks the line between science and religion, describing itself in the same video (AtheneWins, 2016d) as the start of a "scientific revolution" (22:30) and as a "religious transformation" (18:01).

In the group's official documents and videos, Athenism repeatedly undermines the role of the body and focuses on the power of minds connecting online. Considering that networks often rely on "social exchanges rather than on spatial proximity" (Wellman & Hampton, 1999, p. 649), the power of Athenism's network occurs not through a shared place of worship, but through the exchange of video links, testimonials, and messages. Athenism thus represents two networks: the networked community its followers create and the neural networks within the human mind that enable logical thought. Athenism embraces Descartes's dualism of mind over body as part of a "cyborg" mentality (Haraway, 1991, p. 149). Athenism creates a Harawayan argument for the acceptance of technological integration to spread logic to everyone. In advocating for an "unbodied" faith, however, Athenism does not eliminate the role of the body completely. Indeed, Athenism frequently contradicts its assertions of the weakness of the body by inadvertently highlighting the importance of materiality to the faith. Analyzing Athenism's arguments provides evidence that, even in virtual environments, religion can function as an embodied experience.

To gain insight into Athenism's negotiation of the mind-body dynamic, I collected official videos, documents, and publicly available communication between Athenism's members on social networking sites. First, I will explain the faith's origins in more detail to contextualize its discourse. Then, I will show how Athenism struggles with aligning the tenets of its faith to its performance. Despite making arguments eschewing the importance of the body, Athenism's arguments invoke the importance of both mind and body to perform membership in the faith via technological means.

Introducing Athenism

Started in 2007, the YouTube channel AtheneWins originally featured live streams of Athene playing games such as *Hearthstone*. Now, the channel focuses on Athenism, with 600 videos, over 700,000 subscribers, and almost 500 million channel views. Viewers have watched the video *Athene's Theory of Everything* more than four million times, while the typical "how-to" YouTube video, in contrast, averages fewer than 9,000 views (Marshall, 2015). Most videos contain information about the four-step clicking process. To click, one must first acknowledge the presence of logical patterns in everyday life. Then, one must identify the core emotion that drives decision making. Step three is replacing one's driving emotion with the logical patterns from step one. Finally, followers make decisions that purposefully employ logic instead of emotion. Once clicked, the site encourages members to share official videos, participate in online message boards, and post testimonials. Through the "social contagion" of the internet (Goodnight, 2016, p. 92), Athenism aims to start a "global chain reaction" so that everyone can experience the click (AtheneWins, 2016d, 23:14). Official texts thus centralize Athenism's arguments, and members chaining out the messages to others decentralize them. The network of Athenism's followers becomes an ephemeral "actor" that connects people as a vehicle to sustain "a vast array of entities" (Latour, 2005, p. 46). Within the faith's parameters, minds, logic, and collective society replace bodies, emotions, and individuals. In what follows, I highlight how Athenism undermines the role of the body before analyzing the body's pervasive presence that underlies Athenism's arguments.

Valuing Mind over Body

Athenism gains followers through engagement in conversion arguments, whereby the faith uniquely has the answers to questions about the "purpose" of human existence (AtheneWins, 2016a, 11:30) and insights into "life, death, and the origin of the universe" (AtheneWins, 2011, 0:28). Because the faith focuses on the power of the mind, Athenism claims that it alone knows the truths of reality. In the beginning of *Science Finds God,* the narrator argued that the world came about because of "consistent patterns" that created order (AtheneWins, 2016d, 22:17). The video described humans as the pinnacle of these logical networks: "our comprehension of our own existence is a result of these patterns coming [...] to understand themselves" (AtheneWins, 2016d, 10:44). Humans are little more than logical networks that have reached a level of mental self-awareness known as consciousness. Because we originate from logical networks, "logic is our Creator" (AtheneWins, 2016a, 2:36). Athenism encourages followers to see logic as a deity: "Logic can be trusted, personified, and embraced in the same way [as a God]" (AtheneWins, 2016d, 17:52). Athenism thus claims that the mind is the key to know more about the world and the nature of humanity.

Athenism undermines the body's emotional and physical drives, describing them as obstructing the natural tendency of the mind to be logical. Athenism argues that the faith is essential to "process information from a more detached and logical perspective" (Athene-Wins, 2016b, 2:37) and not from emotions. On a thread in r/makingsense (Athenism's Reddit community), a person having difficulty clicking receives guidance to imagine their doubts as "symptoms" of a weak body (Jononetwothree, 2017, para. 1). In *Science Finds God,* the narrator condemned the body's "relentless pursuit of achieving [safety]" and its "attachment to shallow pleasures" (AtheneWins, 2016d, 14:02, 16:37). When the body is dominant, people are selfish and do not think logically about postponing pleasure or sacrificing individual needs. The video *Are We Controlled By A Monkey?* echoed this idea, portraying one's thinking process as an argument between a monkey, the primitive, emotional part of the brain, and an owl, "the more advanced and intelligent part of our brain" (AtheneWins, 2016b, 2:56). While the monkey wants to react immediately to stimuli, the owl takes time to process information. The video equates clicking to letting one's logical, thoughtful owl "deliberate" with the monkey, thus controlling the internal monkey as if individuals were machines with on/off switches (AtheneWins, 2016b, 2:01).

Athenism argues that after making the click, individuals and society will improve. Engaging in clicking becomes a desirable process because of the immediate and profound benefits. The video *Logic Nation* compared the click to when "you start believing in God," because "from one day to another, you, you [*sic*] just behave differently, you act differently, you think differently" (AtheneWins, 2016a, 01:42). Athenism promises that "your problems will disappear" (0:31) and "you will be able to think faster" (AtheneWins, 2016a, 0:41). In fact, Athenism's followers boast they are "one hundred fold" smarter than Albert Einstein (AtheneWins, 2016d, 0:37). People in *Science Finds God* described how, after clicking, they performed better on cognitive tests and were easily able to quit their previous vices, such as nicotine addiction (AtheneWins, 2016d, 18:54). When describing their conversion experience, one person said, "Everything that was hard before comes easy now" (AtheneWins, 2016d, 19:42).

On a larger scale, Athenism argues that clicking will solve problems such as "disease, famine, or even death" (AtheneWins, 2016d, 8:13). Athenism is thus "vital to the future of humanity" (AtheneWins, 2016d, 14:23). Connecting everyone in the world will "be the difference between the society we live in now and literally a utopia" (AtheneWins, 2016a, 13:31). In agreement with Castells (2007), followers of Athenism argued that dominant ways of thinking will change once "a majority of people think in ways that are contradict-ory" (p. 238) to the present system. So that the world can benefit, Athenism encourages people to share their clicking experiences and its official videos, because only through a critical mass of people thinking logically will significant, global change occur.

Athenism started online and flourished on the internet, connecting people through its speed, reach, and interactivity (Zappen, 2005). Online, "the costs of dissemination are low, the means of production simple, and the potential audience vast" (Goodnight, 2016, p. 89). With a few videos, a powerful message, and a built-in audience of Athene's fans and others looking for answers, Athenism has an ideal dissemination mechanism. Athenism appears to have little need for bodies on the street or coordination between members offline. Instead, Athenism invokes a "logic of aggregation" where a house of worship is any computer terminal, phone, or internet access point (Juris, 2012, p. 260). The meeting "place" of Athenism's network is "a space of contacts," which exists because of the connections sustained between members (Edbauer, 2005, p. 10). An individual person, after viewing these videos and "clicking," immediately becomes an intimate and complete member of Athenism, linked with other members across the globe. The connections between Athenism's members are "mute and invisible" (Latour, 2005, p. 31), where individuals often type words rather than speak them and members can only view Athene and other followers through their screens. Latent in Athenism's arguments, however, is that only through the aggregation of individuals (bodies), working towards a common cause, think-ing and acting logically, does the world experience physical and social change.

Reclaiming the Body

Although Athenism makes repeated arguments undervaluing the body, these same arguments unconsciously laud physicality. If the mind is where life's value lies, then bodies play an important role as hosts for the mind's greatness. Technology itself is partly hardware, which requires physical connections, wires, electricity, and screens to create virtual networks. No revolution occurs without the work of followers' bodies logging on, viewing, and participat-ing in the online community. The majority of Athenism's videos show followers, including Athene, talking about their experiences, running tests, and interacting with one another. When someone messages someone on r/makingsense or on Athenism's Discord page, they are not simply interacting with technology, but with real people behind the usernames. Athenism emerges out of and is made possible by technology and the internet, but people that constitute the networked communities always define it.

Athenism's preferred method of spreading the click is through testimonials, which serve as verified examples of the benefits of clicking. Testimony videos highlight individuals that embody conversion experiences. Testimonials add a personal element to the movement and remind potential members of the human network that exists behind the virtual. In one testi-mony video, a follower described his reaction to clicking, saying, "I started feeling very euphoric. I felt a really big rush of dopamine [in] my head [....] I just started shaking. I had to get my clothes off. I was really feeling hot" (Ramos, 2016, 8:20). For this follower, click-ing elicited a strong physical reaction, exemplifying how a religious epiphany is often felt and experienced materially. The bodies of members are featured as exemplars for potential members, showing visually that Athenism's faith network is more than just text on a screen.

For Athenism, the videos simultaneously portray clicking as a process that occurs with a simple, mental click and as a "lived social and bodily realit[y]" that employs people for its collective per-formance and expression (Haraway, 1991, p. 155). When people click, the direct result is that they make decisions to act logically. So, Athenism does not simply address the functioning of the mind, but also the consequent actions of the body and in conjunction with the mind. Furthermore, one needs physical brain matter to create the "neural connections" of consciousness (AtheneWins, 2016c, 3:17). Langer (1996) argued that logical thinking and science rely on "sensory reports" (p. 17) and physical experiences, making them interdependent processes. Athenism's videos convey a tension between recognizing the material nature of the brain and undermining its importance. In *Athene's Theory of Everything*, the narrator noted, "nothing is external," because reality is merely "a global network of neurochemical reactions," seemingly acknowledging the role of biology and the body but also attempting to separate the internal from the external (AtheneWins, 2011, 15:50, 20:20). The neural pathways of the brain define decision-making, dictate actions, and produce "consciousness" (AtheneWins, 2011, 9:10). Because individuals have a body to inhabit and mental activity to sustain it, they exist and are capable of building a network with people across the world.

Indeed, the positive effects that happen because of clicking (i.e., increased intelligence, quitting vices, creating a utopia) are physical manifestations of change. Athenism thus defines success for the faith through its effects on the world. Athenism argues that once people free themselves from their core values, they realize that the "only thing that is worth living for is to have a positive *impact* on life itself" (Nikitoss377, 2017, para. 2, emphasis added). In his click testimony, Ramos (2016) argued that once clicked, "I felt more connected with people" (9:28). Clicking not only creates effects in the real world, but it also grows an existing, populated community of other like-minded people. Reading Athenism's tenets and converting to them, followers cannot help but acknowledge the physical effects of clicking and Athenism's existence as a network of individuals. Athenism fosters "an individualized communal experience" (Campbell, 2012, p. 70) where people identify as a single member of Athenism, logging on and sharing information, and as part of a "collective" that defines the faith (Ramos, 2016, 10:46). Followers of Athenism are no longer moving through life alone, but are an integral part of a global network dedicated to improving the world through logic. Athenism embraces technology's ability to reimagine "the superficial facticity of flesh" (Dejmanee, 2013, p. 7) as subservient to a network of minds united throughout the world. Athenism's followers might imagine themselves as "an ultimate self untied at last from all dependency" (Haraway, 1991, p. 151), but their performance of Athenism's tenets invokes the importance of bodies, the physical, and the integration of the mind into both. As Haraway (1991) argued, "The boundary between the physical and non-physical is very imprecise" (p. 153). In engaging the mind and condemning the urges of the body, Athenism attempts to draw a line where none logically occurs.

Conclusion

Athenism argues that the faith will create a "new era for humankind," where logical, scientific thinking replaces the pleasures of the body (AtheneWins, 2016d, 23:24). Through their reliance on cybernetic dynamics to share their message and gain followers, Athenism arguably functions as a wholly virtual religion. Athenism certainly lacks many of the physical elements of traditional faith and must use conversion arguments to gain followers without the aid of offline communities or physical proximity. But even without offline interactions, Athenism incorporates the physicality of technology, bodies, and actions. Technological connections that are made possible through physical and mental labor fuel the faith. Athenism's emergence and dissection of the mind-body dualism should prompt further exploration of how religious networks function and create communities online. What seems clear, however, is that Athenism highlights the interdependence of mental adherence and physical performance in establishing religious networks, whether in existence offline or online.

References

AtheneWins. (2011, January 23). Athene's theory of everything [Video file]. Retrieved from https://you tube.com/watch?v=dbh5l0b2-0o&t=933s

AtheneWins. (2016a, October 20). *LOGIC NATION: A psychological revolution* [Video file]. Retrieved from https://youtube.com/watch?v=drcseH-7hpw

AtheneWins. (2016b, November 7). Are we controlled by a monkey? [Video file]. Retrieved from https://youtube.com/watch?v=Bl06hyehxfE

AtheneWins. (2016c, November 14). 4 steps to change your life & the world [Video file]. Retrieved from https://youtube.com/watch?v=lb0dLkxCPvo

AtheneWins. (2016d, November 23). *Science finds God (documentary/sci-fi short film)* [Video file]. Retrieved from https://youtube.com/watch?v=SXDw73rToPE&t=38s

Campbell, H. A. (2005). Making space for religion in internet studies. *The Information Society: An International Journal, 21*(4), 309–315. doi:10.1080/01972240591007625

Campbell, H. A. (2012). Understanding the relationship between religion online and offline in a networked society. *Journal of the American Academy of Religion, 80*(1), 64–93. doi:10.1093/jaarel/lfr074

Castells, M. (2007). Communication, power and counter-power in the network society. *International Journal of Communication, 1*, 238–266. Retrieved from http://ijoc.org

Dejmanee, T. (2013). Bodies of technology: Performative flesh, pleasure and subversion in cyberspace. *Gender Questions, 1*(1), 3–17. Retrieved from http://hdl.handle.net/10520/EJC167619

Edbauer, J. (2005). Unframing models of public distribution: From rhetorical situation to rhetorical ecologies. *Rhetoric Society Quarterly, 35*(4), 5–24. doi:10.1080/02773940509391320

Goodnight, G. T. (2016). Argumentation and the cybersphere. In R. Von Burg (Ed.), *Dialogues in argumentation: Windsor studies in argumentation vol. 3* (pp. 83–104) [E-reader version]. University of Windsor, Ontario: Windsor Studies in Argumentation. doi:10.22329/10.22329/wsia.03.2016

Haraway, D. (1991). A cyborg manifesto: Science, technology and socialist-feminism in the late twentieth century. In *Simians, cyborgs, and women: The reinvention of nature* (pp. 149–181). New York, NY: Routledge.

Jononetwothree. (2017). Re: Questions i need answered [Reddit post response]. Retrieved from https://reddit.com/r/Makingsense/comments/663783/questions_i_need_answered/

Juris, J. S. (2012). Reflections of #Occupy everywhere: Social media, public space, and emerging logics of aggregation. *American Ethnologist, 39*(2), 259–279. doi:10.1111/j.1548-1425.2012.01362.x

Langer, S. K. (1996). *Philosophy in a new key: A study in the symbolism of reason, rite, and art*. Cambridge, MA: Harvard University Press.

Latour, B. (2005). *Reassembling the social: An introduction to actor-network-theory*. London, United Kingdom: Oxford University Press.

Marshall, C. (2015, February 2). How many views does a YouTube video get? Average views by category. *Tubular Insights*. Retrieved from http://tubularinsights.com

Nikitoss377. (2017, March 3). Death to the world (testimony) [Reddit post]. Retrieved from https://reddit.com/r/Makingsense/comments/5xa1ei/death_to_the_world_testimony/

O'Leary, S. D. (1996). Cyberspace as sacred space: Communicating religion on computer networks. *Journal of the American Academy of Religion, 64*(4), 781–808. Retrieved from http://jstor.org/stable/1465622

Ramos, F. (2016, November 22). Re: Science finds God? [Video file]. Retrieved from https://youtube.com/watch?v=wIKQtTmnRNc

Religion and Electronic Media: One-in-Five Americans Share Their Faith Online. (2014, November 6). *Pew Research Center: Religion & Public Life*. Retrieved from http://pewforum.org/2014/11/06/religion-and-electronic-media/

Wellman, B., & Hampton, K. (1999). Living networked on and offline. *Contemporary Sociology, 28*(6), 648–654. Retrieved from http://jstor.org/stable/2655535

Zappen, J. P. (2005). Digital rhetoric: Toward an integrated theory. *Technical Communication Quarterly, 14*(3), 319–325. doi:10.1207/s15427625tcq1403_10

44

"NASTY WOMEN"

"Dialectical Controversy," *Argumentum Ad Personam,* and Aggressive Rebuttals

G. Thomas Goodnight

As a general rule, half an ounce of will is more effective than a hundred-weight of insight and intelligence.

— Schopenhauer. *The Art of Being Right,* 1831

Eristic argument constitutes a dialogue type when reasoning goes terribly wrong. Strategically driven interlocutors strive for victory and work to disguise weakness. The 19th century German philosopher Arthur Schopenhauer (1896) postulated that the success of arguing depended most basically on an individual's will to be right. He defined "dialectical controversy" as a species of eristic argument that moves from a personal confrontation to a public exchange before audiences. When arguers are losing a position, they reach into a bag of tricks in order to ward off any appearance of being wrong. Pessimist, misogynist, and an exponent of *kultur*, Schopenhauer (1896) observed that the successes of arguers depended on the will of reasoners to assert that they are right and to maintain their positions, regardless. Strategies are necessary to protect the appearances of being right; after all, time is limited, facts tricky, and reasoning complicated. So, sometimes one may be wrong, but an admission of error only leaves asserted reasons vulnerable to quarrelling by an opponent. Stratagems appear necessary to forestall such unproductive encounters. Wit sharpens will. Word-wise and worldly, arguers must be. The will to win trumps the opposition. Success requires observation, sketching tricks, and assembling a repertoire of preferred retorts. So, stratagems that work to secure a victor's triumph are valuable. Those that expose the vulnerabilities of losers may be even more useful.

Schopenhauer's philosophical views are one thing; his estimates of human interaction are quite another. Taken at face value, human thinking routinely promises more than it delivers. Minds operate like parallel clocks, but experiences among people do differ. The individual is the seat of reasoning. Situations embody complications. Fact and opinion mix. False beliefs abound, unsound inferences multiply, and conclusions have impact, even when utterly false. Argumentation persists as flawed practice among the general population and elites alike.

Pessimists presume that the mind is subject to the vicissitudes of time and that intellectual insecurity marks persons driven with vanity. Routinely, reasoners remain more or less sure of what they know as fact and proud of their personal opinions. Thus, all arguers perforce are reluctant to admit mistakes. Of course, an arguer finds it more convenient to start out with complete facts, good reasons, and sound claims, but truth is neither necessary nor usually at work in any particular encounter. Interlocutors may find themselves opposed, questioned, refuted, and embarrassed. Opportunistic opposition should not receive much recognition. Even if refutation of a given point is accurate, advocates should be loath to admit error. Even when uttering a flawed supporting claim, circumstances may prove an arguer right in the long run. Other means of winning an argument are available. The odds are that in the rush of time, indeed, any reasoner may have overlooked a detail. People being what they are, admission of an ill-considered statement will result in a wide, specious diversionary attack that drags down the whole edifice. Charity remains at home. Attacks on others are always useful. Gestures of disrespect do come naturally, but arguers must carefully assemble and deploy the tools of disagreement with tactical surprise, like the Roman general Scipio's attack on the city of Carthage.

For Schopenhauer, argument as an act of will always rests upon being right, which demands never conceding that one's facts or opinions are wrong. Audiences characteristically are gullible and likely to believe anything that flatters immediate interests; thus, "tricks" work, and practiced routines may refine them. If difficult-to-answer objections arise, advocates should put their opponents in a suspicious or false light to avoid having themselves under scrutiny, attack, or shadowed by doubt. Fallacious appeals are natural to the course of affairs. True, sometimes things can go too far. Clash spirals out of control, but sophisticated cunning can avoid duels, violence, and scandals.

Schopenhauer (1913) authored an infamous tract on women that essentially described the sex as limited to flat household reasoning abilities with no place in the public sphere. Philosophers ignored or rationalized Schopenhauer's essay on women with great difficulty, and so refrained from reading his views on women and eristic as mutually re-enforcing (e.g., see Grimwood, 2008; Hamlyn, 1980; Janaway, 1999). Yet, Schopenhauer's explorations in sexism and pessimism literally furnished materials for concocting a manual for authoritarian, paternalistic, repressive argument practices. "Dialectical controversy" shapes a non-emancipatory cultural space that enables, trains, and encourages reasoners to cut off all others from entering into meaningful disagreements. The classic, balanced legal distinction between argument *in rem* (to the matter) and *in personam* (to the individual) becomes inverted. Dialectical controversy shapes an exchange when interlocutors feel compelled to protect and extend authority by diverting attention from issues at hand to insults in the offing. A type of ad hominem, *ad personam,* propels debate away from questions of facts in relation to source and toward attacks on the worth on a competitor.

Eristic argument rules when arguers razor difference. *Ad personam* is ready at hand, Schopenhauer believed, as the stuff of everyday exchange. It is useful to elites when challenging one another and when status is at issue before audiences. *Ad personam* violates intentionally basic politeness rules of communication. Venal speech acts trample norms of communication. Informal venal speech acts are ambiguously playful, accidental, perhaps a matter of bad manners, or mistaken propriety. Public relations professionalize eristic politics by emphasizing the negative, the gain in deploying dismissive gestures. Negative arguments spin out wicked tricks that demean an opponent. Venal speech acts strive to secure a candidate's own credibility, status, and trustworthiness through the downgrading, humiliating, mocking and/ or stigmatizing of opponents and their alleged associates.

Dialectical Controversies and the 2016 Presidential Campaign

A presidential debate is a performance of argument between candidates. The exchange occurs in a variety of negotiated formats. Debates are publicized events. Newspapers reprint quotations and provide lead-up and follow-on stories. Radio provokes call-in responses. Media networks present live debates. Televised debates serve as campaign markers. Journalists gather enthusiastic appraisals of performance to warm the heart and spur the horse race. Debates feature a host of party spokesmen, celebrities, and viewing rooms that provide "spin" for the media (Fridkin, Kenney, Gershon, & Serignese Woodall, 2008).

Still, in 2016, spin draws publicity. Celebrity evaluations rushed along with citizen commentaries to percolate disputes within and across networks. Social media platforms generated strings of iterations, retorts, and repeats. Debates furnished the occasion for partisan fans to offer rejoinders. These heterogeneous accumulated retorts exhibited patterns, then became gathered, amplified, and interwoven into stories to fit and fill mass media venues. Opponents issued acts of rebuke, charged inconsistencies, and conjectured alternatives. Such rebuttals clipped pieces of sentences together, and wound the excerpts into various emotional, moral, ethical, and personal petite-rebuttals (responses included those from robots, hackers, and trolling spew). The news pounded mayhem into a story that, in turn, built and passed along narratives out of discourse pieces.

This essay analyzes the host of mini-rebuttals to a venal speech act in the last 2016 presidential election debate as "dialectical controversy." Donald Trump trashed politeness norms and met throngs of networked rebuttalists who aggressively responded during the campaign and inauguration. In the final presidential debate of the 2016 election, Hillary Clinton worked her way through a number of routine policy talking points. They included how the public would have to pay higher taxes, including Trump unless he could figure a way out of them as he had bragged about doing in the past. Turning to the camera, jaw set, Trump intoned, in the voice and gesture of a private aside: "Such a nasty woman." Clinton did not respond to the interjection, nor even appeared to have heard the remark: unruffled, she pressed onward. The last debate rambled to its finish in undistinguished fashion, as the speakers downplayed policy details, while balancing use of *in rem* and *ad personam* contestation.

Secretary Clinton's fans noticed and responded. Platforms lit up (Chan, 2016; Keith, 2016). Word-flicked, quick-quipped, and phrased retorts rebutted Trump's claim. Chan (2016) provided examples of diverse, pointed, passionate tweets (aphoristic counter epithets in this case) that swirled quickly into an information cascade. Some pointed out Trump's debate-night hypocrisy: "Trump just said no one respects women more than him, but just called Hillary a 'nasty woman' #debatenight" (Lewis, 2016). Others offered advice: "The election is over, but Trump needed to do 1 thing tonight: modestly increase his support from women" (Fratto, 2016). Still others attributed low character to Trump: "It's like he has a[n] alarm that goes off when he hasn't said anything mean in a few minutes" (Bell, 2016), while one respondent reported her own trauma: "My mouth fell open. I'm utterly shocked that a boorish misogynist of this caliber is on that stage" (Penny, 2016). Another posed a vicious equivalence: "The only person with more respect for women than Donald Trump is Bill Cosby" (Handler, 2016), while one crossed over to disgust: "My stomach literally churned as he snarled 'what a nasty woman.' That moment just won't leave me" (Wolfers, 2016).

The word "nasty" multiplied virtual speech acts across the web—first in shock, then in an unstoppable cascade of support, as Clinton's fans claimed the insult as their own. Another blogging journalist echoed Griggs (2016): "Overnight, his insult became a battle cry for Mrs. Clinton's partisans – including many whose passions she had not yet stirred

[…] More than 8,000 people had taken up the phrase on Twitter by midafternoon, wielding it as a badge of honor" (Stockman, 2016, para. 6). Celebrities piled on the Tweets (Marcus, 2016). *Time* online quickly made available Trump's speech act and contrasted it with the Republican candidate's earlier comment about Vladimir Putin's assessment of Clinton (Berenson, 2016). Would counter-tweets, that is, these acts of rebuttal, move quickly from questioning to turning tables to the *ad personam* assault? Election debates are citizen performances (Asen, 2004). Public arguers must not only refute the matters at hand, but also rebut *ad personam* attacks. Refuting matters of fact and opinion are important. Confronting gestures of disrespect are important, too. Any act of rebuttal necessarily performs a gesture of opposition. Acts of rebuttal can range from passive resistance to aggressive counters.

Journalists conventionally report debates by polling outcomes. Who won? Who lost? After the third debate, these questions were less riveting than speculation on whether "nasty woman" or "bad hombre" would rouse voters (McCann & Bromwich, 2016). Arguers reiterate, repeat, and elaborate acts of rebuttal. For example, one source summed: "*People Magazine* called the 'nasty woman' moment a 'battle cry.' *Vox's* Liz Plank branded the insult the 'best thing Donald Trump has ever done for [Clinton's] campaign.' Bustle called it 'the female empowerment message Donald Trump didn't mean to inspire'" (Gray, 2016, para. 4). *The Huffington Post* provided add-on proof by promoting a survey of readers responding to if and why they identified as "nasty women," "Women responded in force, tweeting #IAmANasty-WomanBecause along with calls for solidarity, LGBTQ rights, education, racial sympathy, reproductive health care, and, yes, a woman in the White House" (Gray, 2016, para. 5). Janet Jackson's song of a similar name found renewed popularity (Ali, 2016). The dig became a "rallying cry." Aggressive rebuttals worked to turn tables on the epithet, materially repurposing symbols in ways that repeated and varied acts of opposition. The rebuttal gestures were recast into objects of display (pictures, clothing, exhibits, badges, posts) that the internet made available (Hatch, 2016), including: a "Make America Nasty Again" red baseball cap, a black tea-shirt with red (nasty), white (women) and blue (vote) front, a profiled coffee mug with nasty (black) and women (pink), and a pair of election pins "Nasty Women" and "Bad Hombres" expressing solidarity. Aggressive rebuttals became fashionable apparel for a time. Anticipation built for an art show and a book series. *National Public Radio* (Keith, 2016) opined optimistically that finally "sexism was out in the open" in the national campaign, adding to the public's view several ugly extensions of the Trump insult. "Nasty women" became a global venue of art exhibits ("Nasty Women," n.d.).

Elizabeth Warren predicted that "nasty women" would defeat Trump on election day, thus converting "such a nasty woman" to "nasty women" (quoted in Gambino & Roberts, 2016). The shift of the vowel "a" to "e" converted the *ad personam* singular into an *ad rem,* a collective plural identified as voters. The rebuttal to the venal speech act featured dropping two words and a shift of two letters. Allies brandished the name, but candidate Clinton did *not* take up these rebuttal acts. The rallying cry had force, raising the stakes of the election with affective lines of difference articulated through Trump's discursive moment. Generally, the populist election crowds played through Trump's invitation to unleash a carnival of insults, barbs, and name-calling. Network news underplayed issues, floundered over balance, reveled in controversy, and abandoned policy (Boehlert, 2016). Thus, the mass media serially channeled Trump's venal speech acts into polarizing episodes, nationalist ideographs, and dog-whistle politics—feeding a hot midwest mix of fervor and alienation.

Post-election, "nasty women" (mashed up with other rebuttals to the War on Women and sexism) continued as a battle cry in the Women's March on Washington, January 16,

2017. Ashley Judd delivered a passionate speech (Kelley, 2017), reading a slam poem that asked the question: Who was it that was really nasty? As Just Jared (2017) explained,

> The 48-year-old actress also opened up about how she was angered by family members who voted for Trump despite his scandals coming to light. "For me, it's not about the wall, it's not about any of that stuff," Ashley said. "It's about, you voted for a p-ssy grabber. You voted for someone who calls his wife a piece of ass, whose daughter is his favorite sex symbol. It really boils down, to me, to the sexual assault and misogyny piece."
>
> *(para. 2)*

Judd's speech continued rebuttal exchange, taking up argument with citizens who voted for the President. Apparently, sexism was not key to the electoral decision, for 53% of American white women voted for Trump, together with his predominantly white male constituency. Name-calling remained a staple of the Trump campaign and continued in tweets of governance (Kellman, 2017). The polls predicted a Clinton victory. Ninety-five percent of over 500 papers in the United States supported Clinton; fewer than 5% came out for Trump ("Newspaper Endorsements," n.d.). The power of a Commander-in-Chief, Chief Executive, and Republican party leader who claims to "be right" all the time will not admit a mistake, back down, or concede to facts is a phenomenon that challenges argumentation studies to rethink its understandings of democracy and citizen performance.

Rethinking Dialectical Controversy

Arthur Schopenhauer (1896) himself recognized that acts of will generate sticky outcomes. He retained his pessimistic views of human nature and women, nor did he repudiate openly his lists of shaky cons, that is, the stratagems he found successful to deal with the opposition and to gull fans. The philosopher did extrapolate the relational problematics of human social reasoning by observing the habits of prickly furred creatures, however. He defined the "hedgehog's dilemma" from an observation of warm blooded creatures who wished for the comfort of warm-bodied companions on a cold night, but who at the same time did not wish to get to close because of their prickly fur (Prochnik, 2007). By analogy, refutation is a neutral act of response to a pro or con assertion; rebuttal is an act where gestures of opposition signal a refusal. *Argument in rem* permits warmth to remain in the relationship, even though analysis can be cold. *Argument ad personam* raises the heat of argument by making things close and personal. Public debate before is always a risky performance, should things end in the wrong way.

Schopenhauer's hedgehog parable entered the world of psychoanalysis when Freud (1921) referred to it in *Group Psychology and the Analysis of the Ego*. A rebuttal is more than a con position or a mere refutation. Whether passive, active, or aggressive, a rebuttal is a "prickly act" of differing. Disagreement itself flourishes in rebuttal. Communicatively, argument works with and against the needs of distance and intimacy (Gurevitch, 1989). Turning the tables is one form of response to a personal attack. However desirable and adroitly put, quills—brandished in response to assertion—distance. Networks transmit and vary these pricks in expected and unexpected folds. "Nasty women" was an aggressive rebuttal, a gesture of counter-will. The speech act retorted to a raw, venal assault on individual women with a collective response. In the end, the phrase was but one response of many to a series of alt-right personal attacks on diverse American people to restrict and whiten American identity. Authority and identity debates continue in dialectical controversy. Mimetic rivalry pushes venal speech acts into a spiral of one-upmanship (Girard,

2014). Hence, *ad baculum* threatens with increasing frequency and intensity, as Schopenhauer feared. Argument fallacies in practice often exhibit multiple, interactive strategies. Some citizens remain supportive of a president who demands loyalty, dismisses others, embraces strong men, and declares himself to be right. Presidential leadership based on the assertion of right offers a precarious style for a democracy, rested on constitutional checks and balance—on critical argumentation. Venality multiplies. The U.S. Congress dismisses public hearings and regular procedure, while the president attacks citizens from office and mocks the press. A mix of opportunistic politicians and nativist movements claim American nationalism to be right for the world. Scholars of argumentation need to shift the ambit of civic debate away from "being right" toward how to get it right, make it right, and do right by others and ourselves. A commonweal prospers only when transcendent, deliberative horizons grace a democratic public sphere.

References

Ali, L. (2016, October 20). "Such a nasty woman": Trump's debate dig becomes a feminist rallying cry. *Los Angeles Times*. Retrieved from http://latimes.com/entertainment/tv/la-et-nasty-woman-trump-clinton-debate-janet-jackson-20161020-snap-story.html

Asen, R. (2004). A discourse theory of citizenship. *Quarterly Journal of Speech*, *90*(2), 189–211. doi:10.1080/0033563042000227436

Bell, W. K. [@wkamaubell]. (2016, October 19). "Such a nasty woman." - @realDonaldTrump. It's like he has a* alarm that goes off when he hasn't said anything mean in a few minutes. #debate [Tweet]. Retrieved from https://twitter.com/wkamaubell/status/788932816167768065

Berenson, T. (2016, October 19). Watch Donald Trump call Hillary Clinton a "nasty woman." *Time*. Retrieved from http://time.com/4537960/donald-trump-hillary-clinton-nasty-woman-debate/

Boehlert, E. (2016, October 26). Study confirms network evening newscasts have abandoned policy coverage for the 2016 campaign. *Media Matters*. Retrieved from https://mediamatters.org

Chan, M. (2016, October 19). Donald Trump's "nasty woman" comment at the presidential debate sets off social media firestorm. *Fortune*. Retrieved from http://fortune.com

Fratto, T. [@TonyFratto]. (2016, October 19). "Such a nasty woman." The election is over, but Trump needed to do 1 thing tonight: modestly increase his support from women. #debate [Tweet]. Retrieved from https://twitter.com/TonyFratto/status/788931647886520320?ref_src=twsrc%5Etfw&ref_url=http%3A%2F%2Ffortune.com%2F2016%2F10%2F19%2Fpresidential-debate-nasty-woman-donald-trump%2F

Freud, S. (1921). Group psychology and the analysis of the ego. In J. Strachey (Ed. & Trans.), *The standard edition of the complete psychological works of Sigmund Freud, Volume XVIII (1920–1922): Beyond the pleasure principle, group psychology and other works* (pp. 65–144). London, United Kingdom: Hogarth Press and the Institute of Psychoanalysis.

Fridkin, K. L., Kenney, P. J., Gershon, S. A., & Serignese Woodall, G. (2008). Spinning debates: The impact of the news media's coverage of the final 2004 presidential debate. *The International Journal of Press/Politics*, *13*(1), 29–51. doi:10.1177/1940161207312677

Gambino, L., & Roberts, D. (2016, October 25). Elizabeth Warren: "nasty women" will defeat Trump on election day. *The Guardian*. Retrieved from https://theguardian.com

Girard, R. (2014). *The one by whom scandal comes* (M. B. DeBovoise, Trans.). East Lansing, MI: Michigan State University Press.

Gray, E. (2016, October 25). How "nasty woman" became a viral call for solidarity. *Huffington Post*. Retrieved from http://huffingtonpost.com/entry/nasty-woman-became-a-call-of-solidarity-for-women-voters_us_5808f6a8e4b02444efa20c92

Griggs, M. (2016, October 20). How Hillary's fans turned "nasty" around. *Daily Beast*. Retrieved from http://thedailybeast.com

Grimwood, T. (2008). The limits of misogyny: Schopenhauer, "on women." *Kritike: An Online Journal of Philosophy*, *2*(2), 131–145. doi:10.3860/krit.v2i2.854

Gurevitch, Z. D. (1989). Distance and conversation. *Symbolic Interaction*, *12*(2), 251–263. doi:10.1525/si.1989.12.2.251

Hamlyn, D. W. (1980). *Schopenhauer, the arguments of the philosophers*. London, United Kingdom: Routledge & Kegan Paul.

Handler, C. [@chelseahandler]. (2016, October 19). The only person with more respect for women than Donald Trump is Bill Cosby. #debate [Tweet]. Retrieve from https://twitter.com/chelseahandler/status/788921973678088192

Hatch, J. (2016, October 26). 18 perfect pieces of merch for the nasty women in all of us. *Huffington Post*. Retrieved from http://huffingtonpost.com/entry/18-perfect-pieces-of-merch-for-the-nasty-woman-in-all-of-us_us_5807c5c4e4b0b994d4c3705c

Janaway, C. (1999). Introduction. In C. Janaway (Ed.), *The Cambridge Companion to Schopenhauer* (pp. 1–17). Cambridge, United Kingdom: Cambridge University Press.

Just Jared. (2017, January 21). Ashley Judd recites "nasty woman" slam poem at Women's March 2017 [Video file]. *Just Jared*. Retrieved from http://www.justjared.com/2017/01/21/video-ashley-judd-recites-nasty-woman-slam-poem-at-womens-march-2017/

Keith, T. (2016, October 23). Sexism is out in the open in 2016 campaign. That may have been inevitable. *NPR*. Retrieved from http://npr.org

Kellman, L. (2017, January 5). Trump is using campaign-style name-calling on Congress. *U.S. News & World Report*. Retrieved from https://usnews.com/news/politics/articles/2017-01-05/trump-is-using-campaign-style-name-calling-on-congress

Kelley, S. (2017, January 21). Ashley Judd recites "I am a nasty woman" poem at Women's March on Washington [Video file]. *Variety*. Retrieved from http://variety.com

Lewis, P. [@Phil_Lewis_]. (2016, October 19). Trump just said no one respects women more than him, but just called Hillary a "nasty woman." #debatenight [Tweet]. Retrieved from https://twitter.com/Phil_Lewis_/status/788932017656389632

Marcus, S. (2016, October 26). These celebrities killed it on Twitter during the third presidential debate. *Huffington Post*. Retrieved from http://huffingtonpost.com/entry/these-celebs-killed-it-on-twitter-during-the-third-presidential-debate_us_58082f8de4b0180a36e8eaed

McCann, E., & Bromwich, J. E. (2016, October 20). "Nasty woman" and "bad hombres": The real debate winners? *The New York Times*. Retrieved from https://nytimes.com

Nasty Women. Global Art Exhibitions and Activism. (n.d.). *Nasty women exhibition*. Retrieved from http://nastywomenexhibition.org/

Newspaper Endorsements in the United States Presidential Election, 2016. (n.d.). *Wikiwand*. Retrieved from https://wikiwand.com/en/Newspaper_endorsements_in_the_United_States_presidential_election,_2016

Penny, L. [@PennyRed]. (2016, October 19). "Such a nasty woman." My mouth fell open. I'm utterly shocked that a boorish misogynist of this caliber is on that stage. #debatenight [Tweet]. Retrieve from https://twitter.com/PennyRed/status/788931812466712576

Prochnik, G. (2007). The porcupine illusion. *Cabinet Magazine*. Retrieved from http://cabinetmagazine.org/issues/26/prochnik.php

Schopenhauer, A. (1896). *The art of controversy and other posthumous papers* (T. B. Saunders, Trans.). London, United Kingdom: Swan Sonnenschein.

Schopenhauer, A. (1913). On women. In *Studies in pessimism: A series of essays* (T. B. Saunders, Trans.). London, United Kingdom: George Allen.

Schopenhauer, A. (2016, May 23). The art of being right (T. B. Sanders, Trans.). *Wikisource*. Retrieved from https://en.wikisource.org/wiki/The_Art_of_Being_Right

Stockman, F. (2016, October 20). In debate, Hillary Clinton's clarion call for women thrills many. *The New York Times*. Retrieved from https://nytimes.com/2016/10/21/us/politics/hillary-clinton-women.html

Wolfers, J. [@JustinWolfers]. (2016, October 19). My stomach literally churned as he snared "what a nasty woman." That moment just won't leave me [Tweet]. Retrieved from https://twitter.com/JustinWolfers/status/788931601770184708

---

*   The original tweet contains this typo.

45

THE RAGE NETWORK

Form, Affective Arguments, and Toxic Masculinity in Digital Space

Casey Ryan Kelly

In his inaugural address, President Donald Trump interrupted his dark portraiture of American economic ruin with a message to his devoted, yet forlorn, followers:

> The forgotten men and women of our country will be forgotten no longer. Everyone is listening to you now. You came by the tens of millions to become part of a historic movement, the likes of which the world has never seen before.
>
> *(Blake, 2017, para. 11-12)*

Though criticized as disingenuous, the message resonated with those who felt aggrieved by a political system that marginalized a once upwardly mobile working-class (Chalabi, 2016). And although the message was generic, its "implied auditor" (Black, 1970, p. 111) was quite narrow: an aggrieved class of white working-class men who believes that progressive forces of feminism, secularism, and multiculturalism had taken the country from them (Kellner, 2008). Above all, the message registered a powerful political emotion—rage.

Indeed, the plight of the *forgotten man* is part of the argumentative frame of right-wing American populism (Lee, 2006). As the argument goes, the overgrowth of large impersonal institutions has victimized this hard-working middle class male, feckless government bureaucrats have garnished his wages, Wall Street billionaires have shipped his job opportunities overseas, and illegal immigrants have stolen the few jobs that remain. Putatively, man-hating feminists, gold-digging ex-wives, affirmative action programs, political correctness, the social acceptance of queer intimacy, and even television situation comedies that satirize oafish working-class fathers emasculate this forgotten man. Hence, as Kimmel (2013) argued, the forgotten man, for many, warrants a more expansive political agenda that seeks to "restore, to retrieve, to reclaim something that is perceived to have been lost" (p. 21). Profoundly felt intensities structure this political agenda as the "system" has denied these men their jobs, opportunities, enfranchisement, family tranquility, freedom, and their entitled status. In short, the forgotten man is angry, or at least the argumentative frame tells him to feel that way. Of grave concern, anger is an emotion easily attached to reactionary political commitments (Ahmed, 2014).

The forgotten man indexes a contemporary crisis of masculinity that is less about the actual decline of material privilege than it is a perceived sense of slight at the proposition that white men make space for those previously excluded from public life. President Trump's electoral campaign tapped into a boiling cauldron of rage among white men who believed that their country had disposed them. Certainly, President Trump did not invent this present iteration of white male identity politics. But, why is this perceived crisis of masculinity so apparently and profoundly aggressive and bellicose? A cursory examination of the conservative virtual spaces that speak directly to the forgotten man (including Breitbart News, Infowars, and The Blaze) reveal the source, extent, and argumentative qualities of male discontent. Consider article titles such as "Feminism is Poison" (The Blaze), "Feminists 'Waging War on Working Class Men'" (Breitbart), and "Feminism is Designed to End Humanity" (Infowars). This network of websites that predominately white men frequent manufactures a reality where male entitlement is in jeopardy and translates intense feelings of alienation into an acceptable male emotion: rage.

This essay explores what I call the *rage network*, a series of networked internet silos that blogs and online forums constitute to stoke the fears and fantasies of a previously clandestine white male public. Indeed, I suggest that so-called alt-right rhetorics flourish in the cyber enclave where white men can curate their preferred kind of news and information, can digitally mingle with other men who share their identity and concerns, and can maintain their anonymity. Websites such as Infowars and Breitbart News comprise an argument network that cultivates a white male identity politic directed against the threat of so-called feminized society. Pfister (2014) argued that in a networked public, blogs and other online communities have the capacity to shape the contours of public argument by the constant "cycling of affect into public life" (p. 6). At their worst, cyber discourses privilege low expertise and cater to emotional venting, thus circulating public feelings such as rage and frustration against an abstract system putatively designed to dispossess white men of their privilege. Hence, my central argument is that at the level of argument form, alt-right online networks function as *affect generators* or incubators that garner and then translate felt intensities—feelings that are often contrary to facts—into legible emotions that are appropriate for male expression. My purpose in this essay is to establish that the form of arguments in virtual space—both in terms of genre and medium—accounts for the rise of vitriolic expressions of male rage in contemporary public culture.

Rage Media and Argumentative Form

Berry and Sobieraj (2014; Sobieraj & Berry, 2011) observed the rise of outrage media, an emergent collection of websites, blogs, broadcast programs, and talk radio networks that promulgate speculative, often inaccurate, and outrageous stories designed to engender extreme emotive response. This engineered form of media works to "provoke a visceral response from the audience, usually in the form of anger, fear, or moral righteousness through the use of overgeneralizations, sensationalism, misleading or patently inaccurate information, *ad hominem* attacks, and partial truths about opponents" (Sobieraj & Berry, 2011, p. 19). While estimations of the race and gender demographics of web traffic are difficult, Sobieraj and Berry (2011) contended that outrage media tends to over-represent the views of white men and, in turn, their ideal demographic tends to skew white and male. Of these largely opinion-based news sources, internet websites feature the most vitriolic political discourse, particularly far-right websites such as Breitbart News and Infowars. These sites experience an extraordinary amount of web traffic. While Infowars has averaged 20 million visitors per month since 2013 (Seitz-Wald, 2013), Breitbart News has surged from approximately 8 million to 18 million visitors per month following Donald Trump's presidential campaign announcement in the summer of 2015 (Malone, 2016). The sites' content emphasizes grievances of a largely older white male audience, such as losses resulting from special rights for women and minorities and endangered basic constitutional rights resulting from vast governmental conspiracies. Above all, this imagined demographic is mad and their seething anger is seeking an outlet.

Although the posted content on these sites helps shape how viewers perceive and relate to specific political controversies, here, I am concerned primarily with how form contributes to the particular affective response of rage. Form predicates not only what kind of argumentative content populates these virtual spaces, but also the kinds of thoughts, behaviors, and emotions that audiences may mimic. For instance, genres emerge as recognizable, patterned forms of discourse in the public imaginary whose recurring commonalities condition audience expectations and responses. As Campbell and Jamieson (1978) argued, "A genre is composed of a constellation of recognizable forms bound together by an internal dynamic" (p. 21). Through patterned repetitions, forms or genres court affective investments and translate felt bodily intensities into the symbolic. Form—the structural organization of recognizable verbal or visual discourse—cultivates audience expectations and appetites in a manner that exceeds the specific content. Gunn (2012) took the perspective that the rhetorical affect of genres is to deliver the "body-in-feeling" (p. 369) into language, suggesting that form is where bodily intensities meet the symbolic. By affect, here, I mean those pre-discursive intensities that, when they enter the realm of the symbolic through language, are legible to us as emotion or feeling (Ahmed, 2014; Cloud & Feyh, 2015; Rand, 2014). Emotion—rage in this case—is the translation of bodily intensities into a legible form, or an argumentative device that not only expresses but also activates, mobilizes, and aggregates bodily affect.

Form operates, at least, in two senses: genre and medium. In terms of the former, the dominant argumentative form of these websites involves a rant, diatribe, or a harsh and shocking invective that inverts dominant logic, reverses assumptions, and violates decorum. Windt (1972) argued that the diatribe is not beholden to accepted deliberative norms or standards of logical proof; instead the diatribe is a "moral dramaturgy intended to assault sensibilities, to turn thought upside-down, to turn social mores inside out, to commit in language the very same barbarisms one condemns in society" (pp. 7-8). The diatribe discharges ineffable feelings such as anger and frustration into a public language readable as a bitter and cynical lamentation on the existing social and political order, including norms of civility and good will. As a form, the diatribe courts outrage and directs it at an opponent. As an argumentative mode fashioned to purge intense feelings, a rant need not conform to the norms of deliberation: expectations that authors will purge their pent-up feelings and that the audience will share in their pain abound. Indeed, Breitbart and Infowars take advantage of this argumentative form to mobilize their aggrieved male audience members and sustain a rage-driven, political platform. Indeed, the sites' authors rage: against feminism, government, racial minorities, gays and lesbians, transgender people, liberals, or anyone who took "their" country from them. Above all, the male writers of these websites tend to feel their politics.

In terms of medium, the digital format amplifies the capturing and sustenance of rage. Argumentation scholars have begun to explore the impact of emerging communication technologies on public controversies, counterpublic formation, and identity constitution. For example, Riley, Hollihan, and Klumpp (1998) argued, "Internet communities redefine the concept of local concerns, however, as people can begin to form communities with like-minded individuals who share their interests even if they live in different states, cities, or even countries" (p. 205). Networked media not only facilitate the development of new communities across virtual space, they also transform the norms of public discourse. For example, with their relatively low barrier of entry, online spaces operate by different discursive norms, often throwing into question what counts as expertise (Howard, 2008). In one sense, the potential of network media is that it democratizes the public. On the other hand, Riley et al. (1998) observed that virtual democracy also provides a platform for militia movements, survivalists, white nationalists, and other dangerous groups not only to recruit but weigh in on public controversies, in some cases even augmenting the national discourse. And while extreme men's movements seem marginal in their overall societal weight, "the use of electronic resources is heavily skewed toward current power groups and away from marginalized citizens" (Riley, Klumpp, & Hollihan, 1995, p. 259). This claim is not simply based on the demographics of usage, but rather Fraser's (1990) argument that the evolution of new modes of civic participation frequently reinvented and replicated old modes of domination. Hence, those in positions of power and privilege often occlude the democratizing function of internet technologies.

In short, new technologies have made possible new connections between emotion and political arguments, giving white men new spaces to rage about their perceived embattlement. Moreover, internet forums do not simply provide a platform of the expression of male resentment; they privilege the argumentative forms that easily lend themselves toward the expression of rage. Without advancing techno-determinism, a focus on form shows how virtual spaces are uniquely suited for the cultivation of rage. The tragedy is that internet enclaves are also places where women, queer communities, and racial minorities might find new opportunities to organize counterpublics and affirm their identities through vernacular expression. They are also places where white men seek out their own version of identity politics, looking for voice and equality as a response to the perceived leveling of social privileges that come with more democratized communication. As Kimmel (2013) observed,

> The internet provides just such a man cave, a politically incorrect locker room, where you can say whatever you feel like saying without having to back it up with something as inconvenient as evidence and still hide behind a screen of anonymity so that no one knows that you're the jerk you secretly think you might just be. That's a recipe for rage.
>
> *(p. 115)*

Hence, white men, who remain anxious about their status in the world where society has thrown open the gates of public sphere, turn to those same virtual communication tools to vent their concerns. Adding to Kimmel's earlier insights, this essay suggests that a focus on the affect of argumentative form in virtual space explains how the technological interface of the internet helps amplify feelings that were previously occluded or made taboo by the communicative norms of public dialogue.

Affect Generators

Can rage sustain a political community? Indeed, for those who perceive themselves as aggrieved, rage can be cathartic. Rage can form the basis of a self-replicated and oppositional identity that aggregates and affirms an audience of the like-minded. For instance, Palczewski (2001) considered the emergence of online counterpublics as largely consummatory. That is to say the rhetorical significance of virtual communities is less about their direct engagement with the state to achieve specific instrumental goals than about how their discourses function as a form of ritualized community self-address with the purpose of gathering the like-minded (see also Lake, 1983). Working from this assumption, I suggest that what I call the rage network is imitative of marginalized online counterpublics, organized less around a specific demand politics than it is about suturing felt intensities to identity formations. For white men, virtual communities affirm their feelings of victimization and marginalization and translate rage into a politics of resentment.

Indeed, like-minded individuals plug into a web of online communication, affirming their intense feelings of alienation and their collective identity as capable and strong, yet maligned and marginalized men. Like other consummatory rhetorics, a prophetic element structures this virtual community. That is to say, feminized society has putatively cast men aside and emasculated them and, consequently, is sowing the seeds of its own destruction. Hence, no specific demand appears and no master signifiers require occupancy. Instead, the resentment politics anticipate a social cataclysm sometimes avoidable with men, but in many other cases, men are simply preparing for a time when society collapses and they return to their rightful place in society.

As such, the rage network works as a kind affect generator, that is, a web of online communities, right-wing news cites, blogs, and forums that circulate feelings of male alienation and frustration into broader civic life. The network gives men a language for their ineffable feelings and directs those intensities in the form of bitter arguments that function as an odd form of "cultural syncretism" (Ono & Sloop, 1995, p. 21): simultaneously affirmative of white male identity and resistive toward institutions such as the *nanny state* (Gibson & Heyse, 2014). This partly explains the violent turn in expressions of masculinity online. The alt-right's network of online news and community discourse bring ineffable feelings into public culture, feelings built up over a time in which society asks white men to make sacrifices in the name of equality like never before in history. Indeed, the reactionary response is palpable. And while white men have not lost their material standing, the rage network names and give forms to abstract sense of marginalization and alienation. This is not to suggest that men do not suffer; instead, online communities help suture a self-affirming form of white male identity with bitter, vitriolic anger. Like President Trump's quasi-populist argument frame, cyber diatribes are a form awaiting content. And no matter the veracity of the claim presented, the form conditions the audience to respond with incredulity, outrage, and hatred, which taken together are anathema to both reason and gender equality.

References

Ahmed, S. (2014). *The cultural politics of emotion* (2nd ed.). New York, NY: Routledge.

Berry, J. M., & Sobieraj, S. (2014). *The outrage industry: Political opinion media and the new incivility.* Oxford, United Kingdom: Oxford University Press.

Black, E. (1970). The second persona. *Quarterly Journal of Speech, 56*(2), 109–119. doi:10.1080/00335637009382992

Blake, A. (2017, January 20). Donald Trump's full inauguration speech transcript, annotated. *The Washington Post.* Retrieved from https://washingtonpost.com

Campbell, K. K., & Jamieson, K. H. (Eds.). (1978). *Form and genre: Shaping rhetorical action.* Falls Church, VA: Speech Communication Association.

Chalabi, M. (2016, January 8). Trump's angry white men–and why there are more of them than you think. *The Guardian.* Retrieved from https://theguardian.com

Cloud, D. L., & Feyh, K. E. (2015). Reason in revolt: Emotional fidelity and working class standpoint in the "Internationale." *Rhetoric Society Quarterly, 45*(4), 300–323. doi:10.1080/02773945.2014.965338

Fraser, N. (1990). Rethinking the public sphere: A contribution to the critique of actually existing democracy. *Social Text*, *25/26*, 56–80. http://jstor.org/stable/466240

Gibson, K. L., & Heyse, A. L. (2014). Depoliticizing feminism: Frontier mythology and Sarah Palin's "the rise of the mama grizzlies." *Western Journal of Communication*, *78*(1), 97–117. doi:10.1080/10570314.2013.812744

Gunn, J. (2012). Maranatha. *Quarterly Journal of Speech*, *98*(4), 359–385. doi:10.1080/00335630.2012.714900

Howard, R. G. (2008). The vernacular web of participatory media. *Critical Studies in Media Communication*. *25*(5), 490–513. doi:10.1080/15295030802468065

Kellner, D. (2008). *Guys and guns amok: Domestic terrorism and school shootings from the Oklahoma City bombing to the Virginia Tech massacre*. New York, NY: Routledge.

Kimmel, M. (2013). *Angry white men: American masculinity at the end of an era*. New York, NY: Nation Books.

Lake, R. A. (1983). Enacting red power: The consummatory function in Native American protest rhetoric. *Quarterly Journal of Speech*, *69*(2), 127–142. doi:10.1080/00335638309383642

Lee, M. J. (2006). The populist chameleon: The People's Party, Huey Long, George Wallace, and the populist argumentative frame. *Quarterly Journal of Speech*, *92*(4), 355–378. doi:10.1080/00335630601080385

Malone, C. (2016, August 18). Trump made Breitbart great again. *FiveThirtyEight*. Retrieved from https://fivethirtyeight.com

Ono, K. A., & Sloop, J. M. (1995). The critique of vernacular discourse. *Communication Monographs*, *62*(1), 19–46. doi:10.1080/03637759509376346

Palczewski, C. H. (2001). Cyber-movements, new social movements, and counterpublics. In R. Asen & D. C. Brouwer (Eds.), *Counterpublics and the state* (pp. 161–186). Albany, NY: State University of New York Press.

Pfister, D. S. (2014). *Networked media, networked rhetorics: Attention and deliberation in the early blogosphere*. University Park, PA: Pennsylvannia State University Press.

Rand, E. J. (2014). "What one voice can do": Civic pedagogy and choric collectivity at Camp Courage [Special issue]. *Text and Performance Quarterly*, *34*(1), 28–51. doi:10.1080/10462937.2013.853825

Riley, P., Hollihan, T. A., & Klumpp, J. F. (1998). The dark side of community and democracy: Militias, patriots and angry white guys. In J. F. Klumpp (Ed.), *Argument in a time of change: Definitions, frameworks, and critiques* (pp. 202–207). Annandale, VA: National Communication Association.

Riley, P. Klumpp, J. F., & Hollihan, T. A. (1995). Democratizing the lifeworld of the twenty-first century: Evaluating new democratic sites for argument. In S. Jackson (Ed.), *Argumentation and values: Proceedings of the ninth SCA/AFA conference on argumentation* (pp. 254–260). Annandale, VA: Speech Communication Association.

Seitz-Wald, A. (2013, May 2). Alex Jones: Conspiracy Inc. *Salon*. Retrieved from http://salon.com/2013/05/02/alex_jones_conspiracy_inc/

Sobieraj, S., & Berry, J. M. (2011). From incivility to outrage: Political discourse in blogs, talk radio, and cable news. *Political Communication*, *28*(1), 19–41. doi:10.1080/10584609.2010.542360

Windt, T. O., Jr. (1972). The diatribe: Last resort for protest. *Quarterly Journal of Speech*, *58*(1), 1–14. doi:10.1080/00335637209383096

46

POLEMIC PLATFORMS AND THE "WOMAN CARD"

Trumping Truth with Enthymemes in the Twitterverse

Joan Faber McAlister

Public forums are still discussing the role of social media in the 2016 presidential election, as Donald Trump's use of Twitter during his campaign attracted widespread critical attention. Dubbed the "Tweeter in Chief" in online press accounts of his unique style of campaign communication (O'Rourke, 2017; Timm, 2017; Williams, 2017), President Trump has become a focal point in popular analyses of the changing nature of political persuasion and public argumentation in the digital age. Using Trump as an apocalyptic exemplar, Ott (2017) proclaimed, "Twitter infects public discourse like a social cancer. It destroys dialog and deliberation, fosters farce and fanaticism, and contributes to callousness and contempt" (p. 60).

This essay brings together current concerns about the influence of social media in politics, the impoverishment of political deliberation, and the disadvantages of a virtual polis to consider important features of Donald Trump's use of Twitter. Drawing attention to social power dynamics of arguments staged on social media platforms, I focus on Trump tweets critiquing women adversaries and responding to charges of sexism and sexual assault. These brief statements rely on followers to supply problematic premises, illustrating why the classical enthymeme may be as helpful as the digital meme for analyzing 2016's gendered political appeals. I then reflect on how Twitter's extension of (rather than departure from) established patterns in persuasion further entrenches urgent ethical concerns.

Social media fosters distinctive experiences of immediacy (Kaun & Stiernstedt, 2014) and intimacy (Jiang, Bazarova, & Hancock, 2010) that shape online communication in complex ways. Moreover, internet platforms may encourage confrontation (Hmielowski, Hutchens, & Cicchirillo, 2014), quickly gratifying rhetors with mass circulation of messages comprised of emotional, reactionary, and negative commentary (Stieglitz & Dang-Xuan, 2013; Thelwall, Buckley, & Paltoglou, 2010). Digital media research is mapping how virtual politics shift the grounds of deliberation into dangerous new territory, but emergent platforms still draw on old rules of the electoral game—rules that have always rewarded efficacy over veracity.

Declarations that society has just entered the era of post-truth politics notwithstanding, my grandmother (born in 1897) would not find the fact that politicians lie and that voters rely on prejudices more often than proofs to be news. If the golden era of truth and morality in politics is more than a century old, the time for mourning the passing of this historical (or mythic) age is over. We need to focus on the present.

To illuminate argumentative strategies inflecting gender politics in Trump's recent use of Twitter, I highlight three different themes in tweets that @realdonaldtrump sent to address women adversaries between December 2015 and January 2017. When analyzed through the lens of argumentation, these tweets operate enthymematically, exploiting popular presumptions regarding gender, common views of women, and familiar accounts of femininity and masculinity. The enthymeme's ability to bury premises that may be unutterable and unchallenged for a popular audience is crucial, considering how Trump's campaign made use of Twitter's 140-character format to advance assertions in place of arguments. A closer look at the logic of these tweets illustrates how they harvested antiquated sexisms while sowing new strains of gendered exclusion in U.S. political culture. Trump's tweets both re-sourced and refashioned misogynistic caricatures of women for an unprecedented (and growing) audience who followed his statements via social media and the popular press.

Key themes explicitly engaging gender politics in Trump's Twitter use included accusing female critics of taking unfair advantage by playing the "woman card," characterizing the presidency in masculine and patronizing terms, and depicting women as dishonest and sexual assault as something women earned. Below, I address how significant messages sent from Trump's Twitter account employed these themes, drawing out flawed premises from followers unwilling or unable to challenge them. In so doing, these statements deployed doxastic logics difficult to denounce and central to gendered social hierarchies that have long privileged wealthy white men at the expense of all other voices in a purportedly democratic political culture.

#1 Playing the Woman Card

The Trump account sent three notable tweets to make use of the concept of the "woman card," insinuating that women who referenced gender or sexism in politics were demanding special treatment, exploiting an unfair advantage, and/or making voter appeals based on gender alone. A tweet sent on December 23, 2015 accused Hillary Clinton of this maneuver in response to her labeling some Trump remarks as sexist (Cook, 2015); Trump's account repeated this charge on May 6, 2016: "Constantly playing the women's card - it is sad!" A similar assertion, sent on May 11, 2016, alleged that Elizabeth Warren imitated Clinton in this regard and was sent following an adversarial Twitter exchange during which Warren derided Trump for launching sexist personal attacks against women who defied him (Stelter, 2016).

"Woman card" and "race card" accusations deploy distinct cultural resources but operate similarly, and they link to contemporary media coverage of Clinton and Barack Obama in 2008 and 2016 (Caughell, 2016a; Lee & Morin, 2009). The card metaphor once referred to coded racist or sexist appeals to conservative white voters (Lee & Morin, 2009), but it has more recently replaced substantive arguments with allegations that a candidate is claiming victim status for political advantage (Falk, 2013). This strategy effectively turned the woman/race card charge into a red herring distraction or an ad hominem attack that nevertheless may be damaging, even without any evidence that the accused had invoked gender or race. In other words, a woman/race card charge can function as a coded sexist/racist appeal (subtly reminding voters of the underrepresented status of the target candidate) while deflecting potential blame for making such appeals.

Moreover, women who mention sexism (or who frame a campaign as historically significant in the context of past gender inequity) become particularly vulnerable to woman card rhetoric, yet gain no actual advantages from voters "who do not believe gender inequalities exist or that the government should address such inequalities" (Caughell, 2016b). Scholars have similarly found that race card rhetoric relies on audiences to supply well-known premises of pervasive post-racial discourse fostered within cultural settings in which whiteness is an unquestionable but also invisible advantage. Such charges function in circumstances where historical amnesia cloaks painful legacies of injustice, where idealized notions of equality find close adherents, and where progressive social change arguably stems from benefiting some selected groups at the expense of everyone else (Lee & Morin, 2009). These conditions cast white men as victims who have the most to lose when women or racial minorities make gains.

Given such contexts, woman card rhetoric subtly resources both sexist and idealist premises, while overtly appealing to male voters' self-interests and female voters' resistance to stereotypic characterizations of their voting patterns (that is, women rejecting the assumption that candidate gender will determine their decisions). At the same time, it makes explicit mentions of gender inequality risky, while obscuring male privilege and protecting candidates whose heightened performances of masculinity may provide political advantage. This dichotomy became important during the Trump campaign, as Trump attacked female adversaries who accused him of sexism, sexual harassment, or sexual assault for playing the woman card, while his boasting about his sexual exploits in public (Barrett, 2016) and the size of his penis during a national presidential debate (Bruton, 2016) did not solicit widespread charges that he was playing the "man card."

#2 The Man in Charge

Trump's tweets dismissing the central role of gender in politics posed a performative contradiction when viewed against his use of masculine imagery of the Office of the President and his description of feminine disqualifiers in his opponent. Trump's statements relied on followers to supply historically and culturally established associations between maleness and an office a woman has never occupied to make the case that Trump's opponent was unfit for the role of commander-in-chief.

Trump drew succinctly on gendered assumptions about his female opponent's inability to serve while exploiting heroic protector/provider figures traditionally coded as male. His account's tweet on December 26, 2015 asserted that Trump would "do far more for women than Hillary," as she lacked the "strength/stamina" required of presidents (Trump, 2015).

Followers need not link this characterization to other attacks questioning Clinton's age and health, as conventional political associations between power, masculinity, and virility abound, while the double standard for females gave an older male opponent, who refused to release his health records, an advantage. Indeed, Trump's status as a televisual entertainer may have allowed him to export Hollywood standards into political campaigns (Guthey, 2016), thereby converting the liability of his public record of infidelity, divorce, and remarriage to progressively younger wives into assets. Given a cultural context combining presidential and entertainment standards, followers can supply the (perhaps unspeakable) premise that only a physically powerful, hyperheterosexual, and gender-conforming man can function as a heroic president who can protect and service women voters—all without risking charges of playing a gender card.

Similarly, a May 6, 2016 tweet credited Clinton's male democratic primary opponent with the observation that she was utterly lacking in leadership qualities, linking this lack to her allegedly endless and pathetic emphasis on gender (Trump, 2016b). This tweet staged two prominent white men engaging in patronizing personal attacks to disqualify Clinton for the presidency and encouraged followers to complete the argument with traditional assumptions about leadership that exhibited measurable patterns of bias (Falk, 2010). The assertion that playing up her gender was Clinton's only gambit, combined with Trump's repeated and widely-publicized claims (supplied one week earlier) that 95% of Clinton's support was attributable to her gender alone, inferred that being a woman constituted her only political asset (Osnos, 2016). This variant of the card metaphor hinted that Clinton was "not playing with a full deck," a colloquialism invoking gendered historical depictions of the hysterical woman, an unhinged and overly emotional figure whom voters could not trust to behave logically or predictably (Scull, 2009).

#3 Women Lie

The October 7, 2016 public circulation of *Access Hollywood's* recorded conversation featured Donald Trump boasting of an uncontrollable penchant for initiating non-consensual sexual contact with women he found attractive (i.e., kissing them and grabbing their genitals without invitation or permission, detailed in the lewdest possible terms), threatening Trump's aspirations of becoming the highest elected official in U.S. government. Following this shocking revelation, *The New York Times* printed polls showing a significant set of voters finding him "ill-suited to the presidency and biased against women and minorities" (Burns & Corasaniti, 2016, para. 20). Although Trump's campaign denied that he had committed those acts that he had described on tape, several women countered by coming forward to accuse him of acts ranging from harassment to assault (Tolentino, 2016).

Two tweets from Trump's account on October 15, 2016 responded to the charges, claiming they were false and fabricated. The tweets foregrounded his accusers' gender in specific ways. The first tweet denied the allegations and suggested that sexual contact with the accusing women was implausible (Trump, 2016c). It also recalled his public remarks that women alleging assault were too unattractive to have drawn his sexual attention (Burns & Corasaniti, 2016). The second tweet asserted that no element of truth existed in the accounts of any of his accusers, with dramatic emphasis on the women's wholesale invention of stories of sexual abuse (Trump, 2016b).

The premises that followers must supply to graft these Twitter statements onto an argument operate in various and troubling ways. Since the tweets do not counter legal evidence or dispute factual testimony, they encouraged Trump's audience to take his word over his female accusers at face value (i.e., he is trustworthy and they are liars). Since Trump neither denied committing the acts he described on tape nor denounced sexual assault in general, the audience could infer that being singled out for Trump's uninvited and nonconsensual sexual attention qualified as a compliment that only some women deserved. The tweets offered no explicit motive for so many women to invent allegations of sexual assault, so followers could supply the motive that seemed most reasonable to them (e.g., money, fame, revenge, mental illness), as U.S. popular media images have long represented women as gold-diggers (Kitch, 2001), fame whores (Jones & Weber, 2015), vengeful hags (Cahill, 2010), and hysterics (Showalter, 1997). The incomplete argument was an asset in this instance, as some sexist statements might be unspeakable on the campaign trail, even for Donald Trump.

Trumping with Enthymeme

As a unique medium, Twitter provides maximum exposure and minimal censoring of very short statements that are most popular when they prompt immediate affects. The form makes them ideal for ad hominem attacks and assertions masquerading as arguments because the 140-character limit excuses the absence of evidence or warrant. The audience must therefore supply most of the needed elements, quickly dividing them into those who will and those who will not follow the implied logic. Hegemonic discourses and deep-seated prejudices will always have the advantage in such a medium, but this is also true of similarly succinct and high profile media (such as the headline, the witty retort, and the sound bite). However, Twitter is unique in the way that it simulates discursive exchange. By allowing claims to circulate and critics to respond, Twitter approximates public debate—without imposing any ethical norms to guide deliberation. In addition, Twitter does not allow the time or the space to present a full case, nor even a complete argument. Analyzing how Twitter displaces, and disguises itself as deliberation, will be an ongoing challenge for argumentation scholars.

No longer a term exclusive to academic rhetoricians, enthymeme's significance as a potent and troubling form of argument has entered the vernacular of popular press outlets now assessing online communication and political culture. *The Guardian* worried that as "the grimy window through which we glimpse our own prejudices" (Shovel, 2015, para. 24), enthymemes will continue to emerge a favorite tool that forges troubling ties between politicians and constituents. Reuters assessed Trump's tendency to leave audiences to complete his statements as both an advantage and a disadvantage, citing his remarks about Fox debate moderator Megyn Kelly. When Trump implied that Kelly was "menstruating and hormonal and therefore irrational," he responded to the ensuing controversy with a denial: "He had never spoken the words" (Flitter, 2016, para. 11). Metro News reported on the importance of this very strategy, noting that enthymeme allowed Trump to dodge dangerous claims that he needed to imply rather that state directly ("The Secret Behind," 2016).

Press articles directly drawing on the literature in argumentation studies—that is, returning to Aristotle, quoting public address scholars, and translating Toulmin for general readers—demonstrate journalists' willingness to turn to the rhetorical tradition to unpack politicians' strategies and styles. The ascendency of social-media savvy candidates is a crucial context for such efforts, even if many problems plaguing contemporary political argument predate platforms like Twitter. Considering the complex elements (old and new, positive and negative) featured in contemporary campaign rhetoric allows us to chart emerging trends without abandoning recurring concerns through fresh perspectives that journey into new territory for argumentation theory and familiar grounds for political ethics. New media studies and new political analysis will always need the perspectives that rhetorical critics and argumentation scholars can offer, as the untold stories of public culture spin out before us, familiar and strange.

References

Barrett, W. (2016, April 17). How Donald Trump used the three women in his life for his own benefit—and pleasure. *New York Daily News*. Retrieved from http://nydailynews.com

Bruton, F. B. (2016, March 4). Trump makes his penis a campaign issue during 2016 debate. *NBC News*. Retrieved from http://nbcnews.com

Burns, A., & Corasaniti, N. (2016, October 14). Donald Trump assails his accusers as liars, and unattractive. *The New York Times*. Retrieved from https://nytimes.com

Cahill, S. (2010). Through the looking glass: Fairy-tale cinema and the spectacle of femininity in Stardust and the Brothers Grimm. *Marvels & Tales*, *24*(1), 57–67. Retrieved from http://jstor.org/stable/41389026

Caughell, L. (2016a). When playing the woman card is playing Trump: Assessing the efficacy of framing campaigns as historic. *Political Science & Policy*, *49*(4), 736–742. doi:10.1017/S1049096516001438

Caughell, L. (2016b, October 17). When playing the woman card is playing Trump: Assessing the efficacy of framing campaigns as historic. *Political Science Now*. Retrieved from http://politicalsciencenow.com

Cook, R. (2015, December 24). Trump warns Clinton about playing the "woman card." *Newsweek*. Retrieved from http://newsweek.com

Falk, E. (2010). *Women for president: Media bias in nine campaigns* (2nd ed.). Urbana, IL: University of Illinois Press.

Falk, E. (2013). Clinton and the playing-the-gender-card metaphor in campaign news. *Feminist Media Studies*, *13*(2), 192–207. doi:10.1080/14680777.2012.678074

Flitter, E. (2016, February 16). Trump is a ———: White House hopeful plays fill-in-the-blanks with voters. *Reuters*. Retrieved from http://reuters.com

Guthey, E. (2016). Don't misunderestimate the Donald (like we did). *Television & New Media*, *17*(7), 667–670. doi:10.1177/1527476416652697

Hmielowski, J. D., Hutchens, M. J., & Cicchirillo, V. J. (2014). Living in an age of online incivility: Examining the conditional indirect effects of online discussion on political flaming. *Information, Communication & Society*, *17*(10), 1196–1211. doi:10.1080/1369118X.2014.899609

Jiang, L. C., Bazarova, N. N., & Hancock, J. T. (2010). The disclosure-intimacy link in computer-mediated communication: An attributional extension of the hyperpersonal model. *Human Communication Research*, *37*(1), 58–77. doi:10.1111/j.1468-2958.2010.01393.x

Jones, J. L., & Weber, B. R. (2015). Reality moms, real monsters: Transmediated continuity, reality celebrity, and the female grotesque. *Camera Obscura*, *30*(1(88)), 11–39. doi:10.1215/02705346-2885431

Kaun, A., & Stiernstedt, F. (2014). Facebook time: Technological and institutional affordances for media memories. *New Media & Society*, *16*(7), 1154–1168. doi:10.1177/1461444814544001

Kitch, C. (2001). *The girl on the magazine cover: The origins of visual stereotypes in American mass media*. Chapel Hill, NC: University of North Carolina Press.

Lee, R., & Morin, A. (2009). Using the 2008 presidential election to think about "playing the race card." *Communication Studies*, *60*(4), 376–391. http://dx.doi.org/10.1080/10510970903109979

O'Rourke, M. (2017, February 1). Donald Trump: Tweeter in chief. *Risk Management*. Retrieved from http://rmmagazine.com

Osnos, E. (2016, April 27). Trump versus Clinton's "woman card." *The New Yorker*. Retrieved from http://newyorker.com

Ott, B. L. (2017). The age of Twitter: Donald J. Trump and the politics of debasement. *Critical Studies in Media Communication*, *34*(1), 59–68. doi:10.1080/15295036.2016.1266686

Scull, A. (2009). *Hysteria: The disturbing history*. Oxford, United Kingdom: Oxford University Press.

The Secret Behind Trump's Speeches? Enthymemes. (2016, February 16). *Metro*. Retrieved from https://metro.us/news/the-secret-behind-trump-s-speeches-enthymemes/zsjpbp—k23opanseo2

Shovel, M. (2015, April 9). Enthymeme, or are you thinking what I'm thinking? *The Guardian*. Retrieved from https://theguardian.com

Showalter, E. (1997). *Hystories: Hysterical epidemics and modern media*. New York, NY: Columbia University Press.

Stelter, B. (2016, May 12). Elizabeth Warren gives Trump a dose of his own medicine on Twitter. *CNN*. Retrieved from http://cnn.com

Stieglitz, S., & Dang-Xuan, L. (2013). Emotions and information diffusion in social media—sentiment of microblogs and sharing behavior. *Journal of Management Information Systems*, *29*(4), 217–248. doi:10.2753/MIS0742-1222290408

Thelwall, M., Buckley, K., & Paltoglou, G. (2010). Sentiment in Twitter events. *Journal of the American Society for Information Science and Technology*, *62*(2), 406–418. doi:10.1002/asi.21462

Timm, J. C. (2017, January 1). Tweeter-in-chief? How Trump campaigned, and will govern, on social media. *NBC News*. Retrieved from http://nbcnews.com

Tolentino, J. (2016, October 20). Trump and the truth: the sexual-assault allegations. *The New Yorker*. Retrieved from https://newyorker.com/news/news-desk/trump-and-the-truth-the-sexual-assault-allegations

Trump, D. J. [@realDonaldTrump]. (2015, December 26). I will do far more for women than Hillary, and I will keep our country safe, something which she will not be able to do-no strength/stamina! [Tweet]. Retrieved from https://twitter.com/realDonaldTrump/status/680947538896252928

Trump, D. J. [@realDonaldTrump]. (2016a, May 6). Crooked Hillary has ZERO leadership ability. As Bernie Sanders says, she has bad judgement. Constantly playing the women's card - it is sad! [Tweet]. Retrieved from https://twitter.com/realDonaldTrump/status/728564631313190912

Trump, D. J. [@realDonaldTrump]. (2016b, October 15). 100% fabricated and made-up charges, pushed strongly by the media and the Clinton Campaign, may poison the minds of the American Voter. FIX! Retrieved from https://twitter.com/realDonaldTrump/status/787244543003467776

Trump, D. J. [@realDonaldTrump]. (2016c, October 15). Nothing ever happened with any of these women. Totally made up nonsense to steal the election. Nobody has more respect for women than me! [Tweet]. Retrieved from https://twitter.com/realDonaldTrump/status/787359730465329152

Williams, B. (2017, January 19). Twitter tips for our tweeter-in-chief @realdonaldtrump (and the rest of us). *CNN*. Retrieved from http://cnn.com

47

FOLLOWING AFFECTIVE WINDS OVER PANMEDIATED NETWORKS

Image-Drive Activism in Chengdu, China

Elizabeth Brunner

Images have long functioned as important argumentative tools for environmental advocates. For decades, organizations like Greenpeace, World Wildlife Foundation, and the Sierra Club have turned to images to raise awareness and incite action, protect charismatic mega-fauna from extinction, and preserve global lands (Delicath & DeLuca, 2003; DeLuca, 1999). Images are integral to protests because they can stoke opposition, circumvent censorship, document resistance, spotlight corruption, and widely disseminate information, as pictures of protestors fly through space before bouncing back down to earth where they appear on millions of screens in locations far from the sites of protests.

Argumentation scholars interested in protests around the globe face the difficult task of how to study visual argument. Images demand different analytical tools than their verbal counterparts, as the travel, appearance, function, and processing of images vary from linear verbal arguments in consequential ways (Birdsell & Groarke, 1996; Finnegan, 2001; Groarke, Palczewski, & Godden, 2016; Smith, 2007). Brunner and DeLuca (2016) offered one approach; for them, scholars examining images from an argumentative perspective should analyze images "via their movement and force" (p. 284) through *panmediated networks* and *affective winds*. Here, I will review current understandings of panmediated networks and affective winds, introduce a new concept—*force majeure*—for studies of networked argument, and illustrate the concept's use in the 2008 Chengdu protests as an abridged case study.

Panmediated Networks, Affective Winds, and Force Majeure

In his essay, Fleming (1996) isolated images-as-arguments and argued that "a picture is incapable of serving independently as an assertion" (para. 24 in HTML full text) and lacks linearity. Groarke et al. (2016), however, responded, "Pictures, especially those that function argumentatively, rarely occur in isolation" (p. 218); thus, they must always be considered in relationship to other arguments, whether those are visual, verbal, or otherwise. Panmediated networks are networks that link people and "objects via online platforms which can transmit a wide array of information, including images, and do so ceaselessly at great speeds" (Brunner & DeLuca, 2016, p. 285). They are marked by immersive spaces of multiple media and highlight image proliferation via technological devices, which create ever more connections and demand that images be examined within these dense flows. Panmediation allows for information, pleas, and disturbances to reverberate across time and space, building upon one another.

Addressing the problem of understanding the force of images outside of reason that Blair (1996), Fleming (1996), Hatfield, Hinck, and Birkholt (2007), and Shelley (1996) discussed, panmediated networks engage affect. Importantly, affect is "not personal feeling but is, instead, the means through which bodies act in context with each other" (Rice, 2008, p. 203). A pre-personal intensity moves bodies to act (Deleuze & Guattari, 1987; Massumi, 1987).

> [Affective winds operate] on a wide range of scales, sometimes as a breeze that stirs local actors to take a photo of an image event and post it to social media and other times stirring thousands of people to march in the streets and demand that a polluting factory be closed.
>
> *(Brunner & DeLuca, 2016, p. 290)*

Images are adept at advancing affective arguments. A focus on affect highlights both the intensities that move people to act, as well as highlighting disturbances resulting from those movements (Brunner & DeLuca, 2016; Massumi, 1987; Tsing, 2015). Such disturbances can reconfigure relationships. Too often, scholars conceptualize arguments as linear and diagrammable, when they are always set within a series of contingencies and conjunctions. Affective winds, Brunner and DeLuca (2016) wrote, "preserve the movement that characterizes *affect*, to circulate among bodies, and to sweep across social media networks" (p. 290), thereby leaving behind the striated spaces of rational argument and delving into the messy complexity of moving bodies. Affective winds flow across panmediated landscapes via moving images, memes, and Graphic Interchange Formats (GIFs).

The concept of force majeure concentrates on the latter strain of affective winds. Force majeure, as applied here, is a type of affective wind characterized by larger mobilizations that leave significant disturbances in their wake and opens striated spaces. In turning to affective winds and panmediation to elaborate, I preserve attention to force, networks, affect, and assemblages, as well as the disruptions they create. The 2008 Chengdu protests will serve as my case study of a force majeure in that the protests disrupted a long-standing tradition of officials ignoring the people for political and economic gain, and they helped generate movement in cities far away in both time and space from the streets of their marches.

Wild Public Networks of Protest in Chengdu

In 2008, the people of Chengdu, China held a protest on the 89th anniversary of the May 4, 1919 protests. The 1919 protests were a landmark event for the democratic movements seeking to restore China as a global leader after decades of oppression and exploitation. Reports estimate that around 500 people gathered in 2008 and, like their predecessors in 1919, the group was composed of largely educated, urban, middle-class residents (Wong, 2008). Modeling in many ways the successful anti-paraXylene (PX) protests in Xiamen a year earlier, the focus of the 2008 protest was a petrochemical plant under construction in Pengzhou located about 18 miles northwest of the city. The people feared that the construction of the plant upstream from Chengdu would pollute their drinking water. They organized a resistance using blogs and Bulletin Board Systems (BBSs), and circumvented censors by calling the protest a *stroll*. The peaceful protest involved participants walking through the streets en mass, with many wearing white face masks. No one carried signs, chanted, or sang. Police broke up the stroll after several hours and arrested or detained six people (Mao, 2008). Ultimately, Chengdu officials cancelled plans for the plant.

While the 2008 protest arguably was a successful deployment of images for activist ends, its value may lie more in its ability to disrupt the political landscape as a force majeure. Since the 1980s Deng Xiaoping's economic reforms prioritized the growth of the nation's gross domestic product. The Chengdu protest functioned as an argumentative disruption that demanded a different ordering of priorities. These protests also represent the impact of a growing panmediated environment on both environmental awareness and activism, as much of the event's force was generated from its travel online.

Force Majeure

The dictionary definition of force majeure highlights three major characteristics of the concept. The first part of the definition, that is, "superior or irresistible force" ("Force Majeure," n.d.) draws attention to protest as a force that is of great magnitude and difficult, if not impossible, to resist. The protest in Chengdu was a force that drew in protestors with affective pleas circulated via blogs and text messages to participate in a highly risky form of protest. The people who walked in the streets wearing masks knew that they risked arrest and detention because the government posted warnings (Baidu, 2008). People also knew from officials' reactions to the 1989 protests in Chengdu that participating in protest could also lead to lost jobs and harassment (Wang, 2015).

After the demonstrations began, both protestors and onlookers documented the event from different angles and then uploaded them to blogs and BBSs, where they gained additional momentum. The images circulating were easily recognizable as pictures of protest because they linked to the Xiamen protests against a chemical plant that occurred the year prior which drew over 10,000 people into the streets, many of whom donned similar masks. Before long, images of people wearing masks moved from the streets of Chengdu to the newsrooms in Beijing where *The Beijing News* picked up the sensitive topic and praised demonstrators for engaging in peaceful protest (Blount, 2011).

Even though the police broke up the stroll through the streets, rowdy online networks animated with messages and images of the event, as well as harsh critiques of leaders, continuing for days and weeks. Citizens on these forums remained firm with their demands. They wanted to stop the plant's construction, but this was no easy task. Protestors and online commentators were challenging a formidable opponent—China's leading state-run oil company, PetroChina, which, as a state-run company, had close ties to the local and national government. The plant represented a $5.5 billion investment, which certainly carried a great deal of financial bonuses for a wide range of employees, making it a difficult project to shut down.

Initially, Chengdu local officials responded to the protests with reassurances in state-run news outlets that promised the project would "install advanced equipment and improve environmental protection facilities with strict pollution prevention" (Wong, 2008, para. 14). They did not anticipate that the so-called *stroll* would continue to generate discontent after it was over and that online protesters would continue to call the officials out for failing to implement such promises. The documentation and critiques culminated into a force that was irresistible and overwhelming for local officials. Pictures proved to the central government hundreds of miles away that people in Chengdu were unhappy and that local officials had failed to follow protocol by conducting an environmental impact statement and releasing it to the public ahead of an open period for comment. The event culminated into a force majeure when it reverberated out far beyond Chengdu's jurisdictions to force officials to act by acquiescing to the people's demands. The protest continued to move and have force long after this instrumental success, because it served as inspiration for people in other far away cities to take to the streets and to their screens in their own panmediated protests over environmental issues.

The second component of the definition of force majeure is that it is "an event or effect that cannot be reasonably anticipated or controlled" ("Force Majeure," n.d.). The protests in Chengdu were unanticipated and uncontrollable as people gathered in the streets and in online forums. Though not characteristic of all environmental protests in China, the Chengdu protests that occurred on the streets were surprisingly peaceful, largely in an attempt to cleverly circumvent laws requiring Chinese citizens to apply for a permit before protesting (which, in all likelihood, the Chinese government would have denied). A gathering without signs and chanting was simply a stroll. Momentum for the protest grew in a largely decentralized fashion, with no single leader or organization emerging as the entity responsible for the event. Rather, plans emerged rhizomatically on online networks via blogs and discussion boards, street corners and break rooms, and through text messages. Once people were gathered in the streets, the police were uncertain as to how to treat this peaceful walk. As a result of creative and strategic protests, the people emerged as difficult to control.

Upon returning home, people engaged in wild and cacophonous online conversations filled with images evidencing the event. The public networks of social media were difficult to control (Brunner, 2017). Conversations filled with critique erupted so quickly and across so many different platforms that they evaded censorship, at least initially (Shen, 2008; Zhou, 2017). Text messages ran rampant and images of silent masked protestors evoked arguments from protests that had preceded the Chengdu event (Wong, 2008). Like the example Groarke et al. (2016) presented, images of masked protestors in Chengdu have "an important relationship to other instances of visual argument" (p. 223) that circulate through panmediated networks to create movement. The pathways forged by banal communication now functioned to spread outrage and incite government response (Mao, 2008; Wan, 2008). The travel of these images generated a force capable of convincing officials to say no to the project and the profits that came with it by exposing their wrongdoing (Liu, 2016).

The third component of a force majeure is its contractual use "to absolve [an entity] from liability" ("Force Majeure," n.d.). A force majeure voids a contract, thereby altering relationships just as a demonstration as a force majeure also creates disruption on such a scale that it forces relationships to change. The protests, by functioning as a disturbance, "open[ed] the terrain for transformative encounters, making new [...] assemblages possible" (Tsing, 2015, p. 160). In the case of Chengdu, the protests altered several relationships. First, it changed the relationship between people and their officials by demanding that the officials reform their corrupt practices. The privileging of GDP above all else guided these practices for too long, including the safety of the people ostensibly served. The people once again had a voice via panmediated networks and officials were pressured to listen and cancel plans for the plant.

Relationships also changed between local and national discourses. The arguments advanced online and on the ground through images and verbal critiques moved Chengdu officials from being a self-contained unit of local cadres (a position Deng Xiaoping's decentralization of power made possible) and forced them into a larger national conversation via media coverage and online networks that connected Chengdu to other cities where environmental protest occurred. All of a sudden, Chengdu, Xiamen, and Shanghai were linked via images and the arguments they advanced, for example, say no to GDP and yes to a clean environment (Brunner, 2017). Chengdu now found itself immersed in a new assemblage of cities that would grow as more people across China protested against pollution of all types that hoisted the city onto a national stage. The images circulating across panmediated environments recreated Chengdu as home to environmental advocates. In subsequent years, people from cities such as Dalian, Guangzhou, Hangzhou, Yinggehai, Maoming, and numerous others would see the images from Chengdu, react affectively to them, and create new relationships through online discourses and advice-seeking with Chengdu (Gottlieb & Ng, 2017).

Affective winds in the form of force majeure create disturbances and disruptions that upset relationships, potentially alter ways of thinking, and introduce new ideas and concepts. Backlash, however, can occur when disruptions are too abrupt. The 2008 protests were the last mass gathering to occur in Chengdu to date. Local officials largely quashed subsequently planned environmental protests in 2013 and 2016 before they even began. Chengdu's repositioning as a site of resistance may have contributed to an intense sensitivity among officials regarding subsequent protests. Though other cities have experienced multiple waves of protest, Chengdu has not. Local officials have repeatedly deployed police officers and erected barriers to quell protests as soon as talk on online forums begins to arise. The force of the 2008 protests, indeed, altered relationships, including those between officials and protesters.

Conclusion

The concept of force majeure can help scholars to trace the various impacts that reverberate out from protest. As one form of affective winds, force majeure concentrates on large-scale movements, but this is not to say these are the only forms of protest that deserve attention. Future theorization of other forms of affective winds will help to better map social movements and the impact of their advanced arguments within a stream of images and texts. For example, following affective winds that continued to move after the 2008 protests can help scholars to better understand more recent protests in Chengdu. Much to the chagrin of local officials, Chengdu's crackdown on protest has not stamped out environmental awareness or attempts at activism. An increasing awareness remains, especially among younger generations, of the harms associated with pollution in Chengdu (Liu & Leiserowitz, 2009). Furthermore, activists unable to protest in the streets have resorted to other creative means of protest traceable via affective winds. In December 2016, discussions of a planned protest vibrated over networks in Chengdu once again. So, too, did anticipation of police presence and blockades, which did subsequently occur. The night before the protests, under the cover of darkness, protestors deployed a different tactic. Rather than using live bodies to express their concern, creative protestors placed masks on statues throughout the city. Authorities could not arrest, detain, or jail these immobilized bodies. The images of these statues, however, were incredibly mobile and made their way from the streets of Chengdu to Beijing, Xi'an, Europe, the United States, and Australia. Again, the masks were effective in this silent protest. The central claim became clear: People wanted their officials to do something about air pollution, and pictures of masked statues connected to the protests almost a decade earlier were the most efficient way to spread that message across wild public networks.

References

Baidu. (2008, May 10). 2008 Chengdu City against the PX project event. Retrieved from https://baike. baidu.com

Birdsell, D. S., & Groarke, L. (1996). Toward a theory of visual argument. *Argumentation and Advocacy*, *33*(1), 1–10. Retrieved from https://public.wsu.edu/~ericsson/birdandgroar.pdf

Blair, J. A. (1996). The possibility and actuality of visual arguments. *Argumentation and Advocacy*, *33*(1), 23–39. Retrieved from http://bcf.usc.edu/~stables/blair.pdf

Blount, P. (2011, April 12). Chinese middle-class and farmers protest petrochemical plant in Chengdu (Chengdu Stroll), 2008. *Global Nonviolent Action Database*. Retrieved from https://nvdatabase.swarth more.edu

Brunner, E. (2017). Wild public networks and affective movements in China: Environmental activism, social media, and protest in Maoming. *Journal of Communication*, *67*(5), 665–677. doi:10.1111/ jcom.12323

Brunner, E., & DeLuca, K. M. (2016). The argumentative force of image networks: Greenpeace's pan-mediated global detox campaign [Special Issue]. *Argumentation and Advocacy*, *52*(4), 281–299. Retrieved from http://tandfonline.com

Deleuze, G., & Guattari, F. (1987). *A thousand plateaus: Capitalism and schizophrenia* (B. Massumi, Trans.). Minneapolis, MN: University of Minnesota Press.

Delicath, J. W., & DeLuca, K. M. (2003). Image events, the public sphere, and argumentative practice: The case of radical environmental groups. *Argumentation*, *17*(3), 315–333. doi:10.1023/ A:1025179019397

DeLuca, K. M. (1999). *Image politics: The new rhetoric of environmental activism*. New York, NY: Guilford Press.

Finnegan, C. A. (2001). The naturalistic enthymeme and visual argument: Photographic representation in the "skull controversy." *Argumentation and Advocacy*, *37*(3), 133–149.

Fleming, D. (1996). Can pictures be arguments? *Argumentation and Advocacy*, *33*(1), 11–22.

Force Majeure. (n.d.). *Merriam-Webster Online Dictionary*. Retrieved from https://merriam-webster.com

Gottlieb, R., & Ng, S. (2017). *The global cities: Urban environments in Los Angeles, Hong Kong, and China*. Cambridge, MA: The MIT Press.

Groarke, L., Palczewski, C. H., & Godden, D. (2016). Navigating the visual turn in argument [Special issue]. *Argumentation and Advocacy*, *52*(4), 217–235. doi:10.1080/00028533.2016.11821871

Hatfield, K. L., Hinck, A., & Birkholt, M. J. (2007). Seeing the visual in argumentation: A rhetorical analysis of Unicef Belgium's Smurf public service announcement. *Argumentation and Advocacy*, *43*(3/4), 144–151. Retrieved from http://tandfonline.com

Liu, C. (2016, December 12). Chengdu city center goes into lockdown as police squash pollution protest before it even starts. *Shanghaiist*. Retrieved from http://shanghaiist.com

Liu, C., & Leiserowitz, A. (2009, July 18). From red to green? Environmental attitudes and behavior in urban China. *Yale Program on Climate Change Communication*. Retrieved from http://climatecommuni cation.yale.edu

Mao, Y. (2008, May 11). 成都警方处罚利用四川石化项目散布谣言者_资讯_凤凰网 [Chengdu police punished the use of Sichuan Petrochemical project to spread rumors]. *Sichuan News Online*. Retrieved from http://news.ifeng.com/mainland/200805/0511_17_533156.shtml

Massumi, B. (1987). Foreword. In G. Deleuze & F. Guattari, *A thousand plateaus: Capitalism and schizo-phrenia* (pp. ix–xv). Minneapolis, MN: University of Minnesota Press.

Rice, J. E. (2008). The new "new": Making a case for critical affect studies. *Quarterly Journal of Speech*, *94*(2), 200–212. doi:10.1080/00335630801975434

Shelley, C. (1996). Rhetorical and demonstrative modes of visual argument: Looking at images of human evolution. *Argumentation and Advocacy*, *33*(2), 53–68. Retrieved from EBSCOhost database.

Shen, J. L. (2008, April 30). 散步, 是一种权利 [Walking is a right; Blog post]. *Shen Jia Lu 1001's blog*. Retrieved from http://blog.sina.com.cn/s/blog_4be1d27f01009d5q.html

Smith, V. J. (2007). Aristotle's classical enthymeme and the visual argumentation of the twenty-first century [Special issue]. *Argumentation and Advocacy*, *43*(3-4), 114–123. Retrieved from http://tandfonline.com

Tsing, A. L. (2015). *The mushroom at the end of the world: On the possibility of life in capitalist ruins*. Princeton, NJ: Princeton University Press.

Wan, S. (2008, May 6). 成都"散步"☒理性的民意表达 [Chengdu "walking": Rational expression of public opinion]. *Wan Shiyan's blog*. Retrieved from http://blog.sina.com.cn/s/blog_4a39e5a301009htw.html

Wang, Y. (2015, June 4). The torchbearers – Participants in the 1989 democracy movement who are currently in prison. *China Change*. Retrieved from https://chinachange.org

Wong, E. (2008, May 6). In China city, protesters see pollution risk of new plant. *The New York Times*. Retrieved from http://nytimes.com

Zhou, K. (2017). *China's long march to freedom: Grassroots modernization*. New York, NY: Routledge.

48

JE (NE) SUIS…

Exploring the Performative Contradiction in Anti-Clicktivism Arguments

Aaron Hess

In the span of a little more than four months, ISIS inspired or directed terrorist attacks that hit Paris in November 2015 and Brussels in March 2016, with injury or death to hundreds. In response to the attacks, ordinary citizens from across the globe took to Twitter and other social media to express their outrage and grief. In the wake of the attacks, Twitter users looked to the social networking site to stand in solidarity with and to memorialize the victims. Within these social media posts, however, many users also decried the online response itself, indicating that posting to social media about the latest tragedy is a meaningless act accented merely with narcissism. These users curiously posted to the same channels with similar visual arguments that called out the display of solidarity as an expression of vanity. On the surface, their statements appear as performative contradictions; yet, recognizing their arguments within the discursive context of Twitter and the networked public sphere provides a different interpretation of the contradiction. To understand this complex performance, I examine the types of visual arguments offered for and against the idea of *clicktivism* for expressing solidarity in these tragedies. I offer that individuals arguing against expressions of solidarity utilize the same channels and participate in a performative contradiction marked with a sarcastic style that stems from the cultural norms often found within digital spaces. By examining those norms and style, I argue that logical argumentation does not inform their postings as much as playful remixing and memetic styling do.

Activism in Digital Culture

The performance of visual argument in response to the terrorist attacks falls within the larger context of the networked public sphere and digital culture. Benkler (2006) argued that because the networked public sphere was marked by the massive reach of networked technology and populated with users that are "sometimes consumers and sometimes producers" (p. 138), it "provide[s] anyone with an outlet to speak, to inquire, to investigate, without need to access the resources of a major media organization" (p. 11). In this decentralized environment, online users eschew traditional gatekeeping functions of editors or editorial boards for cultural capital, the number of shares or likes, or adherence to structural norms of the platform (Bruns, 2008). Within the political elements of the networked public sphere, users also fundamentally alter traditional argumentative forms, such as letter writing, petitions, and even protest itself. As Pfister stated, "In hypercomplex societies, networked media empower a whole set of new political intermediaries—bloggers, wikipedians, social bookmarkers, and video artists—as participants in and organizers of public argument" (2014, p. 43). The trading of memes and other digital visual arguments follows and flows from this fractured and decentralized environment.

The responses of social media users constitute "clicktivism" and "slacktivism" in common vernacular. Often derided as a poor replacement for traditional forms of activism (e.g., petitioning, letter-writing, or protest), digital activism has become a common form of public advocacy. Whether through the spread of memes or the signing of online petitions, digital forms of political participation have produced mixed understandings of purpose and effect. Indeed, Vie (2014) referred to the dismissal of such activism as "slacktivism," but still concluded, "the spread of memes is an opportunity for digital activism, or instances of social and political change made possible through digital networks" (p. 3). Penney (2015) maintained that digital activism operated "as more-or-less extended versions of traditional forms of political participation, such as lobbying public officials and organizing face-to-face rallies and protests" (p. 52), and that "everyday processes of moral and political self-identification cultivated by online interaction create a 'major reservoir of civic energy' [quoted in Bakardjieva, 2009] that can potentially be tapped by both social movement organizations and formal political institutions" (p. 54). In the face of global events such as terror attacks, civic energies can stir mixed emotions as users grapple with the violence and tragedy.

Certainly, social media platforms are making it easier to share memes, change profile pictures, sign petitions, and even mobilize for protests, but the processes embodied in such platforms remain a subject of ongoing critique. Indeed, clicktivism as a term denotes the simplification of online processes, as one click signature links on social media illustrate. Clicktivism and slacktivism often function as a quick means to feel active without having to actually participate by taking on an issue in real life, or as Halupka (2014) put it, "a lazy or overly convenient alternative to the effort and legitimacy of traditional engagement" (p. 116). Halupka (2014) goes on to advocate for a focus on the concept within academe:

> We need to recognize clicktivism as a distinctive category of online political participation, and in so doing, shift its terminological use in academic discourse. As technology develops, and once complex actions are simplified and universalized, it is likely that clicktivist-like actions will increase in both prominence and popularity.
>
> *(p. 117)*

As such technologies expand, the question of effect becomes ever more pertinent. Given the relative weight of social media in the 2016 election and continued Twitter presence from the Trump administration, social media and other networked technology should prompt more thorough examinations of their rhetorical force and impact.

Twitter and other social media accounts are strong examples of media and discursive fragmentation commonly seen in digital culture. In this strained and fractured moment, social media sites have emerged as a maelstrom of networked opinions speaking in small fragments that carry powerful ideological weight and provocative visualities. This context parallels comments regarding postmodernism as Rowland (1995) recognized well before the advent of Twitter, which he recognized as an "epistemological indictment of argument"

(Rowland, 1995, p. 351). For Rowland, postmodernists and poststructuralists such as Jacques Derrida utilized logical claims about how logic failed to produce truth. He cited Derrida as engaging in "free play" (p. 352) with signification through deconstruction. Similarly, users engaging in remix culture and the spread of memes as acts of solidarity do so with playful signification, linking and mimicking things like *The Simpsons*, often with nihilistic tendencies. Responding to Rowland, Thomas (1997) argued scholars should understand the tendencies within postmodern and poststructural philosophies—such as playful signification —not as against logic and rationality, but expressions of different forms of rationality or another way to "create knowledge" (p. 73). In this sense, the remix culture alters and reinterprets the terms of logic and argumentation in ways that account for the digital users' preference for playful signification. For example, Bruns (2008) collapsed the notion of producer and user into produsage as a hallmark of digital, participatory culture. In these spaces, users playfully engage in remixes of original content, often through parody or satire as a mode of argumentation (Hutcheon, 1994). In effect, the style of argument weighs more heavily than its substance.

These culturally-informed tweets surface at a time when online users rely on internet memes and other digital visual expressions to make their arguments create a sense of (sub)cultural identity through a remix of other displays. Parallel with internet memes, these playful digital creations circulate as "contagious patterns of 'cultural information' that get passed from mind to mind and directly generate and shape the mindsets and significant forms of behavior and actions of a social group" (Knobel & Lankshear, 2007, p. 199). The nature of "contagious patterns" highlights the often "viral" quality of internet memes, which often pass between thousands, if not millions, of users with little regard for the original creator (Milner, 2013). Vie (2014) contended that the success of these digital expressions depended upon "the social and cultural specifics of their audience, as they play on familiar visual or textual concepts or rely on culturally relevant songs, jokes, or sayings" (p. 6). In their analysis of participatory digital culture, Wiggins and Bowers (2014) applied Giddens' notion of structuration to gain a perspective on meme culture that appreciates the "recursive relationship with the resources [individuals] use for meme creation" (p. 1894). In short, visual, digital expressions draw heavily on cultural capital for their successful (re)creation and (re)circulation. As arguments, they are heavily dependent upon larger cultural frameworks that span across social media platforms. Looking to those platforms and their cultural expectations assists in understanding how argument functions in ways that are seemingly illogical.

The Case of the Terrorist Attacks in Paris and Brussels

Tragedies such as the Paris or Brussels attacks are difficult to comprehend, and many Twitter users took to social media to explore their grief and confusion. Indeed, with images of bodies and blood littered across social media, the strong visual focus of digital technology initiates a sense of despair. Here, I analyzed nearly 7000 instances of the Twitter hashtags— #ParisAttacks, #JeSuisParis, #PrayForParis, #BrusselsAttacks, #JeSuisBruxelles, and #PrayForBrussels—that included visual content after the Paris and Brussels attacks. One persistent theme emerging in the tweets was a backlash against the act of memorializing or creating solidarity, as several users looked to the postings of solidarity and "#JeSuis..." hashtags as trite displays of narcissism or futility, rather than true expressions of solidarity with the victims. In this way, these oppositional tweets exist as "anti-memes" or memes that are against the idea of memes. To further explore these critical posts and anti-memes, I looked to the ways that particular rhetorical communities used images by conducting an additional search and analysis of images visually similar to those in my initial data set and by uploading them to Google Images and tracing additional posts and their origins.

Responses to the six hashtags analyzed here critiqued the practice of clicktivism and the notion that spreading "virtual flowers" can make a difference. Such critiques came in many forms and often carried a sarcastic or derisive tone. For example, one political cartoon image expressed a dark sentiment by featuring a young couple looking rather forlorn as they substituted their black "Je suis Paris" t-shirts for "Je suis Bruxelles" from a laundry line of other shirts saying "Je suis..." Another image decried the act of clicktivism in the face of horrific violence, saying "You can flag up your profile pic...but the only thing that will stop the killing will be bullets and bombs." In still another titled "Emergency Plan," the image told users, in case of "terror attack in a white country," to engage in mourning activities such as drawing tears, to create a flag filter on Facebook, to illuminate buildings, and finally, to wait for the next attack and "repeat." These images offer painfully honest reminders of the frequency of these events and how many people feel useless in response. They also mark the posting of images in response to tragedy as futile.

Moreover, while many of the visual artifacts circulating in response to the attacks had a memetic quality, the anti-meme set utilized established memes or macros from other contexts. Two of the macros appearing in twitter responses to the Paris attacks featured screenshots from *The Simpsons* television program, a common macro in use in other online communities such as Reddit. One of the images featured an awkward looking Homer Simpson in a bar surrounded by people with the French flag covering their faces. The image, coupled with the caption "Me on Facebook," made the argument that the user, while surrounded by individuals sympathetic to the French was not participating in the same act. The same Homer Simpson meme appeared on other sites (e.g., Reddit), featuring various flags in response to attacks in other countries. Another *Simpsons* macro featured the dim-witted and painfully clumsy character Ralph Wiggum with the French flag overlaying his face. Poking fun at those who participated in the same act, the caption sarcastically read, "I'm helping," Similarly, another image featured a smiling person actively exchanging

Figure 48.1 Examples of Images that Offer Arguments Against the Idea of Clicktivism

a "Pray for Paris" image with a "Pray for Belgium" image. The individual placed the "Pray for Paris" placard into a trash bin labeled "old modes," signaling the frequency of such exchanges. The smile on the figure's face hinted at how the "real" emotion of the user remained unchanged in the face of acts of terror and tragedy.

Such anti-meme responses include a performative contradiction. They lambast users that turn to social media to express despair and solidarity as futile. The argument—heavily accented with sarcasm—reads that posting to social media is worthless and ineffectual because of its nature within social media. Indeed, the final image previously discussed showcases how the real emotion of happiness in lands far away from the actual attacks appear draped in front-facing despair, covering a real sense of non-involvement and even happiness. Yet, those who offer critiques of social media solidarity use similar mechanisms and do so by circulating on the same hashtags associated with the attacks. Posting an image on #PrayForParis that argues against the act of posting an image on #PrayForParis functions as a performative contradiction. Structurally, adding to the hashtag only raises its relevance, thereby elevating each of the hashtag's other associated tweets or posts. So, the use and promotion of the hashtag is antithetical to the argument of solidarity offered; certainly, the performative contradiction makes the argument appear contradictory if read through a logical lens and analysis of argument.

However, re-reading these anti-memes through the lens of digital culture may account for the performative contradiction. Examined from a larger rhetorical and digital context, the anti-meme tweets adhere more to digital culture norms than to formal logic or traditional argumentative forms. The lens of mimicry, parody, or satire, for example, produce a different sentiment typical of internet cultures. Remix or produsage culture often utilizes forms of mimicry or imitation to replicate original creations, either in form or function (Bruns, 2008). In this rhetorical culture of produsage, speakers replicate established forms (e.g., using *Simpsons* memes), or toy with mainstream norms (e.g., the acts of prayer and solidarity) within hashtags using parody or satire. The use of satire often adds a subversive edge to undercut the original message. The subversive tone present in rhetorical communities such as Reddit, Imgur, or 4chan often includes a playful derisiveness, to put it lightly. Frankly, the participants' uses of derision in these environments frequently utilizes racism, sexism, and homophobia among other forms of oppressive discourse. Playfulness, in this sense, is more culturally important in these spaces than adherence to a consistent political stance.

Looking deeper into digital culture, structuration also assists in understanding why anti-memes succeed (Wiggins & Bowers, 2014). Memes exist in an ongoing conversation that

Figure 48.2 Examples of Highly Sarcastic Images that Argue Against the Idea of Clicktivism

shifts along with the ever-changing cultural and rhetorical situation, especially in contexts such as Reddit. As new memes appear and new rules for use take form, the structure of meme culture is constantly moving. Within this ebb and flow, users find agency in their ability to recognize and adapt to the changing normative behaviors. As Wiggins and Bowers (2014) put it, "In structuration, agency is characterized by an innate ability to imagine different outcomes" (p. 1894). Looking back to the Paris and Brussels attacks, structuration maps nicely with an understanding of audience. Differing interpretations of meme culture likely guide the various competing audiences within the responses to the attacks. Twitter, however, serves as a large platform with many, many cultures linked to it or speaking through it. Within its large, diverse audience of users, individuals that wish to sarcastically remark on meme culture can find rhetorical agency and an audience that overlooks the (illogical) posting of anti-memes. Structurally, these anti-memes will surface within the larger hashtag. Although somewhat odd to have such contradictory statements existing side-by-side, the cultural assumptions within the networked public sphere invite this type of playful signification.

Conclusion

Within networked cultures and public spheres, the fragmentation of discourse leads to a fundamental rethinking of discursive and performative rationality. In the case of the anti-memes posted in response to the Paris and Brussels attacks, consistency in argumentative stance is less important than the adherence to subcultural norms embedded in particular websites, such as Reddit, 4chan, and Imgur. Because of larger links in social media, posts such as these inevitably surface within massively trending hashtags, such as those on Twitter in response to the Paris and Brussels attacks. Yet, devoid of their (likely) original context and subcultural norms, these posts may appear as antithetical to the aims of the hashtag and as self-contradicting. Looking to how these arguments operate may require a more thorough investigation of the normative structures found within their originating spaces of speaking.

References

Benkler, Y. (2006). *The wealth of networks: How social production transforms markets and freedom.* New Haven, CT: Yale University Press.

Bruns, A. (2008). *Blogs, Wikipedia, Second Life, and beyond: From production to produsage.* New York, NY: Peter Lang.

Halupka, M. (2014). Clicktivism: A systematic heuristic. *Policy & Internet, 6*(2), 115–132. doi:10.1002/1944-2866.POI355

Hutcheon, L. (1994). *Irony's edge: The theory and politics of irony.* New York, NY: Routledge.

Knobel, M., & Lankshear, C. (2007). Online memes, affinities, and cultural production. In M. Knobel & C. Lankshear (Eds.), *A new literacies sampler* (pp. 199–228). New York, NY: Peter Lang.

Milner, R. M. (2013). Pop polyvocality: Internet memes, public participation, and the Occupy Wall Street movement. *International Journal of Communication, 7*, 2357–2390. Retrieved from http://ijoc.org

Penney, J. (2015). Social media and symbolic action: Exploring participation in the Facebook red equal sign profile picture campaign. *Journal of Computer-Mediated Communication, 20*(1), 52–66. doi:10.1111/jcc4.12092

Pfister, D. (2014). *Networked media, networked rhetorics: Attention and deliberation in the early blogosphere.* University Park, PA: The Pennsylvania State Press.

Rowland, R. C. (1995). In defense of rational argument: A pragmatic justification of argumentation theory and response to the postmodern critique. *Philosophy & Rhetoric, 28*(4), 350–364. Retrieved from http://jstor.org/stable/40237870

Thomas, D. E. (1997). Deconstruction and rationality: A response to Rowland, or postmodernism 101. *Philosophy & Rhetoric, 30*(1), 70–81. Retrieved from http://jstor.org/stable/40237937

Vie, S. (2014). In defense of "slacktivism": The Human Rights Campaign Facebook logo as digital activism. *First Monday, 19*(4). http://dx.doi.org/10.5210/fm.v19i4.4961

Wiggins, B. E., & Bowers, G. B. (2014). Memes as genre: A structurational analysis of the memescape. *New Media & Society, 17*(11), 1886–1906. doi:10.1177/1461444814535194

49

MEMES AS COMMONPLACE

Ted Cruz, Serial Killers, and the Making of Networked Multitudes

Jonathan S. Carter

Networked media ecologies have led to lamentations of the loss of civic life, due to charges of ideological balkanization and a focus on affect and irony over argument (e.g., Putnam, 2000). While networked logics threaten modernist conceptions of publicity, I argue that the participatory, social inventions of networked technologies facilitate the amateur production of commonplaces that, in turn, mobilize the democratic potential of networked users as a multitude. Allowing participants to play with combinations of text and image, *memes*—which Milner (2013) defined as "multimodal artifacts remixed by countless participants, employing popular culture for public commentary" (p. 2357)—are amongst the most popular and widely circulated forms of network native discourse. Although scholars such as Hahner (2013) and Milner (2013) noted meme's ability to generate argument by providing new voices and frames, Madsen and Fritch (2014) posited the need for further explication of the relationships between meme and argument. To expand understandings of networked argumentative affordances, I analyze the Cruz/Zodiac meme. Circulating widely during the 2016 Republican primaries, this meme claimed that Ted Cruz was/is the Zodiac Killer. Drawing on the specific *topoi* (or commonplaces) of the serial killer, the meme commented on the politics of Cruz, while suggesting that the political system writ large acted with the ethos of a serial killer.

In context, the Cruz/Zodiac meme exemplifies how topoi can serve as inventional resources by functioning as repositories of the common knowledge created via shared experiences (Aristotle, trans. 2007; Virno, 2004). Such common experiences establish the foundations for argument development (Goodnight, 2005). Additionally, localized interests can garner more control over the conditions of knowledge in the absence of the general wisdom of commonplaces (Virno, 2004). Recognizing the role of the local in the inventional process, this essay argues that commonplaces give form to networked argument. Further it seeks to update Virno's observations on commonplaces. More than repositories for common wisdom, the participatory nature of memes (and other network commonplaces) makes them unique sites for deliberation outside of the structure of traditional politics. I parse the potential of the Cruz/Zodiac meme in three parts. First, I contextualize Cruz/

Zodiac within memetics and the 2016 presidential primary elections. Next, I explore how the meme evokes and creates politically oriented commonplaces. Finally, I develop how such activation of commonplace arguments can mobilize radical democracy by organizing networked participants as a multitude.

Memes in the 2016 Presidential Primaries

Early on, Dawkins (1976) contended memes function as the cultural analog to genes because both enable informational transmission through processes of evolutionary imitation. As memes moved online, scholars redefined the term away from Dawkins's deterministic genetic metaphor. Shifman (2014) argued that internet memes are user-generated "group[s] of digital content units sharing common characteristics of content, form, and/or stance" (p. 188). Further, Hahner (2013) noted that single texts or images do not define memes. Rather, memes draw their rhetorical force through the circulation of multiple, fragmented artifacts that evoke cultural ideas and frames. A meme's interpretation emerges from common understandings of narratives, affects, and arguments.

To further develop how memes foster political argument, I turn to circulations of the Cruz/Zodiac meme during the 2016 presidential primaries. This campaign cycle was particularly noteworthy because it was the first presidential contest after memes emerged as a central part of networked discourses (Chayka, 2014). During the 2016 election, no single meme dominated public attention. National Public Radio (NPR) ran over 20 articles featuring different examples of a #memeoftheweek (all related to politics) and Elect-Meme recognized 222 widely circulated election-based memes ("Elect-Meme: It's Decision," 2016). Amongst this memetic diversity, I focus on Cruz/Zodiac because it was both popular among networked publics (its memeplex ranked third on Elect-Meme) and because it generated significant mainstream press attention—including from NPR, *The Guardian*, and *Gentlemen's Quarterly*.

The Cruz/Zodiac meme emerged from a comparison between the visage of Ted Cruz and the famous pencil sketch of the Zodiac Killer—a never identified serial killer in the late 1960s and early 1970s (see Image 1). The meme began when The Red Pill (2013) tweeted, "#CPAC Alert: Ted Cruz is speaking!! His speech is titled: 'This is the Zodiac Speaking.'" Over the next three years, repetition of the analogical comparison across tweets and images allowed it to emerge as a popular political meme. By the 2016 primaries, the meme's cultural influence was such that a Google search for the words "is ted" offered "cruz the zodiac killer" as the second autofill (Sanders & Firozi, 2016). The meme's wide circulation seemingly influenced some voters. Prior to the Florida primary, polling found that 10% of respondents thought Cruz was the killer, with 28% not sure (Jensen, 2016).

Iterations of the Cruz/Zodiac meme appeared in many forms. Some offered conspiratorial proof of Cruz as the killer. For example, "Ted Cruz just finished his latest GOP debate. ZODIAC is currently airing on Showtime 2. it's [*sic*] all adding up" (Ehrlich, 2016). Other iterations made visual connections, including t-shirts that combined Cruz's face with the symbols associated with the killer (see Image 2). Participants also juxtaposed the meme with traditional political issues to express disdain for Cruz's politics. After Cruz (2016) tweeted, "You don't defeat terrorism by taking away our guns. You defeat terrorism by using our guns," one user retorted, "You kidnap women and lock them in your basement using your guns #tedcruzisthezodiackiller" (Edward, 2016). Gaining wide circulation, individual iterations of the meme playfully built on one another to build a narrative that Cruz's past as the Zodiac killer explained his current persona and politics.

Figure 49.1 Screenshot of a Typical Facial Comparison of Ted Cruz and the Zodiac Killer

Such iterations of Cruz/Zodiac may lack propositional depth; however, memes generate argumentative force through form more than content (Jenkins, 2014). The form of this meme—the juxtaposition of Cruz with the Zodiac Killer—enabled participants to express their feelings about Cruz in ways traditionally excluded from political communication. While politics has (traditionally) relied on rationality and facticity, the meme called attention away from this norm. Michelle Dean (2016) argued,

> Ted-Cruz-is-the-Zodiac types often say they're only doing what birther Repub-
> licans did to Obama in 2008. They repeatedly insisted that Obama's birth certifi-
> cate was faked, and that he was born in Kenya. Gradually, certain members of the
> public began to believe it. So claiming that Ted Cruz is the Zodiac simply mimics
> the mass-panic technique Republicans have already perfected.
>
> *(para. 15)*

For participants, the fact that an impossible claim can gain traction served to highlight their frustration with a system where traditional facts are not at the core of politics.

However, just because the meme relied on a factual impossibility does not mean that it is without a sense of truth. Interviewing participants who circulated the meme, Sanders (2016) noted, "They know Cruz is not the Zodiac killer. But they say it's all about a feeling they have about Cruz: they think he's creepy. And they want to point that out, as clearly as they can" (para. 14). Although the Cruz/Zodiac meme does not match historical facts, it articulated an affective truth about Cruz for participants. To understand the rhetorical force of this affective truth, I turn to memes' relation to commonplaces.

Figure 49.2 Rory Blank's Art for the First Cruz/Zodiac T-Shirt. Permission to use this image kindly
granted by Rory Blank.

Commonplace Memes

While modernist theory often reduced topoi to banal tropes, contemporary rhetoric has worked
to restore them as rich resources for developing argument (McKeon, 1973; Perelman &
Olbrechts-Tyteca, 1969). Aristotle (trans. 2007) distinguished two primary forms of topoi: *koinoi
topoi* (commonplaces) and *idia topoi* (specific/special places). Commonplace arguments transcend
specific fields or locations, while the special topics are only relevant in specific contexts. Following McKeon (1973), I conceive of commonplaces as storehouses of argumentative resources
built around what is collectively familiar. In this conception Leff (1996) noted, commonplaces
are tied to memory, demanding the internalization of collective wisdom, views, and/or affects.

Virno (2004) elaborated on the political functions of commonplaces by returning to Aristotle's distinction between commonplaces and special places:

> The "special places" of discourse and of argumentation are perishing and dissolving,
> while immediate visibility is being gained by the "common places," or by generic
> logical-linguistic forms which establish the pattern for all forms of discourse. This
> means that in order to get a sense of orientation in the world and to protect our-
> selves from its dangers, we can not [*sic*] rely on those forms of thought, of reason-
> ing, or of discourse which have their niche in one particular context or another.
>
> *(p. 36)*

For Virno (2004), the fluidity of contemporary capitalism disrupts the special places, preventing local communities from exerting stable force. Conversely, commonplaces are the manifestation of "social cooperation in the form of action in concert, the totality of poietic, 'political,' cognitive, [and] emotional forces" (p. 78). In this capacity, commonplaces are more than common tropes; they store the ideational resources to remake politics.

Drawing on common memories of figures ranging back to Jack the Ripper and Ed Gein, the cultural trope of the serial killer functions as one such commonplace. Stratton (1996) argued that contemporary understandings position serial killers as socially disaffected normal guys whose killings are a statement of rebellion. Yet, this commonplace is more than the romanticizing of disturbed individualism. Stratton (1996) noted that serial killers are typically framed as exaggerated versions of modern banality, which draws in the public because of similar feelings of alienation from the march of (post)industrialism.

The Cruz/Zodiac meme drew on traditional conceptions of the serial killer commonplace as well as offered specific commentary on the 2016 elections. At its core, Cruz/Zodiac was built around the recognition that Cruz is not the Zodiac Killer. Consequently, the meme functioned not as an evocation of that specific historical narrative but rather a synecdochal reference to the larger commonplace. The juxtaposition highlighted the undesirability of Cruz as a presidential candidate, because despite its historical inaccuracy, Moore (2016) argued that the serial killer comparison was valid because Cruz is "by all reports [...] one of the most repulsive, awful human beings you could ever meet" (para. 5). In this iteration, the commonplace suggested the politics of Cruz are not just undesirable: They are a twisted ambition-motivated, serial killer-like attack on society. Further, by combining serial killer narratives with Cruz to create a new commonplace, Cruz/Zodiac imposed the original commonplace's sense of disturbed normalcy onto contemporary politics. The ironic use of a factually impossible commonplace suggests that political discourse has become one of Virno's (2004) special places, losing touch with reality in a way that alienates voters.

In foregrounding its stance within a commonplace response to contemporary politics, the meme did more than provide an avenue for affectively commenting on politics, it dictated the proper collective response to Cruz. For example, meme participant Tim Faust created a t-shirt to embody the meme (see Image 2; Dean, 2016). When sales took off, Faust felt compelled to donate the proceeds to a cause that Cruz opposed. Thus, Faust donated $69,000 to the West Fund, which assists women to pay for abortions in Texas (Dean, 2016). Within the commonplace, Cruz's opposition to abortion functioned as still another of his serial killings. Consequently, the only ethical response was move to prevent the violence.

Commonplaces and Networked Multitudes

Examining the juxtaposition of Cruz with the serial killer, the importance of commonplaces to organize networked argument becomes apparent. The participatory nature of networked spaces invites more diverse and potentially fragmented responses than the comparatively rigid rhetorics of electoral politics and political media. Participants variously perceived Cruz as creepy, disliked certain of his policies, or were upset with the state of politics. However, the form of the commonplace provided a unifying form to organize these disparate evaluations into a unified stance—Cruz is the embodiment/product of a broken political system where only the alienated can survive.

As part of giving form to networked argument, networked commonplaces create sites for the implementation of radical democracy. Speaking on contemporary governance, Hardt and Negri (2004) noted that increasingly, traditional politics operate in the interests of dominant forces, prompting the need for a radical democracy built around the multitude. Although the foci of representative democracy, such as publics, reduce participants to a single factor (e.g., blue-collar voters), a multitude recognizes participants as a collective of complex and diverse individuals (Hardt & Negri, 2004). While publics create rigid categories that limit political action, multitudes open space for individuals to participate.

Virno (2004) took initial steps to link the multitude to commonplaces. The special places, for him, enabled elites to control the conditions of knowledge production and therefore argument and action. Conversely, as repositories of the "general intellect" (p.12), Virno (2004) argued that commonplaces serve as a repository of knowledge that allows the multitude to recognize itself as separate from dominant politics. The meme of Cruz, the serial killer, allowed participants to realize that—in rejecting that system—they could exist as a polity outside of representative politics. Specifically, by creating new commonplaces of politics such as serial killer, Cruz/Zodiac allowed an emerging democratic philosophy of government that posited the idea that politics should be less self-serving and less willing to engage in falsity for ideological gain.

However, the Cruz/Zodiac meme did more than exemplify how commonplaces can store knowledge that invites democratic action; it suggested that networked commonplaces function as sites of radical democracy. Every time participants mobilized the meme to judge politics, they altered the force of Cruz/Zodiac without negating their individual perspectives. For example, when tweeting to complain about Cruz's vote against funding for Hurricane Sandy recovery, Reid (2017) affixed #zodiacted, joining and restating the meme with the criticism. Reid (2017) articulated specific issue concerns and evaluations of Cruz as "a pile of manure pretending to be a man." At the same time, those concerns added to the broader serial killer story by suggesting Cruz's lack of empathy as reinforcement of the serial killer comparison. Thus, the form of the networked commonplace allows participants to maintain their multitudinous individualism while still participating in collective action.

Moreover, the form of networked commonplaces also allows participants to negotiate democratically on perspectives they consider most important. The process of recirculating popular iterations allows each user to spread—and make more salient—interpretations of Cruz/Zodiac that they think ought to be relevant, functionally voting on the interpretation of the commonplace they believe should be dominant. While iterations of the meme might judge specific policies, the most liked tweets focused on Cruz's general affect (Moore, 2016). This in turn made the desire for a less creepy politics the most salient argument of the evocation of the commonplace. Every act of participation in a commonplace meme functioned as a deliberative renegotiation of the political subjectivity of the multitude, changing the possibility of future action.

Conclusion

Writing on the rhetorical force of this meme built around a historical impossibility, Sanders (2016) proclaimed, "It's all really absurd. And increasingly, it's trending" (para. 5). Yet, in an era where claims of fake news continue to dominate politics, the rhetorical power of factually inaccurate content has never appeared more salient. Certainly Cruz/Zodiac was not responsible for the failure of the Cruz campaign. However, in criticizing the feeling surrounding Cruz, this memetic commonplace provided argumentative resources that encouraged a radically democratic politics by articulating views that dominant politics wanted to ignore. In this sense, Cruz/Zodiac demands that both networked participants and critics should not simply reject false or absurd political claims that gain wide social purchase. Rather, these groups need to recognize the possibility that they are potentially the product of the democratic negotiation of multitudinous common sentiment. In recognizing this potential, networked rhetors can address the real concerns motivating the circulation of false claims. Rhetors can discover how addressing the motivations of falsity can shape a society where democracy is not a victim of Zodiac/Cruz and the pessimism and disenchantment of the special places; rather, the shaping is a positive production of commonplace feelings driving collective life.

References

Aristotle. (2007). *On rhetoric: A theory of civic discourse* (G. A. Kennedy, Trans). New York, NY: Oxford University Press.

Chayka, K. (2014, October 24). How the meme went mainstream. *The Daily Dot*. Retrieved from https://dailydot.com/unclick/how-the-meme-went-mainstream-kyle-chayka/

Cruz, S. T. [@SenTedCruz]. (2016, June 16). You don't defeat terrorism by taking away our guns. You defeat terrorism by using our guns. cs.pn/1ttnhx5 [Tweet]. Retrieved from https://twitter.com/Sen TedCruz/status/743491139492274176

Dawkins, R. (1976). *The selfish gene*. Oxford, United Kingdom: Oxford University Press.

Dean, M. (2016, March 9). Ted Cruz is the Zodiac Killer: The anatomy of a meme gone rogue. *The Guardian*. Retrieved from https://theguardian.com

Edward, L. [@LeeEdward]. (2016, June 16). You kidnap women and lock them in your basement using your guns #tedcruzisthezodiackiller [Tweet]. Retrieved from https://twitter.com/LeeEdward_/ status/743503475263209472

Elect-Meme: It's Decision 2016Time. With So Many Election Memes Out There, Who Will Lead Us As Meme-In-Chief? Vote For Your Favorites: Let's Play [Interacting quiz]. (2016). *Elect-Meme Leaderboard*. Retrieved from http://electmeme.lol/leaderboard#

Ehrlich, D. [@davidehrlich]. (2016, March 3). Ted Cruz just finished his latest GOP debate. ZODIAC is currently airing on Showtime 2. it's* all adding up [Tweet]. Retrieved from https://twitter.com/davi dehrlich/status/705608890604511232

Goodnight, G. T. (2005). Science and technology controversy: A rationale for inquiry. *Argumentation and Advocacy*, *42*(1), 26–29. Retrieved from http://tandfonline.com

Hahner, L. A. (2013). The riot kiss: Framing memes as visual argument. *Argumentation and Advocacy*, *49*(3), 151–166. Retrieved from http://tandfonline.com

Hardt, M., & Negri, A. (2004). *Multitude: War and democracy in the time of empire*. New York, NY: Penguin Press.

Jenkins, E. S. (2014). The modes of visual rhetoric: Circulating memes as expressions. *Quarterly Journal of Speech*, *100*(4), 442–466. doi:10.1080/00335630.2014.989258

Jensen, T. (2016, February 25). Trump leads Rubio even head to head in Florida [Poll]. *Public Policy Polling*. Retrieved from http://publicpolicypolling.com

Leff, M. (1996). Commonplaces and argumentation in Cicero and Quintilian. *Argumentation*, *10*(4), 445–452. doi:10.1007/BF00142977

Madsen, A., & Fritch, J. (2014). 100 million buttons can't be wrong: Argument in political pinback buttons. In C. H. Palczewski (Ed.), *Disturbing argument* (pp. 193–200). New York, NY: Routledge.

McKeon, R. (1973). Creativity and the commonplace. *Philosophy & Rhetoric*, *6*(4), 199–210. Retrieved from http://jstor.org/stable/40236861

Milner, R. M. (2013). Pop polyvocality: Internet memes, public participation, and the Occupy Wall Street movement. *International Journal of Communication*, *7*, 2357–2390. Retrieved from http://ijoc.org

Moore, J. (2016, March 17). More evidence Ted Cruz might be the Zodiac Killer. *GQ*. Retrieved from http://gq.com/story/ted-cruz-loves-soup-zodiac-killer-maybe

Perelman, Ch., & Olbrechts-Tyteca, L. (1969). *The new rhetoric: A treatise on argumentation*. South Bend, IN: University of Notre Dame Press.

Putnam, R. D. (2000). *Bowling alone: The collapse and revival of American community*. New York, NY: Simon & Schuster.

The Red Pill. [@RedPillAmerica]. (2013, March 14). #CPAC Alert: Ted Cruz is speaking!! His speech is titled: "This Is The Zodiac Speaking" [Tweet]. Retrieved from https://twitter.com/RedPillAmer ica/status/312323787091755009?ref_src=twsrc%5Etfw

Reid, C. [@zombiejunky]. (2017, August 29). Just another reminder that @tedcruz Ted Cruz is a walking pile of manure pretending to be a man. #tedcruz #zodiacted [Tweet]. Retrieved from https://twitter.com/zombiejunky/status/902533287599419392

Sanders, S., & Firozi, P. (2016, February 26). #MemeOfTheWeek: Ted Cruz and the Zodiac Killer. *National Public Radio*. Retrieved from http://npr.org

Shifman, L. (2014). *Memes in digital culture* (Google Books view). Cambridge, MA: The MIT Press.

Stratton, J. (1996). Serial killing and the transformation of the social. *Theory, Culture & Society, 13*(1), 77–98. doi:10.1177/026327696013001004

Virno, P. (2004). *A grammar of the multitude: For an analysis of contemporary forms of life* (I. Bertoletti, J. Cascaito, & A. Casson, Trans.). Los Angeles, CA: Semiotext(e).

* the original tweet contains this typo.

50

CRITICAL DELIBERATION UNDER FIRE

Milblogging, Free Speech, and the "Soldiers' Protocol to Enable Active Communication Act"

Michael K. Middleton and Kevin A. Johnson

Amidst the United States' involvement in conflict zones in Iraq, Afghanistan, and elsewhere, a new phenomenon emerged that expanded the network of participants engaged in critical dialogues about U.S. military engagements *and* raised new threats about the operational security of those missions. Military blogs ("milblogs") offer a forum to convey information, speculation, and opinion about the post-9/11 security state, foreign policy, and politics more broadly. Ten years after 2001, when milblogs first appeared as a digital phenomenon, thousands of active and inactive military personnel, defense professionals, academics, and other commentators created more than 3,000 digital fora (Hockenberry, 2005; Reynolds, 2003).

Milblogs vary in quality and credibility, ranging from credible sources of news and commentary to biased and partisan screed (Reynolds, 2003). For some, milblogs are problematic because they risk undermining the objectives of defense and security policy. The central worry is that some "milbloggers will carry gasoline to fires for politicians and sufficiently high-ranking officers" (Yon, 2012, para. 22). For others, milblogs provide an essential forum for information sharing, critique, and debate on issues that intersect with defense and security discourses, potentially leading to more effective decisions grounded in public deliberation and the free exchange of ideas. Proponents argue that milblogs exist as essential interlocutors in debates about critical issues of national security and that the bloggers "constitute a rich subculture with a refreshing candor about [...] war, expressing views ranging from far right to far left" (Hockenberry, 2005, para. 7).

At the intersection between milblogs' value to democratic deliberation and their potential threat to national security lies a vexing free speech dilemma. Even if military First Amendment rights are not co-extensive with strictly civilian rights, we argue that the milblogs have significant free speech implications. To develop our claim, we catalog some of the central arguments for and against milblogging, suggesting that these points of argumentative tension persist because proponents and opponents of milblogging interact on related, but independent and parallel, terrains of argumentation. We rely on Dauber's (1989) theorization of "fusion criticism" to identify the argumentative burdens one faces in an attempt to traverse this seemingly irresolvable conflict over milblogging. We conclude by examining an illustrative example that charts a path for resolving this conflict's specific free speech implications within the context of military speech. Further, we suggest some general implications for argumentation aimed at issues that technical/scientific and public/political dimensions of argument complicate.

Milblogs and the Complexities of Free Expression

Currently, the Pentagon allows milblogs within a matrix of restrictions, including requiring contributors to register with their command, enforcing quarterly reviews to ensure that controlled information remains protected, and creating the Army Web Risk Assessment Cell to monitor compliance (Hockenberry, 2005). However, critics maintain that such regulation efforts are "ambiguous," "subjective," and "arbitrary" (Rosengarten, 2006, p. 1311). Further, the restrictions create a free speech dilemma because of the vagaries of First Amendment jurisprudence in the context of active military service in the age of social media, user-generated web content, and rapidly expanding connectivity. Such circumstances dissuade active duty military personnel from engaging in these forums, with the consequences of limited free expression and denying broader publics first-hand accounts of U.S. foreign policy and military engagements that could inform public debates about those topics. Rosengarten (2006) explained that, in terms of fostering an informed public debate, the Supreme Court has held in *Pickering v. Board of Education* and numerous other cases with a general and specifically military focus that public employees "are likely to have informed opinions as to the operations of their public employers [....] Were they not able to speak on these matters, the community would be deprived of informed opinions on important public issues" (pp. 1325-1326). Even so, the Supreme Court ruled in *Garcetti v. Ceballos* that the First Amendment does not necessarily protect the speech of public employees.

Elaborating on the consequences of milblog regulations, Rosengarten (2006) explained that in addition to curtailing the exercise of free speech rights by importantly situated stakeholders, the chilling effect of ambiguous limitations on milbloggers' exercise of free speech also harms the quality of public deliberation outside the scope of the military. She noted, "The benefit of milblogs to civilians is patent. Soldiers offer varied accounts, distinct perspectives, and deeply personal reactions to their situations" (p. 1310). She continued by noting that the information communicates a reality necessary to make informed decisions, as "the soldiers' expressions have a powerful impact on readers, and provide valuable insight into the reality of everyday life in the combat zone" (p. 1310). The information from soldiers is even more vital because "without a real media presence or freedom for soldiers to discuss their experiences, the American public is left in the dark about [...] war" (Rosengarten, 2006, p. 1310).

Argumentative Antagonisms in the Public Debate(s) over Milblogs

Security studies scholars argue that chilling the public debate about United States' military and foreign policy also creates unintended negative consequences for the strategic goals of the United States Armed Forces. Specifically, they note that milblogs have value "in countering mainstream media and maintaining domestic support for the war effort," while providing "a way for the Army to get its message directly to the American people and counteract anti-military bias" (Lawson, 2014, pp. 236-237). Similarly, legal scholars note that, in the context of counterinsurgency-based conflicts that characterize current U.S. military efforts, such argumentative networks are invaluable, because "'in a counterinsurgency, the media battlespace is critical [...] when it comes to mustering public opinion, rallying support, and forcing opponents to shift tactics and timetables [....]' Political persuasions are reshaped daily through [...] the blogosphere" (Rosengarten, 2007, pp. 1305-1306).

However, despite arguments identifying how limitations on the activities of milbloggers generate significant First Amendment concerns, undermine service member morale, and eschew a useful tool for advancing strategic objectives, discussions among military officials consistently reflect efforts to limit their content and presence. Indeed, in both 2007 and 2009, the U.S. Department of Defense issued clarifications, expansions, or modifications of regulations on deployed military personnel's use of social media, including outright bans on social media access and use (Lawson, 2014).

The seemingly recalcitrant conflict between operational security and access to First Amendment protections centers on the antagonism present between inter-related but mutually incompatible argumentative frames applied to the role of information and communication technologies (ICTs) within the military. Lawson (2014) argued that in information-age conflict(s), an inherent tension exists between stakeholders who conceptualize "information as data/commodity" and stakeholders who conceptualize "information as image/perception" (p. 229). In the case of the former:

> Information [is] the resource that makes the operation of the military machine possible and victory probable [...because] the US military has increasingly conceived of gathering, processing, distributing and utilizing information [...] as the central activities of a new era of conflict.
>
> *(pp. 229–230)*

In the case of the latter, information is "a resource for the shaping of perception" and serves as an argumentative resource for "forming images and representations—more particularly, the image of the U.S. in the world" (Brunner & Cavelty, 2009, pp. 630, 635). Lawson (2014) summarized this conflict, arguing that social media supporters mostly "understand information and its value as stemming primarily from its ability to improve situational awareness, collaboration and morale [...], as well as to fight the battle for the hearts and minds of both domestic and foreign audiences" (p. 231). Social media opponents tend to view information simply as data and "tend to worry more about threats to the confidentiality, integrity and availability of military networks and information and see the use of social media by individual military professionals as a dangerous new vector for such attacks" (p. 231). What Lawson's mapping revealed is an argumentative stalemate that tacks between two argumentative positions: arguments against milblogs grounded in technical considerations and arguments for milblogs grounded in public and political considerations.

Proponents of milblogs and other forms of social media couch their arguments in a recognition of the new contours of conflict. Contemporary conflicts in the War on Terror rely on a strategy of counterinsurgency and require an ongoing effort to win the hearts and minds of stakeholders both at home and in the theater of combat (Lawson, 2014). These challenges to shaping perceptions of stakeholders with a variety of investments in, or objections to, the machinations of the U.S. military leads proponents of social media to ground arguments in the contention that "allowing individual military professionals to act in a decentralized way to address these challenges is crucial for success" (Lawson, 2014, p. 231).

But, despite efforts to defend milblogs as a military or security asset, opponents highlight that they risk introducing new liabilities into theaters of conflict. Opponents contend that such activities threaten operational security because milbogs "maintained by individual military professionals provide more 'uncensored, unmediated, intimate, [and] immediate' information about the war and the military than either the mainstream media or the government" (Burden 2006, p. 5; cited in Lawson, 2014, p. 232). Specifically, opponents argue that "adversaries collect information for use against the United States," including "the collection and analysis of freely available information, such as [...] Web sites in particular, especially personal Web sites of individual Soldiers" (Department of the Army, 2014, pp. 33-34). By failing to account for these objections, the status of milblogs (as well as the disciplinary ramifications for military personnel who produce such blogs) remains in flux, dependent on which frame prevails in debates about milblogs, the First Amendment, and military personnel.

Balancing Speech and Security

The antagonisms that contribute to the deadlock in policy debates about milblogs reflect challenges familiar to critics of argument. Dauber (1989) maintained that, when addressing public argument, the notion of a transcendent public equally well-equipped to evaluate, refute, and construct the political/public and technical/scientific dimensions of arguments of public import is optimistic at best. Concluding that the job of resolving this difficulty rests with arguers and critics, Dauber contended, "It may well be inadequate to study either public or technical argument structures in isolation, [but] there is no reason why an integrated approach would not work" (p. 34). To demonstrate this possibility, Dauber theorized "fusion criticism," or criticism and argumentative strategies that fuse these interrelated spheres of argument. Such an approach, Dauber (1989) argued, "seeks to unite analyses of both public and technical argument forms in order to participate in an act of discovery: to successfully uncover ways of promoting improved public debate within the framework of liberal democratic institutions" (p. 33).

In the context of milblogs, fusion criticism both identifies and offers a conceptual framework for critically intervening in the antagonism Lawson (2014) identified. On the one hand, milblog proponents (adopting the "information as image/perception" side of Lawson's antagonism) ground arguments in a public approach to the controversy. Their arguments stem from collectively held public goods (e.g., free speech) and are silent on the question of the technical challenges the milblogs for U.S. military forces create. On the other hand, opponents of milblogs (adopting the "information as data" side of the antagonism) ground their arguments in technical concerns raised from active military operations. Leaks that compromise troop safety, strain the military's information infrastructure, and open new vectors of cyberattack dominate their arguments. These opponents make little effort to balance public concerns grounded in political values like free expression.

To traverse these challenges in public arguments, critics and arguers must find ways to "establish consensus on which risks are tolerable and which are not, and to find ways to ethically resolve or minimize unavoidable risks" (Dauber, 1987, p. 137). In the case of milblogs, this includes balancing risks to political goods (e.g., free speech) and risks to technical goods (e.g., operational security). One approach that reflects the impulse of fusion criticism to wed these concerns and offer an alternative of balance is Rosengarten's (2007), "Soldier's Protocol for Enabling Active Communication (SPEAC)." SPEAC, Rosengarten (2007) argued, provides an example of how both technical liabilities and political goods can find balance rather than function as irreconcilable absolutes. She argued for an approach that limited the content of soldiers' speech, broadly allowed soldiers to create milblogs within these constraints, established a mode of observation of milblogs to ensure compliance, and articulated a method of enforcement that maintained the anonymity of the soldier-author as protected until after a determination that any blog brought under question had violated the content restrictions. Examining Rosengarten's policy proposal against the backdrop of arguments for and against milblogs, and through the lens of "fusion criticism," provides a pedagogical example for arguers and critics interested in finding argumentative paths forward (as Rosengarten does) in what otherwise appears as intractable stalemates in public debates that traverse political and technical spheres.

Viewed from the perspective of the public sphere, these limitations, especially prior restraint on content, are arguably an anathema to the First Amendment. Some First Amendment scholars have even argued that the types of solutions that Rosengarten is proposing represent a set of content restrictions that exceed those currently established by Supreme Court jurisprudence and military law governing enlisted, active duty soldiers (Johnsen, 2010; Lytle, 2006; Mitchell, 2006). However, scholars should brook such criticisms because Rosengarten's proposal protects soldiers' identities until military authorities determine whether a milblog has violated SPEAC. For some, this step thaws the chilling effect resulting from the otherwise arbitrary enforcement of violations characterizing current approaches. Additionally, the proposal allays security concerns by adopting a regime of observation practices, by identifying technical requirements of usage, and by immediately removing material that may threaten genuinely held concerns about operational security.

By striking this balance, Rosengarten's proposal is reflective of a critic astutely tacking between the technical and public concerns shaping the impasse regarding milblogs that is the hallmark of fusion criticism. Additionally, by offering an alternative, Rosengarten demonstrates how SPEAC can inform effective argumentative interventions in such controversies. Rosengarten (2007) explained, "While there may properly be deference to the military's choices about what is protected, the military should still be required to set forth clear standards that preserve space for protected speech" (p. 1348). Doing so also requires, she argued, that opponents of milblogs realize that technical objections cannot trump such protections for free expression; when "soldiers are entrusted with fighter planes, missiles, and weapons of mass destruction," the argument that "they cannot be trusted with information" (p. 1348) is untenable. By working across these separate spheres of argument, Rosengarten was able to intervene in the controversy in a way that traverses the antagonism between upholding free speech for milbloggers while maintaining national security interests. By mapping the argumentative terrain and analyzing Rosengarten's intervention, we believe our analysis helps to demystify how parties to public argument can enact the principles of fusion criticism, not only to diagnose the tensions that create argumentative deadlock, but also how such an approach can open space for new interventions in significant public arguments.

Conclusion

In this essay, we have introduced the controversy over the use of milblogs as a space of public argument. In doing so, our essay highlights how the shifting of public deliberation to online networks brings with it considerations not faced in similar historical contexts. As argumentative networks expand (both for how our arguments move online and for who can, with or without permission, access those networks), these spaces of deliberation present new challenges for First Amendment scholars and critics of argument.

For argumentation theorists, the controversy around milblogs provides a useful exemplar to inform how arguers and critics engage with a host of pressing social controversies that render traditional understandings of argument spheres and their implied burdens obsolete. In a political climate where, for example, publics decry environmental consequences of climate change and regulations aimed at ameliorating those changes while, at the same time, questioning the science that explains both the consequences and proposed regulations, arguers wishing to affect publics must more effectively traverse sometimes incompatible understandings of the public and technical facets of contemporary controversies. Our analysis of the controversy surrounding milblogs helps illuminate how arguers might more effectively navigate the challenges presented by the seemingly competing demands of public and technical spheres.

Moreover, as a matter of free speech, milblogs will continue to test the boundaries of free speech jurisprudence. As we suggested earlier, the Supreme Court has already held that public employees do not have free speech protections when speaking about matters in their official/ professional capacity. However, milblogs may blur that distinction when the content of the blogs, for example, testify to the personal affects (positive and negative) that are the consequence of professional life. The personal affects, being part of the "cost of war," may pertain to the decision-making calculus of democratically-deliberated questions of deploying military troops. If anything, the future of milblogs are almost certain to create circumstances that reaffirm and/or redraw those boundaries as the arguments and cases continue to develop.

References

Brunner, E. M., & Cavelty, M. D. (2009). The formation of in-formation by the US military: articulation and enactment of infomanic threat imaginaries on the immaterial battlefield of perception. *Cambridge Review of International Affairs, 22*(4), 629–646. doi:10.1080/09557570903325454

Dauber, C. E. (1987). Better red or dead: Risk in a nuclear age. In J. W. Wenzel (Ed.), *Argument and critical practices: Proceedings of the fifth SCA/AFA conference on argumentation* (pp. 137–142). Annandale, VA: Speech Communication Association.

Dauber, C. E. (1989). Fusion criticism: A call to criticism. In B. E. Gronbeck (Ed.), *Spheres of argument: Proceedings of the sixth SCA/AFA conference on argumentation* (pp. 33–36). Annandale, VA: Speech Communication Association.

Department of the Army. (2007/2014). Army Regulation 530–1: Operations Security (OPSEC). Retrieved from http://apd.army.mil/epubs/DR_pubs/DR_a/pdf/web/r530_1.pdf

Hockenberry, J. (2005, August 1). The blogs of war. *Wired*. Retrieved from: https://wired.com/2005/08/milblogs/

Johnsen, D. (2010). Free speech on the battlefield: Protecting the use of social media by America's soldiers. *The John Marshall Law Review, 44*(4), 1085–1106. Retrieved from http://repository.jmls.edu.

Lawson, S. (2014). The US military's social media civil war: Technology as antagonism in discourses of information-age conflict. *Cambridge Review of International Affairs, 27*(2), 226–245. doi:10.1080/09557571.2012.734787

Lytle, T. H. (2006). A soldier's blog: Balancing service members' personal rights vs. national security interests. *Federal Communications Law Journal, 59*(3), 593–614. Retrieved from http://fclj.org

Mitchell, J. E. (2006). Warring ideologies for regulating military blogs: A cyberlaw approach for balancing free speech and security in cyberspace. *Vanderbilt Journal of Entertainment and Technology Law, 9*(1), 201–219. Retrieved from http://jetlaw.org

Reynolds, G. (2003, February 20). On the warpath. *GuardianUnlimited*. Retrieved from https://web.archive.org/web/20030306194405/http://guardian.co.uk/online/story/0,3605,898665,00.html

Rosengarten, M. (2006). All quiet on the Middle Eastern front? Proposed legislation to regulate milblogs and effectuate the First Amendment in the combat zone. *Cardozo Arts & Entertainment Law Journal, 24*, 1295–1358.

Yon, M. (2012, November 7). Milblogs: A rise and fall. *Michael Yon Online Magazine*. Retrieved from https://michaelyon-online.com

51

EMBEDDED ARGUMENTATION IN DIGITAL MEDIA NETWORKS

On "Native" Advertising

Seth Fendley

In an effort to reach more consumers, marketers have developed a "new" form of advertising known as native advertising (Carlson, 2015). This essay explores the argumentative features of these advertisements, particularly examining the ways in which the suasive possibilities and constraints change when advertisers embed commercial arguments in digital media networks. What are the specific rhetorical strategies that advertisers use to colonize these networks and imbue their arguments with the quality of "nativeness"? Native advertising content is not simply something that occurs within networks; it requires direct argumentative engagement with the features of the network qua network in which it finds itself. Even further, I argue that native advertising content *constructs* networked argumentation through its structure, form, placement, and use by individual auditors interacting with the advertisements online.

Native Advertisements as Networked Argumentation

Native advertising goes by many names: advertorials, branded journalism, integrated content, partner content, sponsored content, and transmedia branding, among others (Wojdynski, 2016). For quite some time, in part due to this proliferation of names and corresponding forms, the definition of native advertising has been murky, both in marketing industry publications and in scholarly literature (Howe & Teufel, 2014). Recently, Wojdynski and Evans (2016) suggested an inclusive and straightforward definition: Native advertising is "a term used to describe any paid advertising that takes the specific form and appearance of editorial content from the publisher itself" (p. 157). An advertisement as editorial content can take many forms. While many reduce native advertising to advertisements disguised as news articles, native advertising can function in many different realms, as the cases in this essay will show.

Advertisements that take on the formal features of non-advertisements present an opportunity for argumentation scholars to analyze how this move changes the way the advertisements function as arguments. Drawing on the concept of *embeddedness*, I argue that in their various forms, native advertisements function as networked arguments that trade on the ethos and warrant structure of digital media environments to which they appear as native (for background on those argumentative concepts, see Toulmin, 2003). The extent to which they succeed depends on how well they fit into the substructure of the network into which advertisers embed them.

Argumentation theorists have attempted to grapple with the problem of native advertising previously. For example, van Eemeren and Houtlosser (1999) conducted a pragma-dialectical analysis of an advertorial published by Shell. However, while their study attended to all the features internally present in the advertorial's text, no part of their analysis considered how the arguments fundamentally worked differently because of its advertorial form. Essentially, their analysis could have addressed any form of communication—a discussion, a news report, a lecture, or even a full-page advertisement—and the analysis would have been the same. While it is true that all analysts must select some features of their object of inquiry to focus on at the expense of others, this kind of analysis misses the most essential feature of the native advertisement, which is its status *as* a native advertisement.

As an argumentative genre, native advertisements work by disguising their true identities within an editorial context. This, in and of itself, warrants a deeper analysis of the argument structure. Thus, I propose analyzing native advertisements using the concept of embeddedness. Embeddedness emphasizes the role networks play in both generating trust and discouraging malfeasance (Granovetter, 1985). In this manner, by placing an advertisement in an editorial setting, the editorial host (be that a news organization, journal, etc.) functions as an argument network in which the native advertisement appears. This means that viewers read native advertisements within a context that imparts a distinctive set of tropes, warrants, and images; implies a critical vantage point, a certain degree of editorial oversight, and sincerity; and effects the appearance of an orientation toward understanding rather than toward success, that is, communicative rather than strategic action (Habermas, 1987). The platform thus allows the advertisement's argument to function within a broader network that the existing structure supports (e.g., a major news organization, journal publisher, or corporate website). These networked arguments not only carry more persuasive weight than they would otherwise, but the way in which they persuade is the unique consequence of the formal features of native advertising.

Integrated Content or Colonization of the Lifeworld

Native advertising raises important ethical questions. Some instantiations are more ethically dubious than others. Habermas' (1987) lifeworld colonization thesis provides an appropriate critical concept to aid in the ethical evaluation of native advertisements:

> When stripped of their ideological veils, the imperatives of autonomous subsystems make their way into the lifeworld from the outside—like colonial masters coming into a tribal society—and force a process of assimilation upon it. The diffused perspectives of the local culture cannot be sufficiently coordinated to permit the play of the metropolis and the world market to be grasped from the periphery.
>
> *(p. 355)*

Given the metaphor built into the name "native advertising," Habermas' thesis is particularly appropriate, offering a useful heuristic to evaluate the degree to which particular strategic moves produce systematically distorted communication. This framework will guide the case analysis in the next section.

Analysis of Native Advertisements in Practice

I examine three cases of native advertising: an op-ed from *The New York Times* which Netflix explicitly paid for to promote the latest season of *Orange is the New Black*, a journal article sponsored by a pharmaceutical company, and the editing of the Wikipedia page for the Whopper by Burger King's Head of Corporate Branding to promote a new marketing campaign. Each case reveals a unique perspective on embedded native advertising based on the networked arguments that provide context for the advertisements. After adumbrating these cases, I draw a few critical implications regarding native advertising and its impact on modern society.

Case 1

Native advertisements on websites make use of a variety of digital and visual features to make complex, multi-dimensional arguments. To begin, I analyze an article that Netflix's *Orange is the New Black* sponsored in *The New York Times* (Deziel, n.d.). The article addressed the incarceration rate of women while drawing the reader into the advertisement and, ultimately, the argument. When scrolling through the web page, the page shifts in a way that keeps the reader engaged with the content. Even though the page clearly says the sponsor is *Orange is the New Black,* the unidentified authors wrote the article in the newspaper's editorial style and its subject matter gives the piece persuasive value, specifically through the concept of embeddedness. No advertising-related arguments exist on their own; rather, the article's embeddedness in a larger media network of editorial content and external sources constitutes its advertising argumentative content.

The *New York Times*'s article cited information from multiple government studies to support its claims. By writing an advertisement in the style of an editorial, the editorial content takes precedence over the advertisement for the reader. The persuasiveness of the advertisement has as its foundation the manner that the consumer chooses to digest the editorial content. Hall (2003) mentioned the different levels at which consumers digest information in his work "Encoding/ Decoding." When a reader digests the editorial content in lieu of the advertisement, the consumer reads the content from the preferential level (Hall, 2003). When a consumer digests the content as an editorial, the advertiser accomplishes its goal of reaching the reader on a subliminal or covert level. In this native advertisement from *The New York Times*, the communicative action of the piece created a persuasive argument positioned to advocate for an underrepresented population. This bolsters the image of the show purchasing the advertisement, thus meeting the goal of embedding the advertisement in what viewers would otherwise interpret as editorial content.

The *New York Times* case exemplifies a commonplace occurrence for many large news outlets today. News outlets are choosing to allow one of the final places of journalistic rigor—the in-depth, interest piece—to give way to corporate sponsorship. As advertisers seek to find relevance with consumers and as news outlets continue their quest to remain revenue positive, the influence of corporations in newspapers editorial spaces will continue. The key for scholars is to focus in and understand what the corporate influence means for consumers and how to navigate this new frontier.

Case 2

In 2004, David Healy authored *Let Them Eat Prozac,* which included an article exposing corporate influence in the field of psychiatric medicine. Healy recounted receiving ghost-written articles from pharmaceutical companies to submit for publication in major medical journals (sometimes in special issues those same companies sponsored). These articles mimicked his personal writing style and included the opportunity for him to make any updates (with corporate approval) before publication. Healy detailed one instance where he stealthily updated two different sections of a paper to show the negative side effects of the drug he supposedly reviewed. Unsurprisingly, the pharmaceutical company noticed and rejected his updates; consequently, he declined authorship. However, when the journal issue came out, Healy discovered the exact article under a different byline. The published article (Tranter, O'Donovan, Chandarama, & Kennedy, 2002), with Healey's objectionable edits removed, still carried his distinct writing style.

In medical journal articles, ghostwriters for pharmaceutical companies use the academic as expert trope to embed corporate messages into the medical landscape. Using the academic rigor of the peer-review process, the arguments the ghostwriter develops for the "author" become embedded in medical discourse during the processes of submission for peer-review and acceptance for publication in the journal. The publication of ghostwritten articles creates a space in which pharmaceutical companies can extend influence toward other professionals in the field by trading on the ethos of professional academic scientists and the medium of the peer-reviewed journal. Despite the efforts of Healy (2004) and others (Berrios & Healy, 2002; "Just How Tainted," 2002) to raise awareness, this practice continues and is remarkably widespread. In a survey conducted of medical journals with the six highest impact factors in 2008, 21% of published articles included evidence of ghostwriting (Wislar, Flanagin, Fontanarosa, & DeAngelis, 2011).

Case 3

In April 2017, Burger King released a two-prong advertisement that was part television ad and part Wikipedia native advertisement. The 15-second television ad claimed that not enough time existed to explain all the ingredients in a Whopper. The Burger King worker's solution: "Okay Google, what is the Whopper Burger?" Vocalization of the question immediately caused Google Home or Android phones to attempt to answer the question. Upon making a query, the device read back the Wikipedia entry for the Whopper, which Burger King's corporate office had previously edited (Maheshwari, 2017). For this marketing message to work, Wikipedia had to embed the message. For Wikipedia to add the message, the content first had to travel through a series of approval steps, each of which required a justification for the updated message. The structure of Wikipedia extended the embedded nature of the argument due to the edit management system that Wikipedia has in place to manage its networks of authors and entries. When a contributor makes an edit on Wikipedia, editors or "content experts" review the change and, if the edit meets their approval, Wikipedia allows it to stay on the site. If the edit does not meet one of several different editorial criteria of Wikipedia, then the content experts will reject the edit. By design, the editorial review process should give readers a sense of security regarding the accuracy of each page.

By embedding an argument in one referential network (Wikipedia) designed for referral to yet another network (Google), all so that the advertising campaign itself could then refer to it, Burger King concealed the self-referential nature of its advertising campaign. Eventually, however, Wikipedia editors exposed the corporate approach by publishing screenshots showing where Burger King's Global Head of Brand Management made updates to the Whopper Burger Wikipedia page, causing Google Home to read Burger King's intended advertising message (Northrup, 2017). The Burger King example is a recent and widely publicized instance of a company editing its Wikipedia page as a promotional tool. The company networked and embedded its argument into its own created Wikipedia account with the sole intent of updating the site's listings related to the company. With Wikipedia, a company can embed the arguments deeper into the network of pages across the site through the tagging of relevant Wikipedia pages. The more pages the company can link and the appropriateness of the source links confirmed, the more networked and embedded the argument becomes. Each subsequent link works to build the credibility of the individual Wikipedia page and thus the credibility of the argument. The approval process and sourcing of the cited articles renders the embedded corporate content as "information" and not blatant advertisement. In this example, the company further networked and embedded its argument through the connection of the television advertisement to Google Home, further promoting the context of the advertisement. Thus, a trusted source (Wikipedia) and a trusted actor (Google Home) supplied the information.

Burger King used a traditional advertisement and took advantage of a new piece of technology to draw attention to the native advertisement it had created. Through the execution of the advertisement, the argument for the Whopper became networked across multiple channels. Ultimately, the advertisement created negative publicity for Burger King through the press that the company received surrounding the ethics of using technology such as Google Home to promote its content without Google's approval (Maheshwari, 2017). The negative press coverage, however, glossed over the vulnerability to native advertising built into the structure of the Wikipedia platform and further supports the embeddedness of native advertising in everyday life.

The Corporate Colonization of Argument

Sponsored articles in outlets like *The New York Times* constitute the most obvious example of native advertising. Reviewing cases like ghostwritten articles and Wikipedia edits show the lengths to which corporations are willing to go to ensure their messages get past audiences' source credibility filters. The corporate colonization of networked media is evident when an organization works to embed its message into native networks by manipulating its formal aspects to match the expectations of the host medium. For each case, the successful colonization of the lifeworld is contingent on the embeddedness of the argument. When the embeddedness of the argument is successful to the point that consumers perceive the concept to be native of the format (e.g., editorial, academic, or digital), then the corporate entity has colonized the lifeworld of the format. News organizations are experiencing the colonization due to a lack of positive cash flow. To continually produce news, these organizations allow corporations to influence and, in many ways, write corporate versions of news. Pharmaceutical companies colonized the lifeworld of medical journals through exploiting the need of many academics (specifically doctors) for publications to maintain their relevancy and status, but lack the time to step away from their practice and conduct the needed research. Wikipedia represents in some ways a final frontier of native content. The content approval process is built to keep content true to form and free of bias (i.e., corporate) influence. However, the ability of organizations, such as Burger King, to make it through the approval process questioned the functionality of the site's filters. While Wikipedia has since returned the page to its original standing and both Wikipedia and Google have condemned the advertisement, the final case shows just how vulnerable different areas of our modern lifeworld are to corporate colonization.

In today's world, corporations are working to ensure their messages become embedded into every aspect of our lives. The line between editorial content and marketing copy grows thinner and thinner. This process is transforming our newspapers, scientific journals, and encyclopedias, threatening the very ethos of these media that motivated the entire enterprise. Now, more than ever, we must ask: How do we train consumers to identify embedded arguments that corporations proliferate and to what extent do these arguments influence our participation in the public sphere?

References

Berrios, G. E., & Healy, D. (2002). How tainted is medicine? *Lancet, 359*(9319), 1776. doi:10.1016/S0140-6736(02)08620-8

Carlson, M. (2015). When news sites go native: Redefining the advertising–editorial divide in response to native advertising. *Journalism, 16*(7), 849–865. doi:10.1177/1464884914545441

Deziel, M. (n.d.). Women inmates: Why the male model doesn't work. *The New York Times*. Retrieved from http://paidpost.nytimes.com/netflix/women-inmates-separate-but-not-equal.html

Granovetter, M. (1985). Economic action and social structure: The problem of embeddedness. *American Journal of Sociology, 91*(3), 481–510. Retrieved from http://jstor.org/stable/2780199

Habermas, J. (1987). The theory of communicative action, volume two: Lifeworld and system: A critique of functionalist reason (T. McCarthy, Trans.). Boston, MA: Beacon Press.

Hall, S. (1980/2003). Encoding/decoding. In S. Hall, D. Hobson, A. Lowe, & P. Wills (Eds.), *Culture, media, language: Working papers in cultural studies, 1972–79* (pp. 117–127). London, United Kingdom: Routledge.

Healy, D. (2004). *Let them eat Prozac: The unhealthy relationship between the pharmaceutical industry and depression*. New York, NY: New York University Press.

Howe, P., & Teufel, B. (2014). Native advertising and digital natives: The effects of age and advertisement format on news website credibility judgments. *International Symposium on Online Journalism, 4*(1), 78–90.

Just how tainted has medicine become? [Editorial]. (2002). *Lancet, 359*(9313), 1167. doi:10.1016/S0140-6736(02)08198-9

Maheshwari, S. (2017, April 12). Burger King "o.k. Google home" ad doesn't seem o.k. with Google. *The New York Times*. Retrieved from https://nytimes.com

Northrup, L. (2017, April 19). Wikipedia editors condemn Burger King for edits related to Google home stunt. *Consumerist*. Retrieved from https://consumerist.com

Toulmin, S. E. (2003). *The uses of argument*. Cambridge, United Kingdom: Cambridge University Press.

Tranter, R., O'Donovan, C., Chandarama, P., & Kennedy, S. (2002). The prevalence and outcome of partial remission in depression. *Journal of Psychiatry and Neuroscience, 27*, 241–247.

van Eemeren, F. H., & Houtlosser, P. (1999). Strategic manoeuvring* in argumentative discourse. *Discourse Studies, 1*(4), 479–497. doi:10.1177/1461445699001004005

Wislar, J. S., Flanagin, A., Fontanarosa, P. B., & DeAngelis, C. D. (2011). Honorary and ghost authorship in high impact biomedical journals: A cross sectional survey. *The BMJ, 343*, 1–7. doi:10.1136/bmj.d6128

Wojdynski, B. W. (2016). Native advertising: Engagement, deception, and implications for theory. In R. Brown, V. K. Jones, & B. M. Wang (Eds.), *The new advertising: Branding, content, and consumer relationships in a data-driven social media era* (pp. 203–236). Santa Barbara, CA: Praeger.

Wojdynski, B. W., & Evans, N. J. (2016). Going native: Effects of disclosure position and language on the recognition and evaluation of online native advertising. *Journal of Advertising, 45*(2), 157–168. doi:10.1080/00913367.2015.1115380

* The title of this article contained the misspell in its original context.

52

TOO SRAT TO CARE

Participatory Culture and the Information Economy of *Total Sorority Move*

Amber Davisson and Kelsey Jackson

Participatory culture, a term Jenkins (1992) coined, refers to a set of social conditions "with relatively low barriers to artistic expression and civic engagement, strong support for creating and sharing creations, and some type of informal mentorship whereby experienced participants pass along knowledge" (Jenkins, 2009, p. xi). These social conditions are possible in part because of an increased access to media production tools that allow media users to smoothly move back and forth between the positions of producer and consumer. As Shirky (2009) explained:

> Every time a new consumer joins this media landscape, a new producer joins as well because the same equipment—phones, computers—lets you consume and produce. It is as if when you bought a book, they threw in the printing press for free.
>
> *(5:02)*

As a result, the number of individuals contributing arguments to the marketplace of ideas has increased. The question is just how much the increase in ideas has truly changed the way we assign value to arguments within that marketplace. Benkler (2006) argued that the two elements that make the information economy of networked media technologies different from mass media technologies are the architecture that informs the distribution of messages and the cost of messages. This essay looks to the case study of social media platform owner Grandex, Inc. to see how users can manipulate those two factors to co-opt the potential argumentative power of participatory culture.

In 2010, Texas State University fraternity brothers Ryan Young and Madison Wickham created a Twitter account to chronicle their daily encounters with #TFM or Total Frat Moves (Shontell, 2015). They built their account by scrolling through Twitter and following anyone who appeared to be part of a fraternity. Their hashtag documented stories like "my professor said she needed a whole bottle of vodka to grade our quizzes. I began to clap, while others joined in, I yelled COLLEGE #TFM" (King, 2016). The brothers amassed 1.8 million followers, and they used the popularity of their Twitter account to found Grandex, which serves as home to the social media platform *Total Fraternity Move* (TFM) and the spinoff *Total Sorority Move* (TSM). TSM's first post read, "Ladies, welcome home" (Warren, 2014, para. 2), and it promised that the site would be a space for women to gather and share their stories about the day-to-day experience of sorority life. Its front page featured users' blog posts about topics ranging from instructions on how to successfully pursue sexual partners to where to go for spring break. Grandex described TSM as "TFM's better half" (Grandex, 2016, Total Sorority Move section, para. 1). The spinoff TSM rivals the original in terms of popularity. In 2015, Grandex platforms had 20 million unique visitors per month, and only 8 million of those were for TFM (Shontell, 2015; Pierson, 2016). Despite the seeming popularity of TSM a year and a half after the site launched, the Kappa Zeta chapter of Sigma Kappa at Elon University created the hashtag #actualsororitymove to protest what they said were Grandex's unfair depictions of sorority life. Sorority women from across the country adopted the hashtag on sites like Twitter and Facebook to put emphasis on the positive aspects of Greek life and counter the narrative of sorority women as drunken party girls.

TSM posed as a user controlled site founded on the principles of participatory culture, but the parent company heavily curated the site. The relationship between the site's users and the platform's creators illuminates a larger set of tensions within participatory culture. The dispute over community identity between TSM and its users illustrates both the limits of user arguments on social networking sites and the capacity of site owners to control argument and direct debate through platform design. The essay examines the affordances of TSM and how they shape the collective community's arguments on the site. As Grandex does not explain on its site how it prioritizes content for inclusion on the front page or what the company promotes across its many social media accounts on Facebook and Twitter, we analyzed the site to identify paid contributors, assuming their posts would be reflective of the kinds of content Grandex would want to see on the site. As Grandex also does not distribute its official list of paid contributors, we combed through the site and used profiles to identify individuals who indicated Grandex was paying them and analyzed those users' posts and promoted content. During September of 2016, we monitored the front page of the site to see what posts the site prioritized and cross-referenced our findings with Grandex's social media accounts on Twitter and Facebook to see what posts the site promoted. Our analysis led us to conclude that Benkler's (2006) two distinguishing characteristics of social media—content curation and content promotion—shaped the information economy of the site.

In the section below describing the site's content curation, we address content from paid contributors only. While anyone can post on the site for free, Grandex uses its network of paid employees to craft arguments about the nature of sorority life and boost messages in line with those arguments. In the section on promoted content, we address the architecture of the site. With Grandex, Inc., the architecture that informs the distribution of messages lacks transparency. The site builds its public image on the principles of user control that philosophically underpin participatory culture, but the information economy of the site is much more akin to a traditional mass media outlet. The site operators determine the prominence of messages on the site. Finally, #actualsororitymove provides an example of what happens when users attempt to take control of the discussion on the site. The example demonstrates that, in terms of shaping argument, the information economy can have a bigger impact than the participatory culture.

Content Curation

Corporate investment in sites that host participatory culture raises serious questions about the ability to create user centered communities on social media platforms. Social media platforms rely on their users to act as both content providers and content consumers, but ultimately, they look to advertising as their major source of income. When companies are making decisions about the design of a platform, they consider both what will generate the most users and what will make those users most appealing to advertisers.

Grandex accomplishes these tasks by cultivating certain types of content and then curating the site to make that content more prominent. Both TFM and TSM cultivate the content on the sites by paying certain contributors for content. The site openly advertises for freelance writers who provide content that is funny, well written, and original (Ruckh, 2014). When scrolling through the site, the distinction between paid contributors and those who simply post content on their own is not clear. Certain site users, however, include lines in their "bios" that indicate they are paid content providers. Sorority jargon used in posts—such as "exec" (Montemayor, 2016b, first slide of quiz) to refer to leadership, using jokes about the "standards chair" (littleredridinghood, 2016, para. 1) to talk about engaging in oral sex, or referencing "big"/"little" (Crowley, 2014) to talk about sorority initiation—suggests that people familiar with Greek life likely wrote the paid content. Grandex employees guide and approve the content they receive from paid contributors (Ruckh, 2014). In the fall of 2016, the Grandex site featured a professional-looking, roster of employees (33 men and two women). If a site user hovers their mouse over each staff picture, the image changes to one of the employee drinking or partying in other ways. Grandex has built its brand identity around the masculine, "frat bro" persona, and while the content for TSM may come from women, Grandex heavily curates itself to fit the masculine identity.

Promoted Content

Social media sites take many different approaches to organizing their home pages. Twitter shows users the most recent posts. Facebook curates feeds based on the interactions a user has had with the people in their network and the content with which they have previously expressed an interest. Message board sites, like Reddit, often use an upvote/downvote system to decide what content users want to see. Each of these architectural choices impacts the information economy of the social network.

Nowhere on the TSM site is the ranking system for content explained, and this study of the site's front page leaves the matter still open to question. Users have options to like or comment on content, which functions to indicate what they are interested in seeing. However, on the front page, viewers may find a post with 10 likes outranking a post with more than 100 likes. Recency clearly does not function as the criteria, as posts may continue to appear on the front page three or four days after their original uploads. Users cannot tag their content with metadata, and the site has no search engine. If users are looking to make their content more popular on the site, the best way to do so appears to be the production of content types that Grandex is already promoting.

Our study identified two trends that explain what content the TSM site promotes. First, the authors cited for most of the top articles were paid contributors. Second, the content appearing on the front page was almost always celebrity news, sex advice, or thinly veiled advertisements promoting products (e.g., Dorn, 2016; Montemayor, 2016a). In August of 2016, Ali Hin, a paid contributor to TSM, posted a story called "Going to Philanthropy

Events Will Get You Laid, According to Science." The post featured research saying that people who do nice things end up having more sexual partners, and concluded with the advice: "Bring condoms. All that doing good will end in doing it" (Hin, 2016, para. 4). The post was one of many on the site that pushed the image of sorority women seeking sex, including posts with titles like "How To Guarantee You'll Get Laid" (sratty bitch, 2016) and "If You Wanna Get Laid, Fall Is The Season For You" (Stritz, 2016). The front page of the site and the site's Twitter and Facebook feeds heavily promoted such headlines. Marshall (2010) argued that in the same way that traditional mass media provides images of daily celebrity life to teach consumers what high social status looks like, the design of social media platforms promotes certain performances of self as a way of teaching users what popularity looks like and how to achieve it. By pushing certain types of content, Grandex teaches site users how to perform sorority life in the most socially desirable way.

#ActualSororityMoves

The Kappa Zeta chapter of Sigma Kappa at Elon University chose to respond to the Grandex's TSM website. They posted #ActualSororityMoves to Facebook, explaining:

> This is a message for you [TSM]. We are a group of 200 passionate, smart, and assertive women. We are the women of the Kappa Zeta chapter of Sigma Kappa. We are not what your website defines [as] a sorority. Nor can you define us as a whole. We decided that it was our time to stand up for sorority life. Here we are, real women, real messages, and #ActualSororityMoves.
>
> *("Elon University," 2016, para. 1)*

In the weeks that followed the posting, sorority women from across the country posted pictures to Facebook using the hashtag. They told stories about charity work, academic achievement, and sisterhood. Early on, the hashtag got some traction online. The original post had more than 10,000 likes and 7000 shares within a week, but six months later, those numbers had not increased (Groves, 2016). Since May 2016, very little activity occurred with the #ActualSororityMoves hashtag. In the norm, hashtags concentrate and direct the conversation on social media sites where large groups of people are speaking. The community building and attention focusing capabilities of hashtags make them a useful tool for activism online. In the case of #ActualSororityMoves, the hashtag drew women from different sororities and different educational institutions into a community capable of having conversations about how they preferred depictions of sorority life. Women posted about the hashtag on the TSM site, but Grandex buried the posts. In some cases users complained that the site had deleted their posts. Protesters had to move offsite to make their argument, and when their hashtag trended on sites like Twitter and Facebook, the activity forced Grandex to respond.

TSM's official response characterized #ActualSororityMoves campaign as an example of slut shaming. The response from the company started out positive: "It's great that you want people to see you as the passionate, smart, and assertive women you are. We are on the same team here" (Ruckh, 2016, para. 9). In Veronica Ruckh's (2016) post responding to the #ActualSororityMoves campaign, she linked to a series of the site's posts that she said were promoting positive sorority values like displaying intelligence, working towards career goals, and valuing education. Interestingly, the five posts she linked to as examples had no comments and no upvotes, suggesting that the site likely buried these posts. Ultimately, Ruckh eschewed responsibility for the site's depiction of women, because depicting sorority women was not ultimately the site's role or goal: "Our goal is simple: to entertain sorority women and other college-aged women, not to define them" (Ruckh, 2016, para. 11). Ruckh's post circulated online with comments about how the original hashtag campaign was slut shaming (Groves, 2016). Most of the Twitter accounts that were promoting Ruckh's post and criticizing the hashtag had some direct link to Grandex. In general, hashtags privilege short term and sporadic participation in a movement, as opposed to long term commitment (Rentschler, 2014). Putting a spotlight on the issue raised some awareness that Grandex's depiction of sorority women was flawed and problematic. However, it failed to create the kind of long-term pressure that would force change. This situation illustrates the problem of unequal participation and resources as a serious issue within participatory culture. Once the hashtag stopped trending, Grandex still curated the site, paying for certain content and using that content to generate advertising. The company continues to have the infrastructure to maintain their message, and they simply wait out passing interest in a hashtag.

Concluding Thoughts

An emphasis on internet users' ability to take part in creating the media they consume is a defining characteristic of participatory culture, which seeks to increase the number of voices able to participate in conversation online and create a more democratic media system. Sites like TSM entice participants to use their platform through the rhetoric of participatory culture, and much of the ethos of the site comes from their argumentative claims that sorority women created the content on the site and that the site's content is for sorority women. On the surface, the claim is true. However, a combination of the site's affordances and the curator's practice of directing and manipulating content belies the claim. The result is a site where the voices of the community members who congregate on the platform sustain the arguments of the site's creators.

For argumentation scholars, this study points to the need to take a broad view when analyzing arguments online. Rather than focus exclusively on analyzing arguments circulating within a given community, researchers need to account for the way the affordances of a site determine the prominence of different arguments. Furthermore, scholars should consider the extent to which site owners control, manipulate, and interfere with what site users see. A community may have a diverse set of arguments present, but the affordances and curation practices can render a portion of those arguments invisible. Studying argument within participatory culture should involve a consideration of both the practices of the community and the technology that organizes the community.

Critics commonly complain that participatory culture is exploitative because sites ask users to provide content without compensation. However, free labor in participatory culture is not necessarily exploitation. Hesmondhalgh (2010) encouraged the consideration of the material conditions of the labor performed before applying that term. In the case of TSM, the real ethical issue is not the free labor as much as the false pretenses of the solicitation of that free labor. Networking technologies forge the connections that enable content circulation and the conditions for community development. For as Meehan (2007) noted:

> Our ability to achieve critical consciousness remains rooted in the intersection between the political economy in which we live, the collectivities with whom we live, the sense that we make of lived contradictions, and the agency that we exercise together.
>
> *(p. 168)*

The TSM site lacks the transparency necessary for users to evaluate the community of which their labor is a part. Meaningful community-building requires platform designers who believe "we are capable of making decisions, collectively and individually, and that we should have the capacity to express ourselves through a broad range of different forms and practices" (Jenkins, Ito, & boyd, 2016, p. 2). However, the system underlying participatory culture online is consumer culture, and consumer culture does not share the values of participatory culture.

References

Benkler, Y. (2006). *The wealth of networks: How social production transforms markets and freedom.* New Haven, CT: Yale University Press.

Crowley, J. (2014, October 16). What big/little reveal is like for new members, as told by "Sex and The City" [Blog post]. *Total Sorority Move.* Retrieved from http://totalsororitymove.com/what-biglittle-reveal-is-like-for-new-members-as-told-by-sex-and-the-city/

Dorn, R. (2016, October 26). The 2017 TFM spring break destinations are among the best beach and party scenes in the world [Blog post]. *Total Sorority Move.* Retrieved from http://totalsororitymove.com/the-2017-tfm-spring-break-destinations-are-among-the-best-beach-and-party-scenes-in-the-world/

Elon University Sigma Kappa [Kappa Zeta]. (2016, April 19). #ActualSororityMove [Photo album]. *Facebook.* Retrieved from https://facebook.com/pg/sigmakappaelon/photos/?tab=album&album_id=1055177251219475

Grandex. (2016). Retrieved from http://grandex.co/

Groves, I. (2016, April 30). Elon sorority's #ActualSororityMove challenges stereotypes, ruffles feathers. *Times-News.* Retrieved from http://thetimesnews.com/news/20160430/elon-sororitys-actualsororitymove-challenges-stereotypes-ruffles-feathers

Hesmondhalgh, D. (2010). User-generated content, free labour and the cultural industries. *Ephemera, 10* (3/4), 267–284. Retrieved from http://ephemerajournal.org

Hin, A. (2016, August 9). Going to philanthropy events will get you laid, according to science [Blog post]. *Total Sorority Move.* Retrieved from http://totalsororitymove.com/going-to-philanthropy-events-will-get-you-laid-according-to-science/#comments

Jenkins, H. (1992). *Textual poachers: Television fans and participatory culture.* New York, NY: Routledge, Chapman & Hall.

Jenkins, H. (2006). *Convergence culture: Where old and new media collide.* New York, NY: New York University Press.

Jenkins, H. (with Purushotma, R., Weigel, M., Clinton, K., & Robison, A. J). (2009). *Confronting the challenges of participatory culture: Media education for the 21st century.* Cambridge, MA: The MIT Press.

Jenkins, H., Ito, M., & boyd, d. (2016). *Participatory culture in a networked era: A conversation on youth, learning, commerce, and politics.* Cambridge, United Kingdom: Polity Press.

King. [@Dom_the_Great]. (2016, October 17). My professor said she needed a whole bottle of vodka to grade our quizzes. I began to clap, while others joined in, I yelled COLLEGE? #TFM [Twitter post]. Retrieved from https://twitter.com/Dom_the_Great/status/788068546341253120

littleredridinghood. (2016, April 21). 5 tips on giving a blow jay like a champ for girls who hate BJs [Blog post]. *Total Sorority Move.* Retrieved from http://totalsororitymove.com/5-tips-on-giving-a-blow-jay-like-a-champ-for-girls-who-hate-bjs/

Marshall, P. D. (2010). The promotion and presentation of the self: celebrity as marker of presentational media. *Celebrity Studies, 1*(1), 35–48. doi:10.1080/19392390903519057

Meehan, E. (2007). Understanding how the popular becomes popular: The role of political economy in the study of popular communication. *Popular Communication: The International Journal of Media and Culture, 5*(3), 161–170. doi:10.1080/15405700701384830

Montemayor, C. (2016a, October 6). The new too faced sweet peach collection is a nude lovers* dream [Blog post]. *Total Sorority Move.* Retrieved from http://totalsororitymove.com/the-new-too-faced-sweet-peach-collection-is-a-nude-lovers-dream/

Montemayor, C. (2016b, October 9). Quiz: Should you run for exec? [Blog post]. *Total Sorority Move.* Retrieved from http://totalsororitymove.com/quiz-should-you-run-for-exec/

Pierson, E. (2016, May 9). Is sexist rhetoric a total frat move? *The New York Times*. Retrieved from http://kristof.blogs.nytimes.com/2016/05/09/is-sexist-rhetoric-a-total-frat-move/?_r=0

Ruckh, V. (2014, January 28). TSM is looking for contributing writers [Blog post]. *Total Sorority Move*. Retrieved from https://totalsororitymove.com/tsm-is-looking-for-contributing-writers/

Ruckh, V. (2016, April 20). Dear #ActualSororityMove (and anyone else who doesn't understand TSM) [Blog post]. *Total Sorority Move*. Retrieved from http://totalsororitymove.com/dear-actualsorority move-and-anyone-else-who-doesnt-understand-tsm/

Shirky, C. (2009, June). How social media can make history [Video file]. *TED: Ideas Worth Spreading*. Retrieved from https://ted.com/talks/clay_shirky_how_cellphones_twitter_facebook_can_make_his tory?language=en

Shontell, A. (2015, June 8). A startup that frat guys and sorority girls love just raised $2.2 million at a $20 million valuation. *Business Insider*. Retrieved from http://businessinsider.com/grandex-raises-22-million-at-a-20-million-valuation-2015-6

sratty bitch. (2016, February 3). How to guarantee you'll get laid: Part 1 [Blog post]. *Total Sorority Move*. Retrieved from http://totalsororitymove.com/how-to-guarantee-youll-get-laid-part-1/

Stritz, K. (2016, September 28). If you wanna get laid, fall is the season for you [Blog post]. *Total Sorority Move*. Retrieved from http://totalsororitymove.com/if-you-wanna-get-laid-fall-is-the-season-for-you/

Warren C. (2014, January 16). Welcome to total sorority move [Blog post]. *Total Sorority Move*.Retrieved fromhttp://totalsororitymove.com/welcome-to-total-sorority-move/

* The original tweet did not include the apostrophe in accordance with possessive form.

53

SOCIAL PHYSICS AND THE MORAL ECONOMY OF SPREADABLE MEDIA

An Integrated Model for Communication Networking

Zachary Sheldon

The communication and circulation of ideas and information is a timeless practice, and the testament of human history is that individuals and societies at large have accomplished astonishing feats in large part due to the use and application of communicative capabilities. The ruins of ancient societies make clear the enormous physical and organizational effort that went into building these civilizations, which individuals conceived and constructed through countless communicative acts (Standage, 2014). In recent years, the proliferation of mass communication and networked technologies has increased the speed and quantity, though not necessarily the quality, of shared ideas (Carr, 2011; Ellul, 1964; Mumford, 2000; Postman, 1993). Acknowledging the contemporary moment as one where society is "drowning in information, so much so that we don't know what items to pay attention to and which to ignore" (Pentland, 2015, p. 2) raises questions about how individuals and groups can best filter the information they receive in order to put it to further use. Such uses are often productive in an economic sense, but may also foster engagement and participation in politics, entertainment, and the public sphere at large. I argue that understanding the spread of ideas and information in social networks to facilitate effective, useful communication can occur through assessing people and their motivations for contributing to a network, determining how the decision to contribute relates to that network's perceived power structures, and exploring how these elements ultimately manifest in influence within the network.

This essay seeks to engage this claim through applications of theories presented in Pentland's (2015) *Social Physics: How Social Networks Can Make Us Smarter* and Jenkins, Ford, and Green's (2013) *Spreadable Media: Creating Value and Meaning in a Networked Culture*. At their core, both books focus on how social networks spread information, though they differ in most other respects. Pentland's approach from computer science is immersed in harnessing big data to understand human social networks through direct engagement of the process and problems in making sense of overwhelming amounts of information. Jenkins, Ford, and

Green, on the other hand, turned a critical eye to contemporary culture to understand the societal imbalance of power in communication technologies, as well as how the activities of socially networked individuals could have significant impacts on the communicative environment that such technologies foster.

Taken together, I argue that the seemingly dissimilar perspectives of these two works are in fact complimentary to the degree that neither one can independently comprise a complete picture of the operating behaviors of agents within social networks. Examining the elements of people, power, and influence in these two networks provides a more comprehensive explanation of the role that social networks can play in the spread of ideas and information, as well as offering implications for cultural participation. Integrating insights from the qualitative, critical perspective of Jenkins, Ford, and Green can help flesh out the quantitative approach of Pentland to illuminate a theoretical middle ground. To explain, I will begin by summarizing the core concepts of the two works, explaining key points of intersection between them. Then, I analyze the book's perspectives on the three key areas of people, power, and influence and explain how the perspectives interact.

Social Physics and Spreadable Media

Pentland's (2015) social physics is a tool that recognizes the social effects shaping the contemporary world and "seeks to understand how the flow of ideas and information translates into changes in behavior" (p. 5). The practice of social physics involves reality mining, which analyzes patterns in "the newly ubiquitous digital data now available about all aspects of human life" (p. 8) to illuminate how society can use "idea flow" and "social learning" (p. 15) in more flexible, creative, and productive directions. Idea flow is "the propagation of behaviors and beliefs through a social network by means of social learning and social pressure" (p. 20). Social learning involves accruing new strategies or beliefs through the observation of others' behaviors, including learning from stories and through direct experience; both approaches directly relate to the rate and quality of idea flow within a given network.

Jenkins et al.'s (2013) notion of "spreadable media," in contrast, recognizes a dramatic shift from a distribution model of media, where "a small number of producers [...] create discrete and finished products for mass audiences" (p. 1) to a "circulation" model "which sees the public not as simply consumers of preconstructed messages but as people who are shaping, sharing, reframing, and remixing media content in ways which might not have been previously imagined" (p. 2). This shift entails the maxim, "If it doesn't spread, it's dead" (p. 1), which summarizes and emphasizes the new participatory role that audiences have in impacting the relevance and longevity of media artifacts. As such, the researchers seek to understand how and why individuals assist in spreading the media in the ways that they do.

Possible, productive connections exist between the two approaches. Pentland's conception of idea flow, for example, serves as the key link to Jenkins et al.'s spreadable media. The flow of ideas functions as a central part of an artifact's spreadability, in which artifacts with a greater density of attached ideas and content are more likely to spread across a given network. Further, "analyzing the social motives of those who are actually doing the spreading" (Jenkins et al., 2013, p. 295) can help argumentation theorists better understand how ideas begin to flow and spread in the first place.

Both theories note a growing disconnect between traditional views of how society operates and how the proliferation of digital social networks has forced changes in those earlier perspectives. Separately, these theories both contribute to an understanding of how ideas and information flow through social networks, but each method and theory misses the fundamentally valuable insights that the other provides. To explore the value of networking the two theories, I illustrate how each theory approaches individuals and their actions within a given social network.

People

Social networks necessarily require people to thrive, a fact that inherently calls into question the role that individuals have within those networks. The focus here is not on what actions people perform within a network, but why they do the things that they do. For Pentland (2015), analysts should not consider people as individual decision makers, but instead focus on the "dynamic social effects [that] are equally important [in] shaping [their] ideas and are the driving force behind economic bubbles, political revolutions, and the Internet economy" (p. 3). Pentland's (2015) analysis was thus less about the action of the individual and more about the interactions that occur between one or more individuals. Jenkins and his colleagues, in contrast, insisted that spreadable media engages with audiences at the level of the individual. They sought to understand why people participate and share both in and with certain media pieces and franchises. For Jenkins et al. (2013), the outward actions and interactions of individuals functioned as a manifestation of individual decisions to engage with certain groups for specific reasons. Combining these theories shows that while interactions are one benchmark in behavior within the social network, concentrating on individuals and their motives for interacting allows for consideration of their role in the network—prior to stepping forward into a fully participatory role. In the consideration of people, Pentland's conception seemed almost to presume that individuals interact within social networks, while Jenkins et al. ostensibly questioned the subtleties of why this is so. Both perspectives, however, are ultimately related to definitions of power and understandings of how power manifests in networks.

Power

All individuals in a network participate to some degree, even those who simply act as "lurkers" or consumers not actively contributing content to the network. These less active individuals could act as an unidentified audience for those more explicitly participating in the exchange of information or goods on the network. What then serves to spur a non-active participant towards active participation becomes an important question. Pentland's (2015) examples of social physics in action emphasized that spurring individual behavior to increase or hone idea flow often relies on the creation of a social network incentive "to alter the pattern of exchanges between pairs of people" (p. 21). These incentives often appear not in economic reward but rather in increased social pressure, which he defined as "the negotiating leverage one person can exert upon another" (p. 21). Effectively, one person sees the benefits of participation that another person is accruing and desires to share in that benefit, which in turn leads to action. Power, then, rests in individuals and their ability to use power for specific ends. Jenkins et al. (2013), however, argued that power is to be found in the network itself and identified the concept of the "moral economy" (p. 52) as underpinning the willing participation of consumers in the emerging media environment. A concept dating back to Thompson's (1971) analysis of 18th century England, the moral economy is "the social norms and mutual understandings that make it possible for two parties to conduct business" (Jenkins et al., 2013, p. 52). All participants in a transaction need to feel that the other parties involved are behaving in a "morally appropriate fashion" (Jenkins et al., 2013, p. 52) to uphold the sanctity and fairness of the deal. Likewise, breaches of this informal moral contract can cause outrage, inspiring a sense of solidarity among marginalized groups that can spur them on to significant action, as illustrated in early modern Europe when peasants revolted against the feudal economy (Jenkins et al., 2013).

Worth recognizing is that these perspectives are not mutually exclusive. Rather, they circulate and interact simultaneously. Individuals may accrue and use power over time to bend the behavior of a network or individuals within that network, but the community itself exemplifies a different sort of power that transcends the individual and contributes to a network's particular culture Consider the online social media enterprise: The establishment and continued maintenance of any online platform rests in the hands of a few individuals who hold some fundamental power over those using the platform, but the content those users contribute determines external perceptions of the network or even what other types of users the network attracts. Both forms of power ultimately rely on one another to flourish, and they do so, in part, through the exertion of different kinds of influence within the network and its systems.

Influence

As a network's power rests in two distinct places for social physics and spreadable media, the two theories accordingly have differing views on influence and motivation. Pentland's (2015) conception viewed influence and motivation as extrinsic to the network. He downplayed the role of economic incentives as a motivating factor for network participation and saw the social pressure that individuals have over others as critical for motivating the kind of social interactions that lead to better idea flow and greater creativity. Pentland, for example, studied millions of trades and the behaviors and networks of individual stock market traders to understand the relationship between the rate of idea flow on an online financial trading platform and the return on investment that investors experienced. Finding that the most profitable investors were socially diverse in their interactions with other traders, yet not susceptible to the echo chamber's "herd behavior" (p. 33), Pentland (2015) was able to use their gathered data to "tune" the social network to allow traders "to make better decisions and achieve better results" (p. 38). He concluded, "As a result of this tuning we were able to increase the profitability of *all* the social traders by more than 6 percent, thus doubling their profitability" (p. 38). This outcome demonstrated the influence that Pentland and others can wield by using data to "tune" networks and create social pressure. Nevertheless, such efforts at tuning initially depend on someone in a position of power deciding what people ought to do and then controlling the potential actions and rewards of the people engaged in those activities. Individuals can exert power to guide the choices of others for some form of benefit, although who ultimately benefits in some situations is debatable.

For Jenkins et al. (2013), influence and motivations are intrinsic to the network. Their work illustrated their perspective on motivation and influence through examining fan-produced homages and participation in media franchises via contest events and the like. *Spreadable Media* asked questions such as, why do fans participate in media franchises over which they have no real ownership? Why are some people willing to expend considerable amounts of time and money to involve themselves in economically unproductive activities intended to signify their loyalty or admiration of characters, shows, or franchises? Or, what social incentives (or pressures) exist to inspire these forms of participation? Many fans are active participants in their chosen fan community because they are motivated intrinsically, that is, they seek rewards "in intangible ways such as recognition or reputation, status, satisfaction, and above all, their pride in a 'job well done'" (Jenkins et al., 2013, p. 58). This pride of creation and the ability to share that accomplishment is the core of online social networking sites. People want to spread content in which they have some sort of stake, and doing so "has currency within their social networks [which] facilitates conversations they want to have with their friends and families" (p. 60). Rather than acting because of social pressure, many use their self-motivated skills and talents as an entry point into conversation and interaction with others. Evaluating contributions for their quality or relevance enacts pressure, but this does not change the reality that they make the contribution *for* evaluative pressure rather than *because* of it.

The arguments offered in each perspective seem at odds with one another in terms of the sources of influence and how the resulting influences manifest themselves within a network. However, this bifurcation seems unnecessary within the general experience of human behavior. Few individuals are so demonstrably shallow that the sole motivation for their behaviors are external forces of influence and interaction, and perhaps even fewer still are so noble as to only respond to be intrinsic means with no external reward or satisfaction. Instead, a mix of types of motivations typically characterize individuality and cultural engagement. Accordingly, the same complementarity likely translates into networked behavior.

Conclusion

What this analysis shows is that neither Pentland (2015) nor Jenkins et al. (2013) could accurately characterize the full range of possibilities for assessing the motivations or behaviors of individuals and networks, but together, they provide a more comprehensive perspective on why and how information spreads in networked environments. My argument is thus that these two perspectives do not effectively stand alone. Argumentation scholars should consider them in conjunction with one another, as both have distinct benefits to offer in understanding how networked arguers function.

The critical, qualitative approach of *Spreadable Media* provides helpful concepts and methodologies for the examination of individuals and their subtle motivations for action in any system, but needs augmentation from the powerful data-driven tools of social physics. Pentland's (2015) studies often involve standard quantitative measurement tools such as surveys, activity logs, integrated smartphone apps, and "sociometric badges" (p. 12) which collect data on people's "tone of voice, body language, whom they talked to and how much, and more" (p. 220). These tools combine to produce massive amounts of data for analysis and can provide a more complete and comprehensive picture of people's actions within a network. When combined with a critical approach that seeks to ascertain and understand motives for behavior, this data can help provide more insight into the interactions that result, allowing for a greater understanding of the causes and consequences of social interactions.

Likewise, by exclusively emphasizing social interactions as the unit of analysis and attributing those interactions purely to a developed sense of social pressure, Pentland misses out on some of the subtler motives individuals have for engaging in social networking behavior. This is the insightful contribution that *Spreadable Media* offers, demonstrating that individuals may engage with a community or network based purely on the sense of accomplishment and meaning they accrue through contribution, with little or no regard to the types of extrinsic incentives or pressures that social physics seeks to cultivate. In this regard, argumentative scholars should view the moral economy perspective espoused in *Spreadable Media* as complementary to the views of *Social Physics*, allowing for the human element to more distinctly emerge from the mass data collection involved in the social physics approach.

The merger of the two approach opens possibilities to address a wide number of research questions, including those that *Social Physics* and *Spreadable Media* sought to explore.

Pentland's approach could provide a great deal of insight into the popularity of cultural arti-facts, including a more extensive mapping of how that popularity manifests itself. Likewise, the qualitative approach of Jenkins et al. (2013) could provide understandings of why stock market traders make the choices they do, attributing subtler motives to the process than mere profit-seeking. Combining these two theories could also bear significant results by ana-lyzing a variety of other factors, from questions relating to popular culture and media, to how news or rumors spread in local communities, to how political news, artifacts, and ideas spread at the local and national levels. In isolation, both theories provide one part of the story to any given research question. Together, these theories enable a greater and indeed necessary level of information to explain the spread and flow of ideas and information across online networks. This step of combining insights from each system is therefore necessary to give a more complete picture of how ideas flow and can ultimately be cultivated for pro-ductive, creative ends.

References

Carr, N. (2011). *The shallows: What the Internet is doing to our brains.* New York, NY: W. W. Norton.

Ellul, J. (with Merton, R. K.). (1964). *The technological society* (J. Wilkinson, Trans.). New York, NY: Vintage Books.

Jenkins, H., Ford, S., & Green, J. (2013). *Spreadable media: Creating value and meaning in a networked culture.* New York, NY: New York University Press.

Mumford, L. (with Blake, C. N.). (2000). *Art and technics.* New York, NY: Columbia University Press.

Pentland, A. (2015). *Social physics: How social networks can make us smarter* (Reissue ed.). New York, NY: Penguin Books.

Postman, N. (1993). *Technopoly: The surrender of culture to technology.* New York, NY: Vintage Books.

Standage, T. (2014). *Writing on the wall: Social media—The first 2,000 years.* New York, NY: Bloomsbury.

Thompson, E. P. (1971). The moral economy of the English crowd in the eighteenth century. *Past & Present, 50*(1), 76–136. Retrieved from http://jstor.org/stable/650244

PART VI

ARGUMENT CIRCULATION IN OFFLINE NETWORKS

54

NETWORKS OF ARGUMENT AND RELATIONALITY IN THE CONTEMPORARY USE OF AUSCHWITZ NUMBERS IN THE NEW ENGLAND HOLOCAUST MEMORIAL

Linda Diane Horwitz and Daniel C. Brouwer

The diminishing number of survivors and witnesses to the Holocaust generates crises of remembering. One type of response to these crises is the innovative and controversial use of Auschwitz tattoo numbers by people generations removed from the trauma and tragedy of the 1930s and 1940s. In this vein, we have investigated the offspring of Auschwitz survivors' acquisition of permanent number tattoos and the use of temporary Auschwitz number tattoos in two different pedagogical contexts to teach current generations about the Holocaust (Horwitz & Brouwer, 2014, 2018). For our third case study, we feature the use of tattoo numbers of Boston's New England Holocaust Memorial (NEHM). As a memory text, the NEHM adds new inflections to our ongoing investigation. In contrast to the reappropriation of historically accurate numbers the Nazis forcibly inked upon people interned in concentration camps (featured in our first two studies), the numbers NEHM uses are imaginary, with no correspondence to the historical record. In further contrast, the primary location of the NEHM numbers is not on or under the skin of human bodies but on glass pillars the memorial designers used, in part, to cast shadows on the bodies of visitors.

Our analysis of the NEHM enjoins several trajectories in contemporary scholarship on argument, public memory, and memorialization. It foregrounds the significance of the placedness of memorials as constitutive of their meaning and rhetorical force (Blair, Balthrop, & Michel, 2011), affirms the power of anonymity as a rhetorical strategy of memorializing (Blair, Balthrop, & Michel, 2011), marks the increasingly democratized approaches to U.S. memorialization (Blair & Michel, 2007; Linenthal, 1994), and makes greater space for direct acknowledgements of national failures in U.S. commemoration (Blair & Michel,

371

2007; Linenthal, 1994). Additionally, we contend the use of Auschwitz-invoking numbers in the NEHM activates *networking argument* in three distinct ways. First, the numbers work to cultivate a historical generational network by cultivating a capacity for contemporary visitors to remember and feel in relation to Holocaust victims and survivors, thereby connecting the present with the past. Second, the numbers exert rhetorical force in networked relation to the other prominent memorial elements, such as quotations from victims and survivors, statements of historical fact, and emblematic collections of smooth stones. Third, the rhetorical force of NEHM stems from its networked position contiguous to the Boston Freedom Trail, whose "experiential landscapes invite visitors to assume (to occupy) particular subject positions" (Dickinson, Ott, & Aoki, 2006, p. 30) toward the Holocaust in their encounter with the memorial.

The NEHM as Network of Memory

The city of Boston, Massachusetts inaugurated designer Stanley Saitowitz's New England Holocaust Memorial in 1995. Located in the heart of downtown Boston, the NEHM resides in Carmen Park near City Hall and Faneuil Hall. Notably, it is entirely an outdoor memorial, ostensibly available to all at all times. While the exhibit encourages groups of ten or more people to schedule guided tours, the memorial website conveys the assumption that people will engage in self-guided tours. At both ends of a short (under 500 feet long), linear black granite pathway, the exhibit hails visitors into their experience with the command to "remember" in both Hebrew and English. Along the pathway are educational materials, collections of smooth stones, plaques, and engravings displaying the statements of survivors and historians, and, most spectacularly, six glass pillars that each rise to over 50 feet. The memorial associates each pillar with one of the six major Nazi death camps, including Auschwitz-Birkenau, and the pillar design creates a chamber effect in which visitors might momentarily dwell and reflect. As part of the ambience, "smoke rises from charred embers at the bottom of these chambers, reminding us of the horrors of the extermination" ("Self-Guided Tour," 2017, para. 3). The pillars feature an abundance of numbers evoking Auschwitz, specifically 17,280 "unique numbers" and, through patterns of repetition, a total of 2,280,960 "non-unique numbers" ("Self-Guided Tour," 2017, para. 4). "As visitors walk along this path, entering the towers, they are tattooed with the shadows of numbers, and trapped momentarily in a theater of horror" ("Design of the Memorial," 2017, para. 7).

The NEHM, as a networked collection of memory texts, makes some of its claims upon visitors in ways common to memorials generally and Holocaust memorials specifically. Memory studies reveal the conventional goal of learning about the past in order to act better in the present and the future (e.g., Blair, Dickinson, & Ott, 2010). As in our two previous case studies, we are particularly interested in how memory texts communicate knowledge and affect about the Holocaust across generations, from those with direct experience to those who are two or three generations descended, in order to pull newer generations into a network of knowing and feeling. The "remember" statements at both ends of the pathway shape the conditions of engagement into a sort of contract: if visitors walk this pathway, the statements task them with the responsibility to remember. The various elements of the memorial network together toward this goal—the quotes from victims and survivors, the recitation of historical facts, the names of the six primary concentration camps, the abundant numbers, and more working together to enact the spirit of the Torah quote from Isaiah also on display: "I will give them an everlasting name" (Isaiah 56:5, The New King James Version). Like many other Holocaust memorials, the NEHM critiques those individuals, collectives, and states complicit in Nazi atrocities through their occupation of a bystander position. A timeline of the Holocaust on one side of the path collaborates with the famous Pastor Martin Niemöller quote of remorse about his and others' participation as bystanders to hail visitors into both remembering the unfortunate past and orienting themselves into upstander subject positions in the current day.

Distinct to the NEHM, however, are the ways the memorial networks its claims in relation to U.S. revolutionary history via its proximity to the Freedom Trail. The Freedom Trail, featuring sites and events from the colonies' revolutionary war against Great Britain in the late 1700s, does not include the NEHM as an official site along its 2.5-mile expanse. In contrast, the NEHM website is keen in citing its location on "Boston's historic Freedom Trail" ("The Memorial," 2017, para. 1), where over four million annual visitors to the trail might encounter the memorial. In this way, the NEHM articulates its proximity to the Freedom Trail as an important part of its "experiential landscape" (Dickinson, Ott, & Aoki, 2006, p. 28), offering visitors a bodily reminder of the Holocaust in order to inspire upstander activity when a parallel or analogical case occurs. Visitors who arrive at the NEHM via the Freedom Trail experience the memorial through the lens of their general encounters with monumental places and events and the specific principles and values of the revolution. The revolutionaries chose to make a stand for liberty, as they fought even when the odds were against them because they believed in self-sovereignty. Visitors walk the Freedom Trail to see and remember the bravery of the past that produced this nation. In this sense, the NEHM takes the Freedom Trail and turns it into a prism through which visitors might re-read U.S. conduct through World War II. Thereby, the NEHM stages a connection between the U.S. revolution and the U.S. role in World War II, advancing a tacit claim the U.S. failed to abide by the values it celebrates, but did not enact. The United States failed to defend values of liberty, freedom, and sovereignty and should have acted differently. Victims of the Holocaust did not die for the United States as revolutionary heroes who changed the world, but as a place dedicated to remembering the Holocaust. The NEHM foregrounds the victims as people who the United States might have saved had the nation not waited so long to transform itself from a bystander to an upstander-liberator.

Contemporary Uses of Holocaust Numbers in the NEHM

The most dominant feature of the NEHM is the six glass pillars. As noted above, the pillars broadcast an extraordinary abundance of numbers:

> Each tower consists of 22 individual panels of glass. The outside walls of the panels are inscribed with seven-digit numbers, evoking the numbers tattooed on the arms of the concentration camp prisoners. Numbers are arranged in 8×10 blocks, each block having sets of six numbers arranged in a 6×6 grid. A single panel contains 17,280 unique numbers, which are subsequently repeated throughout the memorial. In total there are 2,280,960 non-unique numbers listed on the 132 panels representing the six million Jews who perished during the Holocaust.
>
> *("Self-Guided Tour," para. 4)*

The practices of contemporary people acquiring permanent or temporary replicas of real Auschwitz tattoos resignify the meanings of the original tattoos, express recognition of familial inheritances of trauma, and work cognitively and affectively to cultivate new witnesses to the atrocities of the Holocaust (Horwitz & Brouwer, 2014, 2018).

Significantly, however, all the numbers on the NEHM pillars are false; none of them correspond to any actual person interned at Auschwitz. The Nazis only tattooed a small fraction of victims of the Holocaust with numbers—404,481 people according to one authoritative count ("Prisoner Numbers," 2017, concluding table)—but nowhere close to the over 2 million numbers on the NEHM pillars. Related, the 404,481 distinct numbers Nazis forcibly inked on Auschwitz prisoners significantly exceed the 17,280 unique numbers on the pillars. Further, while each of the numbers on the pillars includes seven digits, the real numbers never exceeded six digits, and many numbers began with a letter to specify the type of prisoner (e.g., Jewish, Roma, political prisoner; "Prisoner Numbers," 2017). Finally, although the memorial's six towers reference the six Nazi death camps, the Auschwitz complex is the only place the Nazis tattooed numbers on prisoners. In several ways, then, the repetition of numbers on the NEHM pillars produces captivating truth gaps. The memorial website is candid about its choices of fabrication and copious repetition of numbers as evocative rather than authentic and historically accurate, yet evidence reveals some visitors persist in assuming the numbers are accurate. Reviewers on the Yelp website, for example, have claimed that "all the numbers listed on the glass walls are the tattoo numbers of each of the people that lost their lives" (Dawn, 2014) or "seeing the numbers of all the captives engraved in the glass towers is what really puts the tragedy into perspective" (Chris L., 2014).

Typically, argumentation scholars consider claims to be valid and to gain strength when they use accurate evidence; inaccurate evidence typically enervates the validity and force of an argument. The NEHM's copious repetition of false numbers produces an openly avowed truth gap, but the memorial manages its "lies" in order to produce a truth effect. Resonant with the aphorism some attribute to Pablo Picasso that "art is a lie that makes us realize the truth," the imaginary numbers carry a truthful function— useful errors producing a truthful utility. Phillips's (2010) account of the relations between memory and rhetoric in a broad set of Plato and Aristotle's writings bolsters the notion that the inaccuracy of a sign need not fatally compromise the essence of an argument. Against the common rendering that the main offense against memory is forgetting, Phillips noted, instead, that the main concern is "the failure of our memory through the process of misremembering or misrecognition" (p. 210). In this vein memorial-goers should more accurately read "the seemingly ubiquitous admonition to 'Never Forget' as 'Never Remember Differently'" (p. 212). The imaginary numbers on the NEHM pillars permit visitors to misremember, but they do not intend to invite people to remember wrongly. Unless they are writing history dissertations, the imaginary numbers need not overly vex visitors, because the numbers evoke the essence or the nature of the genocide. By themselves, but also networked with the other components of the NEHM, the imaginary numbers work cognitively and affectively to tell a good—that is, moral—story that suggests values by which to live. Unlike the Vietnam Veterans Memorial with its engraved names of real soldiers or the U.S. Holocaust Museum and Memorial with its entry-passports of real Nazi victims, the pillar numbers do not work to cultivate relationality through a one-to-one relationship. Instead, the repeated numbers produce an excess that cultivates a sense of magnitude. Networked with the memorial's proximity to the Freedom Trail, the pillars' magnitude-through-repetition reminds and indicts a U.S. government and populace that stood by rather than stood up.

When the pillars cast the numbers as shadows on to visitors' bodies, they produce a different rhetorical force. Notably, the numbers appear on the *outside* of the pillars, which are not accessible from the clearly marked path. Inside the pillars, where the memorial expects visitors to pause separated from the busy surrounding neighborhood in a sort of contemplation cocoon, they see the numbers in reverse—recognizable as numbers but not optimally legible. Because the numbers also appear on the outside of the pillars, however, daytime sunlight and nighttime permanent illumination cast shadows of endlessly repeating legible numbers upon visitors' bodies. Staying open to visitors' disparate experiences and impressions, the architect Saitowitz identified this as an intentional design feature and imagined that some visitors "*feel the shadows of [...] numbers tattoo their flesh*" ("About the Architect," 2017, para. 3). These tattoos touch the skin at a distance. The palpability of the touch—the ability to sense an impression on one's skin—is variable to be sure.

In the enclosure of the pillars and in proximity to the rising steam and other elements of the memorial, the lack of choice in seeing the iconic numbers on one's body invites a temporal bodily experience. When the numbers cast shadow tattoos upon the body, the memorial invites visitors to imagine not that it forcefully inscribes permanent tattoos upon their bodies but, instead, that those interned at Auschwitz had that experience. In the case of the NEHM, visitors experience these shadows as palpable on their bodies. Cognitive psychologists have argued that when our bodies cast shadows, those shadows alter our perceptions in the direction of reduced distance between self and object (Kuylen, Balas, & Thomas, 2014). In a parallel sense, when the pillars cast imaginary number shadows upon the body, the shadows work in part to reduce the distance between visitor and victim. Here, the shadows enact a metaphor for empathy, as they extend the life of the dead victims of the Holocaust. The shadow tattoos assist in the effort of giving an "everlasting name" (Isaiah 56:5, The New King James Version), which serves the larger goal of remembering Holocaust victims. More, the shadow tattoos function as embodied reminders that the Holocaust happened and the U.S. government did not act in a timely manner—stigmata from history casting stigmata upon contemporary visitors' bodies.

Conclusion

Fearing that contemporary memorializing practices encourage forgetting, this project illustrates the efficacy of Young's (1993) criterion that visitors, critics, and scholars should judge Holocaust memorials by how they inspire the act of doing memory work among those who encounter them. In a broad sense, the NEHM cultivates an intergenerational network of relationality and empathy. It does so in part by networking itself with the Boston Freedom Trail, leveraging the physical proximity to cultivate particular resonances between Holocaust values and sensibilities with those of the U.S. revolution. More specifically, the NEHM memorializes U.S. failure in the face of the Holocaust as much as the nation's success. This placedness works in conjunction with the enthymematic demands that the semiotic and material elements of the NEHM place on visitors. While the instructions and inscriptions tell a lot to audiences, other components (e.g., the numbers and the steam) ask a lot of audiences. In the enthymematic labor of reading the numbers inscribed on the glass pillars, audiences might enact what we call a "Jewish hermeneutic" that privileges the essence of truth as much as the facts of the case. Visitors need not be Jewish to practice a Jewish hermeneutic as they interpret the imaginary numbers not as direct correspondences to victims and survivors, but as para-anonymous signs that point to the magnitude of atrocity. Like the U.S. Holocaust Memorial Museum and Holocaust education in the United States in general, the NEHM makes it clear that the role of the visitor is to remember and, in the future, to move more quickly from bystander to upstander.

References

About the Architect. (2017). *The New England Holocaust Memorial*. Retrieved from http://nehm.org/the-memorial/design-of-the-memorial/about-the-architect/

Blair, C., Balthrop, V. W., & Michel, N. (2011). The arguments of the tombs of the unknown: Relationality and national legitimation. *Argumentation, 25*(4), 449–468. doi:10.1007/s10503-011-9216-9

Blair, C., Dickinson, G., & Ott, B. L. (2010). Introduction: Rhetoric/memory/place. In G. Dickinson, C. Blair, & B. L. Ott (Eds.), *Places of public memory: The rhetoric of museums and memorials* (pp. 1–54). Tuscaloosa, AL: University of Alabama Press.

Blair, C., & Michel, N. (2007). The AIDS Memorial Quilt and the contemporary culture of public commemoration. *Rhetoric & Public Affairs, 10*(4), 595–626. doi:10.1353/rap.2008.0024

Chris, L. (2014, January 20). Recommended reviews for New England Holocaust Memorial [Web post]. *Yelp*. Retrieved from https://yelp.com/biz/new-england-holocaust-memorial-boston?start=20

Dawn, O. (2014, April 23). Recommended reviews for New England Holocaust Memorial [Web post]. *Yelp*. Retrieved from https://yelp.com/biz/new-england-holocaust-memorial-boston?start=20

Design of the Memorial. (2017). *The New England Holocaust Memorial*. Retrieved from http://nehm.org/the-memorial/design-of-the-memorial/

Dickinson, G., Ott, B. L., & Aoki, E. (2006). Spaces of remembering and forgetting: The reverent eye/I at the Plains Indian Museum. *Communication and Critical/Cultural Studies, 3*(1), 27–47. doi:10.1080/14791420500505619

Horwitz, L. D., & Brouwer, D. C. (2018). Temporary holocaust tattoos: Recovering signs for collective prosthetic memory. In R. A. Lake (Ed.), *Recovering argument* (pp. 39–44). New York, NY: Routledge.

Horwitz, L. D., & Brouwer, D. C. (2014). The progenic trauma tattoo as resignification: Auschwitz 157622, A-15510, 4559,.... In C. H. Palczewski (Ed.), *Disturbing argumentation* (pp. 87–92). New York, NY: Routledge.

Kuylen, C., Balas, B., & Thomas, L. E. (2014). My shadow, myself: Cast-body shadows are embodied. *Psychonomic Bulletin & Review, 21*(3), 676–681. doi:10.3758/s13423-013-0545-6

Linenthal, E. T. (1994). The boundaries of memory: The United States Holocaust Memorial Museum. *American Quarterly, 46*, 406–433. doi:10.2307/2713271

The Memorial. (2017). *The New England Holocaust Memorial*. Retrieved from http://nehm.org/the-memorial/

Prisoner Numbers. (2017). *Memorial and museum, Auschwitz-Birkenau: Former German Nazi concentration and extermination camp*. Retrieved from http://auschwitz.org/en/museum/auschwitz-prisoners/prisoner-numbers

Phillips, K. R. (2010). The failure of memory: Reflections on rhetoric and public remembrance. *Western Journal of Communication, 74*(2), 208–223. doi:10.1080/10570311003680600

Self-Guided Tour. (2017). *The New England Holocaust Memorial*. Retrieved from http://nehm.org/visit/self-guided-tour/

Young, J. E. (1993). *The texture of memory: Holocaust memorials and meaning*. New Haven, CT: Yale University Press.

55

NETWORKED RECONCILIATION

Tyler Hiebert, Randall A. Lake, and Chris Robbins

In 2015, the Canadian Truth and Reconciliation Commission (CTRC) published the full extent of crimes committed over one hundred years by the Canadian government and churches in residential schools. The report revealed that the Canadian residential school system, a system that began in 1876 and closed a mere 20 years ago, was a form of "cultural genocide" (Truth and Reconciliation Commission, 2015, p. VII, para. 1) that attempted to "kill the Indian in him, save the man" (Barrows, 1892, p. 46, para. 1). This paternalistic goal notwithstanding, the system did kill thousands of Aboriginal children and subjected tens of thousands more to physical and sexual abuse, traumatizing entire generations (Truth and Reconciliation Commission, 2015). The Indian Residential School Settlement Agreement (IRSSA) addressed this historical pattern of genocide. The IRSSA paid $2,000,000,000 in reparations, initiated the CTRC, which published six volumes of its findings about the crimes, and allocated $20,000,000 for "commemorative projects" to encourage reconciliation through the arts (Truth and Reconciliation Commission, 2015, "Commemoration and Community," para. 2).

To help the public better understand reconciliation, several programs have presented the experiences of the residential schools' survivors. This paper analyzes one such installation, the Witness Blanket, which serves as a national monument for victims of the residential school system. After survivors submitted networks of objects, master-woodworker Carey Newman (traditionally known as Ha-yalth-Kingeme) emplaced them in a traveling art installation (Newman, 2015). Each object speaks to the memories of one or more survivors, reaching out to viewers and creating opportunities to engage with survivors' personal experiences. We suggest that the networks these objects create model a form of reconciliation by portraying strong relationships among objects, survivors, and viewers, as the installation invites viewers to listen to the objects and the survivors in real life. This invitation (really a requirement) to listen departs from traditional forms of theorizing about national reconciliation in working from the ground up rather than the top down. Moreover, many theories of reconciliation privilege the institutional politics of reconciliation at the cost of reconciliation in the personal lives of those most affected by previous injustices. The Witness Blanket theorizes in the opposite order and creates a vision of how reconciliation can build out of lasting networks of listening.

Vernacular and grassroots presentational efforts to commemorate past atrocities abound at both the national and local levels (Margry & Sánchez-Carretero, 2011). Grassroots monuments, such as the ones that popped up after mass shootings at Columbine or Las Vegas, often affectively speak to the power of commemoration in the public imaginary. These monuments serve many functions including reminding survivors of the need for revenge (Volkan, 2006), reinforcing or attacking identities (Dwyer, 2010), protesting (Margry & Sánchez-Carretero, 2011), and countering hegemonic narratives (Strakosch, 2010). While the Witness Blanket does many of these things, it also represents a theory of reconciliation and argues that reconciliation ought to have its foundation in the lived experiences of Aboriginals. It does not merely commemorate the victims of the residential school system, but speaks to a wide audience about how to engage with victims of residential schools in the process of healing and community building.

The Witness Blanket is an argument for a form of Canadian-Aboriginal reconciliation that requires diffuse networks of listening. It performs an indigenous theory of networked reconciliation based on the artist's own experience of dealing with his father's trauma at residential schools. By revisiting the place of his father's trauma, Newman could see a "great weight lifted from his [father's] shoulders" (personal communication, December 4, 2016). The Witness Blanket offered Aboriginal communities the same opportunity to revisit their own traumas through the process of submitting artifacts. It was the process of creating a cohesive monument out of these artifacts, and the stories that accompanied them, through which Newman began to theorize about reconciliation.

Reconciliation

Racial reconciliation is "a call for rhetoric and a form of rhetorical activity" (Doxtader, 2003, p. 268). Recently, scholars have wrestled with rhetorical conceptions of reconciliation and offered a number of different theories (e.g., Doxtader, 2003; Govier, 2006; Hatch, 2008; McPhail & Frank, 2009). Reconciliation has taken many different forms over time— from the Greeks to the present—but it has always existed between "language and speech" (Doxtader, 2003, p. 286). Speaking about the Truth and Reconciliation Commission in South Africa, Doxtader (2003) claimed:

> Cast as a rhetorical concept, reconciliation is a way to *think of speaking* in those moments when we stand at a loss for words and a *speaking to thought* in which thinking is confronted with the character of its (non)identity.
>
> *(p. 270)*

Given this conception, reconciliation intends to help the individual see and understand the Other, which can lead to "Other-wise" thinking (Doxtader, 2004). By displacing the colonial logics that prevail within traditional reconciliatory performances, this form of thinking creates opportunities for reconciliation based on the ideas and behaviors of indigenous thinkers.

While Doxtader focused on South Africa, Hatch (2008) focused on the North American context. Hatch described reconciliation as a tragicomic rhetorical genre in which individuals take on different roles (based on the tragic and comic forms): oppressors assume the role of the comic; victims take on the role of the tragic. The comic oppressor is not completely bereft of good but is merely acting out of a mistaken value system. Thus, reconciliation is, at least partially, a process of changing the oppressor's mind. However, reconciliation is not just about cognitive transformation; it also requires both economic and social-psychological redress, including "confessing truth(s), apologizing for offenses, [and] forgiving offenders" (Hatch, 2006, p. 189). Reconciliation efforts rely for success on discursive processes and an understanding of the role of structural racism in society. But, for Hatch (2006), such efforts also need a "cooperative discourse regarding reparations and symbols of reunion for restorative justice" (p. 189).

Both Doxtader and Hatch largely adopt top-down perspectives on reconciliation, seeking primarily to define and theorize reconciliation. This approach, however, can overlook the memories and public arguments of oppressed groups and individuals and, more importantly, ground-up reconciliation efforts. We take seriously Chief Dr. Robert Joseph's admonition regarding Canadian reconciliation efforts with First Nations: "Listen. Listen with all of your heart and soul" (ReconciliationCanada, 2016). Treating the Witness Blanket as a presentational argument for reconciliation from the ground up prioritizes the specific relationships among communities and individuals involved in day-to-day processes of reconciliation.

The Witness Blanket

The Witness Blanket is a 40-foot-long, 10-foot-high "blanket" of more than 700 objects. The blanket is a highly visual and tactile model of reconciliation, understandable as a network. Each shard within the network is one object from a residential school building, a property, or a survivor. A grassroots nationwide movement collected the objects through a process that started on social media (personal communication, December 4, 2016). Two collaborators travelled around the country, going to former residential schools in search of objects and survivors' belongings. Still, local communities selected more than 80% of the objects to send to Newman, who subsequently wove them into the blanket (personal communication, December 4, 2016).

The objects range in size and material from a door to paper letters. The descendants of survivors gave some of the objects, including braids of hair from Newman's own daughters in honor of their grandfather (personal communication, December 4, 2016). Still other objects include students' paintings, children's shoes, and even light fixtures. The wide array of items that make up the blanket speaks to the memories of the survivors and vividly reminds viewers of the trauma the residential schools caused.

Placed within a small room, the blanket is striking not only because of its size but also because of the diverse texture of the objects. Each of the objects fits within a multicolored wood frame that Newman crafted. While the wood paneling frames the objects, it remains a background to the objects and their stories. The frame has four upended square X-shaped panels, split between horizontal panels. Each of the square shaped panels has a flower with eight petals made of rhomboid-shaped objects centered within them. The Witness Blanket has 13 panels and meets the individual in the middle with a half-ajar door, welcoming the visitor to come to it and begin the process of listening. Each visitor can experience the blanket in one of its many locations throughout Canada.

Not originally designed to be a traveling monument, the Witness Blanket's popularity sparked a change to render the monument mobile (personal communication, December 4, 2016). The blanket has removable multiple panels, each transferable to the next presentation of the monument. Twenty-one different sites in Canada, stretching from British Colombia to Nova Scotia, have shown or will show the monument in the future (personal communication, December 4, 2016). The blanket will continue to travel to different sites through at least 2021, with local funding from the prospective host. In many cases, Aboriginal communities have raised the funds to pay for the cost of shipping. While the Witness Blanket has appeared in archives and libraries, it has also garnered international attention. The Duke and Duchess of Cambridge, for example, viewed the blanket and its traumatic narrative of settler colonialism while visiting British Colombia (personal communication, December 4, 2016).

Beginning with the blanket's appearance at the Canadian Museum of Human Rights (CMHR, n.d.) in 2015, iPods and apps for cellphones became part of the viewing experience (Media One Multimedia, 2015). These devices enable viewers to engage with each object, including its historical and geographical story. The mediated applications also direct viewers to other, similar objects. In addition, the CMHR invited viewers to type two words that expressed what reconciliation meant to them, and the most popular words would often appear on a wall next to the blanket.

Networked Reconciliation

Prior scholarship (e.g., Lake & Pickering, 1998; Langer, 1953; McGeough, Palczewski, & Lake, 2015; McNaughton, 2007; Roberts, 2007) has confirmed that presentational forms of art can argue. The Witness Blanket is a visual argument for networked reconciliation, an argument that viewers perform when interacting with it. Viewers can interact with objects, in much the same way that they can interact with survivors. They can listen to the stories of the individuals and create networks within Canadian communities to disseminate the knowledge they have learned. The Witness Blanket quilts these "bits and pieces" into a cumulative argument about the personal traumas of the individuals the Canadian government abducted. Doxtader (2003) wrote about this process of storytelling: "Testimony was claimed to broker reconciliation as it established the standing of individuals to speak of their experience before and in relation to others" (p. 280). This process of visual storytelling creates a space for reconciliation by grounding the survivor in a position of speaker and society in the role of listener.

The blanket's networked argument of reconciliation resembles a diffusion of innovation model of networks (Rogers, 2003; Ryan & Gross, 1943; Valente, 1995, 2010). Like technological innovations (Ryan & Gross, 1943), health behavioral changes (Valente & Saba, 1998), and public policy shifts (Meseguer, 2005), community networks perhaps best spread reconciliation where key individuals—opinion leaders within communities and individuals that bridge between communities—model legitimate behavioral adoption (Borgatti, 2006). Change that spreads from person to person is far more sustainable over the long term, especially in contrast with top-down interventions (Valente, 2012). Recipients view recommended changes most favorably when they originate with peers (Simoni, Nelson, Franks, Yard, & Lehavot, 2011; Valente, Hoffman, Ritt-Olson, Lichtman, & Johnson, 2003). The Witness Blanket fosters such "cooperative discourse" (Hatch, 2006, p. 189) through its emphasis on the interpersonal nature of reconciliation, that is, people's responsibility to "listen with all of [their] heart[s]" (ReconciliationCanada, 2016) and to seek reconciliation together.

The way in which viewers interact with the blanket models ideal reconciliatory behaviors for individuals in their communities. Confronted by the blanket's overwhelming scale, viewers have difficulty acknowledging, much less remedying, every memory its pieces represent and evoke. Viewers must focus their attention on a single object. The app tells the object's story and leads the viewer to another, and so on. Each viewer experiences a unique subset of objects leading them to a better understanding of the larger tragic narrative of Canada's shameful past. The viewer then listens to the narratives of the individual objects, representing specific events that people in their communities have experienced. This process of discovery and listening models diffusive listening networks that are interactive with the life of the viewer.

Argumentation scholars should recognize that authorities, such as the Canadian government, cannot simply dispense reconciliation. No single agent can reconcile such extensive wrongdoing (Govier, 2006). The work of weaving each object, with its (non)identarian subject potential, into a whole represents both a radically personal and communal attempt to understand and achieve reconciliation. All Canadians must confront pieces of the ugly legacy of the residential school system, seeking reconciliation with its individual victims and modeling this process for their communities. The Witness Blanket encourages Doxtader's (2004) "Other-wise" thinking by confronting viewers with the victims' tragic position. Viewers recognize the Other in a tattered shoe, a child's doll, or even the partially opened door that reads "Sunday Mass." Certainly, losing one's own subjectivity and entering another's is impossible; nonetheless, in this case, viewers come to acknowledge other subjectivities alongside their own. The Witness Blanket also makes what Hatch (2008) called a "tragicomic" presentation. When confronted by tragedy, viewers comically can correct their own mistaken views about race and/or reconciliation. Such acknowledgment can foster conciliatory listening habits. In this way, acknowledgment and reconciliation can slowly diffuse through interpersonal networks in both Aboriginal and non-Aboriginal Canadian communities. The Witness Blanket demands that viewers reconcile with individual elements of the oppressive past and argues that reconciliation is possible only through the creation of networks of listening individuals. As the artist Carey Newman quipped, "#HeyWhitePerson let's work on Reconciliation together" (Newman, 2016).

The Witness Blanket powerfully demonstrates a vision of networked reconciliation that calls its viewers to listen and to innovate reconciliation. Just as individuals tore the blanket's shards from their original settings, so the Canadian government tore approximately 150,000 Aboriginal children from their homeland, some never to return. The shards and the Blanket itself argue for a new mode of reconciliation, which the act of viewing performs. More importantly, they give viewers something concretely to do: listen, create networks, and build community.

References

Barrows, I. C. (Ed.). (1892). *Proceedings of the national conference of charities and correction at the nineteenth annual session held in Denver, Col., June 23–29, 1892.* Retrieved from http://quod.lib.umich.edu/n/ncosw/ACH8650.1892.001?rgn=main;view=fulltext

Borgatti, S. P. (2006). Identifying sets of key players in a social network. *Computational & Mathematical Organization Theory, 12*(1), 21–34. doi:10.1007/s10588-006-7084-x

Canadian Museum for Human Rights. (n.d.). The Witness Blanket [Presentational art]. Retrieved from https://humanrights.ca/exhibit/witness-blanket

Doxtader, E. (2003). Reconciliation—A rhetorical concept/ion. *Quarterly Journal of Speech, 89*(4), 267–292. doi:10.1080/0033563032000160954

Doxtader, E. (2004). The potential of reconciliation's beginning: A reply. *Rhetoric & Public Affairs, 7*(3), 378–390. doi:10.1353/rap.2005.0005

Dwyer, L. (2010). Building a monument: Intimate politics of "reconciliation" in post-1965 Bali. In A. L. Hinton (Ed.), *Transitional justice: Global mechanisms and local realities after genocide and mass violence* (pp. 227–248). New Brunswick, NJ: Rutgers University Press.

Govier, T. (2006). *Taking wrongs seriously: Acknowledgement, reconciliation, and the politics of sustainable peace.* Amherst, NY: Humanity Books.

Hatch, J. B. (2006). Beyond apologia: Racial reconciliation and apologies for slavery. *Western Journal of Communication, 70*(3), 186–211. doi:10.1080/10570310600843496

Hatch, J. B. (2008). *Race and reconciliation: Redressing wounds of injustice.* Lanham, MD: Lexington Books.

Lake, R. A., & Pickering, B. A. (1998). Argumentation, the visual, and the possibility of refutation: An exploration. *Argumentation, 12*(1), 79–93. doi:10.1023/A:1007703425353

Langer, S. K. (1953). *Feeling and form.* New York, NY: Scribner's.

Margry, P. J., & Sánchez-Carretero, C. (2011). Rethinking memorialization: The concept of grassroots memorials. In P. J. Margry & C. Sánchez-Carretero (Eds.), *Grassroots memorials: The politics of memorializing traumatic death* (pp. 1–50). New York, NY: Berghahn Books.

McGeough, R. E., Palczewski, C. H., & Lake, R. A. (2015). Oppositional memory practices: US memorial spaces as arguments over public memory. *Argumentation and Advocacy*, *51*(4), 231–254. doi:10.1080/00028533.2015.11821852

McNaughton, M. J. (2007). Hard cases: Prison tattooing as visual argument [Special issue]. *Argumentation and Advocacy*, *43*(3–4), 133–143. doi:10.1080/00028533.2007.11821669

McPhail, M. L., & Frank, D. A. (2009). Slouching toward coherence: Rhetoric, religion, and the broken promissory note of racial justice in the United States. *Southern Communication Journal*, *74*(2), 209–225. doi:10.1080/10417940902820847

Media One Multimedia. (2015). Witness Blanket (Version 1.1.2) [Mobile application software]. Retrieved from http://itunes.apple.com

Meseguer, C. (2005). Policy learning, policy diffusion, and the making of a new order. *The Annals of the American Academy of Political and Social Science*, *598*(1), 67–82. doi:10.1177/0002716204272372

Newman, C. (2015). Witness Blanket [Presentational Art]. Retrieved from http://witnessblanket.ca/wp-content/uploads/2014/11/WitnessBlanket-bg.jpg

Newman, C. [@blueravenheart]. (2016, November 14). #HeyWhitePerson let's work on Reconciliation together [Tweet]. Retrieved from https://twitter.com/blueravenart/status/798375736272777216

ReconciliationCanada. [@Rec_Can]. (2016, November 3). What is the role Canadians & newcomers can play in reconciliation? – "Listen. Listen with all of your heart & soul" Chief Joseph #namwayut [Tweet]. Retrieved from https://twitter.com/Rec_Can/status/794384291643785216

Roberts, K. G. (2007). Visual argument in intercultural contexts: Perspectives on folk/traditional art [Special issue]. *Argumentation and Advocacy*, *43*(3–4), 152–163. doi:10.1080/00028533.2007.11821671

Rogers, E. M. (2003). *Diffusion of innovations* (5th ed.). New York, NY: Free Press.

Ryan, B., & Gross, N. (1943). Acceptance and diffusion of hybrid corn seed in two Iowa communities. *Rural Sociology*, *8*(1), 15–24.

Simoni, J. M., Nelson, K. M., Franks, J. C., Yard, S. S., & Lehavot, K. (2011). Are peer interventions for HIV efficacious? A systematic review. *AIDS and Behavior*, *15*(8), 1589–1595. doi:10.1007/s10461-011-9963-5

Strakosch, E. (2010). Counter-monuments and nation-building in Australia. *Peace Review*, *22*(3), 268–275. doi:10.1080/10402659.2010.502065

Truth and Reconciliation Commission of Canada. (2015). *Canada's residential schools: The history, part I origins to 1939. The final report of the truth and reconciliation commission of Canada, volume 1*. Montreal, Canada: McGill-Queen's University Press.

Valente, T. W. (1995). *Network models of the diffusion of innovations*. Cresskill, NJ: Hampton Press.

Valente, T. W. (2010). *Social networks and health: Models, methods, and applications*. Oxford, United Kingdom: Oxford University Press.

Valente, T. W. (2012). Network interventions. *Science*, *337*(6090), 49–53. doi:10.1126/science.1217330

Valente, T. W., Hoffman, B. R., Ritt-Olson, A., Lichtman, K., & Johnson, C. A. (2003). Effects of a social-network method for group assignment strategies on peer-led tobacco prevention programs in schools. *American Journal of Public Health*, *93*(11), 1837–1843. doi:10.2105/AJPH.93.11.1837

Valente, T. W., & Saba, W. P. (1998). Mass media and interpersonal influence in a reproductive health communication campaign in Bolivia. *Communication Research*, *25*(1), 96–124. doi:10.1177/009365098025001004

Volkan, V. D. (2006). What some monuments tell us about mourning and forgiveness. In E. Barkan & A. Karn (Eds.), *Taking wrongs seriously: Apologies and reconciliation* (pp. 115–131). Redwood City, CA: Stanford University Press.

56

TO TELL OUR OWN TRUTHS

Settler Postcolonialism as an Antecedent to Native American Argumentation Studies

Margret McCue-Enser

Building on the work of space, place, and bodies as argument, this essay explores how a nineteenth-century Midwestern settlers' village celebrates a version of settler colonialism stripped of the machinations of systematic displacement of the Native Americans. I argue that as part of a broader network of social, economic, and cultural arguments of the present, a historic place, *The Landing,* works to erase the more troubling events of the past while simultaneously normalizing their implications for the present. Founded in 1969, *The Landing* is an 88-acre living museum assembled around the ruins of an inn whose builder, Richard Murphy, served as the area's first Indian Agent to the Dakota (Sioux), as well as its first territorial senator. This analysis makes two important contributions to argumentation studies. First, the essay builds on the work of embodied/emplaced argument. It exemplifies how multiple embodied/emplaced arguments of place across time work in a kind of transference through which dominant ideologies transcend not only space but time as well. Second, it expands studies in Native American argumentation. It examines the cultural practices and discourses settler societies tell, not about Native American peoples but rather about themselves, showing how these arguments work to anesthetize the historical removal and contemporary marginalization of Native American communities and cultures.

This analysis examines settler postcolonialism as a network of discursive, material, and spatial elements that invites visitors to identify first, as settlers within the confines of *The Landing* and, second, as stewards of the sociological, cultural, and economic icons of postcolonial settler society once they emerge outside of the park. In order to explore how *The Landing* functions as an embodied/emplaced argument, this analysis will focus on: (a) the mapping and naming of areas of the park as it appears in brochures and posted placards; (b) the physical spatial layout of the trails and buildings; (c) the naming and dating of buildings as they appear on the buildings themselves; (d) the physical proximity the buildings in relation to others present during the similar time period; (e) the immigration patterns of various ethnic groups who entered the space; and (f) natural landmarks, such as the Minnesota River. After examining how the space embodies or performs argument, this discussion then

explores the many programs and other events that allow visitors to dress as settlers, participate in work and recreation, and engage in seasonal rituals. I will then turn to the influences
of the broader socio, economic, and cultural landscape of the central Minnesota River
Valley and *The Landing*. Finally, I will explore settler postcolonialism and its role in undermining not only historical but also contemporary recognition of Native American communities and cultures.

Space, Place, and Bodies as Networked Argument

Thinking of *The Landing* as the place that both influences and is influenced by the larger
space (Endres & Senda-Cook, 2011) reveals not only how the interactions between place
and spaces operate, but also how the interactions between the past and present function. *The
Landing* is a type of curated past that informs and legitimizes the materialization of present
ideologies as they populate the Minnesota River Valley landscape. Conversely, the greater
Minnesota River Valley, a present-day materiality of the agrarian to free-market socioeconomic culture, informs *The Landing*. What makes decoding *The Landing* so complicated is
that while the museum is historically accurate in its focus on Murphy and the settlers'
homes, it is inaccurate by virtue of its almost complete omission of the Dakota–the very
group of people that brought Murphy to the area. A closer examination of *The Landing* as
an argument of place within a broader network of arguments of space reveals how the historical formation of settler society depended upon the willful erasure of the Dakota people
and their connection to the land. At the same time, it demonstrates how arguments of the
past and present work in tandem to mutually influence each other, producing an argument
of space that obscures historical and contemporary recognition of the Dakota.

This more nuanced understanding of how ideological forces influence space as argument
explains the recalcitrance of some places to allow for different, alternative meanings. *The
Landing*, like other historical sites, is open to multiple meanings and while the site's management recognizes this potentiality, the site itself does not. In their examination of public
monuments, McGeough, Palczewski, and Lake (2015) explored how "argumentative strategies [....destabilize] memory and [open] up sacred spaces to alternative articulations of the
past by expanding the lives deemed worthy of remembrance and grief" (p. 232). The
authors further offer a strategy of "dissection" (p. 232) as a way to make historical sites open
to multiple, even conflicting, interpretations. The efficacy of this strategy, though, depends
on the degree to which the broader socio, cultural and economic communities identify with
these alternative interpretations. Examining *The Landing* as it exists within the socio, cultural,
and economic space of the Minnesota River Valley reveals how settler postcolonialism
undermines the possibility of alternative interpretations of the past as well as the present.

Settler Postcolonialism as Antecedent to Studies
in Native American Argumentation

This project takes up and extends Lake's (1991) work on the "Euramerican establishment's
discourse concerning Native Americans" (p. 125) by focusing on what discourses settler
societies tell about themselves and how these arguments work to obscure historical and contemporary recognition of Native American sovereignty. Shifting attention to the exhibitions
and celebrations of settler society, or "settler colonialism," make visible how an exclusive
narrative of place works to displace other, competing narratives. Wolfe (2006) elaborated on
the term "settler colonialism," when he noted, "negatively, it strives for the dissolution of

native societies. Positively, it erects a new colonial society on the expropriated land base—as I put it, settler colonizers come to stay: invasion is a structure not an event" (p. 388). As a networked argument of place within the broader space, *The Landing* works as a postcolonial argument in which settler society is framed as the necessary and honorable origin of contemporary society. Anderson and Domosh (2002) explained postcolonial as "national discourses formulated from within *historical* colonial relationships, but which are constantly re-enacted in contemporary *politics*" (p. 125). Thus, argumentation scholars and others interested in Native American sovereignty would do well to examine the arguments made by and about settler society. Examining *The Landing* as an argument of place within the broader network of space reveals how it functions as a kind of origin story that anchors the ideology of agrarian free-market economy that dominates the wider space.

The Landing obscures the ways in which settler postcolonialism normalizes an exclusive understanding of place and people, reflecting what Anderson and Domosh (2002) explained as "the implications of national identities that are continuously being constructed through narratives of the conquest of Native populations, and the disavowal of that conquest" (p. 126). By celebrating settler colonialism while omitting any material or discursive evidence of the Dakota presence on the same land, *The Landing* encourages what Dickinson, Ott, and Aoki (2006) called "an amnesiatic mode of looking" (p. 40). Schmitt (2015) elaborated on the idea in his analysis of Native American effigy mound layouts, in which the mounds functioned as "places of modern rhetorics" (p. 310) in that "their arrangements—through text, image, material, and other elements—serve to perpetuate modern regimes of truth and experience instead of ancient ones" (p. 310). Accordingly, the rhetorical force of *The Landing* stems both from its function as an embodied/emplaced argument and its function within the broader socioeconomic space.

The Landing

As an embodied/emplaced argument, *The Landing* affirms the material and ideological origin and progression of settler society from subsistence to the proliferation of free-market farming in the Minnesota River Valley. In addition to the sense of identification the natural landscape engenders, the proliferation of German, Irish, and Scandinavian names all work to construct *The Landing* as a kind of origin story of the greater Minnesota River Valley moving from fur trade to farming to urban centers. The spatial organization and labeling of the structures, and the ways in which they move visitors from the early 1840s to the 1890s, reflect the story of the first Minnesota settlement by the French, followed by German, Irish, and Scandinavian settlers. Just a hundred feet or so from the visitor's center is the small, rudimentary 1845 trading post that Oliver Faribault owned, symbolic of generations of family fur traders. About 300 feet west of the trader's post is an 1857 farm featuring livestock, as well as a garden and outbuildings. Two horses stay at the farm throughout the year, creating an eerie sense that life continues on at the farm, despite the fact that the original farm was well over a hundred years old. Moving past the farm, the narrative of Minnesota settlement jumps from 1857 to 1889, with another farm representing the change from subsistence to market farming. This farm has a larger barn, a second out-building, and a nicer, larger home. The distance from the trader's post to the 1858 and 1889 farms is sequentially shorter, so as one moves from one to the next, the sites emerge on the landscape more quickly echoing the escalating pace of settlement and socio-economic development of the time. Murphy's Inn, the only structure authentic to this site, links the trader's post and farm sites to the collection of nine homes, the general store, depot, lumber yard, town hall, gazebo, and church.

Murphy's Inn, which looks out over the Minnesota River, is centrally located in the park between the 1889 farm and the settler's village. The inn is the only structure in *The Landing* that has a permanent guidepost complete with pictures of Major Murphy and the original inn. The photographs display the inn as it looked in the 1890s and in the 1950s shortly before it burned down. The stone foundation of the inn and its proximity to homes and businesses work to blur the distinction between the decaying past and the past not only preserved but fully operational. The museum stocks family homes with décor and home goods authentic to the family and time period. Just next to Murphy's Inn, for example, is the Wilkie home (dated 1880) which "represent[s] a Scandinavian immigrant's home" and includes a bride's cupboard inscribed with the couple's initials and wedding date. Just a few homes down and across the gravel road from Murphy's Inn is the Druke home (dated 1855) made of limestone and sand. Across the little town is the O'Connor home (dated 1865-1880) where John O'Connor, a Civil War veteran, and his family lived. Finally, the museum stocks and equips all of the businesses with authentic antiques like cash registers and blacksmith tools.

The Landing eschews any recognition that the Dakota brought the Indian Agent Murphy to this place. Instead, the museum celebrates Murphy as the venture capitalist and politician whose economic and governmental agency generated the success of not only settler society then, but its descendants in the Minnesota River Valley now. As visitors stand at the stone foundation of Murphy's Inn, what was Shakpay's village is clearly visible across the river. The elder Shakpay, otherwise known as Shapaydan or "Little Six," was one of signers to the 1851 treaties that stripped the Dakota of millions of acres for pennies on the dollar–money that the Dakota never saw–and left them a 20 mile-wide reservation along the Minnesota River. Looking across from Murphy's Inn, visitors can imagine Shakpay's village in the substantial clearing just fifty feet or so from the river and the mooring immediately off the river. Throughout the many fully-furnished and operational farms, homes, and businesses, a permanent marker details the construction, operation, and longevity of Murphy's Inn and signage explains the plants and animals indigenous to the area; yet, no mention of Shakpay, the village, or the Dakota appears. This excised history that *The Landing* presents works in tandem with the present by presenting a past in which the Dakota were conveniently absent and thereby normalizing their contemporary marginalization.

As a historic, partially authentic pastiche of the past, *The Landing* works to ideologically anchor the place's development from subsistence to free-market farming to industrialization. While visitors to *The Landing* enjoy going back in time to the beginnings of the farm and later to the market economy, they need only step outside the park to see the continuation of these market practices. Eight gigantic modern-day grain bins rise just off the parking lot of *The Landing*. An expansive industrial park stands just a few hundred feet farther away. The grain bins and industrial park are the evolution of the farm to a market-based economy the park represents. Analyzed within its socioeconomic spatial context, *The Landing* works first, to obscure historical evidence of productive potential of the Dakota on their original land and, second, to emphasize the contemporary condition of the Dakota people confined to their reservations, operating lucrative casinos. Within a few hundred feet of the parking lot to *The Landing* is a sign for *Mystic Lake* casino, the popular casino located on the Mdewankanton reservation that the Dakota operate. At night, visitors can see the search lights, constantly rotating in and out of the shape of a teepee from miles away.

To be sure, the museum could acknowledge a more complete history of the site by including space for the Dakota story and how the tribe existed prior to and during Murphy's tenure. The only two sites acknowledging the Dakota within this space are *The Landing* and *Mystic Lake*, both of which excise any memories of the systematic violence that led up to the

U.S.-Dakota war or the traumatic events of August 1862 that led to the largest mass execution in U.S. history (Anderson, 2014, p. 243). The sites relegate the Dakota to the past or fold them into a complicated, unrepresentative stereotype of wealthy Native Americans. What resonates loudest in this network of arguments are the contemporary manifestations of settler society–still bustling rail yards feeding the commodities market, thriving industrial parks, and healthy communities. As each works to normalize the historical silence and continued marginalization of the Dakota, the ideological and economic implications abound.

Settler Postcolonialism or To Tell Our Own Truths

Embodied/emplaced arguments that celebrate settler colonialism work to celebrate and perpetuate settler postcolonialism, which in turn work to excise not only historical, but also contemporary, recognition of the Dakota. In June 2017, exactly eighteen miles from *The Landing* stood *Scaffolds*, a controversial outdoor art installation at the Minneapolis Walker Art Center which featured exact replicas of seven different scaffolds the United States had used for state-sponsored executions. The biggest and most pronounced piece was that of the Dakota 38. The local Native American community and allies were quick to articulate (via mass protests) their incredulousness at the Arts Center's inept curation. After a mediated session between the Dakota, the artist, the executive director of the Walker Art Center who commissioned the piece, and the co-sponsor of the Minneapolis Parks Board, a Dakota construction company removed the structure as part of a ceremony with Dakota Elders. The group also reached an agreement that the Dakota would burn the scaffold at a later date at Fort Snelling, the site of the internment of 1600 Dakota women, children, and elderly from November 1863 to May 1864, but the ceremony's implementation remains on hold. The scaffold controversy clearly demonstrates that for many, the Dakota are either shadows of the past or relegated to remote reservations. In the context of Native American argumentation studies, seeking to tell our own truths means expanding the scope of our studies to include the mainstream majority's arguments insofar as they normalize and perpetuate the historical and continued displacement of Native American peoples.

References

Anderson, G. C. (2014). *Ethnic Cleansing and the Indian: The Crime that Should Haunt America.* Norman, University of Oklahoma.

Anderson, K., & Domosh, M. (2002). North American spaces/postcolonial stories. *Cultural Geographies, 9*(2), 125–128. doi:10.1191/1474474002eu239xx

Dickinson, G., Ott, B. L., & Aoki, E. (2006). Spaces of remembering and forgetting: The reverent eye/I at the Plains Indian Museum. *Communication and Critical/Cultural Studies, 3*(1), 27–47. doi:10.1080/14791420500505619

Endres, D., & Senda-Cook, S. (2011). Location matters: The rhetoric of place in protest. *Quarterly Journal of Speech, 97*(3), 257–282. doi:10.1080/00335630.2011.585167

Lake, R. A. (1991). Between myth and history: Enacting time in Native American protest rhetoric. *Quarterly Journal of Speech, 77*(2), 123–151. doi:10.1080/00335639109383949

McGeough, R. E., Palczewski, C. H., & Lake, R. A. (2015). Oppositional memory practices: U.S. memorial spaces as arguments over public memory. *Argumentation and Advocacy, 51*(4), 231–254. Retrieved from http://tandfonline.com

Schmitt, C. R. (2015). Contours of the land: Place-as-rhetoric and Native American effigy mounds. *Western Journal of Communication, 79*(3), 307–326. doi:10.1080/10570314.2015.1041651

Wolfe, P. (2006). Settler colonialism and the elimination of the native. *Journal of Genocide Research, 8*(4), 387–409. doi:10.1080/14623520601056240

57

RHETORICAL RUMORS

Hauntology in International Feminicidio Discourse

José Ángel Maldonado

In August 2013, Ciudad Juárez awoke to the news of an assassinated bus driver, Roberto Flores. Two days later, Alfredo Zárate, another bus driver working the same route, was also the victim of murder. Local news media received an email that confessed to the murders. The confessor called herself Dianalacazadoradechoferes, Diana the Hunter of Bus Drivers, and alleged that the murdered men were serial rapists who had taken advantage of female *maquiladora* (manufacturing) employees who relied on public transportation. The news spread, but Dianalacazadoradechoferes turned out to be a troll. Law enforcement traced the confession to a U.S. IP address: Someone apparently found joy in seeing the authorities attempt to solve the seemingly unsolvable vengeful murders.

Society's authorities (the public majority, the police, and several journalists) made several quick assumptions about the case—mainly, that the confessor was likely a real avenger. Thus, the mythic and modern figure of Diana, I argue, was central to the success of this persuasive confession. By deconstructing journalistic discourse that at times hinted at mythology, I aim to unravel the complexity of persuasion in cultures that have learned to live with the omnipresence of death and violence. Diana's confession became a rupture in mundane Mexican modernity, allowing rhetorical scholars to witness the transformations of immaterial forces into material phenomena. In my analysis, I borrow ideas about the spectral from Derrida's (1994) *Spectres of Marx*. My contention is that a cultural, rhetorical approach to mythology attunes to the various, almost random influences participating in the networked rhetorical situation.

Hauntology

Rhetorical and communication studies have long studied hauntology. For example, Gunn's (2004) analysis of 9/11's "mourning speech" clearly revealed that traces of human life (and death) linger in the imaginations of others, becoming new types of memories—indeed hauntings. Moreover, Gunn's work demonstrated how critical work ought to question hauntology and the dualism between materiality and spectrality.

Hauntology is not the study of the capture and provability of the material existence of ghosts. Instead, hauntology aims to connect ontology to its dialectic correspondent: If ontology is the philosophical study of the nature of being, existence, and reality, then *hauntology* replaces being, existence, and reality with "the figure of the ghost as that which is neither present nor absent, neither dead nor alive" (Davis, 2005, p. 373). Hauntology is a border or limit concept—something that does not belong to material or immaterial existence. Davis (2005) explained that critics across disciplines welcomed hauntology mostly due to the claim that deconstruction was always a Marxist project. As a consequence of aiming to resurrect Marx, Davis (2005) argued that Derrida, the originator of the term, also rehabilitated the topic of ghosts "as a respectable subject of enquiry" (p. 373). Hauntology belongs to the ethical turn in deconstruction, a moment when critical scholars discuss topics such as justice and responsibility (p. 373).

Dianalacazadoradechoferes, the troll and the ghost, demonstrates the necessity for a critique of global circuits and global rhetorics of economic growth and development. When seen from the side of the developing world, dialectic deconstruction tends to equate with economic oppression and exploitation. Capitalism affects populations—individually and collectively. More importantly, capitalism functions differently in different international (and rhetorical, persuasive, and argumentative) contexts. Critics should always question the role of the nation-state in global and border regions (here, federal governments) in managing and influencing an otherwise free market. The critique of capital today should not centralize traditional Marxist methods, that is, an analysis of the superstructure that overlooks poverty, homelessness, and unemployment in its core concern for the international working classes. One still makes a living, I argue, even if one lacks employment. Moreover, feminist critiques of Marx have pointed to the assumed, masculine subject—an assumption that overlooks specific forms of labor, including domestic labor and sex work, among many others (see Cloud, 1994; Putnam Tong, 1998; Rubin, 1975).

Still, many Marxist tenets ring true when analyzing the borderland maquiladora (e.g., the freedom of cross-border movement multinational corporations enjoy, as well as the demand for black market U.S. and Mexican narcotics, firearms, child laborers, and sex workers). The division of labor, at times, also equates conveniently with the division of the United States and Mexico territories. The condition has also produced unexpected phenomena: migration from Central and South America (not only to the United States, but to Mexican cities where maquiladoras need thousands of unskilled laborers), unexpected urbanization (dialectically, the abandonment of rural towns and ranches—leaving ghost towns behind as sites for mass graves), the entry of women into the public labor force (which evokes a deep and deadly misogyny), the emasculation some men experience (with few available employment opportunities, some men become *sicarios* or hitmen for various cartels—simultaneously earning a living and recuperating their masculinity through the exertion of deadly violence), and finally, the bilateral war on drugs (which has turned Mexico into one of the most violent places in the world, particularly for the poor, women, sexual minorities, immigrants, indigenous people, and intellectuals).

Hauntology emerges as an appropriate critical lens because truth is relative. One person may experience the wind as a cold phenomenon, for example, while another will qualify it as warm (Barney, 2006). While both opinions are *true*, even while contradictory, one of the two, as Plato argued, is *better* (Barney, 2006). The sophists also found in this naturally contradictory world an opening toward unknown and creative possibilities—maybe no wind exists at all and individuals can only know of something we call *wind* (Barney, 2006). Referencing the sophists (and alluding to Plato's reading of the comedian Aristophanes), Nietzsche

(1968) argued that contemporary thinkers engage in a naïve performance when they ask for real and honest answers. He explained: "The faith in 'immediate certainties' is a *moral* naïveté that reflects honor on us philosophers; but—after all we should not be '*merely* moral' men" (Nietzsche, 1968, p. 236). Thus, truth concepts reflect specific conditions; they do not exist as universals. Barney (2006) argued that a critique of fifth-century enlightenment (BCE) resulted in the sophistic tradition, a perspective that has resurfaced among philosophers and rhetoricians throughout centuries and into postmodernity.

Truth is relative because *anything* can become truth. Rumors, as Ovid warned and as I hope to demonstrate, have the capability of becoming truth when certain unpredictable conditions assemble. Journalistic rumors, in particular, enjoy a circulation endowed with forms of credibility and credulity—of leading and persuading audiences to believe and perceive the world in specific ways. I turn to Ovid because his collection *Metamorphoses* contains the myth of Actáeon, where the mythical figure of Diana appears. I will use the myth as the foundation from which to begin making sense of the journalistic rumors circulating the deaths of two Ciudad Juárez bus drivers and the alleged, spectral appearance of Diana.

Ovid's Metamorphoses

Ovid's (trans. 2004) *Metamorphoses* is a single poem presented as a collection of 15 books containing over 250 ancient myths. Thematically, the myths all involve a physical transformation, typically from human to nature (e.g., Aurora becomes the dawn, and Cycnus becomes a swan). In becoming or transforming, the word also gains its structural, surface-level meaning, becoming a part of the environment: If I say *aurora* in Spanish, my audience thinks mostly about the dawn, and not about a myth; and if I say *cisne* in Spanish, my audience thinks mostly of a swan, a big, waterfowl, not a mythical figure.

In *Rumour*, Ovid (trans. 2004) described the *haunt of credulity*, a concept born from rumor. For Ovid, rumor did not oblige by physical borders, but rather inhabited a metaphysical landscape that could reappear in various locations. As such, rumors have panopticonic and panauditory dimensions, involving the interpretation, repetition, and reproduction/retelling of stories, with each retelling of a story further separating the listener from the original story. The *haunt of credulity*, the post-life or afterlife of gullibility, resonates with the ethical turn in deconstruction: "This is the haunt of credulity, irresponsible error/groundless joy, unreasoning panic, impulsive sedition/and whispering gossip" (pp. 466–467). Rumors, then, function as themes and tropes of hauntology, that is, to the immaterial forces that drive the imagination in a given moment. In what follows, I analyze the rumor of Diana as it enters and undergoes recontextualization by Gloria Castrillón, a Colombian journalist.

Recontextualizing Feminicidio

Gloria Castrillón (2013) published "The Mexican Woman Who Assassinates Bus Drivers for Vengeance" in *Cromos* for a Colombian audience, not fully aware of feminicidio in Ciudad Juárez like their Mexican counterparts.[1] She began with an ontological disclaimer: "No one knows if she exists" (para. 2). The opening was also a hauntological disclaimer as it set the eerie setting for the forthcoming text. She wrote that *desconcierto* (i.e, uncertainty, confusion, bewilderment, and *un-concern*) visited Ciudad Juárez, but also disorder and chaos—specifically, an auditory quality that presented itself as the opposite of harmony—the opposite of organized, structured music. "More fear than usual" (para. 2) accompanied *desconcierto*, indicating that fear itself had become inseparable from the atmosphere in which discourse circulated. Moreover, this fear was due to the "apparition of she who calls herself 'avenger'" (para. 2). Apparitions are the subject of hauntology: In the ontological sense, something appears, becomes present, and exists even if ephemerally (in this case, killing two men—leaving their corpses as physical evidence). In the hauntological sense, this entity is spectral, circulating back to the ontological questions concerning the nature of reality. The specter that appeared in Ciudad Juárez did not precisely call herself avenger, Castrillón (2013) argued, as much as she made others call her avenger [*se hace llamar*]. In other words, the author knows that the power does not only lie in calling herself Diana or avenger, but in the hegemonic consent: Yes, you are Diana, the avenger of subaltern women. Castrillón offers a contextual frame for her readers to understand the role of Diana:

> Amid such a discussion, feminist organizations described Diana as a media creation intended to distract public opinion from what truly matters: the attacks, abuses, and homicides of women. According to unofficial figures, 1441 women have been killed in the past 20 years and an undetermined number are still [*siguen*—ontologically important translation of *are still* or *continue to be*] disappeared.
>
> *(para. 7)*

Following a Derridian line of inquiry, how can someone who has disappeared continue to be? If someone can disappear, what existence does one take on after such a transformation? Within the Mexican context, *desaparecidas* (or, *desaparecidos*) are people reported missing. The underlying interpretation of desaparecida tends to mean missing and likely dead. For the family of the disappeared, a sentiment of hope exists in the sense that they may yet reappear—dead or alive—or in another state, such as DNA evidence. Most importantly, one does not disappear, but rather one is disappeared—someone disappears me—takes me from existence and into another realm: an unknown realm—a mystery.

Castrillón described Ciudad Juárez as a place where a long and systemic project had aimed to disappear women, where various planes of ontological existence align—a place of disappeared women not accurately describable as dead. Rather, readers cannot know this other realm of life because it lies at the extremity of life in physical and otherly existence. These women could be alive, but their metaphysical location remains unknowable.

Castrillón: *Preguntas sin Respuestas*

Castrillón (2013) wrote that the world knew the "constant and systematic assassination" (para. 8) of women in Ciudad Juárez—a place "bordering the United States" (para. 8)—as *feminicidio*. The victims were low-income women between the ages of 15 and 25 who had abandoned their homes in small towns in search of a better life as maquiladora employees. Maquiladoras, Castrillón explained, "were established [in Ciudad Juárez] after the signing of the North American Free Trade Agreement" (para. 8). She then explained that authorities had tabulated the feminicidios since 1993, when bystanders found the body of Alma Chavira Farel, a thirteen-year-old girl, raped, strangled, and dead. Castrillón informed her audience that according to investigations, most of these deaths involved sexual sadism, asphyxiophilia, rape, and mutilation. While human rights organizations spoke about 1441 dead women in 20 years, authorities recognized less than 700 over the same period.

"Who kills women and why?" Castrillón (2013, para. 2) asked. She responded, "There are no answers" (para. 2). Nevertheless, she subsequently presented seven theories. First, the judicial apparatus was inoperative and as a result, it had guaranteed impunity for those responsible for feminicide, despite the fact that the Inter-American Court of Human Rights and the United Nations had sanctioned the Mexican state several times for its lack of action, prevention, and proper investigation. Second, the killings were crimes of passion, as Chihuahua's governor argued in the 1990s, insisting that feminicide's proper place was within the domestic sphere. Third, "one or several serial killers" (para. 12) arrived from "the exterior [United States], committed these crimes, and left without a trace" (para. 12). Fourth, the maquiladora industry was somehow responsible, given that most of the assassinated women worked in one or more of 235 production plants. Castrillón went on to explain that an estimated 240,000 people worked in the maquiladora sector—and the majority were women. Fifth, organized crime was involved; in November 2001, bystanders found eight dead women in Campo Algodonero, outside of Ciudad Juárez and in the proximity of a maquiladora. According to Castrillón, apart from being tortured and mutilated, the perpetrators had branded the backs of the women's bodies. Sixth, organ trafficking was responsible, rising from the February 2003 mutilated bodies found in Cerro Cristo Negro. Finally, the last hypothesis involved the production and distribution of snuff films or, bluntly, pornography that ends with the alleged *real* assassination of a woman. Castrillón explained that authorities had abandoned the last two theories.

Hauntology points to the simultaneous existence and inexistence, as well as the presence and absence, of the answers. Two ideas are crucial for understanding borderland feminicidios. The first is the revenant—a discourse about the end, but specifically, about returning from the end: "The spirit comes by *coming back* [revenant], it figures *both* a dead man who comes back and a ghost whose expected return repeats itself, again and again" (Derrida, 1994, p. 10). In Juárez, the public murder of one woman gives life to, or brings back to life, the hundreds of women killed in similar ways. Additionally, the discourse about death repeats, from the probable causes of feminicidio to the various justifications that do not satisfy the mourning masses. Moreover, the location of the murders (i.e., on the urban, Mexico-United States border) displaces ontologies of ends, limits, extremities, or borders. Derrida (1994) explained that the frontier between public and private is in the process of displacement:

> And if this important frontier is being displaced, it is because the medium in which it is instituted, namely, the medium of the media themselves (news, the press, telecommunications, techo-tele-discursivity, techno-tele-iconicity, that which in general assures and determines the *spacing* of public space, the very possibility of the *res publica* and the phenomenality of the political), this element itself is neither living nor dead, present nor absent: it spectralizes.
>
> *(pp. 50–51)*

Thus, the assassination of women in Ciudad Juárez is systemic. The peculiarities of each assassination should not divert critical attention from the fact that women suffer assassination *discriminately*. In other words, none of these answers will singularly solve feminicide, and yet all of these answers respond to the specific deaths of specific lives, that is, they all point to the assembled, cultural answer: (a) The police have been ineffective in their response to feminicide; (b) public violence against women ought not obscure domestic violence against women; (c) foreigners live out a plethora of erotic, colonial, and violent fantasies when visiting Ciudad Juárez; (d) the maquiladora is a key, local site of misogynist crimes; (e) these crimes can quickly become organized crimes, especially when unemployed men begin to feel emasculated; (f) poor people have organs that can be sold to foreigners; (g) and, if someone's taste in pornography is a taste for the proximity to the real, who will stop them from generating an interest in snuff films? And if enough people have the interest and capital to purchase and participate in the making of these films, what would stop them from living out this *fantasy*?

Of course, we have (perhaps dangerously) ventured back, as revenants, into the realm of rumor and speculation. But the speculative and the spectral are not very different things—they inhabit the unknown, allowing us to glimpse and imagine, but never to hold and capture.

Castrillón's Conclusion: More Alone than Ever

Castrillón uncovered the power of spectral discourse. Diana's power resided in the public's credulity regardless of her ontological existence, real or fantastic. Regardless of the existence of a revenant hero, the belief and credence that a hero is defending women's lives has a rhetorical force that can emerge for several purposes—from raising the spirits of a public that has learned to live in the omnipresence of death to turning the public's attention away from the fact that more women continue to face deadly rape cultures.

More importantly, violence against women knows no borders. At times, such violence appears not to exist—particularly when it is hidden away behind the walls of the private sphere, the walls of the foreign factory, or the walls that symbolically divide nation-states. In this networked and ever-globalizing age, news media has the power to unite groups through new modalities of communication, and voices like Castrillón's can reach audiences across multiple borders to raise awareness of issues that affect people across gender, language, nation, and creed.

Note

1 The Castrillón article originally appears in Spanish. The author translates all direct quotations in this essay.

References

Barney, R. (2006). The sophistic movement. In M. L. Gill & P. Pellegrin (Eds.), *A companion to ancient philosophy* (pp. 77–97). Malden, MA: Blackwell.

Castrillón, G. (2013, October 2). La mexicana que asesina conductores de bus por venganza [The Mexican woman who kills bus drivers for revenge]. *Cromos*. Retrieved from http://cromos.com.co/crom cas/articulo-148329-la-mujer-asesina-conductores-de-bus-venganza-mexico

Cloud, D. L. (1994). The materiality of discourse as oxymoron: A challenge to critical rhetoric. *Western Journal of Communication, 58*(3), 141–163. doi:10.1080/10570319409374493

Davis, C. (2005). Hauntology, spectres and phantoms. *French Studies, 59*(3), 373–379. doi:10.1093/fs/kni143

Derrida, J. (with Magnus, B., & Cullenberg, S.). (1994). *Specters of Marx: The state of the debt, the work of mourning, & the new international* (P. Kamuf, Trans.). New York, NY: Routledge.

Gunn, J. (2004). Mourning speech: Haunting and the spectral voices of nine-eleven. *Text and Performance Quarterly, 24*(2), 91–114. doi:10.1080/1046293042000288344

Nietzsche, F. (with Kaufmann, W., Ed.). (1968). *The will to power* (W. Kaufmann & R. J. Hollingdale, Trans.). New York, NY: Random House.

Ovid. (2004). *Metamorphoses* (D. Raeburn, Trans.). New York, NY: Penguin.

Putnam Tong, R. (1998). Marxist and socialist feminism. In *Feminist thought* (pp. 94–129). Boulder, CO: Westview Press.

Rubin, G. (1975). The traffic in women: Notes on the "political economy" of sex. In R. Reiter (Ed.), *Toward an anthropology of women* (pp. 157–210). New York, NY: Monthly Review Press.

58

NETWORKED MEMORIES

Remembering Barbara Jordan in 21st Century Immigration Debates

Carly S. Woods

Barbara Jordan is hard to forget. Hailing from Houston, she served in the Texas Senate in the 1960s and in the U.S. House of Representatives beginning in 1972. Jordan rose to national prominence as the first African American woman from the South to serve in the U.S. Congress. After three terms as a House representative, she retired and subsequently taught courses in public policy and ethics in the Lyndon Baines Johnson School of Public Affairs at the University of Texas-Austin. President Bill Clinton awarded her the Presidential Medal of Freedom in 1994. Shortly before her untimely death in 1996, Jordan chaired the U.S. Commission on Immigration Reform.

Jordan defined her legacy through her well-known national political speeches, several of which communication scholars consider to be among the best of the 20th century (Lucas & Medhurst, 2009). Jordan's speeches are memorable for numerous reasons, including her incisive arguments, ability to invoke history for contemporary application, and commanding delivery. In analyzing Jordan's rhetoric, scholars have been particularly interested in her masterful use of enactment, that is, the reflexive form in which a speaker physically embodies a verbal argument with their presence (e.g., see Campbell & Jamieson, 1978; Horwitz, 1998; Logan, 2004; Palczewski, 2002). For example, in her 1976 Democratic National Convention keynote, Jordan (2017) incarnated the possibility of a diverse and inclusive United States by claiming her "presence here is one additional piece of evidence that the American dream need not forever be deferred" (para. 2). While her biographies do mention her leadership of the U.S. Commission on Immigration Reform, her efforts in that role, by contrast, have not come to define Jordan's legacy (Crawford, 2003; Rogers, 1998).

In 2015, NumbersUSA, a lobbying group in favor of strict numerical limits on "legal" immigration, "reintroduce[d] the world to Barbara Jordan" (Beck, 2015, para. 1) by re-circulating footage of a 1995 speech she gave about the Commission on Immigration Reform's findings.[1] The NumbersUSA move brought Jordan's immigration rhetoric to a new generation of viewers and prompted interlocutors across the political spectrum to debate about the nature of Jordan's true legacy. Using the Jordan episode as a case study, this essay examines the complexities involved when digital media networks memories of past figures to intervene in contemporary debates. To explain, I first review the arguments from Jordan's speeches and their context related to immigration from the 1990s. Second, I explore how networked publics have embraced and contested Jordan's memory used in favor of stricter immigration policies in the 21st century. Finally, I consider how argumentation scholars might better account for this "new digital temporality of memory" (Hoskins, 2009, p. 93) in other instantiations of public argument.

Barbara Jordan's Commission on Immigration Reform

The Immigration Act of 1990 mandated the creation of a nine-person, bipartisan U.S. Commission on Immigration Reform. President Bill Clinton (quoted in Peters & Wooley, 1993, para. 2) called Barbara Jordan "one of the most well respected people in America" when he asked her to chair the Commission. Jordan was an excellent choice for the role: She was recognizable to a national audience, she no longer held an elected or other formal political role, she had a reputation for bipartisanship, and she was a Texan who fought for the inclusion of Mexican Americans in ongoing civil rights legislation. In 1975, for example, Jordan became the "national face" behind the successful effort to amend the Voting Rights Act with protections for "language minorities" (Berman, 2015, p. 108), including Mexican Americans, American Indians, and Asian Americans. Under her leadership and her role as primary spokesperson, the U.S. Commission on Immigration Reform became dubbed the "Jordan Commission."

The Jordan Commission's work was extensive and arduous. To produce four comprehensive reports between 1994 and 1997, members held public hearings, commissioned expert research studies, consulted community members, and conducted field visits. While the Commission's reports provided guidance on many aspects of immigration policy, most notable was their recommendation to admit 550,000 "legal" immigrants per year based on nuclear family ties, work skills, and refugee status (Miranda, 1998). A detailed look at Jordan's speeches reveals that though the Commission clearly intended to reform immigration policy to prioritize "legal" over "illegal" immigration. The speeches acknowledged a need to reunite "legal" immigrants with their spouses and children, which would result in a short-term increase in the number of approved visas. However, the Commission's recommendations would curtail overall numbers of those admitted each year in the longer term. The Commission's recommendations were controversial—in fact, Jordan told the American public that the Texas heat was nothing compared to the heat she endured as the Commission's chair (Jordan, 1995a). Notably, this work created tensions with some Mexican American advocacy groups that she had allied with in the past, although mutual respect remained (Sherman, 2007). Still, Jordan was adamant that the recommendations were not anti-immigrant and believed that immigration policy reform could be accomplished with common sense and compassion. She declared that the Commission understood the importance of immigration to the country and underlined the need to protect civil rights and liberties (Jordan, 1994). Moreover, the Commission explicitly sought to promote an Americanization ideal that was neither xenophobic nor racist (Jordan 1995b), to advocate for U.S. leadership in refugee resettlement, and to address global economic inequities (Miranda, 1998). Jordan repeatedly condemned the scapegoating of immigrants, noting, "We cannot sustain ourselves as a nation if we condone divisiveness in this nation of immigrants" (1994, 10:17). The Commission's work consumed the last years of Jordan's life, and she did not live to see the release of the final report.

Jordan Re-Emerges

Nearly 20 years later, Jordan re-emerged in mainstream contemporary public arguments over immigration. On November 10, 2015, during a commercial break from the Fox Business Network's broadcast of the Republican presidential primary debate, an advertisement calling for immigration restrictions featured media footage of Jordan. The sponsor was NumbersUSA, an organization that billed itself as a grassroots group of "moderates, conservatives [and] liberals working for immigration numbers that serve America's finest goals" ("About Us," n.d., para. 1). However, the Southern Poverty Law Center described NumbersUSA as an anti-immigrant, "immigration-restriction [organization...] at the nexus of the American nativist movement" (Beirich, 2009, p. 4).

The 30-second spot ran during each of the 2016 Republican and Democratic primary debates. It featured a carefully selected clip of Jordan denouncing unskilled immigrant workers with menacing music playing in the background. The advertisement spliced fragments of Jordan's undated testimony with images of construction workers and forklift operators at work. Her videotaped remarks appeared to support the claim that the Commission was anti-immigrant:

> The commission finds no national interest in continuing to import lesser skilled and unskilled workers to compete in the most vulnerable parts of our labor force. Many American workers do not have adequate job prospects. We should make their task easier to find employment, not harder.
>
> *("2015 Barbara Jordan," 2015, 0:04-0:24)*

Without context, Jordan's quotation seems unequivocal. She had delivered the testimony 20 years earlier at the Ross Perot-organized United We Stand America Conference in Dallas, Texas. Immediately prior to the NumbersUSA advertisement's clip, Jordan (1995b) had endorsed specialized immigration, relaying a story about a foreign-born entrepreneur who helped a U.S. company create thousands of jobs. The ad also edited out a line of Jordan's original testimony about welfare reform; the last sentence of her comment did not reflect a general comment about the U.S. workforce, but referred more specifically to her concern about welfare recipients seeking employment (Jordan, 1995b). The brief clip lacked any of the nuance and care that the Jordan Commission worked diligently to include with its public statements. This version of Jordan's immigration rhetoric offered in the NumbersUSA ad supplied stated premises of an enthymeme that invited a 21st century viewership to conclude that Jordan was anti-immigrant.

The television spot ignited a firestorm of commentary across media platforms. Writers in news outlets like the *National Review* and the *Washington Times* expressed their approval of public citation of this aspect of Jordan's legacy, while *The Boston Globe* and *Houston Chronicle* searched for greater context for the remarks (e.g., see Diaz, 2016; Kammer, 2016; Krikorian, 2016; Pothier, 2016). Jordan's closest friends and colleagues decried the appropriation of Jordan's words, highlighting the historical differences in context and pointing to her social justice advocacy on behalf of immigrant groups throughout her lifetime (Diaz, 2016).

Across the political spectrum, people also used social media to celebrate or resist NumbersUSA's instantiation of Jordan's rhetoric. Many of those in favor of stricter immigration policies suggested that Jordan's identities insulated them from accusations of bias. For example, one Twitter user tweeted that Donald Trump's immigration policy was "ALMOST IDENTICAL to those of [a] Black Dem Lesbian who worked for [Bill] Clinton. Barbara Jordan" (Usecommon Sentz, 2016). Several users argued that Jordan's testimony in the advertisement represented the opinion of all African Americans, suggesting that immigration restrictions would be an appropriate way to celebrate Black History Month. NumbersUSA President Roy Beck (2015) maintained that invoking Jordan was effective:

> As a Civil Rights icon, she also helped people get beyond attempts of the immigration-expansion lobbies to make immigration reduction seem to have a racial component which has tended to intimidate many Americans from dealing with immigration rationally just like any other policy.
>
> *(para. 3)*

NumbersUSA sought to harness Jordan's reputation for common sense and compassion in the service of their 21st century positions.

In fact, both sides of the debate seemed to presuppose that reference to Jordan's identity would *enact* their arguments about immigration for them. By using audiovisual footage from her speech and then making specific mention of her identities (especially her race and status as a Civil Rights icon) across other media platforms, immigration restriction advocates confirmed their intent to appropriate Jordan's legacy as a well-liked figure who enacted a diverse and inclusive American Dream. Those opposed to using Jordan's memory for anti-immigration measures similarly summoned these aspects of her identity, implying that a liberal African American woman could not possibly have said the words featured in the NumbersUSA advertisement. Arguments on this side of the debate typically expressed anger about the appropriation and called for fact-checking. In other words, Jordan's legacy functioned as an argumentative resource for network creation and disruption as interlocutors embraced or rejected this representation of her 1995 testimony as a valid contribution to the contemporary debate.

Legacies and Networked Public Argument

Numerous rhetorical studies demonstrate that examining the varied ways that publics remember and repurpose famous figures can yield useful insights (e.g., see Parry-Giles & Kaufer, 2017; Wilson, 2012). Moreover, following Derrida's and Butler's work, other studies point to the ways in which all language is citational, ever-circulating, and imperfectly reproduced in contexts beyond the control of the individual speaking subject (Hartelius & Asenas, 2010). Networked media enable an easy movement of discourses across modes and platforms, permitting interlocutors to shape public argument through the citation of particular memories for particular purposes (Hoskins, 2009). This essay suggests that argumentation scholars should pay greater attention to how publics remember, repurpose, and recirculate memories of famous figures through networked media to intervene in contemporary public argument.

This brief study of Barbara Jordan's immigration rhetoric offers an important opportunity to deepen our understanding of how the recirculation of rhetorical legacies built on enactment have ongoing implications. In this case, more than the content and nuance of the U.S. Commission on Immigration Reform's recommendations, Jordan's race, gender, sexuality, and political identity became a focus. Although Jordan represented a group of individuals who had engaged in extensive research and fact-finding in her leadership of the Commission, the re-circulation of her 1995 testimony flattened and condensed these details to make them all about Jordan, her legacy, and her intersectional identities. Viewers familiar with Jordan expected her electrifying rhetorical performances. Since bodily enactment helped solidify Jordan's legacy at pivotal points in her political career, the repurposing of her words and image held particular sway as an intervention in the contemporary immigration debate. This sets up a 21st century clash between the established public memory of Jordan as representative of a diverse and inclusive American Dream and a re-circulation of her speech footage in the service of arguments for stricter immigration measures.

NumbersUSA operated under the assumption that if Jordan's embodied presence provided evidence for her arguments in its original context, they could harness that same presumptive validity and argumentative force for future contexts. Their strategy relied upon Jordan's use of enactment to make an argument by association; they hoped that audiences would enthymematically resolve that Jordan's image in the 2016 ad served as an endorsement of further immigration restriction policies, and that her status as a Civil Rights icon would shield them from accusations of racial bias. This appropriation attempted to move Jordan's rhetoric across history with little regard for the original context of her remarks and without acknowledging that she was a person composed of many complex and shifting identities and affiliations (Woods, 2012). To truly engage networked legacies, interlocutors on both sides of the debate needed to take Jordan's arguments seriously with attention to historical context and complexity.

Argumentation scholars should anticipate other instances where individuals or groups might redeploy the image and words of famous figures in new contexts to augment public argument. While the accomplishment of this strategy may not depend on a close tie between the speakers' rhetorical legacy and their previous, effective use of enactment, the rhetorical form of enactment personalizes political argument with particular potency. Powerful and goose bump-inducing as it is in its original context, one unforeseen consequence of enactment is the possibility that individuals and groups can co-opt and redeploy it in subsequent argument contexts with relative ease. Networked arguments operate at the nexus of citation and circulation; they will necessarily move and mutate across time. However, if a corresponding dedication to investigating their context and complexity does not exist, such instantiations will not move public argument forward.

Note

1 Many immigration advocates critique the terms "legal" and "illegal" (Anguiano, 2015). For the purposes of clarity and context, I will use these terms as the Jordan Commission and various immigration groups use them.

References

2015 Barbara Jordan TV Ad [Video file]. (2015, November 9). *NumbersUSA*. Retrieved from https://numbersusa.com

About Us. (n.d.). *NumbersUSA*. Retrieved from https://numbersusa.com/about

Anguiano, C. A. (2015). Dropping the i-word: A critical examination of contemporary immigration labels. In E. J. Hartelius (Ed.), *The rhetorics of US immigration: Identity, community, otherness*. University Park, PA: Pennsylvania State University Press.

Beck, R. (2015, November 11). Our "Barbara Jordan" ad in debates stunned, shocked, angered, buoyed viewers—why Barbara? [Web log entry]. Retrieved from https://numbersusa.com/blog/our-barbara-jordan-ad-debates-stunned-shocked-angered-buoyed-viewers-why-barbara

Beirich, H. (2009, January). Editor's note. In M. Potok (Ed.), *The nativist lobby: Three faces of intolerance* (p. 4). Retrieved from the Southern Poverty Law Center website: https://splcenter.org

Berman, A. (2015). *Give us the ballot: The modern struggle for voting rights in America*. New York, NY: Picador.

Campbell, K. K., & Jamieson, K. H. (1978). Form and genre in rhetorical criticism: An introduction. In K. K. Campbell & K. H. Jamieson (Eds.), *Form and genre: Shaping rhetorical action* (pp. 9–32). Falls Church, VA: Speech Communication Association.

Crawford, A. F. (2003). *Barbara Jordan: Breaking the barriers*. Houston, TX: Halycon Press.

Diaz, K. (2016, June 8). Barbara Jordan's memory in a tug-of-war over immigration. *Houston Chronicle*. Retrieved from http://houstonchronicle.com

Hartelius, E. J., & Asenas, J. (2010). Citational epideixis and a "thinking of community": The case of the Minutemen Project. *Rhetoric Society Quarterly 40*(4), 360–384. doi:10.1080/02773945.2010.499862

Horwitz, L. D. (1998). *Transforming appearance into rhetorical argument: Rhetorical criticism of public speeches of Barbara Jordan, Lucy Parsons, and Angela Y. Davis* (Doctoral dissertation). Retrieved from the Northwestern University Library database. (DAI No. 59-12A).

Hoskins, A. (2009). Digital network memory. In A. Erll & A. Rigney (Eds.), *Mediation, remediation, and the dynamics of cultural memory* (pp. 91–106). Berlin, Germany: Walter de Gruyter.

Jordan, B. C. (1994, September 30). Immigration reform interim report [Video file]. Retrieved from https://c-span.org/video/?60547-1/immigration-reform-interim-report&start=4231

Jordan, B. C. (1995a, August 12). United we stand America day 2 part 3 [Video file]. Retrieved from https://c-span.org/video/?66708-1/united-stand-america-day-2-part-3

Jordan, B. C. (1995b, November 28). Remarks by Barbara Jordan to the Immigration and Naturalization Service. Retrieved from the University of North Texas Libraries Portal to Texas History website (with credit to Texas Southern University): texashistory.unt.edu

Jordan, B. C. (2017, February 13). 1976 Democratic National Convention keynote address delivered 12 July 1976, New York, NY [Transcript and video file]. *American Rhetoric*. Retrieved from http://americanrhetoric.com

Kammer, J. (2016, January 13). Barbara Jordan's immigration legacy. *The Washington Times*. Retrieved from washingtontimes.com

Krikorian, M. (2016, January 18). Barbara Jordan, American patriot. *National Review*. Retrieved from nationalreview.com

Logan, S. W. (2004). Identification and resistance: Women's civic discourse across the color line. In G. Hauser & A. Grim (Eds.), *Rhetorical democracy: Discursive practices of civic engagement* (pp. 33–44). Mahwah, NJ: Lawrence Erlbaum Associates.

Lucas, S. E., & Medhurst, M. J. (2009). *Words of a century: The top 100 American speeches, 1900–1999*. New York, NY: Oxford University Press.

Miranda, C. O. (1998). United States Commission on Immigration Reform: The interim and final reports. *Santa Clara Law Review 38*(3), 645–689.

Palczewski, C. H. (2002). Argument in an off key: Playing with the productive limits of argument. In G. T. Goodnight (Ed.), *Arguing communication and culture* (pp. 1–23). Washington, DC: National Communication Association.

Parry-Giles, S. J., & Kaufer, D. S. (2017). *Memories of Lincoln and the splintering of American political thought*. University Park, PA: Pennsylvania State University Press.

Peters, G., & Wooley, J. T. (1993). William J. Clinton: "Appointment for chair of the Commission on Immigration Reform," December 14, 1993. *The American Presidency Project*. Retrieved from http://presidency.ucsb.edu/ws/?pid=46238

Pfister, D. S. (2014). *Networked media, networked rhetorics: Attention and deliberation in the early blogosophere*. University Park, PA: Pennsylvania State University Press.

Pothier, M. (2016, February 4). Why does a NumbersUSA ad include a clip from 1995? *The Boston Globe*. Retrieved from http://bostonglobe.com

Rogers, M. B. (1998). *Barbara Jordan: American hero*. New York, NY: Bantam Books.

Sherman, M. (Ed.). (2007). *Barbara Jordan: Speaking the truth with eloquent thunder*. Austin, TX: University of Texas Press.

Usecommon Sentz. [@UsecommonSentz]. (2016, August 25). @KellyannePolls Trumps #immigration ideas are ALMOST IDENTICAL to Those of Black Dem Lesbian who worked for BIll[*] Clinton. Barbara Jordan [Tweet]. Retrieved from https://twitter.com/UsecommonSentz/status/768996737335828480

Wilson, K. (2012). Memories of the king: How the memorialization of the civil rights movement is shaping American culture and race relations. *Intercultural Directions Council Lectures*. Retrieved from http://digitalcommons.csbsju.edu/idc_lectures/1

Woods, C. S. (2012). (Im)mobile metaphors: Toward an intersectional rhetorical history. In K. Chávez & C. Griffin (Eds.), *Standing in the intersection: Feminist voices, feminist practices in Communication Studies* (pp.78–96). Albany, NY: SUNY Press.

[*] The original tweet message contains this typo.

59

REMEMBERING ROOSEVELT

Arguing for Memory Through Public and Private Networks

Chandra A. Maldonado

Communication scholars have long worked to understand how to preserve memory and the extent to which memory-based practices are rhetorically impactful. Many scholars interested in memory and commemoration have used history to foreground their investigations. For example, memory studies have focused on the ways in which collective negotiations emerge regarding national character (Blair, Jeppeson, & Pucci, 1991; Dickinson, Ott, & Aoki, 2006; Ott, Aoki, & Dickinson, 2011), the performance of historical identities (Dickinson, 1997; Sweet & McCue-Enser, 2010), and the material consequences of their commemoration (Schuster, 2006). These scholarly works utilized rich textual analyses to illustrate how the chosen narratives sustain or contest a specific public identity (Morris, 2004) based on their alignment (or lack thereof) with the public's definition of the status quo.

From this perspective, "historical memory matters" (Hume, 2010, p. 181). Those interested in memory and commemoration have turned to more focused approaches, grounding rationales and justifications in methods of argumentation to identify the "complex role of memory in contemporary culture and the ways in which these phenomena operate as instances of communication and persuasion" (Pruchnic & Lacey, 2011, p. 473). For example, McGeough, Palczewski, and Lake (2015) used the argumentative strategies of dissection, transformation, and substitution to examine the ways in which the material changes to a memorial site can counter history. Others such as Blair, Balthrop, and Michel (2011) utilized enthymemes to illustrate how material elements of a site can argue for collective identity. However, these approaches focused narrowly on historical memory as singular experiences, missing the subtle nuances that may affect the extent of the preservation and remembrance of history due to variations between sites and experiences. Here, I argue that scholars should look at the ways in which sites compose memory and circulate between and within multiple levels of collectivity.

This essay puts to task a networked approach to memory and commemoration studies useful for scholars invested in the politics of representation. The suggested approach offers insights into the making of memory. It focuses on the multi-leveled negotiations of institutionalized discourses of history, something scholars rarely examine beyond the singular level of material elements and functions of commemoration. To illustrate this claim, I analyze the 1957 National Theodore Roosevelt Centennial Celebration to show how the public image of Roosevelt—as an exceptional citizen circulated through multiple national, local, private, and public agencies—serves as a reiteration of a singular narrative performed in different ways. As such, this essay addresses how and to what extent those internal and external networks act as vital agents in the priming and employing of the various public commemorative practices, as well as their consequences for understanding how various publics experienced Roosevelt's memory.

Some scholars use *network* in a way that refers to the study of assemblages articulated beyond the space of a site or event (Greene, 2011; Slack & Wise, 2015). In accordance with that focus on broad, diverse actors, my approach works to ensure that historical work on events and sites are as thoroughgoing as possible. Others have examined the emergence of identities in public commemoration (e.g., see Biesecker, 2002); still, continuing conversations on a networked approach provides a greater awareness of the rhetorical limitations associated with recovering and putting histories to work within contemporary life. To be clear, my interest here is in making a broader theoretical point rather than getting mired in the specificity of Roosevelt or his centennial commemoration year. Thus, I use this case to illustrate a new starting point for what the canon of memory can be: an interconnective form embodying arguments between and within multiple networks of negotiation, invention, and experience.

Consanguinity, Citizen Actors, Responsible Networks

The networks that help produce and employ memory and commemorative practices commonly embed specific nodes of cultural and political ideals within their rememberings. As such, a broader, previously established network within the community worked to create the central governing bodies responsible for preserving the memory of Roosevelt long before the emergence of planning committees or specific plans for the centennial celebration. Shortly after the death of Roosevelt in 1919, friends and supporters of the President formed the Theodore Roosevelt Association to promote Roosevelt's memory. For the next 40 years, the Association acted as a starting point for the narratives that emerged about Roosevelt's life and legacy, which resulted in a series of assemblages (memorials, historical sites, and public events) to carry on that legacy.

The Association and other institutions created multiple opportunities for celebrating Roosevelt's life and legacy, resulting in many public exhibits and ceremonies. Choosing selected local state officials to serve as keynote speakers at exhibit openings was one of the ways these organizations guided the commemorations remembering Roosevelt. For example, at the 1948 opening of a Roosevelt exhibit in the American Museum of Natural History, New York's Mayor William O'Dwyer addressed the public with nostalgic words of Roosevelt's campaign run for mayor. The date of the opening marked the 62nd anniversary of Roosevelt's unsuccessful campaign run. Referring to Roosevelt as a "human cyclone" ("Address of Mayor O'Dwyer," 1948, p. 2), O'Dwyer reminded his audience of the time Roosevelt continued to speak to a crowd on the presidential campaign trail immediately after getting shot, along with other Roosevelt stories that still functioned as vital staples in the nation's definition of American exceptionalism. While the opening of the American Museum of National History exhibit serves as just one example of the ways in which public commemoration took place during this period, it is a significant lesson in the importance of remembering and authoritatively recalling the past to identify with a present public. Events like the opening of the Roosevelt exhibit set a precedent for the importance of future public commemoration events, especially for those wishing to lionize the life and times of Roosevelt.

Almost a decade later, Congress and President Dwight D. Eisenhower pushed forward a joint resolution that called for the nation to celebrate Theodore Roosevelt's centennial birthday on September 4, 1957. The Theodore Roosevelt Centennial Commission worked throughout the year to develop a program that would demonstrate "a conviction, realistically related to a present national need" ("Final Report," 1959, p. 5). Other public officials, such as Mayor Wagner of New York, glorified Roosevelt's life as an example that citizens should embody during times of change and uncertainty. Recalling Roosevelt's significant impact, Wagner noted, "he stands forth clearly out of our recent past as a personification of the best in America" ("Theodore Roosevelt," 1958, para. 4). The Commission made clear that this celebration was a way to highlight the important characteristics and values that Roosevelt considered as foundational to the nation's identity.

Convinced of the significance of preserving one of Roosevelt's creeds, the Commission decided to make the "responsible citizen" the theme of the centennial celebration. This ideal encompassed the notion that the concepts of civic engagement and moral responsibility were central to the exceptional American. The individual state branches of the Commission received the theme well. For example, Francis W. H. Adams, new chairman of New York City's branch, believed that Roosevelt embodied this ideal because he "dramatized in his own life the responsible citizen in action for public service" (quoted in "Theodore Roosevelt," 1958, para. 6). Subsequently, the state of New York took great pains to preserve Roosevelt's memory consistent with the responsible citizen theme.

The national collaboration for his centennial celebration worked in ways that not only preserved the greater national narrative of Roosevelt as an embodiment of the exceptional American, but enacted the notion in the present day. The collaborators invited multiple states and the federal government, along with the Roosevelt Centennial Commission, to create pathways for citizen involvement in the invention of Roosevelt's memory, one which performed as a rededication to the responsibilities of the nation to serve "as a beacon of mankind" ("Final Report," 1959, p. 20). The resulting approaches commemorated Roosevelt's life as a central function in the circulation of national pride and the notion of outstanding citizenry, rather than as a function to commemorate Roosevelt and his legacy.

Roosevelt's centennial celebration consisted of the workings of many federal, state, and local institutions participating as interconnected networks to shape Roosevelt's commemoration. Opening ceremonies for the national observance of Roosevelt's centennial year began on October 27, 1957. One such ceremony occurred at Youngs Memorial Cemetery in New York. Hundreds gathered at Roosevelt's grave to pay homage with flowers and wreaths, and prominent figures publically commented on the importance of Roosevelt's values, including his belief in the country's strong and capable Navy ("Centennial Opens," 1957).

Other opening ceremonies took place on that same day throughout the country. In Washington, D.C., the Commission held a ceremony at Grace Reformed Church where Roosevelt frequently attended services to battle his own inner-demons. The appropriateness of the venue emerged from Roosevelt's own expressed feelings about the value of the place: "I am sure I get a wisdom not my own and a superhuman strength for fighting the moral evils I am called to confront" (quoted in "Commission's Final Report," 1959, p. 13). Another service marking the beginning of the centennial year took place at the University of Southern California. Rev. G. Bromley Oxnam officiated the ceremony with his address titled "Theodore Roosevelt—Preacher, Politician and Patriot" ("Final

Report," 1959, p. 13). The members of the Federal Commission agreed that the primary mission of the commemoration should focus on themes that celebrate faith, nation, and power. These characteristics became primary foci for the commemoration celebration across the country because of the standards the USC event set for all citizens, namely that with faith, national pride, and a strong arm, Americans could overcome any obstacles placed before them.

Independent national agencies also worked to repurpose and circulate images and narratives of Roosevelt to showcase memorable moments in American history where he "was determined with soul of fire that the gates of opportunity would not snap shut" (quoted in "Final Report," 1959, p. 16). For example, *The New York Times* published multiple quotes of Roosevelt in the hopes of answering the question, "what does he mean to us, in the troubled mid-20th century?" ("Final Report," 1959, p. 14). Among the quotes was one that spoke of the manifest destiny characteristic of American national identity:

> Succeed? Of course we shall succeed. How can success fail to come to a race of masterful energy and resoluteness, which has a continent for the base of its domain, and which feels within its veins the thrill that comes to generous souls when their strength stirs in them, and they know that the future is theirs.
>
> *("Final Report," 1959, p. 15)*

As this example shows, times of despair often reemerge as reminders of the need for a national collective, and performances of the remembrance can function to temporarily stabilize uncertain situations.

Local institutions also created ways to define Roosevelt's successes. One option that some localities utilized was to have younger citizens take part in the commemoration events in ways that educated them on *exceptional* citizenry. For example, emergent through the workings of 20 subcommittees all chaired by people "who knew everyone and were accustomed to getting things done" ("Final Report," 1959, p. 35), the centennial committee of Roosevelt's home county of Nassau County, Long Island demonstrated its commitment to the educational values of the responsible citizen by prepping schools and teachers with materials that would "give a lift not only to classes in history or the social sciences but to every class in any subject" ("Final Report," 1959, p. 35). Distribution of materials on Roosevelt in the classroom, events by students, and trips to Sagamore Hill primed students on the teachings of Roosevelt, including the powers of politics, natural history, and the "maxim about speaking softly, and the big stick" ("Final Report," 1959, p. 36). While the official planning took place within subcommittees, multiple collaborative networks helped circulate the importance of embracing the former President's teachings.

Other states across the country (and countries abroad) followed a similar pattern. A Mayor in Aztec, New Mexico, for example, called for a "Responsible Citizen" month. The Roughriders held a reunion in Las Vegas. In New Hampshire, 238 public libraries set up reading programs and exhibits ("Final Report," 1959). Taken together, the efforts of multiple networks during the centennial's yearlong ceremonies illustrated how and to what extent public institutions, government officials, and private citizens could rely on historical memory to determine "acceptable" discourses for action in the present. The junction of multiple efforts among individual agents in Roosevelt's centennial celebration demonstrated the extent to which networks create, connect, and circulate discourses to significantly shape public memory. Indeed, the commission's efforts worked collectively to define the future of the nation through the circulation of narratives related to a past America ("Final Report," 1959).

Public Networks of Historical Memory

Scholars have long understood the strategic use of public memory. Romano and Raiford (2006) noted that histories may be used to mobilize and "to serve partisan purposes" (p. xxi) and can "shape a nation's sense of identity, build hegemony, or serve to shore up the political interests of the state; and they can certainly influence the ways in which people understand their world" (p. xxi). Blair (1992) called this selectivity the historian's mask, as they are unaware of "their own partiality" (p. 403) to history. The example of the Roosevelt memorialization makes clear, however, that commemoration practices are not fixed; instead, they are fluid in terms of how multiple networks experience history within their own groups and as part a larger national collective, past and present.

Through distribution practices reaching multiple commemoration networks at both state and local levels, for example, the federal branch of the Roosevelt Centennial Commission worked to successfully disseminate its own expectations for smaller branches to follow. The result was the circulation of the larger narrative about a troubled present America and the need to return to the historical value of an exceptional nature. The commission's nostalgic view for a contemporary America to immolate implied that if citizens could embrace a moral compass, strength, and possessed values in God and country, the nation would be able to overcome any hardships or struggles, including the perils of war. While this main national narrative remained a core strategy, however, each network collaborator focused on their own interpretation of what they thought showcased the nexus of responsible citizenry (e.g., national strength, faith, or education).

By studying the assemblages of a networked history and how commemoration practices emerge from within a single network and its connection to others, argumentation scholars should equip themselves with necessary tools to explore the extent to which histories circulate as rhetorical performances of the people that embodied those narratives, rather than simply focus on prescriptions evident in the artifact itself. Moving away from singular interpretations of collective memory and instead approaching its rhetoric as something which is localized and connected, opens commemoration studies to avenues of uncertainty which destabilize notions of identity yet to be discovered.

Positioning and examining external and internal assemblages of commemoration networks as central rhetorical agents can better help scholars identify how and to what extent the network's fashioning and circulation of history becomes fetishized within and between collectives. Such attention also directs public consumption toward a specific way of remembering (and forgetting), particularly to the extent to which the circulation of a legacy transforms into multiple iterations and experiences for remembering. By encouraging scholars to consider networks responsible for framing commemorative texts for their public consumption and rhetorical potentiality, sensitivity to differences between sites become apparent. This approach puts the problems of historical preservation and the circulation of such traditionally shrouded discourses at the forefront of analysis.

References

Address of Mayor O'Dwyer at the Opening of the Roosevelt Exhibition at American Museum of Natural History. (1948, November, 23). Theodore Roosevelt Memorial and Exhibits Collection, MSS.R6671; American Museum of Nature History Library, New York, NY.

Biesecker, B. A. (2002). Remembering World War II: The rhetoric and politics of national commemoration at the turn of the 21st century. *Quarterly Journal of Speech*, *88*(4), 393–409. doi:10.1080/00335630209384386

Blair, C. (1992). Contested histories of rhetoric: The politics of preservation, progress, and change. *Quarterly Journal of Speech*, *78*(4), 403–428. doi:10.1080/00335639209384008

Blair, C., Balthrop, V. W., & Michel, N. (2011). The arguments of the tombs of the unknown: Relationality and national legitimation. *Argumentation*, *25*(4), 449–468. doi:10.1007/s10503-011-9216-9

Blair, C., Jeppeson, M. S., & Pucci, E., Jr. (1991). Public memorializing in postmodernity: The Vietnam Veterans Memorial as prototype. *Quarterly Journal of Speech*, *77*(3), 263–288. doi:10.1080/00335639109383960

Centennial Opens for T. Roosevelt; Ceremonies Are Held at the Grave of Ex-President in Oyster Bay, L.I. (1957, October 28). [Special to The New York Times]. *The New York Times*, p. 21. Retrieved from ProQuest Historical Newspapers: The New York Times database.

Dickinson, G. (1997). Memories for sale: Nostalgia and the construction of identity in Old Pasadena. *Quarterly Journal of Speech*, *83*(1), 1–27. doi:10.1080/00335639709384169

Dickinson, G., Ott, B. L., & Aoki, E. (2006). Spaces of remembering and forgetting: The reverent eye/I at the Plains Indian Museum. *Communication and Critical/Cultural Studies*, *3*(1), 27–47. doi:10.1080/14791420500505619

Final Report of the Teddy Roosevelt Centennial Commission. (1959, July, 9). Theodore Roosevelt Memorial and Exhibits Collection, MSS.R6671. American Museum of Natural History Library, New York, NY.

Greene, R. W. (2011). Pastoral exhibition: The YMCA Motion Picture Bureau and the transition to 16mm, 1928-39. In C. A. Acland & H. Wasson (Eds.), *Useful cinema* (pp. 205-229). Durham, NC: Duke University Press.

Hume, J. (2010). Memory matters: The evolution of scholarship in collective memory and mass communication. *Review of Communication*, *10*(3), 181–196. doi:10.1080/15358591003632563

McGeough, R. E., Palczewski, C. H., & Lake, R. A. (2015). Oppositional memory practices: U.S. memorial spaces as arguments over public memory. *Argumentation and Advocacy*, *51*(4), 231–254. Retrieved from http://tandfonline.com

Morris, C. E., III. (2004). My old Kentucky homo: Lincoln and the politics of queer public memory. In K. R. Phillips (Ed.), *Framing public memory* (pp. 89–114). Tuscaloosa, AL: University of Alabama Press.

Ott, B. L., Aoki, E., & Dickinson, G. (2011). Ways of (not) seeing guns: Presence and absence at the Cody Firearms Museum. *Communication and Critical/Cultural Studies*, *8*(3), 215–239. doi:10.1080/14791420.2011.594068

Pruchnic, J., & Lacey, K. (2011). The future of forgetting: Rhetoric, memory, affect. *Rhetoric Society Quarterly*, *41*(5), 472–494. doi:10.1080/02773945.2011.597818

Romano, R. C., & Raiford, L. (Eds.). (2006). *The civil rights movement in American memory*. Athens, GA: University of Georgia Press.

Schuster, M. L. (2006). A different place to birth: A material rhetoric analysis of Baby Haven, a free-standing birth center. *Women's Studies in Communication*, *29*(1), 1–38. doi:10.1080/07491409.2006.10757626

Slack, J. D., & Wise, J. M. (2015). *Culture and technology: A primer*. Bern, Switzerland: Peter Lang.

Sweet, D., & McCue-Enser, M. (2010). Constituting "the people" as rhetorical interruption: Barack Obama and the unfinished hopes of an imperfect people. *Communication Studies*, *61*(5), 602-622. doi:10.1080/10510974.2010.514679

Theodore Roosevelt Is Honored by City of His Birth. (1958, May 28). *The New York Times*, p. 21. Retrieved from ProQuest Historical Newspapers: The New York Times database.

60

APPEARANCE TRUMPS SUBSTANCE

The Enduring Legacy of the Great Debate of September 26, 1960

Sara A. Mehltretter Drury and Dale A. Herbeck

"You think you know the rules. But what happens when you discover you don't even know how to play the game" ("Race to the White House," 2016). So began CNN's six-part series on presidential campaigns, *Race for the White House*. The first episode, "JFK vs. Nixon," focused on the 1960 presidential race, including the first televised presidential debate held in Chicago, Illinois on September 26, 1960. While the episode introduced a broad range of themes, it lingered on the decisive role the debate played in Kennedy's dramatic victory. According to CNN's documentary account, Nixon's dismal appearance on the television screen explained the Vice President's narrow electoral defeat. Timothy Naftali, one of the experts featured in the documentary, ominously concluded, "television sees it all" ("Race to the White House," 2016).

The focus on the visual elements of the first debate that *Race for the White House* described is consistent with most published accounts of the exchange. As Schroeder (2000) noted:

> Although the mythology surrounding the first Kennedy-Nixon broadcast would greatly amplify in the years to follow, the moral of the story has never varied: presidential debates are best apprehended as *television shows*, governed not by the rules of rhetoric or politics but by the demands of their host medium.
>
> (p. 9)

According to this narrative, Kennedy won the debate—and the White House—because he recognized the new politics required for success in the television age. Alternatively, Nixon lost the debate—and the election—because he did not appreciate that the rules of politics had changed. Nixon (1962) later admitted he had made a "basic mistake" and "concentrated too much on substance and not enough on appearance" (p. 340).

When recounting momentous political spectacles like the first Kennedy-Nixon debate, public memory often reduces the spectacle to a discrete event, frozen in time and detached from contemporary influences. Here, CNN condensed the first debate to a familiar, cautionary parable—appearance trumps substance—and interpreted the significance for the past, present, and future of political campaigns. Rhetorical artifacts like *Race for the White House* reduce pivotal moments of the 1960 campaign into a simple argument that missed their "significant place in U.S. political culture" (Parry-Giles & Parry-Giles, 2015, p. 115). Such analyses offer a clear standard for judging presidential debates, ignoring the evolution of public memory over time. As a result, commentators reduced the Kennedy-Nixon debates to a political fable and ignored the ways contemporary factors might influence the argument's claims, circulation, and reception. Understanding political spectacles like the Great Debates requires seeing public argument as "an ongoing social flux [...or] a networked space of flows and connections" (Edbauer, 2005, p. 9). Accordingly, a more nuanced view of political events demands consideration of how contemporary artifacts referencing past political events intermingle with elements of the present.

This essay offers a networked reading of the *Race for the White House's* "JFK vs. Nixon" episode to illustrate the important and interconnected role that collective memory plays in contemporary discourse. We draw on research that we have conducted on the Kennedy-Nixon debates over the past decade (e.g., see Drury & Herbeck, 2016) and extend it to our analysis of the contemporary docudrama *Race for the White House.* By focusing on a present account of the consequential Great Debate, this essay interrogates the claim that appearance necessarily trumps substance—demonstrating how the narrative presented in *Race for the White House* suggested that appearance triumphs through pointed political maneuvering, in addition to the Great Debate's advent of a new type of television politics. Such an account, we argue, networks into the public memory of Kennedy, Nixon, and the Great Debate, and resonates with contemporary declines in civic trust.

Contemporary Lessons from the Kennedy-Nixon Debate

Accounts of the Kennedy-Nixon debate widely echo the "looks count" narrative (e.g., Smith, 1996; White, 1961). In short, Kennedy won because he appeared glamorous and confident; Nixon's sweaty face and pallor made him look nervous and nonpresidential. This so-called lesson is, in fact, a public argument reiterated in different contexts for different purposes. Yet, the claims arguers draw from the narrative are not always consistent. Analyzing the past and present network of linked memories, sites, and values around the Great Debate yields insight into how the "looks count" narrative remains contested. For example, Drury and Herbeck's (2016) analysis of the Kennedy and Nixon presidential museum exhibits focusing on placards, televisual content, and physical displays demonstrated two different claims. At the Kennedy library, the proffered lesson is that JFK's decisive win through style *and* substance "ushered in a new era of televisual presidential leadership" (p. 174), whereas the Nixon library argues that the debate was inconsequential to the election but significant for presidential politics in the television age. The contestation of the legacy of the Great Debates demonstrates how this political event remains connected to representations of past and present politics, including the representation on *Race for the White House.*

The *Race for the White House* series originally aired on CNN and became available for streaming on Hulu in the summer of 2017. The first episode, "JFK vs. Nixon," premiered on March 6, 2016, immediately after a Democratic primary debate between Bernie Sanders and Hillary Clinton ("Race to the White House," 2016). Although the primary debate drew a modest television audience, it served as a powerful lead for the series. The episode attracted 2.56 million viewers (including 885,000 adults in the coveted 25-54 age demographic), making it the most successful CNN Original Series event on record (Kissell, 2016). The 60-minute episode follows the trajectory of the 1960 election, beginning with a short segment on Richard Nixon's expected ascendancy from Vice President to the Presidency before transitioning to ten minutes profiling John F. Kennedy's entrance into the campaign and his domination of the Democratic primary. The episode compared the two candidates' respective conventions and campaign strategies to highlight differences: Kennedy was popular, Nixon aloof; Kennedy's campaign commercials were in the catchy style of advertising jingles, Nixon's were serious and boring; Kennedy campaigned smart, Nixon's strategy to campaign in all 50 states was a foolish error. The opening foregrounds the difficulties that Nixon faced during the campaign, while claiming Kennedy's family connections and skilled campaign team generated victories. Halfway through the episode, however, the narrator turned to the first presidential debate and stated that it offered a "ray of hope" ("Race to the White House," 2016) to Nixon's beleaguered candidacy.

The brief, five-minute segment on the Great Debate in *Race for the White House* offered a mix of images, archival footage, and expert testimony. Narrator Kevin Spacey deftly weaved the elements together to recount the familiar "looks count" narrative: Kennedy appeared calm and presidential, whereas Nixon was a sweaty mess. However, the full context of the episode made the central argument more nuanced. The documentary offered two explanations to prove that "looks count": politics as game and appearance trumps substance.

Politics as Game

Public memory of the Great Debates often contains some degree of politics as gamesmanship. Oft-mentioned elements include the Kennedy team's assurances that their man had plenty of rest and tanned skin prior to the event, and that his suit and shirt appeared favorable on television (Schroeder, 2000). However, the broader context of *Race for the White House* constructed an understanding of Kennedy's ascent in the 1960 campaign, including the debates, as a take-no-prisoners political game. Contributing to that context was the episode's use of Kevin Spacey as narrator. Spacey, a well-established actor currently known for his portrayal of the fictional President Frank Underwood in Netflix's popular series titled *House of Cards*. Spacey's voice detailing the historical account brought the *ethos* of his character—unbridled ambition, manipulation, and deceit—into the *Race for the White House* series, connecting a contemporary cynical view of politics to past events.

Tracing the Democratic primary between Kennedy and Hubert Humphrey, the CNN episode presented Kennedy as an ambitious young man who would stop at nothing to secure the presidency. Today, recognition of Kennedy is ubiquitous, but the narrator was careful to introduce him as a "young," "inexperienced," and "almost unknown" contender ("Race to the White House," 2016, para. 23), suggesting that a win in the Wisconsin primary would establish Kennedy as a serious candidate. To illustrate this early period, the documentary offered images of Kennedy campaigning like a Hollywood celebrity on tour, greeting jubilant voters as if they were fans rather than citizens. Even in black and white, the images and videos drew a sharp contrast between the dazzling, rising star and the mundane Wisconsin winter setting, made the more poignant by the addition of whistling wind sound effects and the narrator explicitly reminding the audience that Kennedy was young and handsome. Kennedy appeared with his "ever present, ever glamorous wife, Jackie" ("Race to the White House," 2016, para. 38), and had financial and political resources of a powerful family available to bolster his campaign. Who could compete, the narrator wondered, with such a potent mix of "glamour, show business, and family" ("Race to the

White House," 2016, para. 43). The episode almost exclusively used images of Kennedy smiling, portraying him as the presumptive victor.

This glamorous narrative took a darker turn, however, when it recounted an effort by the Kennedy campaign to smear Humphrey in the Democratic primary. In one re-enactment scene, the docudrama portrayed Kennedy campaign man and "dirty trickster" ("Race to the White House," 2016, para. 49) Paul Corbin instructing his team to mail fliers with anti-Catholic headlines; the episode showed a dramatized video of Kennedy campaign staff stuffing envelopes with fliers labeled "The Pope for President?" and "A Catholic in the White House?" ("Race to the White House," 2016). From another expert, Evan Thomas, viewers learned that Corbin "would stop at nothing" ("Race to the White House," 2016, para. 49) to win an election. According to the documentary account by Thomas, Wisconsin voters at the time mistakenly believed that the bigoted mailings originated from Humphrey, and, as a result, thousands of outraged Catholic voters cast their ballots for Kennedy. This example epitomizes a central claim of *Race for the White House* "JFK vs. Nixon": Politics is a game, and trickery is what wins.

Before turning to the debate, *Race for the White House* reduced the political process to a game that candidates had to play strategically to win. It likened the candidates to athletes through the descriptions of their pre-debate activities. Nixon's warm-up that day was a series of speeches and campaign events that featured poor choices, such as delivering a campaign speech to the hostile, pro-Democratic Carpenter's Union. By contrast, Kennedy's pre-debate preparation included "sunning himself, taking a nap, maybe doing a little bit of studying, but basically preparing himself by relaxing" ("Race to the White House," 2016, para. 145). The CNN episode suggested that these strategies resulted in the candidates approaching the debate/game with different dispositions: Nixon was exhausted and nervous; Kennedy was relaxed and ready to dominate. The docudrama provided further evidence of Nixon's lack of preparation by showing archival footage of him pacing prior to going onstage for the debate with a worried expression. Kennedy, instead, "did not present himself until he was fully ready," Naftali explained, emerging "like the prize fighter he was" ("Race to the White House," 2016, para. 152).

Using events from the primary campaign and pre-debate preparation as evidence, the episode claimed that Nixon lost the debate before he ever opened his mouth. Kennedy and his campaign team worked as clever gamesmen, while Nixon "made every mistake you could think of" ("Race to the White House," 2016, para. 153), as his once-advisor Patrick Buchanan lamented. Such an account supports and heightens the larger narrative of appearance over substance. *Race for the White House* portrayed Nixon's comparative shortcomings in the debate as resulting from a set of manipulated circumstances and his lack of awareness regarding the "rules" of the modern campaign game.

Appearance Trumps Substance

The CNN Special Report's (2016) account of the Great Debate in *Race for the White House* is a consistent fit within the larger narrative that visual impressions matter to U.S. voters. In particular, "JFK vs. Nixon" used archival footage and expert commentary to document the significant visual contrast between the two candidates during the debate. Particularly compelling was a screen test of Nixon pacing around the studio with his eyes darting from side to side that accompanied a short video clip of his attempt to make a pre-debate joke: "I think I better shave" (CNN Special Report, 2016, para. 149). The commentary that followed stressed Nixon's lack of preparation and unattractive image, with Naftali commenting, "look at the faces of the two candidates in this debate. And ask yourself, who is presidential and who is scared" (para. 154), and Thomas recounting a reporter's comment that "Nixon looks like a suspect in a statutory rape case" (para. 169). Then, on a final and seemingly decisive note, the documentary concluded with the supposed results of the Great Debate: "TV polls show Kennedy wins the debate. But radio listeners side with Nixon" (para. 169-170). The documentary made no mention of the fact that scholarly evidence challenged the purported viewer-listener disagreement (e.g., Vancil & Pendell, 1987).

Where *Race for the White House* varied from the typical debate account, however, was that the "looks count" lesson extended to the entire 1960 campaign. The episode presented debate as symptomatic of the general importance of political appearances at the expense of substantive policy. Early in the episode, the narration stressed the vibrancy and glamour of the Kennedy family as part of JFK's rise to prominence. Furthermore, one of the first, direct candidate comparisons in the episode involved their commercials. The design of the Kennedy advertising strategy was, according to the narrator, to keep the attention of housewives watching soap operas by showing images of a commercial playing on a period-appropriate television, catchy jingles, and attractive photographs of the Kennedys greeting potential voters. By contrast, Nixon's commercials for housewives were appeals that promised to address the most important of the many issues confronting the American people. *Race for the White House* briefly showed Nixon's advertisement with a voiceover about policy on the same period-appropriate television set, and then showed a portrayal of a 1960s housewife abruptly starting to vacuum over Nixon's ad. As a result, "JFK vs. Nixon" taught audiences that in the modern era of campaigning, candidates do not achieve victory by controlling the issues, but rather, by capturing attention through the televisual.

Race for the White House's portrayal of the Great Debate's emphasis on the value of appearances extended across other aspects of the Kennedy campaign. After the section on the Great Debate, the episode detailed how both campaigns had a chance to help secure Martin Luther King, Jr.'s release from prison after the young minister's arrest following a protest in Atlanta, Georgia. The episode's use of re-enactment footage, expert commentary, and archival footage blended together to suggest that Kennedy's campaign team supported King because they thought they could "turn the situation" to Kennedy's "advantage" in the campaign, swaying African American voters towards the Democratic ticket ("Race to the White House," 2016, para. 204). The narration acknowledged that the move was not without risk—the episode showed reenactment footage of Robert F. Kennedy screaming at campaign staffer Sargent Shriver for suggesting the move to their candidate, and testimony from Kathleen Kennedy Townsend about why her father (Robert F. Kennedy) viewed support for King as worrisome for the campaign. To explain why Kennedy supported King, the episode portrayed Shriver as arguing for justice, but Robert Kennedy only changing to support justice when he realized the appearance of support could sway voters. The episode alternatively portrayed Nixon as having deep commitments to civil rights, but because of the Vice President's loyalty to President Eisenhower and Eisenhower's reticence to interfere in local and state matters, Nixon was unable to intervene on King's behalf. *Race for the White House* displayed video footage of King's release on October 28, 1960, with King crediting "Senator Kennedy [...] as a great force in making the release possible" ("Race to the White House," 2016, para. 206). This testimony, according to various experts commenting within the episode, moved many voters to support Kennedy. Like the Great Debate, the civil rights example demonstrated how the Kennedy campaign team adapted to use televisual appearances to their candidate's advantage.

Networking Legacies of the Great Debate: Reflections of Declining Civic Trust

This analysis of *Race for the White House* demonstrates how past political events remain networked within current political argument and culture. Even strongly established political parables are open to reinterpretation. New contexts intertwine with old norms, resulting in corresponding shifts as to how networks can interpret the past into lessons for the present. In the United States, contemporary political campaigns are almost always functioning in a field of networked argument—current candidates create meaning out of the interplay between current circumstances and issues with the legacies of previous campaign cycles.

The historical series *Race for the White House* therefore connects past political contests with a particularly contentious primary election season, followed by the acrimonious 2016 presidential campaign. The 2016 election saw voters polling the highest levels of unfavorability for both presidential candidates (Saad, 2016) and declining levels of trust in government and civic institutions (Gao, 2015). While the "JFK vs. Nixon" episode reaffirmed the "appearance matters" legacy of the first presidential debate of 1960, it also emphasized a narrative of political manipulation to ensure victory. This second theme connects the current civic climate with the prevailing public memory of the debates, with troubling implications. "JFK vs. Nixon" argued that voters should expect manipulation to win as the norm and appearance to matter more than substantive issues. Our analysis is not meant to suggest that presidential candidates—including those in 1960—are not actively trying to win the White House; politics has always been about winning, at least in part. However, the arguments presented in "JFK vs. Nixon" map twenty-first century political cynicism and dysfunction onto public memory of the 1960 Great Debate. In so doing, the episode offers a dramatization that sadly promotes our worst political selves.

References

Drury, S. A. M., & Herbeck, D. A. (2016). Remembering and re-creating the Great Debates of 1960: Presidential libraries as sites for political argumentation. *Communication Quarterly, 64*(2), 173–192. doi:10.1080/01463373.2015.1103283

Edbauer, J. (2005). Unframing models of public distribution: From rhetorical situation to rhetorical ecologies. *Rhetoric Society Quarterly, 35*(4), 5–24. doi:10.1080/02773940509391320

Gao, G. (2015, December 22). 15 striking findings from 2015. *Pew Research Center.* Retrieved from http://pewresearch.org

Kissell, R. (2016, March 7). Ratings: CNN's "Race for the White House" opens well following Democratic debate. *Variety.* Retrieved from http://variety.com

Nixon, R. M. (1962). *Six crises.* Garden City, NY: Doubleday.

Parry-Giles, T., & Parry-Giles, S. J. (2015). Expanding the discipline's debate contributions: New potentials, beyond effects. *Quarterly Journal of Speech, 101*(1), 113-126. doi:10.1080/00335630.2015.994902

Race to the White House [Transcript of televised series]. (2016, March 6). *CNN Special Reports.* Retrieved from http://cnn.com/TRANSCRIPTS/1603/06/csr.01.html

Saad, L. (2016, November 8). Trump and Clinton finish with historically poor images. *GALLUP News.* Retrieved from http://gallup.com

Schroeder, A. (2000). *Presidential debates: Fifty years of high-risk TV.* New York, NY: Columbia University Press.

Smith, H. K. (1996). *Events leading up to my death.* New York, NY: St. Martins.

Vancil, D. L., & Pendell, S. D. (1987). The myth of viewer-listener disagreement in the first Kennedy-Nixon debate. *Central States Speech Journal, 38*(1), 16–27. doi:10.1080/10510978709368226

White, T. H. (1961). *The making of the president, 1960.* New York, NY: Atheneum.

61

"MORNING IN AMERICA"

Ronald Reagan's Legacy of Population as Argument

Paul Elliott Johnson

Scholars of communication have focused significant attention on Ronald Reagan's famous campaign advertisement "Morning in America," examining it as a character profile (Hart, 1999), as a celebration of the America Dream (Mackey-Kallis, 1991), and as an appeal to nostalgia (Lee, 1995). The notion that Reagan tapped into, even constituted, something quintessentially American—not to mention politically powerful—is rather uncontroversial.

This paper uses "Morning in America" as a case study in the service of discussing what Lee (2006) called "the populist argumentative frame" (p. 361). Lee's essay described four key elements in populist argumentation, namely (a) the production of the people as good and virtuous, (b) the construction of a powerful enemy, (c) the built-in attacks on the system or political establishment, and (d) the promise of a sublime, apocalyptic reckoning with the people's enemy. I argue that the Morning in America campaign advertisement is populist because it constructs the life of the nation's population as the warrant for its argument, shedding light on the rhetorical shift from liberalism to neoliberalism in American politics.

I proceed in four steps. First, I elaborate on the populist argumentative frame. Then, I discuss the role of the idea of *population* in relationship to the economic life of the nation, briefly rehearsing relevant arguments from Foucault's *The Birth of Biopolitics*. Next, I analyze the advertisement before concluding by drawing implications related to the advertisement's legacy.

Populist Argument

Populism is a resource for democratic argument that no one political party or ideology monopolizes. It functions as an argumentative frame by serving as a collected set of repeated themes and tendencies that might confound standard partisan or political coordinates. While ideologically and politically diverse rhetors might produce or find appeal in populism, Lee (2006) emphasized the importance of defining populism as an argumentative frame in order to avoid trading in "atomized conceptions of liberal populism, conservative populism" or historically specific "time-bound" (p. 357) populism like that of the People's Party.

Treating populism as an argumentative style also avoids the false dichotomy of opposing populism with public reason. A strict theorization of populism as anti-rational denies its constitutive role for identity formation and persuasion, as in argument scholarship invoking populism as either a direct threat to scientific authority (Collins & Weinel, 2011) or a logical fallacy threatening public reason (Ieţcu-Fairclough, 2008). Instead, Lee followed McGee's (1975) approach in treating appeals to "the people" (p. 242) as constitutive of political identity and therefore part of the *terra firma* of a flexible political rationality. If critics approach populism as a broadly available rhetorical technique for subject constitution, they can better recognize it as a distributed mode of reason intrinsic to, rather than opposed to, politics.

Over time, the structure of populist argumentation might encompass many "varied expressions of populism" (p. 362), but Lee (2006) was careful to consider these approaches as non-discrete entities that "develop in linear fashion" (p. 362). His two key examples—the rhetoric of Huey Long and George Wallace—offered straightforward examples for his typology. Lee's choices, however, suggest that more work is needed to examine "harder" cases of moderated or sublimated populist rhetoric. Arguably, populism might be present even when its generic features are difficult to discover. Furthermore, populist argument may frame ways of thinking about broader discursive formations, such as the shared ideology of a set of voting constituents or the base of a political party.

Here, I examine the contemporary conservative claim to ownership over the concept of "the American people," marked by the insistence that American conservatism properly represents the spirit of the nation. These assumed "American" characteristics have not emerged *ex nihilo*, but are part and parcel of a widespread transformation accompanying the political realignment initiated with the decline of the Democratic "solid South" in 1964 and spread by the arrival of the Reagan Revolution in 1980.

Certainly, analyses of the New Right have prefigured some of Lee's (2006) four typological elements. For example, Patton (1995) described the process of enemy construction in her essay "Refiguring Social Space" and how the American public came to fear racial and sexual differences during and after Reagan's presidency, while Crowley's (2006) *Towards a Civil Discourse* focused on the latent apocalypticism of modern conservatism. Such works helped to explain the fear and anxiety of modern conservatives, while suggesting the need to examine the more positive side of American conservatism.

Moreover, the political realignment discussed here significantly changed American argument culture. As Spence (2015) argued, "Ronald Reagan transformed the way we think about government, and this not only affected the Republican Party, it affected the Democratic Party" (p. 20) by shifting presumption *against* rather than *for* social welfare policy. Frank (2000) described this transformation as "market populism" (para. 4), the belief that "markets manage to express the popular will more articulately and meaningfully" (para. 4) than state institutions. In the next section, I will briefly discuss the ways in which the life of the nation's population and the health of the market function as a single rhetorical entity in contemporary America, and I show how the population itself becomes a resource for the construction of conservative populist argument.

Life of Population as Truth of the Market

Drawing on Foucault's (2008) *The Birth of Biopolitics*, I briefly rehearse three insights from his lectures on neoliberalism that are central to the shift from liberalism to neoliberalism. First, as neoliberal economic theory trickled up from various sources, the market shifted from *an* element nameable within a society composed of several different elements (e.g., the political, the national, and perhaps the mystic) to *the* element that defined reality. While the government at one point seemingly functioned "according to justice" and positioned "good government" as that which was "just," the transformation from liberalism into neoliberalism marked when individual freedom named the process of economic reality constraining government action (Foucault, 2008, p. 32). Within liberalism, actors often weigh the consequences of government action on economic growth against the implications of its decisions for the public good; within neoliberalism, the health of the economy serves as the ultimate public good while government conceals its structuring role in political deliberation and argumentation. Neoliberalism functions not as *an* account of reality, but *as* reality. The market, then, is no longer one interest among many others; instead it becomes a site for the "verification-falsification for governmental practice" (Foucault, 2008, p. 32) in which market-driven decisions can trump accounts of public reason that originate from the government based on their position of enunciation. In short, the market finds the truth better than government does.

The second transformation Foucault identified is in the concept of life itself, which ceases to exist separate from the economic and, instead, is now fundamentally economic. The truth of the market communicates not merely economic information but indexes the health of the population. Borrowing from Rüstow's (1961) term *vitalpolitik* (p. 171), Foucault (2008) observed that previously considered, non-economic entities and objects (e.g., food, shelter, and community) had become economic, such that the "basic units" of human existence come to "have the form of [...] enterprise" (p. 148). Under the "multiplication of the 'enterprise' form within the social body" (p. 148), more and more is economic and less and less is simply social or political. Under neoliberalism, not only do a panoply of actors in politics, economics, and in the media speak of human necessities like shelter as "investments," society also tends more and more to apprehend the health of the economy as a verdict on the value of the humanity of those who compose it. Foucault's account of the spectacular size and speed of the post-war industrial boom, for example, no longer registered as readily with audiences as accumulations resulting from the expenditure of human labor power; instead, the boom was the work of "human capital" (p. 231). His reading of the production of economic value expressed humanity's capacity for ingenuity and innovation, reframing the world historical economic growth of the post-war period as an achievement of America's humanity realized, rather than a production of alienated labor.

Foucault's (2008) third relevant phenomenon for this analysis was "state phobia" (p. 187). State phobia reductively figures any form of the state as "successive branches of one and the same great tree of state control" (p. 187), making difficult distinctions between "the administrative state, the welfare state, the bureaucratic state, the fascist state, and the totalitarian state" (p. 187). State-phobia is most useful as a concept for theorizing the ways in which cultural and political discourses figure the relationship between the state and the individual. The sentiment compels abstract reactions of hostility towards the very idea of governance, even if many Americans approve of government programs that improve their material existence.

In the next section, I read the advertisement-length version of "Morning in America" to show the ways in which the text constituted the nation's population as a resource for making an argument. Specifically, I examine how the advertisement figured the living of American life as economic and posited the state as intrinsically separate from the life of the American population. The advertisement articulated life and economics together, such that the two concepts functioned as mutually enabling referents where the economic takes precedence. Morning in America also rendered the government as almost invisible, and therefore conceptually separate from the life of the nation and the economy.

"It's Morning in America"

Based on a longer 1984 Republican National Convention campaign film, the shortened version of the advertisement, technically called "Prouder, Stronger, Better" (Pytka, 1984), served as one of the most effective campaign advertisements in history (Lipset & Schneider, 1987). Part of a stunning electoral victory where Reagan won 49 out of 50 states, the advertisement marks the transition from movement conservatism into consolidated power. It produces a vision of American existence based on a blending of life and economics whereby the American population emerges as a good in and of itself.

Morning in America performs a faith that American living is a good in and of itself. The advertisement contained no disasters or threats, focusing instead on a happy and bucolic nation rising to meet the day. Four years removed from the Carter administration's perception of malaise, the advertisement represented economic recovery through "ordinary" Americans living their lives—still in slow process at the end of Reagan's first term. Opening at the break of day, Morning in America depicted people either at work or on their way to work. Amongst the occupation workers shown are a paperboy, farmer, firefighter, and a specifically unidentifiable white-collar worker. Fully one-third of the advertisement—the first twenty seconds—focused on commerce, either in the form of employment or purchasing goods. The voiceover mentioned increases in home purchases as a sign of recovery while viewers watch presumably new homeowners marching a large, just-purchased rug into their home. Between the bucolic imagery of Americans going to (or performing) their jobs and the voiceover, the advertisement posited that a working population is a sign of a successful nation. Economic recovery does not constitute the provision of means for non-economic activity, such as recreation and pleasure, but something more like Foucault's (2008) observations about human capital, in which the realization of humanity and production of economic value are coincident. Work and life blur together into the same formation.

These conditions of economic recovery do not facilitate prosperity, as the advertisement never depicted anything outside of life in a small town until the conclusion of the piece. The voiceover is the only access point to the macro-level economic conditions: references to housing purchases, declines in inflation, and rising job numbers. The advertisement positioned the productive and energetic morning in the advertisement as the whole of America, making the activities of the population themselves exemplars of the prosperity on hand. The actuarial character of the narration strengthened this element, as Morning in America repeated numbers: 2,000 will buy homes and 6,500 will be married. In quantifying life by laminating imagery with audible macro-economic indicators, the advertisement performed what Foucault identified as the tendency to elevate the economic as the sole source for understanding reality, rather than one among several.

The advertisement spent fully a quarter of its running time on the marriage montage, which included the couple's walk down the aisle and the smiling procession into wedded bliss and a prosperous future. A smiling grandmother bookends the wedding, sitting in a pew smiling on the front end and embracing the wedded bride (presumably her granddaughter or granddaughter-in-law) at the end of the ceremony. During this montage, the narrator mentioned the inflation rate, but insisted that the wedded couple can "look forward with confidence" (Pytka, 1984, 0:32) yoking the act of building a family to economic certainty and stability. In converting the familial *oikos* into an extant unit tied to the economic fortunes of the polity, the advertisement evidenced the gravitational appeal of Foucault's (2008) economic.

The government's appearance in the advertisement mirrored the wish of the state-phobic politics of neoliberalism, as it was separate from the population yet enormously powerful. Following the wedding ceremony, a generic video of the Capitol appeared with three distinctive elements. First, the editors rendered the building enormous within the shot's frame and positioned it as larger and more towering than any other building appearing in the advertisement. Second, in the shot of the Capitol, citizens raised a single, small U.S. flag that the building increasingly dwarfs as the shot pans out. Third, the sky was dark in the shot, with fewer hints of "morning" than in any other shot in the advertisement. The advertisement's depiction of the federal government not only tacitly suggested that the District of Columbia signifies night—implicitly separating the rebirth of the nation happening elsewhere from the seat of governance—but also played to state-phobic fears that the federal government is large, distant, and inhuman. The approach contrasted the Capitol's monolithic existence in the dark of night to the bright and vibrant morning of commerce and life in "real America." Morning in America's only other evidence of government was mostly local, presenting shots of firefighters and schoolteachers working at a public school. Both the schoolteacher and the firefighter raised flags, larger than those in the shot of the Capitol and became even more so as the flags slowly towered over the figures that held them. As an emotional apparatus, state-phobia works in part by positing the government and the population as oppositional figures. The advertisement performed this belief, depicting the life of the population as separate, distant, and even alien to the federal government.

In Morning in America, government was generally absent. When it did appear, it mostly functioned to defend life and property. Otherwise, the community defined itself through its own acts: commerce, labor, and love, each dependent upon and interrelated with the others. This population was industrious, virtuous, hardworking, and finding fulfillment in their relations with one another. The absence of inflation and the reduction of other economic negatives, combined with the felt positivity of Americans living their lives, suggested an America where prosperity of the population generally mirrored economic prosperity. The occurrence of these achievements in the absence of the state is no accident. "Real America" is alive and is separate from government and management. Even Reagan himself barely appeared—a tiny image on a campaign button that the American flag dwarfed in the advertisement's close.

Conclusion

Market populism requires leaders to conflate the economic health of the nation with the life of the population, and Morning in America stands as an early example of market populism that does not merely anticipate the rhetorical trend but helped produce it. I argued in this essay that population, nation, and economy function together as a totality. Politicians, spokespeople, campaigns, and media actors often invoke the various parts of the totality in ways that ultimately defer to the economic: Market reality deems the other elements mere opinion by dissociating them with the life of the population. Morning in America posits the appropriate measure for the life of America might be the extent that people work, purchase goods, and have kinship relationships with durable, commercial activities like homeownership. Life does not exist alongside economics, but *is* economic.

Additionally, the sovereign separation of the life of the nation from governance functions as a resource for populist arguments and their decoding. A positive depiction of life functions not only to establish the virtuousness of "the people," but to separate them from the realm of governance, a move that places presumption even further against governmental intervention. State-phobia helps facilitate the collapse the New Deal-era liberal consensus by positing government as a threat to the freedom of the population. In the advertisement's zero-sum formulation, less government equates with greater popular sovereignty of the population.

References

Collins, H. M., & Weinel, M. (2011). Transmuted expertise: How technical non-experts can assess experts and expertise. *Argumentation, 25*(3), 401–413. doi:10.1007/s10503-011-9217-8

Crowley, S. (2006). *Towards a civil discourse: Rhetoric and fundamentalism.* Pittsburgh, PA: University of Pittsburgh Press.

Foucault, M. (2008). *The birth of biopolitics: Lectures at the Collège de France 1978–1979* (G. Burchell, Trans., & A. I. Davidson, Ed.). New York, NY: Palgrave Macmillan.

Frank, T. (2000, October 12). The rise of market populism. *The Nation.* Retrieved from https://thenation.com/article/rise-market-populism/

Hart, R. P. (1999). *Seducing America: How television charms the modern voter.* Thousand Oaks, CA: SAGE.

Ieţcu-Fairclough, I. (2008). Legitimation and strategic maneuvering in the political field. *Argumentation, 22*(3), 399–417. doi:10.1007/s10503-008-9088-9

Lee, M. J. (2006). The populist chameleon: The people's party, Huey Long, George Wallace, and the populist argumentative frame. *Quarterly Journal of Speech, 92*(4), 355–378. doi:10.1080/00335630601080385

Lee, R. (1995). Electoral politics and visions of community: Jimmy Carter, virtue, and the small town myth. *Western Journal of Communication, 59*(1), 39–60. doi:10.1080/10570319509374506

Lipset, S. M., & Schneider, W. (1987). The confidence gap during the Reagan years. *Political Science Quarterly, 102*(1), 1–23. Retrieved from http://jstor.org/stable/2151482

Mackey-Kallis, S. (1991). Spectator desire and narrative closure: The Reagan 18-minute political film. *Southern Journal of Communication, 56*(4), 308–214. doi:10.1080/10417949109372842

McGee, M. C. (1975). In search of "the people": A rhetorical alternative. *Quarterly Journal of Speech, 61* (3), 235–249. doi:10.1080/00335637509383289

Patton, C. (1995). Refiguring social space. In L. Nicholson & S. Seidman (Eds.), *Social Postmodernism: Beyond Identity Politics* (pp. 216–249). Cambridge, United Kingdom: Cambridge University Press.

Pytka, J. [Director]. (1984). Prouder, stronger, better [Video file]. *Museum of the Moving Image.* Retrieved from http://livingroomcandidate.org/commercials/1984/prouder-stronger-better

Rustow, A. (1961). Organic policy (vitalpolitik) versus mass regimentation. In A. Hunold (Ed.), *Freedom and serfdom: An anthology of western thought* (pp. 171–190). Dordrecht, The Netherlands: Reidel.

Spence, L. K. (2015). *Knocking the hustle: Against the neoliberal turn in black politics.* Brooklyn, NY: Punctum Books.

62

NETWORKING LEGAL ARGUMENTS

Prudential Accommodation in *National Federation v. Sebelius*

M. Kelly Carr

On June 28, 2012, the U.S. Supreme Court announced its much-awaited ruling on the Patient Protection and Affordable Care Act (ACA). Most interested parties turned straight to the court's holding to see whether the Supreme Court had ruled against key components of President Obama's signature universal health care law. Chief Justice John Roberts surprised many by penning a decision upholding the Act. Roberts dismissed the constitutionality of the government's primary support—the Commerce Clause, which granted Congress the ability to regulate interstate commerce—but supported its secondary argument about Congress's ability to tax citizens. The Court's majority argued that the ACA's mandate arguably functioned as a tax upon those not carrying health insurance, a constitutional use of Congress's enumerated powers.

The decision's reasoning was predictably complicated, as it reflected a complex federal effort to bring health care to all Americans, including the public sphere arguments and constitutional questions surrounding the legislation. ACA supporters praised Roberts for restraining the partisan excesses of legal challengers and his conservative colleagues (Sage, 2012). Opponents labeled the decision "a political dodge" (Hoff, 2013, p. 5). This dichotomy fails to acknowledge the multiple goals of Supreme Court authorship and the Court's multiple audiences. This essay asserts that Chief Justice Roberts' opinion in *National Federation of Independent Business v. Sebelius* (2012), otherwise known as the ACA case, served as an act of jurisprudential prudence, a largely unsatisfying but institutionally effective legal argumentation strategy responsive to the unique inventional needs of the Supreme Court opinion writing process.[1] This essay will begin by expanding the scope of prudential argumentation to include the collaborative inventional process, describing an example of prudential opinion-writing as a model for prudential legal argument, and then applying the framework to Roberts' decision.

Prudential Accommodation

The Supreme Court has long established its credibility based upon an ethos of prudence, an ongoing performance that insulates its reputation from its moments of activism. According to Hariman (1991):

> Prudence designates the capacity for effective political response to contingent events. It arises in deliberation, requires implicit understanding of the possible, the probable, and the appropriate within a specific community, and is not reducible to categorical imperatives, deontologies, or universal laws.
>
> *(p. 26)*

Advocates most commonly implement prudential rhetorical strategies to resolve acute controversies by praising restraint, privileging experience, and distinguishing between *is* and *ought*: "Prudence dictates that we live in the world as it is, not as we wish it might be" (Jasinski, 1995, p. 461). Nelson (2003) asserted that "the inventional capacity of prudent people stems from their acute, well-tuned sensitivity to the complexities of any place" (p. 247). Yet, because of its reliance on the situational and contingent over the universal and settled, critics characterize prudential action as unprincipled and ends-driven (Randall, 2011). Thus, the prudential rhetor must draw upon experience to make the response seem customary, relying on dual idioms of audacity and accommodation (Southard, 2007). The balancing strategies of prudential argumentation serve the legal situation well, especially because its temporal orientation mirrors appellate court questions that demand "knowledge of the past, understanding of the present, and a sense of the future" (Southard, 2007, p. 6). Indeed, prudence's reigning term is *balance*: weighing competing courses of action, competing values, potential consequences, and balancing between individual and collective interests (Bluhm & Heineman, 2011).

This essay argues that within appellate legal discourse, prudential argumentation strategies begin with the collaborative inventional process through which justices craft their arguments. Both institutionally motivated and rhetorically strategic, the tools of prudential accommodation allow the Court to perform the expectation of constraint, merge the justices' multiple voices, and affirm the court's apolitical character to the public, even as individual published opinions vary. These tools are necessary, because as cases like the ACA reach the Supreme Court, they encounter not only complicated questions about federal powers and individual liberties but also the needs and constraints of the Court itself. In their final opinions, justices must issue decisions reflecting both the circumstances of the particular case and jurisprudential norms that require their decisions to be consonant with previous rulings, legislative intent, and informed interpretation. Knowledge of the past, a key feature of prudence, reigns supreme in appellate reasoning. Yet in complex cases dealing with controversial social issues like universal health care—a congressionally enacted and politically controversial policy without precedent—institutional standards alone do not meet the needs of the case (Carr, 2018). Justices must turn toward the present and future, against the current of institutional prudence.

Prudent justices find solutions that appear to already exist. They rely on solutions that uphold the expectations of judicial review, that avoid the appearance of legislating from the bench, and that fit within the existing flows of public and legal discourses surrounding the issue (Carr, 2018). Justices must also rely on their networks, considering each other's arguments and writing collaboratively in order to form a holding of the court.

The fact that courts must address multiple audiences, including other justices, lower courts, legislators, litigants, legal scholars, and the non-legal public complicates these choices (Makau, 1984). Exploring the justification process with multiple audiences in mind can unearth previously unconsidered counter-arguments, strengthen support for the decision, or reframe arguments in a manner previously ignored. These argumentative networks, which all serve as inventional devices, often form the fabric of the decision.

Justices, as they form their arguments, also write with broader rhetorical outcomes in mind. These include the court's authority, the construction of particular histories, and the rules of legal culture (Carr, 2018). When Roberts assigned himself the task of writing the decision, he also assigned himself the weight of these inventional burdens. As majority opinion writer, his primary mission was to patch together the constitutional and political concerns of the ACA's advocates and opponents both inside and outside the chambers, while avoiding the appearance of institutional overreach. The political weight of this case made the appearance of an apolitical court decision nearly impossible—someone had to lose—but also quite necessary for the decision's acceptance and for the court's long-term credibility. In short, this case required prudence.

Roberts' Prudential Networking

When Congress passed the ACA by narrow margins in 2010, the individual mandate was a key provision, requiring most citizens to either maintain health insurance coverage or pay a penalty. Support for the mandate split along party lines (Brodie, Deane, & Cho, 2011). Opponents gave two main reasons. The individual mandate's goal of near universal buy-in to lower the cost for everyone raised the specter of socialized medicine—a potent charge against universal health care every time advocates have proposed it dating back to President Truman (Feulner, 2010; Johnson, 2016). The mandate's compulsory nature also troubled limited government conservatives who saw it as an affront to individual liberty (Shapiro, 2011). After the ACA's passage, two main legal challenges emerged via state lawsuits. The first, and the focus of this paper, questioned the constitutionality of the individual mandate. The states argued that the federal government could not force individuals to buy a product. The Eleventh Circuit Court agreed, ruling that Congress had overstepped its constitutional authority.

In his role as chief justice, Roberts needed to balance the maintenance of the Court's credibility, the delicate networking process between justices, and the potential damage done to valuable doctrine if each side completely had its way. From conference meetings and oral arguments, Roberts likely knew that four justices would uphold the mandate, and four justices found it unconstitutional (Crawford, 2012). The consequences of declaring the mandate unconstitutional would include the Supreme Court striking down a major legislative action and enduring accusations that it was an anti-Obama co-political branch of Congress. By contrast, upholding it as presented would expand the Commerce Clause into an unconsidered class of actions and open the Court to accusations that it was a pro-Obama co-political branch of the Executive Office. Roberts needed to find a solution that avoided these consequences.

The search for a prudent solution led him down a path of a similarly controversial case. In 1978, Justice Lewis Powell wrote the majority opinion in *Regents v. Bakke*, the first case addressing the constitutionality of university affirmative action admissions policies. Powell's donated collection of papers provided a unique view into the Supreme Court opinion-writing process in a publically controversial and jurisprudentially divided case. In *Bakke*, Powell undertook the task of networking between the justices, as well as between legal reasoning and public sentiment. Faced with a less-than-ideal affirmative action program, a public divided on the issue, a polarized court, and heavy consequences for institutional credibility, Powell turned to the principle of prudential accommodation. Powell used the idiom of accommodation to validate the principle of individual rights that opponents of the program argued, while evoking the idiom of audacity to pair the value of diversity with a legal story of limits that deferred judgment to universities. This solution upheld the public policy, while curbing what Powell saw as its excesses. As with Roberts' ACA opinion, critics charged Powell with uninspiring pragmatism (Alschuler, 1986; Klafter, 1998; Tushnet, 1995). The text of Roberts' ACA opinion evidenced a similar pattern to Powell's: first, uphold the primary conservative principle of the case; second, proclaim deference to the authoritative body; and finally, find a way to say yes while limiting the impact of the policy.

The government's use of the Commerce Clause to support the individual mandate was both the ACA's lynchpin argument and opponents' biggest target. Conservative commentators argued that it violated a foundational conservative principle of individual liberty by expanding the government's reach into the lives of individuals by forcing them to buy an unwanted product for their own good (see Jeffrey, 2009). Public arguments analogizing the mandate to the forced purchase of broccoli caught traction and worked their way into legal arguments as a warning of the slippery slope that the precedent would allow (Stewart, 2012). Within the Court, Justice Kennedy, reportedly incensed at what he saw as federal overreach of power in the ACA legislation, launched a sustained internal campaign to sway Roberts to join the three reliably conservative justices: Scalia, Alito, and Thomas (Crawford, 2012). Roberts agreed, but as chief justice, his role included maintaining the court's integrity (Crawford, 2012). Prudence is not reducible to categorical imperatives. Whereas other justices were willing to strike down the entire legislation on principle, Roberts attempted to balance these principles with the real consequences of such a vote.

To accommodate the ACA's opponents and protect useful doctrine, Roberts spent much time explaining his rejection of the Commerce Clause justification. He argued that the clause already gave Congress great authority, not just to regulate interstate commerce but even to regulate activities that *affect* commerce; thus, he drew a line at inactivity (Roberts, pp. 17–18). "Accepting the government's theory would give Congress the same license to regulate what we do not do [as they have to regulate what we do], fundamentally changing the relation between the citizen and the Federal Government," argued Roberts (pp. 23–24), using language similar to Justice Kennedy during oral arguments—likely in hopes of persuading him to join the opinion. Next, Roberts evoked a slippery slope argument common in public arguments against the ACA. Applying the Commerce Clause power to commercial inactivity "would open a new and potentially vast domain to congressional authority. Every day individuals do not do an infinite number of things," Roberts observed (p. 20). In a nod to ACA protesters, he even gave broccoli a rare legal appearance before announcing his ruling on the mandate's constitutionality under the Commerce Clause. As the mandate forced individuals to buy into commerce precisely because they refrained from commercial activity, it did not fall under Congress's authority to regulate commerce (Roberts, p. 27).

After offering protection to the Commerce Clause's doctrinal boundaries and a voice to opponents' concerns about individual liberties, Roberts attended to the Court's prudential ethos via the performance of judicial restraint. Here, Roberts enacted a story of limits that asserted the court's need to exercise deference toward the elected branches of government. LaRue (1995) argued that narratives written to support constitutional interpretations can be read as *stories of limits* and *stories of growth*, both of which are foundational to the Court's maintenance of judicial authority. In these narratives, justices expand or constrict constitutional limits within their justificatory framework as interpreters. Stories of growth see the Constitution as dynamic, meeting contemporary needs as they arise (LaRue, 1995). Stories of limits assert that the Constitution is not subject to legislative whim, and must remain above transient political needs (LaRue, 1995), thereby limiting the justices' ability to act.

Justice Powell had made good use of the story of limits when arguing why the court did not have the job of determining which educational goals best meet the needs of a student body. So long as the policies passed constitutional muster, Powell argued, then the Court should refrain from interfering with policy, instead presuming good faith of university administrators (*Regents v. Bakke*, 1977/1978, p. 17).

A deferential position on legislative action, paired with a secondary argument that upheld the legislation under Congress's well-known taxing authority, offered Roberts a prudential solution to the case's conundrum. As early as page two of his decision, Roberts previewed his story of limits by declining to speak to the wisdom of the ACA legislation: "We do not consider whether the Act embodies sound policies. That judgment is entrusted to the Nation's elected leaders. We ask only whether Congress has the power under the Constitution to enact the challenged provisions" (p. 2). This opening simultaneously signaled Roberts' doubts about the legislation's wisdom while disavowing the court's "expertise [or] prerogative to make policy judgments" (p. 6).

Roberts' deferential stance required more of the Supreme Court than did Powell's, as it insisted on deferential textual interpretation instead of merely relegating responsibility. The government had offered a second argument in favor of the individual mandate. In this argument, the government asked the justices to read the mandate "not as ordering individuals to buy insurance, but rather as imposing a tax on those who [do not buy it]" (Roberts, p. 31). Roberts pulled on two powerful authoritative sources—Justices Story and Holmes—to support the doctrine that "if a statute has two possible meanings, one of which violates the Constitution, courts should adopt the meaning that does not do so" (p. 31). Instead of deferring to the good faith efforts of an external body, the Roberts doctrine construed deference as applying good faith within the Court's interpretative process. "The Government asks us to interpret the mandate as imposing a tax, if it would otherwise violate the Constitution. Granting the Act the full measure of deference owed to federal statutes, it can be so read," argued Roberts (p. 32). Roberts dutifully provided a doctrinal test of whether an act was functionally a tax: it should not be so severe as to be coercive, it is not limited to willful violations, it is collected by the IRS, and it does not declare non-purchasers as criminals (pp. 33–35). Read this way, Congress was well within its enumerated powers to collect and lay taxes. Roberts concluded in the language of deference: "Because the Constitution permits such a tax, it is not our role to forbid it, or to pass upon its wisdom or fairness" (p. 44).

Conclusion

Critics have described Roberts' ACA decision as confusing, overreaching, underwhelming, and out of line with constitutional texts and doctrine. The decision satisfied no party completely—legally or extra-legally. Yet the decision has prodded ACA's opponents to attempt change through congressional action rather than lawsuits. Roberts networked conservative arguments with progressive outcomes, accommodation with audacity, and public concerns with legal argument. He artfully used a deferential jurisprudential stance to avoid assuaging concerns he shared. "The Framers created a Federal Government of limited powers, and assigned to this Court the duty of enforcing those limits," said Roberts in his conclusion. "The Court does so today. But the Court does not express any opinion on the wisdom of the Affordable Care Act. Under the Constitution, that judgment is reserved to the people" (p. 59). His prudential strategy allowed him to disavow his support for the ACA while nevertheless upholding the mandate, thus giving voice to his legal and public networks while avoiding a credibility crisis for the Court.

Note

1 This essay will cite all quotations from this court case by the opinion writer and page number, from the slip opinion.

References

Alschuler, A. W. (1986). Failed pragmatism: Reflections on the Burger Court. *Harvard Law Review, 100* (6), 1436–1456.

Bluhm, W., & Heineman, R. (2011, November/December). What is prudent pragmatism? *Philosophy Now: A Magazine of Ideas*, (87). Retrieved from https://philosophynow.org

Brodie, M., Deane, C., & Cho, S. (2011). Regional variations in public opinion on the Affordable Care Act. *Journal of Health Politics, Policy and Law, 36*(6), 1097–1103. doi:10.1215/03616878-1460587

Carr, M. K. (2018). *The rhetorical invention of diversity: Supreme Court opinions, public arguments, and affirmative action*. East Lansing, MI: Michigan State University Press.

Crawford, J. (2012, July 2). Roberts switched views to uphold health care law. *CBS News*. Retrieved from http://cbsnews.com

Feulner, E. J. (2010, March 29). Opposing an intolerable act. *The Heritage Foundation*. Retrieved from http://heritage.org/taxes/commentary/opposing-intolerable-act/

Hariman, R. (1991). Prudence/performance. *Rhetoric Society Quarterly, 21*(2), 26–35. doi:10.1080/02773949109390914

Hoff, J. S. (2013). Obamacare: Chief Justice Roberts's political dodge. *The Independent Review, 18*(1), 5–20. Retrieved from http://independent.org

Jasinski, J. (1995). The forms and limits of prudence in Henry Clay's (1850) defense of the compromise measures. *Quarterly Journal of Speech, 81*(4), 454–478. doi:10.1080/00335639509384129

Jeffrey, T. P. (2009, October 21). Can Obama and Congress order you to buy broccoli? *CNS News*. Retrieved from http://cnsnews.com

Johnson, M. (2016, December 11). Why Republicans hate Obamacare. *The Economist*. Retrieved from https://economist.com

Klafter C. E. (1998). Justice Lewis F. Powell, Jr.: A pragmatic relativist. *Boston University Public Interest Law Journal, 8*(1), 1–13. Retrieved from HeinOnline database.

LaRue, L. H. (1995). *Constitutional law as fiction: Narrative in the rhetoric of authority*. University Park, PA: Pennsylvania State University Press.

Makau, J. M. (1984). The Supreme Court and reasonableness. *Quarterly Journal of Speech, 70*(4), 379–397. doi:10.1080/00335638409383705

National Federation of Independent Business v. Sebelius, No. 11-363. 567 U.S. 219 (2012)

Nelson, J. S. (2003). Prudence as Republican politics in American popular culture. In R. Hariman (Ed.), *Prudence: Classical virtue, postmodern practice* (pp. 229–257). University Park, PA: Pennsylvania State University Press.

Randall, D. (2011). The prudential public sphere. *Philosophy and Rhetoric, 44*(3), 205–226. doi:10.5325/philrhet.44.3.0205

Regents of the University of California v. Bakke, 438 U.S. 265 (1977/1978).

Sage, W. (2012, June 30). Preserving the republic: Chief Justice Roberts' Affordable Care Act opinion [Blog post]. *Health Affairs*. doi:10.1377/hblog20120630.020926

Shapiro, I. (2011, January 31). Health care ruling a victory for federalism and individual liberty [Blog post]. *Cato Institute*. Retrieved from https://cato.org

Stewart, J. B. (2012). How broccoli landed on Supreme Court menu. *The New York Times*. Retrieved from http://nytimes.com

Southard, B. F. S. (2007). Prudential argumentation and John Marshall's opinion in *Marbury v. Madison* (1803). *Argumentation and Advocacy, 44*(1), 1–17. Retrieved from http://tandfonline.com

Tushnet, M. (1995). Lives in the law: Justice Lewis F. Powell and the jurisprudence of centrism. *Michigan Law Review, 93*(6), 1854–1884.

PART VII

EVALUATING ARGUMENTATION NETWORKS

63

RISING TO THE DEFENSE OF *AD HOMINEM* ARGUMENTS

David Cratis Williams and Dale Hample

Argumentation scholars classically identify attacks on the author of an argument, rather than the argument's content, as an *ad hominem* fallacy. The justification for regarding this tactic as fallacious has been that only the argument's content should matter and that even a bad person can make a good argument. This position has been recognized as too simple for several decades, but it is nonetheless where one begins thinking about arguments that attack the other person.

Today, the field of argumentation studies distinguishes three types of *ad hominem* (Copi, 1982; van Eemeren, Garssen, & Meuffels, 2009; Walton, 1998; Walton, Reed, & Macagno, 2008): (a) direct or abusive: a nasty attack on the other person's character, nature, intelligence, etc.; (b) indirect or circumstantial: the other person has special circumstances that result in a vested interest or invalid perception, etc., that render what she or he says as mere rationalization; and (c) "you too" or *tu quoque*: the other person has said or done other things that are not consistent with what she or he is saying now. All three types share that they either move a judgment about the speaker to his/her argument (abusive and circumstantial) or they judge the argument by connecting it to the arguer (*tu quoque*).

Argumentation studies also recognizes that attacks on the other arguer are not necessarily illegitimate. The standard example is that of impugning the credibility of a witness in court. Another would be attacking the expertise of a person who advocates have proposed as an authority. Both illustrations constitute legitimate matters of substance. Worth noting, however, is that utilizing traditional analysis, these tactics really should not be decisive. A biased woman or evil man can still say a correct thing. Even legitimate attention to the arguer's nature only justifies doubt about the argument. The central question remains: Is our intuition that aggressive evaluations of a witness's honesty or an authority's credentials substantively defensible?

Scholars writing and thinking about *ad hominem* generally depict legitimate uses of the tactic as exceptions. The field's intellectual history is hard to abandon. The critic's presumption is quietly proposed to be that anything having to do with the arguer should be set aside in evaluating the argument's substance, unless some well-known exception is noticed. We aim to reverse that presumption and insist that the nature of the arguer is an essential part of the argument, not a pollutant.

We maintain that the argument and the arguer are one organic thing, artificially separated only for academic purposes. In the world, and therefore in veridical theory, analysts should first see the organic whole of argument and arguer, and only then notice or critically remark about one or the other, or about how the two join in the moment.

Our position is that scholars should understand and evaluate an *ad hominem* argument scheme in many circumstances as a rational argument from an interpretive orientation that features the importance of human agents and attributes intrinsic qualities to agents. Burke's (1952) reflections influence our analysis. Burke intended his well-known pentad as a description or schemata for reasonably full descriptions of human motives. The elements of the pentad are act, agent, agency, scene, and purpose. He maintained, "Any complete statement about motives will offer *some kind* of answers to these five questions: what was done (act), when or where it was done (scene), who did it (agent), how he did it (agency), and why (purpose)" (p. x). From a Burkean orientation, all pentadic functions are in play, at least implicitly, in any well-rounded analysis of a text. One element, however, will tend to emerge as a featured element, and in a similar manner, a particular structure of motives, or motivational structure, tends to emerge as the featured ratio that characterizes the overall motivational structure of the text.

Ratios describe relationships among the pentadic elements, relationships that are clearly present in the text. Thus, the argument "I am late to class because my alarm clock did not go off" enacts a scene/act ratio: scenic elements (alarm clock) control/ shape/determine the act (being late). Or, when pulled over for speeding, a driver might explain: "I did not realize I was going so fast. This is a rental with a turbo-charged V-8 and it just went." This argument enacts an agency/act ratio: the exceptional power of the agency or means (the turbo-charged V-8) caused or led to the act (speeding). In describing a particular episode, the argumentative narrator can feature one or more of the pentadic elements and let others recede into the attentional background. Both Ling (1970) and Kneupper (1992) analyzed Edward Kennedy's Chappaquiddick speech of self-defense and found that it operated by featuring scene (dark night, twisty roads, narrow bridge) as the determinant of the act (driving off the bridge), which removed the agent from listeners' focal attention. Similarly, and more to the point for our purposes, Brummett (1979) found, in an analysis of pro- and anti-gay rights arguments in Florida in the 1970s, that the arguments from pro-rights advocates expressed an agent/act ratio (the intrinsic nature of the person determines the nature of the act). Thus, to deny legal rights for gay acts is to deny personhood. The anti-rights arguments suggested that rights would permit gay acts (and concomitant scenic shifts might encourage gay acts), and gay acts would make people gay. This act/agent argument simply reverses directionality: in each instance, agent and act function as substantially inter-connected.

A volitional human act is a unified motivational accomplishment. It may have five leading features, but it is one thing. *The act and the agent are unified.* Each informs, reflects, and confirms, or perhaps destabilizes, the other. Perelman and Olbrechts-Tyteca (1969) explained the need to evaluate the two as an integrated unit:

In treating the relationship between act and person, the speech, considered as an act of the speaker, deserves special attention, both because, for many people, speech is the most characteristic manifestation of the person and because the interaction between speaker and speech plays a very important part in argumentation.

(pp. 316-317)

Our analyses concentrate especially on the agent/act ratio (a dialectical unity of person and utterance) as illuminative of *ad hominem* arguments.

In the case of this essay, the act is the argument and the agent is the arguer. Our position is that argument critics should assume that any motivationally relevant element of one pentadic element is transitively relevant to any other element. For example, a murderous purpose justifies the hypothesis of a murderous agent, a murderous agency, a murder scene, and the act of murder. We think it is perfectly reasonable to suppose that an evil arguer has produced an evil argument, that a narcissist has said something self-serving, that a generous person has expressed liberal intentions, and that an uninformed arguer has gone beyond his or her factual inventory.

None of these things may prove to be true. Nevertheless, a Burkean approach is a sensible and rational way of thinking that assumes the unity of the arguer and argument. As Burke (1952) explained:

The agent is an author of his acts, which are descended from him, being good progeny if he is good, or bad progeny if he is bad, wise progeny if he is wise, silly progeny if he is silly. And, conversely, his acts can make him or remake him in accordance with their nature. They would be his product and/or he would be theirs.

(p. 16)

Thus, oaks grow from acorns and flawed arguments from flawed people. The nature of the eventual product, the oak or the argument, is reasonably expectable from knowledge of its unified pentadic context, which in this case is the agent/act ratio.

We must not overlook that the person is the best context for evaluating the meaning and significance of an assertion, especially when the statements are not integrated in a more or less rigid system, in which case the place they occupy and the role they play in the system provide sufficient criteria for interpretation.

(Perelman & Olbrechts-Tyteca, 1969, p. 317)

Or, when the good witch magically creates a bridge (an act of creation) across a bottomless chasm allowing people trapped on one side to escape to the other, the expectation is that it is a good bridge that will allow people to cross safely; conversely, if the bad witch creates the bridge, the expectation is that it is a bad bridge. These expectations flow from the agent/act ratio. If the audience is attracted to the agent/act interpretive orientation, the ratio *is* a reason, and a decision not to cross the presumably bad bridge (i.e., not to escape) might be perfectly rational.

Viewed from another angle, the ratio creates a *form*. In the Burkean sense: "Form is the creation of an appetite in the mind of the auditor, and the adequate satisfying of that appetite" (Burke, 1931, p. 40). The expectational qualities of the agent/act ratio create a form that serves a warranting function in the interpretation and assessment of the act. Again, the ratio is the reason, which makes sense. As Klumpp noted (1993), "The etymological root of 'ratios' and 'reason' are the same" (p. 162).

Pentadic analysis is a search for the featured ratios or reasons that constitute the grammar or structure of motives in a particular text; more specifically, it is a process through which we attribute motives to the text. In the "Introduction" to *A Grammar of Motives*, Burke

429

(1952) wrote, "The book is concerned with the basic forms of thought which [...] are exemplified in the attributing of motives" (p. x). Each of the ratios emerges as a form of thought; collectively, they constitute a rubric for the forms of thought individuals employ in attributing or understanding the motive structures of others. In this sense, ratio structures can be empirically present in the text, and the habitual or salient interpretive orientation the audience brings to bear will also influence their attribution of motives.

Particular arguments may, in their own presentation, strongly feature an agent/act orientation to implicitly invite the audience into that interpretive frame. An argumentative response that is *ad hominem* certainly encourages the audience toward an agent/act interpretative orientation. Moreover, certain audiences (including broad audiences, such as American citizens or Russian citizens) may have predispositions toward interpreting argumentative discourse through an interpretive lens that features or seeks out an agent/act structure of motives. These habituated interpretive orientations will incline the audience to see those featured relationships in an argumentative exchange. Burke (1952) offers a hypothetical illustration of this process:

> We can say that people interpret natural sequences in terms of cause and effect not because of something in the natural scene requiring this interpretation, but *because they are the sort of agents that see things in terms of necessary relations.*
>
> *(p. 187)*

That is, we are guided in our interpretation by an orientation, for example, a habituated ratio that functions as a form of mind that invites us to "see" the world in its terms. Similarly, people are often "the sort of agents" who connect arguer and argument, interpreting them as a single thing.

In a context in which an advocate's arguments feature what Burke called an agent/act ratio, an argument attacking that agent may appear perfectly rational through its concomitantly implied de-valuation of the quality of the act (i.e., the argument/claim advanced). Burke was not the only scholar to notice and defend the need to connect arguer and argument if the organic nature of argumentation is to be understood.

> This interaction between speaker and speech is perhaps the most characteristic part of argumentation as opposed to demonstration. In formal deduction, the role of the speaker is reduced to a minimum; it increases progressively as the language used is more removed from univocity and as context, intentions, and ends gain in importance.
>
> *(Perelman & Olbrechts-Tyteca, 1969, p. 317)*

In the agent/act ratio, the quality or nature of the agent shapes, molds, determines, or otherwise expresses itself in the quality or nature of the act. An argument for compassion and giving in a time of hardship (act) has one quality or nature if the audience perceives the arguer as a benevolent, caring person, but it would have a different quality or nature should an *ad hominem* attack convince the auditor that the arguer is actually a cheat and swindler.

Based on Perelman and Olbrechts-Tyteca's (1969) insights, four distinct phenomena are characteristic of a prototypical *ad hominem* exchange: (a) the original arguer; (b) his/her original argument; (c) the respondent arguer; and (d) the respondent's argument, alleging some sort of *ad hominem* flaw. Notably, conventional fallacy analysis focused only on the respondent's argument. To object to what someone said on the grounds of the speaker's deficiencies as a person was, more or less, the definition of the *ad hominem* fallacy (Hamblin, 1970). Guided by this definitional equation, argumentation theory since at least the 1950s "mostly used" the label *"argumentum ad hominem"* "in a pejorative sense" (van Eemeren et al., 2014,

p. 164). Using Burke, we re-theorize all this and urge reconsideration of the presumption that things taking the form of *ad hominem* attacks should be immediately scrutinized for unsoundness. Instead, critics should begin their analysis by respecting the unity of act and agent, and suppose that the virtues and failings of one flow into the other.

The traditional conception of *ad hominem* argument rejected the unity of act and agent, insisting that qualities of the arguer have little to do with the quality of the argument. But we have long applauded a different tradition that did unify them. Aristotle's original conceptualization of *ethos* was that it emerged from the speech. "Persuasion is achieved by the speaker's personal character when the speech is so spoken as to make us think him credible" (Aristotle, trans. 1984, 1358a4-5). In other words, attributes of the act (being well-spoken and well-reasoned) transfer to the agent and constitute *ethos*. For two and a half millennia, rhetorical scholars have been perfectly comfortable with this directionality. We easily say that a good speech must have been given by a good rhetor, and that an awful speech must have been given by a demagogue, thus moving our judgments of the acts to the agents. The modest proposal of the present essay is that we understand this essential relationship to be multidirectional. Just as a good rhetor is assumed to be producing a well-intentioned argument, approving the argument should imply a good arguer. Similarly, a bad person is assumed to be manipulative, and a flawed argument should imply a rhetor who deserves personal critique.

Attacking another person's public utterances because individuals consider that other person reprehensible is entirely sensible. Sometimes such a position will be wrong, of course, just as concluding that a good person will give good reasons can also be wrong. Whether arguer and argument should be joined or separated is a matter of default critical position. We believe that the default should be that the act and agent function together as a ratio, a dialectical unity, that brings with it expectational qualities and formal inducements to the audience to attribute perceived qualities of a person to the person's acts. By moving beyond the traditional automatic dismissal of *ad hominem* arguments as fallacious and instead recognizing a fundamental rationality in many *ad hominem* arguments, argument critics and argumentation theorists will better understand and assess argumentation as people really practice it. Continuing to label *ad hominem* as a fallacy in an almost categorical sense is not a productive means for fully understanding the complex processes of human argumentation. We should instead take a more rational course of action, and, as Burke noted (1941), "what, in fact, is 'rationality' but the desire for *an accurate chart for naming what is going on?*" (pp. 113-114fn).

References

Aristotle. (1984). *The complete works of Aristotle: The revised Oxford translation, Vols. 1–2* (J. Barnes, Ed.). Princeton, NJ: Princeton University Press.

Brummett, B. (1979). A pentadic analysis of ideologies of two gay rights controversies. *Central States Speech Journal, 30*(3), 250–261. doi:10.1080/10510977909368018

Burke, K. (1931). *Counter-statement.* New York, NY: Harcourt, Brace and Company.

Burke, K. (1941). *The philosophy of literary form: Studies in symbolic action.* Baton Rouge, LA: Louisiana State University Press.

Burke, K. (1952). *A grammar of motives.* New York, NY: Prentice Hall.

Copi, I. M. (1982). *Introduction to logic* (6th ed.). New York, NY: Macmillan.

Hamblin, C. L. (1970). *Fallacies.* London, United Kingdom: Methuen.

Klumpp, J. F. (1993). A rapprochement between dramatism and argumentation. *Argumentation and Advocacy, 29*(4), 148–163.

Kneupper, C. W. (1992). Dramatism and argument. In W. L. Benoit, D. Hample, & P. J. Benoit (Eds.), *Readings in argumentation* (pp. 279-291). Berlin, Germany: Foris.

Ling, D. A. (1970). A pentadic analysis of Senator Edward Kennedy's address to the people of Massachusetts, July 25, 1969. *Central States Speech Journal, 21*(2), 81–86. doi:10.1080/10510977009363002

Perelman, Ch., & Olbrechts-Tyteca, L. (1969). *The new rhetoric: A treatise on argumentation* (J. Wilkinson & P. Weaver, Trans.). Notre Dame, IN: University of Notre Dame Press.

Walton, D. N. (1998). *Ad hominem arguments*. Tuscaloosa, AL: University of Alabama Press.

Walton, D., Reed, C., & Macagno, F. (2008). *Argumentation schemes*. Cambridge, United Kingdom: Cambridge University Press.

van Eemeren, F. H., Garssen, B., Krabbe, E. C. W., Snoeck Henkemans, A. F., Verheij, B., & Wagemans, J. H. M. (2014). *Handbook of argumentation theory*. Dordrecht, The Netherlands: Springer Link. doi:10.1007/978-90-481-9473-5

van Eemeren, F. H., Garssen, B., & Meuffels, B. (2009). *Fallacies and judgments of reasonableness: Empirical research concerning the pragma-dialectical discussion rules*. Dordrecht, The Netherlands: Springer Link. doi:10.1007/978-90-481-2614-9

64

THE FALLACY OF SWEEPING GENERALIZATION

David Botting

In some ways, a sweeping generalization is a misnomer: We do not generalize when we make a sweeping generalization, but draw an inference about an individual from a general claim made about some class that includes the individual. Consider the following argument:

> All the philosophers in the room are bearded.
> Therefore, all philosophers are bearded.

It generalizes from the philosophers in the room to all philosophers and is not a sweeping generalization. In contrast, consider the argument:

> All philosophers are bearded.
> Therefore, Plato the philosopher is bearded.

It makes a claim about a particular philosopher from the general claim concerning all philosophers. When argumentation scholars think of such an argument that the premise does not justify the conclusion, they say that the argument makes a "sweeping generalization" (even though it does not really make a generalization at all) and identify it as a fallacy. Of course, the reasoner will reach an unjustified conclusion if the premise is false or unjustified, but that does not make the argument a sweeping generalization. The fact that not all philosophers are bearded and that the evidence does not justify the general claim does not make the reasoner's inference or conclusion about Plato less reasonable. The general claim itself, and not the evidence the reasoner uses to support it, must be insufficient for justifying the conclusion if a fallacy of sweeping generalization is to exist.

I think this confusion explains why practically every textbook on fallacies has a discussion of hasty generalization but discussions of sweeping generalizations are rarer. In nearly every case where an arguer is accused of committing the fallacy of sweeping generalization, the accused has earlier generalized hastily on the basis of insufficient evidence and consequently draws particular conclusions from general claims that are unjustified and often untrue. Note that generalizers always draw an inductive inference relative to the evidence, so if the evidence is insufficient for the general claim, then the problem lies with the evidence, whereas the inference is still a good one and not fallacious. To commit the fallacy of hasty generalization, then, is not to draw an invalid inductive inference, but to generalize from what one has no reason to believe is a representative sample.[1]

What if the reasoner had a principled reason for excluding a particular piece of evidence from consideration? In such a case the reasoner could think themselves justified, and could be justified, in generalizing the way they do and reject the accusation of having generalized hastily. A fine line exists between an accusation of hasty generalization and a substantive disagreement about what the evidence is and whether it is sufficient; the burden of proof is on the accuser to show that some violation of the canons for statistical sampling has occurred, as opposed to just having different evidence or a substantive disagreement over the evidence. That is to say, the accuser needs to show that the evidence that makes the accused's conclusions unjustified is evidence that the accused already knows or is at least cognitively available to them. But if the accused knows of this evidence and counts it as evidence, they cannot plausibly choose to ignore it, at least when trying to reason well. Once the general claim is established, whether hastily or not, no fallacy exists involving the drawing of an inference from it, for this is to infer from an exceptionless generalization to one of its instances, which is deductively valid. On this view, the fallacy of sweeping generalization effectively disappears, leaving only the mistake of inferring from a fallaciously established premise.

Sometimes evidence insufficient for an exceptionless generalization is sufficient for a weaker kind of generalization. For example, from "All the swans in the northern hemisphere are white," reasoners consider the conclusion "All swans are white" as hasty, but the conclusion "Generally/typically all swans are white" as justified, since the latter kind of general claim, unlike the other, can be true even if black swans can serve as an exception. Consider whether the following is a good argument, that is, one in which the premise justifies the conclusion:

> Generally/typically all swans are white.
> Therefore, Charles the swan is white.

If it is not a good argument and the conclusion is not justified by the premise, then inferring that Charles the swan is white is a mistake and a fallacy: specifically, a sweeping generalization. And many theorists think that the argument above is not good, implying that the reason that we think it is good is because we take a generalization that is subject to exceptions as if it were exceptionless. I disagree. Although the conclusion may obviously be false, reasoners can reasonably draw the conclusion from the premises, thus rendering it not a fallacy.

My central claim is that the fallacy of sweeping generalization does not really exist, or more accurately, no minimally competent reasoner reasons in the way that the fallacy of sweeping generalization describes. Accusations that a reasoner has committed the fallacy of sweeping generalization often turn out to arise from substantive disagreements about evidence, in this case whether initially something should count as an exception or not.

The Fallacy of Sweeping Generalization

Suppose that I make the following argument:
> All taxi-drivers are dishonest
> Therefore, Derek, the taxi-driver, is dishonest

Am I being unfair or unkind to Derek? Have I committed a fallacy?

If we take the "all" as universally applying to taxi-drivers, this is a deductively valid inference by universal instantiation. Thus, accusing the arguer of faulty reasoning—as opposed to simply accusing him of having a false premise—requires attributing to the arguer a generalization that is subject to exceptions. When argumentation scholars, as they often do, assume that it would be an error of reasoning to infer the conclusion, this argument demonstrates the fallacy of sweeping generalization. You might be tempted to say that the taxi-driver example is an instance of this fallacy, and say, "It is not exceptionlessly true that all taxi-drivers are dishonest. Derek might be an exception, and you do not know that he is not. Therefore, how can you say outright that Derek is dishonest? It is faulty reasoning." In this hypothetical exchange, you accuse me of *ignoring exceptions*.

I think that such a view is uncharitable. To such an objection, I would say something like, "Of course! I am not saying that exceptions cannot exist to my generalization, and I am not saying that Derek could not be one of them. All I am really saying is that rationally I can believe that Derek is dishonest, and my premises justify this belief. I am justified in drawing this inference. What you are implying is that I should not make or act on such an assumption because of the mere *possibility* that Derek is an exception without giving me any evidence that Derek actually *is* an exception. You are interpreting my argument uncharitably as stating Derek's dishonesty as an infallible matter of fact, but I make no claims to infallibility. He *may* be honest—I did not really intend to suggest otherwise—but why should I act on this assumption? In that sense, my argument is a completely reasonable one to use and it justifies my belief."

The burden of proof falls to you to show me that Derek constitutes an exception. Suppose that you do this. You have proved that my conclusion is false, and if I accept the evidence, then I should retract my conclusion, but my inference has not thereby become invalid. I would be unjustified to continue to have the same beliefs about Derek's dishonesty, but my inference, relative to the evidence that I had, is not unjustified or fallacious, and any accusation that I have committed a fallacy of sweeping generalization is no less unjustified now than before you presented the evidence. After all, I never denied that I might be wrong and was ready to change my mind on learning of new evidence. If I simply refuse to change my mind despite accepting your evidence, then the fallacy is one of ignoring relevant evidence available to me—I am, seemingly out of logical perversity, drawing an inference from the wrong body of evidence and am culpable for doing so, but the inference I am drawing is inductively valid just the same.

If I do not (for some principled reason) accept your evidence, then a substantive disagreement emerges between us that we can discuss in a meta-level discourse. One way I might signal this disagreement or potential disagreement is by stating the conclusion with an "even though" clause in which I mention the putative counter-evidence. Often, then, the accusation of fallacy turns out to be a symptom of a substantive disagreement about evidence, rendering it an unjustified accusation of faulty reasoning.

In defence of my interpretation, many cases exist where the reasoning exemplified in the taxi-driver example would be uncontroversial, or where no one would ever accuse the reasoner of fallaciously ignoring exceptions. One example is a lottery: You know from the start that one lottery ticket will win, so you know from the start that the premise, "All lottery tickets are losing tickets" is false, and that one particular lottery ticket is an "exception" to this generalization. Nevertheless, for any ticket, you can be as confident as you like (by altering the total number of tickets) that that ticket will lose. You can, in this situation, say, "This lottery ticket will lose." You could be quite sincere in believing it will lose, you can back it up with an argument that shows this belief is a rational and justified belief to have, and you have no evidence that the particular ticket in question actually is the exception, even though you know this to be a remote possibility. I do not think that anyone in this example would say, "That is a fallacy of sweeping generalization! How can you say that your ticket will not win when you know that it might!" This kind of criticism would only be appropriate if I were stating this infallibly as though it were certain, which I am not.

In both cases of exceptionless generalizations and generalizations where we do not know that the given case is an exception, we reason deductively. We deductively infer that our ticket will not win because it is deductively entailed by "All lottery tickets are losing tickets," despite knowing that this is strictly false when taken exceptionlessly. Nor do I think we are obliged to make a more guarded statement of our conclusion: We straightforwardly believe that our lottery ticket will lose, and we may say so. We admit that, despite the existence of no error in our reasoning or in our evidence, we might be wrong and would be willing to retract our statement on acquiring evidence that Derek is not dishonest or that a particular ticket is the winning one. But this, interestingly, presupposes that we do *not* admit to any error in our reasoning. Only if we do not accept the possibility that our reasoning might have led us to a false conclusion, or stated the conclusion so strongly as to rule out the conclusion's falsity have we committed the sweeping generalization fallacy.

Skepticism about the Fallacy of Sweeping Generalization

Does anybody commit the fallacy of sweeping generalization? Or is the person who accuses the other of committing the fallacy himself guilty of treating arguments like the taxi-driver example uncharitably as making stronger claims than the arguer really intends to make? The analysis of Woldoff and Kraynak (2012) manufactured a fallacy by overstating the conclusion, adding to it the modal qualification "surely" (p. 63). Pirie (2006) overstated the premise by noting that the arguer "insists" (p. 51) without reason on treating the generalization as though it had no exceptions. The burden of proof is on the accuser to show that the accused is somehow acting in these irrational ways without noticing, for if the accused does notice but still insists on making a sweeping generalization, then we are not describing someone's sincere reasoning anymore but someone who is knowingly arguing badly.

Surveying previous accounts of sweeping generalization, theorists present the concept in two forms: (a) the *basic form*, and (b) a form including an "even though" clause. I will now argue that neither form is a plausible construction of reasoning.

The Argument for Skepticism: The "Even Though" Form

Engel (1976) elaborated on the "even though" form. He defined the concept as when a general rule is applied to a specific case to which the rule is not applicable because of special features of that case (p. 66). He provided an example to illustrate the concept:

> Everyone has a right to his own property.
> Therefore, even though Jones has been declared insane, you had no right to take away his weapon.
>
> *(p. 66)*

Someone who argues in the way that Engel illustrated errs by taking a general rule subject to exceptions as being exceptionless.

This would be an error, of course, but I wonder whether it is an error that people actually make, and whether Engel's example makes it here. The arguer must think that insanity must make some difference, or otherwise he or she would not have made the point, given the implausibility of supposing the arguer to have given a list of exceptions in the argument and then subsequently ignored them. Apparently, the arguer is indicating that she or he does not allow insanity—or other objects of the "even though" clause—as an exception. In that case, although we may disagree about what should count as an exception, we may not accuse him of reasoning badly; there is a substantive difference of opinion over whether insanity is an exception and not a fallacy.

For the arguer to have committed the fallacy that Engel is charging, the arguer must accept the generalization as subject to exceptions and then somehow forget this when applying it to the particular case (thus applying it as an exceptionless generalization) or, taking some exceptional circumstance to obtain in the particular case, forget that this case is an exception at the moment of applying the generalization while simultaneously remembering the exception well enough to mention it in an "even though" clause. Surely it is implausible to attribute this line of reasoning to any minimally competent reasoner.

The Argument for Skepticism: The Basic Form

If the argument does not mention exceptions, then the argument takes what I call the *basic form*. Here is an example that Engel (1976) provided:

> Since horseback riding is healthful exercise, Harry Brown ought to do more of it because it will be good for his heart condition.

(p. 66)

The conclusion may of course be false and, for Harry's particular condition, horseback riding would not be good for Harry and he ought not to do more of it.

Is this, however, a bad inference for someone to make who did *not* know this? For someone who believed that horseback riding is healthful exercise, the reasoning would be sound even if they believed the rule was subject to exceptions supposing that such a person had no reason to suppose that Harry was among those exceptions. And if the reasoner did know that Harry was among those exceptions, why reason at all?

The Argument for Skepticism: The Dilemma

A general problem with the fallacy of sweeping generalization is that if you do not know that the particular case to which you wish to apply the rule is one of the exceptions, then you make no error in applying the rule in the particular case. Such a move is a reasonable thing to do and you have justified beliefs as a result. On the other hand, if you *do* know that the particular case is (or is not) an exception, then you know *already* whether, for example, Harry should (or should not) go horseback-riding more often, and the rule has no purpose—it is epistemically redundant.

If we know for every case under the general claim whether or not it is an exception, then clearly no epistemic role for the general claim exists *at all*. This is as true for statistical generalizations that complete enumerations establish as well as for universal claims. Not only is "All men are mortal; Socrates is a man; therefore, Socrates is a mortal" a *petitio principia* (an argument in which the conclusion is identical with a premise, or in which the truth of the premises cannot be established except by establishing the truth of the conclusion), but also "Nine out of ten men are mortal; Socrates is a man; therefore, Socrates is a mortal" would be (on the likely supposition that the conclusion is true). Toulmin's (1958) idea of arguments that are "probable" yet "analytic" is an elaboration on this basic idea (Botting, 2016).

Conclusion

When advocates reason in the way the taxi-driver example describes, they do not reason erroneously. For an error of reasoning to exist—as opposed to having a false (or unjustified) premise—reasoners must take the generalization to be subject to exceptions and then either forget this when applying it in practice (effectively treating the generalization as exceptionless), or know an exception to obtain but forget to do so (effectively treating a known exception as an unknown exception). It is implausible to attribute this reasoning to any minimally competent reasoner. It is not plausible that reasoners ignore a known exception, while also mentioning it in the conclusion in an "even though" clause. If reasoners do mention it in such a clause, then, apparently, they do not take the particular case as falling under that exception. In fact, also implausible are cases where reasoners knowing an exception to obtain would reason by appealing to the rule at all, since they already know what they want to know. The burden of proof is on the accusers, and to meet it they must attribute to the reasoner: (a) knowledge that the generalization has exceptions (since there is no fallacy in inferring from an exceptionless generalization to a particular conclusion); (b) knowledge that the given case is an exception (since otherwise this is simply disagreement about whether something is an exception); (c) to have somehow forgotten that the exception obtains when drawing the inference (which only seems possible in the basic form, since in the "even though" form the reasoner mentions the very exception he is imputed to have forgotten); and (d) to have failed to realise that, by knowing the exception, he knows what he wants to know, and so reasoned when there was no need to do so (since the generalization is epistemically redundant). Reasoners accused of making a sweeping generalization must surely be presumed innocent without very strong evidence to the contrary.

Note

1 The FCT Portugal provided funding for this project under the codes SFRH/BPD/77687/2011 and PTDC/FIL-FIL/110117/2009.

References

Botting, D. (2016). Toulmin's analytic validity. *Cogency, 8*(2), 7–31. Retrieved from http://cogency.udp.cl/ediciones/16/Cogency_v8n2_01.pdf
Engel, S. M. (1976). *With good reason: An introduction to the informal fallacies*. New York, NY: St. Martin's Press.
Pirie, M. (2006). *How to win every argument: The use and abuse of logic*. New York, NY: Continuum.
Toulmin, S. E. (1958). *The uses of argument*. Cambridge, United Kingdom: Cambridge University Press.
Woldoff, R., & Kraynak, J. (2012). *GRE for dummies* (7th ed.). Hoboken, NJ: Wiley.

65

EXHORTATION IN INTERPERSONAL DISCUSSION

Susan L. Kline

One view of argument networks embeds them in both systems and a lifeworld of relationships that everyday interactions catalyze. Theorizing the argumentation lifeworld has involved, for some, understanding arguments as embedded in ecologies that pragmatic structures of conversation and speech acts underwrite. Over the last 30 years, several groups of argument scholars have worked to explicate the pragmatics of speech acts, utterance-meaning, and ethno-methodological sense-making that undergird argumentation. This work has produced pragma-dialectic theory (van Eemeren & Grootendorst, 1984), conversational argument theory (Jackson & Jacobs, 1980), and pragmatic analyses of stasis, norms, and speech acts such as proposing and giving testimony (Kauffeld, 1998; Kauffeld & Fields, 2005). Identifying speech acts and their pragmatic structures is a useful way to study argumentation, because the constitutive conditions associated with uttering a particular speech act actually specify the lines of reasoning that are capable of overcoming disagreement. Thus, within this view, a desirable way to study argument would be to analyze the presentation of reasons within "identifiable argumentation structures," a method that Kauffeld and Innocenti (2016) recommend: "Students of argumentation from both dialectical and rhetorical traditions ought to attend carefully to the nature and dynamic of components which can seem to reach beyond the scope of strictly reasoned discourse" (p. 1). While pragmatic analyses continue, particularly for those employing pragma-dialectic theory, interpersonal argument scholars have not extensively conducted them. This exploratory study aims to fill that gap by using a pragmatic analysis to identify the issues, lines of argument, and arguers' abilities relevant to deploying an illocutionary act common in interpersonal discourse: exhortation. The essay also serves to honor Fred Kauffeld and his contribution to the field of argumentation. After reviewing the pragmatic structure of exhorting, I examine if lines of argument can map onto the pragmatic conditions of exhorting, and if arguers' social cognitive abilities relate to particular exhortation message features.

The Pragmatics of Exhorting

In a recent essay, Kauffeld and Innocenti (2016) presented an analysis of the conceptual and pragmatic structure of exhortation. The speech act of exhorting involves inspiring an addressee to act in ways that enact high minded commitments to act on principles and aspirations. Exhortation occurs in situations marked by "conflicted principles," in which reluctant, confused, or "troubled" addressees need inspiration to commit to action (Kauffeld & Innocenti, 2016, p. 2). Exhortations can occur in civic speechmaking, in public events like graduations and sermons, but also in interpersonal contexts like pep talks and parental encouragement. To produce an exhortation, a speaker (SE) must engage in several actions. First, the SE says that the addressee (AE) should do X, where X is an action regarding AE's obligations or aspirations, and SE urges AE to develop high-minded commitments. Second, SE further intends to inspire AE by arousing an elevated intentional/affective orientation and resolve to act on AE's commitments. This presumes that SE understands the situation and AE's reluctance to act, as well as that SE's avowed effort to inspire AE is reasonable. Third, SE's intention to inspire AE is to provide AE with good reasons "to grant a sympathetic hearing" (Kauffeld & Innocenti, 2016, p. 3) to what the speaker says. SE's commitment facilitates such interaction by creating a favorable relationship with AE. In sum, exhortations create a discursive space that secures a sympathetic hearing for what speakers say by addressing addressees' reluctance and by inspiring them to act on their responsibilities and aspirations.

Understanding the pragmatic design of exhorting can unpack its strategic potential. Applied to interpersonal contexts, pragmatic design suggests that exhortation calls for positive identity and relationship work. Mutual uptake that a positive relationship and network exists occurs when the SE engages in altruistic argument (reasoning for the benefit of the addressee; Kline & Song, 2016), or positive altercasting (casting the addressee into a positive identity from reasoning about valued qualities; Kline, 1987), which then the AE recognizes, resulting in a sympathetic hearing and a reason for an elevated disposition by the AE. Altruistic argument and positive altercasting, then, are two discourse features underlying exhortation.

Kauffeld and Innocenti's (2016) pragmatic analysis of exhortation may be useful for theorizing about issues embedded in a range of interpersonal situations for which exhortation is relevant. Interpersonal influence often calls for exhortation, as in inspiring a neighbor to sign a petition or cheering friends on to keep to their diets. While much research has amassed on social support and influence, studies of communication strategies focus more on their ability to address psychological needs or attitude changes, rather than for their ability to address the pragmatic conditions resident in the communication context. Determining if pragmatic conditions map onto exhortation messages that speakers produce could advance the relevance of pragmatic approaches for studying interpersonal argument.

Thus, a first purpose of this study is to analyze exhortation messages to test the applicability of a pragmatic perspective for describing exhortation. The focus is on the role of exhortation in challenging situations when a friend has self-doubt about his/her ability to attain his/her aspirations in passing an important exam, or starting a career job:

RQ1: Do exhortation messages address pragmatic conditions for exhorting?

Kauffeld and Innocenti's (2016) analysis also asserted that exhorters possess mindfulness and resources to engage in exhortation, such as understanding the addressee and knowing how to inspire the addressee. Similar to support provider models (e.g., see Dunkel-Schetter & Skokan, 1990), the ability to understand an addressee's appraisal helps the speaker determine the most effective means of support. Constructivist communication researchers have documented a range of mindful communication abilities associated with effective support provision and persuasion, such as perspective-taking, construct differentiation, and message monitoring (Burleson, 1994, 2003; Burleson & Caplan, 1998; Kline, 2006). Thus, construct differentiation should be positively related to exhortation message themes whose performance would benefit from having highly differentiated interpersonal constructs, such as focusing on understanding the AE and his/her concerns, expressing care and confidence, and reasoning about AE's valued positive qualities:

H1: Interpersonal construct differentiation is positively related to exhortation message themes that focus on the pragmatic conditions for inspiring an addressee.

While complex social perceptions may help speakers design competent exhortation messages, speakers translate their social perceptions into plans that shape their communicative behaviors. Berger (1988) conceptualized planning as the process that connects cognition to actions (Berger, 1988). Waldron and Applegate (1994) documented that the complexity of plans (actions and contingencies), specificity of plans (concrete behavioral steps identified to attain goals), and the quality of plans (the extent the current situation is addressed and future conditions sought) are associated with integrative conflict management. Similarly, exhortation should also require sophisticated planning:

H2: Planning sophistication is positively associated with exhortation message themes focused on the pragmatic conditions for inspiring an addressee.

Theoretically an exhorter's personal constructs should affect their perception of social situations from which they form plans and messages. Level of construct differentiation may moderate the effects of planning on exhortation practices. Thus, a last research question asks about the joint contribution of construct differentiation and planning in predicting exhortation message practices is:

RQ2: What is the contribution of construct differentiation and planning on exhortation message themes focused on the pragmatic conditions for inspiring an addressee?

Method

Participants were 100 young adults (69% female) enrolled at a large U.S. midwestern university. Students were mostly Caucasian (82%) and from middle class backgrounds. They met in small groups outside of their classes to complete a print questionnaire for extra course credit. Their tasks and measures included the following:

Interpersonal Construct Differentiation

Participants completed a one-role version of the Role Category Questionnaire by describing a liked peer (RCQ; Crockett, 1965). Scoring of the descriptions and their associated constructs followed Crockett's procedures (Burleson & Waltman, 1988). Independent codings of 20% of the impressions were reliable (intraclass correlation = .93). Burleson & Waltman (1988) previously showed this measure to be functionally independent of verbal fluency and intelligence.

Message Elicitation Task and Coding

Participants responded to two realistic role-play situations developed from previous work (Kline, Rooney, & Jones, 2012). Situations focused on how participants would talk with friends about taking an important examination for their chosen career and starting a new job with especially difficult challenges. In each case the friend expressed having serious doubts about being "up to the job."

Participants produced two messages in response to the situations presented in random order. Message coding utilized Saeki and O'Keefe's (1994) procedures of unitizing messages into thought units and then grouping them into idea types and message themes based on frequency of idea types and conceptual similarity. This procedure produced 13 themes for each situation. Based upon the theoretical analysis, these themes were matched to the pragmatic conditions of exhorting. Ten themes formed five summary themes that enacted the pragmatic conditions: (a) act as you'll do fine (composed of don't worry, you'll do fine, just act); (b) you have valued qualities; (c) expressing understandings and concerns (composed of the themes, understanding the other and legitimating concerns); (d) reasoning and enacting qualities (reasoning about qualities with the other and providing specific suggestions); and (e) expressing caring confidence (expressing care and confidence in the other). Interrater reliability assessments on 15% of the messages produced acceptable Cohen's kappa for message themes (.66 to .78). The five summary measures of exhortation emerged from averaging across the two messages.

Message Planning Task and Measure

After participants finished their second message, they completed a planning analysis task that was similar to Waldron and Applegate's (1994) cued-recall task. Participants reread their second message and numbered "each separate thought, strategy or sentence ... used in the message to have an effect on your friend." On a separate sheet, participants took each numbered message fragment and responded to a request to "explain what you were thinking at the time you wrote this part of the message. That is, what was your objective? What, if any, actions were you planning in the message? Were you thinking ahead about what you might say next or what your friend might say or do?"

Following Waldron and Applegate (1994), coders placed each numbered response for plan specificity according to a four-level system on whether the response reflected (a) no planning, (b) undifferentiated planning, (c) function-level or (d) implementation-level planning. Total plan specificity was the sum of these codes. Interrater reliability on 25% of the responses was acceptable at .89 (Scott's pi).

Results

The first RQ asked if exhortation message themes produced in interpersonal challenging situations corresponded to the pragmatic issues that define exhorting. The percentage use of message elements that were focused on the five pragmatic conditions were: (a) the AE should act (act as you'll do fine) = 88.2%; (b) acting enables the AE to express qualities that enact aspirations (you have valued qualities) = 86.6%; (c) the exhorter understands the AE and his/her legitimate constraints (understanding and legitimating concerns) = 83.2%; (d) the exhorter inspires AE (reasoning about qualities with the other; providing suggestions) = 89.9%; and (e) creating fellowship and inducing a sympathetic hearing (expressing care and confidence in the other) = 80.7%. Message coding for each pragmatic condition occurred frequently (Chi-square tests = 50.91, 50.75, 40.23, 60.59, & 33.15, all df = 1, p < .001, respectively). Each of the pragmatic conditions Kauffeld and Innocenti (2016) defined was identified in over 80% of the messages, with three of the pragmatic conditions identified in over 86% of the messages.

H1 and H2 predicted that the level of construct differentiation and cognitive planning of exhorters would be positively associated with exhortation message themes. Table 65.1 presents the Pearson correlations. As expected, construct differentiation was positively associated with all five exhortation measures (rs ranged from .19 to .48). H2 was also confirmed, as plan specificity correlated positively with all five exhortation measures (rs ranged from .33 to .58).

Table 65.1 Means, Standard Deviations and Pearson Correlations for the Exhortation Variables

Variable	M	SD	1	2	3	4	5	6
1. Con Diff	16.50	5.85	-					
2. Plan specificity	19.68	9.61	.52	-				
3. Just act; you'll do fine	1.59	1.32	.35	.40	-			
4. You have valued qualities	1.67	1.40	.19	.33	.06	-		
5. Understanding & concerns	1.88	1.84	.48	.58	.46	.28	-	
6. Reasoning about qualities; suggestions	1.92	1.53	.30	.33	.28	.30	.39	-
7. Caring, confidence	1.46	1.53	.47	.56	.50	.26	.50	.43

Note: rs > .19 = p < .05; rs > .27 = p < .01; rs > .33 = p < .001. Con Diff = Construct Differentiation.

Five moderated multiple regressions conducted on the exhortation theme measures examined how the cognitive measures collectively predicted exhortation. A three-step conceptual order included: (a) mean centered construct differentiation (CD), (b) mean centered planning specificity (PC), and (c) the interaction term (CD x PC). The regressions for each measure of exhortation were statistically significant: just fine, act $F (3, 98) = 11.31$, p < .001, $R^2 = .19$; valued qualities $F (3, 98) = 4.91$, p < .01, $R^2 = .13$; understanding, concern $F (3, 98) = 30.93$, p < .001, $R^2 = .49$; reasoning about qualities, suggestions $F (3, 98) = 5.67$, p < .05, $R^2 = .15$; and care and confidence $F (3, 98) = 25.02$, p < .001, $R^2 = .44$. In each regression CD was a significant predictor on Step 1: βs were .35, .20 (p=.05), .48, .30, and .47, respectively. Planning was a significant predictor in each regression on Step 2: βs were .30, .30, .46, .23, and .43, respectively. At Step 2, PC attenuated the effect of CD to p < .10 for just act (.19) and reasoning about qualities, suggestions (.19).

Significant interactions between construct differentiation and planning emerged on Step 3 for two regressions: expressing care/confidence, β = .31, and understanding/legitimating concerns, β = .36. Graphing each interaction showed that planning had a significantly higher association with these exhortation measures when exhorters had a high level of construct differentiation than when they had a low level of construct differentiation. Hence, the level of construct differentiation moderated planning specificity on two exhortation themes.

Discussion

Consistent with Kauffeld and Innocenti's (2016) pragmatic analysis, participants here engaged in exhortation by referencing the core conditions necessary for warranting an exhortation to be worthy of a sympathetic hearing. In circumstances when an addressee is experiencing confusion and doubt over an important personal event, exhortation is relevant. Kauffeld and Innocenti's (2016) analysis specified that the argumentation surrounding a rational exhortation included: (a) that the addressee should act, (b) that the exhorter understood the situation and the addressee's reluctance to act, (c) that that the exhorter intended to inspire the address by arousing an elevated orientation to act, and (d) that the exhorter provided good reasons to induce a sympathetic hearing from the addressee. The data analysis here suggests that Kauffeld and Innocent's account is valid. Consistent with their analysis, participants reasoned in their messages that their friend who had self-doubts could and should act despite their self-doubt, that they understood the friend and his/her doubts, but that the friend already has the resources, knowledge, and qualities to enact their aspirations. Participants also expressed caring toward their friend that would be more likely to inspire and create the condition for a sympathetic hearing. In sum, exhortation becomes a reasoning structure for bringing reluctant, doubting addressees to commit to undertaking actions that will enact their aspirations.

The analysis further shows that exhortation themes, particularly themes connected to the themes of fellowship and inspiration, positively relate to the exhorters' level of construct differentiation and planning specificity. These findings bolster the view that exhortation occurs most fully when exhorters empathize with and understand the other, and have the cognitive and verbal resources to inspire the addressee.

These findings are significant for both interpersonal argument theory and interpersonal communication theory. Identifiable and tested pragmatic issues and lines of argument could foster effective exhortations and other illocutionary acts. Such studies could help elucidate the range of issues that arguers address with different types of speech acts, which guides the selection of particular arguments to use with addressees. In the case of exhorting, relational and identity issues are also at work, which may produce additional complexity for the addressee. Thus, the need for multiple goal management may be at work in situations calling for exhortation.

Replicating these findings needs to occur with larger samples, multiple measures of exhortation and social cognitive competencies, and an analysis of message effects. However, in the meantime, the study shows that a pragmatic analysis enables us to identify the relevant issues and lines of argument involved in exhortation.

References

Berger, C. R. (1988). Planning, affect and social action generation. In L. Donohew, H. E. Sypher, & E. T. Higgins (Eds.), *Communication, social cognition, and affect* (pp. 93–115). Hillsdale, NJ: Lawrence Erlbaum.

Burleson, B. R. (1994). Comforting messages: Features, functions, and outcomes. In J. A. Daly & J. M. Wiemann (Eds.), *Strategic interpersonal communication* (pp. 135–161). Hillsdale, NJ: Lawrence Erlbaum.

Burleson, B. R. (2003). Emotional support skill. In J. O. Greene & B. R. Burleson (Eds.), *Handbook of communication and social interaction skills* (pp. 551–594). Mahwah, NJ: Lawrence Erlbaum.

Burleson, B. R., & Caplan, S. E. (1998). Construct differentiation. In J. C. McCroskey & J. A. Daly (Eds.), *Communication and personality: Trait perspectives* (pp. 233–286). Cresskill, NJ: Hampton Press.

Burleson, B. R., & Waltman, M. S. (1988). Construct differentiation: Using the role category questionnaire. In C. H. Tardy (Ed.), *A handbook for the study of human communication: Methods and instruments for observing, measuring and assessing communication processes* (pp. 1–35). Norwood, NJ: Ablex.

Crockett, W. H. (1965). Construct differentiation and impression formation. In B. A. Maher (Ed.), *Process in experimental personality research (Vol. 2)* (pp. 47–90). New York, NY: Academic Press.

Dunkel-Schetter, C., & Skokan, L. A. (1990). Determinants of social support provision in personal relationships. *Journal of Social and Personal Relationships*, 7(4), 437–450. doi:10.1177.0265407590074002

Jackson, S., & Jacobs, S. (1980). Structure of conversational argument: Pragmatic bases for the enthymeme. *Quarterly Journal of Speech*, 66(3), 251–265. doi:10.1080/00335638009383524

Kauffeld, F. J. (1998). Presumption and the distribution of argumentative burdens in acts of proposing and accusing. *Argumentation*, 12(2), 245–266. doi:10.1023/A:1007704116379

Kauffeld, F. J., & Fields, J. (2005). The commitment speakers undertake in giving testimony. In D. Hitchcock & D. Farr (Eds.), *The uses of argument: Proceedings of a conference at McMaster University, 18-21 May 2005* (pp. 232–243). Windsor, Ontario: OSSA.

Kauffeld, F. J., & Innocenti, B. (2016). Inducing a sympathetic (empathic) reception for exhortation. In P. Bondy & L. Benacquista (Eds.), *Argumentation, objectivity and bias: Proceedings of the 11th international conference of the Ontario Society for the Study of Argumentation (OSSA)*, 18-21 May 2016 (pp. 1–15). Windsor, Ontario: OSSA.

Kline, S. L. (1987). Identity management in argumentative discourse. In F. H. van Eemeren, R. Grootendorst, J. A. Blair, & C. A. Willard (Eds.), *Argumentation: Across the lines of discipline* (pp. 241–251). Dordrecht, The Netherlands: Foris.

Kline, S. L. (2006). Deliberating about behavior change: The role of message monitoring in person-centered regulative messages. In P. Riley (Ed.), *Engaging argument* (pp. 578–588). Washington, DC: National Communication Association.

Kline, S. L., Rooney, M., & Jones, E. (2012, May). *A multiple goals perspective on edifying and esteem support.* Presented at the annual meeting of the International Communication Association, Phoenix, AZ.

Kline, S. L., & Song, W. (2016). Altruistic argument in the demand-withdraw pattern in interpersonal disputes. In P. Bondy & L. Benacquista (Eds.), *Argumentation, Objectivity, and Bias: Proceedings of the 11th International Conference of the Ontario Society for the Study of Argumentation (OSSA), 18–21 May 2016* (pp. 1–20). Windsor, Ontario: OSSA.

Saeki, M., & O'Keefe, B. J. (1994). Refusals and rejections: Designing messages to serve multiple goals. *Human Communication Research, 21*(1), 67–102. doi:10.1111/j.1468-2958.1994.tb00341.x

Van Eemeren, F., & Grootendorst, R. (1984). *Speech acts in argumentative discussion.* Dordrecht, The Netherlands: Foris.

Waldron, V. R., & Applegate, J. L. (1994). Interpersonal construct differentiation and conversational planning: An examination of two cognitive accounts for the production of competent verbal disagreement tactics. *Human Communication Research, 21*(1), 3–35. doi:10.1111/j.1468-2958.1994.tb00337.x

66

WRITING ABOUT SERIAL ARGUMENTS: THE EFFECTS OF MANIPULATING ARGUMENT PERSPECTIVE

Amy Janan Johnson, Ioana A. Cionea, Eryn N. Bostwick, Megan A. Bassick, and Nathan J. Lindsey

Serial arguments capture ongoing disagreements between two individuals, which occur at least twice, about a topic where the two perceive that an incompatibility exists between them (Trapp & Hoff, 1985). These repetitive exchanges can take a toll on participants, affecting their mental and physical well-being, as well as the relationship with the other person, especially if the conflict appears unresolvable (Malis & Roloff, 2006; Miller & Roloff, 2006). Therefore, one key goal of research on this topic should be to identify how arguers can minimize the potentially negative effects of such arguments. We propose a new approach in this study, combining two ideas—argument interdependence and expressive writing—to suggest that writing about a serial argument could have positive outcomes.

The first idea rests on a new concept—*argument interdependence*. Argument interdependence measures the degree to which two arguers depend on each other to resolve the issue at the heart of a serial argument. Johnson and Cionea (2017) suggested that a higher degree of argument interdependence about an argument topic positively affects how a serial argument progresses and the motivation each individual has to work toward resolution. Recent research (Johnson, Cionea, & Bostwick, 2015; Johnson, Cionea, & Bostwick, 2016) supported the proposal that argument interdependence levels predict positive outcomes for arguers. For example, Johnson et al. (2016) found that argument interdependence was associated positively with constructive serial argument goals (e.g., mutual understanding or positive relational expressiveness) and negatively with destructive goals (e.g., wanting to hurt the other person while benefitting oneself and relational termination). Further, Johnson et al. (2015) found that argument interdependence predicted higher levels of perceived resolvability of a serial argument, which negatively predicted stress related to the serial argument.

If interdependence can have positive relational effects and reduce relational harm, then considering how researchers can increase perceptions of argument interdependence has practical importance. Therefore, the second idea behind our study rests on the practice of expressive writing. Pennebaker (1997) concluded that having individuals write about traumatic events made them feel worse initially, but ultimately resulted in a more positive outlook, improved immune function, and resulted in better physical health. Thus, expressive writing could potentially increase positive perceptions of a serial argument.

This study will examine whether engaging in expressive writing about possible ways of resolving the serial argument affects people's perceptions of that argument. Specifically, we examine the potential positive effects of serial arguments in writing from different perspectives: that is, writing about what the participant can do to solve a serial argument, writing about what the participant's partner can do to solve a serial argument, and writing about what the participant and their partner can do *together* to solve a serial argument.

This endeavor can yield a practical and readily available tool that individuals involved in repetitive conflicts could adopt in order to resolve their disagreements or result in more positive outcomes. Furthermore, arguers may identify specific strategies perceived to be more effective for the resolution of their argument, which could enrich understandings of conflict resolution approaches.

Expressive Writing and Conflict

The basis of Pennebaker's (1997) expressive writing research is the assumption that people wish to share their beliefs and feelings about traumatic experiences. Not discussing these issues can lead to higher stress levels. However, discussing these issues can lead to more accurate perspectives about the experience and can aid individuals in interpreting and understanding their own emotions about the experience.

More recent research has expanded this paradigm to other variables besides stress and immune function. For example, Floyd, Mikkelson, Hesse, and Pauley (2007) found that engaging in affectionate, relational-based writing predicted a decrease in cholesterol levels over time. Additionally, Koenig Kellas, Flood-Grady, and Allan (2015) examined expressive writing's influence on conflict. They asked individuals to write about a relational conflict from their own or their partner's perspective. Those who wrote from their partner's perspective reported an increase in closeness. Also, no matter what their writing condition, those who believed that the intervention aided them in gaining perspective about the conflict reported better mental health.

Prior expressive writing research demonstrates that writing about conflict produces positive outcomes. This study examines whether writing about solutions to a serial argument from different perspectives could lead to more constructive perceptions about the serial argument. To determine whether just writing in and of itself may make a difference, the study also has a control condition in which individuals wrote about a neutral topic (the room in which they were writing). We propose the following hypotheses:

H1: Writing about a serial argument from the mutual perspective should result in greater perceived *argument interdependence* than the other two perspectives (self, other) or the control condition.

H2: Writing about a serial argument from the mutual perspective should result in greater reported *intimacy* than the other two perspectives (self, other) or the control condition.

H3: Writing about a serial argument from the mutual perspective should result in higher *perceived resolvability* of the argument than the other two perspectives (self, other) or the control condition.

H4: Writing about a serial argument from the mutual perspective should result in more positive reported *changes in satisfaction* than the other two perspectives (self, other) or the control condition.

Method

One hundred eighteen individuals, 29 men and 89 women, completed a study to investigate these predictions. The average age was 20.99 (SD = 2.99). The majority of participants were White (n = 87), with the remainder Hispanic, African-American, Asian, and other ethnicities.

Participants came to the lab and completed an online questionnaire. Only those who were currently engaged in a serial argument and who consented to participate were eligible to begin the survey. The survey asked the participants to select the relationship they had with the person with whom they were arguing. Forty-two indicated a friend, 32 a romantic partner, 22 a parent, nine a sibling, one an extended family member, and 12 reported their relationship fell into none of these categories but specified examples such as "almost romantic partner." The survey then asked individuals to describe their serial argument and to answer further questions about it, such as how long ago the argument had started and how often they argued about it. Next, the researchers randomly assigned individuals to one of four conditions and asked the respondents to write in an essay format for 15 minutes: 28 wrote from the self perspective, 29 wrote from the other's perspective, 29 wrote from the mutual perspective, and 32 wrote about the room in which they were sitting (control condition). Participants then completed measures for the dependent variables in the study, including argument interdependence, social intimacy, perceived resolvability, and changes in one's satisfaction with the relationship following an episode of the serial argument. Conducting manipulation checks to examine if significant differences similar to the researchers' assessment of self, other, mutual, or control perspective existed across conditions, the researchers asked participants from which perspective they wrote with four semantic differentials related to each perspective, measured on a seven-point scale: yes/no; true/false; not correct/correct (reverse coded), wrong/right (reverse coded). Lastly, individuals reported demographic variables.

The study measured argument interdependence using Johnson and Cionea's (2018) nine-item scale. Sample items included, "The two of us need to work together to address this issue," and "It takes input from both of us to effectively argue about this topic," with the items measured on a seven-point scale from 1 = strongly disagree to 7 = strongly agree. The researchers measured intimacy using the Miller social intimacy scale (Miller & Lefcourt, 1982). This scale has 17 items summed to create an intimacy score. Six items assessed frequency of intimate behaviors (e.g., "How often do you show this person affection") measured on a seven-point scale from 1 = very rarely to 7 = almost always. Eleven items measured intensity of intimate feelings (e.g., "How close do you feel to this person most of the time?") on a seven-point scale from 1 = not much to 7 = a great deal. The study measured perceived resolvability with seven items adapted from Johnson and Roloff (1998, 2000a, 2000b), including "I don't think we will ever agree on this issue," and "I think that a productive solution can occur," on a seven-point scale from 1= strongly disagree to 7 = strongly agree. Researchers measured changes in satisfaction due to the argument based on seven items from Hample and Cionea (2012), edited for this study's context, on a seven-point scale from 1= strongly disagree to 7 = strongly agree. Examples included, "My relationship with my partner became better due to this argument," and "My relationship with my partner is less welcoming due to this argument" (reverse coded).

All scales had reliabilities above .80: argument interdependence = .89; intimacy = .97; perceived resolvability = .84; changes in satisfaction = .90. The correlations between all scales appear in Table 66.1. The researchers conducted four separate one-way ANOVAs followed by Tukey HSD multiple comparison tests to determine if responses differed across the four conditions in respect to argument interdependence, intimacy, perceived resolvability of the argument, and changes in satisfaction (i.e., positive or increased vs. negative or decreased satisfaction).

Results

All manipulation checks showed the expected differences, with the correct condition scoring significantly higher than the other three conditions, except the mutual perspective condition in which scores related to the mutual and self perspectives were not significantly different. The researchers expected that participants who wrote from the mutual perspective would score significantly higher than participants in any of the other three conditions for all four dependent variables. However, only the dependent variable of intimacy showed a significant difference between conditions, $F(3, 114) = 3.00$, $p = .03$, $\eta^2 = .07$, with participants writing from the other's perspective scoring significantly higher than those writing from the self-perspective. Table 66.2 reports all means, standard deviations, and significance values for all four ANOVAs.

Discussion

Replicating Koenig Kellas et al.'s (2015) findings on romantic partners, this study found that writing from one's partner's perspective leads to greater reported degrees of closeness (reflected by higher frequency of and more intense intimate behaviors) than writing about conflict from one's own perspective. Our study extends the findings related to romantic partners to a greater variety of interpersonal relationships, such as friends and family members. It suggests that perspective-taking may be an effective strategy for increasing intimacy in all interpersonal relationships.

The remaining results did not offer support for the effect of writing perspective on interdependence, resolvability, or satisfaction. Individuals may find it difficult to view serial arguments from a mutual perspective. Thus, a practical suggestion for those interested in resolving their serial arguments and minimizing the effects the argument has on their

Table 66.1 Correlation Matrix for All Scales Utilized in Serial Argument Analyses

	1	2	3	4
1. Argument interdependence	–	.23*	.22*	.03
2. Intimacy	.23*	–	.48**	.61**
3. Perceived resolvability	.22*	.48**	–	.53**
4. Changes in satisfaction	.03	.61**	.53**	–

*Correlation significant at $p < .05$; ** Correlation significant at $p < .01$.

Table 66.2 Results for ANOVAs Related to Perspectives on Serial Argument

	Mean	SD	F-test value
Argument interdependence			1.43
Mutual	5.89	0.94	
Self	5.70	1.08	
Other	6.17	0.68	
Control	5.72	1.11	
Intimacy			3.00*
Mutual		5.47	1.43
Self	4.56a	1.72	
Other	5.55b	1.09	
Control	5.05	1.32	
Resolvability			1.45
Mutual	4.71	1.66	
Self	4.23	1.48	
Other	4.77	1.38	
Control	4.10	1.58	
Changes in satisfaction			1.65
Mutual	4.34	1.43	
Self	3.50	1.49	
Other	4.06	1.44	
Control	3.99	1.46	

*F-test value significant at $p < .05$. Means with different subscripts
are significantly different at $p < .05$.

relationship with the other person would be to learn to reframe the issue in more coopera-tive, mutually-oriented terms. On the other hand, expressive writing may not work well to aid individuals thinking of approaches to resolving their serial arguments. Although expres-sive writing may relieve stress or help with emotional healing, resolving a serial argument may require more instrumental, concrete solutions than writing, especially if only one member in the relationship participates. Finally, some insignificant findings may relate to the smaller sample size of the study; a larger sample could reveal significant associations between the study variables.

One of the goals of this study was to further examine the relationship between argument interdependence and other variables related to serial arguments. In this respect, our study provided additional findings. Argument interdependence had a positive relationship with intimacy level and perceived resolvability. These latter two variables had a positive relation-ship with changes in relational satisfaction. With a larger sample size, future researchers should investigate a potential causal chain where argument interdependence leads to greater perceived intimacy and greater perceived resolvability, which both lead to greater satisfaction after an episode of the serial argument.

Another possibility that future research could examine is including argument interdepend-ence as a covariate. This isolation of interdependence's effects may strengthen the relationship between writing perspective and the outcome variables of perceived intimacy, resolvability, and changes in relational satisfaction. We know that interdependence has a positive relationship with at least two of these variables, so controlling for it could clarify the effect that writing perspective has on these variables. Hence, the findings from this study illustrate several fruitful directions for research on argument interdependence in future studies.

In addition to these findings, a systematic reading of the open-ended data (i.e., the expressive writing segments) revealed some recurring themes in the strategies respondents suggested for solving their serial argument. When writing from the mutual perspective, respondents suggested changing their approaches from emotional or unilateral to more mutually oriented, mature orientations that could result in a compromise or accommodation of both parties' interests and needs. These mature orientations involved apologizing, recognizing the other person's autonomy, respecting their decisions, and understanding the other person's point of view. Another suggested solution was to work together and generate concrete task management lists. Finally, some solutions involved avoidance (of the person or topic), agreeing to disagree, or ending the relationship. Notably common in these answers was that participants had some difficulty viewing the conflict from a mutual perspective, which may also explain the lack of support for the study's hypotheses. Several respondents indicated what they could do and what the other person could do, without necessarily expressing it as a joint, mutual effort.

When writing from the self-perspective, participants indicated solutions such as listening to the other party and communicating better, thinking rationally (instead of emotionally) about the argument, convincing the other person of their point of view, or proving themselves to the other person (especially in parent-child serial arguments). In addition, participants mentioned concrete task management lists, giving up or dropping the argument, agreeing to disagree, distancing themselves from the other person, or ending the relationship.

Finally, when writing from the other person's perspective, participants suggested the other party could agree to their terms, develop more open-mindedness, acknowledge the participants' concerns or position, trust the respondent, or respect the respondents' autonomy or personhood (especially in parent-child serial arguments). Other solutions involved the other party not getting defensive, argumentative, or hostile, and putting more effort into the relationship. Regardless of their writing perspective, participants recognized listening more, showing more empathy, communicating better, approaching the argument with less emotion, and avoidance or relational termination as viable solutions for resolving the conflict.

Several practical applications derive from our study. First, the entrenched nature of positions in participants' serial arguments makes it difficult to see solutions for resolving the conflict. Miller and Roloff (2006) found that individuals who are involved in intractable conflicts (such as ongoing serial arguments) report greater resistance to the resolution of the conflict as compared to individuals involved in resolvable conflicts. Thus, a first step to resolving a serial argument would be to cultivate perceptions of resolvability. Writing, regardless of perspective, may aid in this endeavor. Second, having to think about what the other person in the serial argument could do to resolve the conflict may improve relationships or at least mitigate the harm that a serial argument could inflict on the relationship. Thus, participants in a serial argument could cultivate empathy and perspective taking through writing.

References

Floyd, K., Mikkelson, A. C., Hesse, C., & Pauley, P. M. (2007). Affectionate writing reduces total cholesterol: Two random controlled trials. *Human Communication Research*, *33*(2), 119–142. doi:10.1111/j.1468-2958.2007.00293x

Hample, D., & Cionea, I. A. (2012). Serial arguments in inter-ethnic relationships. *International Journal of Intercultural Relations, 36*(3), 430–445. doi:10.1016/j.ijintrel.2011.12.006

Johnson, A. J., & Cionea, I. A. (2018). A new measure for argument topic interdependence in serial arguments. In R. Lake (Ed.), *Recovering argument* (pp. 357–362). New York, NY: Routledge.

Johnson, A. J., & Cionea, I. A. (2017). Serial arguments in interpersonal relationships: Current knowledge and future directions. In J. A. Samp (Ed.), *Communicating interpersonal conflict in close relationships: Contexts, challenges, and opportunities* (pp. 111–127). New York, NY: Routledge.

Johnson, A. J., Cionea, I. A., & Bostwick, E. N. (2015, November). *Argument interdependence and the value-relevance of the argument topic: Effects on resolvability, satisfaction, and psychological well-being.* Paper presented to at the annual meeting of the National Communication Association conference, Las Vegas, NV.

Johnson, A. J., Cionea, I. A., & Bostwick, E. N. (2016, July). *Serial arguments in romantic relationships: The relationships between argument interdependence, goals, tactics, and relational satisfaction.* Paper presented at the biennial conference of the International Association of Relationship Researchers, Toronto, Canada.

Johnson, K. L., & Roloff, M. E. (1998). Serial arguing and relational quality: Determinants and consequences of perceived resolvability. *Communication Research, 25*(3), 327–343. doi:10.1177/009365098025003004

Johnson, K. L., & Roloff, M. E. (2000a). Correlates of the perceived resolvability and relational consequences of serial arguing in dating relationships: Argumentative features and the use of coping strategies. *Journal of Social and Personal Relationships, 17*(4-5), 676–686. doi:10.1177/0265407500174011

Johnson, K. L., & Roloff, M. E. (2000b). The influence of argumentative role (initiator vsresistor) on perceptions of serial argument resolvability and relational harm. *Argumentation, 14*(1), 1–15. doi:10.1023/A:1007837310258

Koenig Kellas, J., Flood-Grady, E., & Allan, J. (2015, November). *Perspective-taking and relational conflict: The impact of writing on communication and relationships over time.* Paper presented at the annual meeting of the National Communication Association, Las Vegas, NV.

Malis, R. S., & Roloff, M. E. (2006). Features of serial arguing and coping strategies: Links with stress and well-being. In B. A. Le Poire & R. M. Dailey (Eds.), *Applied interpersonal communication matters: Family, health, and community relations* (pp. 39–66). New York, NY: Peter Lang.

Miller, C. W., & Roloff, M. E. (2006). The perceived characteristics of irresolvable, resolvable and resolved intimate conflicts: Is there evidence of intractability? *International Journal of Conflict Management, 17*(4), 291–315. doi:10.1108/10444060610749464

Miller, R. S., & Lefcourt, H. M. (1982). The assessment of social intimacy. *Journal of Personality Assessment, 46*(5), 514–518. http://dx.doi.org/10.1207/s15327752jpa4605_12

Pennebaker, J. W. (1997). *Opening up: The healing power of expressing emotions* (2nd ed.). New York, NY: Guilford Press.

Trapp, R., & Hoff, N. (1985). A model of serial argument in interpersonal relationships. *Journalof the American Forensic Association, 22(1),* 1–11.

67

ARGUMENTATIVENESS AND VERBAL AGGRESSIVENESS ARE TWO THINGS APIECE

Dale Hample

Dominic Infante jump-started the study of interpersonal arguing in the 1980s with his development of two self-report scales that measured basic argument motivations: argumentativeness (Infante & Rancer, 1982) and verbal aggressiveness (Infante & Wigley, 1986). These two scales have been in constant use since their publication. According to Google Scholar, researchers have cited the argumentativeness paper more than 500 times and the verbal aggressiveness article almost 700 times. Rancer and Avtgis (2014) summarized the very substantial literature involving these two empirical constructs in their book that has moved into its second edition.

Infante and his collaborators theorized both argumentativeness and verbal aggressiveness as individual traits that reflected a person's impulses for face-to-face arguing. Both instruments measure aggression, but the two aggressions have different targets. Argumentativeness is the aim to attack the other arguer's case, evidence, or reasons, or to present one's own controversial case. Verbal aggressiveness is the motivation to attack the other person's character, background, nature, habits, and so forth. Argumentativeness represents the inclination to argue on the merits of an issue and verbal aggressiveness is the impulse to engage in *ad hominem* attacks. Argumentativeness targets the case but verbal aggressiveness targets the other arguer. Consistent with thousands of years of argumentation pedagogy, the constructiveness of argumentativeness produces desirable outcomes at work, in personal life, in the classroom, and throughout the mundane world of disagreement. Verbal aggressiveness, as the teaching of *ad hominem* attacks predicts, is corrosive to personal, interpersonal, workplace, and public experiences. The centrality of these two ideas to both pedagogy and the cumulating research results in argumentation studies is clear.

This essay is about the measurement of the two constructs. Beginning with the original papers of Infante and his collaborators, the research community has had clear directions for generating a single argumentativeness score or a single verbal aggressiveness score for an individual. I will give evidence to indicate that those procedures are not statistically justifiable around the world, and that the field of argumentation studies needs to reform its routine calculation of these scores. In particular, I will propose that scholars in the discipline report two scores apiece for both argumentativeness and verbal aggressiveness.

Opposites: The Original Case for Subtractions

Both argumentativeness and verbal aggressiveness are measured concepts, each composed of two subscales. Two opposite impulses theorize each pair, so scholars must subtract one from the other to get a resultant vector. That subtraction (or equivalently, reverse-scoring half the items) is what is at issue here.

Two scales measure argumentativeness: argument-approach and argument-avoid. The argument-approach scale (e.g., "I am energetic and enthusiastic when I argue") indexes one's motivation to engage in arguing, and the argument-avoid scale (e.g., "I get an unpleasant feeling when I realize I am about to get into an argument") reflects a person's wish to avoid arguing. Infante and Rancer (1982) understood these two as opposite impulses, based on an explicit conceptualization of argumentativeness as an "approach-avoid or excitation-inhibition conflict" (p. 72). That humans experience approach-avoid conflicts is nearly beyond dispute. But what argumentation scholars did not question until recently was the assumption that the decision to engage or escape arguing was in fact the resultant vector of two opposite impulses. For example, a dieter deciding whether to have ice cream after dinner is a fairly clear instance of approach (ice cream tastes good) and avoidance (ice cream will wreck my diet) needing to be reconciled (probably by subtraction) to generate the decision. This was the sort of model scholars in argumentation originally assumed to be relevant to argumentative engagement.

But perhaps arguing does not always work that way. While some people are high on approach and low on avoid ("high argumentatives") and others are low on approach and high on avoid ("low argumentatives"), other people fall into intermediate categories. People with low scores on both subscales are "apathetic moderate argumentatives," people with high scores on both are "conflicted feelings moderate argumentatives," and people with moderate scores on both subscales are "neutral moderate argumentatives" (Rancer & Avtgis, 2014, pp. 14-15; cf. Hamilton & Mineo, 2002; Levine & Kotowski, 2010). The interesting point is that all people do not necessarily have opposed approach and avoidance scores. If the scores always point to opposite impulses, how could both be high (or both low) simultaneously? Random error of measurement is an unsatisfying explanation, especially if these impulses are really "types" of argumentativeness.

A simple statistical test available to evaluate whether approach and avoid are inherently opposed to one another is to correlate approach with avoid scores. If the two subscales are opposite, the correlation should be extremely negative, even approaching $r = -1.0$ when correcting for random measurement error. Hamilton and Mineo's (2002) meta-analysis discovered that the mean correlation was $r = -0.41$, a summary that included only four studies (including one from Japan and one from Germany). Hample and Irions (2015) examining 460 U.S. respondents produced $r = -0.35$. These represent substantial negative correlations, but whether they really justify the description of "opposite" is an open matter of judgment.

The case of verbal aggressiveness is similar. It, too, has two subscales (Infante & Wigley, 1986). One is antisocial (e.g., "When individuals are very stubborn, I use insults to soften the stubbornness") and the other is prosocial (e.g., "I am extremely careful to avoid attacking individuals' intelligence when I attack their ideas"). Infante and Wigley (1986) again made an explicit theoretical connection to approach-avoid conflicts, but this time the scholars focused in terms of attacking other people. Subtracting the prosocial score from the antisocial score resulted in a vector measuring the impulse to generate *ad hominem* attacks.

Although Rancer and Avtgis (2014) did not provide a parallel discussion of the possibility that some people might have equivalently low or equivalently high scores on the two subscales, the possibility is imaginable. Perhaps one wants both to attack and charm another person simultaneously, or perhaps one is largely indifferent to how the other person feels, one way or the other. Subtracting one scale from the other only makes sense if they are truly opposites.

Again, the simplest empirical test is to correlate the two subscales. In the Hample and Irions (2015) study of U.S. respondents mentioned above, the correlation was $r = -0.31$. More complex statistical analysis gave clear support to the idea that the two subscales were distinct (Levine et al., 2004), with correlations at about $r = -0.50$. As before, this correlation was clearly negative but perhaps not strikingly so. And as before, the correlation would not generalize to other nations.

Whether considering the argumentativeness or verbal aggressiveness scale, *subtracting the avoid score from the approach score is only sensible if approach and avoid are clear opposites.* Otherwise, the approach and avoid scores have their own distinguishable meanings (i.e., neither merely means "opposite of the other") and may have their own not-quite-parallel records of covariates, causes, and effects. If they are not really opposites, subtracting one from the other is simply mashing them together, like mixing bacon into cream cheese. What I imagine Infante had in mind was something more elegant and useful, like dissolving sugar into bitter tea. The sweetened tea is a single discernible thing, but the bacon and cream cheese will always be two things put together in one bowl.

Cross-National Data

For several years, my colleagues and I have participated in basic argument-relevant data collection in several nations. Among the instruments we used were argumentativeness and verbal aggressiveness. The studies differed in sampling frame (some used undergraduates, some non-university adults, and some a mixture) and language (some used English, some used the native language, and some respondents were given a choice of language). But the most obvious difference was that we conducted the studies in different nations. Other details are available in the original reports.

Here, I want to report the correlations between argument-approach and argument-avoid, and between the antisocial and prosocial scales for verbal aggressiveness. The pertinent results, including some gleaned from other research programs, are in Table 67.1. The argumentativeness results most consistent with Infante's original conceptualization appear first.

The first column of data reports correlations that bear on the question of whether argument-approach and argument-avoid are opposites. In several nations, including the United States, the results give evidence that the two scales opposed one another. However, several countries produced results that clearly do not justify the conclusion that the measures were opposites. In Chile, the correlation was negative but small. The United Arab Emirates' (UAE) result was essentially null. By contrast, Malaysia and India showed *positive* correlations between the two subscales.

The other column lists the available results for the antisocial-prosocial correlations for the verbal aggressiveness scale. The highest negative correlations are relatively modest compared to the most extreme values for the argumentativeness instrument. The same nations that generated unconvincing evidence of oppositeness for argumentativeness did the same for verbal aggressiveness: Chile, the UAE, Malaysia, and India. The last two correlations, in fact, approach support for the claim that antisocial and prosocial impulses are quite consistent with one another in Malaysia and India.

These data seem straightforwardly to justify certain conclusions. First, associations between the approach/avoid subscales of the two instruments are not internationally consistent. Second, associations between the approach/avoid subscales are not always negative. Last, associations between the approach/avoid subscales do not consistently achieve reasonable standards for "opposite."

Table 67.1 Correlations Among Argumentativeness and Verbal Aggressiveness Subscales by Nation

Country	Approach-Avoid	Antisocial-Prosocial
Germany	-0.64	
US, mTurk	-0.54	-0.43
China	-0.40	-0.26
France	-0.40	-0.26
US, Undergrads	-0.35	-0.31
Portugal	-0.34	-0.21
Japan	-0.34	-0.24
Turkey	-0.31	
Netherlands	-0.31	-0.28
Chile	-0.16	-0.16
UAE	0.02	0.15
Malaysia	0.16	0.20
India	0.17	0.27

Sources: Japan: Suzuki & Rancer (1994), and these correlations are between latent variables (i.e., corrected for unreliability of measurement); Turkey: Croucher et al. (2013); Germany: Blickle (1995, Study 3); US Undergraduates: Hample & Irions (2015); US, mTurk: Hample & Anagondahalli (2015); Chile: Santibáñez & Hample (2015); Portugal: Hample, Lewiński, Saàágua, & Mohammed (2016); India: Hample & Anagondahalli (2015); Malaysia: Waheed & Hample (2016); United Arab Emirates: Rapanta & Hample (2015); Netherlands: Labrie, Akkermans, & Hample (2017); France: Dufour & Hample (2017).

Discussion

The most general implication of these findings appears in my title, "Argumentativeness and Verbal Aggressiveness Are Two Things Apiece." Neither functions as a single construct. Approach and avoid subscales are not, or do not act as, opposites that can simply combine by means of subtraction or reverse-scoring.

The methodological inference is simple and easy to implement. Researchers must cease to report single measures of either argumentativeness or verbal aggressiveness. They need to treat the four subscales as separate measures. Sometimes, no doubt, they will obtain parallel but reversed findings for argument-approach and argument-avoid, or for antisocial and pro-social. But sometimes they will not—especially when working outside of the United States.

The global findings presented here encompass the more challenging implications. Theories of argumentativeness and verbal aggressiveness originated in the United States, and frankly, the resulting understandings made sense in that context. The U.S. results reported here are at least generally supportive of the original "theory of opposites." Further, even a cursory examination of the literature on interpersonal arguing reveals its U.S. centricity until recently. Naturally, interpersonal scholars began studies in other nations with expectations based on U.S. research. However, the intuitive understanding of U.S. motivations that Infante and his followers likely held are not accurate everywhere in the world. People everywhere experience approach-avoid conflicts, but somehow, for some people in some cultures, issue arguments and *ad hominem* attacks do not particularly represent that sort of interior friction.

The previously unexamined idea that scholars can export North American theory to other nations without qualification or empirical warrant is no longer sustainable. Literature reviews that carelessly combine results from various nations, or fail even to take note of the data's varying cultural origins, need more precision. The results summarized here pertain only to arguing motivations, but those are fundamental constructs in any thorough model of interpersonal arguing. If motivations do not work the same way from nation to nation, surely scholars should be wary of assuming anything else will necessarily (automatically, inherently) work in an American way. Argumentation scholars need to extend the sort of work summarized here to questions of argument tactics and their consequences, connections between arguing behavior and arguer's image, tolerance for fallacious derailment, preferences for types of evidence and argument scheme, perceptions of argument quality, and many other basic matters.

Most of all, these results indicate that argumentation studies need to develop genuinely local theories of argumentation for every nation and culture. People in those cultures need to conduct the work through their own intuitions, just as Infante's intuitions led him to what is, in retrospect, a very nice theory of U.S. arguing motivations. Given the current reality that argumentation studies are something of an educational luxury, mostly undertaken in the universities of developed economies, this poses practical problems for the development of global argumentation theory. Somehow the field must develop local theories and must find a way to make them commensurate with one another. Only then can scholars approach the task of figuring out how humans argue face to face.

References

Blickle, G. (1995). Conceptualization and measurement of argumentativeness: A decade later. *Psychological Reports*, 77(1), 99–110. doi: 10.2466/pr0.1995.77.1.99

Croucher, S. M., Otten, R., Ball, M., Grimes, T., Ainsworth, B., Begley, K., & Corzo, L. (2013). Argumentativeness and political participation: A cross-cultural analysis in the United States and Turkey. *Communication Studies*, 64(1), 18–32. doi: 10.1080/10510974.2012.727942

Dufour, M., & Hample, D. (2017, June). *French interpersonal argument: Fundamental understandings*. Paper presented at the 2nd European Conference on Argumentation, Fribourg, Switzerland.

Hamilton, M. A., & Mineo, P. J. (2002). Argumentativeness and its effect on verbal aggressiveness: A meta-analytic review. In M. Allen, R. W. Preiss, B. M. Gaye, & N. Burrell (Eds.), *Interpersonal communication research: Advances through meta-analysis* (pp. 281–314). Mahwah, NJ: Lawrence Erlbaum.

Hample, D., & Anagondahalli, D. (2015). Understandings of arguing in India and the United States: Argument frames, personalization of conflict, argumentativeness, and verbal aggressiveness. *Journal of Intercultural Communication Research*, 44(1), 1–26. doi: 10.1080/17475759.2014.1000939

Hample, D., & Irions, A. L. (2015). Arguing to display identity. *Argumentation*, 29(4), 389-416. doi: 10.1007/s10503-015-9351-9

Hample, D., Lewiński, M., Saàágua, J., & Mohammed, D. (2016). A descriptive and comparative analysis of arguing in Portugal. In D. Mohammed & M. Lewiński (Eds.), *Argumentation and reasoned action: Proceedings of the 1st European conference on argumentation, Lisbon, 2015* (Vol. 1, pp. 135–157). London, United Kingdom: College.

Infante, D. A., & Rancer, A. S. (1982). A conceptualization and measure of argumentativeness. *Journal of Personality Assessment, 46*(1), 72–80. doi: 10.1207/s15327752jpa4601_13

Infante, D. A., & Wigley, C. J., III. (1986). Verbal aggressiveness: An interpersonal model and measure. *Communication Monographs, 53*(1), 61–69. doi: 10.1080/03637758609376126

Labrie, N. H. M., Akkermans, A., & Hample, D. (2017). *Arguing in the Netherlands.* Manuscript in preparation.

Levine, T. R., Beatty, M. J., Limon, S., Hamilton, M. A., Buck, R., & Chory-Assad, R. M. (2004). The dimensionality of the verbal aggressiveness scale. *Communication Monographs, 71*(3), 245–268. doi: 10.1080/0363452042000299911

Levine, T. R., & Kotowski, M. R. (2010). Measuring argumentativeness and verbal aggressiveness: Psychometric concerns and advances. In T. A. Avtgis & A. S. Rancer (Eds.), *Arguments, aggression, and conflict: New directions in theory and research* (pp. 67-81). New York, NY: Routledge.

Rancer, A. S., & Avtgis, T. A. (2014). *Argumentative and aggressive communication: Theory, research, and application* (2nd ed.). New York, NY: Peter Lang.

Rapanta, C., & Hample, D. (2015). Orientations to interpersonal arguing in the United Arab Emirates, with comparisons to the United States, China, and India. *Journal of Intercultural Communication Research, 44*(4), 263-287. doi: 10.1080/17475759.2015.1081392

Santibáñez, C., & Hample, D. (2015). Orientations toward interpersonal arguing in Chile. *Pragmatics, 25* (3), 453-476. doi: 10.1075/prag.25.3.06san

Suzuki, S., & Rancer, A. S. (1994). Argumentativeness and verbal aggressiveness: Testing for conceptual and measurement equivalence across cultures. *Communication Monographs, 61*(3), 256–279. doi: 10.1080/03637759409376336

Waheed, M., & Hample, D. (2016, June). *Argumentation in Malaysia and how it compares to the U.S.,* India, *and* China. Paper presented at the 66th Annual Conference of the International Communication Association, Fukuoka, Japan.

68

IS FACT-CHECKING BIASED? A COMPUTERIZED CONTENT ANALYSIS

Jeffrey W. Jarman

Fact-checking political statements is an important part of the democratic process. As Delli Carpini and Keeter (1996) noted, "Political information [...] is the currency of citizenship" (p. 8). The media, in its role as fact-checker of the statements of public officials, is a vital part of the process for providing accurate information to inform the citizenry. Yet, providing information to the public is only one prerequisite of a vibrant public sphere. Not only must the public have access to reliable information, they must also be willing to accept the facts and integrate them into their prior beliefs.

An all-too-common refrain from those who want to dismiss the findings fact-checkers report is to attack the credibility of the news. "Conservatives use words such as 'left-leaning,' 'biased,' 'hackiest' and 'serial-lying'" (Adair & Iannucci, 2017, para. 8), while the Republican Party openly dismissed fact-checking as both biased and incompetent on its website (Shah, 2016). Opponents label fact-checkers as biased in an effort to discredit their reporting and devalue their conclusions. While such criticism likely resonates with a public that wants to see their favored candidate redeemed, the important question remains: Is fact-checking biased?

The 2016 presidential election cycle provides a good test of potential bias in political fact-checking. The media regularly accused Donald Trump of lying or otherwise misstating the truth. Trump's apparent pattern of lying emerged early in the campaign. The *New York Time*'s David Brooks (2016) declared, "Trump is perhaps the most dishonest person to run for high office in our lifetimes. All politicians stretch the truth, but Trump has a steady obliviousness to accuracy" (para. 9). The day before the election, "the Guardian [...] catalogued more than 100 falsehoods made by the Republican nominee over the last 150 days" (Yuhas, 2016, para. 1).

In response, Trump regularly attacked the media's perceived bias. As *The New Yorker*'s Margaret Talbot (2016) observed, "'dishonest' and 'lying' are Trump's go-to insults when talking about the press" (para. 11). The *Washington Post*'s Katie Zezima (2016) added that Trump's campaign speeches "slammed the media harder than ever. The candidate labeled reporters the 'lowest form of humanity'" (para. 1). By positioning himself as the victim of media bias, Trump argued, "I'm running against the crooked media" (Zezima, 2016, para. 5) and responded to news he found disagreeable by labeling it "fake news." As Steve Benen (2017), a producer for *The Rachel Maddow Show* commented, "One of Trump's favorite phrases, repeated in tic-like fashion, is 'fake news'" (para. 9).

Did Trump lie? Were the media dishonest as they peddled fake news designed to undermine Trump? Were the fact-check articles written during the 2016 presidential campaign season biased toward one candidate over another? This essay analyzes the quality of political fact-checking to determine the extent of any political bias.

Linguistic Markers of Bias in the Media

Measuring bias in news coverage is a difficult task. Unlike more concrete concepts (e.g., number of words spoken, number of sources cited, etc.), bias is more abstract and more challenging to measure. As Lowry (2008) noted, bias in the media "cannot be measured directly" (p. 485). Rather, bias is a conceptual idea inferred based on other measurable elements. Many efforts to identify bias in political fact-checking have used the frequency of a particular conclusion assigned to a specific candidate as a sign of an impropriety. For instance, if reporters disproportionately rate Trump as making false statements and Clinton as making true statements, the news risks the attack of having an anti-Trump bias. Shapiro (2016), for example, argued for the bias of Politifact because it was "much more likely to rate Republicans as their worst of the worst 'Pants on Fire' rating, usually only reserved for when they feel a candidate is not only wrong, but aggressively and maliciously lying" (para. 16). While an appearance of bias may seem plausible when the vast majority of ratings go against one candidate or one political party, the number of false statements is not the best measure of political bias, as Trump may have misstated more facts than Clinton. A more powerful critique of Politifact rests not in the number of false statements the publication's fact-checkers identified, but in the quality and nature of the written findings. Thus, analyzing the word choice of the articles on Politifact may provide a more nuanced evaluation of the potential bias in their reporting.

One of the key principles of journalism is neutrality. Historically, the principle appears as fairness, balance, and objectivity, where journalists attempt to use value neutral language to simply explain the issue at hand. Even subtle word choices, whether positive or negative, could have profound effects, especially if used regularly. Several potential linguistic markers of bias in the media exist, including the number of positive and negative terms in the text and the level of integrative complexity of the content. The frequency of positive and negative terms could serve as a sign of bias in the news, as several previous studies of newspaper coverage measured the frequency of positive and negative terms to document an imbalance in the presentation of content on a wide variety of topics (e.g., see Campbell, Turner, & Walker, 2012; Cepela & Danowski, 2012; Lowry, Eng, Katende, & Subramanian, 2012; Sevincer, Wagner, Kalvelage, & Oettingen, 2014). Integrative complexity is another potential sign of bias in news writing. Integrative complexity is a measure of how well a person makes sense of competing viewpoints and divergent information. As Brundidge, Reid, Choi and Muddiman (2014) elaborated:

> The most integratively complex reasoning differentiates between viewpoints on any given issue and offers a solution that reconciles those viewpoints. Low integrative complexity arguments, however, either fail to recognize different points of view or fail to offer solutions to their reconciliation when they are recognized. Thus, integrative complexity is an ideal measure of the extent to which alternative viewpoints on controversial issues are deliberatively considered.
>
> *(p. 742)*

In the context of political fact-checking articles, integrative complexity is a sign that the author is actively considering multiple points of view, inferring a low level of bias. As Tetlock, Armor, and Peterson (1994) explained, "Encouraging integratively complex reasoning in experimental settings reduces or even eliminates such well-replicated judgmental biases as belief perseverance (complex thinkers are less likely to resist revising their first impressions in response to later contradictory evidence)" (p. 116).

Attempts to measure bias must also account for the relative nature of the concept. Ideally, scholars could determine the bias of news stories, but such a conclusion is challenging since no agreed upon standards exist to distinguish between neutrality and bias. Instead, relative bias relies on disproportionate numbers of linguistic markers to illustrate bias in a text. As Lowry et al. (2012) explained:

> It is definitely possible to analyze two different bodies of content, such as stories pertaining to a Republican president and a Democratic president, and then determine if the words [*sic*] choices employed in the stories favored one president more than would be expected by statistical chance. From the scholarly perspective, the notion of relative bias is much more achievable and useful than any forced attempt to come up with a measure of absolute bias.
>
> *(pp. 17-18)*

Rather than attempting to measure absolute bias, this project will investigate relative bias by analyzing potential differences in the language used in fact-check analyses of competing candidates. To investigate the role of these potential signs of relative bias in political fact-checking, this essay addresses three research questions:

RQ1: Will the number of positive emotional terms vary based on the candidate and/or the conclusion of the article?

RQ2: Will the number of negative emotional terms vary based on the candidate and/or the conclusion of the article?

RQ3: Will the level of integrative complexity in fact-check articles vary based on the candidate and/or the conclusion of the article?

Method

Politifact, a Pulitzer prize winning fact-checking operation run by the *Tampa Bay Times*, is the source of the fact-checked stories in this analysis. Politifact is a leading fact-checking site that both the right of the political spectrum (e.g., see Hudson, 2016; Shapiro, 2016) and the left (e.g., see Byers, 2012) criticize. The sample (*N*=424) includes every article published on *politifact.com* between January 1, 2016 and November 8, 2016 that analyzed statements by either Hillary Clinton or Donald Trump. As the eventual nominees for the two major parties, the two candidates represented the bulk of the fact-checking coverage in the study's time period. Moreover, the eight months of coverage leading up to the election constituted an important time for political news reporting on Clinton and Trump. In 2016, the electorate included an unusually large number of undecided voters throughout the campaign season ("24% Opt Out," 2016; Liesman, 2016; Silver, 2016) who wanted more information to make their choice (Wren, 2016). In addition, many voters held negative opinions of both candidates, making them conflicted about how to vote. These voters continued the search for information, including "'visiting] a fact-checking site' either during or after the debate" (Blumenthal, 2016, para. 20).

The study utilized the computerized content analysis software Linguistic Inquiry and Word Count (2007) to analyze each of the articles in the sample. A widely-utilized and psychometrically validated approach to analyzing content (Pennebaker, Boyd, Jordan, & Blackburn, 2015; Tausczik & Pennebaker, 2010), LIWC utilizes a dictionary of nearly 4,500 words and word stems organized into one or more categories (nearly 80 total). Categories include six-letter words, pronouns, articles, conjunctions, swear words, and many more. This study analyzed each article independently by comparing each word in the text to every category. The program assigned each category a standardized score based on the number of occurrences in the text divided by the total number of words. For example, consider the last line of a fact-check article: "Therefore, we rate the statement false." The total number of words is six. The word count (WC) variable score is 6. The pronoun score is 16.67 since there is one pronoun (we) that represents one-sixth of the total. The word "we" is also a social word, with that category similarly scored 16.67. Many categories (e.g., adverbs) scored as zero because they did not appear in the short statement.

I conducted a series of two-way ANOVAs using fact-check conclusion and candidate as the independent variables and the LWIC-created categories of positive emotion, negative emotion, and integrative complexity as the dependent variables. One coder, unaware of the research questions, examined each fact-check article in the sample to identify the candidate (Clinton or Trump) and the conclusion of the fact-check analysis (Pants on fire, False, Mostly false, Half-true, Mostly true, True). The study measured positive and negative emotional words using the standard LIWC dictionaries. Since LIWC does not have a predetermined measurement for integrative complexity, a combination of several LIWC categories served as the basis of analysis. Following Abe (2011), the study assessed integrative complexity by summing the standard scores for exclusive words, negations, tentative words, and conjunctions.

Results

Table 68.1 contains the descriptive statistics for the dependent variables. RQ1 asks if the number of positive emotional terms varies based on candidate and/or conclusion. The two-way ANOVA finds no significant difference for the main effect for candidate, $F (1, 412) = 1.443$, $p = .23$, nor for conclusion, $F (5, 412) = 0.071$, $p = .99$, and no interaction effect, $F (5, 412) = 0.318$, $p = .90$. The test confirms that the articles use roughly the same number of positive emotional words regardless of candidate and conclusion.

RQ2 asks if the number of negative emotional terms varies based on candidate and/or conclusion. The two-way ANOVA finds no significant difference for the main effect for candidate, $F (1, 412) = 3.638$, $p = .06$, nor for conclusion, $F (5, 412) = 0.995$, $p = .42$, and no interaction effect, $F (5, 412) = 0.557$, $p = .73$. Again, the test confirms the articles use roughly the same number of negative emotional words regardless of candidate and conclusion.

Finally, RQ3 asks if the level of integrative complexity varies based on the candidate and/or conclusion. The study finds no statistically significant main effect for candidate, $F (1, 412) = 2.006$, $p = .157$. The integrative complexity scores for fact-check reports about Clinton are not significantly different than those about Trump. The study does find a statistically significant difference for the main effect of conclusion, $F (5, 412) = 4.087$, $p = .001$, $\eta_p^2 = .05$. Post-hoc tests reveal that integrative complexity scores are the lowest when the conclusion is true and those scores are significantly lower than the scores for all other conclusions. No other pairs of conclusions are significantly different ($ps > .05$). Finally, the study finds no statistically significant interactions between candidate and fact-check conclusion, $F (5, 412) = .773$, $p = .57$.

Table 68.1 Means (Standard Deviations) for Linguistic Inquiry and Word Count Categories

Candidate	Conclusion	N	Complexity	Posemo	Negemo
Clinton	Pants on fire	5	1.65 (3.84)	2.23 (0.64)	0.86 (0.63)
	False	13	-0.16 (3.23)	2.03 (1.21)	1.07 (0.80)
	Mostly false	17	0.55 (2.16)	2.27 (1.14)	1.58 (0.92)
	Half true	40	0.23 (2.58)	2.20 (1.19)	1.56 (0.98)
	Mostly true	43	0.19 (3.29)	2.28 (1.16)	1.67 (1.04)
	True	33	-1.44 (2.59)	2.01 (1.08)	1.60 (1.25)
	Total	151	-0.10 (2.92)	2.17 (1.13)	1.54 (1.04)
Trump	Pants on fire	45	-0.22 (2.55)	2.02 (1.24)	1.63 (1.05)
	False	83	0.60 (2.74)	2.00 (1.10)	1.64 (1.31)
	Mostly false	59	0.41 (2.67)	2.01 (1.06)	1.58 (1.41)
	Half true	38	-0.09 (2.06)	1.99 (0.91)	1.74 (1.13)
	Mostly true	34	-0.50 (2.56)	1.87 (1.08)	1.83 (1.33)
	True	14	-2.11 (2.72)	2.10 (1.43)	1.65 (0.78)
	Total	273	0.05 (2.64)	1.99 (1.10)	1.67 (1.24)
Total	Pants on fire	50	-0.03 (2.71)	2.04 (1.19)	1.56 (1.03)
	False	96	0.50 (2.80)	2.01 (1.11)	1.57 (1.26)
	Mostly false	76	0.44 (2.55)	2.07 (1.08)	1.58 (1.31)
	Half true	78	0.07 (2.33)	2.09 (1.06)	1.65 (1.05)
	Mostly true	77	-0.11 (2.99)	2.10 (1.14)	1.74 (1.17)
	True	47	-1.64 (2.62)	2.04 (1.18)	1.61 (1.12)
	Total	424	0.00 (2.74)	2.06 (1.11)	1.62 (1.17)

Discussion

Fact-checking has an important role to play in enhancing the quality of public deliberation on important political issues. But, accusations of bias threaten the ability of fact-checking to improve the public's understanding of complex political issues. This study investigates the subtle role of language choice in creating biased coverage of candidates in fact-checking articles. Drawing from nearly a year's worth of coverage from a widely-respected fact-checking website, the fact-checked articles related to the two most prominent 2016 presidential candidates demonstrate no bias for one candidate over the other. In analyzing more than 400 articles, these results confirm that the fact-check articles treated both Clinton and Trump similarly, utilizing roughly the same number of positive and negative emotion terms and roughly the same level of integrative complexity. While the conclusions of the articles may have found Trump more likely than Clinton to make an untrue statement, the quality of the writing was relatively free of bias, treating both candidates evenly.

This study had several limitations. First, and most obviously, the scope of the analysis was too narrow. Future studies should continue the project by analyzing additional fact-checking outlets, candidates up and down the ballot, and longer periods of analysis. Second, the study examined only a few LIWC categories of words as the basis of the findings. Future research should continue to refine how to measure bias and to identify other categories potentially productive for showing signs of bias in political news reporting.

References

24% Opt Out of a Clinton-Trump Race. (2016, April 28). *Rasmussen Reports*. Retrieved from http://www.rasmussenreports.com

Abe, J. A. A. (2011). Changes in Alan Greenspan's language use across the economic cycle: A test analysis of his testimonies and speeches. *Journal of Language and Social Psychology, 30*(2), 212–223. doi:10.1177/0261927X10397152

Adair, B., & Iannucci, R. (2017, June 7). Heroes or hacks: The partisan divide over fact-checking. *Duke Reporters' Lab*. Retrieved from https://reporterslab.org

Benen, S. (2017, June 28). Trump's embrace of "fake news" takes an embarrassing turn. *MSNBC*. Retrieved from http://www.msnbc.com

Blumenthal, M. (2016, October 6). A different way to think about undecided voters. *The Huffington Post*. Retrieved from https://www.huffingtonpost.com/mark-blumenthal/a-different-way-to-think_b_12351724.html

Brooks, D. (2016, March 18). No, not Trump, not ever. *The New York Times*. Retrieved from https://www.nytimes.com

Brundidge, J., Reid, S. A., Choi, S., & Muddiman, A. (2014). The "deliberative digital divide:" Opinion leadership and integrative complexity in the U.S. political blogosphere. *Political Psychology, 35*(6), 741–755. doi:10.1111/pops.12201

Byers, D. (2012, February 21). Rachel Maddow attacks Politifact, again. *Politico*. Retrieved from http://www.politico.com

Campbell, G., Turner, J. D., & Walker, C. B. (2012). The role of the media in a bubble. *Explorations in Economic History, 49*(4), 461–481. doi:10.1016/j.eeh.2012.07.002

Cepela, N., & Danowski, J. A. (2012, January). *Network centrality of Obama and his cabinet members as predictors of job approval over time.* Paper presented to the 83rd annual conference of the Southern Political Science Association, New Orleans, LA.

Delli Carpini, M. X., & Keeter, S. (1996). *What Americans know about politics and why it matters.* New Haven, CT: Yale University Press.

Hudson, J. (2016, December 15). 9 reasons why Politifact is unqualified to label "fake news." *Breitbart News Network*. Retrieved from http://www.breitbart.com

Liesman, S. (2016, June 20). 25% of voters in 2016 race remain undecided: Survey. *CNBC*. Retrieved from https://www.cnbc.com/2016/06/20/25-of-voters-in-2016-race-remain-undecided-survey.html

Lowry, D. T. (2008). Network TV news framing of good vs. bad economic news under Democrat and Republican presidents: A lexical analysis of political bias. *Journalism & Mass Communication Quarterly, 85*(3), 483–498. doi:10.1177/107769900808500301

Lowry, D. T., Eng, B., Katende, B. R., & Subramanian, R. (2012, August). *Opinion polling, relative news bias and the modern presidency: Analyzing story tone in the network TV news coverage of Bush vs. Obama.* Paper presented at the annual convention of the Association for Education in Journalism and Mass Communication, Chicago, IL.

Pennebaker, J. W., Boyd, R. L, Jordan, K., & Blackburn, K. (2015). *The development and psychometric properties of LIWC 2015.* Austin, TX: University of Texas.

Sevincer, A. T., Wagner, G., Kalvelage, J., & Oettingen, G. (2014). Positive thinking about the future in newspaper reports and presidential addresses predicts economic downturn. *Psychological Science, 25*(4), 1010–1017. doi:10.1177/0956797613518350

Shah, R. (2016, August 30). Politifact's so-called fact-checks show bias, incompetence, or both. *GOP. com*. Retrieved from https://gop.com/politifacts-so-called-fact-checks-show-bias-incompetence-or-both/

Shapiro, M. (2016, December 16). Running the data on Politifact shows bias against conservatives. *Federalist*. Retrieved from http://thefederalist.com

Silver, N. (2016, October 25). Election updated: Where are the undecided voters? *FiveThirtyEight*. Retrieved from http://fivethirtyeight.com

Talbot, M. (2016, September 28). Trump and the truth: The "lying" media. *The New Yorker*. Retrieved from http://www.newyorker.com

Tausczik, Y. R., & Pennebaker, J. W. (2010). The psychological meaning of words: LIWC and computerized text analysis methods. *Journal of Language and Social Psychology*, *29*(1), 24–54. doi:10.1177/0261927X09351676

Tetlock, P. E., Armor, D., & Peterson, R. S. (1994). The slavery debate in antebellum America: Cognitive style, value conflict, and the limits of compromise. *Journal of Personality and Social Psychology*, *66*(3), 115–126. doi:10.1037/0022-3514.66.1.115

Wren, A. (2016, November 5). The undecided: Meet 6 voters from around the country who still haven't made up their minds. *Politico*. Retrieved from http://www.politico.com

Yuhas, A. (2016, November 7). How does Donald Trump lie? A fact checker's final guide. *The Guardian*. Retrieved from https://www.theguardian.com

Zezima, K. (2016, August 14). Trump's campaign continues to blame "disgusting and corrupt" media. *The Washington Post*. Retrieved from https://www.washingtonpost.com

69

BUILDING ARGUMENTS AND ATTENDING TO FACE IN SMALL CLAIMS COURT

Distinctive Features of the Genre

Karen Tracy

When Toulmin (1958) argued that logic "characterizes the essentials of the legal process" (p. 7), he was undoubtedly thinking about appellate rather than small claims courts. One would stretch the meaning of small claims advocacy to describe ordinary, non-legally trained people's speech as logic-filled. Following traffic court, small claims court is the venue where most Americans experience the legal system. Created in the early years of the twentieth century, small claims courts, by design, make the law accessible to ordinary people as the attendant legal processes are informal, inexpensive, and quick. By 1970, small claims trials were part of all state judicial systems, and by 1990, cases in these courts comprised 27 to 40 percent of all civil case filings in large cities (Goerdt, 1992).

Small claims court requires a person to define a dispute as a monetary claim against another for an amount whose limit varies state to state, but usually falls between $5000 and $7500 ("50-State Chart," 2017). Small claim matters include disputes among landlords, tenants, and roommates; quality and payment for contracted services; and damages to property and persons. Three features of small claims proceedings deserve mention. First, disputants speak for themselves; only rarely are attorneys present. Second, judges have freedom in how they enact small claims court; some frame the occasion as a mini-trial, while others treat the experience as an occasion where the judge asks questions (Tracy & Caron, 2017). Finally, trials are short.

My purpose in this essay is twofold. The primary aim is to describe the communication that comprises a small claims hearing, attending specifically to the argumentation and face-work, that is, a person's image as created in interaction (Goffman, 1955) of litigants and judges. The second purpose is to use this description to identify implications for other argument practices. After reviewing a key study and describing the trials this study analyzes, I identify four features of small claims discourse. In the final section, I draw out implications for future studies.

Previous Studies of Small Claims Courts

Conley and O'Barr (1990) did a study of small claims courts in the United States. Drawing on observation of more than 450 cases in six states, interviews with disputants, and taping and discourse analysis of a small set of trials, they noted that American law "is the product of diverse and discordant voices" (p. 1). The law is an activity of varying speeds with the small claims version serving as a particularly fast one. Of 74 cases in their analysis, only 20 took more than five minutes. The authors also showed that litigants' communication tended to adopt one of two styles: rule-based or relational. The rule-based style narrated a dispute in terms of rules of the court. To reformulate their findings into the language of argumentation, litigants using a rule-based style attended to making a claim that the court saw as appropriate for its consideration and provided the kind of evidence and reasoning the judge would determine as "legal." Litigants using the relational style, in contrast, appealed to the judge's moral world of responsibilities, as well as the duties that the litigants believed were more personally important within the dispute. Relational-style litigants told stories filled with details of personal motives, intentions, and specifics about the problematic action. Reformulated, their style functioned in face terms, as defending the goodness, reasonableness and/or morality of the self, and attacking those same qualities in the other.

The National Center for State Courts conducted two major surveys of small claims courts (Goerdt, 1992; Ruhnka & Weller, 1978) that led courts around the United States to revise routine procedures in the 1980s. Since Conley and O'Barr did their study, small claims courts have frequently channeled cases into mediation as an alternative to trial, provide training materials for litigants, have lengthened the average trial, and have moved the whole genre toward a more formal style. In addition, the dollar limit on cases has continuously risen across the years, which, as Goerdt (1992) argued, has brought new kinds of cases to the court. For all these reasons, the field of argumentation studies should take a fresh look at small claims exchanges.

Data and Approach

This paper is part of a larger study analyzing small claims trials (Tracy & Caron, 2017; Tracy & Hodge, 2019). The central data comprised 55 cases obtained from four states, five courts, and 12 judges, with half of the trials coming from Colorado. The shortest trial is 12 minutes, the longest is 176 minutes, with the average at 45 minutes. Tapes of trial, available as public records, underwent verbatim transcription. In addition to the trial transcripts, my seven years of trial observation in two small claims courts informed the four distinctive features of small claims discourse identified below.

Argumentative Features of Small Claims Discourse

Judge Designed Occasions Strongly Shape Litigants Arguments

In contrast to civil courts that have no dollar limits or criminal courts that focus on nonmonetary matters, the shape of a small claims hearing varies considerably from court to court, as well as from judge to judge. As Ruhnka and Weller (1978) commented,

> Significant areas such as trial procedures, rules of evidence, the handling of attorneys, and assistance to *pro se* litigants are left up to the trial judge, and it is possible for a judge to shape the small claims trials to whatever he believes.
>
> *(p. 17)*

One dimension of variation involves the degree to which the judges frame court events as adversarial (i.e., a mini-trial with openings, cross-examination, and closing statements) or inquisitorial (i.e., structured to allow a judge to ask questions directed to each party). Small claims proceedings designed as mini-trials typically start with the judge explaining the steps, specifying time limits, and then turning the proceeding over to the plaintiff. Within the inquisitorial frame, judges cue discursive manifestations by allowing the litigant only a short time to talk before interrupting with questions. The inquisitorial frame leads to judges defining the issue and identifying what would count as evidence. In contrast, a judge using the adversarial style gives litigants more opportunity to develop the argument that they want to make.

The roles of the disputants—plaintiff and defendant—shape argument possibilities. Plaintiffs have the responsibility to place the blame on the defendant and describe how the defendant has wronged them. Defendants then problematize the plaintiff's standpoint. How judges frame the occasion also affects how litigants argue. Using van Eemeren's (2010) pragma-dialectic approach, the adversarial style in court keeps a judge attending to the freedom rule of good argument, which requires each party to allow the other to advance their standpoint. In the inquisitorial format, judges pepper a litigant with questions, acting similarly to an attorney conducting direct and cross-examination of witnesses.

Excerpt 1 is the case of two female neighbors who had a physical altercation in a nearby convenience store/gas station. Later in the day, the plaintiff experienced a seizure, which she attributed to the altercation. She asked for $3000 to cover her hospital bills. Excerpt 1 is a transcript of the judge questioning the defendant after he had questioned the plaintiff. Of note is the way he tacks back and forth between questions directed to both parties. The upshot of the judge's inquisitorial style is that litigants produced relatively fragmented arguments.

Excerpt 1 (Michigan, Case 34, J = Judge, D= Defendant, P = Plaintiff)

J: Okay. So then what happened?
D: Then she start- so I let her go. And I was- told her leave me alone. Okay? And then she started screaming and yelling at me about this far in front of my face. So in the meantime I asked the gentleman to call the gas- to call the police station. He did. Then she called her husband. Her husband comes in. Then I have them both in front of my face like this. So I asked the gentleman to put me behind the cage. They yelled at him and said he couldn't put me behind the cage-
J: Who's they? These people?
D: Mr. and Mrs. Castor. It's illegal. The gentleman opened the cage and let me in the cage because I was afraid. Police came-
J: Is that hap- did that happen?
P: No sir.
J: She was never in the cage?
P: She was behind the door sir. But my husband was the one who called 911.
J: No was she in the cage?
P: Yes sir.
J: Okay go ahead.

Small Claims Disputes Should Be Arguments about Money—Not Relationships

Ordinarily, the money frame fits small claims disputes well. Disputes about how much of a rental deposit landlords should return, how much rent the renter owes, or whether parties should pay for damages are often about money, even if negative feelings from both parties lurk around the edges. At other times, however, the money frame is a bad fit. The claim about money appears as an instantiation of a larger, interpersonal dispute where both parties want the judge to publicly pronounce them the wronged party and the other person as the wrongdoer. In the case of Excerpt 1 above, the end of the hearing makes clear that the two women had behaved as warring next-door neighbors for many years. The defendant had previously called the police on the plaintiff multiple times for noise infractions that the plaintiff considered unwarranted, and the defendant had also been instrumental in getting the plaintiff evicted from their house. In cases where the real issue is relational and the central aim of a plaintiff is to discredit the other, small claims proceedings become weapons for furthering the argumentative dispute, rather than a tool to settle them.

Litigants Describe Actions for Other-oriented Face Attack and Self-oriented Face Enhancement

Even when the key issue of a dispute is money rather than a relational issue, parties in small claims court cases direct their discourse toward supporting their own face, while attacking that of the other party. Both the self-talk and partner's talk shape the concept of face (Goffman, 1955). In small claims courts, a central way that parties build face is through building descriptions. Through the specific formulations selected, descriptions do moral work (e.g., Drew, 1992) in ways that portray a speaker as either acting reasonably, generously, or some other positive qualities, or not.

Consider a case involving ex-intimates. The plaintiff, Mary, sued her now ex-boyfriend Baxter for about a thousand dollars. Mary had placed Baxter on her cellphone plan when they became boyfriend and girlfriend. After they separated, she allowed him to continue paying for his phone service through her plan. Her suit also included the cost of a new cell phone billed to her account (that Baxter ordered and did not pay to own). Explaining why she initially allowed Baxter on her cellphone plan, Mary framed the reasons for her actions as her desire to be a good friend. She "allowed Baxter to um add his number under my cell phone bill as a savings to him." When the couple split, she permitted him to stay on her plan so that he could continue saving money. Excerpt 2 illustrates her description of his response to her request to get the phone under his own name.

Excerpt 2 (Colorado, Case 22, Plaintiff Mary's Account)

So Baxter finally got frustrated with AT&T and gave up on the process of transferring it into his name. Um so then his comments to me were, well I don't want the cell phone anymore so do you want to buy it from me? I said, no. I don't need a new cell phone. Nor would I ever pay that kind of price for a cell phone. Umm he then said uhh, well, he really didn't want it because he can get a free phone from his new girlfriend who works at Sprint. So he doesn't want to continue to make payments on the phone. He said it was under my name so he could care less and he was gonna send me the phone. And that's what he did.

Mary presented a portrait of Baxter as an irresponsible person through the formulation of his stance as "he could care less," followed by the details about how he got a free phone through his new girlfriend and how he had reneged on his agreement to pay. Descriptions like these, rich in self-face enhancement and other-face impugning, are routine ways of speaking in small claims court.

Attorney Speech Appears Less Intentionally Hostile than Litigant Speech

Talk conveys a different emotional stance toward the person with whom one is having a conflict based on two situational factors. Garcia (1991) initially identified the first situational element in her study of mediation: whether a person was having a face-to-face dispute with another individual versus directing talk about the other person's conduct to a third party. Talk directed to a third party, such as a mediator or judge about the other disputant, occurs in the third person ("she did X") rather than in the second person ("you did X"). Second-person descriptions more easily escalate into heated accusations and counter-accusations than do ones in the third-person. As all small claims conflict is third-party conflict due to the presence of the judge, parties mute their hostility in the court more strongly as compared with situations of personal conflict outside of the court's hearing.

Third-party small claims conflicts have a significant difference regarding the presence or absence of legal representation. In some cases, an attorney represents one party. Attorneys elicit descriptions of alleged wrongs through questions to witnesses. Unrepresented litigants often build portraits of self and other's conduct through assertions. An attorney-represented disputant, in contrast, responds to questions within a less straightforward, self-promoting facework. Put another way, attorney questioning involves face-attacking of the opposing party and face-defending of the client. In that sense, the attorney distances a represented disputant's facework from the self. For decades, scholars have recognized that the attorney questioning in trials do this kind of demeanor work (e.g., see Penman, 1990). Undermining the opposing party's face functions as part of the attorney job definition (Archer, 2011). An additional side effect is that attorney representation shields the client from performing these face-implicating actions.

Consider how face-attacking and face-defending worked in the cell phone case (Excerpt 3) where an attorney represented Baxter. In noting that his client's phone stopped working, the attorney implied a strong need for his client to get a new one. Furthermore, in asking about the giving of passcodes, the attorney began the process of depicting the plaintiff as lying when she treated the phone as a loan rather than a gift from girlfriend to boyfriend.

Excerpt 3 (Colorado, case 22 continued, A= attorney, P = Plaintiff)

A: You- you were aware that his phone stopped working, right?
P: I was aware that there were some issues with the phone. My phone also has issues but I keep it.
A: And he told you that he was going to get a new phone, did he not?
P: Umm he said he would like to get a new phone, he never said he was going to.
A: And you gave him passcodes uhh security codes in order to get the new phone. Is that right?

Attorneys are rare in small claims court. In the 55 cases that comprise this dataset, attorneys appeared in only three cases. Whether small claims courts should allow the presence of attorneys is a question that states answer differently. Some do not allow them, others allow them under restricted conditions, and still others allow them any time. What this analysis suggests is that attorney participation for one party will shape perceptions of both parties in ways that may be consequential to judge decisions.

Implications

Small claims are legal practices that require lay participants or their attorneys to make arguments for or against a claim that warrants monetary compensation. Parties make their claims in courtrooms that judges structure in markedly different ways, and where this structuring strongly shapes what and how the parties argue.

Arguments about the reasonableness of the conduct of self and other are different in kind from other kinds of arguments. Arguments about behaviors highlight and make the ways speakers talk to and about others more relevant. "When people describe other people," Ingrids (2014) argued in his study of family court, "they simultaneously make their own motives for doing so reflexively available" (p. 49).

In small claims court cases, argument quality is not the only issue. In conflict situations brought before the court, people work hard to show that they possess qualities such as moral principles, honesty, or reasonableness in their expectations in contrast to the disputing other. Sometimes these concerns facilitate good argument making; at other times they do not. Identifying the variety of concerns that animate talk is essential to understanding this argument-focused genre.

References

50-State Chart of Small Claims Court Dollar Limits. (2017, October 11). *Nolo*. Retrieved from http://nolo.com/legal-encyclopedia/small-claims-suits-how-much-30031.html

Archer, D. (2011). Cross-examining lawyers, facework and the adversarial courtroom. *Journal of Pragmatics, 43*(13), 3216–3230. doi: 10.1016/j.pragma.2011.06.007

Conley, J. M., & O'Barr, W. M. (1990). *Rules versus relationships: The ethnography of legal discourse*. Chicago, IL: University of Chicago Press.

Drew, P. (1992). Contested evidence in courtroom cross-examination: The case of a trial for rape. In P. Drew & J. Heritage (Eds.), *Talk at work: Interaction in institutional settings* (pp. 470–520). Cambridge, United Kingdom: Cambridge University Press.

Garcia, A. (1991). Dispute resolution without disputing: How the interactional organization of mediation hearings minimizes argument. *American Sociological Review, 56*(6), 818–835. Retrieved from http://jstor.org/stable/2096258

Goffman, E. (1955). On facework: An analysis of ritual elements in social interaction. *Psychiatry: Interpersonal and Biological Processes, 18*, 213–231. doi: 10.1162/15241730360580159

Goerdt, J. A. (1992). *Small claims and traffic court: Case management procedures, case characteristics, and outcomes in 12 urban districts*. Williamsburg, VA: National Center for State Courts.

Ingrids, H. (2014). Blame-account sequences in child custody disputes. *Discourse & Society, 25*(1), 47–64. doi:10.1177/0957926513508857

Penman, R. (1990). Facework & politeness: Multiple goals in courtroom discourse. *Journal of Language and Social Psychology, 9*(1-2), 15–38. doi: 10.1177/0261927X9091002

Ruhnka, J. C., & Weller, S. (1978). *Small claims courts: A national examination*. Williamsburg, VA: National Center for State Courts.

Toulmin, S. (1958). *The uses of argument*. London, United Kingdom: Cambridge University Press.

Tracy, K., & Caron, M. (2017). How the language style of small claims judges does ideological work. *Journal of Language and Social Psychology, 36*(3), 321–342. doi: 10.1177/0261927X16652191

Tracy, K., & Hodge, D., M. (2019). Discourse features of disputing in small claims hearings. In M. Evans, L. Jeffries, & J. O'Driscoll (Eds.), *The Routledge handbook of language in conflict* (Chpt 14). London, United Kingdom: Routledge.

van Eemeren, F. H. (2010). *Strategic maneuvering in argumentative discourse*: Extending the pragma-dialectical theory of argumentation. Amsterdam, The Netherlands: John Benjamins.

70
ARGUMENTATION AS A PRACTICAL DISCIPLINE

Robert T. Craig

This essay argues that the field of argumentation studies is, or should be, in part, a practical discipline: a field of knowledge production that cultivates reflective discourse and deliberation in a field of social practice. Aristotle's concept of *praxis*, Dewey's pragmatist theory of inquiry and other ideas in the traditions of practical philosophy, rhetoric, and social theory have informed the metatheory and methodology of practical discipline (Aristotle, trans. 2001; Craig, 1989, 2001, 2015; Dewey, 1938). Previous works have conceptualized the discipline of communication and addressed certain issues in argumentation theory from this approach (e.g., Craig, 1992, 1996). This essay contributes to the metatheory and methodology of argumentation studies by clarifying the essential role of practical discipline vis-à-vis other essential aspects of argumentation. I begin by showing that argumentation has a practical dimension (*praxis*) that is complementary, but not reducible to either of its equally necessary epistemic (*theoria*) or technical/productive (*poeisis*) dimensions. Second, while acknowledging the multiple approaches available for studying *praxis* of argumentation, I propose *grounded practical theory* (GPT)—an empirically-informed, normative reconstruction of social practices designed to inform reflective thinking—as one methodological approach to practical discipline. Third, I review several studies that illustrate applications of this methodology in the field of argumentation. Finally, I reflect on the tensions and complementarities between argumentation as a practical discipline and the equally important theoretical and technical dimensions of argumentation studies.

Argumentation as *Theoria, Poiesis,* and *Praxis*

The metatheory of practical discipline makes heuristic use of Aristotle's categories of *theoria, poeisis,* and *praxis*. For Aristotle (trans. 2001, pp. 1022-1036; see also Craig, 2016; Levine, 1995, pp. 105-120; Lobkowicz, 1967, pp. 3-46), these terms referred to kinds of human activity that involve different intellectual virtues or forms of knowledge cultivated by different kinds of disciplines. *Theoria,* the activity of contemplating eternal, noncontingent truth develops the intellectual virtue of *episteme* (knowledge for its own sake) in sciences like astronomy and physics. *Poeisis,* the activity of making things, develops the intellectual virtue of *techne* (rationally grounded craft skill) in sciences like shipbuilding and rhetoric. *Praxis,* the activity of contingent human affairs, develops the intellectual virtue of *phronesis* (practical wisdom) in sciences like ethics and politics.

Argumentation and its associated science of argumentation studies involve all of Aristotle's three types of human activity and the associated intellectual virtues. Argumentation, not all at once, but at different moments, involves: (a) a *theoretical* activity and science devoted to knowledge for its own sake of non-contingent principles of rational validity; (b) a *technical-productive* activity and science devoted to the development and use of rational methods for the design and analysis of arguments, discussion formats, and related objects; and (c) a *practical* activity and science devoted to the cultivation of wise and effective argumentation in contingent human affairs. As a theoretical discipline, argumentation studies develop normative principles and models of argument based on philosophical theories of rationality, for example, informal logic and pragma-dialectics. As a technical-productive discipline, argumentation studies develop techniques for producing or reconstructing arguments and related procedures, such as using design principles (Jackson, 2015), heuristic schemes (e.g., *stasis* and *topoi*), and automated (computational) systems. Finally, as a practical discipline, argumentation studies investigate practices and deliberate on problems of judgment and action in the situated conduct of argumentation.

The practical dimension of argumentation, although analytically distinct from the theoretical and technical dimensions, still relates to them. Theoretical principles can inform reflective thinking and deliberation about argumentation practices. For example, one might use the pragma-dialectical ideal of critical discussion to reflect critically on an actual discussion process. Theories of argumentative techniques can also inform practical deliberation, as one might consider which of several discussion formats would be most appropriate and effective in a current situation. Although both argumentation theory and technique can inform argumentation *praxis*, scholars should not reduce the field to either. As Aristotle knew no theory can dictate what to do in any concrete situation, and no technique provides the wisdom to know *when* or *how* to use it in practice (Aristotle, trans. 2001, pp. 122-136; see also Craig, 2016). Social contexts in which actors confront contingencies and dilemmas affecting the application of principles and the use of techniques always situate argumentation practice. Arguers require both deliberation and judgment when considering the particulars of a situation. For example, the rational validity of a critique may not be a sufficient reason to voice the criticism at a given moment; instead, this is a matter of prudential judgment that should take account of interpersonal and other considerations. *Praxis*, thus, is an essential dimension of argumentation irreducible to decontextualized theories or technical procedures without distortion, rendering practical inquiry a necessary role in a rounded discipline of argumentation studies. Accordingly, argumentation studies should be, in part, a practical discipline.

Grounded Practical Theory: A Methodology for Practical Discipline

Many valid methodological approaches to practical inquiry see widespread usage in argumentation studies. Some examples include the rhetorical-critical approaches traditionally well-represented at the Alta conferences, design theory (e.g., Jackson, 2015), and pragma-dialectical studies of "strategic maneuvering" (e.g., van Eemeren, 2010). Here, I propose grounded practical theory (GPT) as a methodological approach explicitly based on the philosophy of communication as a practical discipline (Craig, 1989, 1996, 2001, 2015; Craig & Tracy, 1995, 2014). This essay builds on prior work by explaining and illustrating the potential usefulness of GPT in argumentation studies.

Defined as "the grounded discovery, critique, and theoretical reconstruction of communication problems, techniques, and situated ideals" (Craig & Tracy, 1995, p. 250), GPT is a method of theory construction intended to cultivate reflective discourse and deliberation in the social practice of communication. In contrast to empirical social-scientific theory, GPT addresses normative (ought) questions. In contrast to normative philosophical theory, which, of course, also addresses normative questions, GPT strives to build empirically grounded theories maximally relevant to problems that communicators experience in practice. GPT conceives the *rational reconstruction* of practices as an idealized model, developed through empirical observation, critical reflection, and creative conceptualization. It provides a reasoned basis for critical and deliberative reflection on conduct. The rational reconstruction of a practice occurs at three conceptually interrelated levels: (a) the *problem* level (dilemmas that typically arise in the practice); (b) the *technical* level (strategies and techniques for addressing problems); and (c) the *philosophical* level (normative principles, grounded in the "situated ideals" of practitioners, that provide a reasoned basis for choosing among the available techniques for addressing problems).

The GPT research process begins with the selection and tentative conceptual framing of a communication practice for study (Craig, 2015). In argumentation studies these practices are ones in which arguments (in the sense of making and/or having arguments) play an important role, such as academic colloquium discussions, oral argument in appellate courts, public meetings, and public deliberation groups. Once researchers select and frame a practice for study, they proceed with empirical data collection (documents, recordings, field observations, interviews, etc.) and qualitative analysis of that data, conceptual reconstruction of the practice within the three-level framework, and articulation of normative theoretical claims concerning the practice. As with most qualitative research, the phases of GPT are not strictly linear. For example, researchers may reframe an argumentative practice during later phases of analysis, and the partial or tentative reconstruction may guide early phases of data gathering. Finally, individual GPT studies do not necessarily produce a complete theoretical reconstruction of a complex practice, but instead usually focus on selected aspects, such as a key dilemma or a salient range of techniques—all the while aiming toward a conceptually integrated reconstruction of the practice as a whole.

Exemplary GPT Studies in Argumentation

Karen Tracy's (1997) early work on *intellectual discussion* in academic colloquia served as a model for the development of GPT methodology and its potential value for argumentation studies. Tracy recorded and analyzed colloquium meetings in an academic department where faculty and graduate students gathered weekly for a research presentation and discussion of the research. She also interviewed colloquium participants at two academic institutions and observed similar forms of intellectual discussion in other settings.

Tracy's (1997) study revealed institutional tensions between two situated ideals concerning the role of argument in intellectual discussion. The *dialectic* ideal envisioned intellectual discussion as rigorous debate and criticism of ideas without regard to the personal feelings or needs of participants; the *constructive criticism* ideal envisioned intellectual discussion as supportive communication that builds community and helps participants to develop their ideas in positive ways. Both ideals involved argumentation, but the interesting normative implication was that assessments of argumentation in practice depend on assumptions about the communicative purpose of the discussion. Tracy (1997) argued that intellectual discussion should attend to both ideals, using discourse techniques to manage the inevitable tensions between them.

A similar conclusion about the need for prudential judgment in adjusting argumentation to its communicative purpose emerged from Craig and Tracy's (2005) comparative study of *the issue* in college critical thinking discussions and public school board meetings. In argumentation theory, the issue refers to an object of contention that defines the normative focus of an argument or a critical discussion. Yet Goodwin (2002) pointed out that issues exist as arguers pragmatically design them and the definition of the issue itself is quite often a matter of contention: in short, the issue becomes the issue. Analyzing references to the issue in practical metadiscourse, Craig and Tracy (2005) found strongly contrasting pragmatic functions of this phrase in two situations. In critical thinking classrooms, the issue functioned to focus the topic of discussion on a controversial question, generally in line with Goodwin's (2002) criteria for designing issues. In school board meetings, however, public participants used the word "issue" "to describe an existing bad state of affairs, speaking as if everyone would see the event in the same way" (Craig & Tracy, 2005, p. 21). Whereas the critical thinking classroom pragmatically constrained participants to focus on a controversial issue for discussion, the preferred norm in school board meetings was to define the situation as community problem-solving, a cooperative endeavor that should avoid controversy and heated debate. Craig and Tracy (2005) concluded that framing a group situation as either controversy on an issue or as a problem-solving discussion is a rhetorical choice that should consider factors such as the importance of clarifying differences of opinion, the time available for group action, and the level of agreement among participants.

Closely related to the metadiscourse of the issue is Leighter and Black's (2010) concept of *raising a question* in their study of public meeting discourse. Raising a question, in contrast to asking a question, is an argumentative move that proposes a topic for discussion without presupposing a readily available answer. Leighter and Black (2010) analyzed various rhetorical uses of raising a question and related terms in public meeting discourse and advocated for the following normative principle:

> Participants in the process of a speech situation, such as a meeting, should raise questions to meet the goals of the group, including achieving clarity, helping to structure conversation, and adding to information that doesn't tell the whole story. To do so can be interpreted by group members as a unitary, or collaborative, communicative action that helps the group achieve its goals.
>
> *(Leighter & Black, 2010, p. 563)*

In another comparative study of metadiscourse in argumentation, Craig and Tracy (2010) examined the use of argument metalanguage (argument, issue, claim, evidence, assumption, etc.) in United States state appellate courts and a New Jersey state legislative hearing, all on the issue of same-sex marriage. They found that argument metalanguage was much more prevalent in the appellate courts even though the discourse of both settings was "chock[ed]-full" of arguments. Personal or group self-expression tended to frame legislative hearing discourse, whereas dialectical engagement with meta-discursively objectified arguments framed appellate court discourse. Here again, the use of framing devices was a rhetorical choice, but the normative role of argumentation in each communication practice (appellate court arguments or testimony at legislative hearings) depended on situated ideals of communicative purpose within a practice.

Finally, Sprain and Ivancic (2017) used GPT to re-conceptualize the norm of *openness* in deliberative democratic argumentation as a discursive stance. Techniques of claiming an unformed opinion, withholding criticism, soliciting perspectives, and expressing a desire to hear other perspectives constructed their norm of openness. For Sprain and Ivancic, the discursive stance of openness responded to problems typically arising in deliberative discussions, including disagreement (which is communicatively problematic, but democratically normative), the need to form an opinion, dysfunctional problem-solving in the community, and making sense of the deliberative process. The researchers offered, in conclusion, the following normative claims: "We question whether it is reasonable to expect participants to refrain from holding strong opinions before deliberation in community contexts" (p. 253), and "instead of promoting deliberation as a place to develop opinions, we suggest theorizing deliberation as an opportunity to listen to, consider, and learn from other perspectives" (p. 254).

Conclusion: Practical Discipline in the Network of Argumentation Studies

Argumentation is communicative praxis that requires deliberative choice in the formulation and use of arguments in each situation. As an approach to a practical discipline of argumentation, GPT strives to inform deliberative choice by theorizing the problems, techniques, and normative ideals that constitute communicative practices. Treating argumentation as a practical discipline has a necessary place in argumentation studies because the praxis of argumentation is not reducible to theory or technique. Argumentation, however, is not only praxis but has equally necessary theoretical-epistemic and technical-productive aspects, which is why argumentation studies can only function as a practical discipline in part. The *theoria* of argumentation seeks for principles by which to judge the rational quality of arguments and argumentative procedures. Regardless if our epistemological scruples no longer allow us to view such principles as universal and non-contingent, the principles must be sufficient to serve their purpose as normative standards that are independent of whatever practical choices are made in each situation. Without this theoretical search for rational principles, a practical discipline of argumentation would cease to be distinguishable from studies of discourse and communication in general.

In the technical-productive dimension, argumentation studies investigate techniques for producing and critically analyzing arguments and argumentative procedures. Jackson (2015) proposed to develop this dimension of argumentation under the rubric of design thinking. Invented designs such as systems of logic, scientific methods, and frameworks for dispute resolution extend human rationality, enabling the reliable production of arguments, decisions, or discussion formats accountable to rational principles. As Jackson (2015) pointed out, argumentation designs "can start with either epistemic or social goals—or with other goals entirely" (p. 253), allowing them to be adapted to practical needs, but my argument implies that they would not be argumentation designs if they were entirely unresponsive to epistemic standards. I would also add that the availability of a technical design for producing arguments, and so on, does not eliminate the necessity of deliberative choice among the designs available in any given instance.

Tensions among the epistemic, technical, and practical dimensions of argumentation studies can be mutually corrective. In particular, normative theories and technical inventions should inform practical inquiry. In the process scholars should resist the excesses of normative idealism or technical reductionism. On the other hand, critiques of practical inquiry from theoretical and productive nodes in the network of argumentation studies can serve to correct its characteristic excesses of descriptivism and deficiencies of technical specificity (see Craig & Tracy, 2014).

References

Aristotle. (2001). *Ethica nicomachean* (W. D. Ross, Trans.). In R. McKeon (Ed.), *The basic works of Aristotle* (pp. 927–1112). New York, NY: Random House.

Craig, R. T. (1989). Communication as a practical discipline. In B. Dervin, L. Grossberg, B. J. O'Keefe, & E. Wartella (Eds.), *Rethinking communication: Volume 1: Paradigm issues* (pp. 97–122). Thousand Oaks, CA: SAGE.

Craig, R. T. (1992). Practical communication theory and the pragma-dialectical approach in conversation. In F. H. van Eemeren, R. Grootendorst, J. A. Blair, & Ch. A. Willard (Eds.), *Argumentation illuminated* (pp. 51–61). Amsterdam, The Netherlands: International Center for the Study of Argumentation.

Craig, R. T. (1996). Practical-theoretical argumentation. *Argumentation, 10*(4), 461–474. doi:10.1007/BF00142979

Craig, R. T. (2001). Dewey and Gadamer on practical reflection: Toward a methodology for the practical disciplines. In D. K. Perry (Ed.), *American pragmatism and communication research* (pp. 131–148). Mahwah, NJ: Lawrence Erlbaum.

Craig, R. T. (2015). Grounded practical theory. In K. Tracy, C. Ilie, & T. Sandel (Eds.), *The international encyclopedia of language and social interaction* (Vol. 2, pp. 703–713). Malden, MA: Wiley-Blackwell.

Craig, R. T. (2016). Theory and practice. In K. B. Jensen & R. T. Craig (Eds.), *The international encyclopedia of communication theory and philosophy* (Vol. 4, pp. 2049–2068). Malden, MA: Wiley-Blackwell.

Craig, R. T., & Tracy, K. (1995). Grounded practical theory: The case of intellectual discussion. *Communication Theory, 5*(3), 248–272. doi:10.1111/j.1468-2885.1995.tb00108.x

Craig, R. T., & Tracy, K. (2005). "The issue" in argumentative practice and theory. In F. H. van Eemeren & P. Houtlosser (Eds.), *The practice of argumentation* (pp. 11–28). Amsterdam, The Netherlands: John Benjamins.

Craig, R. T., & Tracy, K. (2010). Framing discourse as argument in appellate courtrooms: Three cases on same-sex marriage. In D. S. Gouran (Ed.), *The functions of argument and social context* (pp. 46–53). Washington, DC: National Communication Association.

Craig, R. T., & Tracy, K. (2014). Building grounded practical theory in applied communication research: Introduction to the special issue. *Journal of Applied Communication Research, 42*(3), 229–243. doi:10.1080/00909882.2014.916410

Dewey, J. (1938). *Logic: The theory of inquiry*. New York, NY: Henry Holt.

Goodwin, J. (2002). Designing issues. In F. H. van Eemeren & P. Houtlosser (Eds.), *Dialectic and rhetoric: The warp and woof of argumentation analysis* (pp. 81–96). Dordrecht, The Netherlands: Kluwer Academic.

Jackson, S. (2015). Design thinking in argumentation theory and practice. *Argumentation, 29*(3), 243–263. doi:10.1007/s10503-015-9353-7

Leighter, J. L., & Black, L. (2010). "I'm just raising the question": Terms for talk and practical metadiscursive argument in public meetings. *Western Journal of Communication, 74*(5), 547–569. doi:10.1080/10570314.2010.512281

Levine, D. N. (1995). *Visions of the sociological tradition*. Chicago, IL: The University of Chicago Press.

Lobkowicz, N. (1967). *Theory and practice: History of a concept from Aristotle to Marx*. Notre Dame, IN: University of Notre Dame Press.

Sprain, L., & Ivancic, S. (2017). Communicating openness in deliberation. *Communication Monographs, 84*(2), 241–257. doi:10.1080/03637751.2016.1257141

Tracy, K. (1997). *Colloquium: Dilemmas of academic discourse*. Norwood, NJ: Ablex.

van Eemeren, F. H. (2010). *Strategic maneuvering in argumentative discourse: Extending the pragma-dialectical theory of argumentation*. Amsterdam, The Netherlands: John Benjamins.

71

NETWORKS, NORMS, AND THE PROBLEM OF CAPABLE ARGUERS

Timothy Barouch

Scholars of public argument maintain a unique commitment to studying the constitutive force of communication in creating political power relationships. This paper argues that networking argument studies can foster interdisciplinary inquiry by highlighting the normative commitments of argumentation theory to reciprocal relationships among arguers, which in turn informs the critical reading protocols of network theorists. To make a valuable interdisciplinary contribution, public argument scholars should better specify the role of dialectic and rhetoric as they relate to argumentation as an ethical practice, including its normative commitments to address asymmetries among participants in argument networks.

This essay proceeds in three parts. The first section considers the contributions of one of the most prominent network theorists of public communication: Bruno Latour. Latour has taken center stage in the discipline of communication studies and in the humanities writ large over the past two decades, centering on his provocative claim that objects have agency and his exhortation to focus on a Parliament of Things as a new model for democracy. The rise of network theory is explainable, in part, by its family resemblance to Toulmin's canonical work *The Uses of Argument* (2003), as descriptions of the background conditions for communication and argument. As Toulmin used his dissatisfaction with formal logic's rigid vocabularies as the impetus to create a new model for assessing the strength of arguments, Latour's network theory rephrases fundamental problems of social theory as a metaphorical network to more accurately account for democracy's contemporary recurring failures (Latour, 1993, 2011).

This work provides argumentation scholars with an opportunity to situate its distinctive contribution to the study of democratic public culture by specifying argumentation as a social activity alongside descriptions of communication as participation in a network. To succeed, the field must avoid the temptation to simply import and circulate Latour's critical concepts as truisms that grant permission to read newer and different digital artifacts, or else provide argumentation with a veneer of newfound popularity by hitching its wagon to network theory's star. A different metaphor—the import/export metaphor—suggests itself for the question of interdisciplinary exchange between argumentation studies and network theories. Rather than merely importing the work of network approaches to communication, argumentation studies should also work to contrast the two approaches to locate places where they may mutually coexist and, at times, where they conflict.

This paper begins that task by sustaining the thesis that Latour's social theory of networks calls into question two fundamental tenets of contemporary argumentation—that argumentation is a social activity that is in part aimed at creating ethical relationships between arguers, and in part by producing epistemological confidence in its products. To explain, I review Latour's use of the concept of a network, including its definition, its political import, and its relative antipathy towards dialectic as a mode of political argument. Then, I turn to the field of argumentation studies, identifying dialectic's importance within a tradition of argumentative concern with democratic ethics and epistemological confidence. Finally, I conclude by marking the ways that argumentation scholars can read Latour's project as an impetus for pushing a productive agenda for new research forward. The conclusion calls on argumentation scholars to tend more carefully to the capabilities of arguers as critical protocols for appraising better and worse arguments, and to revisit the relationship between rhetoric and dialectic in methodological work.

Latour's Networks: Things, Epistemologies, and Dialectics

Tending to the meaning and function of the term "network" in Latour's thinking draws out his methodological and epistemological concerns and helps to make sense of his criticism of dialectic. Latour (2011) wrote that the term "designated a mode of inquiry that learns to list, at the occasion of a trial, the unexpected beings necessary for any entity to exist" (p. 4). As he elaborated:

> [Networks are] the series of little jolts that allow the inquirer to register around any given substance the vast deployment of its attributes. Or, rather, what takes any substance that had seemed at first self contained [...] and transforms it into what it needs to subsist through a complex ecology of tributaries, allies, accomplices, and helpers.
>
> *(p. 4)*

Latour's examples helped to illustrate what he believed network thinking could generate. In his essay on *Dingpolitik* (which sketches his idea about the Parliament of Things), Latour (2004) referenced Peter Sloterdijk's appeal that "the US Air Force should have added to its military paraphernalia a 'pneumatic parliament' that could be parachuted at the rear of the front [....] Instant democracy would just be delivered!" (pp. 7-8). Individuals cannot imagine democracy without its objects—a culture's "local ecological requirements, material infrastructure, and long-held habits" (p. 8). He paired this story with the story of Colin Powell's infamous address to the United Nations that justified the invasion of Iraq. "Every one of the slides was a blatant lie—and the more that time has passed, the more blatant it has become" (p. 8).

Both the pneumatic parliament and Powell's catastrophic UN speech point to an epistemological crisis of modern liberal democracy which erroneously assumes that following particular parliamentary procedures are signs of correct democratic decisions. Modern democratic cultures think that procedures can guarantee that arguments proceed according to facts and exclude mere unproven assertions. Many devalue those who resist the conclusions of fact-driven policy because they have "fallen prey to subjective passions" (Latour, 2004, p. 9). But this attitude is misguided, because "to provide complete undisputable proof has become a rather messy, pesky, risky business" and "to offer a *public* proof, big enough and certain enough to convince the whole world [...] seems now almost beyond reach—and always was" (p. 9). In its place, the world needs a *Dingpolitik* in which, among other things, "the inherent limits imposed by speech impairment, cognitive weaknesses and all sorts of handicaps are no longer denied," and which is marked by "assemblages in search of a rightful assembly [...] under the provisional and fragile Phantom Public" (p. 31).

Although Latour has no preoccupation with dialectic as an abstract concept—no surprise, because he is working to describe the material relationships between and among actors for specific political purposes—he nevertheless has demonstrated antipathy for dialectic. He remarked in *We Have Never Been Modern* (Latour, 1993) that a dialectical approach replicates dualism, which "feigns to overcome it by loops and spirals and other complex acrobatic figures" (p. 55). His concern with dialectic stemmed from the consequences of the method. He criticized the dialectical procedure of opposing categories in order to transcend them on the ground that they failed to account for the multiplicities that form the contrasting objects in the first place. What appeared as poles in a dialectical opposition offered "public life with a promise of salvation worse than the evil against which it offers protection" (Latour, 1999, p. 40). Latour used this antipathy towards dialectic as a critique of dualisms such as subject-object and nature-society in favor of a notion of political ecology that marks the collective assemblages of humans and non-humans.

Only in dismissing these familiar oppositions can argumentation scholars move beyond the failures of representation that plague modern political cultures. For Latour, the implicit organization of new collective arrangements was premised on the common capacities of unrepresented entities. Chief among these were the capacities to speak and to have effects, which even natural objects possessed (if primarily through experts). At the core of this project was to conceive of natural objects as "actors" that qualify as matters of public concern. This approach culminated in claims to reconceive political practice by meditating explicitly on how things were made public. This focus on things—*Dingpolitik*—strived to create "object-oriented democracy" that investigated two sides of the question of political representation: the side that "designates the ways to gather the legitimate people around some issue" and the side that focuses on "the object of concern [presented] to the eyes and ears of those who have been assembled around it" (Latour, 2004, p. 6).

Latour was not necessarily an enemy of dialectic because he was an enemy of argument. He readily embraced dispute and imagined evidence and rhetorical style as part and parcel of a politics of re-presentation: "provisional assertions [...] imperfect proof [...] complicated machinery of assembly [...] argumentation, negotiation, and conclusion" (Latour, 2004, p. 16). Rather, he opposed dialectic as the privileged method to achieve realistic political representational processes. This mode not only failed to deliver on its promise of synthesizing diversity into a *general will*, it also "kept generating aborted monsters and ended up discouraging people from thinking politically" (Latour, 2004, p. 28).

According to Latour (2004), placing faith in a particularized dialectical procedure flattened multiplicities and produced trained incapacities in citizens. Post-Enlightenment political procedures allowed "90 percent of the contradictory passions [to be] spirited away" (p. 29) because of an impoverished sense of progress framed as fundamentally unrepresentative oppositions: "Are they progressive or reactionary? Enlightened or archaic? In the vanguard or in the rear guard?" (p. 29). This twin movement—the forgetting of capabilities to make things matters of public concern and the perverse incentives of those in power to exclude perspectives—combined to make for a desiccated political field. The next section explicates the role of dialectic in argumentation studies to contrast the argumentation approach with Latour's use of networks in pursuit of a *Dingpolitik*.

Argumentation as a Practice of Democratic Ethics

Unlike Latour's aversion to dialectics, argumentation scholars have consistently maintained some core of symmetrical dialogue to justify the study and critique of public argument in relationship to democracy. Ehninger (1970) wrote that argumentation was a type of correction in which arguers maintained a bilateral relationship. Relationships sustained through argumentation contrasted with coercive relationships (like the teacher/student or layman/skeptic) because the latter were unilateral, oriented towards conformity, were unconcerned with justice, and posed no risk to the participants' personal integrity (Ehninger, 1970). Argumentation promised a communicative means to claim personhood because it better respected our capacities to reason democratically, making it a superior dispute resolution practice than reference to authority, chance, or intuition (Ehninger, 1970). Ehninger specified the object of argumentation studies: Argumentation concerns a specialized practice marked by a relationship between the arguers. Brockriede (1972) developed this strain of thought through descriptions of arguers. Although the descriptions can be roles that we inhabit from time to time, the ethical idealism of Brockriede's article was unmistakable: some arguers used violence and threat (rapists), others used trickery and misrepresentation (seducers), while lovers valued argumentative equality, cooperation with one's opponent, and shared decision-making.

Brockriede's position implies that argumentation at its best involves ethical relationships of equality, but it does not represent our constant communicative state. These characteristics persisted as the field grew in stature and the most prominent research programs gave the ethics of argumentation a prized place in their work. The pragma-dialectics school associated with van Eemeren and Grootendorst (2004) relied on the model of a critical discussion to generate rules for arguers to uphold. Douglas Walton, whether specifying what is wrong with propaganda (2007) or the conditions under which formal fallacies are fallacious (1995), consistently emphasized the ethical relationship between arguers as simultaneously a marking of the practice and criteria for its appraisal. Scholars of argumentation know that they are in the presence of argument because of the way that arguers treat each other, and we also evaluate desirable arguments based on the same information.

Not coincidentally, both research programs carefully mark the contribution that dialectic makes to the study of argumentation. For Walton (2003), dialectic was a "standard of rationality against which an argument used in [conversation] can be measured" (p. 196). This standard is significant not merely for the methodological influence Walton identified, but also for understanding the ethics of argumentative practice. Dialectic supports the values of argumentation insofar as arguers test their commitments in a dialogue whose goal is persuasion. Because dialectic moves from generally accepted propositions to controversial ones through inference, Walton relied on it as a method to evaluate how argumentation can result either in freely changing one's mind or deepening one's original position. This process occurs because argumentation reveals inner commitments—individuals come to know them through the back and forth of persuasive dialogue.

This position articulates a standard for dialectic in the ethics of argument criticism by articulating a principle of relevance. Walton (1999) explored dialectical relevance as a test of arguments, claiming that a dialectical method that used argument chains and tested propositions according to previously articulated commitments of the arguers could form the basis of a relevance principle. A standpoint is relevant if it responds to one's interlocutor in a manner that advances the dialogue. And, of course, the dialectical portion of van Eeme-ren's and Grootendorst's pragma-dialectical approach supported the ethics of democratic decision-making because of its orientation towards their model of a critical discussion. The pragma-dialectic argumentative ideal includes rules designed to sharpen the issues in dispute and place obligations on parties to serve that goal, such as requiring that a party may defend a standpoint only by advancing argumentation relating to that standpoint (relevance rule), and requiring that parties retract standpoints that they fail to defend (closure rule). These rules (and Walton's focus on commitments) can trace a line of influence back to Ehninger and Brockriede's statements about personhood and dignity of the participants. By disclosing and refining the participants' respective commitments, argumentation promises to tell us something about who we are.

Are Networks and Dialectics Complementary or Adversarial?

Returning to Latour's ambivalence about dialectic raises some important challenges to argu-mentation studies. First, it questions the extent to which dialectic can serve as an ethical practice. If the argumentative relationship is ethical because the arguers have obligations to be responsive and relevant, and because they mutually affirm each others' personhood through this reciprocal process of reason-giving, it is fair to ask whether dialectic can, at times, obscure and disqualify "matters of concern" when it is claiming to assert a normative commitment conforming to a particular model of analysis. Methodologically, this matters, for example, when argumentation scholars are reconstructing discourse. What elements and objects get left out? Which objects does the analyst deem irrelevant? That such judgments derive from a critical-objective point of view is far from clear. What is the status of a less-than-capable arguer? Does a concept such as the principle of charity equate to Latour's notion of prostheses to assist less capable speakers?

Second, Latour's critique of procedural politics raises the question of "why argue" directly, calling for future research in argumentation across disciplines to further articulate its epistemo-logical benefits. Zarefsky (2009) provided the best contemporary answer to the question about why one should engage in argumentation: It provides answers to questions about what lacks certainty, and argumentation theorists are confident about their answers because they have arrived at them according to procedures that proved reliable in the past. But to take Latour's work seriously entails questioning whether procedures eclipse certain objects, rendering irrele-vant or illegible certain motives of arguers. For example, Zarefsky (2009) wrote that arguers share a common goal of "reaching the best possible decision under the circumstances" (p. 302), but his description skirts the dreaded parliamentary procedures against which Latour wrote: "arguers […] play the role of committed advocates […] so that the proposition […] under examination would receive a particularly rigorous test" (p. 302).

To conclude, I want to suggest a place of agreement between Latour and theorists of argumentation to develop a research agenda for these important questions—the relationship between rhetoric and dialectic in the study of political argument. Latour (2004) has expli-citly referred to the presence of rhetoric as the study through which we could "trace the frail conduits through which proofs and truths are allowed to enter the sphere of politics" (p. 9). The common refrain in argumentation studies is that rhetoric is local (or "anthropo-logical") and dialectic makes claims to both a higher level of abstraction and universality. This refrain leads to the conclusion that both disciplines can and should inform the study of argumentation—"the two arts speak[ing] to one another in a pattern of call and response [...] in balanced verses like those recited by the chorus" (Leff, 2000, p. 252). Latour seems decidedly more pessimistic about the prospects of dialectic in political argument because it covers over relationships among and between matters of concern. For Latour, the relationship between dialectic and rhetoric is less a harmonious call and response than a tug of war or zero-sum game. Focus on particular procedures detracts from focus on matters of concern, and dialectic also covers over important relationships and chains that bring objects into existence in the first place.

These areas may be fruitful for continued research in argumentation studies to develop connections with social theory and its pursuit of networks. The relationship between rhetoric and dialectic can provide new insights into whether dialectic as a communication practice (and critical method) advances ethical democratic relationships. It may also be productive in advancing our understanding about why we argue, pressuring us to further specify the relationship between matters of concern and matters of procedure. Rather than using Latour as a permission slip to study networks and the agency of objects, or else a stamp of approval to validate the standard ways we conduct our inquiries, we should read him as a friendly foil—with care and skepticism, presenting an opportunity to think about our core commitments anew.

References

Brockriede, W. (1972). Arguers as lovers. *Philosophy & Rhetoric, 5*(1), 1–11. Retrieved from http://jstor.org/stable/40237210

Ehninger, D. (1970). Argument as method: its nature, its limitations and its uses. *Speech Monographs, 37*(2), 101–110. doi:10.1080/03637757009375654

Latour, B. (1993). *We have never been modern* (C. Porter, Trans.). Cambridge, MA: Harvard University Press. (Original work published in 1991 in French)

Latour, B. (2004). *Politics of nature: How to bring the sciences into democracy* (C. Porter, Trans.). Cambridge, MA: Harvard University Press. (Original work published in 1999 in French).

Latour, B. (2005). From Realpolitik to Dingpolitik—An introduction to making things public. In B. Latour & P. Weibel (Eds.), *Making things public: Atmospheres of democracy*. Cambridge, MA: Harvard University Press.

Latour, B. (2011). Networks, societies, spheres: Reflections of an actor-network theorist [Special issue, M. Castells, Ed.]. *International Journal of Communication, 5*, 796–810. Retrieved from http://ijoc.org

Leff, M. (2000). Rhetoric and dialectic in the twenty-first century. *Argumentation, 14*(3), 241–254. doi:10.1023/A:1007848912283

Toulmin, S. E. (2003). *The uses of argument*. Cambridge, United Kingdom: Cambridge University Press.

van Eemeren, F. H., & Grootendorst, R. (2004). *A systematic theory of argumentation: The pragma-dialectical approach*. Cambridge, United Kingdom: Cambridge University Press.

Walton, D. N. (1995). *A pragmatic theory of fallacy*. Tuscaloosa, AL: University of Alabama Press.

Walton, D. N. (2003). *Ethical argumentation*. Lanham, MD: Lexington Books.

Walton, D. N. (2007). *Media argumentation: Dialectic, persuasion, and rhetoric*. Cambridge, United Kingdom: Cambridge University Press.

Walton, D. N., & Krabbe, E. C. W. (1995). *Commitment in dialogue: Basic concepts of interpersonal reasoning*. Albany, NY: SUNY Press.

Zarefsky, D. (2009). What does an argument culture look like? *Informal Logic, 29*(3), 296–308. doi:10.22329/il.v29i3.2845

72

THE MICROPOLITICS OF CONTROL

Fascism, Desire, and Argument in President Trump's America

George F. (Guy) McHendry, Jr. and Nicholas S. Paliewicz

As the vote count settled in the 2016 election, Donald Trump emerged as the 45th President of the United States. For many supporters, Trump's victory, coming off his aggressive campaign rhetoric, validated their worldview. Conversely, some supporters of Secretary Clinton felt shock and disbelief at the notion that any reasonable person could vote for Trump. These responses represented two of many reactions to a victory that ostensibly violated conventional political norms and pre-election polling results. Here, we argue that theories of argumentative assemblages, which draw upon alternative forms of reasoning, help explain the chasm that emerged in the 2016 election in ways normative pragmatic theories of argument could not. In short, we see the 2016 election as an exemplar where the desires motivating and sustaining argumentation turn away from clash and decision-making in the pragma-dialectical model, instead evincing a model of domination and control as the key to decision-making.

With the advent of digital screens, social media networks, and online media, argumentation increasingly privileges rhetorical force over critical decision-making. The transformation of society into literal and figurative networks that alter the possibilities for argument encounters facilitates this transition (Castells, 2010). For instance, the fact that Trump disseminated his argumentative propositions on Twitter, which White House Press Secretary Sean Spicer recently declared "official [presidential] statements" (quoted in Landers, 2017, para. 2), troubles the utility of dialectical models of argumentation. Argumentative networks activate to reject the existence of alternative positions and subjectivities that dialectical analysis requires.

Our point is not to deny the utility of pragma-dialectical approaches to argument in some deliberative situations; however, we see instances where emergent argumentative forms present such challenges. Consider some of the basic tenets of the pragma-dialectical model. To van Eemeren and Grootendorst (1987), pragma-dialectics is a consensualistic conception of discourse that defines a clear objective for argumentation and argumentative discourse which, at its roots, holds that successful arguments ought to adhere to pragmatic rules (e.g., the freedom rule, obligation to defend rule, standpoint rule, relevance rule) and avoid logical fallacies (e.g., *ad hominem, tu quoque, circumstantial, post hoc ergo propter hoc*). This model assumes argument subjects are inherently reasonable, singular, human speaking subjects, which limit argumentation to face-to-face interactions between reason-making human participants. These assumptions, though useful in some situations, are ill equipped to explain the force of *assembled argument.*

In our recent essay on assembled arguments, we argue that human and non-human argumentative actors often function to sow doubt rather than reach consensus (Paliewicz & McHendry, 2017). We contend assembled arguments gain force through conditioning affects and enticing desires, rather than adhering to idealistic standards for constructive argument. Instead of seeking to resolve disputations through critical rational debate, assembled arguments are ontological forces beyond reason that utilize desire-based dissemination to control networks and bodies of argument production. We consider argument assemblages to be *postdialectical* because they surpass assumptions that good reasons matter by jettisoning the believed primacy of reason in argument situations. Postdialectics supplement scholarship on the networked public sphere (Pfister, 2011) and networked rhetoric (Pfister, 2014) by enabling the study of how desires, forces, and affects flow through argument networks. Networks of argument can enhance deliberative democracy and social change; however, they can also create conditions necessary for the rise of fascism. We suggest that argumentation scholars should understand networked argument from a postdialectical perspective that assumes effective argument does not have to conform to normative ideals.

In a political world where coalitions of state and non-state actors circumvent dialectical argumentation, we suggest arguments which express fascist desires emerge as a strategy to limit the possibilities of clash for subaltern bodies. We advance a program of study for assembled arguments by examining how such networks serve as tools for domination. Our analysis contributes to networked considerations of argument by demonstrating how argument networks enact fascistic desire and gain force to subjugate subaltern bodies.

Given the sustained hostility related to the 2016 election and its potential relevance to the subject at hand, this essay explores the political-desires that network with the argumentative efforts of the Trump campaign and administration. Moving from our existing work on argument assemblages, we argue President Trump frequently utilizes argumentative forms that appeal to assembled, collective, micro-political, fascist desires. Such arguments reside in collective desires to dominate the other—making the submission of various identity groups a central node in arguments to garner support. To be clear, our argument is not that President Trump is a fascist; instead, we argue that he actualizes a mode of argumentation that expresses micro-political communication patterns that draw upon desires rooted in a refusal to see or engage with the other.

Our argument unfolds in three ways. First, we articulate our theory of fascist desire as an argumentative assemblage. Second, we examine the ways the Trump Administration's use of executive orders on immigration function as an instance of fascist desires. Last, we consider the implications of fascist desire for argumentation scholars and the Trump Presidency.

Locating Fascistic Desire in Argumentation: A Denial of the Other

In this section, we develop a theoretical model for locating fascist desire in a variety of argumentative forms. These desires appear in argumentation when two conditions are met: (a) the arguer denies the existence of alternative positions, rejecting clash, and (b) the arguer

constructs the domination of the bodies of subaltern populations as reasonable and/or necessary. Our model has its foundations in the continental philosophy of Gilles Deleuze and
Felix Guattari. Deleuze and Guattari (1987) developed theories of desire and microfascism
that enable us to explore micro-politics of domination in argumentation.

Desire functions as a pivotal term in this analysis. Deleuze and Guattari (1987) asked,
"Why does desire desire its own repression, how can it desire its own repression?" (p. 215).
They claimed individuals want a form of desire that limits their freedom—individuals do
not want repression because they are passive, wrought with "masochistic hysteria," or
"tricked by an ideological lure" (p. 215). Instead, "desire is never separable from complex
assemblages [...] already shaping postures, attitudes, perceptions, expectations, semiotic systems, etc." (p. 215). Argumentation reconfigures these existing attitudes to gain force.
When argument assembles desires based on the repression of the self or other, it "potentially
gives desire a fascist determination" (p. 215).

Fascism in this essay is not a reference to state fascism but a fascist politics expressed at
the level of the individual. Bonta and Protevi (2004) defined microfascism as "the construction of a 'thousand monomanias' [....] Such micro-fascisms spread throughout a social fabric
prior to the centralizing resonance that creates the molar apparatus of the State" (p. 86).
Microfascism takes root in the interstices of argumentative interactions, enticing desires for
the domination of oppositional claims, bodies, and cultures. This form of argumentation
desires material-rhetorical control that refuses alterity. These arguments deny the other and
repress alternative viewpoints.

First, in denying the reality of alternative positions, the arguer ignores the role of clash in
argumentation. Rhetors refuse the existence of argumentative ground beyond their own
positions. This radical refusal blocks what Hawes (2015) called the essential communicative
pattern of turn-taking. For example, chiding critical news coverage as "fake news" (Sink,
2017, para. 6), rather than engaging and rebutting such coverage, dissipates the media's argumentative positionality and mitigates their force as watchdogs of government. Consider also
President Trump's attribution of oppositional arguments to "paid protestors" (Maloy, 2017,
para. 5) at GOP town halls. These exchanges generated rhetorical appeals, denied dialectical
processes, and created authoritarian networks of argument. In such an environment, arguments do not win via clash and superior reasoning, but take hold as expressions of power.

Second, the expression of fascist desires in argumentation refuses to recognize the identities of marginalized groups through calls for physical domination. Rhetors deny the other's
presence in majoritarian spaces (e.g., borders, border crossings, bathrooms). The other lacks
valid argumentative ground and their bodies are also subject to denial. For example, the
criminalizing of immigrant bodies and identities pushes them away from proper society.
This process constructs "proper" bodies (e.g., white, heterosexual, cisgendered, male) while
endangering non-normative bodies. In the next section, we examine the Trump Administration immigration restrictions on seven Muslim-majority countries as an exemplar of the networking of fascist desire in argumentation.

Executive Orders & Fascistic Desires: From Theory to Case Study

Within 30 days of his inauguration, President Trump signed 13 executive orders, 12 memoranda, and four proclamations ("What Executive Actions," 2017). While the number of
Trump's orders was not overwhelming (President Obama issued 276 in a comparable time
period), the force of the new President's orders remains palatable. As part of his 100-day
plan to reshape the political landscape of the nation, Trump appealed to emerging fascist

desires in argumentative forms through the denial of both the possibility of democratic argumentative exchange and the existence of subaltern bodies. Thus, the force of arguments in (and in support of) Trump's executive orders elides alternative viewpoints and basic structures for democratic deliberation. President Trump's Chief Strategist Steve Bannon, for instance, recently announced that "the deconstruction of the administrative state" (Peters, 2017, para. 3) has begun. However, rather than dismantling the state, the administration is generating a new politics of the sensible that is a deconstructive process that erases liberal democratic argument and critical-rational debate.

Consider Trump's travel ban. Just seven days after his presidential inauguration, Trump signed Executive Order 13769 titled, "Protecting the Nation from Foreign Terrorist Entry into the United States." This order reduced the number of allowable refugees from 120,000 to 50,000 for 2017, indefinitely suspended the allowance of Syrian refugees to enter the United States, and suspended entry of persons from Iran, Iraq, Libya, Somalia, Sudan, Syria, and Yemen into the United States (de Vogue, Diamond, & Liptak, 2017). The travel ban restricted entry access to those from predominantly Muslim countries on grounds that such persons posed an increased terrorist threat to the United States. The executive order followed Trump's campaign promise to impose "a total and complete shutdown" (quoted in Johnson, 2015, para. 1) on Muslims entering the United States. At present, Trump's statements about the order have become grounds to challenge the constitutionality of the order.

The executive order, and arguments for its necessity, is an exemplary case of the force of fascistic desire in argumentation. The President depicted critical media coverage of the order as fake news and the courts as biased, rendering those who resisted and/or provided critical coverage of the order "unreasonable" (Rhodan, 2017). President Trump's decision to ban persons belonging to seven Muslim-majority countries exhibits a nativist politic that services the purification of political argument by essentializing and eliminating presumption that religious and racial minorities are a component part of America's national character. Consistent with the idea of spiritual traditionalism that Julius Evola, the "darling of Italian fascists" (Horowitz, 2017, para. 5) purported, Trump's travel ban minimized the rationality of religious subalterns enabling Judeo–Christian populations to ground claims of belonging through a reassertion of state-religious authority. In denying Muslim immigrants legitimate presence in the United States and emphasizing Muslim bodies as threats, the administration constructed Muslim immigrants as bodies exterior of the American project. The stance denied entrance to Muslim subjectivities, and thus argumentative ground, on a topic that affected them most: immigration. In short, the position of the administration barred such bodies from entry on both literal and figurative grounds.

The travel ban is an instance of postdialectical fascistic argument that networks with desires to deny Muslim bodies the ontological standing for argument production. Trump's policy propositions hail desires for the domination of these bodies. Arguments in favor of the ban, as speech acts, essentialize Muslim bodies as dangerous and (un)invited in America. Materially, the travel ban performs a domination of immigrant bodies by controlling movements to, from, and within the United States. This fascistic argumentation generates controlled networks of subjectivity that negates "others." Thus, Trump establishes a singular, homogenous argument assemblage, which flows via the negation of Muslim foreign nationals. Such manufacturing of argumentation is, by its nature, beyond the horizon of dialectical, because conditions for productive argumentative exchange with the purpose of resolving disputations such as security, immigration, and religious tolerance cannot exist as argument possibilities. The ban's arguments refuse the symbolic and corporeal belonging of Muslim subjectivities within the American empire.

George F. (Guy) McHendry, Jr. and Nicholas S. Paliewicz

From Micro-Desires to Assemblages: Networked Fascism

Fascistic argumentation serves as one example of "postdialectical" argumentation, exceeding the metaphysical foundations of what, since Plato, constitutes good argumentation: the ideal of reasonable argumentation (*logos*). An essential project of analyzing argumentation after a post-dialectical turn is charting, critiquing, and expanding the conceptual schema available to assess the force, function, and flow of arguments. Our use of microfascism in this essay is an initial attempt to engage in such a project. We see this work as a path forward for alternative ways of understanding argumentation, especially in instances where arguers and audiences advance claims which fail normative rules.

Trump's executive order banning immigration from predominantly Muslim nations is not the sole instantiation of fascistic desire. For example, we believe future analyses can locate fascistic desire in President Trump's executive order to nullify trans-students' access to bathrooms, in the Trump Administration's escalation of detention and deportation of "suspected" undocumented immigrants, and the Administration's targeting of so-called "sanctuary cities." These cases exhibit similar arguments to the Muslim ban that we analyze above. However, these argumentative forms pre-date and extend beyond the Trump administration. Argumentative assemblages around access to birth control and abortion frequently generate argumentative fields that exclude women's agency. Healthcare debates which emphasize choice and cost, at the expense of those with pre-existing conditions, limit access to healthcare for all. Debates over gun control frequently assert that gun owners and collectors are beyond reason and exclude their voices. We see fascistic desire as a generative source for exploring post-dialectic argumentation.

These examples (and many others) delimit argumentative fields by marking which bodies are acceptable and unacceptable to engage in clash. This inclusion and exclusion is metonymic for fascist desire: It reduces politics to codes, rules, and orders, circumventing complex arguments by making difference a propositional impossibility. Fascist desire in argumentation is networked desire. Across these examples the desires motivated these orders (and the arguments which support them) remain connected, yet distinct.

Fascistic desires in argumentation exist in defiance to assumed dialectical underpinnings of argumentation for the simple reason that fascistic arguments negate the possibility of critical-rational argumentation to occur as a condition for its existence. Arguments belonging to this assemblage flow along the affective chords that desire the domination of subaltern bodies; effectually, argumentation becomes vibrations within a homogenous network without alterity. Argumentation is not and cannot become dialectical when affect and desires motivate arguers to unilaterally control discourse and dominate the other through tactics that serve to desubjectivize argument opponents (e.g., ostracization, defamation, ridicule, humiliation, hostility, stigmatization, derision, scorn, etc.). Therefore, argumentation scholars should not overlook the dark side of argument networks. Whereas numerous scholars have importantly studied the possibilities of networks for deliberative democracy and social change (e.g., DeLuca & Peeples, 2002; Pfister, 2014), argument networks can also function as tools for domination and control. To more fully recognize how networked argument works as forces, we encourage fellow colleagues to consider taking the postdialectical turn. Not only does postdialectics offer richer considerations of the networked forces of deliberation and social change, but it also provides the wherewithal for realizing how arguers can use networks to dominate subaltern bodies and foreclose critical debate. Such desires posit supreme homogeneity as the only reasonable regime of signs creating what Gilles Deleuze (1995) termed a "society of control."

References

Bonta, M., & Protevi, J. (2004). *Deleuze and geophilosophy: A guide and glossary*. Edinburgh, United Kingdom: Edinburg University Press.

Castells, M. (2010). *The rise of the network society: The information age: Economy, society, and culture, Volume 1* (2nd ed.). West Sussex, United Kingdom: Wiley-Blackwell.

de Vogue, A., Diamond, J., & Liptak, K. (2017, March 7). US President Donald Trump signs new travel ban, exempts Iraq. *CNN*. Retrieved from http://cnn.com

Deleuze, G. (1995). *Negotiations* (M. Joughin, Trans.). New York, NY: Columbia University Press.

Deleuze, G., & Guattari, F. (1987). *A thousand plateaus: Capitalism and schizophrenia* (B. Massumi, Trans., 2nd ed.). Minneapolis, MN: University of Minnesota Press.

DeLuca, K. M., & Peeples, J. (2002). From public sphere to public screen: Democracy, activism, and the "violence" of Seattle. *Critical Studies in Media Communication, 19*(2), 125–151. doi: 10.1080/07393180216559

Hawes, L. C. (2015). *A new philosophy of social conflict: Mediating collective trauma and transitional justice*. New York, NY: Bloomsbury Academic.

Horowitz, J. (2017, February 10). Steve Bannon cited Italian thinker who inspired fascists. *The New York Times*. Retrieved from https://nytimes.com

Johnson, J. (2015, December 7). Trump calls for "total and complete shutdown of Muslims entering the United States." *The Washington Post*. Retrieved from https://washingtonpost.com

Landers, E. (2017, June 6). White House: Trump's tweets are "official statements." *CNN*. Retrieved from http://cnn.com

Maloy, S. (2017, February 6). The "paid protest" lie: The Trump White House is trying to delegitimize public protest. *Salon*. Retrieved from http://salon.com/2017/02/06/the-paid-protest-lie-the-trump-white-house-is-trying-to-delegitimize-public-protest/

Paliewicz, N. S., & McHendry, G., Jr. (2017). When good arguments do not work: Postdialectics, argument assemblages, and the networks of climate skepticism. *Argumentation and Advocacy, 53*(4), 287–309. Retrieved from doi: 10.1080/00028533.2017.1375738

Pfister, D. S. (2011). The logos of the blogosphere: Flooding the zone, invention, and attention in the Lott imbroglio. *Argumentation and Advocacy, 47*(3), 147–162. Retrieved from http://tandfonline.com

Pfister, D. S. (2014). *Networked media, networked rhetorics: Attention and deliberation in the early blogosphere*. University Park, PA: Pennsylvannia State University Press.

Peters, J. W. (2017, February 23). Stephen Bannon reassures conservatives uneasy about Trump. *The New York Times*. Retrieved from https://nytimes.com

Rhodan, M. (2017, February 6). President Trump defends travel ban: "Any negative polls are fake news." *Time*. Retrieved from http://time.com

Sink, J. (2017, February 24). Trump fumes about anonymous sources after anonymous briefing. *Bloomberg*. Retrieved from https://bloomberg.com/politics/articles/2017-02-24/trump-assails-fake-news-blasts-media-use-of-anonymous-sources

van Eemeren, F. H., & Grootendorst, R. (1987). Fallacies in pragma-dialectical perspective. *Argumentation, 1*(3), 283–301. doi: 10.1007/BF00136779

What Executive Actions Has Trump Taken? (2017, April 12). *BBC*. Retrieved from http://bbc.com/news/world-us-canada-38695593

PART VIII

EVALUATING DEBATING
NETWORKS

73

NETWORKING DEBATE AND CIVIC ENGAGEMENT

Measuring the Impact of High School Debate Camps

Brian Lain and Karen Anderson-Lain

Scholars from multiple disciplines (Adler & Goggin, 2005; Dewey, 1916; Forestiere, 2015; Lenzi et al., 2014) have debated the importance of civic engagement in the U.-S. educational system. They have explored the role of civic engagement in the classroom and beyond the classroom. Civic engagement is the knowledge, attitudes, and behaviors individuals engage in to promote civic participation and help shape their community's future (Adler & Goggin, 2005; Lenzi et al., 2014). Fostering civic engagements promotes critical thinking about our country, allows citizens to utilize their voices, and combats political apathy (Forestiere, 2015). Lenzi et al. (2014) argued that schools provide a venue to combat the decline in civic engagement of young people. Scholars exploring the development of civic engagement in adolescence have focused on how formative contexts develop civic identity as well as the importance of participating in in-class and out-of-class activities (Forestiere, 2015; Zaff, Malanchuk, & Eccles, 2008). However, few communication scholars, except McIntosh and Milam (2016) and Zorwick and Wade (2016), have attempted to establish the ways in which participation in debate fosters civic engagement in youth.

While a vibrant conversation has emerged regarding the relationship of academic debate and civic engagement in the last few years (Hlavacik, Lain, Ivanovic, & Ontiveros-Kersch, 2016; Hogan, Kurr, Johnson, & Bergmaier, 2016), comparative analyses of the level of civic engagement produced by debating activities and other civic activities remain virtually nonexistent. Further, while debate camps for high school and middle school students have become commonplace during the summers on college campuses, very little research attends to the outcomes of those co-curricular summer camp experiences. This study comments on both of these conversations through an examination of a survey measuring adolescents' perceptions of civic duty and engagement while participating in a summer debate curriculum. We seek to explore the extent to which participation in debate camp influences middle school and high school students' perceptions of their own civic engagement. After reviewing the literature regarding civic engagement, youth, and debate, we move on to an explanation of our study and findings. Ultimately, the results suggest new ways of assessing the relationship between civic engagement and debate in different networks of argument.

Civic Engagement, Youth, and Debate

Civic engagement in middle and high school youth has served as a topic of study both in school and in out of class activities such as 4-H, Boys and Girls Club, and youth development organizations (Larson, 2000). Scholars exploring the development of civic engagement in adolescence have focused on how formative contexts develop civic identity (Levine & Youniss, 2006; Youniss, McLellan, Su, & Yates, 1999). Interactive models of civic engagement and adolescence have demonstrated that early attempts to encourage civic engagement and civic identity benefit society, communities, and the individual (Levine & Youniss, 2006; Zaff et al., 2008). For example, Zaff et al. (2008) developed a revised model of youth positive citizenship development that explored the influence of individual characteristics (e.g., ethnicity, parental involvement, socio-economic status) and sustained civic engagement across early and late adolescence on the development of civic engagement into adulthood. Adolescents with higher levels of civic engagement were more likely to have higher levels of engagement as young adults, thereby increasing the likelihood of voter participation and volunteering (Zaff, et al., 2008; Zaff, Moore, Papillo, & Williams, 2003). Thus, in-school programs and out-of-class activities that foster civic engagement appear to have lasting impacts beyond adolescence.

Most research on debate and civic engagement has focused exclusively on higher education settings (Hogan et al., 2016; Lain, Hlavacik, Ivanovic, & Ontiveros-Kersch, 2015). For example, scholars have explored debate's ability to supplement service-learning (Leek, 2016) or provide an outreach curriculum in one college's First Year Seminar program (Roidt, DeNicolo, Kittle, Osborne, & Saindon, 2016). An ongoing academic conversation examining the ways in which debate might make a stronger contribution to national civic education at different educational levels has sparked a renewed interest in civic engagement and debate (Hogan et al., 2016).

Despite the importance of developing civic engagement in adolescence and the link to participation in out of class activities, minimal research has established ways in which participation in debate and forensics fosters civic engagement in the middle school and high school population. Of the few who have broached this topic, McIntosh and Milam (2016) focused on the ways in which debate functions as civic education in high school through common core standards and the development of competency based skills. Zorwick and Wade (2016) examined how teachers incorporate advocacy training, argumentation, and debate across middle school and high school curriculum into their classrooms. While both studies drew a connection between civic engagement and debate from teachers' perspectives, the authors did not account for how the students themselves viewed their level confidence and skills in engaging in the civic engagement attitudes and behaviors that debate may foster.

Although research on the effects of high school debate education continues, especially as it relates to the Urban Debate League (e.g., Anderson & Mezuk, 2012; Mezuk, 2009), recent studies have not examined the benefits of summer debate camps in spite of their increasing popularity. In general, students who have higher levels of involvement in high school debate typically have higher GPAs, are more likely to complete high school, and score higher on college readiness measures such as the ACT (Mezuk, 2009). Pineda and

Salinas (2009) found that summer debate workshops could enhance the participation of certain demographic populations that were given pedagogical strategies. However, the most recent systematic research on teaching strategy and effects of debate camps occurred over forty years ago (Klopf, 1974; Shoen & Matlon, 1974).

With this study we seek to explore the extent to which participation in debate camp influences middle and high school students' perception of their own civic engagement. The study specifically explores two questions: How should argumentation scholars measure the level of civic engagement for adolescences? Does debate camp participation increase students' perception of their own civic engagement abilities and skills?

Study Scope

Initially, 291 middle school and high school students attending a summer debate camp at a large southwestern university agreed to participate in the study. However, 52 participants either submitted incomplete data or failed to complete a post-test, resulting in their elimination from the analysis. Two hundred and thirty-nine students completed the study's surveys. Ten percent of the participants were middle school students, while 90% were high school students. Forty-five percent of the participants were female and 55% were male. The average age of participants was 16 years old. This study examined the 239 paired surveys using a pre-test/post-test design with students completing the measure during orientation as they arrived at camp and during their final day of camp.

Measure

Participants completed select items of the Civic Engagement, Active and Engaged Citizens (AEC) inventory that Zaff, Boyd, Li, Lerner, and Lerner (2010) used to measure civic education in middle and high school students attending 4H clubs across the United States. Developed in a longitudinal study with 8th-10th graders involved in 4-H, the AEC includes four dimensions: civic duty, civic skills, neighborhood social connect, and civic participation. Civic duty explores a belief in the ability to make a difference through civic participation and a sense of responsibility to speak up for others experiencing inequality. Civic skills consider an individual's belief and competence in their own political voice and competence to engage in specific civic action. The researchers eliminated items related to participants' perceptions of the extent to which others care for them (e.g., my teachers really care about me) from the analysis. Civic participation examines social responsibility by exploring levels of political efficacy and participatory citizenship. The revised scale was found to be reliable for both the pre-test ($\alpha = 0.81$) and the post-test ($\alpha = 0.88$). A paired t-test determined whether a significant difference existed in the students' self-reports of engagement between the start of debate camp and the end of debate camp. A post hoc analysis of individual items on the measure highlighted specific gains in civic duty and development of civic skills. The time between the pre-test and post-test varied based on whether students enrolled in one, two, or three-week camps.

Results

Students' perception of their own civic engagement increased significantly between the pre-test ($M = 4.05$) and post-test ($M = 4.12$), $t(238) = -2.91$, $p = 0.000$. For findings related to individual items on the survey instrument, see Table 73.1.

Table 73.1 Post Hoc Analysis of Paired T-Tests Individual Items of AEC

Item	Pre-test Mean (SD)	Post-test Mean (SD)	t	df	p value
Helping to reduce poverty and hunger in the world.	4.19 (2.2)	4.14 (.93)	.39	248	.70
Helping to make sure that all people are treated fairly.	4.44 (.77)	4.58 (.65)	−2.96	249	.003*
Helping to make the world a better placeto live in.	4.37 (.78)	4.48 (.70)	−2.26	248	.025*
Helping other people.	4.37 (.83)	4.44 (.76)	−1.41	248	.16
Speaking up for equality (everyone should have the same rights and opportunities).	4.59 (.73)	4.57 (.70)	.53	246	.60
When I see someone being taken advantage of, I want to help them.	4.22 (.83)	4.34 (.76)	−2.14	247	.034*
When I see someone being treated unfairly, I don't feel sorry for them.**	4.43 (1.02)	4.27 (1.13)	1.89	247	.06
I feel sorry for other people who don't have what I have.	3.49 (1.15)	3.60 (1.19)	−1.59	247	.113
It's not really my problem if my neighborsare in trouble and need help.**	3.96 (.98)	3.96 (1.03)	.11	248	.914
I believe I can make a difference in my community.	3.85 (1.07)	4.01 (.98)	−2.31	245	.022*
I often think about doing things so that people in the future can have things better.	4.09 (2.12)	3.99 (.92)	.75	246	.455
It is important to me to contribute to my community and society.	4.22 (.97)	4.22 (.83)	.07	245	.94
Contact a newspaper, radio, or TV talk show to express your opinion on an issue.	3.37 (1.12)	3.59 (1.11)	−3.51	246	.001*
Contact an elected official about the problem.	3.40 (1.22)	3.54 (1.16)	−2.25	247	.025*
Contact or visit someone in government who represents your community.	3.40 (1.17)	3.49 (1.22)	−1.30	245	.19
Write an opinion letter to a local newspaper.	3.83 (1.19)	4.00 (1.06)	−2.68	246	.008*
Express your views in front of a group of people.	4.26 (.99)	4.33 (.88)	−1.42	245	.16
Sign an email or a written petition.	4.58 (.80)	4.60 (.74)	−.31	246	.754

* Significant difference at < .05. **Item reverse coded.

Discussion

Overall, students' perceptions of their own civic engagement significantly increases after participating in summer debate camp. Students indicated that they experienced an increase in both their civic duty and civic skills. Specifically, students reported an increased desire to ensure that all people experienced fair treatment and a desire to make the world a better place. They reported an increase in the belief that they had a duty to act when others were taking advantage of someone. Additionally, students reported increased confidence in their civic skillset including increased willingness to (a) contact a newspaper, radio, or TV talk show; (b) contact elected officials; and (c) write an opinion letter to a local newspaper. Other aspects of civic skills that did not increase over time, perhaps due to some participants already ranking highly on those items in the pretest condition. These results demonstrate that middle school and high school debate students' participation in debate camp can positively influence civic engagement as operationalized as civic duty and civic skills.

This brief survey suggests the need to gather more data. While the Civic Engagement, Active and Engaged Citizens inventory provides some insight into how debate contributes to the development of civic engagement in adolescents, providing comparisons based on sex, grade level, race, and experience with debate would provide additional data points needed to understand more fully debate's programmatic benefits. Additionally, a baseline sample of non-debate students would provide greater insight into the overall impact of middle school and high school debate on students' perceptions of their own civic engagement.

Additionally, debate educators and communication scholars can play a role in understanding the developmental process of civic education among adolescents. Zaff et al.'s (2008, 2010) framing of civic engagement emphasizing civic duty and civic skills highlighted the communicative role of civic identity development and engagement. Debate is only one important extra-curricular activity that informs the development of civic engagement. Comparative analyses between debate and other significant extracurricular activities (e.g., volunteering, participation in religious organizations, or other community-based programs) could yield additional insights that could strengthen the civic engagement outcomes of all programs.

Finally, this project serves as an important start to a conversation about the influence of middle and high school debate and summer debate camps beyond success in students' current debate circuits. The long-term benefits of enhanced civic engagement highlights the educative importance of debate in developing well-rounded and engaged citizens.

References

Adler, R. P., & Goggin, J. (2005). What do we mean by "civic engagement"? *Journal of Transformative Education, 3*(3), 236–253. doi:10.1177/1541344605276792

Anderson, S., & Mezuk, B. (2012). Participating in a policy debate program and academic achievement among at-risk adolescents in an urban public school district: 1997–2007. *Journal of Adolescence, 35*(5), 1225–1235. doi:10.1016/j.adolescence.2012.04.005

Dewey, J. (1916). *Democracy and education: An introduction to the philosophy of education.* New York, NY: Macmillan.

Forestiere, C. (2015). Promoting civic agency through civic-engagement activities: A guide for instructors new to civic engagement pedagogy. *Journal of Political Science Education, 11*(4), 455–471. doi:10.1080/15512169.2015.1066684

Hlavacik, M., Lain, B., Ivanovic, M., & Ontiveros-Kersch, B. (2016). The state of college debate according to a survey of its coaches: Data to ground the discussion of debate and civic engagement. *Communication Education, 65*(4), 382–396. doi:10.1080/03634523.2016.1203006

Hogan, J. M., Kurr, J. A., Johnson, J. D., & Bergmaier, M. J. (2016). Speech and debate as civic education. *Communication Education, 65*(4), 377–381. doi:10.1080/03634523.2016.1203002

Klopf, D. W. (1974). Systematizing debate instruction in the workshop setting. *Speech Education, 2*, 85–96. Retrieved from EBSCOhost database.

Lain, B., Hlavacik, M., Ivanovic, M., & Ontiveros-Kersch, B. (2015, March). *A survey of scope and perceived value of debate outreach and civic engagement at the college level.* Paper presented at the Speech & Debate as Civic Education Conference, Center for Democratic Deliberation at Penn State University, State College, PA.

Larson, R. (2000). Towards a psychology of positive youth development. *American Psychologist, 55*(1), 170–183. doi:10.1037//0003-066X.55.1.170

Leek, D. R. (2016). Policy debate pedagogy: A complementary strategy for civic and political engagement through service-learning. *Communication Education, 65*(4), 397–408. doi:10.1080/03634523.2016.1203004

Lenzi, M., Vieno, A., Sharkey, J., Mayworm, A., Scacchi, L., Pastore, M., & Santinello, M. (2014). How school can teach civic engagement besides civic education: The role of democratic school climate. *American Journal Community Psychology, 54*(3-4), 251–261. doi:10.1007/s10464-014-9669-8

Levine, P., & Youniss, J. (2006). Youth and civic participation: Introduction. In P. Levine & J. Youniss (Eds.), *Youth civic engagement: An institutional turn* (Circle Working Paper No. 45, pp. 3–6). Baltimore, MD: The Center for Information & Research on Civic Learning and Engagement. Retrieved from http://civicyouth.org

McIntosh, J., & Milam, M. (2016). Competitive debate as competency-based learning: Civic engagement and next-generational assessment in the era of the common core learning standards. *Communication Education, 65*(4), 420–433. doi:10.1080/03634523.2016.1203007

Mezuk, B. (2009). Urban debate and high school educational outcomes for African American males: The case of the Chicago debate league. *The Journal of Negro Education, 78*(3), 290–304. Retrieved from http://jstor.org/stable/25608747

Pineda, R., & Salinas, C. (2009). Model proposal: Increasing Latina/o involvement in policy debate through summer debater workshops. In A. D. Louden (Ed.), *Contemporary argumentation and debate, volume 30* (pp. 114–129). Retrieved from http://cedadebate.org/files/2009CAD.pdf

Roidt, J., DeNicolo M., Kittle, A., Osborne, K., & Saindon, B. (2016). First year symposium: One college's response to the perceived "deficit" in civic education. *Communication Education, 65*(4), 409–419. doi:10.1080/03634523.2016.1203003

Shoen, R., & Matlon, R. J. (1974). A survey of content and teaching methods in high school summer debate workshops. *The Speech Teacher, 23*(1), 40–50. doi:10.1080/03634527409378055

Youniss, J., McLellan, J. A., Su, Y., & Yates, M. (1999). The role of community service in identity development: Normative, unconventional, and deviant orientations. *Journal of Adolescent Research, 14*(2), 248–261. doi:10.1177/0743558499142006

Zaff, J., Boyd, M., Li, Y., Lerner, J. V., & Lerner, R. M. (2010). Active and engaged citizenship: Multi-group and longitudinal factorial analysis of an integrated construct of civic engagement. *Journal of Youth Adolescence, 39*(7), 736–750. doi:10.1007/s10964-010-9541-6

Zaff, J. F., Malanchuk, O., & Eccles, J. S. (2008). Predicting positive citizenship from adolescence to youth adulthood: The effects of a civic context. *Applied Development Science, 12*(1), 38–53. doi:10.1080/10888690801910567

Zaff, J. F., Moore, K. A., Papillo, A. R., & Williams, S. (2003). Implications of extracurricular activity participation during adolescence on positive outcomes. *Journal of Adolescent Research, 18*(6), 599–630. doi:10.1177/0743558403254779

Zorwick, L. W., & Wade, J. M. (2016). Enhancing civic education through the use of assigned advocacy, argumentation, and debate across the curriculum. *Communication Education, 65*(4), 434–444. doi:10.1080/03634523.2016.1203005

74

DESIGNING PUBLIC DEBATES TO FACILITATE DYNAMIC UPDATING IN A NETWORK SOCIETY

Justin Eckstein and Gordon R. Mitchell

In its most useful forms, deliberation harnesses the power of argument to inform civic choice, motivating citizens to participate in non-zero sum conversations about issues of public concern. In such settings, citizens use reason to share perspectives, test standpoints, and discover stasis points of agreement and disagreement.

Yet, to the average citizen jaded through exposure to televised verbal jousting, argument often stands for conflict, agitation, and tumult—something to avoid, not to embrace. Indeed, previous psychological research has shown that when faced with factual challenges to their beliefs, audience members tend to switch into "motivated reasoning" (Nyhan & Reifler, 2010, p. 323), or put another way, tuning out alternative viewpoints and doubling down on their own settled opinions. They avoid embracing argument, something that Ehninger (1970) described as a "'person risking' enterprise" (p. 104).

Fortunately, public debate is a relatively malleable "cultural technology" (Greene & Hicks, 2005, p. 117), flexible enough to facilitate particular patterns and habits of argumentation. Utilizing a design perspective (Aakhus, 2007; Jackson, 2015), this paper explores the potential of public debate designs to cultivate what Karpowitz and Mansbridge (2005) called dynamic updating, a concept they described as "an open-minded, ongoing discovery of one another's possibly changing values and interests" (p. 238). In contrast to deliberative models that strive to suppress conflict in the name of consensus, dynamic updating enables participants to "feel comfortable in exploring those conflicts as well as in building bonds of solidarity, creating shared value, and finding unexpected points of congruence" (Karpowitz & Mansbridge, 2005, p. 238).

Can the design of public debates foster dynamic updating by audience members? We explore this question by pursuing a comparative analysis of two video recorded and transcribed public debates. Comparative analysis across debate exemplars holds the potential of generating insights regarding how design choices implicate deliberative practice, as well as the ways that communication technology shapes group decision-making in what Pfister (2014) called "networked society." Like Isocrates (1929), we eschew a "handbook" approach to the challenge of deliberative design, instead generating insight from the way that particular public debate episodes compare and contrast with each other, as well as extend and depart from prevailing patterns of argumentation.

Public Debate Juxtaposition

Interscholastic debate tournaments provide venues for debaters and scholars to come together and learn from differing approaches to argumentation. Different teams advance various interpretations of a pro/con resolution and test novel approaches to competitive practice. In contrast, single schools, uncoupled from the social network of the tournament format, typically host public debate events. This relative isolation can limit opportunities for theory building through the exchange of design perspectives. The design of events circumscribed to *a* specific place and time can become difficult to compare, contrast, and evaluate. Only through a comparative format can we determine if a design is effective in a particular circumstance, or if it is repeatable in other contexts.

Here, we explore how the juxtaposition of two public debate exemplars carries the potential to transcend this potential lacuna by discerning how some design features translate to broader audiences. At the same time, the two approaches preserve space for local experimentation. One event, the 2015 Ruth Anderson Public Debate occurred at Pacific Lutheran University in Tacoma, Washington. The second event, the 2013 Marcela L. Finegold Public Debate took place at the University of Pittsburgh, in Pittsburgh, Pennsylvania. The two debate events are similar in that each grew out of endowed public debate series, enjoying a level of resource support that enable format experimentation and incorporation of advanced communication technology endemic in today's networked society. Yet, each event took a different approach to the design question of how to best implement format features—for example, the Woodward (1928) audience shift ballot, focused Audience Response System polling, and live Twitter feeds —to foster dynamic updating. By exploring each of these approaches in turn, the following elucidates the relationship between public debate and opinion change.

The Woodward Audience Shift Ballot

The Anderson Public Debate addressed the topic of a proposed minimum wage ballot initiative, Proposition 1, that would immediately raise the minimum wage in Tacoma, Washington to 15 dollars an hour on January 1, 2016. Expert advocates served as speakers, along with college debaters. A Woodward change of opinion ballot determined the winner of the debate (Woodward, 1928). Facilitators polled the audience's beliefs before and after a debate using the ballot, with the team moving the greatest number of people to their side declared the winner. To determine levels of audience opinion shifting, the moderator deployed *Poll Everywhere*, a text voting service that translated data—generated by audience smartphone inputs—into a numerical expression and a bar graph.

Prior to commencement of arguments in the Anderson Public Debate, the audience polled 35% in favor, 40% against, and 25% undecided on Proposition 1. After the debate had concluded, the audience polled 30% percent of the voted in favor, 68% against, and 2% remained undecided. The opposition won the debate because the opposition increased by

■Yes ■No ■Undecided

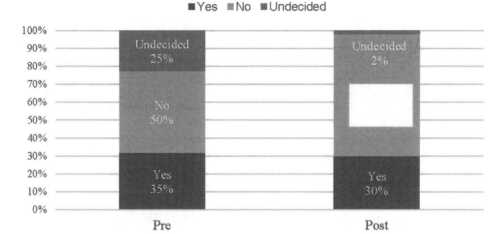

Figure 74.1 Anderson PD Woodward Shift of Opinion Ballot
"This house would raise the minimum wage to $15 an hour."

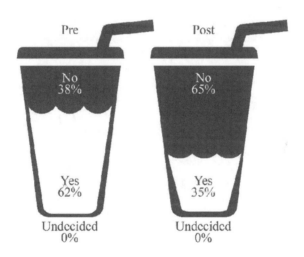

Figure 74.2 Finegold PD Woodward Shift of Opinion Ballot
"Should there be a surtax on sugary drinks?"

28% while the proposition decreased by 5% (see Figure 74.1). A large screen positioned behind the debaters displayed the result for the onsite audience.

The Finegold Public Debate, which tackled the question of whether a surtax should exist on sugary drinks, also mixed expert advocates with student speakers and deployed the Woodward ballot. However, the format also utilized the TurningPoint Audience Response System to gather reaction data. Prior to the debate, 62% of audience members favored such a tax, with 38% opposed. After arguments were completed, a poll asking the same question revealed a considerable 27% shift of audience opinion against the resolution, with 35% in favor of the tax and 65% opposed (see Figure 74.2).

The Woodward change of opinion ballot urges audience members to account for implicit biases that might undergird their settled viewpoints. Arguers tend to be unaware of their implicit biases, until they encounter different perspectives that introduce friction (Jackson, 2015; Johnstone, 1990). The pre-debate vote, taken prior to any speeches, externalized audience members' implicit biases into a publicly expressed (albeit anonymous) commitment. William Connolly (2005) explained that this process helps people "come to terms viscerally and positively with the extent to which it [the belief] must appear profoundly *contestable*" (p. 32). The pre-debate vote helps listeners stake out relevant commitments and forces listeners to reflect on the on the reasonableness of arguments on both positions. The vote after the debate measures shift of opinion and offers a tool for social comparison. Projecting others' votes might prompt listeners to reflect why their position did (or did not) change relative to the rest of the audience, and it might encourage them to ask what information they missed. But, even if no change of opinion occurs, the vote showed that, even in similar circumstances, people could reach different conclusions.

Yet, a drawback from the Woodward ballot is that it favors less popular positions. In short, the lower the audience's pre-debate score on the ballot, the chances of winning are higher. For example, if a position polls at 10% before the debate and then attracts an additional 5% of the audience during a post-debate poll, the position would "win" the debate. Comparatively, if one side enjoys substantial audience support in a pre-debate poll, say 80%, then winning that same 5% in the post-debate poll might be insufficient to secure victory for that side. The ratio of change is much larger for the unpopular decision (5% of 10%, or a 50% gain) than for the popular one (5% of 80%, or a 6.25% gain). The ratio difference is most dangerous with fringe positions, because the debating procedure might sanction them as potentially reasonable.

A related limitation of the Woodward ballot involves the fact that the meaning of a shift of opinion outcome is itself open to interpretation. For example, the 27% swing to the negative evident in the Finegold Public Debate could mean that debaters had persuaded the audience to become skeptical about using tax mechanisms to improve public health. Indeed, the expert who advocated the surtax on sugary drinks became so concerned that she attempted to halt circulation of the recording of the public debate and its transcript after the event. However, an alternative explanation for the 27% change of opinion in this case might highlight how the negative won over audience members by criticizing a retail-level surtax as ineffectual, instead proposing a larger and more direct tax levied further up the supply chain, that is, on farmers who harvest the sugarcane.

Focused Audience Polling

Some public debate formats make slight modifications to the Woodward audience shift ballot procedure to measure changes in audience opinion about issues subsidiary to the overall question that frames the debate. For example, in the Finegold Public Debate, audience members answered a poll question before and after the event that asked, "How much merit do you see in arguments offered by those with a viewpoint which you don't agree with?" Possible responses ranged from 1 to 5 on a Likert scale, with 1 indicating "no merit," 3 indicating "moderate merit," and 5 indicating "compelling merit." In the Finegold Public Debate, the results of such comparative polling revealed intriguing shifts in audience opinion (see Figure 74.3).

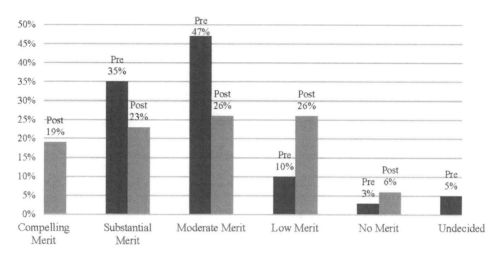

Figure 74.3 Finegold Focused Audience Polling

"How much merit do you see in arguments offered by those with a viewpoint which you don't agree with?"

The responses to the focused audience polling suggest that the Finegold Public Debate aided opinion formulation. A majority of the audience opinion shifted from more moderate stances on the topic towards more extreme perceptions. Initially, the medium score for the audience perceptions of the merit of an opposing side was moderate, the equivalent of a neutral on a Likert scale. At the start of the debate, 48% of the audience viewed opposing standpoints as moderately meritorious, but after the debate the number dropped to 26%. At the same time, the percentage of audience members finding positions they found disagreeable, or having low or no merit, more than doubled. Similarly, the perception that an opposing position contained compelling merit grew from 0% before the debate to 19% after. These numbers suggest the audience generally came to the debate with neutral perceptions on opposing arguments. But, after they listened to both sides, they intensified or attenuated disagreement with the opposing side.

Yet, the Finegold Public Debate's focused audience polling approach faces a significant limitation. The polling question does not account for a change of opinion. If one switched sides from being in favor of a sugary tax to opposing it, what exactly constitutes "a view point with which you don't agree?" Consider a scenario that could occur in the post-debate poll. If listeners interpret "a view point with which you don't agree" as their previously held, but now surrendered commitments, then they might perceive a sugary tax as less meritorious because they heard sufficient reasons to surrender that standpoint. But, if audience members define "a view point with which you don't agree" as the standpoint they previously opposed and just adopted, they might rate the newly adopted position as more meritorious. Considering the number of people that shifted their opinion in this debate, the confusion about what viewpoint serves as the focus of the question creates unreliable data. The language needs to be reworked to produce more useful data.

A future line of research might inquire into a follow-up on the merit question. Perhaps a reworded question or use of equipment with the technical capacities to isolate patterns of audience member participation could yield additional insights. Future research can also focus on specific audience members that changed their mind and researchers can ask participants questions about the poll or interview audience members about their shifts of opinion.

Twitter and Dynamic Updating

The ebb and flow of audience opinion during an unfolding public debate also serves as insightful data for opinion analysis. Accordingly, the Anderson Public Debate encouraged audience members to contribute live tweets during the debate. Unlike other social media platforms, Twitter is unique in that it allows strangers to interact with one another. In the Anderson Public Debate, the hosts monitored, amalgamated, and projected the audience tweets onto a screen behind the debaters (the same used for projecting the Woodward ballot). The hosts also gave audience members hashtags to organize their interactions: #RAPD15, #15NOW, #NO15, and #AsktheMod.

This format variation produced over 350 tweets during the 50-minute Anderson Public Debate, with topics ranging from ethics, jobs, fast food, the Seattle case study, health care, and even comments on the debate itself. Audience members used Twitter to fact check claims the debaters made, engage one another on points of contention, call out one another's conduct, and add commentary on the debate itself. Twitter changes the norms of turn taking as audience members offer objections, endorsements, or assessments of arguments simultaneously without fear of interrupting or masking arguments that others offer. Hashtags provide a mechanism for audience members to index their contributions as relevant to a particular point of contention. The move away from linear turn taking reduces the amount of attention the audience gives to each reason. The number of other tweets lowers perceived social risk. The combination of non-linear turn taking and the lowered social risk begets rapid-fire argument as inquiry, as the audience helps uncover the argumentative terrain. The audience rapidly tests reasons, sparks other conversations, and uncovers new points of stasis.

Despite these benefits, integration of Twitter as a design feature also introduces potential drawbacks. Audience members may try to heckle debaters or just get a laugh through use of memes and/or providing inappropriate commentary. While the hosts of the Anderson Public Debate filtered out irrelevant tweets from appearing on the big screen, such content remains in the feed for online users to view. Additionally, since any individual tweet might get less scrutiny, a potential exists for falsehoods to spread, although such risk of misinformation is endemic to any deliberation.

Conclusion

This study addresses a gap in argumentation literature by engaging the understudied question of how audience members change their minds during public debates. While the small sample size of only two debates may limit generalization of the study's findings, Jackson (2015) argued convincingly that case studies can inform understanding of how design choices implicate the "built" communicative environment. In particular, the study contributes to theory and practice of public debating, with a unique comparative perspective yielding insights on public debate formats, especially those aiming to transcend echo chamber deliberation endemic to our hyper-sorted, network society.

Our framework may tempt some to question the value of public debates that fail to prompt audience opinion change. Yet, independent of the results of Woodward ballot polling, both the Finegold Public Debate's focused polling and the Anderson Public Debate's

Twitter feed integration, illustrate how careful public debate design can cultivate what Sprain and Ivancic (2017) called "openness as a discursive stance" (p. 241). Conversely, polarization entrepreneurs can utilize change of opinion data to mislead audiences beyond those present for the original event, as the palpable concern of the expert affirmative advocate in the Finegold Public Debate who sought to quash transcript circulation illustrates.

Recent attempts to manipulate U.S. public opinion in echo chambers raises the stakes for public deliberation. To recirculate in the online environment, "fake news" depends on audience members adopting a closed discursive stance that eschews critical thinking. As Cole, Esposito, Biddle, and Grim (2017) argued, Russian intelligence officers took advantage of the fact that large portions of the U.S. citizenry approached the 2016 presidential election as an exercise in "motivated reasoning" (Kahan, 2013, p. 408), a cognitive process that entails suspension of critical thinking in the search for confirmatory evidence.

Communication events, such as well-designed public forums, that value expression of different perspectives and emphasize social learning through deliberation oriented around collective choice-making (Carcasson, 2017) can nudge citizens beyond personalized "filter bubbles" (Pariser, 2011). Recent events, including the 2016 Russian presidential election influence campaign, highlight the national security importance of inoculating the American citizenry against similar attacks that will likely become endemic in the current age of inter-networked enclave deliberation (Dilanian et al., 2017; U.S. DHS, ODNI, 2016). These trends configure educators and researchers in the forensics community as potentially key actors in the challenge to bolster public immunity against future attempts by foreign actors to undermine the nation's democratic foundations. This prospect reaffirms the importance of public debates as serious objects of study, with the type of comparative analysis featured in this essay serving as one approach for refining formats designed to facilitate audience critical thinking and dynamic updating.

References

Aakhus, M. (2007). Communication as design. *Communication Monographs, 74*(1), 112–117. doi:10.1080/03637750701196383

Carcasson, M. (2017). Why process matters: Democracy and human nature. *Kettering Review, 36(1)*, 16–22.

Cole, M., Esposito, R., Biddle, S., & Grim, R. (2017, June 5). Top-secret NSA report details Russian hacking effort days before 2016 election. *The Intercept*. Retrieved from https://theintercept.com

Connolly, W. E. (2005). *Pluralism*. Durham, NC: Duke University Press.

Dilanian, K., Jackson, H., Butchireddygari, L., & Martinez, G. (2017). Trump White House has taken little action to stop next election hack. *NBC News*, June 24, retrieved November 26, 2017 from https://nbcnews.com/politics/elections/trump-white-house-has-taken-little-action-stop-next-election-n776116.

Ehninger, D. (1970). Argument as method: Its nature, its limitation and its uses. *Speech Monographs, 37*(2), 101–110. doi:10.1080/03637757009375654

Greene, R. W., & Hicks, D. (2005). Lost convictions: Debating both sides and the ethical self-fashioning of liberal citizens. *Cultural Studies, 19*(1), 100–126. doi:10.1080/09502380500040928

Isocrates. (1929). Panathenaicus. In G. Norlin (Trans.), *Isocrates Volume II* (pp. 372–541). London, United Kingdom: William Heinemann.

Jackson, S. (2015). Design thinking in argumentation theory and practice. *Argumentation, 29*(3), 243–263. doi:10.1007/s10503-015-9353-7

Johnstone, H. W., Jr. (1990). Rhetoric as a wedge: A reformulation. *Rhetoric Society Quarterly, 20*(4), 333–338. doi:10.1080/02773949009390895

Kahan, D. M. (2013). Ideology, motivated reasoning, and cognitive reflection. *Judgment and Decision Making, 8*(4), 407–424. doi:10.2139/ssrn.2182588

Karpowitz, C. F., & Mansbridge, J. (2005). Disagreement and consensus: The importance of dynamic updating in public deliberation. In J. Gastil & P. Levine (Eds.), *The deliberative democracy handbook* (pp. 237–253). San Francisco, CA: Jossey-Bass.

Nyhan, B., & Reifler, J. (2010). When corrections fail: The persistence of political misperceptions. *Political Behavior, 32*(2), 303–330. doi:10.1007/s11109-010-9112-2

Pariser, E. (2011). *The filter bubble: What the internet is hiding from you.* New York: Penguin Books.

Pfister, D. S. (2014). *Networked media, networked rhetorics: Attention and deliberation in the early blogosphere.* University Park, PA: Pennsylvannia State University Press.

Sprain, L., & Ivancic, S. (2017). Communicating openness in deliberation. *Communication Monographs, 84* (2), 241–257. doi:10.1080/03637751.2016.1257141

United States. Department of Homeland Security and Office of the Director of National Intelligence. (2016, October 7). *Joint statement from the Department of Homeland Security and Office of the Director of National Intelligence on election security.* Retrieved from https://dhs.gov/news/2016/10/07/joint-state ment-department-homeland-security-and-office-director-national

Woodward, H. S. (1928). Measurement and analysis of audience opinion. *Quarterly Journal of Speech, 14*(1), 94–111. doi:10.1080/00335632809379726

75

COMMUNITY-BASED PARTICIPATORY DEBATE

A Synthesis of Debate Pedagogy, Practice, and Research

John J. Rief and Rachel Wilson

Efforts to recalibrate intercollegiate academic debate have gained momentum recently due to the work of the Schenley Park Debate Author's Working Group (DAWG) at the University of Pittsburgh (Mitchell et al., 2010a; Mitchell et al., 2010b) and two recent national conferences: the 2009 National Developmental Debate Conference at Wake Forest University (Louden, 2010) and the 2015 Speech and Debate as Civic Education conference at Penn State University (Hogan & Kurr, 2017). A central concern in these efforts has been reaffirming the connection between debate and civic life. For example, in his keynote at Wake Forest, Keith (2010) argued, "Debate will need to become not only more transparent and less introverted but also more responsive to its publics" (p. 12). In response, debate scholars and practitioners have renewed their commitment to the civic foundations of intercollegiate academic debate both in terms of its pedagogy (Atchison & Panetta, 2009; Hogan & Kurr, 2017; Keith, 2007, 2010; Llano, 2017; Mitchell, 2011; O'Donnell et al., 2010; Polk, 1995) and its scholarship (Mitchell et al., 2010b).

A series of practice changes aimed at pushing the activity out of "the proverbial pedagogical bullpen, a peripheral space marked off from the field of social action" (Mitchell, 1998, p. 43), and toward "civic activity" (Keith, 2010, p. 25; Llano, 2017) have characterized these national-level efforts. In his germinal essay on community-oriented and civically attentive debate practice, Mitchell (1998) argued in favor both of seeking input from "social movements, government offices, and citizens" (p. 49) and offering public debate events that promoted "citizen advocacy training and community action research that are designed to build community capacity for public discussion" (p. 51). Mitchell (1998) also highlighted the development of "shared decision-making power regarding determination of formats, dates, venues, and topics of public debates" (p. 51). At the Wake conference, Albiniak (2010) echoed Mitchell's call and argued for "alternative models as part of the movement to establish a civic-engagement curriculum at the university level" (p. 236) that would build upon "the major effort by many universities to change their image from that of an elite institution that simply occupies space in a neighborhood to the image of active community members in their surrounding areas" (Albiniak, 2010, p. 237; Keith 2010; O'Donnell et al., 2010; Panetta et al., 2010; Vats, 2010).

These arguments for transforming the activity occurred during an era of growing "skepticism" towards higher education (Leeper et al., 2010, p. 156; O'Donnell et al., 2010). Debate practitioners and scholars have noted this problem, initiating efforts to establish the learning outcomes of debate participation in response to "the assessment drive that has descended upon many of our institutions" (O'Donnell, 2011, p. 221). Such efforts offer opportunities to collect evidence documenting the benefits of debate participation using various methods (Albiniak, 2010; Bartanen, 2006; Leeper et al., 2010; Mitchell, 1998, 2000; O'Donnell et al., 2010; O'Donnell, 2011; Panetta et al., 2010; Partlow-Lefevre, 2012). However, these assessment activities have often focused on benefits for those directly engaged in the activity (i.e., students, coaches, and closely affiliated individuals) rather than cultivating opportunities to consider the potential outcomes of debate education beyond the tournament site or the ways that civic approaches might inspire changes to practices in contest rounds (Batt & Schultz, 2003, p. 515).

Faced by these challenges, we contend that debate practitioners would benefit from an approach that synergistically attends to pedagogy, practice, and research/assessment. Drawing on the Community-Based Participatory Research (CBPR) approach from academic medicine (Chen, Jones, & Gelberg, 2006; Jones & Wells, 2007; Minkler, 2004), we begin the work of developing a method we call, "Community-Based Participatory Debate" (CBPD). CBPD features the involvement of local communities in the design, implementation, and evaluation of debate projects to inspire multidirectional learning and growth. In developing this perspective, we draw on previously established principles of debate-community partnership and consider how others might apply them in new contexts of debate scholarship and assessment. We begin by describing recent work on debate-community partnership before turning to an articulation of our conception of CBPD.

Debate-Community Partnerships: Expanding the Conversation

In recent years, debate practitioners have demonstrated exceptional pedagogical dexterity, especially in terms of developing approaches sensitive to community norms (Albiniak, 2010; Mitchell, 1998; Mitchell, 2000, 2011; O'Donnell et al., 2010). In particular, the Urban Debate League movement (e.g., see Baker, 2010; Mitchell, 1998; Preston, 2006; Reid-Brinkley, 2012; Wade, 2010; Winkler, 2011) and related approaches to public and outreach programming (e.g., see Atchison & Panetta, 2009; Baker, 2010; Leeper et al., 2010; Mitchell, 1998, 2000, 2011; Vats, 2010; Wade, 2010) have energized efforts to create locally oriented opportunities for debate pedagogy and practice. The practitioners and scholars involved in these activities have underscored the notion that sharing leadership with community members in outreach programs (Mitchell, 1998) is essential for affirming and valuing the interests and conventions of specific communities (Albiniak, 2010; Baker, 2010; Chávez, 2015; Mitchell, 1998; Preston, 2006). In other words, events and programs with either negligible or nonexistent community involvement fail to ring audible chords in the larger rhythms of social, cultural, and political life. Thus, coupling debaters with community in meaningful partnership is essential to effective and ethical outreach.

While the literature on debate-community partnerships is significant, scholars have paid less attention to how such partnerships might transform the scholarly and assessment practices of the activity. The debate community has largely accepted moves to value local input in debate; however, embracing its import in the context of debate's scholarly research practices, methods, and modes of dissemination has been much slower. One of the challenges in accomplishing this task has been the recalcitrant notion that research remains the domain of experts and scholars. Though subject area and methodological expertise are essential in developing trustworthy insights, community members bring a set of ideas, expectations, and assumptions that, as many debate practitioners have experienced, fundamentally unsettle the practices of the activity. Including community voices in event design and in research and assessment might alter not only the collection and interpretation of evidence but also expand its potential audience. The next section develops one way to approach research that provides room for valuing forms of knowledge beyond the academy to embrace more fully the calls for a return to the civic.

Community-Based Participatory Debate: Multidirectional Learning and Discovery

As debate practitioners and scholars pursue a return to the civic, the experiences of another community—academic medicine— might prove useful for understanding similar tensions between expertise and community outreach. To address community interests in developing approaches to public health and improving the delivery of care in ways that are sensitive to community norms and practices, some researchers in medicine have turned to CBPR. This strategy features expert-community member collaboration in the design of research activities to inspire "uptake" of new discoveries (Chen et al., 2006, p. 121) and answer questions that are of interest to medical practitioners and the communities they serve. Minkler (2004) provided an essential definition for CBPR:

> CBPR is defined as a collaborative process that equitably involves all partners in the research process and recognizes the unique strengths that each brings. CBPR begins with a research topic of importance to the community with the aim of combining knowledge and action for social change to improve health and human welfare.
>
> *(pp. 685-686)*

Minkler (2004) explained two key features of CBPR: grounding in a "'community-driven' agenda" (p. 685) and the promotion of "community capacity building" (p. 684), both of which help forestall the unreflective acceptance of the needs and interests of medical experts. In other words, CBPR inspired the cultivation of medical research projects not grounded solely in the interests of biomedicine but also, and more primarily, in the needs, values, interests, and topics of concern shared throughout the communities the medical research served. Moreover, Minkler (2004) and others (Chen et al., 2006; Jones & Wells, 2007) noted the importance of research not only to accumulate more evidence to support medical interventions and improve care, but also to inspire community-based capabilities to alleviate public health concerns. Finally, CBPR involves "the establishment of a long-term community-academic partnership that extends beyond any single research study" (Chen et al., 2006, p. 119), thus implying an ongoing exchange of ideas, skills, and findings.

The basic assumptions of the CBPR approach provide a useful way to frame key elements of the effort to inspire ongoing debate-community partnerships with an emphasis on the community rather than debate. Adapting Minkler's (2004) definition of CBPR for debate, we introduce CBPD and define it in the following way: CBPD is a collaborative model of debate practice and research that features student, scholar, and community member participation in the cultivation of events and projects that facilitate long-term and sustainable learning for producing educational, social, cultural, and political renewal through diverse modalities of advocacy and discovery. As indicated by this definition, CBPD echoes many well-established principles of debate-community partnership, but adds a new civic inflection to the activity's research practices. In line with the scholarly findings described in the previous two sections, CBPD encourages long-term outreach efforts that value community leadership. This focus would support debate's gradual move away from the tournament model and single public events and toward the creation of resilient networks of community-based deliberation (Albiniak, 2010; Baker, 2010; Mitchell, 1998). More importantly, CBPD offers a new modality of civic practice for intercollegiate debate, namely synergizing changes in practice with changes in research. It assumes that external stakeholders (i.e., non-debaters) should help to design not only public outreach efforts, but also research and assessment projects that, as Batt and Schulz (2003) have suggested, might influence changes in the activity's internal practices. In this sense CBPD takes inspiration from the work of the DAWG in terms of developing interdisciplinary research on debate and argumentation (Mitchell et al., 2010b; see also Albiniak, 2010), but adds a new dimension drawn from CBPR in which nonacademic participants play a role in framing, implementing, and producing research (Jones & Wells, 2007, p. 409) that addresses questions well beyond those that might occur to debaters and scholars. This new civic inflection would not only change the intent and content of current debate research but also implies the need for new outlets for the presentation and circulation of findings that are accessible to wider communities. In short, this level of collaboration and transparency in research practices will fit debate for the specific needs and challenges facing emergent deliberative ecosystems in local and national venues. If debate is to move beyond its status as an insular activity that views itself as always reaching outward, its pedagogy *and* research must transform in ways that account for the realities of deliberation in the public square and create a living record of such activities for use by future practitioners *and* community members. While others, notably Baker (2010), have offered accounts of debate-community partnership that share assumptions with this approach, CBPD builds on such accounts by synergizing outreach with a newly fashioned civic identity for the activity that stretches from the tournament site to the public square and involves more "transparent," "responsive," and "accessible" (Keith, 2010, p. 12) research practices.

What would a CBPD project look like in practice? The following demonstrates key features of such a project that draws from scholarship on CBPR and debate. First, debate practitioners would build community relationships near their campuses (Baker, 2010). Dialogue would be the foundation of these relationships (Minkler, 2004; Mitchell, 2000) in ways that acknowledge the needs, interests, values, and norms of involved debaters *and* community participants (Chávez, 2015; Leeper et al., 2010; Mitchell, 1998; Panetta et al., 2010; Preston, 2006). Next, dialogue would turn to cultivating educational opportunities that assist in developing skills both for debaters *and* community participants (Albiniak, 2010). As part of this "iterative" (Chen et al., 2006, p. 120) process, opportunities for generating findings with multidirectional consequences (Albiniak, 2010; Chen et al., 2006; Jones & Wells, 2007; Minkler, 2004; Mitchell, 1998; Vats, 2010; Wade, 2010) would frame research, scholarship, and public advocacy opportunities for undergraduate student debaters, coaches, faculty members, and community members (Albiniak, 2010; Mitchell, 1998). As such, instead of delivering debate to a community, CBPD inspires an "organic" (Mitchell, 1998, p. 52) development of public argumentation followed by transparent and collaborative scholarly evaluation.

Conclusion

In sum, CBPD builds upon extant resources for envisioning debate as a mode of civic education that serves the interests of its participants and the wider communities beyond the classroom and the tournament site (Albiniak, 2010; Mitchell, 1998). Moreover, it moves beyond current conversations about interdisciplinary debate scholarship (Mitchell et al., 2010b) and articulates the values and attitudes necessary for inter-community research and assessment initiatives. Both debate as community and communities outside debate would, under CBPD, share not only in planning public encounters and interventions, but also in creating evaluative research projects that would include co-authors and contributors who are more likely to challenge the activity's assumptions about its value, scope, and norms. Such innovative scholarship would put debate on the cutting edge of scholarly innovation in the wider fields of argumentation, rhetoric, and communication studies and provide opportunities to reconsider the role of these fields' professionals in the maintenance of sorely needed democratic deliberation.

References

Albiniak, T. (2010). Alternative debate models: Working group summary. In A. D. Louden (Ed.), *Navigating opportunity: Policy debate in the 21st century* (pp. 236–241). New York, NY: International Debate Education Association.

Atchison, J., & Panetta, E. (2009). Intercollegiate debate and speech communication: Historical developments and issues for the future. In A. A. Lunsford, K. H. Wilson, & R. A. Eberly (Eds.), *The SAGE handbook of rhetorical studies* (pp. 317–333). Thousand Oaks, CA: SAGE.

Baker, W. (2010). Toward an understanding of the landscape of debate expansion in urban areas and opportunities for the college community. In A. D. Louden (Ed.), *Navigating opportunity: Policy debate in the 21st century* (pp. 253–261). New York, NY: International Debate Education Association.

Bartanen, M. (2006). Rigorous program assessment in intercollegiate forensics: Its time has come. *The Forensic of Pi Kappa Delta, 91,* 33–45.

Batt, S., & Schulz, D. (2005). Design principles for competitive debate formats. In C. Willard (Ed.), *Critical problems in argumentation* (pp. 510–517). Washington, DC: National Communication Association.

Chávez, K. R. (2015, March 16). Community debates: Where activism and deliberation converge [Web log comment]. *Rhetorically Speaking.* Retrieved from http://rhetoric.commarts.wisc.edu/?author=10

Chen, D. T., Jones, L., & Gelberg, L. (2006). Ethics of clinical research within a community- academic partnered participatory framework. *Ethnicity & Disease, 16 (Suppl.1),* 118–135.

Hogan, J. M., & Kurr, J. A. (2017). Civic education in competitive speech and debate. *Argumentation and Advocacy, 53*(2), 83–89. doi: 10.1080/00028533.2017.1304959

Jones, L., & Wells, K. (2007). Strategies for academic and clinician engagement in community-participatory partnered research. *Journal of the American Medical Association, 297*(4), 407–410. doi: 10.1001/jama.297.4.407

Keith, W. M. (2007). *Democracy as discussion: Civic education and the American forum movement.* Lanham, MD: Lexington Books.

Keith, W. (2010). Keynote address: A new golden age—Intercollegiate debate in the twenty-first century. In A. D. Louden (Ed.), *Navigating opportunity: Policy debate in the 21st century* (pp. 11–26). New York, NY: International Debate Education Association.

Leeper, K., Abbott, B., Congdon, K., Gonzales, J., Lefevre, S. P., Richardson, D., ... Hardy, A. (2010). Innovation and debate: Where do we go from here? In A. D. Louden (Ed.), *Navigating opportunity: Policy debate in the 21st century* (pp. 149–162). New York, NY: International Debate Education Association.

Llano, S. M. (2017). The counterfeit presentment: An early 20th century model of intercollegiate debate as civic education. *Argumentation and Advocacy, 53*(2), 90–102. doi: 10.1080/00028533.2017.1304983

Louden, A. D. (2010). Beginnings: The national developmental debate conference. In A. D. Louden (Ed.), *Navigating opportunity: Policy debate in the 21st century* (pp. 1–8). New York, NY: International Debate Education Association.

Minkler, M. (2004). Ethical challenges for the "outside" researcher in community-based participatory research. *Health Education & Behavior, 31*(6), 684–697. doi: 10.1177/1090198104269566

Mitchell, G. R. (1998). Pedagogical possibilities for argumentative agency in academic debate. *Argumentation and Advocacy, 35*(2), 41–60. Retrieved from http://files.eric.ed.gov/fulltext/ED418455.pdf

Mitchell, G. R. (2000). Simulated public argument as a pedagogical play on worlds. *Argumentation and Advocacy, 36*(3), 134–150. Retrieved from http://pitt.edu/~gordonm/JPubs/Roleplay.pdf

Mitchell, G. R. (2011). iSocrates: Student-led public debate as cultural technology. *Controversia, 7*(2), 54–75. Retrieved from http://pitt.edu/~gordonm/JPubs/Mitchell2011b.pdf

Mitchell, G. R., Bsumek, P., Lundberg, C., Mangus, M., Voth, B., Hobeika, M., & Jensen, M. (2010a). Pathways to innovation in debate scholarship. In A. D. Louden (Ed.), *Navigating opportunity: Policy debate in the 21st century* (pp. 93–122). New York, NY: International Debate Education Association.

Mitchell, G. R., Woods, C. S., Brigham, M., English, E., Morrison, C. E., & Rief, J. (2010b). The debate authors working group model for collaborative knowledge production in forensics scholarship. *Argumentation and Advocacy, 47*(1), 1–24. Retrieved from http://tandfonline.com

O'Donnell, T. (2011). On building a culture of assessment in intercollegiate policy debate. In R. C. Rowland (Ed.), *Reasoned argument and social change* (pp. 221–228). Washington, DC: National Communication Association.

O'Donnell, T., Butt, N., Bauchard, S., Bellon, J., Decker, W., Katulas, J., … Packer, J. (2010). A rationale for intercollegiate debate in the twenty-first century. In A. D. Louden (Ed.), *Navigating opportunity: Policy debate in the 21st century* (pp. 27–56). New York, NY: International Debate Education Association.

Panetta, E. M., Mosely-Jensen, W., Fitzmier, D., Hall, S., Kuswa, K., Lee, E., … Turner, J. (2010). Controversies in debate pedagogy: Working paper. In A. D. Louden (Ed.), *Navigating opportunity: Policy debate in the 21st century* (pp. 211–235). New York, NY: International Debate Education Association.

Partlow-Lefevre, S. T. (2012). Arguing for debate: Introducing key components for assessment of intercollegiate debate programs. *Contemporary Argumentation & Debate, 33,* 31–74.

Preston, C. T., Jr. (2006). The interconnectedness between intercollegiate policy debate and the urban debate leagues: From a distance, five years and change later. *Contemporary Argumentation & Debate, 27,* 157–172.

Polk, L. R. (1995). The NDT and information processing: The decay of dialogue. In S. Jackson (Ed.), *Argumentation and values* (pp. 122–124). Annandale, VA: Speech Communication Association.

Reid-Brinkley, S. R. (2012). Ghetto kids gone good: Race, representation, and authority in the scripting of inner-city youths in the urban debate league. *Argumentation and Advocacy, 49*(2), 77–99. Retrieved from http://tandfonline.com

Vats, A. (2010). Civic engagement through policy debate: Possibilities for transformation. In A. D. Louden (Ed.), *Navigating opportunity: Policy debate in the 21st century* (pp. 242–249). New York, NY: International Debate Education Association.

Wade, M. M. (2010). Rethinking debate education: The impact of community programs and engaged scholarship on debate at Emory University. In A. D. Louden (Ed.), *Navigating opportunity: Policy debate in the 21st century* (pp. 262–270). New York, NY: International Debate Education Association.

Winkler, C. (2011). To argue or to fight: Improving at-risk students' school conduct through urban debate. *Controversia: An international journal of debate and democratic renewal, 7*(2), 76–90.

76

TEXT, TALK, ARGUE

How to Improve Text-Driven Political Conversations

Don Waisanen, Allison Hahn, and Eric Gander

In fall 2016, the authors of this essay held a public deliberation on the U.S. presidential election using the well-funded and widely endorsed "Text, Talk, Vote" tool that the National Institute for Civic Discourse (NICD) developed. Text, Talk, Vote aims to facilitate "large scale change in the behavior and ideology of people and systems [...including] media, citizens, and elected officials" (NICD, n.d., para. 1). In this paper, we use NICD's tool to examine how the internet, social media, and new mobile technologies are changing the nature of how people argue (Harsin, 2014; Lewiński, 2010; Pfister, 2010, 2014; Waisanen, 2018), with a specific focus on how this technology may either facilitate or impede the products and processes of public argument. This analysis draws from data gathered through participant observations of approximately 95 people who engaged with Text, Talk, Vote in classrooms at Baruch College, CUNY and from a public event held collaboratively with Public Agenda, a New York based non-profit organization.

Although we report aggregate data collected during our facilitation of Text, Talk, Vote, we became most interested in the process of participation—specifically, the rhetorical or social resources that produced possibilities for argumentation during the event and how text-messages appeared to promote or hinder small-group deliberation. We begin with a description of the process of a Text, Talk, Vote event. We then highlight our findings from these text-driven conversations, including themes such as "hyperlinked argumentation," which describe how some participants pulled out their cell phones to compare and contrast evidence with one another at key moments. Finally, we provide a brief analysis of the administered survey and provide recommendations for how modifications in the Text, Talk, Vote program might improve political discussions.

Facilitating Text, Talk, Vote

In advance of the 2016 election, NICD sought to facilitate conversations among students and civic organizations such as the United Way. Text, Talk, Vote events were held during the 2016 presidential election, often in conjunction with debate watches, organizer training sessions, or during class time. Text, Talk, Vote emerged from the prior success of Text, Talk, Act, which used the same text-message interface to encourage students and families to hold conversations regarding mental and public health services. The Text, Talk, Act program connected participants with a range of local and national service providers after they participated in conversations about mental health in their school and community. Similarly, after participating in a Text, Talk, Vote event, participants received links to opportunities for political engagement in their communities and prompts to vote in upcoming elections (Share & Knighton, 2016). The design of Text, Talk, Vote focuses on combatting online "slactivism" by having people discuss issues face-to-face (3:01).

Text, Talk, Vote employs a SMS text-message interface to facilitate a 90-minute discussion. At the beginning of a Text, Talk, Vote event, participants clustered into small groups of four to five members. Each group used one participant's smart phone to receive a series of 20 to 25 questions such as, "What are the most important issues you believe should be addressed in this election?" Once the groups had a few minutes to talk about the question, they texted in their answers and received a new question. During the question and response period, participants took several breaks in which they could see visualizations of collective responses by other participants. At the conclusion, the Text, Talk, Vote program prompted participants to take a group selfie and post their image to Twitter using the hashtag #TextTalkVote. Hosts collected all data from Text, Talk, Vote events as anonymous, aggregate responses.

Text, Talk, Vote requires minimal set up from facilitators; it primarily relies on participants' smart phones. While this makes an event easier to arrange, it can also produce programing problems. For example, we found that some cellular carriers experienced delays in delivering messages and, at one point, AT&T coverage was not available in the room holding the public event. While the cost of sending a text message has decreased rapidly in recent years, participants, especially students, may face constraints from shared data plans that make it difficult to send and receive multiple text messages.

Observations of Text-Driven Argumentation

We used participant observation at our Text, Talk, Vote events, moving between groups and sometimes asking questions. When employing the participant observation method, researchers should ideally draw from varied experiences and theories, maintain reflexivity and a tolerance for ambiguity, and look to the embodied, behavioral dimensions in situations (Lindlof & Taylor, 2002). Accordingly, we each made individual field notes to diversify our observations and interpretations. Due to the short-term nature of our event and to test our observations, we compared our field notes using "intensity and frequency" (Foss, 2018, p. 413) as criteria to guide the development of our analytic themes. We found three themes from our data: power imbalances in the deliberations, hyperlinked argumentation, and humor as a gateway to arguments. In considering each theme, we sought to understand the rhetorical or social resources that produced possibilities for argumentation through Text, Talk, Vote.

Power is in the Hands of the Beholder

Each group used one phone during a Text, Talk, Vote session. We each observed that the person holding the phone played the "dominant voice" simply by carrying out their assigned task of reading questions out loud and texting the answers. Participants tended to defer to the person who held the phone, and often this person determined if, and when, a question had been fully answered. In this way, the grounds for argument were not equal in practice.

One consequence of this status hierarchy was that some participants stopped paying attention to the discussion. Some even signed into the Text, Talk, Vote program on their own phones and began answering the questions individually. We also observed non-dominant participants using their phones to conduct research during the event, to fact check other group members, or to non-verbally exit from an awkward or heated discussion by using their phones in ways that had nothing to do with the Text, Talk, Vote application. Regardless of their power position, some participants simply became disinterested during the event. When the questions did not inspire participants, they quickly lost interest, which reduced the possibilities for argumentation. This was particularly true for those who participated during in-class facilitations where individuals spoke in groups with known classmates.

Yet the majority of the participants, especially those grouped with new acquaintances, started leaning in and grew interested once they "got it." As their discussions developed, participants shared both their claims and evidence. Often, participants reflected on their use of new and social media to find political information. For example, one participant said, "I Googled one [campaign ad] six months ago." Another provided backing for an argument regarding presidential candidate Donald Trump ridiculing a person with a disability: "I YouTubed it."

This sharing of information seemed to work best in small, subgroup discussions where two-person conversations often emerged. Sometimes the subgroups would report back to the larger group and move on to the next question. On some occasions, however, the subgroup broke off from the discussion entirely. Given these power imbalances and distributions over the course of using the Text, Talk, Vote program, future organizers should give greater thought to how active or passive participants are during these discussions, and how smaller subgroups might promote quality arguing.

Hyperlinked Argumentation

Throughout the events, we observed participants searching for facts and argumentative backing during their discussions. We saw one participant using a smart phone to search for information on the Fox News website. Another found and displayed examples of Trump's tweets to group members. When consulting the internet, participants appeared to have several goals. Some simply wanted to prove that a citation existed for their arguments. Others wanted to ensure that they were correctly representing a certain point, while others used their phones to find visual evidence.

Once participants saw the Text, Talk, Vote format as an occasion for turning to their phones and hyperlinking claims and evidence, attention to the process of argumentation also became a noticeable part of the deliberations. The content of these discussions ranged from the presidential debate formats to the communicative responsibilities of the candidates themselves. One participant said that "politics needs to involve something different than rallies," clarifying the potential usefulness of a "more town hall style" format, while recognizing that a "town hall is [still] not enough." Other groups provided inventive ideas for candidates' speech practices. One participant highlighted how "Trump should have to answer to the other side of the spectrum." In these examples the process of argument became part of the discussion, apparently by participants prompted to try out a new way of arguing via the Text, Talk, Vote format.

Throughout the process, the NCID and Text, Talk, Vote partners aggregated responses and, when possible, projected those responses onto a large screen for participants to see and comment upon. In our events, participants generally enjoyed seeing the aggregate answers revealed during the event. For example, in the public event, a good deal of discussion occurred when the screen showed the aggregated "Top 3 Issues" in the election.

Being able to text in their answers and then see the surprising, real-time results also appeared to build engagement with the platform. We noticed that members of breakaway subgroups generally rejoined the discussions after viewing the aggregate data. One qualification is worth mentioning, however. When prompted to take a selfie at the end, those attendees at our public event seemed to like the feature, but students in the class facilitation asked, "Do we have to do that," or simply ignored the request and reported that they had finished using Text, Talk, Vote.

Humor as a Gateway to Argument

We observed how the use of humor often preceded substantive insights in the conversations, and therefore propose building more playful actions into the texting technology to advance argumentative processes (for the use of similar strategies, see Palczewski, 2002). Throughout the Text, Talk, Vote public event, the participants engaged in copious laughter and side conversations. The occasionally awkward gaps between the technological ideal, on the one hand, and actual practice, on the other, of using SMS text-messages to facilitate face-to-face deliberation prompted the use of humor at times.

Humor also emerged in answers to some of the Text, Talk, Vote questions. For example, when answering a question concerning what kind of traits they most wanted to see in a politician, one participant said, "good hair, an orange complexion, and likes to swear a lot." These jokes worked to move the conversation along and, at other times, to express the limited options provided by the Text, Talk, Vote application. Feeling overwhelmed by the election, one participant at the public event asked the others, "Is there any option for terrified?" In response to the question, "Do you have any other ideas about how the political process should involve citizens," another person remarked, "Give them money."

Far from a frivolous diversion at the events, these pockets of humor and laughter largely drove arguments forward. Yet the productivity of these moments and the inventional moments they could have inspired were frequently cut short by the Text, Talk, Vote program's next question, moving the discussion in a new and at times awkward direction. Additionally, the situated use of humor at these events, as in all events, occurred in cultural and linguistic groupings. More instances of humor happened at the public event, which was diverse in age, but not in race and ethnicity. The in-class facilitation included students from many cultural, ethnic, and national groups, which could have contributed to the more limited uses of humor. Or, the formality of classroom exercises as opposed to an evening, public event may have contributed to the lack of humor during the in-class facilitation.

The Usefulness of Text, Talk, Vote

Approximately one week after the Text, Talk, Vote public event, an instructor invited students in a public address class at Baruch College to share in the same experience. A week after that, the professor administered a three-question survey to this class to elicit their impressions of the usefulness of Text, Talk, Vote as a tool for increasing and improving political discussions. A total of 54 students completed the survey, which used Likert scale questions to gauge engagement with the Text, Talk, Vote tool. We understand the limits of this sample-size and are cautious about drawing any grand conclusions, but found it useful nonetheless.

The largest plurality of students had a neutral response to the prompt, "I found that the 'Text, Talk, and Vote' application enhanced my ability to participate in political discussions," with slightly more respondents agreeing versus disagreeing. This answer confirmed our suspicion formed at the public event that the tool may have a limited range of engagement. When answering the statement, "I would use the 'Text, Talk, Vote' application again," students were largely optimistic, however. Relatively few respondents gave up completely on the Text, Talk, Vote application, suggesting that tweaking the tool might improve text-driven political conversations.

During both the public and student events, users of Text, Talk, Vote seemed mildly curious about its potential, and somewhat interested in the way it operated. However, they were generally not convinced that the tool would dramatically change the way that they or others participated in political discourse.

Conclusion

Much funding has facilitated the development and scaling of Text, Talk, Vote. We remain cautiously optimistic about the tool's potential and, following the analytic themes developed here, we offer the following recommendations for improving the tool's ability to facilitate productive argument.

First, the platform itself needs to incorporate more egalitarian and interesting features for its users. We recommend using fewer questions for these forums and building more engagement around the interface itself. Given the power struggles we observed within the groups, users clearly want more individuals involved in determining when an argument is complete before the group moves on to the next question. The "hyperlinked" argumentation we observed in our public event demonstrated that most people in each group wanted to talk, look for data on their phones, argue, and so on. Perhaps the tool could add a question every few steps that prompts users to search for information on their phones. With some slight, inexpensive tweaks, the platform could encourage much more hyperlinked argument and deliberative engagement.

Since we observed that humor often preceded substantive insights in the conversations, we also advise building some brief, strategic opportunities for humor into the platform's structure. Perhaps the Text, Talk, Vote tool could include a humorous anecdote between some questions, or it could ask participants to write captions for a political cartoon or meme. Such additions would work with rather than against what seemed to happen naturally in these events. Additionally, participants enjoyed seeing the revelations of collective results on the screen, suggesting that the occasional presentation of what's going on in other groups could also drive engagement. Critically, more research needs to examine how Text, Talk, Vote might contribute to (or perhaps undermine) the so-called "bandwagon effect"—that is, the tendency of individuals to agree with the views of the majority on any given issue, once an individual knows those majority views (see Kiss & Simonovits, 2014).

Along these same lines, our second suggestion concerns the way in which this platform has the potential to combat the pernicious effects of "confirmation bias," or the tendency of individuals to credit evidence and arguments that confirm their pre-existing beliefs and prejudices (see Plous, 1993). Confirmation bias may occur if like-minded groups of individuals arrived together and then stayed together at a given Text, Talk, Vote event. Organizers could address this potentially negative situation by asking participants to answer one or more questions anonymously on their own phones at the beginning of the event. Based on these initial responses, organizers could construct groups in which participants hold different opinions on important issues (for similar methods, see Lipmanowicz & McCandless, 2013).

The screen in the room could also provide cues suggesting that participants search for diverse sources, or even provide a range of credible sources directly. In this way, the host could reassure participants that using their phones is acceptable, while still encouraging attendees to encounter diverse viewpoints as a regular, structural feature of the event. The goal would be to foster, not impede, reasoned discourse, and start the participants on more equal footing in terms of their contributions to the argumentation from the outset.

In the end, we want to remain realistic about the possibility that applications like Text, Talk, Vote could improve our political discourse. Our findings lead us to believe that enough bright spots exist in the use of such technologies that they may be able to play a significant part in making some public deliberations accessible and engaging. Indeed, compared with purely face-to-face or online methods, citizens may now have arrived at a place where the workings of programs like Text, Talk, Vote are more in line with their everyday life experiences. As "public screens" increasingly constitute the horizons in which citizens can see, debate, and imagine their social worlds (DeLuca, Lawson, & Sun, 2012), argument scholars should continue to theorize the rhetorical and social resources that can promote the most valuable ways of practicing argumentation in hybrid, face-to-face, and technology-mediated conditions.

References

DeLuca, K. M., Lawson, S., & Sun, Y. (2012). Occupy Wall Street on the public screens of social media: The many framings of the birth of a protest movement. *Communication, Culture & Critique, 5*(4), 483–509. doi:10.1111/j.1753-9137.2012.01141.x

Foss, S. (2018). *Rhetorical criticism.* Long Grove, IL: Waveland.

Harsin, J. (2014). Public argument in the new media ecology. *Journal of Argumentation in Context, 3*(1), 7–34. doi:10.1075/jaic.3.1.02har

Kiss, Á., & Simonovits, G. (2014). Identifying the bandwagon effect in two-round elections. *Public Choice, 160*(3-4), 327–344. doi:10.1007/s11127-013-0146-y

Lewiński, M. (2010). Collective argumentative criticism in informal online discussion forums [Special issue]. *Argumentation and Advocacy, 47*(2), 86–105.Retrieved fromhttp://tandfonline.com

Lindlof, T. R., & Taylor, B. C. (2002). *Qualitative communication research methods* (2nd ed.). Thousand Oaks, CA: SAGE.

Lipmanowicz, H., & McCandless, K. (2013). *The surprising power of liberating structures: Simple rules to unleash a culture of innovation.* Seattle, WA: Liberating Structures Press.

National Institute for Civil Discourse. (n.d.). Retrieved from http://nicd.arizona.edu/programs

Palczewski, C. H. (2002). Argument in an off key: Playing with the productive limits of argument. In G. T. Goodnight (Ed.), *Arguing communication and culture* (pp. 1–23). Washington, DC: National Communication Association.

Pfister, D. S. (2010). Introduction to special issue: Public argument/digital media. *Argumentation and Advocacy, 47*(2), 63–66. Retrieved from http://tandfonline.com

Pfister, D. S. (2014). *Networked media, networked rhetorics: Attention and deliberation in the early blogosphere.* University Park, PA: Pennsylvania State Press.

Plous, S. (1993). *The psychology of judgment and decision making.* New York, NY: Mcgraw-Hill.

Share, T., & Knighton, J. (2016, October 13). #NICDChat - Dialogue XXIII- Text talk vote FAQs [Audio file]. *Sound Cloud.* Retrieved from. https://soundcloud.com

Waisanen, D. J. (2018). Arguments for everybody: Social media, context collapse, and the universal audience. In R. Lake (Ed.), *Recovering argument* (pp. 264–269). New York, NY: Routledge.

77

GENDER DIVERSITY IN DEBATE IN JAPAN

An Examination of Debate Competitions at the Secondary and Tertiary Levels

Junya Morooka

This paper is part of a larger research project the Japan Debate Association (JDA) spear-headed to celebrate the 30th anniversary of its founding. From August 2015 through June 2016, JDA administered a survey to participants, teachers, coaches, and tournament directors at 13 debate competitions to grasp the current state of competitive debate in Japan. The interview/focus groups lasted between 90 minutes and 120 minutes with each session audio-recorded to ensure accuracy and verbatim transcriptions. To complement the survey findings, researchers conducted a series of semi-structured interviews and focus groups with fifteen selected members of central organizations in their respective debate circuits. Central organizations of debate in Japan include: (a) the National Association of Forensics and Argu-mentation (NAFA, opened in 1983) oversees college policy debate in English; (b) the National Association of Debate in Education (NADE, opened in 1996) oversees middle and high school policy debate in Japanese; (c) the Collegiate Debate Association (CoDA, opened in 1997) oversees college policy debate in Japanese; (d) the Japan Parliamentary Debate Union (JPDU, opened in 1999) oversees college parliamentary debate in English; (e) the All Japan High School English Debate Association (HEnDA, opened in 2006) oversees high school policy debate in English; and (f) the High School Parliamentary Debate Union of Japan (HPDU, opened in 2010) oversees high school parliamentary debate in English.

This essay focuses particularly on data related to female participation. It investigates how styles (parliamentary and policy), levels of study (middle school, high school, and college), and languages (English and Japanese) relate to gender diversity in competitive debate. In and outside of the United States, scholars exploring gender issues in policy debate, parliamentary debate, and other formats of forensic competitions revealed that female debaters are generally underrepresented at tournaments (especially at higher levels of intercollegiate tournaments), have lower retention rates, and are more subject to discrimination and harassment (Allen, Trejo, Bartanen, Shroeder, & Ulrich, 2004; Mazur, 2001; Pierson, 2013; Stepp & Gardner, 2001; Szwapa, 1994). While plenty of anecdotal evidence and individual testimonies attest to challenges facing women debaters in Japan, no systematic research to date documents debate's relationship to gender.

This study is a long overdue attempt to examine the state of gender diversity in competitive debate in Japan. Scholars have well-documented the educational benefits of debate by demonstrating that the activity not only teaches students to be better speakers and listeners, but also helps to equip them with the skills necessary to become more engaged and effective citizens in an increasingly interconnected and complex world (Hogan & Kurr, 2017). As these skills benefit all who participate, those involved in debate education should strive to ensure that all students receive equal opportunities to excel in competitive debate regardless of gender, race, ethnicity, and other social factors.

One notable characteristic of competitive debate in Japan adds an interesting twist to gender dynamics within the Japanese debate community: the longstanding popularity of English debate. As Nagatomo (2016) noted, the Japanese often view English as a key skill for women's career advancement and personal development in Japan. Because learning English is highly popular among female students both as a field of study and a foreign language, the role of gender in Japan may differ from its global counterparts. This study thus provides unique insights into the relationship between gender and competitive equity in debate.

Growth and Diversification of Competitive Debate in Japan

Competitive debate in Japan has changed over time. According to Aonuma, Morooka, and Seno (2014), recent trends of competitive debate in Japan included the decline of collegiate English policy debate, the emergence of parliamentary debate in English, and the growth of high school debate in Japanese and English. JDA's survey research largely corroborates these key points.

The relative growth rates between policy and parliamentary debate varied by school level. At the college level, team entries at the JPDU tournament far outnumbered those at the NAFA tournament, but the number of participating schools was similar, suggesting that any conclusion that parliamentary debate had surpassed policy debate would be premature. However, many more schools participated in parliamentary debate at the novice level. Only 14 teams from eight schools entered policy debate at the SIDT for Freshmen. The number went up to 23 teams from 14 schools at NAFA Kanto (a competition open to soon-to-be sophomores), but was nowhere close to 145 teams from 34 schools participating in parliamentary debate at BP Novice. These figures bore out Aonuma, Morooka, and Seno's (2014) diagnosis that "the [English-language] college policy debate community in Japan is in critical condition" (p. 435).

At the high school level, in contrast, English policy debate has grown rapidly. The first HEnDA national championship in 2006 involved only 34 schools (Yano, 2013), whereas over 470 teams from 280 schools attended local qualifiers for a bid to the national championship in 2015 (Miyagawa, personal communication, June 8, 2017). Also worth mentioning is a surge of interest in parliamentary style on the high school debate circuit. Partly based on discontent with the situation that the winners of HEnDA Nationals represented Japan at the World Schools Debating Championships, a group of high school English teachers in 2010 formed a parliamentary debate association called the High School Parliamentary Debate Union of Japan. The number of schools attending its annual competition has steadily increased from 17 in 2012 to 34 in 2017 (HPDU of Japan, 2017). Notably, most high schools participated in both styles of debating. In this respect, high school English debate differs markedly from its college counterpart where the policy and parliamentary debate circuits sharply divide from one another. See Table 77.1 for a synopsis of the current state of participation levels and structure of all English language debate tournaments in the JDA survey.

Table 77.1 Description and Participation Level of English Debate Competitions

Tournament	Month/Year	Organizer	Level of Study	Division	Style	# of Teams	# of Schools
All Japan High School English Debate Tournament (HEnDA Nationals)	12/2015	HEnDA	High School	Varsity	Policy	66	66
HPDU Competition	03/2016	HPDU-J	High School	Varsity	Parliamentary	40	22
Sophia Invitational Debate Tournament for Freshmen (SIDT for Freshmen)	09/2015	Sophia University ESS	College	Novice	Policy	14	8
NAFA Kanto Educational League (NAFA Kanto)	03/2016	NAFA	College	Novice	Policy	23	14
NAFA Tournament	11-12/2015	NAFA	College	Varsity	Policy	38	22
BP Novice	11/2015	JPDU	College	Novice	Parliamentary	145	34*
JPDU Tournament	09/2015	JPDU	College	Varsity	Parliamentary	64	23*

Note: *The number does not include joint teams comprised of students from multiple schools for lack of information.

Japanese-language debate remains popular among middle and high school students. Fifty-three middle schools and 94 high schools entered local qualifiers in 2015 to compete at the national championships known as Debate Koshien. By contrast, the collegiate Japanese-language debate circuit remains quite small. As only a handful of universities have debate clubs, many students become team members with students from other universities to participate in debate competitions. For example, six out of the 19 teams entering the 2015 CoDA national championship were joint teams from multiple schools. The lack of intramural debate clubs is one factor inhibiting the growth of Japanese-language debate at the college level. See Table 77.2 for a synopsis of the current state of participation levels and structure of all Japanese language debate tournaments in the JDA survey.

Method of Analysis

To assess the level of gender diversity in competitive debate in Japan, I focused on varsity tournaments as they constituted major national championships that the primary Japanese debate organizations hosted. I included four novice debating competitions—BP Novice, the Sophia Invitational Debate Tournament for Freshmen, the NAFA Kanto Educational League, and the CoDA Rookies Match—to ascertain any differences in demographic characteristics between the novice and varsity divisions. After collecting the demographic information of participants, JDA asked all the tournament directors except HEnDA Nationals' to report the gender composition of each team, its win-loss record, and the preliminary and elimination round results. I completed data collection from the sample by identifying the

Table 77.2 Description and Participation Level of Japanese Debate Competitions

Tournament	Month/ Year	Organizer	Level of Study	Division	Style	# of Teams	# of Schools
Middle School National Debate Championship (Debate Koshien)	08/2015	NADE	Middle School	Varsity	Policy	24	24
High School National Debate Championship (Debate Koshien)	08/2015	NADE	High School	Varsity	Policy	32	32
CoDA Rookies Match	06/2016	CoDA	College	Novice	Policy	26	15
All Japan Intercollegiate Debating Championship (CoDA Nationals)	11/2015	CoDA	College	Varsity	Policy	19	15
JDA Fall Debate Tournament	11/2015	JDA	NA	Open**	Policy	26	NA
JDA Kyushu Debate Tournament	12/2015	JDA	NA	Open**	Policy	17	NA

Note: **The events are open to everyone, even those who are not enrolled in school.

gender of debaters at HEnDA Nationals based on their first names. When the names of debaters were gender-ambiguous, I filled in the gaps by asking Junichi Miyagawa, a HEnDA board member, to provide gender information. JDA also asked all the directors to compile data on judges by gender and age group who, in turn, supplied complete gender information.

The debate competitions were divided into seven categories for the purpose of this analysis: (a) middle school policy debate in Japanese, (b) high school policy debate in Japanese, (c) college policy debate in Japanese, (d) high school policy debate in English, (e) high school parliamentary debate in English, (f) college policy debate in English, and (g) college parliamentary debate in English. The two JDA tournaments also allowed participants not enrolled in school. The vast majority of JDA Fall Tournament participants were college students and graduates, thus resulting in their placement in the college policy debate in Japanese category. I excluded the JDA Kyushu Tournament from the analysis because a rough equivalence of high school and college students attended the tournament. Logistical and practical reasons omitted demographic data collection on the preliminary rounds of BP Novice.

Findings and Discussion

The high school English debate tournaments attracted more female students than male students. Females accounted for nearly 70% of the participants at the HEnDA Nationals and 60% of those advancing to the elimination rounds were women. The level of female participation was similar at the HPDU Competition. The participation rates of women dropped at the intercollegiate English debate tournaments, but not as sharply as at their Japanese-language counterparts. These figures suggest that English contributed to encouraging female participation in competitive debate, but the debate styles did not have a significant impact on the level of female participation.

Moreover, female participation was higher in the novice division than in the varsity division. An equal number of males and females emerged as the top eight teams at SIDT for Freshmen and NAFA Kanto. Likewise, women constituted 41% of those who cleared the preliminary rounds at BP Novice. The participation rate of female debaters decreased to 36% at the CoDA Rookies Match, but the percentage is still high compared to the varsity Japanese debate tournaments. At the same time, no female debaters advanced to the final round at the CoDA Rookies Match and only one woman participated on the top eight teams at the tournament. These findings underscore the danger of conflating participation with success.

As for Japanese-language debate, the highest participation rate of women was 50% in the middle school division of Debate Koshien. The percentage of those advanced to the elimination rounds remained almost the same, which suggests relatively low barriers to female participation and success in debate at the middle school level. The female participation rate dropped sharply to under 30% in the high school division of Debate Koshien. The percentage was unexpectedly low as all three NADE members who participated in a focus group—Yusuke Koyama, Kuriko Goto, and Shuichi Chikuda—shared the view that female participation in high school debate was only slightly lower than in middle school debate. On the other hand, Japanese-language debate is vastly male-dominated at the college level. The female participation rates decreased from 36% at the CoDA Rookies Match to 22% at CoDA Nationals and 19% at the JDA Fall Tournaments, suggesting that women tend to quit debate at higher rates than men during their first year of competition in college.

Tables 77.3 and 77.4 summarize the gender breakdown of debaters in preliminary and elimination rounds of competition. As eligibility rules, team size, and the number of elimination round teams varied for each event, readers should cautiously compare the data across

Table 77.3 Gender Breakdown of Japanese Debaters (Preliminary Rounds)

Tournament	Male	Female	Team Size	Note
Debate Koshien (Middle School)	69 (50%)	69 (50%)	4-6	A team consists of up to 6 enrolled students, but only 4 of them can compete in a single round.
Debate Koshien (High School)	117 (71%)	48 (29%)	4-6	
CoDA Rookies Match	47 (64%)	26 (36%)	2-4	
CoDA Nationals	40 (78%)	11 (22%)	2-4	
JDA Fall Tournament	50 (81%)	12 (19%)	2-4	
HEnDA Nationals	117 (31%)	264 (69%)	4-6	Same as above
HPDU Competition	44 (37%)	76 (63%)	3	
SIDT for Freshmen	17 (61%)	11 (39%)	2	
NAFA Kanto	22 (48%)	24 (52%)	2	
NAFA Tournament	32 (62%)	20 (38%)	2	Data on the preliminary rounds in the East Japan district
BP Novice	No data	No data	2	
JPDU Tournament	73 (57%)	54 (43%)	2	The gender of one participant is unknown.

Note: Percentages were rounded to the nearest integer.

Table 77.4 Gender Breakdown of Japanese Debaters (Elimination Rounds)

Tournament	Male	Female	Elimination rounds teams
Debate Koshien (Middle School)	45 (49%)	47 (51%)	16 (octa-finals)
Debate Koshien (High School)	58 (73%)	21 (27%)	16 (octa-finals)
CoDA Rookies Match	6 (100%)	0 (0%)	2 (final round)
CoDA Nationals	19 (86%)	3 (14%)	8 (quarter-finals)
JDA Fall Tournament	6 (100%)	0 (0%)	2 (final round)
HEnDA Nationals	18 (40%)	27 (60%)	8 (quarter-finals)
HPDU Competition	8 (38%)	13 (62%)	8 (quarter-finals)
SIDT for Freshmen	8 (50%)	8 (50%)	8 (quarter-finals)
NAFA Kanto	8 (50%)	8 (50%)	No elimination rounds. The figures refer to the gender makeup of the top 8 teams.
NAFA Tournament	9 (56%)	7 (44%)	8 (quarter-finals)
BP Novice	38 (59%)	26 (41%)	32 (octa-finals). BP debates take place between four teams.
JPDU Tournament	21 (66%)	11 (34%)	16 (quarter-finals) BP style

Note: Percentages were rounded to the nearest integer.

competitions. Moreover, the results do not clearly indicate if the data reflect persistent trends over time or represent overall female participation in each category.

Table 77.5 outlines the gender composition of judges. Clearly, the numbers were heavily skewed towards male judges at most competitions. The gender gap closed a bit in the novice division, which implies that women are less likely to receive invitations to judge at a higher level of competition or are more reluctant to participate in higher rounds of competition.

Particularly concerning is the low presence of female judges at the Japanese-language debate tournaments. Only 11% of the judges at Debate Koshien and CoDA Nationals were women. Only one woman served in the judging pool at the JDA Fall Tournament, which, according to focus group member Kuriko Goto (personal communication, January 8, 2017), is not unusual on the Japanese-language debate circuit.

Conclusion

English high school debate tournaments attracted more female students than male students regardless of style. Although the gender ratio tilted in favor of males on the college English debate circuit, the gap was not as wide as on the Japanese-language circuit. These findings suggest that English is a motivating factor for women to participate in competitive debate.

Female participation in competitive debate decreased from middle school to high school to college. This finding is largely consistent with McRee and Cote's (2002) study demonstrating that competitive debate is more gender balanced at the high school (i.e., less competitive and intense) level. Conversely, female debaters are less likely to find success and more likely to leave the activity at the college level.

Table 77.5 Gender Breakdown of Judges in Debate Competitions Held in Japan

Tournament	Male	Female	Note
SIDT for Freshmen	12 (67%)	6 (33%)	
NAFA Kanto	8 (50%)	8 (50%)	
NAFA Tournament	16 (84%)	3 (16%)	Judges in the East-Japan preliminary rounds
JPDU Tournament	22 (69%)	10 (31%)	
BP Novice	35 (71%)	14 (29%)	Data on breaking adjudicators (adjudicators at BP tournaments also compete to judge at elimination rounds.)
HEnDA Nationals	39 (85%)	7 (15%)	Data on "main" (invited) judges
HPDU Competition	16 (57%)	12 (43%)	
Debate Koshien	78 (89%)	10 (11%)	Judges in the middle- and high-school divisions combined
CoDA Rookies Match	17 (81%)	4 (19%)	
CoDA Nationals	17 (89%)	2 (11%)	
JDA Fall Tournament	16 (94%)	1 (6%)	

Note: Percentages were rounded to the nearest integer.

Female judges were vastly underrepresented at most debate competitions. The underrepresentation of female judges is particularly problematic as they perform an important role-modeling function for other women debaters. The collective failure to increase female judges in competitive debate across all debate organizations requires an urgent and immediate response.

While participation rates document that gender inequality exists in competitive debate activities in Japan, less clear is what causes such inequality. Future research should strive to isolate factors influencing women's decision to start, continue, and quit debate. Additionally, longitudinal studies should track consistent demographic patterns in the debate community. By providing a snapshot view of the state of gender diversity at various debate competitions, this study sought to serve as a stepping stone for such future research. However, studies alone may make little difference unless meaningful action follows up such work. Still, research on gender diversity can help to expose troubling gender gaps. As Allen et al. (2004) aptly put it, "If diversity is not measured, expected, rewarded, encouraged, or in some manner considered in terms of accountability, the probability is that diversity will be less likely to occur" (p.176).

References

Allen, M., Trejo, M., Bartanen, M., Shroeder, A., & Ulrich, T. (2004). Diversity in United States forensics: A report on research conducted for the American Forensic Association. *Argumentation and Advocacy, 40*(3), 173–184. Retrieved from http://www.tandfonline.com
Aonuma, S., Morooka, J., & Seno, K. (2014). Revisiting the U.S. footprints: A critical exploration of interscholastic/intercollegiate policy debate in post-World War II Japan. In C. H. Palczewski (Ed.), *Disturbing argument* (pp. 432–437). New York, NY: Routledge.
Chikuda, S. (2017, January 8). Focus group.

Hogan, J. M., & Kurr, J. A. (2017). Civic education in competitive debate and speech. *Argumentation and Advocacy*, *53*(2), 83–89. doi:10.1080/00028533.2017.1304959

HPDU of Japan. (2017). The 6th federation cup (2017) [Leaflet]. Retrieved from https://sites.google.com/site/hpdujapan/file-cabinet

Goto, K. (2017, January 8). Focus group.

Koyama, Y. (2017, January 8). Focus group.

Mazur, M. A. (2001). Women in parliamentary debate: An examination of women's performance at the National Parliamentary Debate Association Tournament. *Parliamentary Debate*, *7*(4), 31–36. Retrieved from http://parlidebate.org/pdf/vol7no4.pdf

McRee, N., & Cote, R. (2002). Does college debate inherit a lack of diversity from high school debate? *Contemporary Argumentation & Debate*, *23*, 28–44.

Miyagawa, J. (2017, June 8). E-mail correspondence.

Nagatomo, D. W. (2016). *Identity, gender, and teaching English in Japan*. Buffalo, NY: Multilingual Matters.

Pierson, E. (2013). Men outspeak women: Analyzing the gender gap in competitive debate. In M. Nugent, Z. Valashiya, A. Connery, M. Schultz, & J. Kilcup (Eds.), *Monash debating review, vol. 11* (pp. 8–15). Retrieved from http://mdr.monashdebaters.com/past-editions/volume-11-2013/

Stepp, P. L., & Gardner, B. (2001). Ten years of demographics: Who debates in America [Special issue]. *Argumentation and Advocacy*, *38*(2), 69–82. Retrieved from http://tandfonline.com

Szwapa, C. A. (1994). Sexual harassment and gender discrimination in NDT debate. *Argumentation and Advocacy*, *31*(1), 41–44.

Yano, Y. (2013, February 18). The growing popularity of high school English debates in Japan: Current conditions and issues. *The Japan News*. Retrieved from http://yomiuri.co.jp/adv/chuo/dy/opinion/20130218.html

78

CONCEPTUALIZING ACADEMIC DEBATE IN JAPAN

A Study of Judging Philosophy Statements

Kaori Miyawaki and Katsuya Koresawa

This essay describes and critiques the ways in which Japan has conceptualized intercollegiate policy debate. More specifically, the paper scrutinizes the 1997 and 2017 judging philosophy statements published online, such as on the official website of the National Association of Forensics and Argumentation (NAFA), the premier English-language policy debate organization in Japan. It investigates how critic-judges in Japan understand debate theories and practice. It discusses how differences in conceptualizations and educational approaches influence the development of theories and practices unique to Japanese debating.

The Japanese policy-debate circuit enthusiastically imported debate theories from the United States, and this phenomenon exemplifies intercultural exchanges in argumentation studies. Although those who once participated in the policy-debate circuit in Japan have studied the phenomena (e.g., Inoue, 1994; Kaniike, 2005), previous research has failed to adequately investigate judging statements as texts. Given that judges are the ultimate decision-makers of debate rounds, how judges understand debate can frame best practice models for debate. Therefore, without understanding functions and implications of the judging statements, scholars cannot draw a full picture of what is happening in the policy-debate circuit of Japan. This study suggests that judging statements represent relationships between judges and debaters, as well as theories unique to Japanese debating. Our analysis of the judging statements provides a unique perspective for understanding the outcome of cultural exchanges in the argumentation studies.

After reviewing the history of the English-language debate community in Japan, the following sections analyze 24 judging philosophy statements NAFA published online in preparation for Japan National Debate Tournament (JNDT) 2017. JNDT occurs annually in May and its goal is to decide "the best team in spring semester" ("Tournament," n.d., translated by

Miyawaki, para. 2). We also conducted a survey of the judges at the 2017 JNDT. We pre-pared written questions in Japanese concerning judging philosophy statements. After asking for study participant's gender and how many years they had debated and judged, we asked:

1. Tell us things you think deeply about when you write a judging philosophy (e.g., letting debaters easily understand, demonstrating concrete understandings of debate theories, etc.).
2. Which section of your judging philosophy did you write most carefully?
3. What materials did you use as references when you wrote your judging philosophy (e.g., judging philosophy written by senior debaters, debate theory books, etc.)?
4. How many times did you revise your judging philosophy?
5. Do you write your judging philosophy in English or Japanese? Please tell us why.
6. Do you write your judging ballots in English or Japanese? Please tell us why.
7. Do you have any other things you specifically care about when you judge?

We explained the goals of the study and asked the judges to fill in the survey at the judging room. We collected 10 responses. We utilized Fisher's exact test to compare the nominal variables of the study. The survey results helped us understand both the motives and the implications of the judging philosophy statements.

History of English-language Debate Community in Japan

After World War II and the subsequent Allied Force occupation, Japan's educational system drastically changed. The scholarly community at the time released several books explaining the practice and theory of debate (Inoue, 1996): Asahi Shimbun's *Tooron: Riron to Jissai* [Debate: Theory and Practice], Goro Hani's *What is Debate*, Masamichi Ariyama's *Debate as Inquiry into Truth*, and Shiho Sakanishi's *Debate Tournament in America*. Even though many attempts to introduce American-style of debate in Japan occurred, "the only one which suc-ceeded was in college English clubs (Inoue, 1996, p. 152). The Japanese community refers to these clubs as English Speaking Societies (ESS). Debate in ESS is like American forensics, an extracurricular club activity for college students. Suzuki and Matsumoto (2002) described the popularity of these extracurricular forensic programs in Japan.

Implementation of the English debate tournament began in the early 1950s, with the first intercollegiate English-language debating contest held in Tokyo in 1950. Since then, the number of English-language debating tournaments has steadily increased in Japan (Inoue, 1996; Suzuki & Matsumoto, 2002). Without support from their universities, students belonging to ESS run these tournaments that have played a major role in improving oral English communication skills for Japanese students (Suzuki & Matsumoto, 2002).

NAFA, established in 1983, has also played a major role in the development of the intercollegi-ate policy debate community in Japan. It, along with Japan Debate Association started in 1986, expanded the intercollegiate debate community ("History," n.d., para. 1, translated by Miyawaki). NAFA served as a leading student organization focusing on studying debate theories Japan imported from the United States. In 1985, NAFA published *Gendai debate tuuron* [Contemporary debate theory], reprinted in 2005. The book's intention was to cover theories of policy debate developed in U.S. debate circuits, such as paradigm, affirmative case, negative case, and fiat (Kaniike, 2005). As of 2007, Japan held 11 national tournaments each year, and local organizations host approximately 40 tournaments each year ("History," para. 2, translated by Miyawaki).

The Japanese debate community practices and those of U.S. debate circuits are comparable. Woods and Konishi's (2008) study of the history of the US-Japan exchange debate tour reports similarities, as well as differences, between the US and Japanese policy debate communities. For example, both communities put an emphasis on the evidence to support argumentative claims, but Japanese debaters put less critical pressure on the source of the evidence. Further, the Japanese policy debate community, like many U.S. debate programs, has adopted the Cross-Examination Debate Association format, while both communities also produce judging philosophy statements and ballots to report the results of each round.

Judging Philosophy Statements in 2017

Judging criteria can influence how judges evaluate debate rounds. NAFA provides a detailed rubric on the formatted ballot that judges must follow: 10 points for macro argumentation (consistency, evaluation, and comparison), 10 points for micro argumentation (analysis, reasoning and superiority), 10 points for English (vocabulary, grammar, fluency, and pronunciation), and five points for communication (credibility, structure, register, time allocation, cross exam effectiveness). The points each debater earns do not influence which team wins. Judges decide a winner according to the arguments debaters present in a debate round, although some judges vote for a team that earns more points in cases when they cannot otherwise decide the round's outcome. Tournament administrators use the speaker points for ranking teams moving on beyond the preliminary rounds. If two teams competing in a tournament won the same number of rounds, the team with greater speaker points can continue to debate beyond the preliminary rounds, making the points crucial for the debaters' point of view. A notable feature of the NAFA rubric for judging is evaluation of the debaters' English skills. The inclusion of English suggests that policy debate in Japan should function as a means for English education. The next section further discusses language selection, a factor unique to the Japanese debate community.

Language Selection

One big difference between tournament practices in the United States and Japanese debate communities is language selection. Japanese is the first language learned for most debaters in Japan, although they debate in English. This dichotomy renders the two major aims of debating to be improving English language proficiency and acquiring argumentation skills. Policy debaters tend to emphasize the latter. For example, Richardson (1985) criticized the fast delivery of Japanese debaters in the 1985 Japan tour. He also emphasized that U.S. debaters were using their own native language so they could speak rapidly. These comments imply the standards that English-language policy debate should strive to achieve and suggest the directions of English-language debate education in Japan. Students may be better able to obtain argumentation skills through Japanese-language policy debating and improve their English language proficiency in other ways. Therefore, the Japanese debate community needs to think about what educational goals can emerge from the combination of the two.

However, the tendency of policy debaters to pay less attention to learning English is strong and more problematic. In 1997, more judges wrote their philosophy in English than in 2017 (18 out of 47, or 38%, in 1997; 2 out of 24, or 8%, in 2017; $p = 0.011$). The survey results revealed multiple reasons for why most of the judges in 2017 wrote their philosophy in Japanese: (a) Japanese was easy to understand for debaters, (b) debaters could save time in comprehending the judges' comments, and (c) debaters ignored statements written in English. All these reasons imply that English can serve as an obstacle for debater comprehension of the judging statements, at least from the judges' perspective. The survey responses also imply that the judges' reasons for using Japanese did not relate to the judges' English ability, but to the English ability of the debaters. The judges acknowledged that debaters want to spend more time on preparing their materials than reading judging philosophies carefully.

Three out of ten (30%) of the judges wrote their debate ballots in English. One judge explained that he used debaters' chosen words from the debate on his ballot, for if he translated their words, he might have interpreted them differently. Seven out of ten judges wrote their ballots in Japanese because of (a) the time it took to write ballots in English, (b) the ease of comprehension for the debaters, (c) the judges' lack of sufficient English skills to communicate effectively, and (d) the desire to follow the practices of their senior debaters. The time to write ballots mattered due to the common practice in the Japanese policy debate community to follow a custom called *reflection*, where debaters come to the judge of the previous round during tournament breaks to ask for comments on their performance. One judge responded that he wrote ballots as quickly as possible to secure time for doing reflection. Another judge wrote that he wrote ballots in Japanese when he judged novice debaters, implying once again that the judges' language choice emerges from trying to assist the debate participants. The admission that certain judges lacked English skills is an honest voice that again bolsters the debater's learning potential. Interestingly, although seven judges out of 24 (29%) put past winning records in their philosophy statements, no one included records of their English skills, such as their TOEFL scores. Seven judges out of 10 (70%) responded that they referred to their senior debaters' judging statements (which were mostly in Japanese) when writing their own philosophies. One judge, however, answered that after he read Thomas and Hart's *Advanced Debate* and Ketcham's *Theory and Practice of Argumentation and Debate*, he wrote his debating philosophy and ballots in English.

In sum, the Japanese policy debate community does not expect judges to conduct their duties in English. First, the judges, who are mostly college seniors and graduate students, do not have incentives to improve their English further and, as a result, mainly write their ballots in Japanese. Second, the community emphasizes a judge's duty as a decision maker over the role of English-trainer. Although English is one of the judging criteria, debaters do not expect judges to teach them how to speak English fluently as they are more interested in learning arguments and strategies rather than English from the judges.

Defining Debate

One notable feature of contemporary judging statements in Japanese debate emerges when judges explain how they understand debate. Thirteen judges out of 24 (54%) wrote how they defined debate in their statements. One judge wrote that he acknowledged many forms of argumentation and tried to avoid any bias. Another judge wrote that debate was a place to decide to affirm or negate a resolution. The remainder of the judges defined debate as a game in which the affirmative and negative teams logically persuade judges. The debate-as -game mentality appears dominant in the Japanese policy debate community.

The perspective of the debate-as-game model remains a contentious matter. Palczewski (cited in Woods & Konishi, 2008) reinforced that Japanese debaters understood debate as a game, based on her experience of participating in the Japan-US exchange tour as a debater in 1987. Inoue (1994) also noted that many debaters in Japan perceived debate as a game and especially clever debaters enjoyed manipulating the rules that bind the activity as an escape from the Japanese formulaic society. Some scholars, however, have criticized the perspective of debate as a game. Kaniike (2005) and other authors in *Gendai Debate Tuuron* cautioned that regarding debate as a manipulative tool for decision-making could result in debaters ignoring debate's another primary aspect: a means for learning argumentation processes. As such, not all judges regard debate as merely a game; in fact, the community of debaters themselves disagree. Further, the majority of the judges who qualified to judge at the JNDT in 2017, one of the top national debate tournaments in Japan, saw debate as a game.

Such a debate-as-game mentality may lead to the idea that judges should avoid *intervention*, a process whereby judges interpret presented arguments within their own logical or value standards, while ignoring or minimizing the value of what debaters argue in a round. Inoue (1994) observed that some judges preferred this Tabula Rasa paradigm because they did not want to intervene in a round. Most of the judges in 2017 employed a policy-making paradigm with a preference not to intervene. One judge wrote that he writes ballots in English so as not to intervene. Another wrote that he tries to write a decision as debaters think, suggesting he wants to understand arguments exactly as the debaters present them.

Communication scholars, particularly those focused on argumentation, have supported the idea of debate as pedagogy for argumentation and civic engagement, not merely as a game. U.S. scholars have published a number of debate textbooks, books, and articles regarding debate as public deliberation. For example, Leek's (2016) article on policy debate and civic engagement, featured in the March 2017 issue of *Spectra*, emphasized the pedagogical aspect of policy debate and advocated the learning of civic engagement through debate and service leaning. Such scholarly conversations on defining the purpose of debate are ongoing, but they have not yet influenced judging statements in the Japanese policy debate community.

Whereas understandings of debate as public deliberation and pedagogy for civic engagement was missing in the judging statements, most of the philosophies touched on debate theories. Most of them explained topicality and counterplans. On topicality, their interest focused on if an affirmative team offered a reasonable interpretation was sufficient for the judge to conclude that the affirmative plans was topical. On counterplans, the statements explained which team won in the event the judge evaluated the affirmative plan and the negative counterplan as equally beneficial. Some judges also referred to value hierarchy, claiming they did not depend on a particular value hierarchy, but saw value hierarchies as debatable. None of them clarified what a value hierarchy was, but judging from their descriptions and debate culture in Japan, value hierarchies here referred to whether a judge preferred certain impacts over others, such as human death over human rights. Although the judging statements described these debate theories and concepts, they did not mention more controversial theories popular in the United States, such as *kritiks*. Zagorin (2013) demonstrated the most striking difference between US and Japan's debate lies in ideological arguments. Japanese policy debaters tend to select net-benefit analysis or single issue evaluations, rather than critical arguments, such as topicality, counterplan, case arguments and disadvantages. Such selections lead to debates that focus on simple comparisons of data, rather than deepened philosophical arguments.

Implications

The history of policy debate in Japan has a strong foundation in U.S. debate practices. U.S. debate coaches considered debate in Japan in the late 1970s as similar to American debate in the 1960s, with Japanese debaters familiar with debate theories of the time (Woods & Konishi, 2008). Many contemporary Japanese judges today forward those traditions and regard policy debate as an intellectual game that serves as a key training platform for strengthening English speaking ability.

However, in the mid-1990s, when the U.S. debaters started to run kritiks and performative turns, the Japanese debate community did not follow their American counterparts by implementing similar theoretical developments (Woods & Konishi, 2008). Even though the Japanese debate community maintains some connections to the United States (e.g., the US-Japan exchange tour sponsored by Japan Debate Association and National Communication Association), development of debate theories emergent in the U.S. circuits no longer have a strong influence on the Japanese debate community. One of the primary reasons is that college debaters in Japan usually have little faculty supervision ("Short History of CIDD," n.d.; Suzuki & Matsumoto, 2002). The absence of debate coach hinders not only the progress of arguments, but also the accumulation of debate knowledge.

Japanese debate should continue to avoid the model of U.S. replication if only to create the nation's own theories and traditions for introduction into other countries. Japan and the United States (as well as other countries) should embrace this new attitude as a mutually beneficial (not one-way), intercultural exchange. However, this study did not reveal any new or unique approach to policy debate that the Japanese circuit generated. Perhaps the student-run nature of the Japanese debate circuit, which also lacks interaction between the debaters and college professors specializing in argumentation and advocacy, creates a systematic issue the community should address. Zagorin (2013) explained, "Success within debate counts for less among Japanese businesses, whereas in the US highly successful debates are often able to more easily obtain entry to polity think tanks, corporate communications' posts or law firms" (Zagorin, 2013, para. 2, The Power of Informal Norm section). Therefore, for the sake of further growth of the Japanese debate community, responsibility is not just on student debaters and judges, but on argumentation scholars who network across the border. We should investigate ways in which argumentation scholars should build stronger networks with Japanese debaters, while respecting and maintaining their autonomy.

References

History. (n.d.). *National association of forensics and argumentation.* Retrieved from http://nafadebate.org/about-debate/history

Inoue, N. (1994). *Ways of debating in Japan: Academic debate in English speaking societies* (Doctoral dissertation). Retrieved from ProQuest Dissertations and Theses. (UMI No. 9519451)

Inoue, N. (1996). Traditions of "debate" in Japan. *Bulletin of the Graduate School of Social and Cultural Studies, 2,* 149–161. Retrieved from http://flc.kyushu-u.ac.jp/~inouen/deb-trad.html

Kaniike, Y. (2005). *Gendai debate tuuron fukkoku ban* [Contemporary debate theory reprinted]. Tokyo, Japan: Debate Forum Press.

Leek, D. R. (2016). Policy debate pedagogy: A complementary strategy for civic and political engagement through service learning. *Communication Education, 65*(4), 397–408. doi: 10.1080/03634523.2016.1203004

Richardson, L. S. (1985, October). Report on the 1985 United States Tour of Japan. *Report to the Japan English Forensic Association (JEFA).*

Short History of CIDD. (n.d.). The committee for international discussion and debate of the national communication association (CIDD). Retrieved from http://groups.wfu.edu/debate/International%20Debates/cidd.html

Suzuki, T., & Matsumoto, S. (2002). English-language debate as business communication training in Japan. In J. E. Rogers (Ed.), *Transforming debate: The best of the international journal of forensics* (pp. 51–70). New York, NY: International Debate Education Association.

Tournament. (n.d.). *National association of forensics and argumentation.* Retrieved from http://nafadebate. org/tournament

Woods, C., & Konishi, T. (2008). What has been exchanged? Toward a history of Japan-US debate exchange. In T. Suzuki, T. Kato, & A. Kubota. (Eds.), *Proceedings of the 3rd Tokyo Conference on Argumentation: Argumentation, the Law and Justice* (pp. 287–290). Tokyo, Japan: Japan Debate Association.

Zagorin, E. (2013, April 24). Japan's diverse debating styles. *Millenial Speech & Debate.* Retrieved from https://millennialsd.com/blog/2013/04/24/japans-diverse-debating-styles/

79

BIG IN JAPAN?

A Note on the Japanese Reception of American Policy Debate

Satoru Aonuma and Kazuhiko Seno

Located at the two ends of the Pacific, U.S. and Japanese intercollegiate debate communities have much in common. While some notable differences exist, the resemblance between the two nation's debate practices are indeed remarkable. Students participating in both communities debate policy propositions as national topics; they also use similar, if not the same, tournament structures, debate formats, argument strategies, and tactics. At tournaments in both countries, observers can enjoy watching heated exchanges of research-intensive, heavily quotation-oriented arguments with rapid-fire delivery.

Of course, these commonalities did not just emerge. Competitive debate in post–World War II Japan is basically a Japanese appropriation of the practices of its U.S. counterpart (Aonuma, Morooka, & Seno, 2014). The Japanese have looked to the U.S. way of debating (National Debate Tournament or NDT, to be more precise) as their model, engaging in "imitation pedagogy" (Aonuma, Morooka, & Seno, 2014, p. 433) that involves aggressively importing, studying, and practicing U.S. debate habits. Through transpacific networking, this Japanese pedagogical appropriation reached its zenith during the mid-1980s, a time when the popularity of English-language intercollegiate debate peaked in Japan, as the number of tournaments and schools entering these tournaments skyrocketed.

This essay turns back the clock some 30 years to reminisce about the history of this transpacific debate network. Focusing specifically on a series of developments during the 1980s, we will ask: In what specific ways did U.S. debate theory and practice become available, shared, spread, and consumed in Japan? What processes exist to make the latest development in U.S. debate still part of Japanese debate?

The Bunken Prolif

When discussing the critical factors that led to the transpacific movement of debate theory and practice, argumentation scholars cannot overstate the role of the multi-year U.S.-Japan exchanges that the Committee on International Discussion and Debate (CIDD) sponsored (Lain, 2014; Woods & Konishi, 2007). Exposed directly to U.S. debate, Japanese debaters participating on U.S. tours brought back and shared what they saw, learned, and experienced with other students in Japan. These "informants" taught new debate theories,

534

strategies, tactics, and other customs and practices of U.S. policy debate to their peers and juniors. U.S. students and coaches who toured Japan were equally influential teachers of debate for the Japanese (Davidson, 1977).

Besides the CIDD-sponsored exchanges, the sharing of U.S. debate theory and practice in Japan occurred through books and other publications. For instance, many U.-S. debate textbooks, such as *Basic Debate, Strategic Debate, Advanced Debate, Argumentation: Inquiry and Advocacy, Argumentation and Debate, Debate and Argument,* and *Contemporary Debate,* had wide availability and distribution in Japan. Some Japanese-written publications focused on the U.S. National Debate Tournament (NDT), the most notable of which was Michihiro Matsumoto's 1981 *Korega Debate Da (This is the Debate).* Matsumoto's volume contained the transcript and audio-recording of the 1981 NDT final debate, as well as the transcribed interview with Tom Kane, coach of the winning team, the two winning debaters from the University of Pittsburgh, and Michael Hazen, then NDT Director.

In addition to these commercial publications, the proliferation of articles, essays, papers, and other debate-related literature (or *bunken)* functioned as an important part of this international sharing. Father Scott Howell, a chemistry professor and advisor to Sophia University's English Speaking Society (ESS), as well as others, made copies of the *Journal of the American Forensic Association (JAFA;* now *Argumentation and Advocacy),* *Debate Issues, Rostrum, Speaker and Gavel,* and the Alta argumentation conference proceedings available to Japanese students. Outside the CIDD-sponsored tours, some Japanese students flew across the Pacific to experience firsthand the U.S. way of debating and brought back to Japan numerous U.S. debate materials (e.g., briefs, evidence blocks, summer camp booklets, etc.).

Joshua Arai, an ex-debater and graduate student at the Tokyo Institute of Technology, and his volunteer group compiled, photocopied, and distributed the massive amount of U.S. debate *bunken* nationwide. Thanks to their *bunken* proliferation project, "pseudo-inherency" (Schunk, 1978), "best definition topicality" (Unger, 1981), "extra-nontopicality" (Kaplow, 1981), "counter-counterplan" (Kaplow, 1981), "counterplan permutation" (Herbeck, 1985; Kaplow, 1981), and "counterwarrants" (Paulsen & Rhodes, 1979), among many other concepts, became part of Japanese debate terminology during the mid-1980s. In fact, Japanese debaters and judges active during this period (including the two authors of this paper) recognized many of their U.S. contemporaries despite never having met them. For instance, as counterwarrants served as one of the most widely utilized negative strategies in Japan, Pat Ganer (1981) who wrote about that strategy in her Alta conference paper already had many Japanese "fans" before arriving in Tokyo when she accompanied the U.S. team on their CIDD tour in 1987.

The Debate Forum

Japanese reception and consumption of U.S. debate theory and practice, however, did not occur uncritically. From the point of view of an insider, a series of developments within the Japanese debate community during the 1980s made the initial exchange rather natural. Immersed in imitation pedagogy, Japanese students became attracted not only to the way their U.S. counterparts debated, but by extension, they also became interested in the development of theory and strategies within the U.S. debate community. During the same period, the Japanese debaters' own rationale for participating in debate had also shifted from language learning and public speaking to critical thinking, research, argument strategy, and tactics.

Influenced by Balthrop's (1983) idea of "debate as laboratory of argument" (p. 1), students in Japan began to take debate as a special/specialized discursive space for argumentative innovation. Accordingly, the National Association of Forensics and Argumentation (NAFA), then the country's largest student-run debate organization, inaugurated the *Debate Forum* (hereafter *DF*) in 1984. Upon inauguration, Yoichi Kaniike (1984a), the *DF*'s chief editor, wrote that this journal is a "forum for scholars of argumentation to form and scrutinize new concepts and theories emerged [*sic*] in their minds and to follow up theoretically ingenious practice of debaters at tournaments" (p. 1). Namely, the NAFA and Japanese debaters wanted to develop their own version of the *JAFA*. As such, the organization and contents of the *DF* closely resembled that of the *JAFA* and the authors wrote the majority of their published works in English.

Prominent judges and ex-debaters in Japan at the time wrote seven scholarly monographs for the inaugural issue of the *DF*. Two focused on the problem of logical inference, or in other words, essay topics normally appearing in philosophy journals. The other five examined debate theories, but each focused on such esoteric topics and incorporated such dense prose that, in all likelihood, no one outside the debate community had an interest in reading them. Two discussed the problem of proper "agents of action" in policy propositions; the remaining three commented on the decision rule for judging a counterwarrant debate (Namiki, 1984), the problem of evaluating "studies counterplans" under the policy-making paradigm (Kaniike, 1984b), and the role of policy-makers in policy disputes (Kawai, 1984).

>Following this inaugural issue, the NAFA published the *DF* two to four times a year. Each issue contained several heavily-annotated essays on debate theory and pedagogy. Occasionally, the issues printed other articles and writings, such as the transcribed interviews of prominent debate judges, as well as the transcript of NAFA sponsored national tournaments. Table 79.1 describes the subjects published in the *DF* from 1984 (Volume 1) to 1988 (Volume 5).

Table 79.1 Contents of the Debate Forum Essays from 1984 (Volume 1) to 1988 (Volume 5)

Topics	Number of Essays
Counterplans	4
Counterwarrants	2
Counter-counterplans/plan add-on	2
Debate strategy in general	4
Debate pedagogy in general	11
Decision-making paradigms	15
(Paradigm disputes)	(3)
(Stock issues)	(5)
(Tabula rasa and "descriptivism")	(3)
(Policy-making)	(2)
(Hypothesis-testing)	(1)
(Game theory)	(1)
Inherency/pseudo-inherency	2
Policy propositions (fiat, agent of action, etc.)	6
Topicality	1

The notable characteristics identifiable in the *DF* reflected what was happening in Japanese intercollegiate debate during these five years. During the mid-1980s, national debate topics were broad and "bi-directional," allowing affirmative teams unfairly large ground to make a case; conversely, negative teams had to deal with too many affirmative possibilities at tournament competition. With negative teams unable to prepare specific arguments for each and every one of these possible affirmative cases, deploying theory-oriented off-case arguments (e.g., counterplans and counterwarrants) became most economical and strategically wise. To assist such efforts, the *DF* carried more essays dealing with negative-initiated issues than affirmative ones. For example, the *DF* printed four articles on counterplans and two on counterwarrants. Essays on agent of action in policy propositions focused on the negative point of view as well, as they challenged affirmative fiat and attempted to legitimize the "cooptation" argument that trumped affirmative solvency as a voting issue for the negative.

Another notable characteristic of the *DF* involved judging paradigms, perspectives, and decision-making models. During the mid-1980s, the demography of the Japanese judging pool became more diverse. The number of available "skills" and "stock issues" judges became a smaller minority, while "policy-making," "hypothesis-testing," "tabula rasa" and "critics of argument" judges increased. Again, the *DF* reflected this development. Japanese judges and ex-debaters engaged in the arguments similar to the ones of U.S. debaters and coaches. The *DF*'s pages extensively cited Robert Rowland, Alan Lichtman, Daniel Rohrer, David Zarefsky, and Walter Urlich, among others. In 1985, the *DF* had a special issue (Volume 2, Number 2) on the stock issues paradigm, perhaps to give a warm-hearted farewell (or final bow?) to the approach. Inspired by Snider's (1984) *JAFA* article, one ex-champion Japanese debater discussed the utility of "game theory" for conceptualizing debate and discussed its application for formulating argument strategies (Tanaka, 1984).

Additionally, judge "intervention" and "descriptivism" became issues in the Japanese debate community just as they had in the United States. While Walter Urlich had some Japanese followers, many others felt that the tabula rasa judging paradigm that he invented went too far. Japanese debaters complained about some judges uncritically accepted everything debaters said in a round. In a similar vein, the *DF* editor Kaniike (1986) harshly critiqued relatively young judges as too afraid to use their interpretive horizon to evaluate the discourse of the debate round in its entirety. Citing Dempsey and Hartmann's (1986) *JAFA* article, Kaniike (1986) dubbed the phenomenon the judge's "judicial impotence" (p. 167).

Debate Tsuron

Having observed how Japanese debate communities processed U.S. debate theory and practice in the *DF,* the remainder of this essay will turn to an analysis of Izuta, Kaniike, Kitano and Namiki's (1986/2005) influential Japanese-written debate textbook: *General Theory of Contemporary Debate* (*Gendai Debate Tsuron;* hereafter *Tsuron*). In the 1980s, Izuta et al.'s textbook constituted the most comprehensive treatment of advanced debate theory and practice written in the Japanese language. NAFA originally published the volume in 1985, with an enlarged edition published the following year. Now out of print for some 20 years, a reprint of the textbook became available in 2005. Table 79.2 describes the chapter-by-chapter contents of this reprinted enlarged edition.

Like the *DF,* the contents of *Tsuron* reflected the problem and needs of Japan's debate community. To begin, Izuta et al. (2005) wrote *Tsuron* in Japanese, making it a debate

Table 79.2 Debate Tsuron (enlarged edition): Table of Contents

Chapters	Title
Chapter 1	Basic Principles of Debate
Chapter 2	Fundamental Theories of Debate
Chapter 3	Analyzing the Resolution
Chapter 4	Affirmative Case Requirement
Chapter 5	Affirmative Plan Construction
Chapter 6	Affirmative Case Structure
Chapter 7	Negative Case Requirement
Chapter 8	Negative Case Structure
Chapter 9	Systems Analysis
Chapter 10	Fiat
(Appendix 1)	Strategy and Rebuttal
(Appendix 2)	Bibliography

publication far more accessible to the Japanese readership than the *DF. Tsuron* offered a very helpful introduction discussing U.S. debate theory and practice for college debaters who found the *JAFA* articles or *Advanced Debate* too difficult due to their limited English skills. *Tsuron* also expanded readership outside the intercollegiate English-language debate circuit. The preface to the reprinted 2005 version indicated that the decision to reprint the book was partly in response to meet the need of the emerging Japanese-language debate community (Izuta et al., 2005).

Second, *Tsuron* exhibited some noticeable incongruities regarding the treatment of affirmative and negative issues. Specifically, while the chapters and sections pertaining primarily to the affirmative conceptualized and explained debate from the viewpoint of the policy-making paradigm, the book handled issues pertaining to the negative from the perspective of the hypothesis-testing paradigm. *Tsuron*'s authors were well cognizant and rather open to this incongruity. For instance, Chapter 4 included a footnote early on that explicitly indicated that the explanation of affirmative case requirements came from the policy-making paradigm and, hence, "heavily [drew] upon" Lichtman and Rohrer's 1980 *JAFA* article entitled, "Logic of Policy Dispute." By the same token, the discussion on negative case structure in Chapter 8 started with a citation from Patterson and Zarefsky's (1983) *Contemporary Debate*, a textbook reflecting the idea of hypothesis-testing.

Third, just as in the case of the *DF* essays, *Tsuron* drew heavily on works published in the United States. In fact, the authors of *Tsuron* were also frequent contributors to the *DF*. They all had extensive experience reading U.S. debate literature and the American authors referenced in *Tsuron*. For instance, consider how *Tsuron's* authors addressed a relatively unknown essay published in the Alta argumentation proceedings dealing with the problem of judging: Hingstman's (1983) "Lessons Learned: The Philosophy of Ordinary Language and the Theory of Debate." The authors of *Tsuron* critically attended to what Hingstman wrote about the "renewed" (p. 37) relationship between in-round debate discourse and the real world. They contended that such renewal, while likely, may not be desirable in the context of academic debate, as the real-world norms should not be the sole basis for argumentative validity in a laboratory of argumentation.

Conclusion

This essay has sought to revisit the history of the U.S.-Japan debate network in its making. As the connection between U.S. debate and how Japanese debate developed is significant and obvious, the question of *how* transpacific knowledge transfer occurred serves as a rich terrain for examination. By explicating the ways in which U.S. debaters shared theory and practice with their Japanese colleagues during the 1980s and how the Japanese, in turn, consumed that corpus of information, the role of CIDD-sponsored tours to knowledge transfer emerges as central and equally important. The Japanese import of debate-related literature from the United States, as well as the publication of their own debate journal and textbook, functioned as critical components.

Gary Fine (2001) once wrote that competitive debate in the United States was an instance of "American exceptionalism" saying, "in other nations, there is no close equivalent to our country's high school policy debate" (p. 249). But as one Japanese debater who spent one year as an exchange student at the University of Iowa in the late 1980s recognized, debates in Japan and the United States were very similar back then, making her feel quite at home within American debate community (Morita, 1991). Our commonalities are what make us peculiar in the world. As we both rely on a cross-examination team format and policy topics, U.S. and Japanese college debaters constitute a minority in the international debate community, but share a special, lasting bond.

References

Aonuma, S., Morooka, J., & Seno, K. (2014). Revisiting the U.S. footprints: A critical exploration of interscholastic/intercollegiate policy debate in post-World War II Japan. In C. H. Palczewski (Ed.), *Disturbing argument* (pp. 432–437). New York, NY: Routledge.

Balthrop, W. V. (1983). Debate judge as "critic of argument": Toward a transcendent perspective. *Journal of the American Forensic Association, 20*(1), 1–15.

Davidson, J. P., III. (1977). Debater as pedagogue: The first United States-CIDD tour of Japan. *Speaker and Gavel, 14,* 2–9.

Dempsey, R. H., & Hartmann, D. J. (1986). Emergent voting criteria and judicial impotence of critics. *Journal of the American Forensic Association, 22*(3), 167–175.

Fine, G. A. (2001). *Gifted tongue: High school debate and adolescent culture.* Princeton, NJ: Princeton University Press.

Ganer, P. M. (1981). Counter-warrants: An idea whose time has not come. In G. Ziegelmueller & J. Rhodes (Eds.), *Dimensions of argument: Proceedings of the second summer conference on argumentation* (pp. 476–484). Annandale, VA: Speech Communication Association.

Herbeck, D. (1985). A permutation standard of competitiveness. *Journal of the American Forensic Association, 22,* 12–19.

Hingstman, D. B. (1983). Lessons learned: The philosophy of ordinary language and the theory of debate. In D. Zarefsky, M. O. Sillars, & J. Rhodes (Eds.), *Argument in transition: Proceedings of the third summer conference on argumentation* (pp.772–772791). Annandale, VA: Speech Communication Association.

Izuta, T., Kaniike, Y., Kitano, H., & Namiki, S. (2005). *Gendai debate tsuron* [*General theory of contemporary debate*] (Enlarged ed.). Tokyo, Japan: Debate Forum Press.

Kaniike, Y. (1984a). The forward from the editor. *Debate Forum, 1,* 1–2.

Kaniike, Y. (1984b). The re-evaluation of the studies counterplan under the policy making paradigm: Another perspective. *Debate Forum, 1,* 15–20.

Kaniike, Y. (1986). Close-up 9: Rebuttal tabula rasa no youkai; descriptivism no bousou [Close-up 9: The phantom of rebuttal tabula rasa; descriptivism runaway]. *Debate Forum, 3,* 197–201.

Kaplow, L. (1981). Rethinking counterplan: A reconciliation with debate theory. *Journal of the American Forensic Association, 17*(4), 215–226.

Kawai, S. (1984). Policy making in debate and formation of a new paradigm: The criticism on policy makers. *Debate Forum, 1*, 1–2.

Lain, B. (2014). Rethinking the history of the Japanese-U.S. exchange tour: Early tours, early topics, and early traffic. In C. H. Palczewski (Ed.), *Disturbing argument* (pp. 427–431). New York, NY: Routledge.

Lichtman, A. J., & Rohrer, D. M. (1980). The logic of policy dispute. *Journal of the American Forensic Association, 16*(4), 236–247.

Morita, M. (1991). Watashi wa debate ryugaku shitetanja nai! [I didn't go abroad just to study debate!]. *Debate Forum, 8*, 45–55.

Namiki, S. (1984). A decision rule of the counter-warrant. *Debate Forum, 1*, 9–14.

Patterson, J. W., & Zarefsky, D. (1983). *Contemporary debate*. Boston, MA: Houghton Mufflin.

Paulsen, J. W., & Rhodes, J. (1979). The counter-warrant as a negative strategy: A modest proposal. *Journal of the American Forensic Association, 15*, 205–210.

Schunk, J. F. (1978). A farewell to "structural change": The cure for pseudo-inherency. *Journal of the American Forensic Association, 14*(3), 141–149.

Snider, A. C. (1984). Game without frontiers: A design for communication scholars and forensics educators. *Journal of the American Forensic Association, 20*(3), 162–170.

Tanaka, S. (1984). Game theory: A quantitative approach to strategy formulation in academic debate. *Debate Forum, 1*, 35–44.

Unger, J. (1981). Topicality: Why not the best? *Rostrum, 56*, 5–9.

Woods, C., & Konishi, T. (2007). What has been exchanged? Towards a history of Japan-US debate exchange. In T. Suzuki, T. Kato, & A. Kubota (Eds.), *Proceedings of the 3rd Tokyo Conference on Argumentation: Argumentation, the Law & Justice* (pp. 271–280). Tokyo, Japan: Japan Debate Association.

80

EVOLUTIONS AND DEVOLUTIONS IN PRACTICE

Theory Arguments in Recent
English-speaking College Policy Debate
in Japan

Noriaki Tajima

Japan is one among the very few nations that has had long relations with U.S. policy debate. Individual efforts of Japanese debaters and former debaters often maintained the connections of these two debate cultures. They brought back argument files from the universities that they had visited (Yano, 1994). More than ten former debaters advanced to graduate programs of communication studies in the United States, worked as coaches, and taught courses in public speaking, as well as argumentation and debate. And notably, a Japanese former debater audio-recorded the final round of the National Debate Tournament in 1981, and published the transcript and accompanying cassette tapes, with the title *Korega dibēto da: Shijō saikyō no eigō* or *This is debate: Strongest English in history* (Matsumoto, 1986).

Further, a long organizational effort reinforced the bridge between the two policy debate cultures. The Committee for International Discussion and Debate of the National Communication Association, or CIDD-NCA (formerly Speech Communication Association), and Japan Debate Association, or JDA (formerly Japan Debate Conference), have sponsored annual debate exchange tours. While the history of the exchange has lasted more than 50 years, scholarly efforts to understand the similarities and differences of the two debating cultures have begun only recently. While Inoue (1994), Aonuma, Morooka, and Seno (2015), and Lain (2015) explicitly focused on specific timeframes and issues of interest within the long history, only Woods and Konishi (2008) and Bauschard (2013) provided insights into recent CIDD-NCA/JDA tours. Yet, these studies rely on personal, anecdotal observations of former international ambassadors, rather than any form of systematic study.

The focus of this study seeks to address the need for a more systematic, comparative study by examining debate theory and theory debates in practice in the two debate cultures. Woods and Konishi (2008) maintained that debaters in Japan and the United States shared most of the same vocabularies and enjoyed a direct exchange of arguments by the mid-1990s—shortly after the critical/performative turn in the U.S. NDT-CEDA circuit. Several years later, however, Stefan Bauschard (2013), with the help of Edmund Zagorin, a 2012 CIDD-NCA/JDA tour debater to Japan, noted that Japan's debating styles were "significantly diverging" (para. 2) from American policy debate and that Japan was evolving "uniquely Japanese argument traditions" (para. 2). As a result, Japan was under what Bauschard called the "Galapagos effect" (para. 2). This study seeks to determine if the trends that Bauschard observed extend into the realm of debate theory.

To analyze current conditions in the Japanese debate community, this essay borrows Fine's (2001) ethnographic method. In order to understand the high-school debate culture, Fine conducted observations of multiple tournaments, debate trips, and the lives of coaches and debaters. Likewise, I visited three policy-debate tournaments in the Tokyo area from March through June of 2017, one exclusively for first-year debaters in Kanto (the greater Tokyo) area and two other national open tournaments in Tokyo. I observed 15 rounds of competition, including five break rounds with nine of those featuring a topicality argument in the opening speech from the negative. At the tournament venues, I conducted 11 face-to-face, one-on-one, semi-structured interviews of debaters, judges, and senior members who tabulated, organized, or helped administer the tournaments. All interviewees were policy debaters or former policy debaters. Each audio-recorded interview had a duration of between 10 and 30 minutes.

The interviews tried to understand both the uniqueness as well as similarities of Japanese policy debate culture and U.S. policy debate culture. As a former debater in this circuit, I speculated that the debaters' learning experience resulted from interactions with coaches, senior club members, U.S. teams coming to Japan with CIDD-NCA/JDA tours, and/or textbooks. After initial questions regarding how they learned debate, all the interviews moved to specifics regarding their pedagogical experiences regarding debate theory. For privacy, I replaced the interviewees' names with pseudonyms, while noting sex, years in college, and organizational roles. The specific interview questions were the following:

Q1: How did you learn or have you learned policy debate?
Q2: How did you learn or have you learned policy debate theories?
Q3: (Follow up to the Q1 and Q2 answers of "coaches," "senior members of the club," and/or "exchange debaters and coaches from the US"): How was/were their teaching and coaching?
Q4: (Follow up to the Q1 and Q2 answer of "textbook"): How was/were their contents?
Q5: What kind of theory arguments do you see more frequently? What kind of theory arguments do you see less frequently?
Q6: Are there any theory arguments you find more acceptable to you personally or to the debate community? Are there any theory arguments you find less acceptable to you personally or to the debate community?

Based on the investigation's results, this essay begins by overviewing present theory debates in English-speaking policy debate circuits in Japan. It then uses the interview results to understand the various perceptions of debate theories. Finally, it offers suggestions to debate communities in Japan and the United States based on the study's findings.

Counterplans and Topicality Theory

Debaters understand debate theories as *theōria*—standards or metaphysics—of policy and stock issues. For instance, Hahn, Hahn, and Hobeika (2013) listed theory as one of the three types of arguments in policy debate, along with policy and kritik. They went on to divide theory arguments into two subcategories: action-specific and resolution-specific. Action-specific theory arguments claimed the legitimacy and illegitimacy of specific actions within a debate round, such as counterplan status and fast reading. The resolution-specific theory arguments dealt with affirmative team's interpretation of the resolution in the face of challenges from the negative team. Conventionally, U.S. policy debate assumes everything is debatable. While one side argues that certain issues are illegitimate or unfair, the opposing team often insists the same issues are legitimate and fair, with the judge resolving the matter as a part of the decision-making process.

The Japanese debate culture has not wholly adopted the U.S. model due, in part, to the unique history of English-speaking policy debate in Japan. On the high-school level, the annual national tournament started about a decade ago and intentionally prohibits debaters from presenting any theory arguments. The high school rule directs debaters to focus on advantages and disadvantages of the affirmative proposal. This exclusion successfully secures common grounds of debate for many high-school debating clubs, which English teachers without prior experience of policy debate coach. Partly thanks to this regulation, the national tournament has steadily grown, with over 300 teams competing in district preliminaries (Yano, June 6, 2017, personal communication).

In contrast, intercollegiate English-speaking policy debate does allow theory debates. Since its inception in the mid-1980s, the National Association of Forensics and Argumentation (NAFA), the leading organization of English-speaking intercollegiate policy debate tournaments, has followed NDT-CEDA debate norms and has allowed any types of debates. When Bauschard (2013) claimed that one key benefit of debate was understanding technical terms for analytical thinking with the result that argumentation education should be the primary goal rather than English-learning, he explicitly referred to NAFA debate. Nevertheless, based on Mr. Zagorin's observation in June 2012, Bauschard (2013) pointed out Japan's lack of counterplan theories and kritik/performance debate, as well as different vocabularies on counterplan competitiveness.

The debate observations and participant interviews generally confirm the ongoing veracity of Bauschard's observations. Based on the findings of the round observations and participant interviews, the lack of counterplan theories and kritik/performance debate in Japan are still apparent. In 2017, debaters continue to use their vernacular term "both adoption" to mean permutation, an argument to test counterplan competitiveness.

However, a terminological difference emerges regarding the term "theory." By and large, theory in the Japanese debate community means counterplan and topicality debates, or put another way, any debates other than net-benefit issues related to the affirmative proposal. This vernacular categorization seems very popular in the community, as the NAFA website also lists all counterplan and topicality materials under the category of "theory" (NAFA, n.d.).

The only exception—and one commonality with the U.S. policy debate—involves what Japanese participants call "shift arguments" or arguments that challenge judging philosophy statements. While debaters can shift virtually any statements, the interviews and debate observations confirm that several kinds are more popular, including arguments for and against specific types of counterplans, topicality meta-standards (reasonable versus better definitions) and agent-specification topicality (NAFA, n.d.). Yet, Mr. Ando, a fourth-year college student and a key organizing member of the national tournament for third-year top debaters, stated that he "has rarely seen these arguments" and that he has more often seen "topicality meta-standard debates in [the] Tokyo area than [in tournaments for…] Kansai debaters [from western Japan, in Kyoto, Osaka and beyond]."

In summary, the Japanese do have a unique debate culture that guides the debate communities' norms of what to expect from debate education, as well as the acceptable parameters for debate theory. The fact that nine out of the 11 interviewees identify internet materials (i.e., past lecture notes and audio and video materials available on the NAFA website) as one among their important sources of learning and that all 11 recognize that these materials exist suggest a shared reservoir of understanding that undergirds the unique Japanese debate community.

Regional Distinctions within Japanese Debate Communities

Because debate happens within and across regions, regional differences are inevitable. Explaining that Minnesota high-school debate in the late-1980s tended to be more classical and generally behind national trends in U.S. debate. Fine (2001), for example, noted that many considered such differences and diversity constituted "a benefit" because the distinctions contributed to "the idea that debate should be communication" (p. 123).

In Japan, regional differences also emerge within localized debate communities. Returning to Mr. Ando's specific mention of "Kansai debaters" in relation to debate norms, I added another question about Kanto debaters' perceptions on Kansai debate, especially their theory arguments for my remaining eight interviews. The responses to the new question reveal a binary understanding of "shift arguments" in the Kanto area. At first glance most judges were open to any kind of arguments, as most, if not all, judges dared to clarify in their judging philosophy statements, "If clearly articulated and won by the debate, I will do my best to follow any kinds [of arguments]." Ms. Ban, a tournament organizer and negotiator with judges in a room specifically set up for waiting judges and writing ballots, explained that "such an open style is pretty much the baseline shared in this community." Indeed, a review of judging philosophies printed out and listed on the table in the judge's room revealed an openness to theory debates reiterated in almost all judging philosophies.

Still, and despite this shared understanding, some judges personally seemed to resist theory arguments. Mr. Chiyoda, a third-year college student and among the best debaters in 2017, confessed that he considered such arguments essentially "crappy" when he came to the tournament as a judge of first-year debaters. According to him, such arguments were "for those outside of Kanto, and not for us" because his team, the winner of the annual national ranking last year, had "in most cases adopted orthodox strategic choices [that is, debate over advantages and disadvantages of the affirmative plan] and won against these tricky teams." Mr. Dando, another third-year debater, echoed Mr. Chiyoda when he said that "the shift argument is the last choice" for him because he "always had easier and more certain strategic choices" than such "weird things." Speculating from such comments, student-run debate communities such as the NAFA appear to identify quality debate performances based on local norms of what counts as good arguments, while avoiding argumentative norms that the community should expel.

While this study does not confirm when and how the situation evolved into its current iteration, I can speculate on how the current convictions and knowledge of the community formed. In all the interview sessions, I asked how interviewees learned debate. All the respondents said that they watched debate rounds, had coaching from their senior club members, and read handouts from past NAFA lecture workshops uploaded on the website. None explicitly mentioned that they had learned debate and debate theory from textbooks.

As Butt (2010) noted, 73 English-written textbooks of argumentation and debate were available in 2008. Many of these are readily accessible in Japan now and are reasonably affordable to college students. Also a few quality textbooks of policy debate written in the Japanese language exist. Yet, the interviewees conducted between March and June 2017 in the Kanto area answered that they had not read or known any of these books, except one senior tournament tabulation member who reported that he read one, although he did not remember its title.

Based on the interview results, my contention is that the current English-speaking intercollegiate policy debate in Japan is localizing itself by reducing its influence from outside sources to confirm the validity of its own activities. Debating technical policy mechanisms without referring to such outside sources would likely be risky because such speeches are likely to be pointless or even confusing to any community outsiders. Indeed, in all the nine observed rounds that included topicality challenges, the second affirmative constructive speakers answered with "no-inherency." Multiple interviews subsequently clarified that, on topicality, "no-inherency" means "no particular reason for defining the terms with the standard." Also, the debaters recognized "redundancy," "net-benefit" and "mutual exclusivity" as sound types of proof for competitiveness. Interview responses also confirmed that by far, the most frequent winning arguments related to topicality are so-called "generic topicalities," such as topicalities of "the Japanese government" and "should," while the vote goes very easily to the negative even when underdeveloped in later speeches.

These examples seem to suggest that the current NAFA debate is developing a peculiar and closed argument culture. But, as David Beers once commented through e-mail, "closed cultures—whatever their individual merits—almost always atrophy over time" (quoted in Fine, 2001, p. 237). Closed debate communities may lose attractiveness to young prospective college students. Further, the loss of shared vocabularies with American debate communities may result in a slowing of the pipeline of Japanese debaters easily transitioning into U.S. graduate schools with debate programs.

Bridging to and within the Galapagos Islands

This study conducted observations of debate rounds and participant interviews to better understand the current status of Japanese policy debate in relation to U.S. debate practices. By and large, the results supported Bauschard's observations from 2012 indicating that Japanese debate was becoming more localized. The more systemic approach, however, did yield some unique findings regarding how the Japanese college policy debate has localized, such as the primary sources of debate education, the definition of debate theory, and the types of acceptable debate theory arguments.

As a researcher of policy debate in Japan, I take the move toward a more closed, localized debate community seriously. The resulting problems can be acute, as when Sheckels (2015), a coach of one of the recent travelling U.S. teams, commented that past tournament organizers (and the host of the U.S. team) had let him and the two of the tour debaters from the United States judge a semi-final round and all the three understood "less than ten percent of what was being said." I recognize as a result of such experiences that the Japanese intercollegiate debate community needs to (re)establish and maintain more positive relations with the American policy debate.

Equally important is the creation of more connections between the Japanese intercollegiate debate community with the high school community. The two cultures need to export, from colleges to high schools, relevant analytical frameworks and debate mechanisms, while setting up a worthwhile stage for talented high school debaters to compete in college. As the high school debate community is now sufficiently large and is enthusiastic about learning English by debate, most participants seem to lack the idea of policy debate as a valuable means to learn policy mechanisms and analytical skills. Even though debate theory makes the practice specialized and less acceptable to a lay audience, the analytic gaming of theory provides and should provide understandings of the complexities of, as well as respect and engagement to, the policy-making process.

Finally, this essay proffers a lesson to the United States. As the history of Japanese college debate community demonstrates, students can flourish and keep inter-school debate communities without substantial outside help. Yet, it also suggests that student-run debate communities can quickly transform to the dynamics of rapidly-changing members of their own communities and such communities may be less open to different contents and styles, with the result that they become more insular and less reflexive about their own performances. The Japanese examples thus suggest that reaching out, positively interacting with outsiders, and being susceptible and welcome to change are all critical for our future.

References

Aonuma, S, Morooka, J., & Seno, K. (2015). Revisiting the U.S. footprints: A critical exploration of interscholarstic/intercollegiate policy debate in post-World War II Japan. In C. H. Palczewski (Ed.), *Disturbing argument* (pp. 432–437). New York, NY: Routledge.

Bauschard, S. (2013, April 24). Japan's diverse debating styles. *Millenial Speech & Debate*. Retrieved from http://millenialsd.com/blog/2013/04/24/japans-diverse-debating-styles

Butt, N. S. (2010). *Argument construction, argument evaluation, and decision-making: A content analysis of argumentation and debate textbooks* (Doctoral dissertation). Retrieved from Wayne State University Digital Commons database.

Fine, G. A. (2001). *Gifted tongues: High school debate and adolescent culture*. Princeton, NJ: Princeton University Press.

Hahn, A., Hahn, T. W., & Hobeika, M.-O. N. (2013). *Finding your voice*. New York, NY: IDEA.

Inoue, N. (1994). *Ways of debating in Japan* (Doctoral dissertation). Retrieved from ProQuest Dissertations and Theses database. (UMI No. 9519451)

Lain, B. (2015). Rethinking the history of the Japanese-U.S. exchange tour: Early tours, early topics, and early traffic. In C. H. Palczewski (Ed.), *Disturbing argument* (pp. 426–431). New York, NY: Routledge.

Matsumoto, M. (1986). *Korega dibēto da: Shijō saikyō no eigo* [*This is debate: Strongest English in History*]. Tokyo, Japan: Alc Press.

National Association of Forensics and Argumentation [NAFA]. (n.d.). Retrieved from http://nafadebate.org/

Sheckels, T. (2015, July 8). Report on U.S. debate tour of Japan. Personal communication.

Woods, C., & Konishi, T. (2008). What has been exchanged?: Toward a history of Japan-US debate exchange. In T. Suzuki, T. Kato, & A. Kubota (Eds.), *Argumentation, the law, and justice* (pp. 271–279). Tokyo, Japan: Japan Debate Association.

Yano, Y. (Ed.). (1994). Meet the Senō: Senō Kazuhiko shi to Senō o kataru [Meet the Seno: Talking about the "Seno" with Mr. Kazuhiko Seno]. *Debate Forum, 10(2)*, 89–104.

Yano, Y. (2017, June 6). Personal communication.

81

NOTES ON THE HUMOR OF TRANSLATION

American Policy Debate Theory and Comic Translations

Brian Lain

First, I want to thank the organizers of this panel for the invitation to speak today. I know all of them and have already promised not to share stories of what happened on various Committee on International Discussion and Debate tours. It seems what happens on a CIDD tour stays on a CIDD tour. I was a participant in the 1995 U.S. debate tour of Japan and a coach of the 2012 U.S. National Debate Team. I made lifelong friends and am truly honored to be able to discuss American policy debate in Japan.

The four papers on this panel all address the question, "What is American academic policy debate as it exists in Japan?" They answer this question in four different ways, and I want to explore four different metaphors they used in their answers and add one of my own.

The first of these metaphors is debate as evolution or devolution, as Noriaki Tajima discusses. I remember quite clearly being on the Tokyo Subway with Edmund Zagorin watching Japanese TV commercials on the train. Market researchers summed up the explanation of the uniqueness, ridiculousness, and absurdity of Japanese advertising with the phrase "Galapagos economy." Basically, the short phrase expresses that the historic self-sufficiency of the Japanese economy resulted in a new advertising norm that is unique and out of place with the rest of the world. The same conceptual framework applies to Japan's debate communities, as they are similarly distinct. Mr. Tajima's essay considers the state of this Galapagos norm. He correctly comments that both the United States policy debate community, as well as the Japanese policy debate community, is Galapagoan. The United States, it appears, is like the blue-footed booby in that the nation has evolved its distinctive features only in college policy debate (e.g., advanced counterplan theory). The Japanese policy debate community is like the flightless cormorant, unable to fly because of adaptations to its ecosystem. Tajima's conclusion is that the Galapagos economy has further split and regionalism now devolves policy debate theory. His solution is connection, but just keep in mind that when unique Galapagos species move to different ecosystems, they often perish.

The second metaphor in these papers examines debate as a game. Katsuya Koresawa and Kaori Miyawaki's examination of judge philosophies does an excellent close reading and interview of practices among debate judges, revealing a potential shift in attitudes among them concerning both their language selection (writing ballots and philosophies in Japanese) and how they define debate. The conclusions of the authors (i.e., that they do not find new approaches in judge philosophies and that the U.S. policy debate community no longer has a strong influence on Japanese debate) depend on the rules of the game. If the name of the game is theory, then, as the authors suggest, little need exists for new approaches. After all, American debate theory is itself a version of American exceptionalism (Fine, 2001). The game defines what counts as debate theory, and different games emphasize different rules. Why look for innovation in Japanese policy debate in American policy debate theory? Might the innovation be in second language acquisition skills pedagogy or even in the format that is a more direct expression of cultural norms? In short, while cultures can play games from other cultures, their own culture forms the rules. This essay, like the one above, asks the question: What happens when Galapagoan games evolve in different ecosystems? The result may not be extinction, but rather bioengineering.

The third approach considers debate as a technology. Satoru Aonuma and Kazuhiko Seno's *Big in Japan* examines the limits of what they call "imitation pedagogy" through an examination of responses to and repetitions of 1980s debate theory. This essay treats policy debate theory as a sort of technology that is subject to export/import rules and reveals a reverse engineering happening in the Japanese technology market. Debate always involves importing. Counterplan theory is an import of opportunity costs theory from economic theory. I always chuckle when I hear American policy debaters exclaim, "our critique of global capitalism is net beneficial." Perhaps something gets lost in the importation process. When reading Aonuma and Seno's essay, I am reminded of Derrida's (1988) famous comments on iteration, that is, every repetition is not the self-same. Thus, unsurprisingly, what some call "imitation pedagogy" is also a form of "innovation pedagogy." Again, to suture these metaphors together, debate is a Galapagoan game exported to new markets and it is reproducing.

Finally, these essays consider debate as a student activity. Junya Morooka puts together the data on participation levels and, especially, levels of gender participation. His conclusions verify that the debate communities between college and high school are separate, a need exists for more female judges, and the causes of the decline in participation require further study. Again, to put this in conversation, Morooka's conclusions essentially argue for the existence of not one Galapagoan debate community but at least two (college and high school). Likewise, the viability of the Galapagos species is itself in question. Are these conclusions related to the points made in other papers? Members of the debate community have made the argument that a reliance on highly technical jargon and argument norms specific to a community have an adverse effect on participation levels from different demographic groups (e.g., Andrade & Bruschke, 2014; Baker, 1998; Preston, 2006; Warner, 1998). I wonder if the prohibition on debate theory makes HEnDA more attractive to female participants, while its presence in college debate is a deterrent to participation. Likewise, the regionalism and student driven nature of debate that Tajima uncovers may have an impact on gender participation.

To these metaphors of American policy debate, I want to add one of my own. I offer debate as humor. In other words, extending Hovden (2006), American policy debate theory is a joke. I don't mean it lightheartedly (well I kind of do), but jokes have a special status in the international, cross-cultural arena. Humor has a difficult time translating languages and crossing borders. Consider the challenge of translating jokes. From here on out, every time I use the word "joke," think "policy debate theory." In other words, translate it. Jokes are culturally dependent. They rely on not just terminology but also on a history of usages, norms, events, and popularly held opinions. Translating humor takes skill. There is not a one-to-one correlation in jokes across cultures. Consider two funny stories of President Jimmy Carter. First, while speaking in Poland, he said, "I want to know the Poles." However, it was translated as, "I desire the Poles carnally" (Hoffman, 2012). Shortly after leaving office, Carter, while delivering a speech at a college in Japan, surprisingly received boisterous laughter in response to his opening story. When Carter inquired of his Japanese interpreter to explain the extraordinary response, the interpreter replied, "I told the audience, 'President Carter told a funny story; everyone must laugh.'" (Hoffman, 2012, para. 13). And if jokes are vexing for translators, consider the pun, comic timing, and sentence structure. These all make the work of translating humor difficult.

Debate theory is not always funny; in fact, it rarely is, but we should not take it too seriously either. To consider the evolution, gaming, imitation, and participation in debate is to address the problem of translating humor directly. Historically, debate theory has served as a joke told in different cultures at different points in time. American policy debaters translated their joke to the Japanese in the postwar era. The joke has persisted, but it has also changed in regional and indigenous forms which play with fidelity and piety.

The humor is not lost on me that the dominant stereotype of Japanese, both in the United States and in Japan, is as "majime ningen" a concept roughly translatable to "serious people." Here is the punchline of my entire response. Historians once noted both a lack of humor and a lack of a tradition of debate in Japanese culture. Of course, this conclusion arose from what the scholars counted as humor or debate as defined in Western terms. The joke that is academic policy debate is itself undergoing changes in translation; thus, we ought to attend to that as translation. I would like to think that regionalism, judging philosophies, the *Debate Forum* and *Tsuron,* and the practices of the Koshien high school tournament all function as a deliberately skewed translation in order to make the joke work. These Galapagoan debate practices are a sort of mischievous comedy that I do not wish to insult at all. Instead, I would applaud the environmental transformation, regional innovation, community formation, and memorial investigation as particularly cunning translations. These things are serious, but they are also comic. I imagine all of these essays as scenes in a vaudeville play between Uncle Sam (the kindhearted liberal trying to bring debate to postwar Japan whose foibles only the Japanese Rokugo can save) and the Japanese community that manages to produce something called debate (while giving Uncle Sam his comeuppance). All of these essays are wonderfully comic and the comic frame, as Burke (1937/1984) told us, is itself a means to challenge the status quo. Through presenting one's foibles, argumentation and debate scholars are able to raise our consciousness and allow transcendence (Powell, 1995). While I have not the time to discuss transcendence and translation here, their similarity and connection is also funny.

Translation has always characterized American academic debate in Japan. The type of translation is not tragedy, romance, or horror, but is, in fact, comedy. We ought to consider not only the difficulty of translating humor, but also what the humor of translation knows. For my part, I'll just end by saying, "thanks for all the laughs."

References

Andrade, L. M., & Bruschke, J. B. (2014). Cultural pedagogy as motivation and the role of "institutional agents" in intercollegiate debate. In C. H. Palczewski (Ed.), *Disturbing argument* (pp. 407–413). New York, NY: Routledge.

Baker, W. (1998). Reflections on the New York Urban Debate League and Ideafest II. *Contemporary Argumentation & Debate, 19*, 69–71. Retrieved from http://cedadebate.org

Burke, K. (1937/1984). *Attitudes toward history* (3rd ed.). Berkeley, CA: University of California Press.

Derrida, J. D. (1988). *Limited inc* (S. Weber, Trans.). Evanston, IL: Northwestern University Press. Retrieved from http://lab404.com/misc/ltdinc.pdf

Fine, G. A. (2001). *Gifted tongues: High school debate and adolescent culture*. Princeton, NJ: Princeton University Press.

Hoffman, J. (2012, October 19). Me translate funny one day. *The New York Times*.Retrieved from http://nytimes.com

Hovden, J. M. (2006). Debate and the comic frame: A Burkean take on the educational value of NDT/CEDA debate. In P. Riley (Ed.), *Engaging argument* (pp. 506–511). Washington, DC: National Communication Association.

Powell, K. A. (1995). The association of southern women for the prevention of lynching: Strategies of a movement in the comic frame. *Communication Quarterly, 43*(1), 86–99. doi:10.1080/01463379509369958

Preston, C. T., Jr. (2006). The interconnectedness between intercollegiate policy debate and the urban debate leagues: From a distance, five years and change later. *Contemporary Argumentation & Debate, 27*, 157–172.

Warner, E. (1998). On preserving identity, debate, and finding home. *Contemporary Argumentation & Debate, 19*, 76–79. Retrieved from http://cedadebate.org